What Do I Do With My Pain?

What Do I Do With My Pain?

PROCLAIM LIBERTY TO THE CAPTIVES

Ann Gwen Mack

WHAT DO I DO WITH MY PAIN?

Copyright © 2017 Ann Gwen Mack

All rights reserved.

No part of this book may be reproduced, distributed or transmitted in any form by any means, graphics, electronics, or mechanical, including photocopy, recording, taping, or by any information storage or retrieval system, without permission in writing from the publisher, except in the case of reprints in the context of reviews, quotes, or references.

Printed in the United States of America

ISBN: 978-0-9993132-0-6

TABLE OF CONTENTS

Preface.. 1

A Dedication To God & Letter Of Apology............... 11

Acknowledgments...................................... 15

SALVATION IS A GIFT FROM GOD! IT IS FREE!

Introduction.. 21

The Pain We Cause Others............................. 39

Proclaim Liberty To The Captives...................... 47

The Meaning Of Faith................................. 57

FROM REVELATION TO REALIZATION

Bittersweet 65

Opposites: No In-Betweens! 77

If Only You Could Walk A Mile In My Shoes! 81

Me The Creation!. 87

Timing Is Everything!. 89

What Is Freedom To Me?. 101

Chosen By God 103

Spiritual Warfare 105

I Believe!. 111

Diversity By Design. 117

Everything Happens For A Reason. 129

Hair Does Not Define Me!. 133

He Who Has Arrived 149

I Get It! 153

Citizen Or Christian? 161

RELATIONSHIPS

Race In America 173

Change: Truth, Fact Or Myth?. 179

I Am Only Human 213

A Father's Love. 219

The Soul Of My Grandfather 229

Family Matters 231

Tribute To A Dear Friend.................................. 237

Love Conquers All.. 239

Assimilation By Association 243

Am I Thy Brother's Keeper?............................... 247

In The World, Not Of The World!.......................... 259

LETTERS TO GOD

Trials And Tribulations................................... 271

Above All Else, Stand!................................... 273

Thank You, God!.. 275

Instant Replay: A Hard Lesson To Learn 277

No Means No! 281

My Family Dilemma.. 283

Ask And You Shall Receive! 287

God, Teach Me Your Ways And Help Me
To Understand.. 291

Coming Together In Praise 293

Spiritual Growth 295

Striving To Live My Purpose 299

Never Ending... 305

Joy On The Inside 307

Juanita Bynum 313

Betwixt 319

Depression Is Not An Option 325

M&Ms 331

Malachi 3:1 Ministries 335

Developing A Personal Relationship With God 345

Baptism 349

Peace 351

A Prayer Request 353

From Revelation To Realization 355

I Am Forever Grateful! 361

Entertaining The Wrong Thinking 369

Judging Or Just Refusing To Accept Iniquity 375

Why Should I Go Along To Get Along? 379

Broken, Mended, And Second Winded 385

TESTIMONIES

The Inner Me 391

Once Was 393

Discerning Of Spirits 395

Help Me! 411

Seeking To Know My Purpose 423

Sharing An Example Of God's Favor In My Life.......... 427

Judging Others... 431

Ignorance 433

Reputation Versus Character.......................... 439

The Assignment....................................... 443

Obedient To God...................................... 453

Messengers Of God.................................... 467

The Grace Of God..................................... 473

Laughter Is Good For The Soul........................ 487

Be Mindful Of What You Ask 489

Touched By God And Led By The Holy Spirit 499

Trust God In Spite Of What You See 517

What Would Jesus Do?................................. 531

Hidden Agendas And Ungodly Motives 535

When The World Spills Over Into The Church!.......... 549

Take Care Of God's Temple 569

THE REALITY OF IT ALL

What Is Your Reality? 581

History: Yours Or Mine? 587

Image.. 591

Transformation 595

Sharing My Thoughts On The Subject Of
My Education, Career And God 599

WORK ENVIRONMENTS

Workplace Bullying And Violence Are Serious Issues! 605

Workplace Bullying Is Unacceptable!.................. 607

What Kind Of Person Are You? 615

Am I Not My Brother's Keeper? 621

A Fact-Finding Investigation......................... 629

To Solve The Big Problems, See The Big Picture......... 637

Attachment 1 677

Attachment 2 683

Awareness... 687

EXIT INTERVIEWS

Icma Retirement Corporation (Rc) 705

Kajax Engineering, Inc. 719

Exit Interview. 721

SCHOOL ASSIGNMENTS

This Is My Story, This Is My Song..................... 731

I Can!. 737

Stress And Its Presence In The Workplace.............. 743

Reparationse. 759

My Idea Of Utopia.................................... 765

Wrongful Termination 773

BONUS

What Is The Nature Of A Scribe? 787

A Deeper Hurt....................................... 803

Born To Die 807

Fight, Take Flight Or Freeze......................... 811

Church Hurt Is Real! 815

Covering.. 821

APPENDICES/LETTERS

Seven Day Adventist 825

Oprah Winfrey. 835

Commissioner of The Salvation Army 857

Oprah Winfrey: Response to letter discussed 900

Mayor Anthony Williams. 901

Department of Employment Services (DOES) 907

City Paper 909

Senate Finance Committee 913

References. 921

About The Author 939

PREFACE

For I know the thoughts that I think toward you, saith the Lord, thoughts of peace, and not of evil, to give you an expected end.

~ Jeremiah 29:11

December 2010
Revised December 2016

This book was written over a period of many years prior to its first release in December of 2010. Early on in my life, I did not realize God had gifted me to be a writer. Nor did I dream I would be able to put pen to paper—like a scribe of old—to share my testimonies with others for His glory while exercising full disclosure, which He also refers to as a spirit of *transparency*. Especially, when I had encountered so many people who did not hesitate to tell me what I could not do, to include doubting my skill to structure a complete sentence! And all along, God was preparing me and encouraging me to record my thoughts in a journal, which included many letters and questions to Him about my struggles (trials and tribulations) in search of spiritual growth.

Moving forward, God has taken me from a place of unbelief to one of belief in ways I never thought or imagined was possible. Being forced to attend church in my younger years by my mother, bless her heart, I was introduced to a form of religion that served to speak of a God who created mankind; however, something was definitely missing. At the time, this was merely a concept that made no absolute sense to me at all! For I lacked the wisdom, knowledge and understanding needed to hold my interest and compel me to want to learn more about this person or entity called God. A God who not only created mankind, but who created the Heavens and the earth, the entire universe as we know it (in general) and all that was in it: living creatures, vegetation, trees, fruit and herbs, as gifted to us to partake of whenever we wanted or needed.

> *And God said, Behold,*
> *I have given you every herb bearing seed,*
> *which [is] upon the face of all the earth, and every tree,*
> *in the which [is] the fruit of a tree yielding seed;*
> *to you it shall be for meat.*
>
> ~ Genesis 1:29

And yet, I was to believe in a higher power—not visible in the natural sense to the naked eye—who sacrificed the life of His only begotten Son to save us from ourselves in the name salvation. The Son, Yeshua or Yahweh, as known to some, and Jesus Christ to many others, was and is God in the flesh, born a man on earth through Immaculate Conception to a woman named Mary. Confusing to say the least, the story concerning Adam and Eve was even more baffling as people or men in general, resulted to blaming all women for Adam's failure in not making the right choice to follow his own mind, to include disobeying God's direct instructions to him as the head of the divine example of a family structure. This was, unfortunately, the beginning of mankind's downfall in so many ways. There was a breakdown in communication, and people allowed themselves to be consumed by lust, greed and selfishness through the influence of all that was outside of the *Will of God*. God loves us so deeply that He actually entrusted us to not only keep His commandments, but He wanted us to appreciate that which He had given to us. He did not intend for us to replace Him with false idols—for He is a jealous God. And yet, He still loves us!

> *So watch yourselves, that you do not forget the covenant of the LORD your God which He made with you, and make for yourselves a graven image in the form of anything against which the LORD your God has commanded you. "For the LORD your God is a consuming fire, a jealous God.*
>
> ~ Deuteronomy 4:23-24 NASB

SALVATION

Strong's Concordance:

- Hebrew

    > 3468[1] - yesha (phonetically pronounced yeh'-shah): deliverance, rescue, salvation, safety, welfare.

- Greek

    > 4982[2] - sózó (phonetically pronounced sode'-zo): I save, heal, preserve, rescue.

    > 4991[3] - sótéria (phonetically pronounced so-tay-ree'-ah): welfare, prosperity, deliverance, preservation, salvation, safety.

As I ventured out in the world and experienced life and all it had to offer (the good as well as the bad), the more confused I became and the more I wondered if God truly existed. Having to interact and develop relationships with others, including those within my immediate family, exposed me to a number of mind-boggling experiences that left me questioning my life's purpose. Not to mention, living in a world that views me as being less important or having less value than a man because I am a woman, which, according to their definition and reasoning, identifies me (and other women) as being a second-class citizen

---

1 http://biblehub.com/hebrew/3468.htm
2 http://biblehub.com/greek/4982.htm
3 http://biblehub.com/greek/4991.htm

on the basis of the control they wish to exert over us. And given the nature of the emphasis on race relations, I am subjected to a world dynamic that further attempts to degrade me on the basis of my skin color and limit my potential for growth! But, I AM who I AM and who I AM is who God created me to be. That includes my gender and the color of my skin, which was purposed by *Him* for a specific reason, time and season!

> *Therefore all they that devour thee shall be devoured;*
> *and all thine adversaries, every one of them,*
> *shall go into captivity;*
> *and they that spoil thee shall be a spoil,*
> *and all that prey upon thee will I give for a prey.*
> *For I will restore health unto thee,*
> *and I will heal thee of thy wounds,*
> *saith the Lord; because they called thee an Outcast,*
> *saying, This is Zion, whom no man seeketh after.*
>
> ~ Jeremiah 30:16-17

Encountering so many hurtful, uncaring and messed up people—each with their own agenda and problems—pushed me into a shell that reinforced my belief that God couldn't possibly exist! How and why would such a God create a diverse population of people who, through an array of misconceived notions and differences, would want to harm one another and destroy the earth through the process of selfish gain? So with each trial and test for living came disappointment after disappointment, leaving me wanting to shield my heart and protect it from becoming bitter, broken and bruised as a result of issues with people. Was no one happy with their life or willing to change it for the better? Their insecurities, for whatever reason, left them wanting to control the world and others! To what end?

> *Why criest thou for thine affliction?*
> *thy sorrow is incurable for the multitude of thine*
> *iniquity: because thy sins were increased,*
> *I have done these things unto thee.*
>
> ~ Jeremiah 30:15

Ironically, as time went on, I started to learn that all of what I had endured was not in vain; it was God's plan to take me through a process to realize my predestined purpose. Knowing me to the depth of my character and personality better than I know myself, He allowed each and every event or encounter to prune me and bring me to a place of belief. Because I needed much convincing, He gave me many chances to commit and surrender my life to Him. As I look over my life, God was always with me, encouraging me and challenging me to move beyond myself to strive to reach my highest potential in Him. And He was more than I had realized. I was simply too busy being consumed by the wrong done to me and allowing the pain to pull me down to notice the intensity of the illuminating light in the midst of the darkness until I acknowledged and accepted my assignment to write this book.

Today, I have declared the Lord to be my God, and I will walk in his ways, keep his statutes, commandments and ordinances, and obey Him (Deuteronomy 26:17); Him who is within me! What a simple yet important request! Walk just as

He has commanded me, so I may live, and all goes well with me (favor); I may live long in the land I AM going to possess (Deuteronomy 5:33). Why? Because *the LORD has commanded us to do all these statutes, to fear the LORD our God, for our good always, that he might preserve us alive, as it is at this day* (Deuteronomy 6:24).

Overall, I lacked "revelational" knowledge and the willingness to be still long enough to hear the voice of the LORD! *So now I can pick out what's true and fair, find all the good trails! Lady Wisdom will be your close friend, and Brother Knowledge your pleasant companion. Good Sense will scout ahead for danger, Insight will keep an eye out for you. They'll keep you from making wrong turns, or following the bad directions Of those who are lost themselves and can't tell a trail from a tumbleweed, These losers who make a game of evil and throw parties to celebrate perversity, Traveling paths that go nowhere, wandering in a maze of detours and dead ends* (Proverbs 2:9-15 MSG). Today, I not only acknowledge revelation as being a vital part of my spiritual growth, but it is my desire to embrace it, accept it and share it with others as God releases me to do so. I strongly believe that there are two kinds of knowledge: 1) man's knowledge and 2) God's knowledge. However, there is only one that really counts. And that is God's knowledge! Man's knowledge comes through his reasoning, but God's knowledge comes through **revelation**. *For I neither received it of man, nor was I taught it, but through a revelation of Jesus Christ* (Galatians 1:11).

Revelation is the knowledge of truth! When you receive revelation knowledge, it's extremely hard for anyone to be able to convince you that what you know, you don't! Although they will try! It is a **divine revealing or uncovering** of something that has always been true but was hidden, locked away or unknown to mankind. In fact, Hosea 4:6 of the Amplified Bible states, *My people are destroyed for lack of knowledge [of My law, where I reveal My will]. Because you [the priestly nation] have rejected knowledge, I will also reject you from being My priest. Since you have forgotten the law of your God, I will also forget your children.*

Strong's Concordance:

- Revelation[4] in the Greek is apokalupsis (phonetically pronounced ap-ok-al'-oop-sis): an unveiling, uncovering, revealing, revelation.

- Knowledge[5] in the Greek is epignósis (phonetically pronounced ep-ig'-no-sis): knowledge of a particular point or thing (directed towards a particular object); perception, discernment, recognition, intuition (a strong gut feeling).

Side Note: While sitting at home one evening, God directed me to a book entitled *The Miseducation of the Negro*[6] and encouraged me to view the content from the standpoint of Hosea 4:6 as referenced above. Then He talked to me about culture and history in comparison to the content of that book, which was written in 1933 by Carter Godwin Woodson to include how things are destined to repeat

---

4 http://biblehub.com/greek/602.htm
5 http://biblehub.com/greek/1922.htm
6 http://www.historyisaweapon.com/defcon1/misedne.html

themselves over and over again; unless, we are awakened to the *truth* to implement and acknowledge the need for change. God went on from there to reference how information was and is deliberately mistaught or kept away from us to keep us in a holding pattern (bondage) in the name of control. And, it is not God's desire for us to be ignorant to the truth. For this reason, I have chosen to use the words **divine revealing or uncovering** because it denotes the disclosure of information through communication from God to His children—if we have an ear to hear. It is He who has given me permission to review and submit a revision to this book since its first publication in 2010 to offer more clarity and revelation as evidence of my spiritual growth. It also adds a greater understanding of who I AM in Him and Him in me from past to present. **As untruths or mistruths are replaced with truths, it is our responsibility to make certain that all information is corrected and revisited in an effort not to stumble our brethren.** (Read 1 Corinthians 10:32, Romans 14:13-23 and 1 Timothy 4:12.)

But if they do not listen,
they perish by the sword and die without knowledge.

~ Job 36:12 ESV

In an attempt to disclose and reinforce my spiritual journey, much of what you will read through these pages may be reiterated in an effort to express my exact feelings of regression and/or progression on any given day as it was journaled. There were times when I thought I had overcome a particular situation only to find out there was much work still needed to be done to move past my pain. So please note that specific dates and times are important!

Nonetheless, after reading this book, I pray each and every individual is blessed enormously by my testimonies to be delivered, healed and set free, as well as encouraged to develop a deeper walk with the Lord. I pray you are compelled to go above and beyond, to push past the boundaries or limitations placed on you by others to reach your destiny. I pray you never get bored or stop seeking God's face to experience *His love* for you to embrace your calling. I pray you never grow weary of doing good or become discouraged in the midst of your trials and tribulations to know **you can do all things through Christ who strengthens you.** Regardless of what it looks like, I pray you are able to keep your focus, hold on and endure to the end to receive your reward in appreciation of your God-inheritance. May you overcome your pain and all your fears to know you are victorious (more than a conqueror) and know in your heart, soul and mind that the battle is already won by Him and through Him for you! You just have to believe and trust the Lord!

No matter what, continue to pray without ceasing and thank Him often! Praise Him in the morning! Praise Him in the noonday! Praise Him in the midnight hour! Praise when you are happy! Praise Him when you are sad! Use your weapon of praise to confuse the enemy! In fact, *I will praise thee; for I am fearfully [and] wonderfully made: marvellous [are] thy works; and [that] my soul knoweth right well* (Psalm 139:14 KJV).

A DEDICATION TO GOD & LETTER OF APOLOGY

Dear God,

Please accept my gracious apology for not receiving Your call on my life so early on in my spiritual journey. In spite of my reluctance, time and time again, You were always there, though I lacked the knowledge of Your presence. So much pain, strife and despair came upon me that I lost all hope of You ever rescuing me from myself to include those in the world who wanted so much to steal my joy and dim my light. Little did I know, You were standing near just waiting for me to take hold of You all along the way!

Deceived by many in my life, especially those I assumed were supposed to love me with no hesitation, I became bitter as I held onto my past and trusted no one. And unfortunately, not even You! Instead of me running toward You and standing firm on Your every word, I let fear grip me and put a wedge between us, mainly because I thought You had turned your back on me! However, loving me as You do, I now know You felt my pain, and

You even hurt with me when I hurt, thus feeling every agonizing imprint. Determined to prepare me by equipping me for the fight, it was necessary for You to take me through a process to get me to this point in my life where I am today. How could I have ever doubted You and Your love for me?

When I once thought You heard me not, I knew nothing about the concept of spiritual warfare. I assumed You were ignoring my prayers, but now I believe each prayer was intercepted and did not make it to Your ears. Also, not knowing or understanding Your ways, I lacked the knowledge of doing things decently in order to receive Your best. But lately, amazingly, You answer every thought in my heart and in my mind more quickly than imaginable. As I learn to forgive myself, I am learning to let go of the memories of the hurt and pain that are stamped on my heart. In doing this, I will also evict those from my mind who have wounded my soul. I will forgive their transgressions against me in the same manner You have forgiven me of my sins, to give me this chance to prove myself once more. You have given me more chances than I deserve and bestowed upon me much love, which is evident by the manner in which You revealed Yourself to me.

Let your conversation be without covetousness;
and be content with such things as ye have:
for he hath said, I will never leave thee,
nor forsake thee.

~ Hebrews 13:5

My second baptism represented the rededication of my life to You as a symbol of my conscious awareness and acknowledgment of a needful relationship with You. I never knew I could reach a place of having such joy and inner peace. You restored me and made my life worth living! Thank You for this opportunity and Your confidence in my ability to carry out the assignment You entrusted to me. Thank You for helping me to understand that my assignment is my assignment until You tell me otherwise by giving me a new one. Because of the anointing of the Holy Spirit that You gifted to me (and many others like me), I know *I can do all things through Christ who strengthens me.* Today, I am totally depending upon You to guide my life as you continue to order my steps!

In openly and boldly saying YES to Your will, I not only dedicate my life to You, but also this book, which honors the presence of Your existence in my life. This book is also a representation of my attempt to impress upon man his purpose here on earth—a lifelong assignment we seem to have overlooked or consistently taken for granted. I pray and hope that those who get the opportunity to read this book will allow You in their lives, see You much differently through my heart and experience You to love You as I do. I will praise You continuously forever more and look forward to developing and sustaining a lifelong relationship with You. Thank You for not giving up on me, for I long to be deeper in You!

For I am persuaded, that neither death,
nor life, nor angels, nor principalities, nor powers,
nor things present, nor things to come, nor height,

nor depth, nor any other creature, shall be able to separate us from the love of God, which is in Christ Jesus our Lord.

~ Romans 8:38-39

Committed to please You,

Your UNIQUE and COURAGEOUS one

ACKNOWLEDGMENTS

Dear Father God

Your persistence in getting my attention has made me whole! I cannot begin to tell You how grateful I am for Your love and the opportunity to serve You. No one but You truly knows just how excited I am to be growing spiritually toward gaining your knowledge, wisdom and understanding in learning and appreciating Your ways! Your confidence and belief in my ability to speak on Your behalf means more to me than I could have possibly imagined. Thank You for Your trust and for saving me from myself as well as rescuing me from the world.

Dear Mom

Thank you for your encouragement and enthusiasm in what God has called me to do.

Dear Mary Bryant

Your patience is amazing! Not once during my seven-year process, upon which time God allowed you and me to become acquainted, did you put me down or ridicule me for being so clueless about my *salvation*. You were always there to offer me words of encouragement and to confirm my God-appointed purpose on the basis of a personality loved by God but rejected by others. In sharing my vision to write and dedicate this book to God, you not only celebrated with me, but you suggested the title (*What Do I Do With My Pain?*) that best describes my walk with God. Thank you!

Dear Jackie Battle

Thank you for being so receptive to hearing God and offering your services in helping me realize a dream in the name of Jesus Christ. God, knowing your heart as well as your commitment to Him orchestrated our meeting by allowing our paths to cross in an unusual place and time. Not once did you disbelieve! Your persistence in seeing this through initially was what I needed to help me stay on target with God's plan for my life. Thank you for offering your editing skills in 2010!

Dear Lorrie Hyatt

Thank you for our long-term friendship and believing in me when others doubted me. Thank you for sharing your loving family; a mother who loved me as her own to open her house to me when solace was much needed!

Dear Family and Friends

Karyn Collins, Angela Shaw

Thank you!

Dear Bishop Raymond and Pastor Vera Horton, III

Unity Life Christian Ministries

Church, for me, had never been what it is now until meeting you. Thank you for sharing your love of the Lord in the manner in which you do! Thank you for hearing the Lord and following through in confirming His plan for my life.

Dear Mr. and Mrs. Porter

My greatest champions!

God does nothing on a whim without purpose! Everything is well thought out and considered down to our street address and chance encounters with others. It has truly been a joy and a pleasure living a few doors from you. You have been a great inspiration! Thank you for your continued encouragement and guidance in the ways of the Holy Spirit.

Dear Apostle Willie E. Bruce

Wife: Rev. Dr. Heather Bruce

World Healing Ministries, International

God always surrounds us with people and friends to help guide us along the way, but not everyone graciously and freely accepts this position like you, Apostle Bruce. Truly dedicated to God's mission of Kingdom building, as opposed to the traditional church-building theology, not once did you place any demands on me to attend your church in exchange for mentoring me about the spiritual things of God whenever there was need. You are the example of what it means to put God first—unconditionally! With the heart of God, your ear was forever close to *His* mouth to hear and to confirm to me the gifting and calling *on* my life. Thank you for challenging me to read the Bible, to study it and to view it literally as a **Citizen of the Kingdom**. I specifically dedicate "Christian or Citizen" under "From Revelation to Realization" to you!

SALVATION IS A GIFT FROM GOD!

IT IS FREE!

INTRODUCTION
GO SHOW THEM WHAT HE TOLD YOU!

Hearing of thy love and faith, which thou hast toward the Lord Jesus, and toward all saints; That the communication of thy faith may become effectual by the acknowledging of every good thing which is in you in Christ Jesus.

~ Philemon 1:5-6

THE PROMISE, PURPOSE AND PLAN

For God to use me, I needed to be receptive to His calling on my life. I needed to unlearn to relearn! To get through to me, it was necessary for Him to renew my way of thinking and take me through a process for healing. My mind needed to be transformed to pursue the will of God. Being separated from God at birth, I had no knowledge of who I was or how special I was to Him. Through years and years of abuse and attacks from the enemy (invisible spirits) through people (lost souls), my mind became clouded, and I became damaged goods. I started carrying around baggage that prevented me from having confidence and trust in God, not to mention, confidence in myself.

> *But without thy mind would I do nothing;*
> *that thy benefit should not be as it were*
> *of necessity, but willingly.*
>
> ~ Philemon 1:14

Seeking to belong and to be accepted, I attempted to figure out who I was, based on my association with others. Those who I thought had my best interest at heart only wanted to control me. Much like an employer whose only need for you is based on what you can do for them to make them wealthier, many people only cling to you based on what you have (perceived or unperceived) to offer or can provide to them and for them with no promise of an even exchange. When the well (your energy and time) or the source of your giving is depleted, you become invaluable and then you are so easily replaced with a newer model.

> *Wisdom is the principal thing; therefore get wisdom:*
> *and with all thy getting get understanding.*
>
> ~ Proverbs 4:7

But God is entirely different! He is loving, kind and gentle. He creates you out of a need (purpose) and gives you a set of instructions (a plan) for carrying out your assignment (according to His will or mandate). He tells you up front, with no hidden agenda, what He expects and how He plans to reward (or prosper) you. Unlike those in the world, God is the same today, yesterday, tomorrow and always. He does not change in the middle of a covenant promise. He is no respecter of persons, meaning He does not discriminate but instead gives everyone the same opportunity to excel and be righteous.

> *Cast not away therefore your confidence,*
> *which hath great recompence of reward.*
>
> ~ Hebrews 10:35

By being persistent and determined to reach me, God healed my mind and my heart as He increased my *faith*. Allowing me to see myself through His eyes, He not only revealed Himself to me by making a believer out of me, but He restored my confidence and trust in Him. He took an ordinary person, absent of fame and fortune (as defined by society, not God), who was no different from anyone else in the world to reach others by giving me an assignment to show you what He told me!

> *For ye have need patience, that, after ye*
> *have done the will of God, ye might receive the promise.*
>
> ~ Hebrews 10:36

Angel on Assignment: A Mission from God

In my pursuit of the Will of God, He allowed me to connect with Him in ways I did not think was possible. What others said I could not do, God told me I was not only going to do, but I was going to do it for Him! I was going to be a living testimony and reveal to others how He was working in my life to bring me to where I am today: deeper in Him! I was to show how I was learning to depend on Him (not man) in my life through the sharing of my testimonies as well as my letters to God with everyone who was willing to listen. Many mornings, God would get me up bright and early to give me titles of topics as well as thoughts He wanted me to write down. God also cautioned me that many may not understand nor agree with what was being written by me or *through* me, as directed by the Holy Spirit, pertaining to my experiences in accordance to His will for my life. Nonetheless, He did not want me to waste time or energy defending myself because it was important not to allow the **Spirit of Offense** to influence my behavior in becoming confrontational; nor did He want me to feel as though there was a need to offer any type of explanation to anyone concerning the assignment or task He had given to me to do! For He knew the plans He had for me.

> *Now go, write it before them in a table, and note it in a book,*
> *that it may be for the time to come for ever and ever:*
> *That this [is] a rebellious people, lying children,*
> *children [that] will not hear the law of the LORD:*
> *Which say to the seers, See not; and to the prophets,*
> *Prophesy not unto us right things, speak unto us smooth things,*
> *prophesy deceits.*
>
> ~Isaiah 30:8-10

Giving in to my flesh and quickly forgetting what was told to me about not attempting to seek approval from others or letting them make me doubt (question) what God gives me to do, I allowed the feedback I received from a coworker after reading my thoughts concerning change to disturb my spirit. I have what one would refer to as a passive agreeable personality. I don't want to be misunderstood and it *was* important for me to be liked or to not be at odds with others. So I was a little unnerved by the divisive tension brought on by my coworker's unwillingness to accept that I was hearing and receiving instructions directly from God because she indicated she was an active Christian in ministry. I often make the assumption that all Christians are operating on the same spiritual level. Not true! Growth is a process, and we all go through different lessons and are given different assignments or tasks to fulfill!

Losing much sleep, I tossed and turned all night long as I replayed the conversation over and over again in my head. I knew I could not allow anyone to undermine what God was doing in my life or how He was using me. I needed to stand strong and not deviate from the direction of my path or purpose in accordance to the *Will of God* for my life. Rising the next morning, Tuesday, November 25, 2008, to prepare for work, I was still disturbed by the comments; so much, in fact, that I had allowed those comments to continuously occupy my mind as I got out of my car to enter the Cheverly Metro Station to board the subway train.

Be not forgetful to entertain strangers:
for thereby some have entertained angels unawares.

~ Hebrews 13:2

◆

For he shall give his angels charge over thee,
to keep thee in all thy ways.

~ Psalm 91:11

Walking toward the elevator, I noticed a woman who was standing tall and walking briskly toward me. I thought, "Where is her coat?" It is too cold not to have on a coat and be in nothing other than a duster that one would wear for lounging around the house. As we made eye contact, I thought, *soldier on a mission*. God, if I don't move out of this woman's way, she is going to knock me down. Approaching closer, I said, "Good morning."

At the same time, she said, "Go show them what He told you!"

Excited and too frozen to move, I knew, without a doubt, she was an angel with a message from God. I turned around to get another glimpse of my angel, but she was gone, as if she had mysteriously disappeared or vanished into thin air.

But let all those that put their trust in thee rejoice:
let them ever shout for joy, because thou
defendest them: let them also that love
thy name be joyful in thee.

~ Psalm 5:11

Getting on the elevator, I began to shout for joy. God was using me through my writing to be the voice of those who were unable to speak for themselves. Just as I was being healed through my writing, others would be healed through the reading of it; therefore, as long as I was pleasing God, I was to give no more thought to what others understood or didn't. I needed to be obedient to Him and follow each command in spite of what others thought! What God has for me is for *me*, and what God has for you is for you. It does not matter whether or not anyone understands or agrees with the directive that is given to me from God, for I was told I owed no one an explanation!

Hear, ye children, the instruction of a father,
and attend to know understanding.

~ Proverbs 4:1

In All Thy Getting, Get Understanding

The churches I attended while growing up did not enlighten me about the extensive power and presence of God through the supernatural. There was no discussion of any kind concerning the manifestation of the Holy Spirit. In fact, I received no information or had no knowledge of the Holy Spirit to prepare me for what to expect when it came knocking on my door. Relying on what was presented by pastors or taught in church, I did not search the scriptures to substantiate or confirm what was being preached and stated to me as being accurate. Conditioned by a culture that was dictated during my upbringing, I was encouraged not to question those in certain positions. And, if they provided the wrong answer, they were still considered to be right. Many days, I walked away needing more clarification or understanding, but I was too afraid to ask any questions. At times, there was much confusion about what I was seeing in comparison to what was being taught, said and acted upon by others. If they demonstrated or displayed a wrong action, I was told to excuse them of that inappropriate action and always act as if there was nothing wrong, regardless if it was immoral or went against the will of God. But as time evolved and I grew older, I found it necessary to question everything.

> *The righteous cry, and the LORD heareth, and delivereth them out of all their troubles. The LORD is nigh unto them that are of a broken heart; and saveth such as be of a contrite spirit. Many are the afflictions of the righteous: but the LORD delivereth him out of them all. He keepeth all his bones: not one of them is broken.*
>
> ~ Psalm 34:17-20

Seeking God and some sort of answer to confirm His plan for my life as well as His existence, I went from church to church in search of something. Anything! Suddenly, I found myself wanting to know everything there was to know about the history of religion and how it came to be that there were so many different denominations. After noting the differences, it also became very important for me to note the similarities. This gave me a greater understanding of diversity. Man observes differences and allows them to dictate his character and actions.

Due to our sinful nature, we often operate outside of the Will of God in developing prejudiced behavior and acting upon it in a negative manner, when we should embrace differences or diversity by learning from one another in love. In the end, God will judge us all the same on the basis of our choices as well as our actions and equally sentence us to Heaven or Hell.

So when they continued asking him, he lifted up himself, and said unto them, He that is without sin among you, let him first cast a stone at her.

~ John 8:7

Jesus died for the sins of us all, whether we all believe in Him or not. God has given us dominion and authority over our sinful nature. There is no "little I" (inferior) or "big I" (superior) in His eyes, regardless of our culture or ethnic background. He sees us all as being the same and possessing the same potential to do great things, no matter the color of our skin, gender, age or denomination. However, society teaches us that we not only need to fit a particular image to be destined for greatness, but our education also determines our level of potential. Not true! Your level of potential can extend beyond your education; there are some who have the education but fail to realize their potential. At any rate, never let yourself believe you are incapable of fulfilling a position because you lack the education others feel you should have to perform a task. When chosen or called by God for an assignment, He blesses you with the gifting to perform any function to accomplish the desired tasks. This gift is the anointing through the Holy Spirit that gives you the grace needed to complete what is required of you by God. To convince me of my calling, as well as the anointing that was upon me, God allowed a public display of the quickening of the Holy Spirit on Wednesday, November 29, 2006. (See the details as explained in the section entitled, "Testimonies."[7])

> *Neglect not the gift that is in thee,*
> *which was given thee by prophecy, with the laying*
> *on of the hands of the presbytery. Meditate upon these things;*
> *give thyself wholly to them; that thy profiting may appear to all.*
> *Take heed unto thyself, and unto the doctrine; continue in them:*
> *for in doing this thou shalt both save*
> *thyself, and them that hear thee.*
>
> ~ 1 Timothy 4:14-16

While I was seeking God like never before, with a great burning passion to have Him materialize in front of me for a question and answer session, Heaven and Hell got stirred up. The more determined I was to have a relationship with God and know Him for myself, the more determined Heaven was to assist me in making that happen, and the less determined Hell was to allow that to happen. Many days and many nights, I cried out to God for his assistance and prayed for wisdom, knowledge, understanding and the ability to discern. Often, I would ask Him to bless me with the wherewithal needed to accomplish my purpose here on earth. Remembering an ability I once had, I asked God to restore my dreams and visions that

---

7 Testify, testimony, testimonies: To bear witness. For more information, see http://biblehub.com/topical/t/testify.htm

I had feared so long ago to help me understand my purpose as I apologized for not appreciating the gift so early on in my life. Needing to know the truth about what was real and what was not in my surroundings, I lived in the library and bookstores, bouncing back and forth from the religion, history, philosophy and self-help to new age sections. If I was directed to it, I read it!

> *Get wisdom, get understanding:*
> *forget it not; neither decline from the words of my mouth.*
>
> ~ Proverbs 4:5

Shielded by God

Once I learned that God uses us according to our personalities and characters, I grew to understand He was pleased about my conquest for mental stimulation and undying thirst for living water; so He indulged me. In fact, I remember explaining to one person that God was teaching me and using me at an accelerated pace—not only in accordance to my willingness but also in alignment with my personality for growth. First, however, it was necessary for Him to awaken certain parts of my brain to be more receptive and spiritually sensitive to the invisible or what others take for granted.

On May 23, 2006, I experienced a transient ischemic attack (TIA), also referred to as a mini stroke, which was brought on by attending an unexpected meeting. This meeting, which disclosed the politics and distribution of money received from donors for tsunami victims, confirmed something I did not want to believe. As I sat and forced myself to continue to capture the notes from the meeting, I thought, *this is organized crime within a religious organization and these are ordained ministers who are not immune to corruption.* The overwhelming pain I felt, which I assumed was the result of no longer being able to stomach what I was hearing and wanting desperately to leave the employment of those who displayed the attitudes of themselves being gods, was actually me experiencing the symptoms of a stroke.

Trust in the LORD with all thine heart;
and lean not unto thine own understanding.

~ Proverbs 3:5

Please always remember! God does not seek to harm us or inflict us with pain. Sickness and disease do not come from God. In an effort to develop us and equip us for the fight, He will use the circumstances of your surroundings to guide you. It is Satan who comes to steal, kill and destroy us. As stated above, my quest for enlightenment stirred up Heaven and Hell. I was getting hungrier every day, every hour and every minute for the presence and power of God while my desire to stay away from people grew stronger. This limited the opportunity for negative influences and fear to control me. Fear is contaminated faith— **f**alse **e**vidence **a**ppearing **r**eal! In breaking away and overcoming strongholds, I was on my way to a breakthrough. Therefore, Satan had to disrupt God's plan to prolong or stop my blessings.

Knowing I was already near a physical breaking point in my life and in desperate need of deliverance or a divine intervention, Satan used the people, circumstances and situations (hypocrisy) in my immediate surroundings to ignite or influence a reaction (stress) for his satisfaction. However, God actually received the glory from allowing it to happen. God, noticing my heart, showed Himself strong on my behalf! Baffled by my medical prognosis, the emergency room doctor who was assigned to me said, "Ms. Mack, the test results confirmed a stroke, but there does not seem to be any physical signs or after effects in comparison to what the tests show. The only thing I can say is, it went as quickly as it came, and you are very lucky."

I responded, "No, not lucky—*blessed!*" That was God.

*Hold your peace, let me alone, that I may speak,
and let come on me what will.*

~ Job 13:13

Throughout this whole ordeal, I held on to the one thing I knew to be true: I believed God! My faith in God would not allow me to disbelieve He was going to see me through. He did not bring me as far as He had to leave me and not intervene on my behalf. I knew He had too much in store for me. Therefore, exiting the building, I kept my mind on God and did not give any thought to my pain. Because my best cure for anything that ails me is to isolate myself for peace of mind and a quiet environment, I was determined to go home, take a nice, hot bath and go to bed; however, not before attempting to access the extent of what was medically wrong with me.

Not accepting assistance from any of my coworkers, I promised I would drive myself to the nearest firehouse to get the opinion of an emergency medical technician (EMT) as to whether or not it was necessary for me to seek emergency medical attention before opting to go home. After explaining the events that had prompted my visit, they took my blood pressure and indicated they were going to take me to the hospital right away. Refusing to believe there was any cause for alarm, I did not allow anyone to drive me to the hospital. I thanked the EMTs and told them I was going to be okay. They cautioned me about the consequences of my actions in getting behind the wheel: should my symptoms persist, I may lose control of the car and possibly kill myself as well as others. After explaining that God was with me, I asked if it was also important for me to stay calm.

They said, "Yes!"

I then responded, "Getting into an ambulance at this point is only going to make me more anxious, but driving myself to the hospital while meditating on God and having a conversation with Him in prayer is going to get me through and keep me calm." I was shielded by God.

> *For thou,*
> *LORD, wilt bless the righteous;*
> *with favour wilt thou compass him as with a shield.*
>
> ~ Psalm 5:12

Signs, Wonders and Miracles

As I became more and more aware of my surroundings, I became spiritually sensitive to the heart and voice of God, but not until I became adamant about wanting to develop and cultivate a relationship with Him. In wanting to know God for myself, I also needed to know my purpose as it related to the Kingdom. "Ask and it shall be given" (Matthew 7:7). Discerning my surroundings, God revealed many things to me; things that were impossible to know in the natural, but through the supernatural, there were no limits. Imagine looking directly at a person (in the natural) and suddenly, you are allowed to see him for who he really is behind the mask (in the supernatural). You are allowed to see the invisible, which is the true heart of that person. Imagine, ironically, standing before you in the natural is a Lieutenant Colonel of The Salvation Army who also happens to be an ordained minister—*a sheep*. However, in the supernatural, standing before you is the Grand Wizard of the Klu Klux Klan (KKK)—*a wolf*. This is the image God used to reveal to me the character and personality of the man standing before me. "Beware of false prophets, which come to you in sheep's clothing, but inwardly they are ravening wolves" (Matthew 7:15).

The truth about this person was being revealed to me. Therefore, this individual was not going to treat me fairly under any circumstances, and I was not to expect to be viewed as being equal or a human being in his eyes. God did not want me wasting any unnecessary time believing him to be something he was not, nor did He want me to be emotionally bound by a situation that could potentially interfere with me not focusing on what He needed me to focus on!

Go your ways; behold,
I send you forth as lambs among wolves.

~ Luke 10:3

Following my stroke and upon receiving what I considered to be my first direct instruction from God to write a letter to the commissioner of The Salvation Army at the national headquarters, I needed to be certain this request was indeed from Him and not my ego. So I told God I was going to need a little more convincing if He wanted me to be obedient. Driving to work one Friday morning, on October 27, 2006, to be exact, at approximately 7:30 a.m., I received that confirmation. In a clear, thunder-like voice, God told me what He wanted me to do and what I was going to write in the letter.

> *Ye shall walk after the LORD your God, and fear him, and keep his commandments, and obey his voice, and ye shall serve him, and cleave unto him.*
>
> ~ Deuteronomy 13:4

My initial reaction to this wonderful experience was not one of fear but of extreme amazement and disbelief. Still surprised by what was happening, I asked God why He had chosen such a moment to speak to me. Why not in the house before leaving for work? While behind the wheel of a car, such a startling experience could have caused me to have a car accident. Speaking again, He commanded I look all around me. Right in the middle of rush hour traffic, in the heart of Old Town Alexandria, Virginia, God isolated me from the rest of the cars. It was as if time was standing still and there was no one on the road but me. I screamed at the top of my lungs, "God, it is you?

I understand! If you had spoken to me before I left the house, I would not have come to work."

Pulling into the parking garage of The Salvation Army National Headquarters, I was hyperventilating and trying desperately to compose myself. Letting my mind get the best of me, I thought, what a request. Not only had God given me a command, but He actually gave me the date I was to have the letter completed. Did God not give any consideration or thought regarding the consequences of me possibly losing my job in honoring His request? God had to take me from one state of being to another to get me to understand and believe that the invisible was more real than the visible. And no one could tell me that this was all in my head, even if they tried!

THE PAIN WE CAUSE OTHERS
EVEN AS CHRISTIANS

*But his flesh upon him shall have pain,
and his soul within him shall mourn.*

~ Job 14:22

September 8, 2008

Dear Father God,

What do I do with my pain? Sitting at the computer this morning, in review of the items I have written, I noted a letter (dated February 28, 1999) that I forwarded to Steve Young, the pastor of the Christian Missionary Baptist Church for All People that I was attending at the time. As I read that letter, it revealed the faith of my understanding. Such fortitude and strength in the midst of troubled times! It was You who instilled that in me! You always attempted to keep me grounded by allowing me to connect with images of You. In spite of my circumstances, You always gave me the determination and the will to go on and push through my pain!

When You envisioned me, You planted the seed that produced me. That seed developed and blossomed into the spirit You needed me to be to fulfill a purpose here on earth for the Kingdom. However, upon my birth, I became separated from You, and I lost my way. Because there was no remembrance of You, I also lost sight of my purpose. Born into a world that was already inhabited by many other spirits seeking to find their way, I knew, deep within my soul, I was different, and I did not belong here. Over time, if we are not careful in allowing our spirit to dominate over our flesh, our flesh can easily dictate our actions negatively. I, unfortunately, adapted to a way of life that was dictated by my flesh to include my way of thinking, which drew me further away from You. Confused about my existence and feeling so out of place, I became consumed by my surroundings, which soon clouded my judgment. I disregarded Your commandments and made choices that robbed me of my joy. *Void of joy, I let pain and grief overtake me!*

For my struggle is not against flesh and blood, but against the rulers, against the (principalities) authorities, against the cosmic powers of this present (world) darkness, against the spiritual forces of (evil) wickedness in the (high) heavenly places (Ephesians 6:12; paraphrased). The adversary, through suggestive subliminal manipulation, and my fears won my mind but not my heart, and I let myself fall prey to spiritual warfare, not knowing who I was or the side I was to choose. Nonetheless, with an aching and wounded heart, I overlooked the spirit that was controlling the flesh of those who wronged me. I then became one of the wounded amongst the walking wounded (spiritually weak and spiritually dead). But I had no desire to be like them. I lacked the desire to hurt others and do to them what they seemed so hell-bent on doing to me and many others in their path. Many nights, I cried out for You to take me home and remove me from this Godforsaken place. Unaware of Your plan for my life, I assumed You had abandoned me and left me here to die.

Through people and their influence, I allowed myself to believe I was incapable of accomplishing great things—to the point of wallowing in self-pity for far too long. So You see, I allowed myself to be deceived by people, places and things that were deliberately put in my path to create situations, circumstances and conditions I felt were too difficult to overcome. They were determined to limit my growth, strip me of my dignity and self-respect, and control me or push me into doing what they wanted me to do with no regard for my sense of integrity or my love for You. With each blow of negativity in the form of unkind words and physical and mental abuse to capture my soul, my pain grew intense! There was an attempt made on my life to kill me and to destroy that essence of You that dwelled within me. And then you reminded me that *He who is within me is far greater than he who is in the world*!

Such cruelty! God, I do not understand how people, Your children, could subject one another to so much pain and feel no remorse. How could a world claiming to be founded upon Your principles be so selfish and ruthless in their approach to humanity? By jockeying to prove one culture, race or individual is better than the other! Your children attempt to classify and label spiritualism by their own levels of importance and call it religion. Religion, simply put, is a man-made concept or system of guidelines, regulations and rules (dogma) to govern how one should worship You. No one should be able to put limits on how another person or individual should worship You! That task, should You choose, should be reserved for You! Unlike man, You don't condemn us; You redeem us and bless us with free will! Today, more than ever, Your children fight over who has the right to dictate another person's belief, which only serves to bring about more pain and destruction to themselves and others. Superficial qualities driven by materialism on the basis of want, lack, greed, racism and all the other characteristics that have nothing to do with You. Truth be told, they do not really know You at all! Wow, they haven't even a clue.

Still seeking to belong and hopefully connect with others, I sought refuge from so-called Christians, only to encounter more devastation that almost crippled me. The greater the pain, the more I wanted to distance myself from others in the world. I grew very tired and weary of those I presumed to have an ulterior motive in wanting to befriend me while using Your name in vain. Oh God, the hypocrisy! My heart felt shattered and broken into a million pieces. Clinching my heart, I cried out to You to protect it from the pain and cruelty that I would be made whole and not succumb to the bitterness. Longing to have You speak to me, I asked You to materialize and pull up a seat so we could talk. I had so many questions and was in desperate need of answers. Determined not to give up or give in, I not only asked You to rescue me. I decided I would stand and take my rightful place to fight for what I believed to be true.

Hearing Your voice was not only pleasing to my ears; it confirmed Your love for me. All these years, from ages seven to forty-seven, I thought You had forgotten me. *And thou shalt remember all the way which the LORD thy God led thee these forty years in the wilderness, to humble thee, and to prove thee, to know what was in thine heart, whether thou wouldest keep his commandments, or no* (Deuteronomy 8:2). After the planting of my seed, time was necessary for the harvest. In revealing Yourself to me, You gave me the evidence and the proof I needed to begin my long overdue healing through my belief in You. **Revelation after revelation, You brought clarity to my realization!** Your plan and purpose for my life was to strengthen and prepare me to walk with You through the death of my flesh over and over again. You renewed my spirit and my mind with the aid of my trials and tribulations.

You subjected me to wilderness experiences to bring me closer to You by opening my eyes to my surroundings. *Be sober, be vigilant; because your adversary the devil, as a roaring lion, walketh about, seeking whom he may devour* (1 Peter 5:8). These experiences gave me insight and knowledge of how not to be; knowledge that man cannot take from me or credit to his concept of education. The teaching You bestowed upon me surpasses man's ideology of education. You gave me wisdom and the courage to conquer my fears! You equipped me to teach others what You taught me in an effort to bring them closer to You. Experience is the best teacher!

You rescued me from a situation I thought was going to be the end of me, but not before giving me an assignment to fulfill. Reluctantly, at first, I allowed my flesh to hinder me from obeying You right away. I thought too much about the consequences of man rather than the consequences of my actions for failing to follow through with Your command. It must have been funny to see me going around in circles trying to figure out how I could disregard Your request. As I look back over that time in my life, I have to laugh too! You were so patient with me, though You were very adamant about what You had asked me to do. Crying and falling to my knees, I yelled out, "Why me!"

In a stern response that not only left me shivering but pierced my soul as you answered, "*Why not you?*"

Wow, that was all I needed! In keeping Your promise to me, it was now my time to prove my seriousness and commitment to You. So I put my procrastination, fears, and "What about me?" syndrome aside and I began to write the letter You asked me to prepare and forward to the Commissioner of The Salvation Army at the National Headquarters.

Through my writing came healing and cleansing. You have given me an assignment that not only benefits me, but it is for the benefit of the Kingdom to promote healing and cleansing for others as well. Through my pain from my experiences, You have given me stories to share with others. And through it all, You have been my rock! So, w*hat do I do with my pain*? I will continue to trust You with my heart, soul and mind, believing You will catch me as You always have, restoring my spirit as You allow me to draw from Your strength. Today and always, I call on the lion of Judah who has also healed my wounds. For I can do all things through Christ who strengthens me! Thank You, for loving me and reaching for me to lift me beyond myself. Thank You, for freeing me and creating me to be the me that I am—diverse, unique and complicated. Thank You, for allowing me to see myself through Your eyes. Thank You, for sustaining me. Radical for You with no regrets! Unwilling to go backwards, but forever forward! Sharing and growing! As You minister to me and through me, I happily minister to others.

With excitement and an open willingness to be a living sacrifice, I rededicated my life to You. *Therefore I urge you, brethren, by the mercies of God, to present your bodies a living and holy sacrifice, acceptable to God, which is your spiritual service of worship. And do not be conformed to this world, but be transformed by the renewing of your mind, so that you may prove what the will of God is, that which is good and acceptable and perfect* (Romans 12:1:2 NASB). As I minister to others, I minister to myself.

Love,
Your Faithful and Willing Pupil

> *Therefore, since Christ suffered for us in the flesh,*
> *arm yourselves also with the same mind, for he who has suffered*
> *in the flesh has ceased from sin, that he no longer should live*
> *the rest his time in the flesh for the lusts of men,*
> *but for the will of God.*
> *For we have spent enough of our past lifetime in doing the will*
> *the Gentiles – when we walked in lewdness, lusts, drunkenness,*
> *revelries, drinking parties, and abominable idolatries.*
>
> ~ 1 Peter 4:1-3 NKJV

PROCLAIM LIBERTY TO THE CAPTIVES

THE UNFOLDING OF MY PURPOSE, MISSION AND VISION

The Spirit of the Lord GOD is upon me; because the LORD hath anointed me to preach good tidings unto the meek; he hath sent me to bind up the brokenhearted, to proclaim liberty to the captives, and the opening of the prison to them that are bound.

~ Isaiah 61: 1 KJV

August 26, 2010

God has created each and every one of us *with a purpose for a purpose* and sent us to earth to carry out our assignments. Jeremiah 1:5-7 AMP states, "'Before I formed you in the womb I knew you [and approved of you as My chosen instrument], And before you were born I consecrated you [to Myself as My own]; I have appointed you as a prophet to the nations.' Then I said, 'Ah, Lord God! Behold, I do not know how to speak, For I am [only] a young man.' But the Lord said to me, 'Do not say, 'I am [only] a young man,' Because everywhere I send you, you shall go, And whatever I command you, you shall speak.'"

When we were in our rightful form (spirit) and mind, we gladly accepted our assignments with honor and gratitude according to the Will of God. But something unexpected happened to us through a chain of events as dictated by this world. *"Be not afraid of them [their faces], for I am with you to deliver you," says the Lord* (Jeremiah 1:8 AMP). The greater the distance or separation from God (who is our light [John 12:35-36]), the greater the void in our *mission*! In allowing our flesh, through the temptations of this world, to rule our decisions, we lost our objectivity (our light) and became blinded by darkness. *To be blinded by darkness is like having a forgotten vision.* This darkness not only consumes our light, it clouds our judgment and threatens to destroy the very essence of who we are by stealing our mind! And should this darkness succeed, Heaven's wrath is against all who *suppress the truth* about God by living as they please (Romans 1:18-25) and falling prey to the enemy through the *captivity of our mind*. Lost identity! God very adamantly tells us to "be not conformed to this world: but be ye transformed by the renewing of your mind, that ye may prove what *is* that good, and acceptable, and perfect, will of God" (Romans 12:2 KJV).

Don't become so well-adjusted to your culture that you fit into it without even thinking. Instead, fix your attention on God. You'll be changed from the inside out. Readily recognize what he wants from you, and quickly respond to it. Unlike the culture around you, always dragging you down to its level of immaturity, God brings the best out of you, develops well-formed maturity in you.

~ Romans 12:2 MSG

Being in the right mind is very important! We should stay alert (be sober), keep our eyes open (be vigilant; watchful) and be ready for spiritual warfare because our adversary (also referred to as the enemy, Lucifer, Satan, the devil or the anti-Christ) is roaming around pacing like a hungry lion, desperate to find anyone he can destroy (1 Peter 5:8). He is an expert at manipulation and trickery! His main objective is to steal your joy, kill your spirit, lead you astray (away from God), hold your mind in bondage and take your body hostage as leverage to have complete control over you. But God has given us something much greater to lead us, guide us and sustain us. He has given us a set of written instructions to live by—the Bible. Then He took time and care in molding that word and giving it life.

The living word, Jesus Christ, through obedience and sacrifice, honorably carried out his assignment with passion and purpose to proclaim liberty to the captives. Never wavering or losing sight of his objective, he spoke with clarity when spreading the gospel of truth and walked boldly as a living testimony in showing us how to escape and conquer captivity, withstand evil (Be not overcome of evil, but overcome evil with good [Romans 12:21 KJV]), and love our neighbors as if loving ourselves (Mark 12:31). Jesus came so we could have a real, eternal life—a better life than we could ever imagine or dream of. He came so we could have abundance (to the full, till it overflows) (John 10:10). *For God so loved the world, that he gave his only begotten Son, that whosoever believeth in him should not perish, but have everlasting life* (John 3:16). Jesus is the good shepherd who giveth his life for (us) the sheep (John 10:11).

It is time to wake up! Follow Christ and do that which He has done. Hear the voice of God and obey. **In Psalm 27:1, David says,** "The LORD *is* my light and my salvation; whom shall I fear? the LORD *is* the strength of my life; of whom shall I be afraid?" True followers deny their own will to obey the commands and teachings, which they hear Him, the Holy Spirit, speak to them from the word in their heart. *For God hath not given us the spirit of fear; but of power, and of love, and of a sound mind* (2 Timothy 1:7).

*My sheep hear my voice,
and I know them, and they follow me.*

~ John 10:27

Accepting the Call

While fellowshipping at 7:45 a.m. with Unity Life Christian Ministries on Sunday, August 15, my heart was overflowing with truth as the word was being preached and came forth through Minister Sharon Capel. Hebrews 11:1 was the topic:

"Now faith is the substance of things hoped for, the evidence of things not seen." Many times, I not only questioned my faith, but I also wanted to understand everything there was to understand about faith. More importantly, I knew I wanted nothing else than to please God and do all of what was asked of me. Listening to Minister Capel, I understood my faith was greater than I had imagined, and I could feel the presence of God all around me. Such power and force emanated through my feet and traveled up my legs and out through my hands. It was like fire shut up in my bones. God was anointing me and preparing to use me in a mighty way.

It is the spirit that quickeneth;
the flesh profiteth nothing: the words
that I speak unto you, they are spirit, and they are life.

~ John 6:63

Joining hands to pray, I could feel an electrifying sensation in my hands and noted an intense increase of heat. I could not help but wonder if the people holding my hands could feel it too. As I let go and prepared to leave, I was given a word from a visiting prophet who spoke to my heart, and the tears began to flow. If you know and understand how God works, you know He does not always give you complete sentences, but he speaks to you in parables: "All these things spake Jesus unto the multitude in parables; and without a parable spake he not unto them" (Matthew 13:34).

> *A **parable** is a short tale or story that illustrates universal truth; one of the simplest of narratives. It sketches a setting, describes an action, and shows the results. It often involves a character facing a moral dilemma, or making a questionable decision and then suffering the consequences.*[8]

Upon being told my gift was healing and my purpose was in my testimony, I was also told to read Psalm 61 or Isaiah 61 to learn more. Exiting the church, my mind desperately tried to recall every word and event that had taken place. I wasn't ready to go home! My spirit was soaring and my excitement was leading me to seek more praise and worship.

Upon sitting to join the fellowship service that was already in progress at Living Word Ministries, Pastor Carter directed the congregation to turn to Matthew 7:13-14. After reading this scripture, I felt God telling me I was on the right path and then I was drawn to Isaiah 61. As I began to read, my mind raced from Isaiah 61:1 and back to Matthew 7:13. At that point, I knew in my heart that I could no longer run from God and deny the calling on my life. God confirmed what I was feeling by bringing to my remembrance a dream I had on December 31, 1999. It was a vision of my future, but this was unbeknownst to me at the time.

---

8   http://www.liquisearch.com/parable/characteristics

> **Vision**: *A dream-like experience that God uses to deliver a message to someone.*

> *Who hath saved us, and called us with an holy calling, not according to our works, but according to his own purpose and grace, which was given us in Christ Jesus before the world began, But is now made manifest by the appearing of our Saviour Jesus Christ, who hath abolished death, and hath brought life and immortality to light through the gospel.*
>
> ~ 2 Timothy 1:9-10

Sharing My Dream: God's Vision for My Life

Background: Prior to the year 2000, the beginning of the millennium, there was much talk about a problem for both digital (computer-related) and non-digital documentation to include data storage resulting from using a four-digit year and changing over to an abbreviated two-digit year. It was believed that computers instrumental in regulating the operation of energy (power), water and sewer plants would cease to function, and people would be without water and electricity.

One minute past midnight and going into January 1, 2000, there is no source of electrical power anywhere in the world. The world is completely void of light and is entirely consumed by darkness. The doors to the prisons, hospitals and insane asylums are disarmed. People are panicking; there are hordes of people stampeding through the streets. There are rats and rodents everywhere.

I, on the other hand, have been given the responsibility to go into each and every area to direct people to safety (higher ground), toward the light. Upon bringing one group to safety and passing the torch to a person to head the group, I go deeper and deeper into dangerous areas, coming out unharmed, only to hand off more people and go in again. The deeper I go, the more difficulty I face in finding my way out of the maze to bring others to safety. Just when I think I have made a wrong turn and meet a dead end, I see someone who escaped the insane asylum that I passed earlier in my rescue mission. Though he is not able to speak, we are able to communicate in spirit. I learn he was sent to help guide me out to safety.

Upon waking from my dream, I felt empowered and spiritually alive! What I did not realize was the unfolding or revealing of my purpose through my dream. God spoke to me about my mission! HE showed me how victorious I was to not only overcome and conquer the captivity of my mind, but I was to assist in reaching others for their breakthrough in this same area.

Lessons Learned

- Don't judge a book by its cover.
- God is Spirit. He is neither male nor female.
- God does think as the world thinks.
- God is no respecter of persons (Acts 10:34). God views us all as being equally important and of value.
- God sees our full potential and wants nothing but the best for us.

Each one, reach one, teach one! As we are freed, it is our responsibility and purpose to help free others for the uplifting and glorification of the Kingdom.

What is your purpose, your mission and your vision?
Are you walking in your destiny? Are you obeying God? Do you know who you are? You are the child of the highest God, and your deliverance is in your praise.

What Is Fear?

False Evidence Appearing Real!

The devil tries to use fear and other forms of roadblocks to control us and keep us from learning who we are in Christ. If he is successful at deceiving us, he is able to keep us from our destiny.

Proclaim:[9]

1. to declare publicly, insistently [with passion], proudly [boldly] or defiantly [in truth and love] and in either speech or writing: announce
2. to give outward indication of: show

Liberty:

Freedom! Give me liberty or give me death!

---

9 https://www.merriam-webster.com/dictionary/proclaim

Captives:[10]

1. taken and held as or as if a prisoner of war

2. kept within bounds: confined

3. limited[11] – confided within limits; restricted or circumscribed; held under control of another but having the appearance of independence

4. mental incarceration – owned or controlled by another concern, thing or entity and not fully operating in the capacity in which you were created. (*Enslaved in your mind by your mind!*)

---

10 https://www.merriam-webster.com/dictionary/Captives
11 http://www.dictionary.com/browse/limited

THE MEANING OF FAITH

*Now faith is the substance of things hoped for,
the evidence of things not seen.*

~Hebrews 11:1

September 2, 2010

Upon birth, we come into this world clinging to those we grow to depend on to protect us and nurture us. Through this connection or union, we not only take on their preconceived beliefs and thoughts; we incorporate the values, norms and thought patterns dictated by the condition of our environment. As we further develop, we become more aware of our surroundings, including the actions of man, as we struggle to choose sides in acknowledging the difference between right and wrong. Noting how different you are from what you have been exposed to, your mind seeks to break free from captivity.

> *You neglected the Rock who begot you,*
> *And forgot the God who gave you birth.*
>
> ~ Deuteronomy 32:18 NASB

Confused by man's teaching through something called education, I once believed I needed to see, touch, feel and taste a thing to know it to be real. If it was not tangible or concrete as dictated by the world, it didn't exist. After questioning and attempting to make sense of what I was seeing and feeling, it did not meet with my approval and only contributed great pain, grief, anger and frustration to my effort toward understanding. In need of hope and refusing to believe I was placed on this earth and left to perish, I told God I had many questions that needed answers, and I wanted so desperately for Him to materialize before me, pull up a chair, and sit with me face to face so we could talk. For I was starting to lose faith and trusted no one to do what was right!

> *Wherefore, if God so clothe the grass of the field,*
> *which to day is, and to morrow is cast into the oven,*
> *shall he not much more clothe you, O ye of little faith?*
>
> ~ Matthew 6:30

Little did I know that my desire to seek God's face was the beginning of a relationship I never knew nor realized was possible! *But seek ye first the Kingdom of God, and his righteousness; and all these things shall be added unto you* (Matthew 6:33). I called on God, and a Spirit I could not see with the naked eye spoke to the measure of my faith, which was the size of a mustard seed. Jesus said to his disciples, "Because of your unbelief: for verily I say unto you, If ye have faith as a grain of mustard seed, ye shall say unto this mountain, Remove hence to yonder place; and it shall remove; and nothing shall be impossible unto you" (Matthew 17:20). That experience and the quickening of the Holy Spirit canceled my disbelief and became the beginning of a walk of faith not based on sight (Corinthians 5:7) but one based on trust and the desire to please God.

> *And without faith it is impossible to please him,*
> *for whoever would draw near to God*
> *must believe that he exists*
> *and that he rewards those who seek him.*
>
> ~Hebrews 11:6 ESV

Because I wanted to see and hear, God not only revealed Himself to me, but He allowed me to see myself through His eyes. Through my out-of-body experience, my spirit separated from my soul and hovered over me for protection as my soul pleaded to God for mercy and deliverance. I have learned and come to know within my heart the very essence of who I am and the necessity of *faith*! To have faith is to have confidence, belief and trust in something or someone, seen or unseen. But that someone is not just anyone; it is God, the Father, the Son and the Holy Ghost. I now know—regardless of the world's view—that which you cannot see *is* more real than that which you can see. You have to be willing to open your heart and your mind to Him who is within you. He who has faith to see shall see. He who has faith to hear shall hear.

> *So then faith cometh by hearing,*
> *and hearing by the word of God.*
>
> ~ Romans 10:17 KJV

In short, faith is about your willingness and ability to shift your state of consciousness. It is about making an attempt or conscious effort to rewind or unwind your mind. Let go of everything you believed to be truth and reprogram your mind to replace that which is false truth with God's truth—the living word. My reward is my deliverance and peace beyond peace to know the Father, my Creator, for myself. It is the faith of knowing and believing that God is the same yesterday, today and always. Faith is the belief in the promise of God, the promise of things hoped for and the *covenant* on the basis of God's unconditional love for us!

> *Therefore being by the right hand of God exalted,*
> *and having received of the Father*
> *the promise of the Holy Ghost, he hath*
> *shed forth this, which ye now see and hear.*
>
> ~ Acts 2:33

This world and everything in it is temporal and put in place to take your mind off of that which is really important. It is set up in a way to redirect your focus, your emotions, your actions and bring about destruction to our being—the very essence of who we are or were meant to be—to keep our soul from waking up and realizing who we are! It is an attempt to keep us from realizing our God-created purpose, which is carrying out our mission (assignment) and connecting to the vision. Yet, we know that God will make everything that happens to us in this life come out to our eventual good, as long as we trust Him and remain true to the purpose for which He called us (Romans 8:28). In the world, not of the world!

> *For everyone who has been born of God overcomes the world. And this is the victory that has overcome the world—our faith.*
>
> ~ 1 John 5:4 ESV

God wants nothing but the best for us! He has given us everything we will ever need to succeed, live and enjoy life. How? *God has predestined those who believe in Him to be like His Son, so He gives us the help we need. Therefore, whoever accepts His Son, He justifies; those whom He justifies, He intends to glorify* (Romans 8:30 Clear Word Bible). We must hold onto our faith and the belief that God is forever with us to walk with us and carry us along the way, if necessary. So shout with joy and claim your victory! I can do all things (done decently and in order) through Christ who strengthens me. *And Jesus said unto him, Go thy way; thy faith hath <u>made</u> thee whole. And immediately he received his sight, and followed Jesus in the way* (Mark 10: 52 KJV).

> *And all things, whatsoever ye shall ask in prayer, believing, ye shall receive.*
>
> ~ Matthew 21:22

The Covenant Promise: First, there is a very distinct difference between a contract and a covenant. Although both are and can be a written or verbal agreement, a contract may specify a particular period to include a beginning and an end date with conditions or agreed upon guidelines; a covenant is a permanent unconditional arrangement between two or more people or groups of people involving promises on the part of each individual or group. A biblically based or divine covenant is an agreement between God and His children as initiated by God, and it covers certain promises made by God to His children. Jeremiah 32:40 states: *And I will make an everlasting covenant with them, that I will not turn away from them, to do them good; but I will put my fear in their hearts, that they shall not depart from me.* The "covenants of promise" as referenced by Ephesians 2:12 are God's guarantees that He will provide salvation in spite of people's inability to keep their side of the agreement because of sin—a true testament of God's unconditional love for us. (For more information, please reference the Nelson's Compact Bible Dictionary, http://www.thomasnelson.com/compact-bible-dictionary, Thomas Nelson, Inc., 2004).

FROM REVELATION TO REALIZATION

BITTERSWEET

This testimony is true. Therefore rebuke them sharply, that they may be sound in faith, not devoting themselves to Jewish myths and the commands of people who turn away from the truth.

~ Titus 1:13-14 ESV

January 15, 2008

Let Me Tell You Why I Love Him!

He loves me in spite of myself—in spite of my pride and the ego that dwells within. He never gave up on me even when I allowed outside influences or challenges in my life to cause me to question His existence. When faced by the worldly actions of so-called Christians and drama in the church, I allowed my faith and belief in Him to lessen, and I turned my back on Him. Titus 1:16 states, "They profess to know God, but they deny him by their works. They are detestable, disobedient, unfit for any good work." But He never gave up on me because He knows me better than I know myself! He believed in me when no one else did. When people made attempts to tear me down, He lifted me; and He keeps lifting me. When man speaks harshly of me, He encourages me to go on. When I am too bruised and tattered to go any further, He carries me! Oh God, how I love Thee. You sacrificed Your only Son for me. Why should I not give my life to Thee? My fire burns brightly!

Oh God, You have taken me through extensive trials, tests and tribulations since what I believed to have been the beginning of my wilderness in January of 1994. That was thirteen years ago, but if I was to include my first unemployment experience, due to no fault of my own, in 1990, that would equate to seventeen years of You molding me. In August of 2000, You placed me in an organization and kept me there for seven years, against my will. "Wherefore seeing we also are compassed about with so great a cloud of witnesses, let us lay aside every weight, and the sin which doth so easily beset *us*, and let us run with patience the race that is set before us" (Hebrews 12:1). However, today, I now know and understand that You have had a profound plan for my life even before I was conceived that included this transition in my life. I could never imagine You loving anyone like me. You are my everything!

> *Before I formed thee in the belly I knew thee; and before thou camest forth out of the womb I sanctified thee, and I ordained thee a prophet unto the nations.*
>
> ~ Jeremiah 1:5

He has touched my life in such a mighty way that there are not enough words in all the universe that I could use to express, explain or describe my gratitude, joy and yes, even sorrow. Bittersweet is how I see thee, but awesome indeed is He! The loss of my hair at the age of fourteen was the beginning of Him using me, strengthening me and preparing me for His Kingdom. He put me in situations I never believed I could defeat. This is what my pastor would refer to as "life-altering encounters" orchestrated by God's hand. For once in my life, I am no longer afraid to say "no" to those who try to control me. So if He is for me, who can be against me?

Formula for Success

Failing to plan is planning to fail!

A recent sermon revealed, (a) you will always be met with opposition in life and (b) it is important to remember, you will always encounter two kinds of people in your journey: those who will help you succeed and those who will hinder you from succeeding or oppose you at every turn. I often wondered if those who oppose you seek to make it their life's mission or if they are so out of touch with God and self that they are unaware of what they are doing. In my heart, I would like to believe that there is a level of unawareness as opposed to believing this is the path they have chosen. Perhaps they have so often succeeded at being the opposer that they have forgotten to examine the morality of their actions, thus rendering their disposition as being second nature. The first would be breathing.

Often, your first instinct or desire in times of trouble may be to join them if you cannot beat them. You stand for something or you fall for anything! Romans 5:2 states, "By whom also we have access by faith into this grace wherein we stand, and rejoice in hope of the glory of God." Because of God and His plan for my life and how He sees me, I would rather lead than follow, unless I am following God. When God puts you in a particular situation, you're there to influence the situation, not to have the situation influence or change you. So in answer of the question, why did I feel the need to get baptized again? It was my way of showing God my love for Him. It was my way of honoring His presence in my life and saying I rather stand for something than for nothing at all. It was and is my personal commitment and rededication of my life to Him—an open acknowledgment of a conscious awareness and understanding of who I am in the Kingdom of God. Not who or what people want me to be! It's about knowing my purpose as it relates to the Kingdom and telling God that I intend to do more than just go through the motions. It's an unbreakable covenant instead of a breakable contract. A new lease on life!

All the paths of the Lord are mercy
and truth unto such as keep his covenant and his testimonies.
The Secret of the Lord is with them that fear him;
and he will shew them his covenant.

~ Psalm 25:10, 14

My Year of Transition: 2007

To whom much is given, much is required. And obedience is the only key. What a simple request from someone who has given so much! To sacrifice Your only Son, who gladly gave His life to bless us with Salvation. Jesus was His name, but He had many responsibilities and held many positions with a title that corresponded to each accordingly. And thou shall call His name, Jesus, Prince of Peace, Mighty God, Wonderful, Counselor, Sanctifier, Root of David, Word of Life, Advocate, Lamb of God, Bread of Life, Great Physician, Author and Finisher of our Faith, Ancient of Days, Daystar, Lord of All, Son of God, Gift of God, Living Stone, Chief Cornerstone, Shepherd and Bishop of our Soul, King of Kings, Righteous Judge, Light of the World, Emmanuel, Restorer, The Vine, Head of the Church, Bright Morning Star, Rose of Sharon, Governor, Sun of Righteousness, Deliverer, Burden Bearer, Lion of Judah, Rock of Offense, The Hope of Glory, The Hidden Treasure, Root of Jesse, The Resurrection and Life, City of Refuge, Strong Tower, Faithful Witness, Prince of Life, The Messiah, Mind of God, Chief Shepherd, Horn of Salvation, Everlasting Father, The Alpha and the Omega, and my favorite one, Savior.

After looking to the wrong source for my validation, yet again, I allowed man to disappoint me and rob me of my joy. Crying out to God, I told Him I needed more and desired more. I needed Him to confirm His existence. I needed Him to speak to me! For example, John 10:1-5 of the message Bible explains it like this, under the caption of He Calls His Sheep by Name: *Let me set this before you as plainly as I can. If a person climbs over* or through the fence of a sheep pen instead of going through the gate, you know he's up to no good—a sheep rustler! The shepherd walks right up to the gate. The gatekeeper opens the gate to him and the sheep recognize his voice. He calls his own sheep by name and leads them out. When he gets them all out, he leads them and they follow because they are familiar with his voice. They won't follow a stranger's voice but will scatter because they aren't used to the sound of it.*

I needed to hear and know His voice. I wanted and needed to know my purpose to move toward fulfilling my destiny. *To every thing there is a season, and a time to every purpose under heaven* (Ecclesiastes 3:1). I felt this was the time and season for me to know how I could serve Him and please Him. If He loved me enough to sacrifice His only begotten Son as well as to give me the desires of my heart, surely it was time for me to seek Him with all of my heart.

> *Delight thyself also in the Lord;*
> *and He shall give thee the desires of thine heart*
>
> ~ Psalm 37:4

I needed to know Him for myself and experience the realness of His presence. I am analytical by nature, so God spoke to me in a language I could understand. *Now concerning spiritual gifts, brethren, I would not have you ignorant* (1 Corinthians 12:1). When He gave me a command, He backed it up supernaturally. Imagine hearing what no one else hears, seeing what no one else sees, and feeling what no one else feels; imagine having a personal, private relationship with God, the

Father, the Son and the Holy Ghost. God, because of You, I not only know what I know when I know it, but I know that what I know, others don't think I know, but I know it when You feel I should know it through the Holy Spirit that dwells within me. So why do I love Thee? Because I can do all things through Christ who strengthens me!

Discovering your Destiny

Discovering your destiny is about digging down deep within yourself to search your heart to see the real you. It is about letting yourself connect to the one who has given you life and breath to cultivate a personal and private relationship with Him outside of your relationship with man. People will attempt to tell you about Jesus, the Father, the Son or the Holy Ghost; however, there's nothing like developing a relationship with Him for yourself to realize your dream. You should never stop dreaming and believing in His purpose for your life. *According to my earnest expectation and my hope, that in nothing I shall be ashamed, but that with all boldness, as always, so now also Christ shall be magnified in my body, whether it be by life, or by death. For to me to live is Christ, and to die is gain* (Philippians 1:20-21). As I am hearing God, believing God and obeying God as He uses me for the Kingdom in carrying out His will, He is honoring His promise as it relates to the purpose of my life. He is propelling me to my destiny. He has allowed my enemies to be my footstool.

For example, as summarized by my pastor, Joseph was hated by his brothers because he was the most loved by his father (Jacob/Israel): *And Joseph dreamed a dream, and he told it his brethren: and they hated him yet the more* (Genesis 37:5). Does not your Father love you? His brothers despised him so much that they sold him into slavery. One night, the wife of Joseph's owner, Potiphar—an officer of Pharaoh and captain of the guard—tried to seduce him. Given the righteous, upstanding gentleman he was, Joseph refused the wife's advances and fled. Potiphar's wife, feeling rejected by Joseph, lied and accused him of rape. Joseph was put in prison for a crime he did not commit, however, the Lord was with him. While in prison, Joseph interpreted the dreams of two of his fellow prison mates, Pharaoh's chief butler and chief baker. When the chief butler and chief baker were released, they mentioned to Pharaoh their knowledge of an interpreter of dreams, Joseph.

> *And Pharaoh said unto Joseph, Forasmuch as God hath shewed thee all this, there is none so discreet and wise as thou art: Thou shalt be over my house, and according unto thy word shall all my people be ruled: only in the throne will I be greater than thou. And Pharaoh said unto Joseph, See, I have set thee over all the land of Egypt.*
>
> ~Genesis 41:39-41

In the words of my former pastor, John K. Jenkins, Sr., of First Baptist Church of Glenarden, life is full of cycles. Do not get depressed or upset when your life is in the low cycle. The low cycles are needed to open your eyes to choices or issues needed to prepare you for your destiny. It's all in how you deal with those issues. Haters in your life indicate that you have God's hand in your life. When somebody does not like you or attempts to hold you back, it's God's way of telling you He does not want you to be conformed to their way of life.

God is your solid rock. Learn to rely on Jesus and draw your strength from the Rock of Offense. God's unchanging plan has always been to adopt us into His family by bringing us to Him through Jesus Christ (Ephesians 1:5). Stand and reach for Him! Wait on the Lord. Be of good courage and He shall strengthen thine heart; wait, I say, on the Lord (Psalm 27:14). He will never make you promises and leave you in the cold. He only wants to help you fulfill your fullest potential by living out your destiny.

> *Jesus answered and said unto them,*
> *Verily I say unto you, If ye have faith, and doubt not,*
> *ye shall not only do this which is done to the fig tree,*
> *but also if ye shall say unto this mountain, Be thou removed,*
> *and be thou cast into the sea; it shall be done.*
> *And all things, whatsoever ye shall ask in*
> *prayer, believing, ye shall receive.*
>
> ~ Matthew 21:21-22

The Breaking of Day

I, like Jacob, have been wrestling with God, and I refuse to let Him go. *And Jacob was left alone; and there wrestled a man with him until the breaking of the day. And when he saw that he prevailed not against him, he touched the hollow of this thigh; and the hollow of Jacob's thigh was out of joint, as he wrestled with him. And he said, Let me go, for the day breaketh. And he said, I will not let thee go, except thou bless me* (Genesis 32:24-26). He has blessed me with new beginnings! Man may demote you, but God lifts you every time and promotes you. Because of God and His love for me, I am seeing the breaking of day.

Imagine receiving a call from a prospective employer. Only this time, (1) you do not hear the customary "you are overqualified" for the position, (2) there are no attempts to offer you a higher position other than what you submitted your resume for, and (3) there are no attempts to offer you a lower paying salary than what you had requested in your cover letter. To your disbelief, you are told to stop referring to yourself as just a clerk, just a secretary or just an administrative assistant. You actually hear, "You are much more than that regardless of the titles that have been affixed to you. In looking at your accomplishments as well as your previous responsibilities from one job to the next, not only are you much more than that, but you have done much more than that!" God was moving on my behalf! I could not hold back the tears; I cried!

Do I need to tell you again why I love Thee? He has given me more than enough proof of His love for me. He challenges me to be the person He knows I can be. He challenges me to be the person He has created me to be. He challenges me to do the things that only I can do as it relates to His purpose for my life. He challenges me to utilize the gifts that He has bestowed upon me through the Holy Spirit in carrying out His will. He challenges me for His Kingdom. His only requirement is obedience. So why would I not be willing to be a living sacrifice for Him? He sacrificed His only Son to save me.

God, I thank You for Your hand in my life and allowing me to see traces of You as You move on my behalf. You only want the best for me, so I'm trusting You with my life. Bittersweet You may be but loving just the same!

Amen

OPPOSITES: NO IN-BETWEENS!

For I am in a strait betwixt two, having a desire to depart, and to be with Christ; which is far better.

~ Philippians 1:23

October 25, 2007
Revised September 20, 2015

Just a Thought

Knowledge through revelation, learning and growing is very important to obtain wisdom! Notice I didn't say "education."

You can accept what others tell you or you can listen to God.
You can rely on your inner emotions/ego/self.
You can read research and seek knowledge.

Ask and it shall be given and received.
There is an opposite for and to everything.

The opposite of Good is Bad.
The opposite of God, who represents Good, is
Lucifer (aka Satan), who represents Bad.
Lucifer was the Angel of Light and God's right hand
Before he decided to attempt to overthrow the Kingdom of God.

God has given us all free will—
The right to choose and make our own decisions or choices.
We can choose God or we can choose Satan.
We can choose to be Good or we can choose to be Bad.

Choosing God for me would mean choosing to be righteous.
Choosing Satan would mean choosing to be evil.

Medicine was created and developed in a laboratory and
Referred to as science or pharmacology.
Medicine is engineered to imitate the properties of herbs,
A natural resource (plant) from God.
Medicine can be used to save a life,
Or it can be used to take a life.

Medicine can be used with the best intentions
Or with the worst intentions.
Therefore, herbs can be used with the best intentions
Or with the worst intentions.
However, herbs are better for us than that which is created in a lab by man.

Medicine is exploited by man,
Controlled by large industries with assistance
From the government and peddled to us
No differently than drug dealers on the street.

One drug dealer has been given a legal right to operate while the
Other is considered to be an illegal merchant committing an
illegal act.
Neither distributes the other (legally or illegally) without an
associated cost.

You can choose to be for God or against Him.
To everything, there are pros and cons.
Opposites, no in-betweens!
Hot or cold, not lukewarm!

In thy getting, get understanding.

Again, just a thought! I'm teaching as I learn.

> *Now therefore go,*
> *and I will be with thy mouth,*
> *and teach thee what thou shalt say.*

~ Exodus 4:12

IF ONLY YOU COULD WALK A MILE IN MY SHOES!

*I indeed baptize you with water unto repentance:
but he that cometh after me is mightier than I,
whose shoes I am not worthy to bear:
he shall baptize you with the Holy Ghost, and with fire.*

~ Matthew 3:11

June 23, 2008

How dare you tell me what to feel or
How to think as if you were me or even a part of me.

How dare you tell me
I don't see what I see,
Feel what I feel, smell what I smell or
Hear what I hear.

Do you know the pain of being judged
By the color of my skin?
Or even being limited by prejudiced
Views that attempt to define who I am?
Do you know me? Really know me?

Do you see the tears in my eyes when
Your actions attempt to reduce me to less
Than the human being that I am?
How dare you belittle me because my skin is different.
I fail to let you continue to humiliate me!

Who are you to say that I deserve
Less than you because you are so determined
Not to accept me for me because of the color of
My skin or the limited views you have of me?

How dare you attempt to silence me
For being willing to speak up and out for myself as you
continue to be determined to keep me in the Rightful place
that you deem so appropriate.

Beyond the color of my skin, have I not flesh that bleeds red when it is pierced?
Like the color of Christ's blood when they pierced his side with a spear!

If only you could walk a mile in my shoes;
You probably wouldn't even last a step!

More than forty years later, no mule or forty acres.
Torn from my mother and never knew my father.

Sold into slavery as spectators probed and prodded.
Wall Street now, but not long ago, a slave trade center with me as a commodity.

Just a constant reminder of the
Struggle of my ancestors as the words of
Martin Luther King, Jr. ring loud
And clear in my inner ear:
"Free at last! Free at last! Thank God
Almighty, I'm free at last."

Free from physical bondage, yet not completely free from persecution
Or the racist views of the past that seem to raise its ugly head whenever it is fed.

Fueled by rage and anger that keeps growing
With ignorance through power and politics.

How can such a tree, used as a form of capital punishment
That took the life of many of my brothers and sisters,
Be more important than justice for the Jena Six and others?

Justice for one and not for all!
Not even equal by far!

If only you could walk in my shoes!
Tarred and feathered, I say not!
Oh, such cruelty!

Strange fruit hanging from a tree with lifeless limbs,
No one bothered to see me as a spirit;
No, not even a human being.
A spirit full of life;
A spirit full of hope;
A spirit just longing to be free!
I AM somebody with a soul!
I AM a child of God,
Regardless of the color of my skin.

Redeemed by His blood and saved by His grace,
I AM more than a conqueror.
Being healed from my past as He sustains me
To be the Queen I was meant to be,
I continue to endure through this unfortunate iniquity!

Loved by Him who created me!
Cherished by Him who dwells within me!
Accepted by Him who is a part of me!
Strengthened by Him who truly cares for me!

For Him, I live and for Him, I die
With Him, not only walking alongside of me;
He feels my pain, He sees my scars and
My scares that others so quickly dismiss or deny!

If only you could walk a mile in my shoes;
Perhaps, it would be more than just an apology!

An apology of truth; an apology of action with
No hint of the past. An apology that shows promise and change,
Not one of broken words for political gain
With no evidence of human change in the name of humanity.

Until then and only then, can you honestly say
You know what it is to walk a mile in my shoes?

ME THE CREATION!

*Even every one that is called by my name:
for I have created him for my glory,
I have formed him; yea, I have made him.*

~ Isaiah 43:7

June 25, 2008

Dear God,

Thank you for creating
The me that I AM!

For years, I cried out in shame
For the me that I was,
Not knowing that you treasured the me that I AM.

Through your eyes, I have not only learned
To embrace the me that I was, but I now love the me that I AM.

Feeling different, I examined my heart and assumed
I needed to be like those in the world to shield
My heart from hurt and pain.

Different is who I AM; different is how you made me.
With no hair to comb and skin aglow, I can be who I AM.

Thank you for creating me to be
The me that I AM.

For I AM *fearfully* and *wonderfully made*!

> *I will praise thee;*
> *for I am fearfully and wonderfully made:*
> *marvellous are thy works; and that my soul*
> *knoweth right well.*

~ Psalm 139:14

TIMING IS EVERYTHING!

Thou shalt arise, and have mercy upon Zion:
for the time to favour her, yea, the set time, is come.
~ **Psalm 102:13**

November 17, 2008

It is my observation that the world we live in, for many years, has been going backwards in time as opposed to moving forward. *But they hearkened not, nor inclined their ear, but walked in the counsels and in the imagination of their evil heart, and went backward, and not forward* (Jeremiah 7:24). Though change has been welcomed in more ways than one, there should be a concerned objective of growth and prosperity for *all*. However, some have become so comfortable with the present situation (to include wickedness and living in sin) that they would prefer for things to remain the same, mainly because they are responsible for manipulating the system in their favor and give no thought to equality or justice for a diverse population (all). Unfortunately, the longer things remain the same, the greater the possibility of it taking too long to undo the wrong to then make a change. Nonetheless, in order for change to take place, it must be perceived and accepted with a willingness to change. *Let him eschew evil, and do good; let him seek peace, and ensue It* (1 Peter 3:11). And that change would have to encompass a shift in the way we think about a committed effort and constitute having an open mind rather than a selfish, narrow-minded viewpoint.

Worthless thinking produces worthless acts. Be transformed by the renewing of your minds (Romans 12:2) and do not be conformed by this world system (operated on the basis of a Babylonian System or Roman Empire) with the objective to divide and conquer on the basis of control through deceit and exploitation. For, without a doubt, these are critical times, and the election of Barack Hussein Obama to the position of the president of the United States could not have come at a better time. However, we must be careful not to view him as being anything other than a man who God has blessed and allowed this victory. Unequivocally, this is the beginning of the change we *all* need, provided President Obama, being influenced by the right spirit, makes the right choices and does not succumb to the influence of false idols or the historical nature of this nation's power base. As referenced in Pastor John K. Jenkins's sermon entitled "A Clarion Call to Prayer," those who have a relationship with God, the Father and Jesus Christ, should pray for the protection and leadership of President Obama. He will be met with many challenges and welcomed as well as unwelcomed. Therefore, I pray that he is able to overcome strongholds with aid from the Holy Spirit through wisdom, knowledge, understanding and discernment and does not succumb to the wearing down tactics of those purposely put in place around him to infiltrate and interfere with a change that will benefit us *all*.

> *Because of the house of the LORD our God*
> *I will seek thy good.*
>
> ~ Psalm 122:9

Being a good leader is not about leading; it is about accountability. Responsibility goes hand-in-hand with integrity, which seems to be lacking in the average person today. Many who have previously taken an oath to lead us through our government have replaced or compromised their integrity by doing evil and wicked things, giving no thought to the consequences of their actions. How can responsibility be taught when so many people in the world (in high places) pride themselves on doing the opposite of what they know to be right, just and fair? Look at the role of our governing body over the years: government officials, executives and major leading corporations have repeatedly encouraged irresponsibility and have referred to it as being business savvy. Some of these same people have questioned Barack Obama's ability to lead this nation and not on the basis of his potential, but out of fear of possibly not being able to persuade him to lead their way. There are others, as in the past, who question his ability on the basis of skin color and refer to it as a lack of experience.

What level of measurement was equated to George W. Bush's ability to lead this nation? Could it be his association or connection to his father? How are leaders of major corporations who are responsible for the collapse of our economy chosen for the positions you deem to be so credit worthy? We seem to give credence to toxic leaders who have misrepresented the truth time and time again, but we fail to give a man who won the election, fairly and outright, the same opportunity that has been given to many others before him. Let's not forget about the election that was believed to have been acquired falsely.[12]

Does President Obama not deserve to receive the same support from *all* who claim to love America? There was an evident and recognizable division that threatened to enslave us all as we headed toward self-destruction under our former presidential leadership. And no one took the chance or was willing to look at the dangers of this world objectively to see the truth, even as it was being presented right before our eyes. And yet, you gave one man your blessing to condemn us all and deny another who wants nothing more than to make things right by attempting to help a nation that is without a soul to recover what was lost.

> *Let every soul be subject unto the higher powers.*
> *For there is no power but of God:*
> *the powers that be are ordained of God.*
>
> ~ Romans 13:1

For the first time in quite a while, not since John F. Kennedy or Jimmy Carter, in my opinion (with no intent of taking anything away from the accomplishments of Bill Clinton), have we had a man in office with whom we could be proud to represent us *all*

---

12   http://www.michaelparenti.org/stolenelections.html

collectively. President Barack Obama set a precedence for others to follow! Though I am sure there are many who would disagree, this man demonstrated through his handling of his election and the charisma of his debates that he is, indeed, spiritual and passionate about leading us in a positive direction. *Blessed is the people that know the joyful sound: they shall walk, O LORD, in the light of thy countenance* (Psalm 89:15). He was unmovable and steadfast; he had an agenda and remained on target. Regardless of his competition and the direction they were trying to impose upon him, he stayed focused. He did not allow his mind to be manipulated, and he did not allow his emotions or the emotions of others to control the situation. *Therefore, my beloved brethren, be ye stedfast, unmoveable, always abounding in the work of the Lord, forasmuch as ye know that your labour is not in vain in the Lord* (1 Corinthians 15:58). Although he is just a man, his candidacy offered hope to many and ignited anger in others. Once again, many of us were reminded of the history of a nation that does not extend equality to us all as we continue to see that racism is alive, striving and well. Similar to the behavior and attitudes of those in our past, those same neverending attributes are present today in those who have condemned the potential of the first elected African American president of the United States before he was officially sworn into office.

> *And whatsoever ye do, do it heartily,*
> *as to the Lord, and not unto men; knowing that of the Lord*
> *ye shall receive the reward of the inheritance:*
> *for ye serve the Lord Christ.*
>
> ~ Colossians 3:23-24

Endless attempts have been made to uncover and even create, if possible, anything that could discredit President Obama to the very last minute of his inauguration. An attorney, Philip J. Berg, alleged that Obama was not a U.S. citizen, thus making him ineligible for the presidency. Berg claimed Obama was either a citizen of his father's native Kenya or became a citizen of Indonesia after moving there as a small child, but there was no initial thought given to his mother's nationality or citizenship in addition to the location and recording of his birth, regardless of the nationality of his father or stepfather. Why would they insult the intelligence of such a man to think he, Obama, would put forth the time and effort to seek the position as president of the United States and not do his homework to ensure the necessary compliance, required in accordance to guidelines and policies, before announcing his intentions to run?

As many conspiracy theories go, in regard to the direction of politics in America, I am sure there was no stone left unturned by those who were opposed to Obama running for president. I can only imagine they spared no expense to have him or those within his family investigated in hopes of finding something to hold over his head that they could use as blackmail to prevent him from succeeding in the election or perhaps hope to use during his reign as president at a more appropriate time. It is also my guess that there was nothing to uncover that was worth using, so much thought and consideration were given to the possibility of linking him to the scandal of Illinois governor, Rob Blagojevich, provided Blagojevich was willing to perjure himself to unjustly implicate President Obama. Why else would so much time lapse in determining a plan of action for bringing federal corruption charges against Blagojevich? There was no time wasted or expense spared when the government authorities decided to set up the former mayor of Washington, D.C., Marion Barry.

Blagojevich was allegedly caught on tape criminally compromising himself. Marion Barry, who was also caught on tape criminally compromising himself, was taken into custody and charged immediately. Considering the history of corruption among government officials in the past, what is the probability of there being a classified report documenting all the indiscretions and illegal activities not only involving Blagojevich but others within the Congressional House of Representatives? I am inclined to believe, truth be told, that not one representative of the House is without spot or blemish; they have put themselves in a category above us all to do what they wish and not necessarily what is right. It may not be publicized, but that does not mean it is not a truth. Yet President Obama openly takes the responsibility and shoulders the blame for the indiscretions revealed about members in his cabinet—something that has nothing to do with him personally! Often, these are people who are in a better financial position than the citizens they serve as a government official; not only are they able to pay their taxes, but they live lavishly with enormous mortgages and no threat of foreclosure. However, they take unnecessary chances like many of their peers because they know they have been able to get away with corrupting the very same government they have been commissioned to service. In the name of crooked politicians, time and time again, we see those who are instrumental in making laws while breaking those same laws, but they enforce the law as it applies to the citizens of the United States.

> *Doth God pervert judgment?*
> *or doth the Almighty pervert justice?*
>
> ~ Job 8:3

In an effort to stimulate the economy, President Obama introduced his stimulus package as a plan to benefit us *all*—unlike the emergency-type government bailouts that only served to rescue major corporations and banks that were in jeopardy of going under but offered no measures to ensure they would apply the funds wisely. Congress's inability or unwillingness to address such issues prior to President Obama being in office is an indication of not only their loyalty to the Bush administration, but it demonstrates a shared responsibility for the corruption that seemed to be prevalent and growing, to include those they seemed more concerned about rescuing than the citizens they should have been serving to protect. In other words, there seems to be a greater loyalty to doing wrong rather than doing what's right in the name of protecting the interest of the wealthy—corporations! Initially, with good intentions, Congress saw the need and aided in devising and developing a plan to create government agencies for protecting the rights and civilities of the people, such as the Equal Employment Opportunity Commission, Environmental Protection Agency, Federal Trade Commission, National Highway Traffic Safety Administration, Department of Justice, Securities Exchange Commission and Regulatory Affairs, just to name a few, as a measure to ensure compliance in certain areas of the government and private sector businesses. Long before the Bernie Madoff and Wall Street scandal, such agencies as the Securities Exchange Commission failed to perform their purpose.

Unfortunately, the rise in unaccountability across the board has damaged us in more ways than one. The United States as a whole failed to serve the citizens, and President Obama is attempting to put us back on track. However, as indicated above, change would have to encompass a change in the way we think for a committed effort to constitute having an open mindset rather than a selfish and closed, narrow-minded viewpoint. An example would be the display by our Congress in not wanting to agree to President Obama's stimulus package. In my opinion, their reluctance is an indication that Obama's plan is viable and would work if put into action. Therefore, the unwritten objective that is most evident through their actions is to keep him from succeeding at doing what they know for certain he is more than capable of doing—being the president the United States needs—especially with all the problems that were handed to him. But time will tell! Nonetheless, in accordance to God's grace, he seems to be up for the challenge even though so many are expecting him to fail, including those who sit with him in Congress! So I ask, where is the integrity?

When thou shall beget children, and children's children, and ye shall have remained long in the land, and shall corrupt yourselves, and make a graven image or the likeness of any thing, and shall do evil in the sight of the Lord thy God, to provoke Him to anger.

~ Deuteronomy 4:25

As a political ploy in the history of America, we have received many promises of change that have never been carried out. We have also been given the illusion of change that never saw the light of day. People, unfortunately, have been more afraid of change than they have been willing to admit. They have allowed themselves to fear the unknown while being held captive in a place and time that showed no evidence of change ever being a possibility. We have been in bondage or captivity for so long that we forget what it is like to be free. Freedom does not come without a price, but the price of bondage that limits the mind and renders us helpless to ignorance is even greater. There is a thin line between influence and control.

How great is your influence? Are you motivated to influence others in a positive manner? Or in a negative manner to incite fear as a means of control? Does your anger and hatred for another go so deep that you are willing to leave nothing for the future of your children? Are you that driven by greed and pride that you are unwilling to work together as a nation to achieve a common goal that would be beneficial for us all in the long run? That sense of selfishness and desire of controlling wealth in limiting others from receiving it contributed to the collapse of our economy. And today, one of the major issues besides the rise in incompetent, cynical, evil, political and corporate leaders, which is the leading root cause of the collapse of the national economy due to what was allowed by those in power, is social injustice on the basis of inequality.

When a world disaster strikes, it affects us all. Hurricane Katrina did not seek to single out victims on the basis of inferiority over superiority. Katrina, and many disasters like it, bring about devastation to all in its path and levels the playing field on the basis of equality. Yet, unlike those affected by the 2004 Sumatra, Indonesia tsunami, the Katrina victims—who are citizens of the United States—did not receive the same level of timely and humanitarian aid. Many suffered horrifically and went without adequate living quarters, food or water due to man's lack of humanity and inequality or double standards as a prevalent and ever-increasing sign of a selfish (me-first) and uncaring population, which is proving to be the norm in this day and age. The role of the government is to *serve the needs of its citizens* as best as the economy will allow, but there seems to be something extremely wrong with that concept in the sense of it being nonexistent. Too often, we have been forced to watch corrupt executives grease the palms of greedy politicians in exchange for written policies and laws that illegally take away the rights of citizens. For the past eight years, the Bush administration has made great strides in condemning us to the past. Blinded by darkness, we have allowed ourselves to be held captive to the past as we continue to wage war against each other based on prejudices that have taken our minds off of the importance of humanity and justice for *all*.

> *But he that doeth wrong shall receive for the wrong which he hath done: and there is no respect of persons.*
>
> ~ Colossians 3:25

Did no one pay attention to President Obama's efforts to bring us all together as a nation during his inauguration through a concept called **unity**? Perhaps we were all too busy condemning his choices to notice the significance of his intent to recognize diversity. In a general sense, diversity is living in a global community that encompasses and embraces differences in characteristics such as age, culture, disability, education, ethnicity or nationality (race), gender, language, religion, sexual orientation and marital or parental status. *Behold, the days come, saith the Lord, that I will perform that good thing which I have promised unto the house of Israel and to the house of Judah* (Jeremiah 33:14).

> *To every thing there is a season, and a time to every purpose under the heaven: A time to be born, and a time to die; a time to plant, and a time to pluck up that which is planted; A time to kill, and a time to heal; a time to break down, and a time to build up; A time to weep, and a time to laugh; a time to mourn, and a time to dance; A time to cast away stones, and a time to gather stones together; a time to embrace, and a time to refrain from embracing; A time to get, and a time to lose; a time to keep, and a time to cast away; A time to rend, and a time to sew; a time to keep silence, and a time to speak; A time to love, and a time to hate; a time of war, and a time of peace.*
>
> ~ Ecclesiastes 3:1-8

WHAT IS FREEDOM TO ME?

*Stand fast therefore in the liberty wherewith
Christ hath made us free, and be not
entangled again with the yoke of bondage.*

~ Galatians 5:1

June 4, 2008
Revised December 11, 2008

Freedom to me or being free
Is being consciously aware of God's love for me in spite of me,
Having the ability to coexist *in* this world and not be *of* the world.

Freedom is not allowing myself to be consumed by dogma
Or the need to prove that I AM better than anyone else
Through the idea of feeling as though I must always
Live my life in constant competition.

Freedom is knowing the definition of being non-pretentious
And truly walking in that freedom to the point of not attempting
To be something that I AM not.
Instead, toward my destiny!

Freedom is being true to myself! But more importantly,
Attempting to live up to the expectations of God, not man.
When God corrects me, He does not condemn me or belittle me,
Making me free to make mistakes yet able to learn through
My mistakes to the point of growth and maturity.
Free from your view of me and free to embrace
The sight of me through the eyes of God.

You call my newfound freedom arrogance;
I call it having confidence in God.
You perceive to limit my value as a human
Being. I perceive to follow God because
With Him, there are no boundaries.
You attempt to trap my mind and enslave my body,
But it is God who frees my mind and saves my soul.

I AM free to accept me, love me
And see me as God sees me
In spite of the limitations of my mind
As my self-esteem is being repaired
By Him who truly loves me
While my mind is being freed
To love you in spite of your negativity toward me.

For all things are possible through the one who has called me!

And I can do all things through Christ who strengthens me.
He who is in me is greater than he who is in the world.

CHOSEN BY GOD

*Ye have not chosen me, but I have chosen you,
and ordained you, that ye should go and bring forth fruit,
and that your fruit should remain: that whatsoever
ye shall ask of the Father in my name, he may give it you.*
~ John 15:16

Man would have me to believe that I AM worthless and Incapable of success. Being worthless would mean my existence Is meaningless and void of purpose with no reason for living.

Being incapable of success would mean
I allowed man to dictate my level of wisdom and
Knowledge that is immeasurable beyond his imagination.

And yet man would have me to believe that my connection
To God is only possible through him as he determines
What I should and should not know
To be the true word of God.

Having a limited connection to God with man as my
only medium
For communication would mean that there is no need for change
Through the renewing of my mind to change or improve my
way of thinking.

Accepting man's interpretation of God's word would mean
I have not spiritually matured to know man is attempting
To deceive me into perverting God's truth
For man's own personal gain.

Chosen by God, I was called to rise to a position
Of being his voice, eyes and ears through the anointing
Of the Holy Spirit. Being chosen by God, rather than
choosing God,
Is far more important than man can even conceive
Or hope I'll realize as he attempts to control me.

Chosen by God, I AM destined for greatness,
But man's lateness for a genuine relationship with God
May cost him an eternity in Hell.

SPIRITUAL WARFARE

*For we wrestle not against flesh and blood,
but against principalities,
against powers, against the rulers of the
darkness of this world,
against spiritual wickedness in high places.*

~ Ephesians 6:12

January 14, 2009

Do I cower into a corner or do I arm myself and fight? You cannot allow the situations of this world or its Babylonian systems of government to dictate your circumstances. Allow yourself *not* to accept the lies through negative influences. *Fight the good fight of faith, lay hold on eternal life, whereunto thou art also called, and has professed a good profession before many witnesses*(1 Timothy 6:12). It is not over until God says it is over. It is not done until God says it is done. Stand firm and be strong, knowing God is with you always. When given an assignment or mandate from God, it is to be carried out until He gives you another or takes you home.

In Every thing give thanks:
For this is the will of god in Christ Jesus concerning you.

~ 1 Thessalonians 5:18

Not having much of a real relationship with God, I allowed negative influences from others to invade my mind. Their issues became my issues as I found myself being consumed and bound by strongholds. Struggling to break free only increased the challenges and deepened my frustration. Determined to control me, they wanted me to believe in their god and question not their doctrines of ill repute. Others like me either gave up or gave in as they made countless efforts to fit in. Joining forces with the evil rulers of the unseen world of darkness who have committed themselves to serving Satan in attacking the children of God in this world, they assisted in my torment to occupy my mind and oppress me. Those I thought knew the word and will of God only deceived me into believing they followed Jesus Christ. Did they realize the price of selling their souls would one day prove to be a fatal choice they would wish they had never made? And yet they pretended to have my best interest at heart, including the heart of God, as they contributed to my pain and rejoiced in my agony. Little do they know, they will be haunted for years to come, with no eternal rest in sight! By falling prey to the tricks of the enemy, they resisted not his temptation for a temporal taste of delusional, instant gratification to lure and capture their flesh.

My flesh and my heart faileth: but God is
the strength of my heart, and my portion for ever.

~ Psalm 73:26

Fighting desperately to hold on, I refused to conform. For I knew in my heart there was something greater than this darkness that wished to draw me in. Coming in the night, many were deceived. Their precious life void of breath and water—near or in sight! Searching for the light, I knew my rescue would be near; if I wouldst thy just believe. So seeking His face with intense determination to escape my strongholds, He drew me closer into the light and away from the darkness to a neverending supply of living water to quench my thirst. Developing a relationship that grew stronger and stronger as I spent more time with Him, I noticed a joyful and peace-filled spirit that surpassed all my understanding.

> *And fear not them which kill the body, but are*
> *not able to kill the soul: but rather fear*
> *him which is able to destroy both soul and body in hell.*
>
> ~ Matthew 10:28

Being showered with His gifts was a confirmation of His love for me and my salvation. With the aid of my spiritual senses (sight, hearing, touch, smell or taste), I was allowed to see beyond what the visible eye could see to know things in the supernatural that others in the natural could only ever dream. I walked from one office to the next, discerning (or distinguishing) of the spirits (see 1 Corinthians 12:10) who were really wolves disguised as sheep fooling the church, to uncover what God knew I must for the edification of the church. With the intensity or change of each foul smell, there was an increased tugging at my soul, which revealed the hierarchy of their ranking sent from Hell to capture souls! Just as there is order in the natural, there is order and hierarchy in the spirit world. And, unfortunately, many camouflaged non-believers hidden amongst believers at different levels and **sifted as wheat** (see Luke 22:31) threatened to take away my armor of Christ, but pleading His blood, I stood steadfast for the fight. Equipped with prophesy, and at first unaware of my calling, I identified ordained ministers not only deceiving the church but bringing souls not to God and steering them away to serve a lifelong sentence of being condemned in Hell.

For thou wilt not leave my soul in hell;
neither wilt thou suffer thine
Holy One to see corruption.

~ Psalm 16:10

Teaching me the art of war, God strengthened my mind as He strengthened my soul. I was blessed to be a blessing to others and later came the speaking in tongues. I was becoming the warrior I was created to be for the uplifting of the Kingdom, as God allowed me to see me through His eyes and heart.

Before I formed thee in the belly I knew thee;
and before thou camest forth out of the womb I
sanctified the, and I ordained thee a prophet unto the nations.
Then said I, Ah, Lord God! Behold, I cannot speak:
for I am a child.
But the Lord said unto me, Say not, I am a child:
for thou shalt go to all

> *that I shall send thee, and whatsoever I*
> *command thee thou shalt speak.*
>
> ~ Jeremiah 1:5-7

Where is your heart? When you are required by God to follow Him and question not, will your heart, soul and spirit say yes? Will you follow Jesus to be like Him who was not only the Son of God, but born a man in the flesh on earth to be an example of how we should live? *Be ye therefore followers of God, as dear children; and walk in love, as Christ also have loved us, and hath given himself for us and offering and a sacrifice to God for a sweet smelling savour* (Ephesians 5:1-2). Oftentimes, we give the illusion to the outside world to be something that we are not and proclaim to be Christians who are void of the character of Christ, thus we are living a lie. One lie often leads to another and another; therefore, over time, living a lie not only makes it harder and harder to separate from the truth, but you may find it harder and harder to conceal it from those you wish to deceive in an effort to project an image for a desired outcome. However, everything you do is seen by God! That which is done in darkness always comes to light.

> *From high in the skies* GOD *looks around,*
> *he sees all Adam's (descendants) brood. From where he sits*
> *(in heaven) he overlooks all us earth-dwellers.*
> *He has shaped (created) each person in turn;*
> *now he watches (sees all) everything we do.*
>
> ~ Psalm 33:13-15 MSG

I BELIEVE!

But I didn't believe the reports until I came and saw it with my own eyes. I wasn't even told half of it. Your wisdom and wealth surpass the stories I've heard.

~ 1 Kings 10:7 GW

January 29, 2009

God attempts to reach you so many times, but your flesh, which seems to be influenced by His adversary, attacks your emotions and creates feelings that control your mind to push you in the opposite direction—far away from Him. You, crying in silence and wanting so desperately to believe in the existence of a higher power (God), envision Him riding to your rescue on a white horse to save the day and set things forever right. Yet, all you notice from day to day is nothing but chaos and immoral decay.

And God looked upon the earth, and, behold, it was corrupt; for all flesh had corrupted his way upon the earth.

~ Genesis 6:12

Striving to do what's right, you stumble across many traps that are set with the intention of destroying your mind to make you docile and mindless like a puppet on a string. Most times, you are successful to avoid the snares, but other times you are greeted by roadblocks and strongholds that keep you at bay for far too long, like getting lost in a maze with no end in sight. Occasionally, you meet people along the way who are genuinely sincere, so you let down your guard in the celebration of hope. With hope in tow, you quickly forget to cover your heart and come across another person who is disguised as a friend. Blindsided by hope and the love for your fellow man, who was actually a wolf pretending to be a sheep, you realize you lowered your guard much too soon without a net to catch you!

They also that seek after my life lay snares for me: and they that seek my hurt speak mischievous things, and imagine deceits all the day long.

~ Psalm 38:12

Feeling hurt and bamboozled, you give in to your emotions while being determined to trust no one—not even God—ever again. Your hurt turns into sorrow and your sorrow into pain. Falling and sinking deeper, you wonder why you bother to do what's right when so many of the unrighteous people around you seem to prosper just the same. You tell yourself to be like the rest, but something inside of you tells you that just ain't so! Tumbling downward, you go deeper into a sea of depression controlled by guilt and anguish. Being down a lot longer than you were up is going to take much healing should you be determined not to revisit your past. Searching for a lifeline, you make several attempts to pull yourself up. Knowing it will take a miracle, you are too ashamed of your actions to call on the one person you know could help you. In your fragile state and afraid to move on, you wallow in self pity all the more, wishing you hadn't blamed God for the confusion in your life.

> *What is my strength, that I should hope?*
> *and what is mine end,*
> *that I should prolong my life?*
>
> ~ Job 6:11

Perhaps hearing the sound of His voice will cause you to come alive, yet hearing that audible voice only makes you more suspicious about your mental state. God's adversary is hard at work in your mind, telling you that it is impossible to trust what you cannot see. God allows you to smell fear and wickedness when you enter a room. Running from one room to the next, you ask yourself, what is that grotesque stench in the air? Trying to make sense of it all, you still run from one room to the next only to detect and feel something different. This time you are not greeted by a smell, but you notice the presence of an all-consuming, unfriendly energy. After thinking back to a series of three books that were written by Dr. Rebecca Brown,[13] I was

---

13 See http://www.harvestwarriors.com/#

inspired to appreciate the blessing of being able to discern (or distinguish) spirits through the gifting of the Holy Spirit that dwells within.

> *But the eyes of the wicked shall fail,*
> *and they shall not escape,*
> *and their hope shall be as the giving up of the ghost.*
>
> ~ Job 11:20

Unfortunately, the darkness surrounding you will not give an opening to any speck of light. Your spiritual insensitivity will not allow you to see beyond the visible to acknowledge the supernatural powers of God. However, if He has any chance at all of bringing you back to Him, He knows He must try with all His might. Attempting to undo the damage of His adversary, He pitches one lifeline after the next. Your pain becomes His pain, and His permissive will release you from an environment you no longer wish to endure. Imagine God loving you so much that He not only anoints you with the Holy Spirit, but He activates the gifts to help you along your journey. *Since we have gifts that differ according to the grace given to us, each of us is to use them accordingly: if [someone has the gift of] prophecy, [let him speak a new message from God to His people] in proportion to the faith possessed; if service, in the act of serving; or he who teaches, in the act of teaching; or he who encourages, in the act of encouragement; he who gives, with generosity; he who leads, with diligence; he who shows mercy [in caring for others], with cheerfulness* (Romans 12:6-8 AMP). Distraught about your disbelief and lack of faith in His existence as a result of all the negative things you have encountered in your life, you start to feel discouraged and God continues to make several attempts to draw you closer still.

> *Now the God of hope fill you with all joy*
> *and peace in believing, that ye may abound*
> *in hope, through the power of the Holy Ghost.*
>
> ~ Romans 15:13

Wrongfully thinking He let you down so many times before, you know you must trust Him, for only He can help you. Putting aside your pride, you reach for faith and ask for God's forgiveness as you believe in love again. I believe!

> *Through faith we understand*
> *that the worlds were framed by the word of God,*
> *so that things which are seen were not made*
> *of things which do appear.*
>
> ~ Hebrews 11:3

◆

> *Who against hope believed in hope,*
> *that he might become the father*
> *of many nations, according to that*
> *which was spoken, So shall thy seed be.*
>
> ~ Romans 4:18

DIVERSITY BY DESIGN

*It seemed good to me also, having
had perfect understanding of all things from
the very first, to write unto thee in order, most
excellent Th-eop-'i-lus. That thou mightest know
the certainty of those things, wherein
thou hast been instructed.*

~ Luke 1:3-4

February 8, 2009

What started out to be a general U.S. Department of Energy, online, on-the-job training course about diversity in the workplace helped to give me a more organized and structured view concerning the issues of cultural differences in America! Sometimes referred to as the melting pot, diversity has been defined in many ways. From a narrow and more legalistic view that focuses on Equal Employment Opportunity (EEO) laws to a broader approach, which is the collaboration of similarities and differences to achieve personal, professional and organizational goals in the workforce, relative to unique perspectives and abilities. Remember, diversity is the reality of living in a global community that encompasses characteristics such as age, culture, disability, education, ethnicity or nationality (race), gender, language, religion, sexual orientation and marital or parental status. The United States is a native-English speaking country; however, to embrace diversity, we must begin to accept and recognize all cultures as well as their native speaking languages. Ironically, we claim America was founded on Christian principles, but we do not attempt to investigate, research or emulate Christian love in favor of all people. We have entered into a period in time where everything seems to be acceptable and no one challenges anything (not even the church that compromises biblical truths to incorporate world views). You can have an awareness of differing viewpoints or enter into a friendship with someone whose cultural beliefs differ from yours without compromising your beliefs at all. The problem arises when you attempt to force your beliefs on someone else by insisting they denounce their beliefs to adopt yours. Free will is a gift that was given to us *all* from God as a confirmation of His love. However, people attempting to play God do not hesitate to strip us of that free will each and every day by subjecting us to a form of control—control on the basis of having and exercising a Jezebel spirit.

> *That Christ may dwell in your hearts by faith; that ye, being rooted and grounded in love, May be able to comprehend with all saints what is the breadth, and length, and depth and height; and to know the love of Christ, which passeth knowing that ye might be filled with all the fullness of God.*
>
> ~ Ephesians 3:17-19

In my opinion, racism, among other isms, has evolved into a form of religion in America that encompasses racial profiling and police brutality. Experiencing racism and discrimination myself on the basis of an individual's misconceived notion on more than one occasion within the workplace for the past thirty-eight to forty years of my life is something you never get used to. Each encounter brought insurmountable pain; pain I wish on no one; pain I am adamant not to inflict upon anyone. As I am reminded of that pain for one reason or another—being a woman (gender), black (race) and bald (physical appearance as a result of a medical condition)—it is my intent not to do to others what has been done to me. I have witnessed many minorities who have been victims of hurtful situations of discrimination discriminate against other minorities, thus condemning them to the same fate all in the name of wanting to be accepted by their abuser. What a vicious web we weave!

*Therefore all things whatsoever ye would
that men should do to you, do ye even so to them;
for this is the law and the prophets.*

~ Matthew 7:12

Extremely disturbed about having to confront prejudiced attitudes and behaviors within an internationally recognized religious organization, I noted numerous civil suits brought against TSA for discriminatory practices with no win in favor of the victims. Given what I presumed to be the nature of their business—soul winning on behalf of God as a church—they have been successful at covering up their indiscretions in addition to having the law on their side as they continue to exploit others. *Now the things which I write unto you, behold, before God, I lie not* (Galatians 1:20).

> Andrew Edimo, a native of Africa who was employed by TSA-NHQ as an information technology assistant, had a very strong accent and heavy tongue. Though I never had any problems understanding him, one person in particular indicated it was not acceptable. As a controlling tactic or strategy that was exercised by the former national treasurer and secretary for business administration, the Lt. Colonel, salary increases or raises were deliberately withheld from Andrew each and every year unless he agreed to take English and diction classes or resign—whichever came first. Having worked within the area of human resources for approximately ten years or more, I not only viewed this as a form of harassment, but it was clearly a case of discrimination. Andrew's immediate supervisor, who was distraught by the decision, explained she valued Andrew's professionalism, loyalty and work ethic. Confiding in me to determine if such a practice was legal, she also indicated Andrew's job performance and level of detail was outstanding. The Lt. Colonel had issues with Andrew's supervisor's nationality as well but not to the extent of Andrew's. Eventually, after more than five years of employment, Andrew resigned and, approximately one to two years later, so did his supervisor.

- Linda, a practicing Jehovah Witness who does not celebrate holidays in the non-spiritual, commercial way, was harassed by the national social services department head for a similar reason: refusing to compromise her religion to attend a Christmas luncheon or birthday celebration. The objective of this department head/officer (ordained minister), under the influence of a Jezebel spirit, was to bully Linda through a means of control to get her to resign or to operate outside of her will to comply with what they wanted. Wanting disparately to assist Linda in any way I could, I suggested she speak to my supervisor, the HR director, to file a formal complaint. But it was I who was asked by my supervisor to stay out of it. It is not my nature, however, to sit back and do nothing upon seeing an injustice being done to another, regardless of the color of their skin, national origin, religion or sexual orientation. That is not who I am. Considering Linda's medical history with multiple sclerosis (MS), I pleaded with her to find other employment as quickly as possible. The stress created by this situation was compromising her health and increasing her symptoms. Realizing this was actually a normal occurrence within the work culture to harass, manipulate and violate the civil rights of their less-than-desirable employees at will, as if it was a type of sport, was what I considered to be a pattern or modus operandi (MO). This prompted me to not only question this less-than-Christian environment but to observe my surroundings more closely.

Side Note: I have had the pleasure of being in touch with each of the above individuals after their departure from the Salvation Army. Andrew still works in the area of computers but has since moved to Ohio. Jane is a successful entrepreneur who owns a gym in the Washington metropolitan area. Linda currently lives in New York near her parents, who have assisted her with her MS. Unfortunately, her bout with MS is up and down. After her departure from The Salvation Army, her health confined her to a wheelchair. She later wrote The Salvation Army National Headquarters for assistance in any way possible; she was refused. Talk about being humble enough to ask the organization that wronged you for assistance. Like for many of us who suffer at the hands of abusive people, especially so-called Christians, it dampens your spirit. However, after much deliberation and time with God as well as family, your spirit is restored.

- Immediately following Linda's departure, there was a need to fill her former position, not to mention a need to prove a point to those who were aware of the situation concerning Linda. So it was the social services department's way of saying, we cannot only do what we want, but we can find anyone to replace her because there are a number of available people with her skills who are just dying to work here. Mila was hired for the position though she lacked the qualifications needed to perform the duties of the job to its fullest potential. Mila was told she would not only be given ample time to learn the position, but she would be given the opportunity to receive the necessary training needed to enable her to do her job. Hearing such a statement during an interview offers a ray of hope and gives you a sense of respect for your new employer that they would encourage growth. However, not knowing the complete truth tends to set you up for a fall. Mila was there just long enough for the suspicion concerning how Linda was harassed and forced to resign was no longer talked about and ceased to exist, but then it was Mila's turn to feel the wrath of not being able to read or write according to the standards of what The Salvation Army deemed was acceptable. Mila was not born or raised in the United States; however, she had been here long enough for her accent not to be noticeable. Unfortunately, she did not grasp the full understanding of the English grammar in her writing, which presented a problem and she did not have the skill level needed to perform the duties of her job prior to her being hired for the position. Mila was terminated and told it was taking her too long to catch on. During her ordeal, Mila and I bonded, as I offered my assistance to prepare her resume while also attempting to counsel her about God and who He really was as opposed to what was being demonstrated to her by this so-called Christian organization.

But when I saw that they walked not uprightly according to the truth of the gospel, I said unto Peter before them all, if thou, being a Jew, livest after the manner of Gentiles, and not as do the Jews, why compellest thou the Gentiles to live as do the Jews?

~ Galatians 2:14

Ethnocentrism, as demonstrated above, is the tendency to look at the world primarily from the perspective of one's own culture with the belief that their way is the best and only way. However, diversity is about differences! Making a conscious effort to objectively view, explore and embrace the differences of others, you would come to know and realize that there are just as many similarities as there are differences. You may find that you have more in common than not, but first, you have to be willing to put aside your ego and superior attitude to extend a sense of mutual respect and consider someone else besides yourself (unselfishness). Today, I have witnessed that same dominating spirit or mindset in many people who feel they are entitled for one reason or another to use exploitation to get whatever they want by any means necessary. That very same self-defeating, self-centered dictatorship attitude is adopted by the children of our future by way of example through their immediate surroundings as well as the world in general.

Even so we, when we were children,
were in bondage under the elements of the world:

~ Galatians 4:3

Though life is a series of choices, there are people in the world who have the belief that you are able to control everything that happens in life. I, on the other hand, would beg to differ; many things happen in your life and often, there is no rhyme, reason or explanation. While enduring the things you encounter in your life, you have the option of choosing how to react or respond accordingly. *I can do all things through Christ who strengthens me* (Philippians 4:13). But nevertheless, you do not have control over everything that happens to you. Otherwise, I would have gladly avoided or dodged a number of obstacles in my life, especially the number of countless times people insulted my intelligence on the basis of their ignorance. You have no control over the ignorance of another who wishes to impose upon you his negative beliefs, misconceived truths or stereotypes that reinforce his prejudiced views about you or others.

> *Am I therefore become your enemy,*
> *because I tell you the truth?*
>
> ~ Galatians 4:16

Growing up, I had difficulty believing God would create a diverse group of people—in a world intended to be inhabited by us all—to wage war against one another because of our physical (visible) differences as a result of our unchanging biology or chemistry. Many nights, I cried about being judged or limited on the basis of my skin color—but not because I viewed myself as others may have wanted me to! I wasn't ashamed of who I was, but I was greatly disappointed, frustrated and hurt by what I was experiencing—time and time again! I was determined to refuse to accept that God would purposely create me to be the person I was: black and female in a man's world to be condemned by others so intensely! I was having a hard time believing and accepting that there was so much cruelty in the world on the basis of prejudices for being so different. Were we not *all* created in the image of God? *And God said, Let us (Father, Son and Holy Spirit) make man in our image, after our likeness: and let them (man) have dominion over the fish of the sea, And over the fowl of the air, and over the cattle, and over all the earth, and over every creeping thing that creepeth upon the earth* (Genesis 1:26).

At what point did we begin to notice our differences and make the determination that one group should rank supreme over the other? How could others who were also created by the same God, in his image, do such horrible things to another human being? How can people justify separating families by taking a child from its mother to be sold as a commodity, removing the father or son from a family to be used for breeding as a means of income, removing the mother or daughter against their will to be used for sexual favors and repeated abuse for entertainment, defiling the body of another human being as a result of beatings, torture, burning, castration, etc., just for sport and feel no remorse? They justify it by nothing other than being allowed to violate the rights of another in accordance to the law as it was written. This is something we were reminded of not that long ago by our former president, George W. Bush, when there was much controversy concerning reparations to blacks for slavery in America. However, enacting a ruling and making it a law does not make it morally right! *Christ hath redeemed us from the curse of the law, being made a curse for us: for it written, cursed is every one that hangth on a tree* (Galatians 3:13). (Ironically, this scripture was perverted and misused during slavery!) In the sense of physical bondage, the institution of slavery in America has existed a lot longer than the concept of free slaves.

> *And that because of false brethren*
> *unawares brought in, who came in privily*
> *to spy out our liberty which we have in Christ Jesus,*
> *that they might bring us into bondage.*
>
> ~ Galatians 2:4

I always wondered about the sincerity of those who go to third world countries to lend a helping hand. I would hope their intentions are admirable and without ulterior motive. Could it be their love for God is directed to people? Could it be more about money than humanity? Going after proposals that are directed toward third world countries is big business. It's a way to get money from the government without having to pay it back. We just have to prove that we are abiding by the contract; no more, no less. Is it an attempt to deny what they know to be true by putting forth an effort to convince themselves that they are void of prejudice feelings because they make such small sacrifices? Look at me, I can't possibly be prejudice; otherwise I wouldn't waste my time helping those people. Or perhaps it is an attempt to be viewed and treated like gods! Upon the return of my coworkers whose responsibilities of their job afforded them the opportunity to travel overseas, I got the distinct feeling they (my coworkers) attempted to identify me in comparison to those they encountered, who as a result of their culture and an economic need, treated my coworkers as if they were royalty. My coworkers, in turn, would attempt to view me as the hired help (a maid or servant). They had no hesitation in asking me to perform duties outside of my job description, such as cleaning the refrigerator, being expected to use my personal vehicle to chauffer others around—even after my normal working hours—lifting heavy objects in the office with no assistance, and, on occasion, being asked by my supervisor to go to his home to help his wife clean up or organize their personal items (closets). Announcing my objection, I would state: How dare you ask me to do things for you outside of my job description that you yourself would not consider or be willing to do for me? Do you not see something wrong with that picture? And they would have the nerve to accuse me of being insubordinate.

I would think their cross-cultural experiences in interacting with individuals who have differing attributes and values would give them more of an advantage to encounter others without prejudice. It is apparent that regardless of one's education or proclaimed sense of religion, their character can be less than favorable toward you as reinforced by false truths and stereotypes contributed by their selfish egos for power and control.

EVERYTHING HAPPENS FOR A REASON

He has made everything beautiful and appropriate in its time. He has also planted eternity [a sense of divine purpose] in the human heart [a mysterious longing which nothing under the sun can satisfy, except God] - yet man cannot find out (comprehend, grasp) what God has done (His overall plan) from the beginning to the end.

~ **Ecclesiastes 3:11 AMP**

October 1, 2010
Revised October 16, 2015

I Truly Believe Everything Happens for a Reason

It is with the *divine connection* and intervention of God that things happen as they do. *Nothing is by happenstance!* We may not know the why or the when, but the most important thing to know is the WHO. *And we know that ALL things work together for good to them that love God, to them who are the called according this HIS PURPOSE* (Romans 8:28). We may seem helpless through it all, but if we are willing to allow God to do what is necessary without any interjection of self or thinking we can do it alone, it will always work out for our good!

You just have to be willing to have an open mind and an open heart to see with your spirit. You just have to exercise patience and seek God's wisdom, knowledge and understanding; do not lean on your own understanding. You just have to wait on God with *faith* in knowing He has your best interest at heart.

Waiting on God does not mean waiting and doing nothing. Waiting on God is about action! Waiting on God is about believing! Waiting on God is about prayer; praying without ceasing; not wavering or giving in to your fears. For God has not given us a spirit of fear but one of power, love and of a sound mind.

Believing is about knowing

- **You can do all things through Christ who strengthens you.**

- **Each of us was created with a purpose for a purpose.**

- **You were created for greatness.**

- **You are more than a conqueror.**

- **Where you are in life has nothing to do with your full potential for greatness!**

Believing is about holding onto the promises of God. He will not leave you nor forsake you! Ask and it shall be given. Knock and the door will be answered. Reach and He will grab you. Seek and He will reward you. Do not allow anyone to limit your abilities. You have limitless possibilities. You just have to believe it, want it, walk toward it and take action.

Now it is up to you.

Be blessed,
Ann

HAIR DOES NOT DEFINE ME!

And let the beauty of the LORD our God be upon us: and establish thou the work of our hands upon us; yea, the work of our hands establish thou it..

~ **Psalm 90:17**

Revised June 25, 2015

In the words of India Arie, "I am not my hair, I am not this skin, I am not your expectations…I am a soul that lives within."

Hair, the outer covering of a human being, may serve to superficially assist in identifying the ethnicity of an individual. It may even serve to assist in identifying the age of an individual, but that may not be altogether accurate. The presence or absence of hair color could be due to a medical abnormality or hereditary in nature. Hair provides warmth during the cold, shade from the sun and protection of the face and scalp from the elements of the air.

Without eyebrows, I am subject to particles getting in my eyes with the possibility of bacteria hijacking a ride as it swims through my sweat to contaminate or evade my body. Nevertheless, it is my spirit that sustains me through all my infirmity (sickness), but a crushed spirit I cannot bear (Proverbs 18:14)! So through the Holy Spirit, I am forever reminded and joyful to know, people do not define me; in the same instance, I am also elated to know, hair does not define who I am, nor does it give me life. *For God so loved the world, that he gave his only begotten Son, that whosoever believeth in him should not perish, but have everlasting life* (John 3:16). Yet sadly, hair is what many people falsely idolize and testify to as being the sole qualifier of a person's beauty in the name of vanity. But beauty is far more than that! Do you know, charm is deceptive and beauty disappears, but a woman who honors the Lord will be praised (Proverbs 31:30)? Beauty on the surface will surely fade, but that which is skin deep is close to God's heart! So see me for me if you will, but your perception of me is not my reality!

Hair does not add to my worth nor does it take anything away, for I am fearfully and wonderfully made! I am a spirit with a soul that inhabits a body made of flesh and blood. My heart defines who I am. *As a man thinketh in his heart, so is he* (Proverbs 23:7). My heart is the beauty of my soul that lives within—not my hair or lack thereof. Thank You, God, for helping me to see the beauty of my heart that You created in the image of You!

> *For we are his workmanship,*
> *created in Christ Jesus unto good works,*
> *which God hath before ordained that*
> *we should walk in them.*
>
> ~ Ephesians 2:10

Living with Alopecia

My mother used to send my younger sister Pamela and I to a beautician approximately every two weeks to get our hair washed, conditioned, pressed, curled or braided. One Saturday morning, when I was approximately thirteen or fourteen years old, the beautician made an unnerving discovery and ran to the back of the shop (out of hearing range so she thought) to call my mother. Hysterically, I heard her say, "Have you seen your daughter's hair? She has some bald spots and her hair is falling out at an alarming rate! You need to get her to a doctor as soon as possible! You may want to try a dermatologist." When she returned to me, she was still very emotional but caring and concerned about not upsetting me. However, she did not realize I heard the entire conversation.

Upon arriving home, my mother said nothing about the incident until she was able to make a medical appointment for me. However, she was not prepared to learn that the medical professionals were not as knowledgeable as she had hoped about this type of hair loss, especially not a loss involving the hair of little girls or women. But my mother refused to give up and she attempted to take me to every hospital or medical facility within the D.C. area, including Johns Hopkins, for a solution. Going from doctor to doctor, there didn't seem to be much information or hope for a cure or treatment. Ironically, one doctor initially told me that I was experiencing a nervous breakdown that resulted in the loss of my hair. And as explained by another doctor, "The body has the ability to repair itself. When the body senses there is a problem, it sends a signal to the brain that something is wrong. Antibodies are released to seek and search out the problem to begin to correct it and heal it."

However, as further explained in my case, "When the antibodies were released, there was no apparent damage or sign of anything being out of place, but the signals from the brain said otherwise." My antibodies began to attack each other, thus causing the body to go into shock and the hair to fall out. What an explanation! I quickly grew tired of receiving false hope and "what ifs" as a possible cause to my dilemma. When my mother wanted to travel to Johns Hopkins in Baltimore, I opted not to go to be poked or prodded and treated like a test case.

Thereafter, my sisters taunted me often about my hair loss whenever they were mad at me about something (you know how sibling rivalry goes). There were days when I would cry an hour each morning before leaving the house. I would agonize about having to go out to be subjected to the ignorance of those who questioned me about my hair or lack thereof or those who threatened to snatch off my wig and my head wrap just to humiliate me. Determined not to feel sorry for myself or let others dictate the outcome of my life, I talked to God often about my anger and disappointment. I asked Him and myself some very hard-hitting questions. Why was I so concerned about what others thought? Why was I allowing people to impose their views upon me concerning how I should see myself? Why was I wearing a wig in the first place? Was I wearing the wig to make life easier for myself or for those who were dealing with their own insecurities and issues of vanity? Was I going to emerge or sink deeper into myself? Giving up or giving in to my circumstances was not an option. I was going to fight and take control of my life by swimming above the current. The first step was to educate myself about my condition.

At age twenty-one, I became a little more diligent about searching for answers for a possible treatment and stumbled across Dr. Knoff. Walking into her office, Dr. Knoff said, "Have a seat and tell me what seems to be your problem." Responding, I said, "This is a wig. I am losing my hair; all with the exception of one braid at the top of my head is gone. In her own sensitive and caring way, she tried to instill confidence by telling me how beautiful and lucky I was to be living in an era that had developed wigs to look more natural or as close to real hair as possible, as opposed to when she was my age. Although I appreciated her attempt to ease my spirit, that wasn't what I wanted to hear. Nonetheless, she was the first doctor to finally enlighten me about the medical terminology used to identify my condition: alopecia. Armed with a name, I decided to conduct my own research in seeking an avenue for accepting and coping with my condition on my own. That search yielded three types of alopecia: areata, totalis and universalis. I happen to be impacted by the latter, alopecia universalis. To help me conquer my fear, which had more to do with the reactions of others concerning my hair loss, I took that research and turned it into a show-and-tell presentation for a final exam grade in my public speaking class at the University of the District of Columbia in 1985. Needless to say, I earned an A+ and I could not believe just how at ease and comfortable I felt. This accomplishment put me well on my way to developing the inner strength and confidence needed to brave the world in 1988, when I decided to venture out for the first time without my wig. From that day forward, I vowed to never again wear a wig as a crutch to hide behind. I was finally finding my way and growing more determined every day about my unwillingness to allow society to impose their insecurities upon me. I thought it was time to start living my life by embracing my baldness—until another roadblock hit me in 1994.

While working for a healthcare provider, I was terminated in January of 1994, while it was in the process of being acquired by another provider. But prior to that, after their failed plan to force me to resign, they harassed me and retaliated against me for an entire year. After refusing to give them my resignation, they attempted to use my performance evaluation against me. However, when that failed, they resulted to other tactics. During the early part of 1993, my supervisor stated she wanted to discuss—with me—my appearance in the eyes of white people. She went on to say that my appearance was viewed as being offensive by her supervisor and others in upper management to include many deeming it as intimidating and militant. Heartbroken and devastated, I fought hard not to lash out or break down into tears. A couple of months later, she called me into her office to discuss a proposition (a forced resignation). She stated she wanted to give me the opportunity to look for another job on a full-time basis. Upon asking her to elaborate, she stated she and the organization were prepared to give me three-months pay in advance in exchange for my resignation. I declined their offer and stated, given the change in the economy and considering the number of downsizing attempts made by other organizations within the past three years, it was not an appropriate time for me to resign without having something already lined up as a replacement and it could possibly take me longer than three months to find another position.

Refusing to resign, I said, "Unless you or the organization is willing to put in writing your proposition to aid me with a possible unemployment claim when and if the time presents itself for me to do so, then I am not willing to give you my resignation. If I resign, I would not be able to claim unemployment benefits." So the following year, as a form of retaliation, which included their numerous failed harassment attempts to get me to quit, I was terminated on January 21, 1994. The reason they gave other than the truth was that I allegedly lied about the death of my grandmother who had sadly passed away on January 6, 1994.

More devastated than ever concerning the circumstances of my situation, I questioned God for allowing such a thing to happen, especially when I was just beginning to adapt to not having any hair! I could not believe that God, who said He loved me, would allow people to continue to decide my fate in such a way when I had suffered enough already and fought often not to lose my sanity when others threatened to snatch my wig or head wrap off of my head and made comments about wanting to slap me across my bald head. Struggling to regain a sense of self, I was extremely angry. But aside from the anger, I was still determined not to regress back to a period of shutting myself in, hiding out or concealing my baldness. I told myself I was strong and resilient! However, feeling defeated and emasculated, I was being drawn closer to the Lord! And God was teaching me how to overcome obstacles by addressing them head-on! He was cautioning me to not allow a temporary setback of any kind to undo what He was attempting to accomplish in me, through me and around me. Yes, I was *fired* from a job! I was wrongfully terminated and discriminated against and my character was assassinated! Defamed! But I left with my dignity and self-respect in order. My character was tried and tested by man, but it was confirmed and approved of by God.

Conclusion

Adversity does not come without challenges! But through the storm of our trials, if we *believe* that there is a God who created us with a purpose for a purpose, then we must also be willing to accept the position in which we have been placed. That includes the consequences surrounding each and every trial and tribulation in accordance to the will of God to bring us to an expected end! He was and is preparing me for His glory. He's been pushing me forward while stretching me and strengthening me from the inside out to be the person He thought of and spoke into existence when He created me! He's been teaching me to love myself, like myself and to appreciate who I am and was called to be in spite of how others see me. It is about me embracing the detours and the challenges to becoming a better me to fulfill the plans He has for me—my destiny. Everything is within His plan to aid me in moving forward. So, I am moving forward by embracing my baldness, seeing the beauty not only inside of me but within others and looking past the imperfections to **try the spirit by the Spirit** in acceptance of each person's unique imperfect perfections to know them by their fruit! *You will know these people because of what they do. Good things don't come from people who are bad, just as grapes don't come from thornbushes, and figs don't come from thorny weeds. In the same way, every good tree produces good fruit, and bad trees produce bad fruit. A good tree cannot produce bad fruit, and a bad tree cannot produce good fruit. Every tree that does not produce good fruit is cut down and thrown into the fire. You will know these false people by what they do* (Matthew 7:16-20 ERV).

No one is perfect; we are all a work in progress! Nothing is by coincidence or happenstance. You are beautiful and wonderfully made in His image, inside and out. You are equipped with a soul and a spirit for conquering your greatest challenges. Therefore, I challenge you to embrace your unique, imperfect perfection as He sees you and created you to be! Love yourself as He loves you. Appreciate yourself as He appreciates you. And more importantly, value yourself as He values you and accept nothing less from anyone else. Allow no one to separate you from what He has gifted to you in being able to see yourself *whole*, with everything and nothing to give without the promise of God and His approval!

> **Side Note:** Because I was told my hair loss was probably triggered by a nutrient deficiency or blood disorder, I

stopped eating red meats, started exercising regularly and cut out dairy products. I even eliminated drinking socially (alcohol). After a year and a half with no change, I decided to go back to eating what I liked. However, today, I still opt to limit alcohol as a lifestyle change and call to ministry. Due to recent tests, I have learned I am extremely deficient in Vitamin D and zinc. Growing up, I always had a history of contracting pneumonia approximately two to three times a year and not one doctor determined the cause. They only treated the symptoms. My continued research confirmed my zinc deficiency. Zinc deficiency may manifest as acne, eczema, xerosis (dry, scaling skin), seborrheic dermatitis or alopecia. There may also be impaired wound healing.

As inspired by a quote I saw on the side of a bus, I would like to leave you with this: I C U 4 U. So please C ME 4 ME. Your perception of me is not my reality! How God sees me is my only reality! And as mentioned to God: I have been without hair for so long that I may not know what to do should it start to grow back. I have adapted and adjusted to embracing my unique identity.

What Is Alopecia?

Alopecia comes from the Greek work *alopex*, which means baldness. Today, alopecia (al-oh-PEE-shah) is widely believed to be a highly unpredictable, autoimmune disease impacting the skin through the lack of nutrients circulating in the blood from cell to cell; this is still suspect. A breakdown in the immune system results in the loss of hair on the scalp and elsewhere on the body. *The actual cause of the disease is unknown and varies from one individual to the next.* As indicated above, there are three types or stages of alopecia.

1. Areata means patches

2. Totalis means total

3. Universalis means complete or universal

Essentially, every individual produces various cell types that fight disease and infection. There are all sorts of immune cells such as lymphocytes (small white blood cells or leukocytes that play a large role in defending the body against disease; lymphocytes are responsible for immune responses), monocytes (a type of leukocyte or white blood cell, which also plays a role in immune system function; as a general rule, a low monocyte count is a good sign and a high count indicates that a problem is present), macrophages (cells that eat other cells) and other cells, all of which have different roles to play in fighting off infection. To fight invading organisms, the immune cells must be able to recognize bacteria as being foreign bodies and not as being part of the body that belongs. The immune cells do this by recognizing structures called antigens. The immune system, as a whole, has the ability to recognize all antigens and function as the body's defense mechanism to repair or heal what's wrong.

Alopecia areata occurs in males and females of all ages and races. It usually starts with one or more small, round, smooth, bald patches on the scalp and can progress to total scalp hair loss (alopecia totalis) or complete body hair loss (alopecia universalis). The affected hair follicles are mistakenly attacked by a person's own immune system (white blood cells), resulting in the arrest of the hair growth stage. Presently, there is no cure. However, researchers believe that several genetic factors may also play a major role in autoimmune disease. The onset of alopecia most often begins during childhood. Although not life-threatening, alopecia areata is most certainly life-altering and unpredictable, thus having a profound psychological impact on the lives of those disrupted by this illness. Unfortunately, I was terminated from a job for not having any hair. This was much more devastating than being bullied and picked on for not having any hair.

This common but very challenging disease affects approximately 1.7 percent of the population overall, including more than 4.7 million people in the United States alone. Many things can contribute to alopecia:

- Anemia
- Autoimmune disorders
- Childbirth
- Crash dieting
- Infections
  - Fungal infections – hair breaks off near the scalp
  - Syphilis
  - HIV
  - Herpes simplex

- Illness or surgery
- Inflammation
- Stress that prompts growing hairs to rest and shed
- Emotional/psychological disorders
- Prolonged fever
- Radiation therapy
- Systemic and discoid lupus erythematosus
- Hair pulled too tightly by:
    - Hair rollers
    - Pigtails
    - Cornrows
- Hot oil treatments (can inflame the hair follicle and cause scarring)
- Twisting and pulling hair out due to psychiatric problems
- Genes
    - Male-pattern baldness is usually inherited.
    - Birth defects can include problems with the hair shaft.
- Hormonal problems

- Overactive or underactive thyroid gland
- Medications:
    - Blood thinners
    - Drugs for gout
    - Chemotherapy for cancer treatment
    - Vitamin A
    - Birth control pills
    - Antidepressants
    - Blood pressure and heart medications
- Allergic reaction to medications

Risk Factors

A risk factor is something that increases your chance of getting a disease or condition.

Examples:

- Family history of baldness or hair loss
- Advancing age (for male-pattern baldness only)
- Pregnancy
- Stress
- Poor nutrition

Possible Treatments

- Cortisone: injections, pills or cream.
- PUVA: ultra-violet light.
- Monoxidile: used for people with high blood pressure but found to grow hair.
- Hair transplant: not guaranteed.
- Consult with an allergist or herbologist.
- Change your eating habits.
- Hormonal change resulting from pregnancy; however, having a baby is no guarantee of regrowth and after giving birth, there is a guarantee the hair may not start to fall out again!

If you wish to learn more, check out the following website: http://www.alopeciaworld.com/.

HE WHO HAS ARRIVED

"When you are cast down and humbled, you will speak with confidence, And the humble person He will lift up and save.

~ Job 22:29 AMP

December 22, 2011

People around me are struggling and attempting to figure out Ann Mack. What they don't know is I too have struggled to figure out Ann Mack. I often wondered why it was so difficult for me to fit in or why my actions, behaviors or norms did not necessarily fit the patterns of those around me. The more I attempted to conform or change myself to mirror those in my surroundings, the more I felt distant and isolated. Why? Because it wasn't me! And it is not who God has created me to be! I AM not expected to fit in!

So I cannot begin to tell you or explain just how excited I AM about the Lord and all He is doing in my life. There is such a great and deep passion that rages within me for who He is, who

I am or have become in Him! It was and is not meant for me to fit into the world's view of who I should be. For God created me with a purpose for a purpose to function in this earth according to His will. He is very adamant about His children fulfilling that purpose as He directs us and guides us to our destiny even if it means standing out away from the crowd. And if I am focused on Him in diligently seeking His face and am willing to hear and listen to His voice, He will reveal things to me by showing me what must be done to forever stay in His will. As I develop questions or thoughts needing answers or clarity of direction that He can only give me, He steps out in front to give me the desires of my heart.

Just this morning, I had thoughts about what it means to have arrived—not according to the interpretation of man's view but as it relates to me and God! And low and behold, I received an article that addresses that very same topic. However, this morning, God told me I was halfway there. My initial step was acknowledging I could do nothing without Him in my life, so I decided to make a conscious commitment to rededicating my life to Him. Then I decided I would attempt to review His ways and restructure my life as well as redirect or change my thought patterns to live my life according to His expectations—not halfway but 100 percent and more. As I took hold and started walking in faith to regain hope and put my trust in Him, I noted a change. What a wonderful change and awesome feeling it is to no longer seek approval from people! But to head in a different direction, not completely absent of people, but no longer giving much thought to the "he said, she said" or feeling less than because people *told me* I was less than. Then I realized just how deeply and joyfully in love I am with the one who is able to see the potential in me that people refuse to see. Then I knew in my heart of hearts that I can do all things through Christ who strengthens me. That's arriving: not measuring yourself according to your net worth or the material possessions that people deem important; not getting caught up in a title or grade that has no reference in getting you to Heaven; not comparing my car or house to the next in size; not looking to obtain a brand-name item that's recognized by many who don't know the name of Jesus.

What is your definition of arriving?

Just sharing my thoughts!
Peace and blessings

I GET IT!

Grace and peace be multiplied unto you through the knowledge of God, and of Jesus our Lord, According as his divine power hath given unto us all things that [pertain] unto life and godliness, through the knowledge of him that hath called us to glory and virtue:

~ **2 Peter 1:2-3**

September 20, 2012

How often have you heard the phrase, "History repeats itself," or "Let the past stay in the past"? If only it were that simple to leave the past in the past, I would gladly choose not to relive over 80 percent of my past ever again. And I definitely would not want to endure the pain and suffering of slavery like so many before me. However, for some reason, I seem to still have some unresolved, deep-rooted issues from my past that continue to rise up and creep back into my present while waging war and wreaking havoc in my life. Every lesson God wants me to learn and conquer, I truly want to do just that to the point of being able to leave the past exactly where it belongs—in the past—but never forgetting those things which are behind me! Nevertheless, with the need to handle each situation according to God's wisdom, knowledge and understanding, it was important for me not to allow any fear from my past to resurface to torment me as I grow and move past it!

Prior to leaving the house for church on Sunday morning, September 16, 2012, I sat down to document that which had plagued me for the last month or so in an effort to not only understand it for myself but to share it with you. After reviewing certain events, I also needed to take into account the number of ministering sisters and brothers God sent my way to give me a word, each coming from a different angle and background but all addressing and sharing their testimonies and points of view to encourage me.

Ministering Saints

On one Friday afternoon, August 24, 2012, to be exact, I felt the pressure of an enormous weight upon my shoulders, a shooting pain in the center of my back and a throbbing headache. I met a dear friend and spiritual sister, Mary, for dinner to discuss my dilemma; I needed to describe my mood to her in addition to sharing the lyrics of a song I was hearing in my mind. With no hesitation, Mary went into action with prayer and reminded me of God's instructions to His children to guard our tongues as well as our minds. And when she referenced that scripture, life and death is in the power of the tongue, I could also hear in my heart to call those things that aren't as though they were in connection to Romans 4:17. Appreciating her wisdom and willingness to listen to me as she encouraged me instead of judging me, I needed her emotional detachment to walk me through my thoughts. For a point of reference, the main lyrics of the song go like this: "Don't push me, 'cause I'm close to the edge. I'm trying not to lose my head. It's like a jungle sometimes, it makes me wonder how I keep from going under."

    I don't know about you, but sometimes I just need to talk out what is on my mind to get to the root of the problem for a solution or remedy in moving forward. Or just hearing it out loud helps me to see things with a different perspective. I do not want to be blind to what I am seeing and, through my ignorance, deny its existence and allow it to overtake me by surprise! Mainly because the *word of the Lord* also calls us to be vigilant and sober at all times. And should you be open to receiving what He has for you, He will reveal things to you to keep you from being blindsided. So although I was truly able to identify with the lyrics of that song, I had no intentions of acting upon my feelings by letting my mind get the best of me. However, I was starting to hear the lyrics of this once very popular song play over and over again as it bounced from ear to ear with a baritone base in my head. Nonetheless, can you relate to what I am saying? Have you ever found yourself too close to the edge?

    As the days and weeks passed, I was struggling to learn what God was trying to tell me and why He had allowed this situation to take place. Why did He give Satan permission to intrude upon me this way? If no one understood my pain and the steps it took to overcome the things in my past, He did! While I was sitting at my desk and searching my mind for answers, the phone rang. It was Pastor Janet Gibson of Cherubim Ministries. She graciously sacrificed her time to listen to my babbling while she attempted to get her point across to me. Like parables, she directed one question after the other at me in trying to get me to see the bigger picture. "Does what you are experiencing really matter?" "Does it matter?" she asked again.

I responded, "Yes and no."

She said, "Why?"

I didn't really have an answer or at least one that made any sense! But, intensely consumed by my issue, I didn't quite understand what she was trying to get across to me at the time. Later, I heard in my spirit, "If pleasing God is of the utmost importance, then nothing else really matters!"

Within the following days after my meeting with Pastor Gibson, I received confirmation after confirmation as other conversations ensued. There was Aleta Clark, who was at home trying to recover from a serious injury she had sustained at work, but she took the time to either text me during the course of the day or to call me and check to see how I was doing. She used to always say, "You have to train people how you want to be treated."

After pondering at my desk, still a little out of sorts, I headed out of the office to the bathroom to pray when I spotted Bishop Horton of Unity Life Christian Ministries in the hallway. Concerned about how I was doing, he had some words of encouragement and reminded me about perception versus deception. Unfortunately, on the basis of ignorance, people tend to typecast or stereotype you. And how they see you has nothing to do with who you really are, mainly because *they do not want to see* who you are! It is all about power, control and influence. Elder Harrison gave me some in-depth information about the rules of engagement as it pertains to spiritual warfare. One other brother in Christ, who wants to remain nameless, spoke to me about seeking assistance from God to reveal the possibility of a family (or generational) curse or the connection to these familiar spirits waging war against me. And God intervened through each person He sent to counsel me in such a mighty way. I GET IT!

Familiar Spirits

Prioritizing and compartmentalizing things as I always have, I realized the most difficult thing to deal with has to do with my workplace and the spirits influenced by God's archenemy. Spirits who knew me better than I know myself! Spirits who knew exactly what buttons to push and would stop at nothing to get me back into their clutches. I was being pushed to the brink by familiar spirits from my past that I thought were no longer an issue. There is nothing more frustrating than having people attempt to limit my growth or progress by dictating my career path, which speaks nothing about who I really am, my potential or what is best for me. People who have decided, selfishly, that I, for some reason, should not be entitled to the same upward mobility opportunities or training for excelling. Satan and his minions are relentless! They will use every able-bodied, willing participant to attempt to take you out! You can run all you want to, but you simply cannot hide! And my plan of action for escape in avoiding any and all conflict or confrontation is and always was to flee quickly—fast and in a hurry.

Like Mary said, these familiar spirits from my past were having fun with me. And can you believe she actually laughed when she said it? Once I thought about it, I had to laugh too! They were all around me and attempting to wear me out! And if I had any hair, I'm sure I would start to pull it out from the stress I was allowing to take hold of me! I wanted so desperately to retreat and isolate myself from everything and everybody. I felt myself wavering and being pulled backwards to that familiar place of doom, gloom and pain. But mostly anger! Because I couldn't believe I was allowing myself to be consumed by this False Evidence Appearing Real. Especially not after breaking free and coming into the realization and revelation of God for who He is and the value He has placed in me regardless of how others within my workplace wish to view me! But God was doing a new thing through this situation. He was attempting to build *nerves of steel and to get me to take a spiritual warrior stand.* To take charge of my inheritance, authority, dominion and power here on earth!

Does It Really Matter?

It does not matter what it looks like! The importance of keeping my eyes focused on God and pleasing Him is the only thing that should matter. Anything outside of your God-ordained purpose does not matter. You just have to stand firm on the shoulders of your heavenly Father in the midst of battle. He is so awesome! Just as people are tempted to manipulate you into allowing them to mistreat you, you are perfectly within your right to attempt to train or retrain them pertaining to how they should treat you. We are to practice treating people in the manner in which we want to be treated—with loving kindness and care—not under the rule of a Babylonian mindset.

If respect is not readily given, you may have to demand it! However, do everything decently and in order with a spirit of excellence. Always remember, as a child of God working unto the Lord, He will take care of everything on your behalf. He will guide and direct you! It is up to you to work within His flow and not against Him. Seek to know how He is using you and how He wants you to conduct yourself in every given situation. Because each person's purpose and assignment is different, how He directs you may not be how He directs someone else. Know who you are in Him and Him in you! Walk in faith with a *holy boldness*, not with pride, self-righteousness or arrogance, but with the assertiveness in knowing "no weapon formed against you shall prosper," as referenced in Isaiah 54:17.

And we know that all things work together
for good to them that love God,
to them who are the called according to [his] purpose.

~ Romans 8:28 KJV

Suggested Reading

Old Testament (Law) vs. New Testament (Covenant under Grace):

- Exodus 20:5, 34:6-7; Numbers 14:17-18; Ezekiel 18:1-4, 18-20
- John 3:17, 8:36, 9:1-3; Romans 8:1-2; Galatians 3:13, 5:1
- Matthew 11:28-30
- 2 Corinthians 5:17-19

Books

1. *Spirit Wars: Winning the Invisible Battle Against Sin and the Enemy*

    > Author: Kris Vallotton

    > ISBN-13: 978-0800794934

2. *Rules of Engagement: Preparing for Your role in the Spiritual Battle*

    > Author: Derek Prince

    > ISBN-13: 978-0800794064

CITIZEN OR CHRISTIAN?

*That ye would walk worthy of God,
who hath called you unto HIS Kingdom and glory.*

~ Thessalonians 2:12

March 22, 2013
Revised March 27, 2013

God has a soundproof way of reaching and using those He has chosen to be a blessing to others. It does not matter what you think or believe to be true or not! It is God the Father who has the last word in deciding upon who He will choose to further His cause (the building and uplifting of His Kingdom). Contrary to popular belief, when God sets His heart on a particular thing or person, He can be quite relentless in His pursuit of you. He may even grant you many opportunities to get it right, to do right and to accept your calling. But He will not and does not do fake or phony. In fact, we live in a world full of hypocrites. And it is becoming increasingly hard to tell who is who: Pharisee or Sadducee, Samaritan or Assyrian, Gentile or Jew, believer or non-believer, *citizen or Christian*! Which are you?

> *So for the sake of your tradition*
> *(the rules handed down by your forefathers),*
> *you have set aside the Word of God*
> *[depriving it of force and authority and making it of no effect].*
> *You pretenders (hypocrites)!*
> *Admirably and truly did Isaiah prophesy of you when he said:*
> *These people draw near Me*
> *with their mouths and honor Me with their lips,*
> *but their hearts hold off and are far away from Me.*
>
> ~ Matthew 15:6-8 AMP

Accepting and looking forward to an employment opportunity with the U.S. Department of Energy (DOE) was a two-year wait. Have you ever wanted something so badly that you could almost taste it and envision it? I wanted a change so badly that my expectations and enthusiasm were running high. The problem with wanting something that badly is you block out the possibility of receiving any messages from God to reveal and prepare you for what is to come and why! From the date of my initial interview in May of 2006 to my start date on January 22, 2008, I needed to complete one training assignment before embarking upon another one (mainly because I was unaware of my extensive battleground training as planned and orchestrated by God)! After leaving one environment of ill repute, it definitely was not my intent to dive directly into another pit of darkness, especially with no promise of career growth amongst those who seemed to have no moral compass for wanting to do what is right. But it is more about my spiritual growth! The phrase "experience is the best teacher" is true indeed and God is determined to make sure I am equipped to do more than just survive.

But when He, the Spirit of Truth (the Truth-giving Spirit) comes,
He will guide you into all the Truth (the whole, full Truth).
For He will not speak His own message [on His own authority];
but He will tell whatever He hears [from the Father;
He will give the message that has been given to Him],
and He will announce and declare to you
the things that are to come [that will happen in the future].
He will honor and glorify Me,
because He will take of (receive, draw upon)
what is Mine and will reveal (declare,
disclose, transmit) it to you.

~ John 16:13-14 AMP

As things began to unfold and much was revealed to me about my current workplace (referred to as the headquarters for demonic activity), I began to question God about the rampant and blatant negativity. Aside from that, I also began to notice the number of Christians throughout the building in the midst of the darkness and wondered why more wasn't being done in the way of prayer and spiritual warfare to combat all the present darkness. The more I questioned God about what I was seeing and experiencing, the more willing He was to enlighten me and connect me with those who were sent by Him to be the light within the darkness—those who had lost their way and became a part of the darkness! And those who were committed to doing the work of the Lord with no hesitation while not allowing themselves to be deceived by the darkness! God never wants us to be in the dark about anything (see 1 Peter 5:8), but we have to be willing to see what needs to be seen, sight beyond sight. Try the spirit by the spirit, as referenced in 1 John 4:1, to discern the characteristics of those within your environment! Whatever we ask in His name (John 15:7), He is willing to give us the desires of our heart (Psalms 37:4) if we abide in Him and Him in us.

> *Ask, and it shall be given you; seek, and ye shall find;*
> *knock, and it shall be opened unto you:*
> *For every one that asketh receiveth;*
> *and he that seeketh findeth;*
> *and to him that knocketh it shall be opened.*
>
> ~ Matthew 7:7-8 KJV

Walking to the fourth-floor deli within DOE, I had the pleasure of encountering Apostle Willie E. Bruce Jr. (Word Healing Ministries), whose light in the presence of darkness shines brightly. He always has a word of encouragement for me each time I see him and this time, he asked me a question and suggested what scripture (Matthew 6) I should review to assist me with my answer. I was so excited about my task and my answer that I didn't know just where to start. With strong reason, I always frowned upon the word, "Christian," especially in the context in which it is regarded by many people in today's society and culture. To be a Christian, for me, is to strive to be *Christ-like*, which is the root word or derivative for its true meaning. However, many people have not taken into consideration the true meaning or expectation of the character one should strive to exemplify when they refer to themselves as being a Christian. It is about diligently working toward embracing and displaying the nine fruits of the spirit, which is centered on who *Christ* is!

> *(for the fruit [the effect, the result] of the Light consists in all goodness and righteousness and truth), trying to learn [by experience] what is pleasing to the Lord [and letting your lifestyles be examples of what is most acceptable to Him—your behavior expressing gratitude to God for your salvation].*
>
> ~ Ephesians 5:9-10 AMP

The word "Christian" should be viewed as an action word, thus calling for us to be and do! Not just saying it but acting upon it. Many people have given the term, Christian, a very bad reputation. If I am consciously seeking to be a Christian, I should seek God's face above all: Seek ye first the Kingdom of God and His righteousness thus taking into consideration all of His commandments (Matthew 6:33). Then, I must unlearn to relearn by replacing all that is false with all that is true concerning my Lord, Master and Savior. I must believe and hold on to hope and faith that He will prevail on my behalf, no matter what and all else will fall into place. As I strive to be a part of and committed to God's Kingdom in full acceptance and obedience, it is more important for me to be a *citizen* of God's Kingdom and not just a Christian (as defined by today's society). An ambassador for Christ! Knowing deep within my heart that God has me covered, I must get to a place of being free of worry and stress, especially if I am clothed in the full amour of Christ, covered in the blood and hedged on all sides! He got me covered!

> *And we have seen and do testify that the Father*
> *sent the Son to be the Saviour of the world.*
>
> ~ 1 John 4:14

Giving no thought to tomorrow.
Giving no thought to what I will wear or eat.
Giving no thought to those within my surroundings
concerning what they do or don't do.
Giving no thought to my care for my life is totally
in the hands of my Lord.
For God will take care of me.

Therefore, I am working on denouncing all my fears and letting myself lean totally on the Lord. I am working on being content in whatever situation I find myself to be in as allowed by God to prosper me. And just this week, God has directed my attention to his stance on hypocrisy in preparing me in advance for this question from Apostle Willie E. Bruce: *Are you a Christian or a citizen?* God frowns upon hypocrisy and so do I. It is impossible for anyone to serve two masters (Matthew 46:24 and Luke 16:13), least of all, be able to devote their all to two opposing forces equally. Oh my goodness, God has spoken to me and brought to my remembrance a number of topics this week alone:

- The difference between being a Christian and a citizen of the Kingdom.

- Letting my YES be YES and my NO be NO (Matthew 5:37 and James 5:12).

- Approximately one month ago, I started to hear the phrase, "the lesson, the quiz and the test," and have heard it repeatedly ever since. That's why I am so excited to get messages from Apostle Bruce that invoke me to think, pick my brain and study to show myself approved (2 Timothy 2:15).

- Prior to seeing Apostle Bruce, the word "recognition" came to my mind.

- Earlier that morning, upon getting off the subway train, I told God that it was my committed desire to please Him and only Him, not man. I was not looking to receive any reward from man in proving to him or her who I am in attempting to fit in or be like others, especially if it was not appropriate or in proper alignment with His will.

- What I do, I do for the Lord, I seek no accolades from man and it is not my intent to boast or brag about what I do in secret for others or on a daily basis. However, God has spoken to me about being transparent. That in itself is amazing to me because I have been assigned to conduct myself with a *spirit of excellence* as one who has no secrets. That means being mindful at all times about what I do or say and having no hidden agenda or meaning but to live for Christ.

> *But while men slept, his enemy came*
> *and sowed tares among the wheat,*
> *and went his way.*
>
> ~ Matthew 13:25

♦

> *But he said, Nay; lest while ye gather up the tares,*
> *ye root up also the wheat with them.*
> *Let both grow together until the harvest:*
> *and in the time of harvest I will say to the reapers,*
> *Gather ye together first the tares,*
> *and bind them in bundles to burn them:*
> *but gather the wheat into my barn.*
>
> ~ Matthew 13:29-30

When you are able to pass the threshold of no return into the Kingdom of God, you have graduated to being a **citizen**. What I have come to note is those who play church and proclaim to be Christians, for one reason or another, do not allow themselves to mature into the things of God long enough to go to the next level of becoming a sold-out citizen of the Kingdom of God. They deny that which is going on around them because they want so desperately to hold on to the things that the world has to offer. And, when you allow any part of darkness to seep in, it acts as a parasite or toxic substance, which threatens to invade your entire body. Then you too begin to display some of the same attributes (non-pleasing, demonic-influenced behavior) while failing to notice the change because it feels good. More importantly, as citizens of the Kingdom of God, each church (or person) is considered to be a community in itself. There are many members, but they are a part of a greater whole (one body), working in *unity* toward the same goal in accordance to the will of God! There are distinctive varieties of operation of working to accomplish things, but it is the same God who inspires and energizes them all in all.

Ephesians 2:19-21

Now therefore ye are no more strangers and foreigners, but fellow citizens with the saints and of the household of God; And are built upon the foundation of the apostles and prophets, Jesus Christ himself being the chief corner stone; in whom all the building fitly framed together groweth unto an holy temple in the Lord (KJV).

Therefore you are no longer outsiders (exiles, migrants and aliens, excluded from the rights of citizens), but you now share citizenship with the saints (God's own people, consecrated and set apart for Himself); and you belong to God's [own] household. You are built upon the foundation of the apostles and prophets with Christ Jesus Himself the chief Cornerstone. 21 In Him the whole structure is joined (bound, welded) together harmoniously and it continues to rise (grow, increase) into a holy temple in the Lord [a sanctuary dedicated, consecrated and sacred to the presence of the Lord] (AMP).

Being a citizen is the difference between wanting to please God and not man. It is having a committed heart for the things of God, meaning that which is important to God should also be important to you. It means having an ear to hear God's voice and doing what is right according to the will of God! Not your will be done, but God's will be done! It means speaking on behalf of God, thus said the Lord, with no emotional attachment. Even if it means losing a friendship with man, it is most important to maintain a friendship with God.

RELATIONSHIPS

> *I Like Your Christ.*
> *I Do Not Like Your Christians.*
> *Your Christians Are So Unlike Your Christ.*
> **~ Gandhi**

RACE IN AMERICA

Injustice anywhere is a threat to injustice everywhere!
~ **Martin Luther King, Jr.**

August 30, 2008

On July 23 and 24 of 2008, CNN presented a segment entitled, *Black in America*. How is it possible to actually cover the plight of blacks in America in a two-hour broadcast with no focus or thought given to how we truly ended up to be where we are today? You must consider from whence we have come in an effort to understand how we landed where we are today in determining where we need to go if we are truly concerned about improving the situation. Otherwise, it is just a lot of talk with no substance or evidence of change. Nonetheless, I must also commend CNN for being willing to make an attempt to openly discuss what others have refused to touch in today's society as well as in the past, though I feel the presentation did us no real justice. You cannot take a safe route when attempting to shed light on the root of a social and inhumane problem in America without addressing the history. The CNN broadcast came approximately two weeks after Barack Obama's speech on responsibility, which was addressed to the NAACP and directed at blacks. I'm sure he may have meant well, however, *responsibility is not a black or white thing, it is a people thing*! And until we as a whole are willing to take responsibility for that which we are truly responsible for bringing to pass, we will never be unified on any front.

> *I don't understand myself at all, for I really want to do what is right, but I don't do it. Instead, I do the very thing I hate. I know perfectly well that what I am doing is wrong, and my bad conscience shows that I agree that the law is good. But I can't help myself, because it is sin inside me that makes me do these evil things. I know I am rotten through and through so far as my old sinful nature is concerned. No matter which way I turn, I can't make myself do right. I want to, but I can't. When I want to do good, I don't. And when I try not to do wrong, I do it anyway.*
>
> ~ Romans 7:15-19

Fortunately, we are not born with feelings of racism or hate. These attributes are considered to be a learned behavior. Do you have any idea of what it is like to live in a world that regards you as being non-existent regardless of your accomplishments? The more I do and the more I accomplish or contribute to the civilization of this world, the more you are determined to limit my accomplishments and dictate my position in the world. Being born into a world that is hell-bent on disliking me based on the color of my skin or nationality, bordering on discrimination and racism, is a very difficult defeat if you do not know who you are. To be subjected to power and influence that dictates your worth not according to your skills, abilities and potential for greatness, but on the basis of your outward appearance and others' willingness to attempt to degrade you by the use of double standards can be crippling, to say the least, if you don't know who you are. Not being regarded by who I am as a person or human being who was created by God to mirror His image because you have allowed yourself to think as the world and not take into consideration the heart of God is not my problem. I know who I am and whose I am, so I will not allow your problem to be my problem.

> *My people are destroyed for lack of knowledge: because thou hast rejected knowledge, I also reject thee, that thou shalt be no priest to me: seeing thou hast forgotten the law of thy God, I will also forget thy children. As they were increased, so they sinned against me: therefore will I change their glory into shame. They eat up the sin of my people, and they set their heart on their iniquity. And there shall be, like people, like priest: and I will punish them for their ways, and reward them their doings. For they shall eat, and not have enough: they shall commit whoredom, and shall not increase: because they have left off to take heed to the Lord.*
>
> *~ Hosea 4:6-10*

As Christians, if you believe God dwells within each of us, then should you not be equally responsible or accountable for your actions to one another as to God? Attached to those actions are consequences. Those consequences are similar to the repercussions of a domino and they impact many people directly as well as indirectly; yet, we go through life giving no thought to both the impact and consequences of our choices. Unfortunately, there are many injustices in the world that have been deliberately orchestrated! The most recent confirmation of all came from Ron Suskind, an investigative journalist, who reveals in his book, *The Way of the World: A Story of Truth and Hope in an Age of Extremism*, the demonstrated lengths to which President Bush and members of his administration lied, misled and deceived the American people to pursue its invasion of Iraq. Was this another genocide attempt that soiled the hands of Americans for the sake of control, oil and greed? And yet, people wonder why Burma refused assistance from the United States when they needed it the most. That assistance never comes without a price. There are racial issues in America that need to be addressed openly across all divides! This world is full of people who lack knowledge concerning the impact of their actions on others and the environment surrounding us.

> *Through faith we understand*
> *that the worlds were framed by the word of God,*
> *so that things which are seen were not*
> *made of things which do appear.*
>
> ~ Hebrews 11:3

While listening to a sermon delivered by Fred Price, he said something that made me run around the house with excitement:

The body of Christ is made up of every ethnic group! As I started to cry, I wondered, Why is there so much division and strife amongst God's children? Have you not given any real thought to the meaning of the word *diversity*? We should be setting an example for the whole world to see, yet we allow ourselves to be consumed by the world. Why do we allow ourselves to entertain characteristics that go against the teaching of God's word? Why do you enjoy and delight yourself in the things that contradict God's word? When God references image, it has nothing to do with ones physical image or outward appearance. It is much greater and deeper than that! It is about the heart of man and his spirit. Those who think they are in control and will stop at nothing to retain that false sense of power in an effort of alienating others through subjectivity have to change, for God is no respecter of persons. When He sees me, He sees my heart. He does not judge me by the color of my skin. It was He who created me to be the person I am. He created us all—a diverse group of people made in his image. Different yet the same!

*We all have sinned
and fallen short of the glory of God.*

~ Romans 3:23 [paraphrased]

The minute I saw myself through the eyes of God and began to conduct myself accordingly by walking boldly, speaking with authority and relieving others of that control they once had on me, I was liberated! I understood the excitement and joy that energized a race of people who yelled, Say it loud, I'm black and I'm proud! From whom the Son sets free is free indeed. What a glorious experience in reclaiming my dignity and understanding that it is okay to say enough is enough as I learn the power of the word "NO." To know the Father is to know who you are! Wow, that day, I stopped allowing myself to be taken advantage of by people who proclaimed to love me as much as they loved God and yet knew very little about what it meant to truly love God with all of their heart and soul to the point of putting His commandments above their egotistical desires. Do you realize that by abusing me, you also abuse God?

CHANGE: TRUTH, FACT OR MYTH?

Do not imitate the way of this world, but be transformed by the renewing of your minds, that you may discern what is that good and acceptable and perfect will of God.

~ Romans 12:2

July 6, 2008

It is truly amazing how easy it is for man to follow a spirit of deceit and embrace it to the point of losing himself to it while still claiming to value the laws of the Lord. Seeing things from the inside out is truly a lot different than seeing them from the outside in. In comparison, it is along the lines of God seeing the end before the beginning and working backwards to the beginning while knowing the outcome will be good. Think about it from the standpoint of Romans 8:28! Although, as creatures of habit, we see the beginning and often worry about how things will end. However, trusting God and not man will give us the advantage every time. For He allows us (His children) to see what others do not see or are not willing to see! He gives us wisdom, which is referred to as vision by some and is called discernment by others.

> *Behold,*
> *thou desirest truth in the inward parts:*
> *and in the hidden part thou shalt*
> *make me to know wisdom.*
>
> ~ Psalm 51:6

From the inside, you are exposed to an array of truth that man not only refuses to see from the outside when that truth is finally revealed to him, but he devotes a great deal of time trying to convince you to be ignorant to the truth even when you do finally see it for yourself. Why? Because he would rather remain ignorant to the truth than to accept it for what it really is for fear of having to see himself for who *he* really is! *A double minded man is unstable in all his ways* (James 1:8) He refuses to see himself objectively for fear of knowing he needs to make a change, for he is not willing to change! His lies become his truth and his truth becomes his way of life. He becomes adamant and indignant in his ways that are centered on untruths and will have no hesitation in forcing them upon you through his self-reasoning (justification) that has nothing to do with the word of God (truth)!

> *Not unto us, O LORD, not unto us,*
> *but unto thy name give glory,*
> *for thy mercy, and for thy truth's sake.*
>
> ~ Psalm 115:1

There are a number of people who are trying to convince us to feel good about being bad, corrupt, dishonest, unjust and operating in an un-Godly way through our actions against others. *There is no peace, saith my God, to the wicked* (Isaiah 57:21). In the words of Creflo Dollar, an American televangelist, pastor and the founder of the non-denominational World Changers Church International based in College Park, Georgia, *you must stay away from people who are framing your way of thinking that goes against the will of God.* It would be in your best interest to stop allowing people to limit your thinking. You are more than your limitations! Stop allowing people to transpose their thoughts into your mind regardless of who they are! That holds true to family members, supervisors, coworkers and even the president of the United States. The position a person holds does not make them qualified to do the job at hand nor is it a justification of their false sense of righteousness. In other words, it does not mean they possess the appropriate skills or knowledge needed to perform the tasks of that position. The position a person holds does not make them the authority of that profession. It may mean, however, that they were in the right place at the right time or connected to the right people or power base to receive favor and were chosen above all others who were more qualified for that position. Or it may simply mean that they stole the election through unjust means. Just as the unjust receive favor, *your covenant with God* will and can give you just as much favor and more over the enemy. God's favor does not last a season, it lasts a lifetime! With that said, you must be careful not to fall for the deception of the unjust. You cannot allow yourself to be moved by what you see or what you hear, especially if it goes against the word of God. Beware of those who twist God's word to justify their untruths!

> *Confess your faults one to another,*
> *and pray one for another; that ye may be healed.*
> *The effectual fervent prayer of a righteous*
> *man availeth much.*
>
> ~ James 5:16-18

Regardless of how much we would like to change the past and rewrite history, it cannot be done. You cannot change what has happened! You can repent and attempt to make a conscious effort to make things right. However, if you refuse to acknowledge history as it has happened—meaning, refusing to acknowledge your wrongdoing—you cannot begin to right a wrong successfully and move forward. For those of us who were affected by history (that which is in the past), we must still address it and confront it, regardless of how painful it is, to allow healing to begin.

> *The power to feel another's hurt and*
> *to want to heal that hurt,*
> *to sense another's need and want to*
> *satisfy that need—this is the root of social justice.*
>
> ~ Harry & Bonaro Overstreet

Oftentimes, I have heard, "hurt people hurt people." Nonetheless, hurt must be confronted and exposed constructively and without violence in order for healing to take place. You cannot put a bandage on it to cover it up while hoping it will just go away! No more than a person who has suffered hurt can lock it away in the deepest corner of their mind hoping to get over the pain and not be affected by it somewhere in the future. The greatest injustice, however, is not only refusing to acknowledge your contribution to the wrong that was inflicted on another in the past, but it is your continued, blatant disregard for your current behavior in the present which tells me you have no desire to change. Irrespective of your deep-rooted desire to avoid the truth or dismiss it, at some point you must take responsibility for your actions—actions I consider to be major contributions to the pollution in this environment we call "America." That mentality has festered and it is referred to as the "American Way," which still exists today! Was America truly built on Godly principles or greed? Or perhaps, have we just confused Godly principles with man's personal crusade for dominance by any means necessary through the concept of religion? This is a time of self-examination and social transformation! *When you allow your mind to be conformed to the world, you then forsake the standard that God has established.*[14] *When you are not connected to the Spirit of Christ, you will assume the world's disposition, conforming to what others dictate.*[15]

---

14 Bishop Noel Jones, *The Battle for the Mind* (Destiny Image Publishers, Inc., Shippensburg, PA, 2006) 89.

15 Bishop Noel Jones, *The Battle for the Mind* (Destiny Image Publishers, Inc., Shippensburg, PA, 2006) 91.

As the Christian church became increasingly corrupted by state power, religious rhetoric was often used to justify imperial aims and conceal the prophetic heritage of Christianity.[16]

~ Dr. Cornel West

Reverend Dr. Jeremiah A. Wright Jr.[17]

Blacks as well as other minority groups have become so familiar with disparity (not being able to enjoy the same equality as whites) that they rarely speak up anymore about the injustice. Those who do speak up come under attack and receive various threats as well as attempts to defame their character! Can you imagine being so frustrated by what you see and convicted by your heart that it makes it impossible not to speak up and out against what you see? Speaking in love with all sincerity, you still find yourself being persecuted for your sense of integrity and desire for truth—a lifelong tactic used to tear you down and shut you up for stepping out of line. Then you become subject to a campaign to put you back in your rightful place to be seen and not heard. However, in the case of many blacks, you are not to be seen or heard. Therefore, your words and intent deliberately get taken out of context. Why put yourself in a position to be

---

16 Cornel West, *Democracy Matters* (Penguin Books, London, England, 2004) 148.

17 Rev. Wright was called by God to preach; he was not called by man. He is responsible to God, not man. Speaking the truth in love is not being divisive. The institution of slavery not only divided us a long time ago; America, through the unconstitutional leadership of vindictive acts, continues to set us apart from the rest of the world in a less-than-favorable way.

the center of the enemy's attention? Satan will stop at nothing to destroy your character. He comes to steal, kill and destroy. However, if God be for you, who can be against you?

> *Integrity will guide the righteous,*
> *but the duplicity of the wicked will (attempt)*
> *to destroy them.*
>
> *~ Proverbs 11:3*

In April or May of 2008, the most talked about person on planet earth was Reverend Dr. Jeremiah A. Wright Jr. I would say that makes him the most important person in the history of all people besides God because he has obtained more than just 30 minutes of fame. Reverend Wright Jr. is a black man who was born on September 22, 1941, in Philadelphia, Pennsylvania. His description alone qualifies him as being a person who can rightfully talk about his point of view from a black experience (or perspective for you educated folks). Are you aware of the events in history as it relates to the black experience as early as 1941?

> *Arise, shine; for thy light is come,*
> *and the glory of the LORD is risen upon thee.*
> *For, behold, the darkness shall cover the earth,*
> *and gross darkness the people:*
> *but the LORD shall arise upon thee,*
> *and his glory shall be seen upon thee.*
>
> *~ Isaiah 60:1-2*

Why should Reverend Wright dismiss his calling and heritage to overlook history and be unwilling to address it because you refuse to accept the truth? *Evil men understand not judgment: but they that seek the LORD understand all things* (Proverbs 28:5). To accept the truth, you must be willing to hear the truth and acknowledge it! Unfortunately, people do not want to hear the truth. Do you want to hear the truth or do you want someone to tell you only what you want to hear? Do you want the truth straight up or do you want it sugar-coated and watered down to be insignificant? Do you want the truth only when it feels good or are you willing to accept the good with the bad?

> *For God does not*
> *withdraw his gift and his call.*
>
> ~ Romans 12:29

To my surprise, for the first time since the beginning of what is now termed a microwave society, we have been challenged to use something called our brain. Is that not a good thing? Some of us have been in the dark for so long that we have lost sight of what it truly means to be able to think for ourselves. We have lost the ability to rationalize, analyze or research the truth for ourselves. Why? Because we have been brought into a way of thinking that voids us of ourselves. You have to be able to think beyond the limitations that have been placed on your mind and in your mind to exercise your mind! You have become a part of the deception! You have allowed yourselves to fall under the spell of a Jezebel spirit. Why is it unbelievable to think that the government could be responsible for the recreation of and the spread of HIV-AIDS as a political form of genocide or population control? Why is affordable healthcare a thing of the past?

> *For ye, brethren, became followers of the churches of God which in Jesus are in Christ Jesus: for ye also have suffered like things of your countrymen, even as they have of the Jews: Who both killed the Lord Jesus, and their own prophets, and have persecuted us; and they please not God, and are contrary to all men:*
>
> ~ Thessalonians 2:14-15

A Little Known Fact

The Tuskegee Study of untreated syphilis in the black male, also known as the Tuskegee Syphilis Study or the Tuskegee Experiment,[18] was a clinical study conducted between 1932 and 1972 in Tuskegee, Alabama. Three hundred and ninety-nine poor—and mostly illiterate—African American sharecroppers, who already suffered from syphilis, were studied to observe the natural progression of the disease if left untreated.

Individuals enrolled in the Tuskegee Syphilis Study did not give consent and were not informed of their diagnosis; instead, they were told they had "bad blood" and could receive free medical treatment, rides to the clinic, meals and burial insurance in case of death in return for participating.

---

18 https://www.infoplease.com/us/race-population/tuskegee-syphilis-experiment

The Tuskegee Syphilis Study[19] *was cited as being "arguably, the most infamous biomedical research study in U.S. history" that led to the* 1979 *Belmont Report*[20].

The American Way or The American Dream

Unfortunately, the ideal American dream has been one based on assimilation. (Let's not forget the episodes of *Star Trek* introducing the "Borg." What was their major mission?) Though we have moved into an age of diversity and have been there for quite some time, since the early 1990s, there are some who not only refuse to share, but they feel they are entitled to more than half of everything, if not all. This mindset stems from what I perceive to be the "good old boy network": a culture or society of a majority of white men who determine truth based on a limited and false sense of knowledge geared at controlling all women and minorities with brute force.

What Is Assimilation?

Depicted by a 58-minute PBS video segment presentation, *In the White's Image,* is a very good example of assimilation. It examines how a humanist experiment gone wrong was really a form of cultural genocide in disguise.[21] In St. Augustine, Florida, in 1875, an ambitious experiment was conceived to teach Native Americans to become imitation white men. With

---

[19] http://www.med.navy.mil/bumed/Documents/Healthcare%20Ethics/Racism-And-Research.pdf

[20] https://www.hhs.gov/ohrp/regulations-and-policy/belmont-report/index.html

[21] https://youtu.be/WpkIsyc0YRU

the blessing of Congress, the first school for Native Americans was established in Carlisle, Pennsylvania, to continue the "civilizing" mission. Native American students had their hair cut short and were forbidden to speak their native languages or to visit home for up to five years. By 1902, there were twenty-six reservation boarding schools.[22]

Today, we live in a very self-centered, selfish society that exhibits what I consider to be a sensate[23] culture. Where is the integrity? We are shown time and time again that an elitist, arrogant attitude is not only good but gives us immunity to the law. Wire-tapping is illegal, but I'm the president, so that gives me the right to be as unjust as I deem absolutely necessary. Why? Because I'm the king of this country; I am god. I do not feel that all people within the world should be entitled to the same treatment, which is why I pardoned I. Lewis "Scooter" Libby. So what if he was convicted of obstruction of justice and perjury for lying to the FBI? He broke the law under my leadership; therefore, he does not deserve to reap one day of punishment for that which he sowed. Yes, we are in a recession and as president, I should be concerned about all people; however, I am only concerned about myself and protecting the wealthy from being affected by a deficit. (A man is literally what he thinks, his character being the complete sum of all his thoughts). Extending unemployment benefits to allow for an additional three to six months, depending upon the circumstances on a case-by-case basis, is neither acceptable nor deserving regardless of whether

---

22   https://www.facinghistory.org/books-borrowing/white-mans-image
23   Perceiving or perceived by the senses; a feeling.

or not it should affect those in the lower class (whites) who voted for me. As quiet as it is kept, my idea of wealthy excludes people of color as well as the many others who are not on my level. I came into office with an agenda—an agenda that calls for a few sacrificial lambs. *The name of the Lord is a strong tower: the righteous runneth into it and is safe. The rich man's wealth is his strong city and as a high wall in his own conceit* (Proverbs 18:10-11). I am, for the most part, a ruthless businessman who is ruled by my flesh and operates under a perverted sense of Christianity with the same mindset as my ancestors over 400 years ago. I know how to market myself to appeal to the little folks to make them believe I truly care about them. I sold them on my faith-based initiative, which has nothing to do with the word of God!

When the wicked are multiplied, transgression increaseth: but the righteous shall see their fall.

~ Proverbs 29:1

What is fear? Fear is a weapon of the enemy! Why has it taken so long to prove weapons of mass destruction do, in fact, exist—if they ever did? Were we manipulated by **fear** (false evidence appearing real) as a result of the events of September 11, 2001, to go along with a war inflicted upon innocent people in an attempt to settle a personal war of vengeance? What have we proven? Really! We have been instrumental as a nation of people to destroy another nation of people, but for what? To repeat history and prove we are better? Superior? Have we succeeded in being a dominant and controlling nation of bullies who unconventionally take what we want because we can? Has no one bothered to research the significance of September 11 to see the connection or pattern to political events? Did no one bother to see the possible connection of the passengers aboard those planes that went down on September 11? Why is it so impossible to believe that such an event could not have been orchestrated by our government? (New money against old money in the name of The New World Order. America is ruled by a corrupt government with many dishonest people deliberately and strategically placed in many positions of power to misguide faith!) Has no one bothered to take a look at the events of our history and note the driving force of our power base? Perhaps you may want to review the nature and character of a Jezebel spirit. *A spirit is neither male nor female; it will attach itself to whomever it can operate in for the best results based on your identity or desire for evil or righteousness.* Whose will are you following? Have you examined your heart lately? Is it that important to follow those in power based on the position they hold, even if they have proven to be morally wrong in their actions? You cannot possibly feel good about the outcome of the events of this nation and consider yourself to be a true Christian.

> *Not every one that saith unto me, Lord, Lord,*
> *shall enter into the Kingdom of heaven;*
> *but he that doeth the will of my Father which is in heaven.*
> *And then will I profess unto them, I never knew you:*
> *depart from me, ye that work iniquity.*
>
> ~ Matthew 7:21-23

We cannot continue as we have in the past and feel as though we are entitled to take what we want without taking responsibility for that which we have done. What goes around comes around. We will reap what we sow in more ways than one. You cannot continue to terrorize people in your own country as well as others in neighboring countries and not give any thought to the consequences. There has been no change because there has been no practice of change—only arrogance and pride! We as Americans have become so comfortable in our sin that we not only fail to recognize truth, we refuse to see it for what it's worth. Yes, *in* our sin, not *with* our sin! We want mercy, but we do not know the first thing about being merciful. *Have mercy on me, O God, have mercy on me, for in you my soul takes refuge. I will take refuge in the shadow of your wings until the disaster has passed* (Psalm 57:1). We have been controlled by negativity for so long that we have reclassified it as justice.

> *He that covereth his sins shall not prosper:*
> *but whoso confesseth and forsaketh*
> *them shall have mercy.*
>
> ~Proverbs 28:13

Ironically, if ignorance according to man's law is, in fact, nine-tenths of the law, shouldn't knowing the truth and doing nothing to correct it make you just as guilty as not knowing the truth? Especially when our judiciary system is structured around this very fact and enforced by men who use it to falsely accuse and sentence individuals for crimes on the basis of not having all the facts or the entire truth. And on the basis of double standards, from where I sit, our judiciary system has also been instrumental in freeing a number of individuals who were entirely guilty, not only in accordance to the truth but with all the facts present as well. How is the truth beneficial if it is not "the whole truth and nothing but the truth"?

> *Then said Jesus to those Jews which*
> *believed on him, If ye <u>continue</u> in my word,*
> *then are ye my disciples indeed;*
> *And ye shall know the truth, and the truth*
> *shall make you free.*
>
> ~ John 8:31-32

Why would the judiciary system allow the men responsible for the bombing of the 16th Street Baptist Church, which took the lives of four little girls (Addie Mae Collins, Denise McNair, Carole Robertson and Cynthia Wesley) on September 15, 1963, to go unpunished and not be determined to seek justice for them until there was talk of reparations for a race of people who were unlawfully enslaved? And yet the current president of the United States would have us believe that such treatment was rightfully justified because it was the law. (*As a man thinketh, so is he in his heart!*) Where else but in America can a man get sentenced to three years for what is considered to be a crime against an animal, while those who take the life of a human being on his wedding day are acquitted? And in a court of law, his death is ruled as being a justifiable accident when he was shot about fifty times by law enforcement officers. If the word of God can be twisted and perverted, why can't the law?

Laws have not been written to protect human rights; they have been developed and redefined to take away human rights. For the most part, there is no rhyme or reason to the actual laws that are on the books.

> Former United States Border Patrol Agents were convicted of shooting an unarmed, illegal alien drug smuggler on the United States–Mexico border near El Paso, Texas, on February 17, 2005.[24, 25]
>
> - Ramos was sentenced to eleven years and one day in prison to include being charged with causing serious bodily injury, assault with a deadly weapon, discharge of a firearm in relation to a crime of violence and a civil rights violation.
>
> - Compeán was sentenced to twelve years and charged with "obstructing justice by willfully defacing the crime scene."

A man goes to trial for murder and is acquitted but not before a member of a law enforcement team deliberately plants evidence in attempting to falsely tie the man to the murder.

---

24 http://www.washingtontimes.com/news/2007/dec/28/justice-for-two/
25 http://www.wlf.org/upload/WLF%20Amicus%20Brief%20in%20 U.S.%20v.%20Ramos.pdf

The law enforcement officer commits purgery and incriminates himself, which is revealed in the court of law. However, the man who is acquitted of murder and found not guilty is later charged with wrongful death for the murder of the same woman. How is this possible? Did the law enforcement officer who committed perjury and violated the law get any time for his crime? Laws are established on the basis of politics in accordance to the biases and possible views of those in power for that term or duration. Now, I am certainly not an attorney or a judge and others would argue that because I lack such credentials that would classify me as one or the other, my knowledge or way of thinking is very limited. I, on the other hand, would argue that when you know better, you must begin to do better! And more often than not, common sense and being self-taught or well-read in many areas of interest carries more weight. What a backwards world we live in; however, it's not the world, it's the *people* in the world who have embraced this negativity and taught it to our children. (*In the world, not of the world.*) Negativity and hate breed negativity and hate! What are we teaching children? What are we saying to the nations outside of the United States when we want them to believe we, Americans, are better than they are?

> *The collapse of the meaning in life—the eclipse of hope and absence of love of self and others, the breakdown of family and neighborhood bonds— leads to the social deracination and cultural denudement of urban dwellers, especially children.*[26]

---

26 Cornel West, Race Matters (Vintage Books, New York, New York, 2001) 9.

Let History Speak for Itself

When Columbus arrived in North America, there was approximately one to three million Native Americans already living here. When white settlers began seizing Indian land, that's when the conflict arose. In 1754, the British government forbade the seizing of Indian land, but the colonists broke this rule or law at every possible opportunity and another plan was devised. Through the American Revolution, treaties with hidden laws and terms were developed. These treaties or agreements (government contracts) were written with the intent to deceive various tribes into believing their rights were being protected. After realizing the opposite had occurred, these tribes were reluctant to accept the government terms that not only placed sanctions on their land, but the terms were also directed at attempting to force them into slavery with the aid of military force. If you know your history, you know New York City was stolen from the Native Americans. (Honestly, it was never obtained for what it was worth!)

If we say that we have no sin,
we deceive ourselves, and the truth is not in us.

~ 1 John 1:8

By 1700, blacks were being delivered from Africa in chains and sold into slavery. Native Americans were too successful at escaping and making their way through the woods to their own people to be forced into slavery. For resisting, Congress decided in 1871 that no Indian tribes would be recognized for purposes of treaties. Instead, they would become wards of the government and later, Public Law 280 was passed to allow state governments to govern Indian reservations. As time went on, the Indian population steadily decreased; this was partly due to contracting diseases from white settlers, being massacred or suffering starvation, which resulted in the deliberate killing of the buffalo by whites for sport and retaliation.

> *The words of his mouth are iniquity and deceit:*
> *he hath left off to be wise, and to do good.*
>
> ~ Psalm 36:3

The History of the Black Experience

From the beginning, the U.S. Federal Government created policies that discriminated against blacks. In Dred Scott v. Sanford (1857), the Supreme Court of the United States declared that blacks could never be citizens of the United States. Free blacks were refused passports by the federal government. Slavery ended in 1865 and was represented through the thirteenth amendment to the Constitution, but the oppression of blacks did not end. Oppression of blacks has a long history in North America and over the years, it has been extended to other races. After the war, the nation adopted two other constitutional amendments: the 14th (1868), making blacks citizens of the United States and prohibiting state laws that denied them equal protection as citizens under the law but failed to enforce it; and the 15th (1870), prohibiting racial discrimination in voting.

> *The NAACP took an active role in organizing a petition and being the voice of us as a race of people to discuss the renewal of*

the 1965 Voting Rights Act. On July 20, 2006, the Senate Judiciary Committee voted in favor of reauthorizing the Voting Rights Act. G. W. Bush addressed the NAACP and seven days later, on July 27, 2006, Bush signed the bill renewing the Voting Rights Act for another twenty-five years. Do you know how close we came to having this ruling not met because there were some who did not feel this was an important issue for us to accomplish—yet again—in the twentieth century? Why is a date or limitation placed on the Voting Rights Act?

> *Think about what it means to*
> *have the mindset of Christ.*
> *You must show evidence of selflessness*
> *and humility while considering the needs*
> *of others as our top priority.*[27]

The Civil Rights Act of 1866 made it a federal crime to deprive a person of color born in the United States of the rights of full citizenship. Both this legislation and the 14th Amendment made civil rights the responsibility of the federal government. However, through the birth of Andrew Johnson's Presidential Reconstruction, the 1865 unwritten laws referred to as the *black codes* were re-enforced by white legislatures in 1866 and beyond. Segregation (Jim Crow) in the United States was a legal and social practice of separating people on the basis of their race or ethnicity. Segregation by law occurred when local, state or national laws made it a requirement. The Supreme Court in *Plessy v. Ferguson* (1896) upheld the constitutionality of separate

---

27   Bishop Noel Jones, *The Battle for the Mind* (Destiny Image Publishers, Inc., Shippensburg, PA, 2006) 158.

railroad cars for blacks and whites. Speaking for the court, Justice Henry Billings Brown argued that as long as the separate facilities for each race were "equal," they were permitted under the Constitution. In dissent, Justice John Marshall Harlan, the only Southerner on the court and a former slave-owner, argued that the "Constitution is colorblind and neither knows nor tolerates classes among citizens." Justice Harlan pointed out that segregation created a psychological sense of superiority among whites while harming blacks. Throughout the South, segregation had the support of the legal system and the police. (*Injustices supported by the legal system and the police. How has this changed?*) Such customs were humiliating and oppressed blacks both emotionally and legally.

The Black Codes

Labor contracts bound blacks to white plantation owners; the black codes were not only established to control blacks and keep them in line, but they were established as an aid to labor contracts. Black codes were a series of laws that dictated rights and restrictions on the freedoms of the newly emancipated slaves with only a few privileges. Among them was the right to own, buy and sell property; the right to sue or testify in court but only in cases against other blacks (not whites); and the restriction that prohibited them to serve on juries. The codes allowed for marriage but didn't permit blacks to marry outside their race; they prohibited blacks to carry firearms or other weapons, as they were reserved for whites. These codes were not only a devastating setback to blacks, who had expected greater freedoms instead of a relapse back into slavery, but they varied from state to state. Black codes, in addition to the Jim Crow laws legalized corporal punishment, maintained black inferiority and established a system analogous to slavery that remained in effect for well over another century. Escalating the situation was the profusion of attacks against blacks as well as other whites who were favorable to justice for all that resulted in cross burnings, lynchings, rapes, beatings and other hostile acts—thus culminating into major riots in Memphis, Tennessee; New Orleans, Louisiana; and Tulsa, Oklahoma.

> *Blessed is the man that walketh not in the counsel*
> *of the ungodly, nor standeth in the way of sinners,*
> *nor sitteth in the seat of the scornful.*
> *But his delight is in the law of the LORD;*
> *and in his law doth he meditate day and night.*
>
> ~ Psalm 1:1-2

Beyond the law, there was always the threat of **terrorist violence** against blacks who attempted to challenge or even question the established so-called order of justice not enjoyed by all on the basis of inequality. During the reconstruction, in the winter of 1865 to 1866, the Ku Klux Klan (KKK), which is the oldest terrorist organization in the world, was formed by a former Confederate general. The objective was to stop both blacks and Northerners from carrying out their government and social reforms along with the Knights of the White Camellia,[28] and other terrorist organizations. These groups or organizations were responsible for the deaths and murders of thousands of

---

28   http://www.knowlouisiana.org/entry/knights-of-the-white-camellia

blacks and some whites as they attempted, through tactics of intimidation, fear and extreme violence, to prevent them from voting and participating in public life. For example, in 1876 and 1877, mobs of whites led by former Confederate generals killed scores of blacks in South Carolina to prevent them from voting or holding office. These white terrorist groups directed their violence toward black landowners, politicians and community leaders, as well as whites who supported racial equality. In some cases, the presence of the U.S. Army prevented mass killings; however, there were never enough soldiers to actually stop the violence, nor was it intended to. Some of the very same men who were disguised as soldiers upholding the law by day were some of the very same men who operated as members of the KKK by night.

> *Let not them that are mine enemies wrongfully*
> *rejoice over me: neither let them wink with the*
> *eye that hate me without a cause.*
> *For they speak not peace:*
> *but they devise deceitful matters*
> *against them that are quiet in the land.*
>
> ~ Psalm 35:19-20

On May 31, 1921, 1,000 to 1,500 whites initiated one of the nation's worst acts of racial violence. It is referenced as being the most horrific race riot in history and known to some as the Black Holocaust—a riot so heinous that it claimed the lives of many blacks in addition to whites who were not in agreement with what was happening. Police with military and combat experience flew airplanes and dropped nitroglycerin and dynamite on 600 black businesses, including churches, two black-owned newspaper establishments, a school, a hospital and a library. Approximately 1,500 homes were burned and looted before they were torched. The Greenwood District in Oklahoma—a 36-square-block black community in Tulsa that was so prosperous that it was nationally known as or referred to as Black Wall Street, with a property value equivalent to $14 million in comparison to today's currency—was destroyed. As of this date, no one responsible for this crime against the Greenwood community has been brought to justice. No monetary compensation for damages to homes or businesses was made by the state or federal government to those who suffered a loss. The longest living survivor is approximately 100 years old. Each year since the 1921 riot, he, along with others (before their death), has attempted to seek justice and restitution. Do you see the irony? Unfortunately, the longest living survivor, after all these years, may not get the opportunity to obtain that restitution!

H.R. 1995: The Tulsa-Greenwood Race Riot Claims Accountability Act of 2007 was enacted on April 23, 2007. **Objective:** provide a mechanism for a determination on the merits of the claims brought by survivors and descendants of the victims of the Tulsa, Oklahoma, Race Riot of 1921 but who were denied that determination in a civil action commencing within five (5) years after the enactment of this Act.[29, 30, 31]

---

29   https://www.congress.gov/bill/110th-congress/house-bill/1995/text
30   https://www.youtube.com/watch?v=NboclI2h-5s
31   https://www.youtube.com/watch?v=QHVQEk8fi2M

Seeing Things as They Are

The Civil Rights Act of 1964 was established to outlaw structured racism and discrimination in the areas of employment and public facilities as well as to create the Equal Employment Opportunity Commission, which was enacted to end segregation in schools. Where else but in America could the confession of two men (Roy Bryant and J.W. Milam, the latter a first lieutenant in the U.S. Army Reserve) who were responsible for the killing of a fourteen-year-old boy, Emmett Till, appear in a story in the January 1956 issue of *Look* magazine for which they actually received compensation? That article, entitled *The Shocking Story of Approved Killing in Mississippi*, by William Bradford Huie outlined the events of such an atrocity in great detail for which justice did not prevail.[32] Adding further insult, because two teachers were planning to have students read a poem about Emmett Till, entitled *A Wreath for Emmett Till*, they were fired from a Los Angeles charter school on March 18, 2007.[33],[34]

> *False witnesses did rise up;*
> *they laid to my charge things that I knew not.*
>
> ~ Psalm 35:11

Unfortunately, discrimination, racism and prejudicial practices are still alive and thriving in the year 2008; for example,

---

32 http://www.pbs.org/wgbh/amex/till/sfeature/sf_look_confession.html
33 http://www.npr.org/templates/story/story.php?storyId=9184608
34 http://articles.latimes.com/2007/mar/19/local/me-newcharter19

the brutal and inhumane treatment of the men who were held captive at the Abu Ghraib prison that uncovered accounts of abuse, torture, sodomy and homicide beginning in 2004.[35] And, what about the issues surrounding the rights of those being held at Guantánamo[36]? Are they not still men—regardless of what we deem their actions to have been? Are they not entitled to their day in court? What evidence of proof was presented to warrant their incarceration? Do you not see a pattern? What have we been reduced to? The Bush administration wanted to limit the rights of the Guantánamo detainees. The practices of injustices are still prevalent but re-disguised and enforced by something called the justice system and religion. Are you spiritual or religious? What does God see or think of you when he is a witness to your actions or views? Our troops are fighting a very senseless war that has nothing to do with justice. The Supreme Court has helped to lead the way with its support of the Patriot Act, an attempt to enforce and exercise more control. Unfortunately, our government and this current administration (Bush) rewrote and broke laws at will to fulfill a personal and political mandate. And, they made many justifications for it by twisting the truth with no accountability. So once again, they have created an environment that encourages dissention against another race fueled by rage, hostility, violence and injustice.

---

35 2004 Taguba Report, a criminal investigation by the U.S. Army Criminal Investigation Command and a U.S. television news-magazine: 60 Minutes II.

36 http://www.cnn.com/2013/09/09/world/guantanamo-bay-naval-station-fast-facts/

For Immediate Release:
March 10, 2008 @11:24 AM

A Report by Krista Minteer, *Human Rights First*, reads:

Tortured Justice: Using Coerced Evidence to Prosecute Terrorist Suspects—released today by Human Rights First, finds the Bush administration has undercut its own intended use of the military commission system to bring those responsible for September 11, 2001 to justice, by allowing the admission of evidence tainted by torture. The administration sanctioned the use of abusive interrogation methods, believing that the need to gather information by any means to prevent future terrorist attacks took precedence over the complications it would cause down the line in prosecuting crimes that had already taken place.[37]

Two to three days after Barack Obama reiterated plans to the nation to bring the U.S. troops home to the United States, within a sixteen-month period following the November 2008 election, an article in the July 10, 2008, issue of the *Express* (a publication of the Washington Post) reads, "Iran Launch Seen as Warning." What a remarkable coincidence! I'm sure his decision was seen as a form of infringement by those who had a personal interest in the oil business! Unfortunately, a great deal of negative talk soon followed concerning thoughts of impeachment and sadly, assignation attempts! With that said, I assume Iran is also tired of being bullied by the United States and has no desire of being

---

37 http//www.humanrightsfirst.info/pdf/08307-etn-tortured-u\ justice-web.pdf

victimized by us anymore—at least not without a fight. As quiet as it is kept, the war in Iraq was never the intended purpose. It was always about oil and Iran. Iraq is simply a means to an end; the back door to Iran! With approximately four months of his term remaining, G. W. Bush needs to move fast to carry out his plans to attack Iran; however, he needs to create probable cause in the eyes of the nation to get support from Congress and the rest of the American people. So yet again, with the assistance of fear, Bush may get that support but at the expense of our troops being put in more danger. The troops are fighting a war for an American people who always fail to take care of them upon their return home. You cannot tell me no one was aware of the appalling conditions of Walter Reed or the many other military medical facilities within the United States before it was made public in the media. They knew, but no one in a position of high importance cared enough to make sure financial provisions were made to ensure funding was appropriately allocated for improving the level of care our military service men and women obtained while making numerous sacrifices for country.

> *But I fear, lest by any means,*
> *as the serpent beguiled Eve through his subtilty,*
> *so your minds should be corrupted from the*
> *simplicity that is in Christ.*
>
> *~ 2 Corinthians 11:3*

Wake up and review things objectively! Unless you are willing to dissect an issue, deal with it objectively and discuss it openly; the fumes from this pollution will continue to ignite and burn as it destroys what little **humanity** we have left. We will continue in the direction in which we began in history by not making an effort to change because we refuse to look at truth as it is today in relation to what it was in the past. You cannot continue to say that you are not and will not address it because it was the law during a period in our American history to commit an unrighteous indignation against another. You cannot and should not justify a wrong action as being right because it was constituted a law! Immoral is immoral; regardless of how you justify it! Many of our laws were written as a double standard! The law was wrong then and it has not improved much now. Only how they are implemented is more sophisticated and strategic!

How much change do you see? Do we really have "freedom of speech"? Why does it matter from where that freedom is spoken, whether inside of the pulpit or outside of the pulpit? Looking at history, all races were not allowed to worship together; in fact, there was a race of people who were forbidden to step foot inside of a church that was occupied by whites unless they were forced to provide the entertainment. Was not the church instrumental in helping to enforce a law that enslaved a race of people in spite of the fact that Christ hath redeemed us from the curse of the law? Nonetheless, it was faith in the Father, Son and the Holy Ghost and the belief that change was inevitable that sustained them!

Jeremiah Asher – Protesting the "Negro Pew"

In the nineteenth century, Asher faced a situation of inherent racism that permeated American culture and shook the very foundations of the ungodly system that existed behind church doors.

I contented that those seats which were made for whites were good enough for blacks; if they did not wish to mix us together, they could give us a certain number of seats expressly for colored persons. But church leaders were aware that, without some visible distinction, whites coming in would often be sitting in the Negro seats and their devotions would be frequently disturbed by the pew-opener, who would be obliged to remove them and regulate all such irregularities ... If me will disenfranchise and separate me from the rest of my Father's children, they shall do it at their own expense, not mine. I cannot prevent, but I will not help them do it. I will lift up my voice against it.

God Has Soul:

Celebrating the Indomitable Spirit of African Americans

African Heritage Series, Honor Books,

Colorado Springs, CO, 2004.

Accept Change!

Embrace Change!

Be Willing to Change!

Be Willing to Implement Change!

I am sure, without a doubt, that there are a number of people reading this who not only fail to see the truth and are consciously unwilling to take a stand for the truth, but they will be quick to call me un-American and in the same breath will call on God to bless America regardless of the truth. However, I, a person who was born in America and currently lives in America as a descendant of a race of people who have been victims of America in the present as well as in the past, pray to God to have mercy on those who find themselves in the middle of a senseless, inhuman society of selfishly motivated people spiraling in an ungodly direction to fulfill a desire for life and death that resembles anything but the character of Christ in an effort to prove they are better in some way.

> *He shall call to the heavens from above, and to the earth, that he may judge his people. Gather my saints together unto me; those that have made a covenant with me by sacrifice. And the heavens shall declare his righteousness: for God is judge himself. Selah.*
>
> ~ Psalm 50:4

At the age of forty-seven, I do not have a whole lot of time to waste. If only I knew at the age of sixteen or seventeen what I know now, I would have been further along in my walk with Christ. Listening to Joyce Myers one morning as I prepared for work, I heard her say, "Your attitude in the wilderness determines how long you will be there. Your attitude during your time of trouble determines how long you will endure." The more negative the attitude or the less productive you are, the longer it will take you to receive your breakthrough! It took Moses and the Israelites forty years to complete an eleven-day journey. Change constitutes you not only changing your attitude, but you must change your way of thinking to see results. Why apologize for something and not mean it? If you plan to continue to conduct yourself as you have and not give any thought to changing your attitude or way of thinking to improve your actions, why exert all that unnecessary energy in being phony? Have you not realized by now that what you do in the dark will eventually come out in the light? You have to take responsibility for your actions and start by changing your demeanor.

> *According to my earnest expectation and my hope,*
> *that in nothing I shall be ashamed,*
> *but that with a all boldness,*
> *as always, so now also Christ*
> *shall be magnified in my body,*
> *whether it be by life, or by death.*
>
> ~ Philippians 1:20

For I know who I am! I know my identity. For God I live and for God I die. I refuse to hate myself in the name of white supremacy that has taken on another identity (Nicolaitanes) to prove myself by condemning others (black, white, purple or yellow) through unjust treatment similar to that of my ancestors who fought for their freedom as well as mine. I will not dishonor the legacy of my ancestors by attempting to deny others a piece of the pie that was not created with me in mind. I will, however, honor them by continuing to fight for my rights as a citizen of the United States as well as the rights of all humans. I will not allow myself to be deceived by the adversary and turn my back on God and all his teachings to fit into a world that has so quickly sold its soul to the devil which is evident by their unjust treatment of others. *If a wise man contendeth with a foolish man, whether he rage or laugh, there is no rest* (Proverbs 29:9). I will not allow myself to be used or tricked by the adversary into oppressing others to mirror the image of those in the world as I have been oppressed. My heart goes out to Ignacio Ramos and José Alonso Compeán, the former U.S. Border Patrol Agents. What a vicious cycle!

God's commandment and will for us is to walk in love! Beware that thou forget not the Lord thy God, in not keeping His commandments, and His judgments, and His statutes, which I command thee this day.

~ Deuteronomy 8:11

Well done thy good and faithful servant!

~ Luke 4:18

I AM ONLY HUMAN

*Be ye therefore perfect,
even as your Father which is in heaven is perfect.*

~ **Matthew 5:48**

September 28, 2008

God the Father loved us so much that He sacrificed His only son. Does that not account for something? *So then every one of us shall account of himself to God (Romans 14:12).* It seems my journaled testimony, dated September 8, 2008, which was shared with many as a handout and blog post, concerning the hurt we cause each other even as Christians, has stirred up much controversy. Some have embraced it and see it as a blessing. Some are indifferent to it and some feel I must be going through something, so they wish to condemn it as well as me. Truth be told, I am going through something. As long as I am here on earth, I will continue to go through something. However, that does not prevent me from listening to God and wanting to follow through with his command. Even here on earth! Yes!

I am here in the world but not of the world. For this is not my home; I am not from here!

Casting down imaginations, and every high thing that exalteth itself against the knowledge of God, and bringing into captivity every thought to the obedience of Christ.

~ 2 Corinthians 10:5

Because I have been determined to not allow myself to be pulled down by those who take on the belief that being human gives them the right to operate in the manner in which they do, there seems to be some question about my salvation. *Neither is there salvation in any other: for there is none other name under heaven given among men, whereby we must be saved* (Acts 4:12). For the most part, after all, they are only human! So what if I treat my fellow neighbor unjustly? I am only human. So what if I, as a manager, approve for some to get a raise while others on my staff who work just as hard within their capability (as allowed) are denied raises? I am only human. So what if I define their net worth or value to be lesser than another human being's on the basis of their identity or social status regardless if they do have more experience? I am only human. So what if I determine they should be treated subserviently based on a class I have equated for them? I am only human. *But thou shalt remember the Lord thy God: for it is He that giveth thee power to get wealth, that He may establish His covenant which He sware unto thy fathers, as it is this day* (Deuteronomy 8:18). How often are we going to attempt to use the justification of our actions as an excuse for being human and not consider what God wants? Did He not give us an example to live by in Christ?

> *For God sent not his Son into the*
> *world to condemn the world;*
> *But that the world through him might be saved.*
>
> ~ John 3:17

Conviction vs. Condemnation

Perhaps the questioning of my salvation by others is a result of my lack of fear and unwillingness to succumb to the control of others who want me to believe that I know nothing about Christianity or what it really means to be saved. Or could this view or way of thinking stem more from a person who lacks knowledge about humanity as well as the concept and need for all to be treated equally? As man condemns us through control, God convicts us through love—without control. Oppression is a form of ungodliness and mind control used by the adversary. God grants us free will to act on what we believe to be right or wrong and I choose not to follow man as it relates to his sense of thinking. Yes, I am human; but that should not be an excuse or justification for wrongdoing! Jesus Christ was human too and let's not forget He was God the Father who ascended to earth in the flesh as a man; God's ultimate ambassador to be a leading example for us all. *So we are Christ's ambassadors; God is making his appeal through us. We speak for Christ when we plead, "Come back to God!" For God made Christ, who never sinned, to be the offering for our sin, so that we could be made right with God through Christ* (2 Corinthinas 5:20-21 NLT). A fact and a truth that many Christians seem so easily to forget as they eagerly misuse the integrity of God.

> *And ye shall be hated of all men for my name's sake:*
> *but he that endureth to the end shall be saved.*
>
> ~ Matthew 10:22

Was I not saved some time ago when Christ died for my sins? In fact, we all were; however, it is up to us to believe, to ask for forgiveness and to be willing to forgive ourselves. Do I believe in the Father, the Son and the Holy Ghost? You cannot believe in one and not the other and consider yourself to be a true Christian. He who dwells within me not only orders my steps, but it is He who guides my hands and my thoughts as I write what is instructed. That is why it is important for each of us to develop a relationship with God and to get to know Him for ourselves rather than accepting what others want us to believe. How often are we going to attempt to use the justification of our actions as an excuse for being human and not consider what God wants? Did He not give us an example to live by in Christ?

> *Blessed are they which do hunger*
> *and thirst after righteousness:*
> *for they shall be filled.*
>
> ~ Matthew 5:6

> From the Dictionary and Concordance of the Holy Bible
>
> **PERFECT:**
>
> *To be whole or complete; also referred to as "mature." The perfection demanded of Christians is a state of spiritual maturity or completeness.*

And when Abram was ninety years old an nine, the LORD appeared to Abram and said unto him, I am the Almighty God;
walk before me be thou perfect. And I will make my covenant between me and thee, and will multiply thee exceedingly.

~ Genesis 17:1-2

◆

Accountability and responsibility goes a long way, even if I AM ONLY HUMAN!

◆

Even as I have seen, they that plow iniquity, and sow wickedness, reap the same.

~ Job 4:8

A FATHER'S LOVE

*For I was my father's son,
tender and only [beloved] in the sight of my mother.*

~ **Proverbs 4:3**

October 26, 2008
Revised September 23, 2015

When I think of a mother's love for her child, I am reminded of the compassion and many sacrifices they often make for their children. Ironically, when a child begins to speak, it seems the word they utter first is "dada," regardless of the presence or absence of the father in the child's life. These questions can be viewed as being rather sexist but significantly bias in relation to my childhood experience with my father:

1. At what point do men actually grow up and consider someone else other than themselves?

2. At what point do they begin to take responsibility for the development of their children and be the father their children need them to be?

Let's look at the definition of the word "development" or "develop"!

DEVELOP[38]

1. To progress from earlier to later stages of individual maturation.

2. To progress from simpler to more complex stages of evolution.

3. To grow, expand or realize the potentialities.

4. To bring gradually to a fuller, greater or better state.

5. To convert to a specific purpose, as by building extensively.

Overall, one could say develop means growth!

Children are very impressionable. They need a very stable environment and people in their life who will give them love. Because there are also many people in the world who prey on

---

38   http://www.thefreedictionary.com/develop

children, they need those who are supposed to love them to also be there to protect them from those who seek to destroy them and abuse them. If your children cannot trust you or rely on you to protect them, then who else do they have? Raising children is about putting in time. Spending time with them and being willing to develop a relationship with them can prove to be more valuable to them than you giving them money. Having time with both parents would be ideal and it could prove to be the difference between a life or death situation.

> *Let all things
> be done decently and in order.*
>
> ~ 1 Corinthians 14:40

Approximately two to three weeks ago, I had the pleasure of hearing an interview involving Madonna. Madonna, due to her celebrity stardom, is known to many as an accomplished singer, actress and writer of children's books, and many news reporters, columnists and the Paparazzi have titled her as being the controversial girl rather than the material girl. However, in my observation, I see her as the very talented individual who has reinvented herself or as T. D. Jakes[39] may put it, has *repositioned* herself many, many times over. Nonetheless, beyond that, I see her as a survivor and strong-willed woman and mother who has taken into consideration the impact of her actions as they relate to her children. If I remember correctly, I distinctly

---

39 Thomas Dexter "T. D." Jakes Sr. is a very prominent pastor, author and filmmaker. He is the bishop of The Potter's House, a Nondenominational American megachurch in Dallas, Texas.

heard Madonna say during an interview that having children has matured her and made her want to be a better person. The thought of being responsible for a life meant she was responsible for their development to include what and how they think. I commend her for wanting to put her children before herself regardless of how the media betrays her to be today.

> *When my father and my mother forsake me,*
> *then the LORD will take me up.*
>
> ~ Psalm 27:10

Exiting the subway on my way to work one Tuesday morning (on October 20, 2008, to be exact), I overheard a conversation between two boys approximately twelve or thirteen years of age. The topic did not include a school assignment; it was about Monday Night Football. As they began to share their excitement about the Washington Redskins' win, one of the boys disclosed the connection he and his father had while watching the game together. Though the boys were facing forward as they rode up the escalator, the boy in the front turned completely around to ask, "You live with your father?" The boy replied, "Yes!" As I looked upon the face of the boy who had asked the question, I knew from the pain that had fallen upon me and the pain my spirit was feeling or sensing from his spirit that his father was absent in his life. Noticing my tears while hoping others around me were not aware of me crying, I began to pray to God that this little boy, whose spirit had touched mine, would be healed of his pain and that the absence of his father would not hinder his growth or his success in the world. I prayed that he would be met with insurmountable strength and courage to overcome any and all issues of adversity to the point of living holy and not being plagued by strongholds in his life. At that moment, I began to think about all the children and people, in general, who were suffering due to the unexplainable absent love of their father (or mother). Even living in the same household with your father could result in the absence of his love. And as you get older, you come to realize that the man you thought you knew, you never really knew at all. So what's worse: not living with your father and never developing a relationship with him or living with your father and still never developing a relationship with him?

> *A father of the fatherless, and a judge of the widows,*
> *[is] God in his holy habitation.*
>
> ~ Psalms 68:5

Having issues of my own concerning my father, I can truly relate to what it feels like to have an estranged relationship with a family member. My father and I never developed a loving daughter-father relationship to the point of me not being able to recognize if such a thing did or could exist at all. I can imagine the thought of a fairy-tale dream to include the ideal father–daughter relationship as portrayed on TV or in the movies; if not accurate, that would only prove to create more trauma in realizing it was just a dream.

Having an actively involved father in my life could have helped me as a female to make better choices when it came to considering a mate. Just as I am sure, had I been a male, the presence of an actively involved father could have taught me how to be a man. However, by allowing the bitterness I developed during my childhood to impact my thoughts, focusing on what I did not want only attracted much of the same: that which I did not want or need in a mate. This not only resulted in many failed relationships, but it added to my pain. Then I realized, after all these years, I had unconsciously been seeking to fill a hollow void of not obtaining a father's love through ungratifying, pseudo relationships, thus replacing one hurt with another.

> *Fathers, provoke not your children [to anger], lest they be discouraged.*
>
> ~ Colossians 3:21

Consider the Scenario

A black male

- The year is 1936.

- *Imagine what was going on during this time and consider the impact of the events on the mind of a black man from 1936 until this date, 2009.*

- *Upbringing: The Deep South; Goose Creek, South Carolina*

- *Occupation: Picking cotton or harvesting tobacco*

- *Many black children missed school depending upon harvest season.*

- *This was also a time before women were liberated. Many men did not have respect for women and treated them like property or second-class citizens. Consider how the culture viewed women overall.*

- *Consider the insecurities of black men during this period as well as the level of control (or lack there of) due to the impact of slavery issues. Some men were fortunate enough to renew the thinking of their mind to replace their negative thinking with positive thinking. Some were not as fortunate and became mentally damaged. These experiences shaped their character and their personality.*

- *The year today is 2009. How much of what they think today is contributed to their thinking thirty, forty or fifty years ago?*

When I attempt to address these issues with my father, a man not that different from most men, who refuses to examine the responsibility of his actions. He also refuses to accept how his absence and lack of active involvement in my life not only crippled me but the family as a whole. My father, a product of his upbringing, is a man who is very set in his ways. It took me some time to understand that the circumstances of a person's environment contribute to how they think and conduct themselves. Exposure to the situations and actions of others as dictated by a culture has helped to contribute to his character. While some people are successful at unlearning a way of thinking that proves to enslave the mind by relearning new thought patterns for growth, others are not so lucky at shedding those limitations.

Being aware of generational curses, I must work extra hard to break any and all cycles that threaten to attack my mind. If I myself am not careful, I could allow my family issues to keep me from my destiny and hinder my relationship with God. But God, determined to keep me on track, decided he would have me reach out to my father to be the daughter he doesn't deserve when he refuses to be the father I need.

Due to God's influence in my life, on September 20, 2000, I agreed to share a house with my father. Feeling distraught one afternoon after having made this decision, I told God I made a very big mistake. Why would I move away from my family at the age of seventeen to escape the drama of a dysfunctional family and allow myself, after all these years, to live with a father who had contributed to my pain? Standing in the middle of my room on the verge of an anxiety attack, I screamed and told God how depressed and unhappy I was to be reliving the past that I ran away from. God spoke to me and said, "I AM using you to convict your father as I use your father to convict you. I use him to teach you the importance of forgiveness to help you heal your heart and I AM going to use you to teach your father the importance of LOVE and family." Needless to say, I cried even more! For I later realized that I was hand-picked by God to serve Him. Not having any choice in picking my family, God purposely birthed me into this family to be the strength He needed me to be.

A couple of months later, while sitting in church, God placed a sermon on the heart of Pastor Tony Brazelton (Victory Christian Ministries International, Temple Hills, Maryland) that spoke to my situation. He talked about God's love being able to fill any void from issues concerning the lack of love from a biological father or parent. Praying for the healing of those who were suffering in this area, he offered to share himself as the father we needed. Upon hearing Pastor Tony say, *God loves you and I love you as he loves me*, I could feel a great releasing.

Humble yourselves therefore under the mighty hand of God,
that he may exalt you in due time;
Casting all your care upon Him;
for He careth for you.

~ 1 Peter 5:6-7

THE SOUL OF MY GRANDFATHER

And the LORD God formed man of the dust of the ground, and breathed into his nostrils the breath of life; and man became a living soul.

~ Genesis 2:7

February 15, 2000

The last conversation I had with my grandfather was a discussion about my decreasing visits to him in South Carolina over the years. When I was younger, my sister and I went every summer. But as I got older, I didn't go as much. Even now, I can hear him say, "Don't let the next time you come to see me be at my funeral." When the call came between 4:30 and 5:00 a.m. on February 9, 2000, I had an immediate ache in my heart because I felt I had let my grandfather down.

Though relationships between family members can prove to be a little strained and distant at times, you never know what tomorrow brings. Needless to say, we don't ever realize just how truly blessed we are to have a family to call upon until it is too late. In listening to the funeral well wishes delivered by family and friends (Deacon Charlie Singleton and my two cousins, Tiffany Mack and Willietta Gibson) describing the life of my grandfather, I realized for the very first time, I knew him not for the wonderful and caring man he was; I only knew him as my grandfather. I felt a sense of great loss while at the same time feeling pleased to have shared his life.

Unfortunately, I believe it is not until certain experiences in your life (trials, tribulations and events) that you really examine your character to the point of observing who you really are or who you were meant to be. Ironically, that day, I understood a connection I didn't realize existed. I was more like my grandfather in character than I ever knew.

If it is possible, as much as lieth in you,
live peaceably with all me.

~ Romans 12:18

FAMILY MATTERS

Let all things be done decently and in order.
~ **1 Corinthians 14:40**

March 5, 2009

Dear God,

Good morning! I want to thank You for this opportunity to spend time with You. There was a time not that long ago when I lacked the understanding as well as the knowledge of such a relationship with You as being possible. As You know, I despise confrontation with a passion, and it is my desire to seek a peace-filled life. In fact, the older I get, the more I strive for complete calmness and peace in my life. Having what I considered to be much drama in my childhood, I do not wish to encounter any drama in my adult life, and today, I feel there is an absence of balance in my life. Being adamant about not going backwards, I need Your help to keep me on track and pray You sustain me through it all.

> *Because strait is the gate,*
> *and narrow is the way, which leadeth unto life,*
> *and few there be that find it.*
>
> ~ Matthew 7:14

After hearing Sunday's sermon concerning the importance of family, I know You were trying to get through to me. Many nights I cried out to You in pain and anger about having to be strong for my family. A family of members, who through their individual pain and need for healing, never bonded or extended love to each other as I had expected or hoped. So to this end, I resented not having a sensible, normal family life. Normal in my mind, at that time, meant having no problems and no drama at all in any way, shape or form. Later, I grew to understand that normal for the most part meant dysfunctional and I should not take lightly the importance of the family You entrusted to me. A family I have unfortunately neglected by limiting my time with them. Although it was not easy, I know You would not have deliberately birthed me into this family or put me in this situation if You did not have a purpose for me or think I could handle it.

> *The book of the law (the Bible which is the word of God)*
> *shall not depart out of thy mouth, but thou shalt meditate*
> *therein day and night, that thou mayest observe to do*
> *according to all that is written therein:*
> *for then thou shalt make thy way prosperous,*
> *and then shalt have good success.*
>
> ~ Joshua 1:8

Many people drown themselves in their work to the point of letting their jobs define who they have become. My job is not my life; my family is my life, and family is important to You. My job is an avenue to a way of life to enable me to live here on earth in accordance to laws set by man. It is my responsibility, however, to do a good job or the best job possible as if working for You during my designated time here on earth, until You call me back home to You. Colossians 3:23-24, from the Good News Translation says it best: *Whatever you do, work at it with all your heart, as though you were working for the Lord and not for people. Remember that the Lord will give you as a reward what he has kept for his people. For Christ is the real Master you serve.* Being mindful of that, I should not allow my job to negatively consume me by draining every ounce of my energy, thus leaving none for You or my family. Before starting this current position over a year ago, a job I am blessed to have by the way, I visited my mother almost every day. Unfortunately, that does not seem to happen much at all anymore, especially not to the extent it did a year ago. This is where the need for balance comes in! If I am not careful to exercise what I consider to be the right mix (balance) in my life, I may find myself focusing on things of the flesh that do not enhance my spiritual growth (complete me) or encourage me in a positive manner.

> *And I gave my heart to know wisdom,*
> *and to know madness and folly:*
> *I perceived that this also is vexation of the spirit.*
>
> ~ Ecclesiastes 1:17

While on the job and earning a living, I must be careful to only concern myself with what I am directly responsible for being able to change. I cannot change others, nor should I concern myself with their individual work ethics or lack thereof. I must be careful not to do to others what I would not want done to me. Each person is different and unique in their own little way, and I have no knowledge of what motivates them or impacts them. I must be careful not to engage in gossip or share things with others who do not show the maturity for handling the information in a positive manner. Therefore, I feel we as individuals have a responsibility to each other while on the job to treat each other with the utmost respect regardless of our personal views.

For in much wisdom is much grief:
and he that increaseth knowledge
increaseth sorrow.

~ Ecclesiastes 1:18

Driven by a competitive spirit, we often tend to tear one another down rather than work as a team to reach the finish line together. And given the nature of people, we are more apt to judge others according to what we ourselves are able to do or are incapable of accomplishing. On the other hand, I have realized I can only work at a pace that is comfortable for me. I should not expect another person to work at my pace, nor should they expect me to work at theirs, and I must be careful not to neglect my health in an attempt to meet the expectations of others. I must, at all times, remember I have a family outside of my place of work that depends upon me and needs me to be healthy for them. My objective should always be to be a part of a solution to the problem. If at any point in time, I feel I am adding to the problem, I must remove myself from the problem immediately and think of my health.

> *Thou wilt show me the path of life:*
> *in thy presence is fullness of joy;*
> *at thy right hand there are pleasures for evermore.*
>
> ~ Psalm 16:11

God, please help me to balance my life! It is my desire to be the best me You created me to be and carry out my assignment and change the things I can in addition to knowing the difference concerning the things I cannot change as I seek to reach my fullest potential in You.

The Serenity Prayer

God grant me the serenity to accept the things I
cannot change; courage to change the things I can;
and wisdom to know the difference.

Living one day at a time;

Enjoying one moment at a time;
Accepting hardships as the pathway to peace;
Taking, as He did, this sinful world
as it is, not as I would have it;
Trusting that He will make all things right
if I surrender to His will;
That I may be reasonably happy in this life
and supremely happy with Him
Forever in the next.

Amen.

~ Karl Paul Reinhold Niebuhr
(June 21, 1892 – June 1, 1971)

American Theologian

TRIBUTE TO A DEAR FRIEND

*A man [that hath] friends
must shew himself friendly: and
there is a friend [that] sticketh closer than a brother.*

~ Proverbs 18:24

I would like to take this time to tell a wonderful person and dear friend of fourteen years just how much I appreciate her kindness, love as a sister, friendship and the use of her mother as a second mother to me.

You, not like most people, are happy for me when I am happy and sad with me when I am sad.

You share my sorrow when I am down and extend joy in an attempt to lift my spirits again. For you understand me as a person—an individual with a soul whose heart breaks deeply. You accept me for me and never look at me as something or someone that I am not.

Please feel free to lean on me in your time of need
as you have let me in mine.

For you have a real friend in me
as I have in you.

I only hope my relationship
with you offers as much reward
as yours has rewarded me.

1980

Although written in 1980 for a very dear friend, on this day, my heart feels the same, and we are still good friends.

Thank you Lorrie (McIlwain) Hyatt!

I love you!

LOVE CONQUERS ALL

*No man hath seen God at any time.
If we love one another, God dwelleth in us,
and his love is perfected in us.*

~ 1 John 4:12

February 3, 2009

Beloved, let us love one another: for love is of God; and every one that loveth is born of God, and knoweth God (1 John 4:7) for the tradition of the family was founded upon agape love. And yet, today, families are trying to survive by way of the wrong foundation, such as selfishness. A selfishness that knows not of love, peace or togetherness. A selfishness that cares not for another to extend a helping hand in all sincerity. The law of life is the love of God. If a man say, I love God, and hateth his brother, he is a liar: for he that loveth not his brother whom he hath seen, how can he love God whom he hath not seen? (1 John 4:20)

While working within the Human Resources Department of the Salvation Army National Headquarters, I had the pleasure of greeting a gentleman named Stephan Solat. As I assisted him during his orientation, it was my responsibility to accompany him and each new employee on a tour of the two National Headquarter buildings and introduce them to each staff member. During that tour, I noted there was something very different about Stephan. At the time, I did not realize that it was God who was allowing my spirit to recognize his spirit. He possessed a very unusual spirit of love, spiritual sensitivity and forgiveness. This was unusual in the sense that I had not encountered such a pull on my spirit in that manner before then; it was not an overpowering pull that induced fear, but it was more of a calming and peaceful feeling that brought tears of joy to my eyes. Returning to my office after the tour, I sat quietly for a few minutes trying to make sense of what I had experienced. Given my personality, I have a tendency to analyze everything for some sort of understanding. Lately, I have come to accept that oftentimes what happens is beyond my understanding in the natural sense, but with God in the supernatural sense, in time, he will make everything clear to me.

> *We are of God:*
> *he that knoweth God heareth us;*
> *he that is not of God heareth not us.*
> *Hereby know we the spirit of truth, and the spirit of error.*
>
> ~ 1 John 4:6

Little did I know, I would be leaving the Human Resources Department to accept a position within another sector, still within the building of the National Headquarters! That new adventure gave me the opportunity to work closely with Stephan in the capacity of a program assistant. Getting to know Stephan, I not only noted his work ethics (e.g., his need to be detail-oriented in the manner in which he completed and submitted his Child Survival reports), but he was an extremely spiritual person. However, because he was believed to be a practicing Muslim, those who followed The Salvation Army doctrine would not allow themselves to see Stephan, the individual. Stephan's wife was Jewish. Through them, I understood for the first time in my life the true power of love: the coming together of two people against all odds, finding love and conquering with love together. Needless to say, Stephan received much persecution from a Salvation Army officer, Major Patricia Kiddoo, who, along with others, failed to see God's love.

> *For if our heart condemn us,*
> *God is greater than our heart, and knoweth all things.*
>
> ~ 1 John 3:20

With religion being a root cause of many of the third world wars, can you imagine a Muslim and a Jew getting past their differences long enough to fall in love and get married? Do you know what that says about their level of maturity? If I could see the beauty in that, why did no one else? Instead of noticing his heart and learning from him, he was persecuted. How did his free will in choosing his right to worship in accordance to his beliefs interfere or affect his ability to do his job? It didn't! And yet they missed the most important message. Love conquers all! It surpasses any and all prejudices that are reinforced through a false sense of thinking that is dictated by our culture and society. *Beloved, let us love one another: for love is of God; and every one that loves is born of God and knows God* (1 John 4:6-7). God's hope and desire for our life is for us to honor his law concerning love. For the most part, we have become so religious that, without thinking, we misinterpret scriptures to mirror our own understanding, which has nothing to do with how God intended us to view and accept His word (truth).

ASSIMILATION BY ASSOCIATION

*My sheep hear my voice,
and I know them, and they follow me.*

~ John 10:27 KJV

March 3, 2014

How often have you heard the phrase, "Birds of a feather flock together"? Have you actually given any thought to the possibility of how much truth that statement holds? Based on the strong influences of people, places and things within our environment and their impact on our mental psyche, if we are not careful, we can indeed pick up on the idiosyncrasies or the characteristics of others. Why? Because spirits are transferable and we seem to be too quick and eager to imitate those in position of power prior to examining or questioning the character they display! Their influence on others or their false sense of control easily seduces the flesh and stimulates our taste for success as defined by society!

> *Examine yourselves,*
> *whether ye be in the faith; prove your own selves.*
> *Know ye not your own selves,*
> *how that Jesus Christ is in you,*
> *except ye be reprobates?*
>
> ~ 2 Corinthians 13:5

And yet, God reminds us repeatedly of the impact of being *in* the world as He cautions us not to be *of* the world. Repeatedly, we disregard His warnings! We refuse to follow His example! We make countless excuses for being human and imperfect as a justification for our actions as if that is okay! Because, in the world, unfortunately, any and everything goes! People make up rules, regulations or laws only to readily break them at will (double standards), thus depending upon the demand of the greatest influences and control of those in the driver's seat. But, have you ever given any thought to how impressionable, naïve and vulnerable children can be? Inquisitively, children tend to observe every move, action or reaction in determining who to follow! In essence, they learn from those within their environment—good, bad or indifferent—while struggling to determine right from wrong!

> *Our wrongdoings pile up before you, God, our sins stand up and accuse us. Our wrongdoings stare us down; we know in detail what we've done: Mocking and denying God, not following our God, Spreading false rumors, inciting sedition, pregnant with lies, muttering malice. Justice is beaten back, Righteousness is banished to the sidelines, Truth staggers down*

the street, Honesty is nowhere to be found, Good is missing in action. Anyone renouncing evil is beaten and robbed.

~ Isaiah 59:12-15 MSG

Different Strokes for Different Folks

As adults, we are nothing more than children in grown-up bodies trying to find our way. Some have matured in becoming more spiritually sound than others to examine themselves in accordance to the example we are *expected* to follow. At the end of each day, we should be able to look at ourselves in the mirror with objectivity in measuring our actions in **alignment** with the **nine fruits of the Spirit**. If we are truly honest with ourselves, it is possible to note what changes are necessary to move from a state of permissive will into God's *perfect will*. Although others could quite simply care less about the consequences of their actions as they seek to follow man and not God, we must be committed to be followers and doers of the word, taking heed to the word of God in total submission! Then there are many who like to push the boundaries by pretending to be followers of the Lord in doing quite the opposite when they think no one is looking or paying them any attention. And some are quite confused and tend to straddle the fence by testing the waters on either side. Those are the ones whose souls I have cried for the most in frustration of them being hypocrites. The act of their arrogance surely outweighs the act of their ignorance, especially when they reluctantly feel or think God is blind to it all!

> *And they say, How doth God know?*
> *and is there knowledge in the most High?*
>
> ~ Psalm 73:11

Amazingly, people seem to deliberately choose what they are willing to believe and deny even if the truth is able to set them free. Yes, from a world view or perspective, everyone is doing his or her own thing to ensure they exceed and happily sail along to the top of the rat race. Everything we have been exposed to all throughout our childhood has helped to dictate the way we think as adults. In other words, that which we have encountered (the good, bad or indifferent) has contributed to who we have become. Our experiences, as unique as they may be, can impose deep-rooted pain we often carry with us like a badge of honor or sorrow. What seems right to a man could be easily tainted by our association with others. As *children of God*, we are expected to impact the atmosphere in being *change agents* to usher in the light—not the other way around in ushering in the darkness!

AM I THY BROTHER'S KEEPER?

*And the LORD said unto Cain,
Where is Abel thy brother? And he said,
I know not: Am I my brother's keeper?*

~ 1 Genesis 4:9 KJV

May 24, 2014

God's word is very clear! He provides us with explicit instructions and principles (the Law of the Lord) in which to follow should we take the time to read and study His word faithfully! The next step would be to meditate on the Law of the Lord day and night (see Psalm 1:2) by applying it and incorporating it into our lifestyle. But first, we must be willing to be honest with ourselves concerning who we are in comparison to who we were created to be. As followers (citizens of the Kingdom), we should be willing to live our lives 24-7 according to God's every command. This would constitute a change of heart—a heart transplant, if you will—to include the renewing of our minds. Romans 12:2 states,

"And be not conformed to this world: but be ye transformed by the renewing of your mind, that ye may prove what *is* that good, and acceptable, and perfect, will of God." Therefore, we should be mindful that, although in the world, we are expected *not* to be of the world in letting it and what it has to offer to influence our actions. *For all that is in the world, the lust of the flesh, and the lust of the eyes, and the pride of life, is not of the Father, but is of the world* (1 John 2:16). But unfortunately, many of us oftentimes get sucked in and lose sight of what's important as we lose our way. We let our love of things in the world create a wedge between us and God as our judgment gets clouded, thus preventing our soul from prospering.

> *Love not the world,*
> *neither the things that are in the world.*
> *If any man love the world,*
> *the love of the Father is not in him.*
>
> ~ 1 John 2:15

This world system, which appeals to our flesh, offers a great number of distractions that are very instrumental and strategic in making us believe that it is not only the right way but the only way—the avenue for gaining happiness and success (fame and fortune)! And some of us are willing to do any and everything possible to receive that fame and fortune to get ahead in life. Even if it means partnering with others (like-minded corruptible seeds) and allowing ourselves to be seduced and influenced by darkness (evil and wicked ways) to destroy others! Especially when God impresses upon us to treat each other in the manner in which we ourselves would want to be treated (Luke 6:31), with loving kindness and compassion! But how can you honestly say you love the Father, whom you do not see and proclaim to be Christians (or spiritual beings) yet you are willing to do any and everything as dictated by the world within your power to display a level of hate directed at tearing down and wounding your brother or sister (another human being) whom you are able to see (1 John 4:20)? And, you attempt to justify those actions within your heart, your mind and your soul as being acceptable? For as a man thinketh in his heart, so is he (Proverbs 23:7)! How do you do that with a straight face and a lack of conscience? There was a time—out of fear, hurt and so much pain from being an outcast—that I wished I could turn off my emotions (or my humanity) and separate myself from my conscience to be able to do and to say to others what they had no problem doing or saying to me as a means of fitting in and being accepted by man! But, the God who lives within me—the God I once doubted and wanted to dismiss—would not let me, to this day, be like the others around me and He continues to push me beyond what may appeal to my flesh to overcome it!

> *Live as children of obedience to God;*
> *do not conform yourselves to the evil desires*
> *that governed you in your former ignorance*
> *when you did not know the requirements of the Gospel.*
>
> ~ 1 Peter 1:14 AMP

Paul, a devoted servant (and slave) of Christ Jesus was called to be an apostle and set apart for the gospel of God, and he stated in Romans 7:21, when I think and know to do good, evil is all around me. However, we *all* have a choice to choose (free will) to do what is right over what is wrong! We just have to dig down deep to be committed to doing the right thing, no matter what! *As the One Who called you is holy, you yourselves should also be holy in all your conduct and manner of living. And if you call upon Him as your Father Who judges each one impartially according to what he does, then you should conduct yourselves with true reverence throughout the time of your temporary residence on the earth, whether long or short. You must know (recognize) that you were redeemed (ransomed) from the useless (fruitless) way of living inherited by tradition from your forefathers, not with corruptible things such as silver and gold, but you were purchased with the precious blood of Christ (the Messiah), like that of a sacrificial lamb without blemish or spot* (1 Peter 1:15, 17-19 KJV).

Everything has a purpose! Meaning, no matter how painful or isolated you may feel, there is a time and season for *all* that takes place in your life to glorify the Lord as He strengthens you and sets you apart from others in moving you closer toward your God-ordained destiny. Being persecuted, hated, lied on, blocked or limited in your career by man should never be enough to make you operate outside of the will of God for your life. No amount of threats or evil intentions should be able to interfere with your faith walk and jeopardize your relationship with God. Whatever gifting and calling on your life as expected or commanded by the Father should be your ultimate concern. *There is salvation (deliverance, healing) in no one else! Under*

ALL *heaven there is no other name for men to call upon to save them* (Acts 4:12 TLB).

I Am Thy Brother's Keeper

After speaking up and out against the unfair and cruel treatment directed at one coworker, I was called into a meeting by an individual who had allowed himself to partner with my coworker's oppressors to chastise me for my compassion. When approached, I was asked why I felt the need to be the abused coworker's protector. To me, this answer was obvious—because it was the right thing to do as instructed by God! And on that day, those in position of leadership and power who set the stage for the entire scenario had intended to turn the situation around on me in an attempt to make me think I had done something wrong; they were even prepared to instigate a legal action against me for their corruptible act to escape having to take responsibility for their part in the matter.

> *If a man say, I love God,*
> *and hateth his brother, he is a liar:*
> *for he that loveth not his brother whom he hath seen,*
> *how can he love God whom he hath not seen?*
>
> ~ 1 John 4:20 KJV

A second coworker, Aleta, who is the inspiration for this topic, suffered a terrible fall on July 25, 2012, in the hallway of the U.S. Department of Energy on her way to a meeting. During her ordeal, I kept hearing in my spirit that God was sustaining her and holding her close to Him. Each time I spoke with her, regardless of the many obstacles she had faced concerning the prolonged workman's compensation process, she was indeed in a good spiritual place. However, physically, she was experiencing a great deal of pain that only worsened while waiting on others within the Office of Human Capital Management to include the Department of Labor to make the appropriate and timely decisions regarding her necessary treatment (and compensation payments). Their reluctance to act or to agree with the diagnosis of her physicians, including the suggested treatment for her recovery and healing, only added insult to injury. Finally, after nearly a year (in August or September of 2013) they accepted the fact that her fall (injury) was not staged and her injuries were very severe and more life threatening than they wanted to believe or were willing to admit. So yet again, out of habit, people are more apt to partner with the prince of darkness as an unhealthy ally rather than choosing to do the right thing immediately for *all* concerned.

> *For if you don't write it,*
> *they will claim I never warned them.*
> *"Oh no," they'll say, "you never told us that!"*
> *For they are stubborn rebels.*
>
> ~ Isaiah 30:9 TLB

When Aleta took that fall in the hallway, which many doubted was serious, she broke her back! And prior to her fall, she extended an olive branch to the leadership of the Office of Human Capital Management in hopes of moving forward in peace and requested a detail for a little solace (relief). But in this environment, you do not speak against any of the negativity or attempt to file a formal complaint without being met with greater opposition and retaliation!

What Qualifies as Retaliation[40]: Retaliation is any adverse action that a company takes against an employee because he or she filed a complaint about harassment or discrimination. Adverse action can include actions such as firing the employee, giving them negative evaluations, disciplining or demoting them, reassigning them or reducing their pay. (Isolation or exclusion[41] and unrealistic work assignments are also forms of retaliation.)

No one was willing to get involved in doing the right thing; they refused to take her harassment (bullying) serious enough to intercede or to intervene on her behalf. The situation, similar to that of a gang initiation or hazing, was talked about and made fun of while others watched from the sidelines and from time to time, joined forces to do her more harm. But I pray the Lord gives her back everything she has lost to the swarming locusts, the hopping locusts, the stripping locusts and the cutting locusts (Joel 2:25). I know deep within my heart that the God I serve will not forsake the righteous nor has He put Aleta in this position to see her suffer greatly at the hands of others so selfishly. The God of miracles, signs and wonders will restore (re-establish) her and heal her completely by righting every wrong that was

---

40 http://smallbusiness.findlaw.com/employment-law-and-human-resources/workplace-retaliation.html
41 http://www.workplaceanswers.com/resources/blog/retaliation-in-workplace-after-compliant/

ever done to her! Don't you realize her suffering (blood) is on your hands?

They Do Not Believe

God's been trying to reach us for a very long time in an attempt to make us aware of not only His existence but Heaven and Hell too! God is capable of using any means necessary, not limited to people, places and things. In Exodus 3, there is a reference to a burning bush being used to speak to Moses. We have been deceived and deliberately taught wrongly to coerce us into disbelieving that the supernatural is more real than the natural. God gives us chances upon chances to get right with Him before we leave this earth (die). He wants to save our souls from being condemned to live out eternity in Hell! Many times, I have asked God to give me an answer for all of this madness, division and strife within and amongst His children to include within and outside of the church. And He answered me by saying, "They don't believe!" Unfortunately, many people do not believe that, should they play with fire, they will be destined to get burned. So they continue to carry on with their lives as if conducting business as usual, committing one immoral act after the other with a seared conscience (1 Timothy 4:2) and jumping from one side to another on the basis of the players involved while developing unfruitful partnerships. But, as indicated above, GOD'S WORD IS VERY CLEAR *AND* IT IS TRUTH. Our actions have consequences whether you believe in the Law of the Lord or not! It is impossible to serve two masters! You are solely responsible for what you put out into the universe. And not only will you reap what you sow, but you will condemn your bloodline to the same for three to four generations to come (see Exodus 20:5).

> *Jesus said,*
> *"Love the Lord your God*
> *with all your passion and prayer and intelligence.*
> *This is the most important, the first on any list.*
> *But there is a second to set alongside it:*
> *"Love others as well as you love yourself.*
> *These two commands are pegs;*
> *everything in God's Law*
> *and the Prophets hangs from them."*
>
> ~ 1 Peter 1:37-40

Closing Remarks

When people attempt to label and ostracize you for whatever reason, it is extremely important to know who you are in Christ and who He is within you. Seek to know your God-given purpose to include the person you were created to be! Having this revelation knowledge, which is a gift from God, will give you the insight and courage needed to resist (walk boldly) and to fight the temptation of giving in to your surroundings. Even if I suffer at the hands of others as their response (retaliation) to my continued unwillingness to operate "outside" of the will of God for my life, what a blessing in itself! For my suffering in being obedient to my God-given assignment will never be in vain (Galatians 3:4)! For that reason and that reason alone, I decree and declare, no weapon formed against me shall prosper, and every tongue that rises against me in judgment my FATHER shall condemn (Isaiah 54:17).

When you know what you know for yourself, no one should be able to convince you otherwise! In other words, they will not be able to tell you that what you know, you don't know; what you feel, you don't feel; what you see, you don't see; or what you have experienced and endured is just a figment of your imagination; but they will surely try! Just like I am sure, without a doubt, that many reading this will be angered by what I have shared. Good! God speaks about anger in Ephesians 4:26! So just how angry are you? Are you angry enough to be remorseful? Are you angry enough to see the error of your ways, to confess with your mouth and to repent in your heart to be committed to changing the obvious patterns of your ways in a more positive direction? Are you angry enough to consider the well-being of someone else to show some compassion to love and to assist your brethren (spiritual sister or brother) when they are in need? What about proclaiming[42] to be baptized and filled with the Holy Ghost in addition to being doers and not just hearers of the word "saints"? Are you angry enough to call those things that are not as though they were? Are you angry enough to join me in petitioning (pulling on) Heaven—in the name of Jesus Christ—to open its windows and doors on behalf of Aleta to bestow upon her so many blessings that there will not be room enough to store it all? Are you angry enough to praise the Lord on her behalf?

---

42 To announce officially or publicly.

The Lord is my shepherd; I shall not want. He maketh me to lie down in green pastures: he leadeth me beside the still waters. He restoreth my soul: he leadeth me in the paths of righteousness for his name's sake. Yea, though I walk through the valley of the shadow of death, I will fear no evil: for thou art with me; thy rod and thy staff they comfort me. Thou preparest a table before me in the presence of mine enemies: thou anointest my head with oil; my cup runneth over. Surely goodness and mercy shall follow me all the days of my life: and I will dwell in the house of the Lord for ever.

~ Psalm 23

IN THE WORLD, NOT OF THE WORLD!

*They are not of the world,
even as I am not of the world.*

~ **John 17:16 KJV**

October 6, 2015

Revised October 7, 2015

There is a very good reason why we are instructed not to look to the left or to the right! In fact, Proverbs 4:23-27 from the Message Bible states, "Keep vigilant watch over your heart; *that's* where life starts. Don't talk out of both sides of your mouth; avoid careless banter, white lies and gossip. Keep your eyes straight ahead; ignore all sideshow distractions. Watch your step, and the road will stretch out smooth before you. Look neither right nor left; leave evil in the dust." In the world, we are surrounded by a number of possible distractions that are intended to derail us from our purpose. And, if you have taken the time to read as well as to study the Bible, it gives you great insight into the war that began in Heaven. Lucifer, whose name means the morning star, shining one, light bearer and son of the dawn, was God's right hand. He, like all the angels, was created by God to include all living things in and outside of the universe. Lucifer and his minions challenged God's position, authority and His love for mankind! So they were tossed out of Heaven (exiled) and fell to earth where they wreak the most havoc! Have you not heard it said many times before that "earth is the devil's playground"? Meaning, people here on earth are influenced primarily by God's adversary more than they are by God Himself.

On another note, do you recall learning about something called Maslow's hierarchy of needs at some point in your life? Abraham Maslow introduced his theory in a paper he wrote in 1943 discussing man's motivation and innate behavioral patterns driving individual wants and needs. Maslow used the terms or categories to identify and distinguish between the basic to the more extreme needs of an individual. Those needs are physiological, safety, belongingness and love, esteem and self-actualization. People can easily be influenced, controlled and misled by the right incentives. And, for that reason alone, we should attempt to keep our focus at **all times** on the LORD and meditate on His word—morning, noon and night. *This book of the law shall not depart out of thy mouth; but thou shalt meditate therein day and night, that thou mayest observe to do according to all that is written therein: for then thou shalt make thy way prosperous, and then thou shalt have good success* (Joshua 1:18 KJV).

Have you considered reviewing Maslow's hierarchy in comparison to your life? For instance, what motivates you? I mean *really* motivates you enough to compel you to go the distance to achieve your desires, good or bad? Is it the need to feel successful, important and accomplished? What does success or being accomplished mean to you? And what are you willing to do to obtain that success? Are you willing to sell your soul to obtain it? Once you achieve what you think you want, will it be enough to truly make you happy? People have a tendency to talk a good game at attempting to prove what they know or believe to others, but it is more for their own benefit as opposed to those around them. Otherwise, they would do more to consider the consequences of their actions! We live in a world full of the walking wounded—people who are trying to find their way. Each person with his or her own agenda attempting to fulfill selfish desires! Some are more desperate than others to carve out a perfect place in which to dwell and exist. *While I was with them, I was keeping them in Your name which You have given Me; and I guarded them and protected them, and not one of them was lost except the son of destruction, so that the Scripture would be fulfilled* (John 17:12 AMP).

When a tragedy like the recent Oregon shooting happens, we do not take the necessary time to consider all impacted parties, including the antagonist (shooter) and the protagonist (victims). Yes, we are always inclined to be sympathetic to the victims, but we rarely sympathize with the antagonist. Well, yesterday evening, upon sitting down to watch television, I flipped through the channels, and I stumbled across the plea of a father, Ian Mercer, who lost a son, Christopher Harper-Mercer, the shooter. In my opinion, Mr. Mercer lost his son to darkness long before this ordeal; however, he wanted nothing more than to apologize to the world for his son's actions in an attempt to share some insight into his son's life to the best of his understanding. On the channel I was watching, before the father could state his point, the focus was rather abruptly interrupted and redirected to the commentator who, with anger in his voice, very rudely criticized the father's love for his son. Can you imagine God's love for us when we repeatedly reject Him time and time again? No matter what, He loves us unconditionally! He does not condemn us and forever leaves the door open for us to return home to Him should we have a change of heart to do so. That is an ultimate example of a gracious and loving father (abba, daddy)! *Beloved, let us love one another: for love is of God; and every one that loveth is born of God, and knoweth God. He that loveth not knoweth not God; for God is love. In this was manifested the love of God toward us, because that God sent his only begotten Son into the world, that we might live through him. Herein is love, not that we loved God, but that he loved us, and sent his Son to be the propitiation for our sins* (1 John 4:7-10 KJV).

No, I AM not dismissing the actions of the shooter, nor am I overlooking the many who lost their lives during this very senseless killing spree! And I AM sure, without a doubt, that this young man's life will be turned upside down as many attempt to show how mentally disturbed, confused, evil and wicked he was to have committed such an unspeakable act. But no one will attempt to explore the root cause of his pain, which triggered such dis-ease to his spirit! Why do I care? *Behold, what manner of love the Father hath bestowed upon us, that we should be called the sons of God: therefore the world knoweth us not, because it knew him not* (1 John 3:1 KJV). Because God put him and many others like him on my heart! As I attempted to watch the father to hear his partial presentation, my heart ached and I cried out in agony while clutching at my heart and stomach. There I was in the middle of my living room, yelling and screaming at the top of my lungs while asking God, why? Although we are born sinners, we are not born damaged or broken into a world that wishes to consume us. We were innocent until we were corrupted, mistreated and abused by those who wanted to silence us. So I have been tasked with a purpose to speak up and out as directed by God to expose injustices in the world. I have been given a platform to speak for those who cannot or are not willing to speak for themselves. I have been allowed to experience great pain and to express that pain explicitly through my testimonies as a vehicle for reaching and connecting with others who are no stranger to pain. With that said, we do not know Christopher Harper-Mercer's story—the complete unadulterated truth—and we probably never will, but God knows the entire truth!

The media often jumps to conclusions to report the news for profit, to boost the ratings and to set up careers. If you were to compare the information presented by various sources all being broadcasted at the same time, you would notice many discrepancies and half-truths. Data is collected and facts are gathered, but the truth is rarely shared! For instance, we heard this young man was specifically targeting Christians or believers. But, once the smoke cleared and witnesses were actually interviewed or questioned, some of them stated he was targeting everybody.

Some things are specifically reported or referenced with the hope of influencing a directed result or outcome, such as fear.

How many remember when the *Washington Star* was in opposition to the *Washington Post*? Well, consider the tone of the two in how they were different! One was more bias toward the Democratic Party and the other was more bias toward the Republican Party, while CNN was noted for investigative reporting to give greater insight into the facts without choosing to sway the reader's thoughts or mindset. I am more interested in knowing what was in the letter that was written by Christopher Harper-Mercer to the police! However, unless I am able to review the letter for myself to know it is the actual product and language as written by Christopher in his own handwriting, we may never know if the letter is the true version (when and if it is released to or shared with the public). That's why I am most grateful and thankful to Jesus Christ for the Holy Spirit. If we are quick to hear and slow to speak, God often reveals what is hidden through the "Gifts of the Holy Spirit."

> *Understand this, my beloved brothers and sisters. Let everyone be quick to hear [be a careful, thoughtful listener], slow to speak [a speaker of carefully chosen words and], slow to anger [patient, reflective, forgiving]; for the [resentful, deep-seated] anger of man does not produce the righteousness of God [that standard of behavior which He requires from us]. So get rid of all uncleanness and all that remains of wickedness, and with a humble spirit receive the word [of God] which is implanted [actually rooted in your heart], which is able to save your souls. But prove yourselves doers of the word [actively and*

continually obeying God's precepts], and not merely listeners [who hear the word but fail to internalize its meaning], deluding yourselves [by unsound reasoning contrary to the truth]. For if anyone only listens to the word without obeying it, he is like a man who looks very carefully at his natural face in a mirror; for once he has looked at himself and gone away, he immediately forgets what he looked like. But he who looks carefully into the perfect law, the law of liberty, and faithfully abides by it, not having become a [careless] listener who forgets but an active doer [who obeys], he will be blessed and favored by God in what he does [in his life of obedience].

~ James 1:19-25 AMP

When we are hurting, we normally attempt to seek refuge or solace from those we think would be the most understanding or likely candidates to help and save us from our troubles! We are not expecting them to be wolves disguised as sheep who take pleasure in inflicting more pain upon us. Can you imagine finding yourself in a compromising position and feeling helpless or at the mercy of others while your dignity and self-respect is being attacked or stripped away? Do you know what it feels like to be powerless and holding on for dear life? Upon incurring scars or wounds as casualties of war, the majority of us are not equipped to handle the trauma. We are not familiar with how to address the actions (cruelty) of others as directed toward us at the onset of every incident or inflicted injury to our self-esteem. In fact, society has been more apt at teaching us how to sweep the many offenses against us under the rug (out of sight or out of mind) to forget or pretend that nothing ever happened.

For the most part, those who have been mistreated, abused or victimized by others have been manipulated into believing that the act of injustice done to them was and is all their fault. That, unfortunately, creates a greater impact on the mental psyche while giving the aggressor more control over us and an opportunity for them to continue to do more damage. When this happens, something on the inside breaks as we die slowly and sink deeper into the darkness and our mind does not quietly convert inwardly all at once. No, it happens gradually over a period of time as we seek avenues for coping with our issues while attempting to simply forget until it becomes unbearable or impossible to push the pain aside anymore. We may even seek to numb our pain by becoming addicts in substituting one problem for another, thus doing more harm to ourselves until we leave this earth or snap and take others into the darkness with us (a permanent death). And then there are others, like me, who lose their focus from time to time but never completely reach the edge of no return while being determined to stay afloat and fight the good fight of faith in knowing and developing a relationship with God. *Thus says the LORD: "Cursed is the man who trusts in man AND makes flesh his strength, whose heart departs from the LORD"* (Jeremiah 17:5). It didn't happen overnight but as part of a beneficial process, the closer I allowed myself to get to God, the better I became in standing my ground and leaning on the Lord to get me through it all! Today, my focus is different, and I have shifted my way of thinking in an attempt to put God first in my life above my wants and needs. *Beloved, I wish above all things that thou mayest prosper and be in health, even as thy soul prospereth* (3 John 1:2).

In the words of Plumb,[43] from a song called "Lord, I'm Ready Now!": *I just let go and I feel exposed, but it's so beautiful. 'Cause this is who I am!* **I've been such a mess!** *Now I can't care less. I could bleed to death. Lord, I'm ready now. All the walls are down. Time is running out and I wanna make this count. I ran away from you and I did what I wanted to, but I don't want to let you down. Lord, I'm ready now! Lord, I'm ready now.* **I was so caught up in who I'm not!** *Can you please forgive me? I've nothing left to hide. No! No reasons left to lie. Give me another chance. Lord, I'm ready now!*

Reference
The Discerning of Spirits
Author: Frank Hammond
ISBN 10: 0-89228-368-8
ISBN 13: 978-089228-368-2

---

43 See, https://youtu.be/EWN3GDuAMM4 and https://youtu.be/nAsTi8kS2SQ

LETTERS TO GOD

TRIALS AND TRIBULATIONS

August 28, 1993

Dear Lord,

Every day I AM tested by the Devil! Sometimes in the image of himself and sometimes in the image of a Christian. But I must often remember that he is not a Christian of this world, nor is he a Christian as we know him. He does not come before me as a follower or worshiper of you but merely as a tool of the Devil to defy my faith and belief in You.

You brought me through many trials and tribulations. You have stood by me through the tests of time. For now I AM strong and I will survive.

Thanks for Your guidance and the will to survive.

Your daughter,

Ann Gwen Mack

> Sometimes trials come on every hand,
> but I feel like going on!

Therefore being justified by faith, we have peace with God through our Lord Jesus Christ: By whom also we have access by faith into this grace where we stand, and rejoice in hope of the Glory of God. And not only so, but we glory in tribulations also: knowing that tribulation worketh patience. And patience, experience; An experience, hope: And hope maketh not ashamed; because the love of God is shed abroad in our hearts by the Holy Ghost which is given unto us.

~ Romans 5: 1-5

ABOVE ALL ELSE, STAND!

August 1, 1998

Hi God,

Lately (in fact, for the past three months … maybe longer), I've had a number of things on my mind. I want so much to speak to you and have you talk back to me. I want to ask so many questions and receive many answers.

As I sit and type this letter, I seem to have a great deal of emotion—unexplainable emotion! I feel pain and heartache. Life seems to be so unfair. I would like to be able to not exactly accept things as they are, but be able to cope with things I see that I feel are not right.

I truly believe that people come in our lives for many different reasons. They provide wisdom, knowledge and growth. I want so badly to be able to discern. I want so badly to be able to face adversity head-on and triumph no matter what. I want to feel a sense of accomplishment in all areas of my life!

I apologize for the rambling. My thoughts seem to be racing from here to there. There is so much to discuss and so much to release! Today, I had a conversation with what I view to be a very spiritual couple. The thing I remember most about the conversation is what was shared with me.

"God allowed a change. The change was to go from one job to another, and although you may not think it was a positive move, God led you to where you are for a purpose. Satan has a way of making us feel that the choices we make in accordance to God's plan are not good choices.

You have to find a way to get through! Pray and ask God to give you the ability to stand. Do not lose focus or sight of what God has in store for you! Satan will always try to intervene and take your mind off God's plan for your life by attempting to steer you off that path."

Dear God, I want to stand. I want to stand tall and remain positive, focused and hopeful. I want to be strong while exercising patience at all times. I AM about to watch a movie that seems to have a spiritual twist. I'll sit again and write down my thoughts as they come. Please be patient with me! Please work with me! Please help me!

Thank You for being You!

THANK YOU, GOD!

September 12, 1998

Hi God,

I want to take this time to say thank You!

Oftentimes, when experiencing adversity, I think that is the most opportune time to chill out and just stand. I know I have a tendency to get upset, frustrated and worried. I think I bring about more discomfort on myself than the actual situation. But I know I AM growing. That's the good part! Especially when you can look back and still feel joy, laugh and cry at the same time while managing to focus on the main objective.

    I do not want to fall apart when trials come. I want to stand firm, look to You and stay encouraged. I want to handle each and every trial or adversity with poise and wisdom while exhibiting professionalism and strength. On another note, I don't want to harbor any negative feelings. I want to be able to overcome, put it behind me, learn from it, grow from it and move forward, staying encouraged and focused. Unfortunately, I AM not particularly fond of what I see, but I know I cannot ponder over it. However, I do notice what I consider to be a difference.

While working at Robbins-Gioia, Inc. (RG), a few of my like-minded coworkers and I would engage in conversation concerning what we noticed as being double standards in the workplace and attempt to identify these differences. More times than not, we noted the salary difference in the offers of employment in comparison to blacks and whites as well as men and women in our working environment. I have heard the statement "What you don't know won't hurt you" so many times that I have lost track. But, for the first time in my life, I truly believe I understand what that statement means. As long as I didn't see with my own eyes of what I believed to be true (confirmation), I could deal with the pain of it much better. But knowing in my gut, through discernment, feeling and actual proof of what others didn't think I knew, was much more painful!

While working at US*internetworking*, Inc., as a Human Resources Assistant, I saw the difference all too clearly on paper each and every day and I was required to enter this information into an HR database, which made it even more difficult to handle the truth. A truth many deny still exists today! However, attempting to honor a sense of professionalism, I tried not to allow the pain of it all to affect me or keep me from doing my job. Discrimination is an evil device. How do a group of people who are discriminated against every day survive? We just do and continue to rely on You! And yes, I know we are all guilty in some form or fashion of something. Even retaliation is a sin. Therefore, God, I will leave vengeance to You. I want to belong, but at what cost? I AM just numb from it all!

INSTANT REPLAY: A HARD LESSON TO LEARN

February 21, 1999

Hi God,

I thought writing about my inner feelings would help me deal with my pain both mentally and physically. On February 16, 1999, I was admitted to the Alexandria Hospital. I've been going back and forth to the hospital to the urgent care unit at Georgetown University Medical Center, the ER in Arlington, Virginia, and the ER in Alexandria, Virginia, since February 10, 1999. How could I be so careless? For that matter, how could I be so stupid?

I took the necessary precautions—birth control and condoms—but abstinence should have been the number one priority. I never really knew if I wanted children, but I did often dream about having a daughter. Now, I may never have that chance. I guess subconsciously I wanted at least one child. But consciously, I don't want to raise a child by myself. Not being able to give birth doesn't mean I can't raise a child or give it life.

Why do I tend to make the same mistakes and the same wrong choices? When does one become wiser or heed to Your will? In 1992, I had an ectopic pregnancy (when the fetus develops outside the uterus) and I was told I could have died; however, I made it through. Seven years later, I'm experiencing the whole ordeal again as if it was an instant replay and ironically, both ectopic pregnancies occurred in the same month (February). According to my doctors, this one nearly killed me too.

> *I will instruct thee and teach thee in the way*
> *which thou shalt go: I will guide thee with mine eye.*
>
> ~ Psalm 32:8

Note Added January 4, 2009: My ordeal did not cause my death because God had mercy on me. It is by the grace of God that I am living today and am able to share my testimonies. Today, much wiser and in a different place, I not only understand the importance of following God's will for my life but the meaning of the scripture concerning not being unequally yoked. I have to accept I have been called by God to do a job for Him. Because of that, there is a price on my head and Satan will stop at nothing to separate me from God's plan for my life. Therefore, I have to accept my position in the body of Christ. I have to accept that I am a Christian and I have a lifestyle that requires me to act accordingly. In giving my life to God, it is important for me to honor His ways. It is important for me to grow up and no longer think like a child. Therefore, it is important for me to put away childish things.

Side Note Added September 24, 2010: Dear God, I truly do not know why I have to experience something more than once before I finally understand and accept the truth. Not once did I experience an ectopic pregnancy but twice. Was the pain of the first ordeal not enough to have not put myself in the same position a second time? And neither conquest measured up to being the mate I deserved.

> This is why all things should be done decently and in order. Lord, being much wiser than in the past, I'm waiting on You! If only I had grasped Your principles earlier, I would have saved myself a great deal of heartache and pain.

> The love of God is different from that of the love of the world. God's love cannot compare to the love of man. People we assume will love us do not necessarily have our best interest at heart. God's love is unconditional! He will not forsake me nor abandon me to face the issues of this world alone. When I am tired and weary, He may carry me and my load, but I must be willing to give it to Him, leave it with Him and never go back to retrieve it! I must be willing to move myself out of the way to allow Him to do His work.

God, I LOVE YOU!

Thank You for always being there when others abandoned me. Thank You for your persistence!

NO MEANS NO!

March 13, 1999

Dear God,

When I woke up this morning, I had a lot on my mind. I know! When have I not had things on my mind? Today was different. I wanted to write down my thoughts and elaborate on them. And today, I actually acted on it without procrastination.

My lifelong goals and definition for success:

- The ability to discern, to have and exhibit wisdom as well as knowledge—a longing for contentment and inner peace.

- I cannot, out of being lonely and desperate for companionship, keep allowing people (men in general) to abuse me. I understand it is better to forgive, but it's hard to forget. And at times, I succeed at forgetting too; at least, until I encounter the next negative occurrence (similar or not) in my life.

I want so much to believe that people are not generally insulting, overbearing, rude, obnoxious or cruel.

Looking Back

Around 5:30 p.m. on Friday, March 12, 2010, while out with my mother, cousin and nephew, I received a page from a gentleman I had been involved with from my past. Once I returned home, I returned the call and explained I had a house full of people and was unable to talk to him at that time. Later on that night around 10:00 p.m., I received a second page at which time I returned the call. *No means no!* We are responsible for our happiness and it is important to exercise your right to say "no" and mean it. **You are responsible for your life, your happiness and your salvation. You are perfectly within your rights to demand that others treat you with respect.**

Note Added September 24, 2010: Never let anyone force you or guilt you into doing something you do not want to do! You must be firm and hold true to your convictions and the will of God for your life. It is better to be alone and pleasing to God than it is to be in a relationship and unequally yoked. I wished I had figured this out much sooner.

Thank you!

MY FAMILY DILEMMA

April 18, 2000

Dear God,

There's a lot I don't seem to understand. I want so much to be the very best person I can be. I'm determined to succeed and be as positive about my life as I can. But sometimes it's very hard. I'm not complaining; I'm just venting.

I truly believe everything happens for a reason. At the beginning of a wilderness or while in the midst of it, I may not see the reason for it, but once my wilderness is over and I've managed to jump over the hurdle or the obstacle, I realize my growth or the positive outcome. For that I'm very grateful.

In looking at my life, I can honestly say that I've grown spiritually. And as I continue to grow, I want to improve the way I handle obstacles in all aspects of my life. I want to denounce anger and frustration. I want to patiently wait on You and trust that my plight is in the scheme of Your plan for me. And when You bring me through, I'm richer and have gained more prosperity.

In order to move forward, you have to leave the past in the past and let go of animosity. Even though I can't change the past, I believe my past contributed to my strengths, weaknesses and faults. And because of my past, I AM who I AM today. I should embrace my past and not dwell on it but learn and grow from it. When it comes to dealing with issues, the one that seems to always haunt me involves my family. For as long as I can remember, I've been the center of that union. That's a great deal of responsibility for a little girl. And even today, at age thirty-nine, I feel overwhelmed and a little frustrated.

Here's my dilemma: I want so much to be able to help my family, but I'm tired. I'm tired of being misunderstood or feeling as though no one takes me seriously. Certain children either connect with their mother or their father. I was always the lone ranger. I don't believe I actually connected with anyone in my family. Does that bother me? It used to bother me a great deal, but as I get older, I'm able to deal with the pain, anger and frustration of my childhood. Sometimes the pain resurfaces, but I try not to think about it.

God, what makes me so different? What was the difference between my siblings and me? What made my mother disbelieve me but believe them? That was my greatest pain and although I can't change the past, that was what I cried about this morning when I realized my nephew was having a similar experience. I truly believe there is nothing more devastating or heartbreaking than being bullied or taken advantaged of by others while not being able to rely on help from those who should love and protect you! So, I needed to offer the best support possible to my nephew because I could relate to his pain. I don't want him to grow up with bitterness and anger. I hope his early experiences in life don't make him weak. I hope they make him a stronger person than his mother. I don't want him to feel that the people he should count on the most are the ones who believe him the least. I want him to believe that anything worth having in life is worth fighting for and nothing in life is free. No matter how tired you get, you must not give up—even if the people you count on the most do!

I want to protect him, but I don't know how. And I certainly can't do it without the help of my mother. How do I convince her to do things differently when she's still holding on to the past herself?

Please teach me how to reach my mother. Please take away her pain, her frustration and anger from her past. Please teach her to live her life from today and begin again. Please give her strength and prosperity. Please give my mother the wherewithal to cope and fight like there's no tomorrow.

Thank You,
Ann

ASK AND YOU SHALL RECEIVE!

May 1, 2000

Hi God,

How are You today? I'm okay. However, I have a lot on my mind. I'm feeling a little discouraged, but I won't give up. I just need to talk and tell You what's on my mind.

    I was excited about the training program and want the opportunity to go back to school. But this time I want to approach it differently. I seem to have a problem with not finishing things. I get started with no problem, but I never seem to see it through. This time, I want to get started and finish. Please make it possible. I think I've covered all the bases. I've met all the requirements. I don't know how, but this time, I want to be a full-time student from beginning to end. I would like to get a part-time job with flexible hours and good pay. A part-time job that would allow me the opportunity to devote the necessary attention to my studies with no interruptions! In addition, I would like to successfully research scholarship programs, loans and grants that would financially benefit my dream. I wish to stay in this apartment and be able to finance school and handle all my expenses. I do not wish to get carried away with my finances or overspend. I do not want to lose sight of my goal or my dream. Please help me!

On another note, You know how I feel about my personal life. It seems I'm having problems finding a mate because I'm not waiting on You. I assumed Laurent was the one, but I thought others before him might be the one as well. This time I thought it was different. However, he and I don't seem to be connecting. I know I have issues and things I need to work on, but he doesn't seem to feel he has any issues. I do not want to be in a relationship without passion or compassion. I do not want to be in a relationship that feels like there's a tug of war. I'm pulling in one direction, and my mate is pulling in the opposite direction. I want a person I can communicate with 100 percent. One who does not agitate me, confuse me or frustrate me. Yes, I know—no relationship is perfect and there will be times when we won't see eye to eye, but it won't be with friction or alienation. Do You understand what I'm trying to say? Sometimes I know what I feel, but I may not know quite how to explain it or relay it to others.

Sometimes I feel I'm in a time warp, if there is such a thing. I've come to believe that we relive (somewhat) episodes in our life because we failed to take heed or learn what You were trying to tell us or teach us the first time. This is my third time being unemployed, and each time was caused by different circumstances at different times. I think there's something in common between each occurrence, but I can't seem to figure it out. The only connection I was able to make is school. Each time, I was either enrolled in classes or thinking about going back to school. That's why it's so important to me that things work out with the D.C. Employment or DOES training program.

I hope with all my might that I not only learn what You're trying to teach me this time, but I pray I get it right!

GOD, TEACH ME YOUR WAYS AND HELP ME TO UNDERSTAND

October 23, 2000

Dear God,

How are You today? Fine I hope.

It seems to be a normal occurrence that I have a number of issues and questions. I wish life were a little simpler. Are there any easy answers?

I want, deep down in my soul, to do the right thing and be the person You want me to be. However, I don't know what that is. A coworker shared a poem entitled *Everything Happens for a Reason*. I want so much to believe that! In fact, for the most part, I do believe it. But it's hard to accept that the negative things that happen are meant to be and do happen for a reason.

I can't seem to get my life together. At least, in my mind, I seem to be having problems. I don't know. Is it possible that I AM where I should be? As I look at my life, I feel I should have accomplished much more by now. And for some reason, when I reach a certain income level, something happens and I find myself starting all over again. And here I AM for the third time in my life, starting over again. I don't mean to be a whiner. I'm just trying to understand.

I know money isn't everything, but in this "world," it is the root cause of all evil as mismanaged or mishandled by man. And as a means of survival here on earth, money is needed. I ask for guidance and understanding. I ask for the ability to be a better financial planner and investor. I ask for the ability to live on what I earn meaningfully, regardless of the amount.

In my mind, I believe I failed a lesson, and until I get it, it's going to be repeated. I need your help! I want to learn and understand what I'm supposed to know.

COMING TOGETHER IN PRAISE

July 24, 2007

Dear God,

You are truly working on me and in me and all around me. You have taught me many things; an avid learner I AM! Unfortunately, I have not done well in keeping those lessons in the forefront of my mind. However, today, like many days, You have allowed me to interact with others as we enlightened one another. It's truly awesome to experience a gathering or worship session of like-minded individuals. As one woman shared her conversation she had with You that threw her into action in servicing others in prayer, the second person shared a song* in her heart about fighting with praise and the armor of Christ. The third one, me, received the message loud and clear as she rejoiced and felt an intense energy that left her bent over and in tears.

    As I focus on a board in that very same room, just minutes before the above encounter, I see a passage: The Lord is my light and my salvation—whom shall I fear? The Lord is the stronghold of my life—of whom shall I be afraid?

Confirmation! I plead the blood of Jesus to be upon me, within me and between me and all evil and the author of evil in Jesus' name.

*I'm a Soldier

I'm a soldier, in God's Army I'm fighting
I'm a soldier, in God's Army, and I'm fighting
Yes, I'm fighting, to pull down strongholds
Fighting to pull down strongholds.
Fighting, fighting with my praise
(repeat)

I got on my armor, my sword and my shield
I'm armed and dangerous, dangerous
I got on my armor, my sword and my shield
I'm armed and dangerous, dangerous
Fighting, fighting with my praise

SPIRITUAL GROWTH

August 23, 2007

Dear God,

Good morning!

August 21, 2007, was the seven-year mark for me here at The Salvation Army. My hope and view of what to expect on day one and the many months following my employment was completely changed in connection with what I have seen and experienced within the past seven years. I embarked on this adventure or journey with the hope of gaining spiritual growth. Without a doubt, I have grown, but not in the manner in which I thought was possible.

For some reason, I put too much stock in people based on their word and my belief of a physical concept and definition. I took to heart "the true meaning" of what a church is and the commitment of ones action in the body of Christ. I assumed there would be a great deal of encouragement and compassion exhibited here, for and by all—not by a few. I assumed a helping hand would be extended as opposed to the need of ego to tear one down. I assumed there would be more togetherness and willingness to work as a team to accomplish Your goals in fulfilling Your will as it relates to the written or otherwise stated purpose, vision, mission and values of The Salvation Army. I assumed the character of Christ would be attempted on a larger scale and those here would be willing to take responsibility for their actions and openly apologize when they were wrong or had wronged another. I assumed there would be nurturing from and by those I assumed not only knew of You but were close to You and committed to following Your example through their way of life (leading by example) and interaction with others. Wow, I guess I made a lot of assumptions.

Nonetheless, I truly know and understand each person is at a different spiritual level and that You deal with each of us accordingly through life's lessons (trials and tribulations). So I understand that what I was hoping to gain during my journey here was and is being obtained through You. I also know and understand the derivative of my strength through the midst of this ordeal. And regardless of what I encounter in my surroundings as I AM met with adversity, I know the importance of faith and Your power.

THANK YOU for not only believing in me and coming to my aid but for the many countless confirmations. My desire and prayer is that I continue to grow in all the ways that count in accordance to Your will, never stooping to the level of others who have lost perspective of the true nature and essence of Christ and the wonders of His work.

Life is like a Journey.
You make stops along the way; they are temporal.
This too shall pass!

GOD does not want us to be timid and fearful,
but through the HOLY SPIRIT,
He has given us power, love and sound judgment.

~ 2 Timothy 1:7 (paraphrased)

Integrity[44] (Honesty)

- A sense of "uncorrupted" virtue.

1. firm adherence to a code of especially moral or artistic values; INCORRUPTIBILITY

2. an unimpaired condition; SOUNDNESS

3. the quality or state of being complete or undivided; COMPLETENESS

Depth of *integrity*, trust, complementary moral values and skill are necessary components.

Good Faith: A term that generally describes honest dealing. Depending on the exact setting, good faith may require an honest belief or purpose, faithful performance of duties, observance of fair dealing standards, or an absence of fraudulent intent.[45]

---

44 https://www.merriam-webster.com/dictionary/integrity
45 https://www.law.cornell.edu/wex/good_faith

Respect[46]:

1. to consider worthy of high regard; ESTEEM

2. an act of giving particular attention; CONSIDERATON

Respect adds general reliability to social interactions. It enables people to work together in a complimentary fashion instead of each person having to understand or even agree with every detail of another's method. And further more, if you dovetail things, you get them working together. It is very important we dovetail our respective interests.

Here's a thought from the publishers of *Bits & Pieces*:

> *Take hope from the heart of a man*
> *and you make him a beast of prey.*
>
> ~ Quote from Ouida - "A Village Commune"

---

46   https://www.merriam-webster.com/dictionary/respect

STRIVING TO LIVE MY PURPOSE

August 31, 2007

Dear God,

I have had a great deal on my mind this past week. Because You are God, I know You know everything without me saying a word. However, at times, I feel the need to spell out exactly what is on my mind or to tell You what is bothering me. First, I would love to have You pull up a chair and appear before me in the physical sense so we can have a face-to-face conversation. There are so many questions I feel I need answered. Yes, I know "want" and "need" are two very entirely different things. What I feel I need is most likely not on Your agenda for what You feel I need. I can respect that, but it doesn't mean I can't dream, hope or look forward to You visiting me for that one-on-one conversation. So for now, I guess I'll just have to settle for putting my thoughts down on paper.

1. It has taken me a while to accept where I AM in my life. You know exactly how I feel about my current place of employment. Upon my arrival, I had such unwavering

enthusiasm about being able to contribute to the growth of The Salvation Army. I expected so much more! It seems I AM on a different page or spiritual level.

I believe in giving my all as well as having the need to accomplish things by implementing positive change. (That's actually funny! My performance evaluation states I don't do well with change. In fact, it actually states that I do not accept change. What a joke! I'm working with a group of people who don't have a clue about the importance of change or flexibility.) Unfortunately, implementing positive change is not possible here. It seems I'm surrounded by a number of people who have no problem with just existing and doing nothing to make things better. There is always room for improvement and with the right team, there is no limit to the potential for growth. God, if You allow me to stay here, I will not be able to fulfill my destiny—whatever that may be. As painful as it is for me, I'm sure my being here fits into your plan, and perhaps I AM succeeding at accomplishing what You intended. That is the most important thing, but it still hurts!

In the physical sense, in respect to what is needed here on earth for survival with the rising cost of living expenses, I do not see myself growing in my career if it is up to those who are in the present positions of leadership and authority. No, not here! They exert energy trying to convince me I AM incapable of doing the things they themselves lack the ability or desire to accomplish. It has nothing to do with education, experience or countless, concrete examples of me proving the opposite. It is about them reinforcing and proving their misconceived notion or false belief they have about people on the basis of race, gender and class.

2. I cannot seem to understand how the Salvation Army World Service Office (SAWSO) managed to stay in business for the past thirty years using the same method of operation as of this date. I'm actually having a hard time believing The Salvation Army has managed to be as successful as it has been with the level of unfairness I have witnessed since the beginning of my employment.

Over the years, I was told that the previous staff was extremely different from this group and worked well together. They had a great deal of passion for the work and each other. Wow, experiencing that would be greatly wonderful. So somewhere along the line, something changed. Perhaps it was the incentive, motivation, drive or commitment? I don't know! What we need is a feasibility study! We need someone to come in and access how we conduct business from the beginning to the end, including our level of interaction with one another. We need a Project Management consulting team similar to my previous employer, Robbins-Gioia, Inc., a company I recommended many times over for their business management concept in determining what was broken in offering solutions to other companies for their services. Taking their own advice and dealing with their issues from within was a different story. Much like The Salvation Army and SAWSO, I'm convinced they are not serious about getting to the root of their problems to make the necessary changes needed. However, a constructive report needs to be generated by an outside company instead of a designated Salvationist or officer for an objective assessment.

3. In spite of the negativity, I have had the pleasure of meeting and becoming close to some very sincere and genuinely spiritually grounded individuals, such as Gladys Fleming, Mary Ndungu, Coreen Watkins, Pat Poe, Thebisa, Macdonald Chaava (and family), Erika Lutz, Mary Bryant and Matthew Smith.

Speaking of Matthew Smith, he doesn't realize just how spiritually good-natured he is; even though he doesn't physically attend church, he has a big heart. I AM going to truly miss not having him around. The more people here attempted to tear me down, the more he did to lift me up and prove them wrong. It's not often in this day and time that you meet someone with such great integrity. In fact, that's what I admire most about each person mentioned above. I can mention a few officers too but not many: Major Shirley Espersen, Major Jerry Duke, The Lewises and the recently departed Swansons. I'm sure there are possibly others; however, these are the ones I can objectively reference based on my personal experience with them.

Dear God, I wish to thank You for allowing me to come in contact with these special individuals as well as others not mentioned (You know who they are; many have touched my life in different ways and will each be remembered and thought of differently!). It confirms that not all people in the world are bad and ruthless, regardless of how cruel this world seems to be. Through their example(s), I AM keeping in mind what it means to be in the world and not of the world. Regardless of what I encounter, my objective is to never fit in or run with the pack. I wish to be a leader—not a follower of the majority unless I AM following You.

I'm striving to live my purpose and always have an open mind!

NEVER ENDING

September 5, 2007

Dear God,

Each day here is truly an adventure. The incorporation of appropriate business practices does not seem to be an option. Why is it so difficult to identify a need for change and express it? You need to also be willing to put it in writing. You schedule a meeting to discuss a new plan of action and solicit ideas from others to get their view(s). Once a mutual agreement is reached, the plan should be outlined or summarized in writing and presented as a final plan of action for all to consider and implement accordingly. It's not hard! If it isn't finalized or put in writing, it's open to interpretation and easily disputable.

To make it all happen and pull it together, there has to be some sort of leadership. Leadership is applicable to all facets of life. The person in this role works best as a leader when he or she (1) is able to manage himself or herself, (2) is not afraid to admit to not knowing everything, (3) understands growth and learning is continuous, and (4) is willing to take responsibility for wrong choices (all actions have consequences).

It seems my area of responsibility is always growing, but no one wants to put it in writing. So I continue to get verbal requests, which makes it easier for them to dispute when the time comes to consider my performance. However, they seem to feel I should not have a problem with things that are asked of me outside of my job description.

> **Side Note:** As of this date, I have yet to receive an updated copy of my job description disclosing my title change from Program Assistant to Administrative Assistant. Should I make a second formal request, I'm sure I'll be given the same response as seven months ago: "It's being formatted." How long does it take to format a document? Let me take seven months to format a document! The games are neverending.

JOY ON THE INSIDE

September 6, 2007

Dear God,

This is a continuation of my letter to you from yesterday (entitled *Neverending*)! In observance of my surroundings, in relation to what I deem to be a normal hiring practice "for some, but not for all," people should not be hired based on their association alone. They should be hired based on their ability to do the job and be expected to carry out every aspect of that position as it relates to the job. If two people who have a personal relationship cannot work together within a business structure to effectively meet the goals of the organization in doing his or her job, then they should not be working together. They must be able to separate the two: business and personal. How can a friend effectively manage and supervise another friend if they are not willing to put things into the proper perspective?

The manager, due to his or her association, should not excuse part of the responsibility of the position/job by eliminating certain functions of the friend's job to give to someone else, thus unloading one to load the other and not take into consideration the difference in the number of tasks as well as the nature of what is involved to execute the requested tasks. If the classification of the position is weighed by the task involved in relation to the compensation, then why does the person being overloaded not receive more compensation and the other receive less as his or her tasks are decreased?

The ones who are here based on their abilities through a real or true selection process are the ones who seem to get more thrown at them and suffer along the way as they continue to be subjected to having to prove themselves daily. Examining the character of Christ, this is not an example of what it means to be just. Christians should be Christ-like or at least strive to get there but like this:

A very good friend, whom I've had the pleasure of knowing since age fourteen from junior high school, managed a division of a Federal government office within the Department of Commerce. In consideration of seeking qualified candidates to fill a position within her division, she contacted me to see if I was interested. Based on our association, I was a little hesitant about applying for and accepting the position. But she told me she had no doubts about my ability to perform in the capacity of assisting her. So needless to say, I accepted the position, and she became my supervisor. On day one, I approached her for a heart-to-heart talk, and I said, "I know who we are and value our friendship, but I do not want our friendship to interfere with what I need to do to perform in this position and be the best Secretary/Administrative Assistant possible. You have been here for a long time, and you have developed relationships with people here. I want you to be you and continue your association with others in the manner in which you have before my employment here in this office with you. Please do not feel like you have to babysit me and include me when you go to lunch. There may be people who do not view me as you do, and I don't want that association to suffer because of our friendship. We will always be friends!"

I didn't realize until now the beauty of being able to separate business and pleasure. True friendship doesn't die; it grows and becomes more. At times, you may find yourself distant from one another, but the ability to reconnect as if you were never disconnected is awesome. That's God! I know it can work with the right perspective. At the end of the workday, my girlfriend and I would connect again on a personal level, and at the beginning of our workday, we would connect on a business level. What a blessing!

When she had the opportunity to move on to another position within a different department, I was asked to accept her position as Office Manager by the Assistant Executive Director. I declined the position because I took into consideration the feelings of the other person who had been working in that office before I started working there. I gave more thought to her needs as opposed to me having the opportunity to not only make more money, but to obtain a permanent position and get back into the Federal government. The Assistant Executive Director had a discussion with me concerning my decision:

"Do you think if the role was reversed, she would turn down the position and consider you? Why would you give up an opportunity like this?" My response was, "It's not about what she would or wouldn't do for me. It's deeper than that! It's about me being able to live with me and much more. She and I would have to work together to accomplish what needs to be done in making this office run smoothly. I don't know if she would be able to come to work every day and objectively give her all to work while being faced by the pain of knowing someone else, who had spent less time at the company, obtained a higher position I'm sure she feels should have been offered to her. I do not want to put her through that."

Looking back, that was a very unselfish act on my part but a bad career move. Perhaps I could have approached her to ask her how she would feel if I agreed to accept the position in addition to her being willing to accept me as her supervisor. I actually never really thought about that segment of my life until now. That means I never looked back and moved forward with no regrets. In fact, if I had accepted the position, it's possible I would have excelled to be promoted to at least a grade 12 or equivalent in earning more money than I currently do right now. Perhaps, I wouldn't be here experiencing what I AM currently. However, I sure have slept well. No sleepless nights for me, at least not about that job I turned down. No—in spite of turning down that position, I still have joy.

> **Side Note (2017):** Since the writing of this letter to the Lord, I have been blessed to grow in my thinking to appreciate each pain-filled trial and tribulation to realize: **Pros-**

perity is not about dollars and cents! Prosperity is about being whole; rich in spirit, health, integrity and character. *Beloved, I pray that in every way you may succeed and prosper and be in good health [physically], just as [I know] your soul prospers [spiritually]* (3 John 2 AMP).

"Great will be the peace and prosperity of a nation when there shall arise within it a line of statesmen who, having first established themselves in a lofty integrity of character, shall direct the energies of the nation toward the culture of virtue and development of character, knowing that only through personal industry, integrity and nobility can national prosperity proceed. Still, above all, is the Great Law, calmly and with infallible justice meting out to mortals their fleeting destinies, tearstained or smiling, the fabric of their hands. Life is a great school for the development of character and all, through strife and struggle, vice and virtue, success and failure, are slowly but surely learning the lessons of wisdom."

~ *The Mastery of Destiny* by James Allen[47]

---

47 https://www.happypublishing.com/marketing/The%20Mastery%20of%20Destiny%20-%20James%20Allen.pdf

JUANITA BYNUM

September 6, 2007

Dear God,

Yesterday, I had the pleasure of fellowshipping with Mary Bryant. Upon my arrival at her home, I had the opportunity to see the last forty-five minutes of a two-hour Juanita Bynum TNB network segment. Through her program, I received one answer after the other. The intensity of those messages had me jumping up and down and running back and forth to the bathroom where I cried, shouted and stomped. Praise! For the first time, I actually know and understand the meaning of "praise" as experienced on this day.

Since that day, I have been extremely giddy. Honestly speaking, my giddiness actually started Tuesday morning, and it was re-ignited on Wednesday by the information passed on through Juanita Bynum. For the first time in her life, she had experienced domestic violence involving her husband. In spite of what she experienced, with the utmost grace, she shared her belief on a televised segment that God allowed this altercation for the necessity of affording her the opportunity to identify with others who have experienced the same thing at one time or another. Because of her personality and who she is through the eyes of God, she was not embarrassed and had no shame in sharing her story as she recognized the importance of healing for herself, her husband, and others who have found themselves in the same position. As I took in what she had to say, the story of Job resonated in my mind.

Oh God, to witness an unrehearsed testimony about a real life event that's unfortunately not discussed openly or viewed by others as being important was awesome to say the least. My heart ached for Ms. Bynum because I, who experienced something similar, understood wholeheartedly how attention is not given to the need for such counseling. And not all women (and in some cases men or people in general) who find themselves in abusive situations at the mercy of someone else are able to bounce back and take control of their lives without sinking into a deeper, darker place of depression in a timely manner. Healing is healing and although there can be no fixed time (and there should be no fixed time) associated with the process or time needed to heal, it could be a lengthy process to which there is no recovery in sight. Mainly, because those who find themselves in this situation are too ashamed to talk about it, so they keep all those feelings bottled inside where they fester and create internal damage, thus compromising the person's health. The hurt increases to encompass physical, mental and spiritual damage.

In fact, given the way society (those who are viewed as the majority and have the ability to sway the direction of a decision, stance or position) dictates the importance of gender, women in some cases are still thought of as second-class citizens and are therefore viewed as property as it relates to the "ancient" way of thinking (old laws, "good old boy network"). Because men occupy many positions within the judiciary system where many domestic cases are heard, women have not received the favorable attention needed to ensure their full protection and safety. Though there has been some change, women still find themselves being viewed unfairly and treated like second-class citizens, throughout history. To that end, many women are not vocal concerning matters of the heart and have been known to live with the knowledge of their abuse in silence, not knowing whom they can rely on for moral support. Juanita Bynum, though her publicly aired domestic troubles were unfortunate to say the least, her willingness to speak candidly (proclaim liberty to the captives) offered encouragement to a number of women.

On Monday, September 3, 2007, I read a series of scriptures recommended to me by Macdonald Chaava. When I rose on Tuesday morning, I had an entirely different attitude because You spoke to me loud and clear through those scriptures. It seemed as though it took me forever to get dressed that morning. I couldn't stop shouting, laughing, crying and praying. I now have difficulty turning the "on" switch "off." But, honestly speaking, I don't think I really want to! I just have to learn how to tone it down a bit, but I'm not sure I want to do that either. I AM bursting with joy! I never really knew until now the difference between being happy and having joy—the joy that comes from the inside and sustains you through the turbulence. That joy that remains the same when you're going through the good and the bad! That unwavering kind of feeling that never lets you down. That feeling one gets from an unrequited love that doesn't want to let you go! (However, this is a sign of true love from God with an intensity of combustible flames.) That feeling that no matter where you are or who you are around, it will not let you hold it at bay!

Arriving to work that day, I entered the elevator and was greeted by a Salvation Army officer who asked how I was doing. I replied, "I'm great. I'm actually feeling better than I thought I ever could. I just want to scream, yell and shout. I'm feeling so good I can't hold it in." That officer backed up in the corner and held onto the metal railing as if he was holding on for dear life; he couldn't wait to get to his floor so he could get off the elevator. Today, while riding in that same elevator, I had the distinct pleasure of riding up with that same officer. He asked if I was going to be crazy today. I told him I was going to make an attempt to contain myself, but when the spirit (Holy Ghost) needs to release, it just comes out. So he said he was going to his office to get away from me. I told him he couldn't hide because the spirit was capable of following him anywhere, and I didn't have to be present. So he asked me to warn him. I told him I wanted to be warned too.

Believing there is a reason for everything, I've had difficulty understanding why I was here in the employment of the Salvation Army and more importantly, why You were keeping me here. For the past seven years, I've been consumed by pain and grief. You know I've been fighting to leave here. I thought You put me in a similar, uncontrollable, pre-Salvation Army situation before to endure alone. I couldn't see beyond the negativity and the adversity. I truly apologize for allowing the enemy (forces of darkness and spiritual principalities) to succeed in getting me off track. I lost perspective of who I AM and the extent of Your power. (Be strong in the Lord and stand in the power of His might!) You are teaching me to stand and hold strong. Please continue to flow through me, around me and in me! Fill me with the Holy Spirit. As I AM emptied or drained, please refresh me! Let my cup runneth over!

I ran from one department (TSA-NHQ Human Resources) to the other (SAWSO) thinking things were going to be better. Not so! That same spirit surfaced, but I know You are teaching me to know thyself and depend on You. Oh God! What a wonderful feeling to know You have always been by my side! You've sent me one sign after another and never gave up on trying to reach me, protect me or console me in spite of myself. I cannot change people according to the way they act or what they may think of me. I can only change myself and my way of thinking by not allowing them to make me think less of myself.

On the way to work in the mornings, I've been listening to Marvin Sapp's *Thirsty* album. My favorite songs have been "Worshipper in Me," "Thirsty," "Praise Him in Advance," and "Never Would Have Made It." Another favorite is Kirk Franklin's *Brighter Day*. I thank You for these artists: Yolanda Adams, Juanita Bynum and many others, who openly share their love of You to encourage others like me. Their gifts help to refuel our souls in assisting us to keep our eyes on You.

Joy on the inside!

BETWIXT

September 23, 2007

Dear God,

Today is my birthday! Happy birthday to You and thank You for allowing me to live to see another year. If, however, it is to be life here and I am to go on living, this will mean useful and productive service for me; so I do not know which to choose [if I am given that choice]. But I am hard-pressed between the two. I have the desire to leave [this world] and be with Christ, for that is far, far better (Philippians 1:22-23 AMP). Indeed, going home to be with You would be better than enduring being told I don't see what I see, feel what I feel, and that what I have to say doesn't matter while my frustration gets misconstrued for having a bad attitude. How easy it is for us to adorn ourselves with labels that make us feel important while deeming ourselves more worthy than another? *He hath put down the mighty from their seats, and exalted them of low degree* (Luke 1:52). Perhaps if more thought was given to the character associated with the label, we would be more mindful of our actions and especially our treatment of others. *Nevertheless, to abide in the flesh is more needful for you* (Philippians 1:24).

Upon waking up this morning, I felt a tug within my spirit to continue what You led me to start yesterday, but I could not finish because the pain was too great. I AM and have been filled with mixed emotions since Tuesday, September 18, 2007, as I attempt to struggle with the realities of life. My life; to include being burdened and overwhelmed by the reality of countless confirmations, such as the Jena Six. And my soul cries out! *And when the Lord saw her, he had compassion on her, and said unto her, weep not* (Luke 7:13). So today, I ask You for Your forgiveness and the strength to carry on (Philippians 4:6). Please give me the ability to deal with this pain in a positive manner and let it not hinder the progress of my spiritual growth. *And having this confidence, I know that I shall abide and continue with you - all for your furtherance and joy of faith* (Philippians 1:25). For I AM a willing participant who wishes to be used by You in spite of the pain! *For unto You it is given in the behalf of Christ, not only to believe on Him, but also to suffer for His sake* (Philippians 1:29).

In the year 2007, I AM still observing the events of history from the 1800s (and as far back as 1619) in which I play a significant role. *Fear ye not therefore, ye are of more value than many sparrows* (Matthew 10:31). How hardening and faith-deadening it is for me to know that I AM or may be surrounded by or come in contact with people—who may occupy the same neighborhood and place of worship—who do not value my existence in the same manner they value their own. To be viewed as being less important due to my nationality, gender, personality, opinionated nature, and religious belief hurts deep down to the bone; there is a piercing through my heart that disturbs my soul. *For by Him were all things created, that are in heaven and that are in earth, visible and invisible, whether they be thrones or dominions or principalities or powers: all things were created by Him and for Him* (Colossians 1:16). So am I not a human being (flesh) and a body that possesses a spirit that has a soul? Should I bleed, does not my blood be the color of red? Does not my blood run warm with life and cold even in death? Am I not the image of You which now inhabits this physical form on earth?

Through a system of government, we devise laws that are written to force some into submission by way of control while others are allowed to break those same laws at will with little to no punishment. Through that same system of government, but on a smaller scale, we institute labor policies (employment law) to qualify some people for positions while discriminating against others. How can two people be given identical job descriptions and a higher classification be given to one and not the other? With the help of human resources—where job descriptions are used to identify an appropriate job candidate with the necessary skills, experience and education to successfully and effectively perform the responsibilities of the position—some are allowed to occupy a position without having any past experience or education. They are given an opportunity to grow into the position as they receive the appropriate training while others are held at a higher standard; this is better known as a double standard. One definition defines double standards as "any code or set of principles containing different provisions for one group of people than for another, especially an unwritten code of sexual behavior permitting men more freedom than women"[48] to include other variations of prejudice, idiosyncrasies and ignorance. For instance, often times, many employees at the lower graded positions are expected to generate a greater output for less compensation with little to no chance of advancement: recognition for growth or opportunities for promotion. Many performance evaluations are deliberately underwritten to minimize the actual accomplishments of an employees' range of potential. Although they, generally, may meet the qualifications for fulfilling the position to accomplish each desired task, they are repeatedly held back because they do not fit the expected image. And, therefore, are subjected to being measured and evaluated according to the invisible yardstick or glass ceiling—never quite hitting the mark. Should you start to climb, the rules always change and you find yourself having to start over, never reaching that imaginary plateau set for you by others as a hindrance and limitation. *I can do all things through Christ which strengthenth me!* (Philippians 4:13) The more you do, the more you are expected to do and your best is never good enough. *Let nothing be done through strife or vainglory; but in lowliness of mind let each esteem the other better than themselves* (Philippians 2:3).

What good is an equal employment opportunity statement or a diversity awareness seminar geared toward addressing the issue if we are not willing to admit that there is a problem? *Fear them not therefore: for there is nothing covered, that shall not be revealed; and hid, that shall not be known* (Matthew 10:26). You

---

48 http://www.dictionary.com/browse/double-standard

cannot put a bandage on the pain, thus attempting to mask it and hope it goes away. Some care needs to be exercised objectively to treat the illness and bring about change to promote individual and universal healing. *Finally, brethren, whatsoever things are honest, whatsoever things are just, whatsoever things are pure, whatsoever things are lovely, whatsoever things are of good report; if there be any virtue, and if there be any praise, think on these things* (Philippians 4:8).

Scenario: Two employees within the same department request to place a petition in the company lunchroom to aid a cause they feel is most important. One employee's aim is to obtain signatures from like-minded individuals who oppose the transfer of ownership of a Christian radio station to a secular radio station. The other employee's aim is to obtain signatures from like-minded individuals who oppose the legal ruling of the Jena Six that, without a doubt, centers on an injustice that clearly identifies a double standard. Both went through the same channels, but one had to get the approval of their department head and the other was granted the opportunity to have his petition displayed without having to obtain approval from the department head. Is the value of saving a radio station more important than attempting to save humanity? More importantly, is not a church in the business of saving souls? All souls!

> **Food for Thought:** Beware of double meanings, which can be the same as double standards. I used to think being told I was **overqualified** for a position was more of a positive statement than it was a negative one until I learned it had a double meaning. Being overqualified is something they

tell you when you don't fit the image or existing culture within a working environment. It doesn't necessarily speak to you being too skilled. How can having more experience than required be a negative thing? Why not say, we would love to hire you, but your salary is too high? However, if I indicated my salary requirement on my resume, why agree to interview me only to tell me my salary is too high? Perhaps it's a blessing from the Lord!

DEPRESSION IS NOT AN OPTION

October 4, 2007

Dear God,

Depression is not an option! For I know from within whom my strength lies. Vengeance is mine, saith the Lord. To me belongeth vengeance and recompence; their foot shall slide in due time, for the day of their calamity is at hand, and the things that shall come upon them make haste. As stated in my previous letter (dated September 23, 2007) that seems to have raised a number of eyebrows, being an individual (flesh and blood) on earth that inhabits a physical form (body) that is sometimes driven (ruled) by emotions and wants nothing more than to see the good in the existence of all that was created by God, I cannot help but be amazed by how easy it is for some to act so unconscionably and not give any thought to You. If we confess our sins, He is faithful and just to forgive us our sins and to cleanse us from all unrighteousness. Nonetheless, it is because of You that I AM able to not only observe my surroundings but see it clearly and objectively without allowing what I see to depress me. Therefore, being depressed would mean I was disillusioned and not walking in truth.

While watching the movie *The Pursuit of Happyness*, I started to cry. At the time, I was extremely unhappy about a situation at work, so the movie touched me deeply. "Never let anyone tell you what you cannot do because—more than likely—they cannot do it themselves." This dialogue from the movie had a great impact on me. For most of my life, I have had people tell me what I cannot do! If we are not careful and do not know from whom our strength comes, we will start to believe what is told to us and unconsciously act on proving them right just so they can feel better about themselves. Though there are moments when the enemy succeeds at entering my mind and accomplishing just that, You intercede and remind me of who I AM. Thank You for gifting me with a personality that drives me to do the opposite of what I'm told I cannot do. The more a person tells me what I cannot do, the more I strive to prove them wrong.

However, upon waking up the next morning to prepare myself for work, I woke up to the sound of Your voice and I have not been the same since. God, I heard You say, loud and clear: "You will not devote any more energy thinking or worrying about what others say you cannot do! You will no longer worry about people not compensating you for what you know you are capable of doing! What I have for you and am calling you to do, is far greater and more valuable than any amount man would be willing to pay you! You can write and you will write for Me! You have nothing to prove to anyone but Me! I AM giving you an opportunity to write about Me through the testimonies I have allowed you to experience. You will encourage others on behalf of Me. *Be not thou therefore ashamed of the testimony of our Lord, nor of me his prisoner: but be thou partaker of the afflictions of the gospel according to the power of God* (2 Timothy 1:8). Are you ashamed of Me?" *Yet if any man suffer as a Christian, let him not be ashamed; but let him glorify God on this behalf* (1 Peter 4:16).

Falling to my face, I cried and shouted to the top of my lungs, I AM NOT ASHAMED, as I thanked You and asked You to forgive me. Oh God, please forgive me for questioning You and asking why You allowed me to be a part of this situation as well as the many countless others that have brought me so much pain here on earth. Forgive me for doubting You and Your will for me. Forgive me for allowing people to come in between me and You because I was having difficulty understanding how those who proclaim to be righteous could sit quietly on the sidelines and do nothing to assist their fellow man or get involved when they see or witness an injustice being done to another. *So justice is far from us and righteousness does not reach us. We look for light, but all is darkness; for brightness, but we walk in deep shadows* (Isaiah 59:9). What a sad world we live in! In fact, it's not the world itself. No, not the beautiful world You created! It's the *people* in the world who have become so accustomed to making excuses for their actions by entertaining the many countless reasons in accordance to their philosophy of a moral code (called justification) as we drift further and further away from You. By not contesting an immoral act in any way, shape or form, are they not just as guilty as if they physically committed that act themselves? I just never understood how we could claim to stand for something yet stand for nothing at all—afraid to get involved, afraid to speak up or out and afraid to encourage or to be encouraged! (Again, what is fear? False Evidence Appearing Real!)

The difficulties, hardships and trials of life and the obstacles one encounters on the road to fortune are positive blessings. They knit the muscles more firmly and teach self-reliance. Peril is the element in which power is developed.

~ William Mathews, Writer (1818–1909)

Oh God, I refuse to believe people do not know what they do. You have given us free will—the ability to make choices. As we get older or get to a certain age, should we not know right from wrong? A number of us are deceitful by nature, and there are some who do what they do to others because they not only feel they can, but because they can get away with it. Still attempting to reach me and console me, You asked me again, Are you ashamed of Me? I answered, No, I AM not ashamed. Do you trust Me? I answered, Yes, I trust You. Then listen to Me! For as a man thinketh in his heart, so is he. I see you. I know you. I know what is in your heart. Trust Me, not man!

Am I depressed? No, not even close! We are troubled on every side yet not distressed; we are perplexed but not in despair; persecuted but not forsaken; cast down but not destroyed (2 Corinthians 4:8-9). To those who question whether or not I hold grudges, I have no bitterness or malice in my heart. That does not mean I AM immune to feelings of hurt or pain. I pray daily in asking God to shield my heart so it does not become bitter or hardened by that which I encounter. My extreme disappointment comes from receiving injustice by the hands of those who—due to hypocrisy, prejudices, cowardliness, and the need to have control over another human being (power)—proclaim to be God-fearing individuals; those who proclaim to have my best interest at heart; and those who believe what they do in the dark is not revealed in the light.

My anger is not fueled by hatred or resentment; it has more to do with being determined not to accept excuses or make any. It's more in line with being true to myself in every sense of the word. It's about believing that each and every person should be held accountable for his or her actions whether the act is committed in secrecy or out in the open—consciously or unconsciously. Otherwise, how else would we learn? But it is not up to me and I do not wish to take on the role of judge or juror. *Therefore judge nothing before the time, until the Lord come, who both bring to light the hidden things of darkness and will make manifest the counsels of the hearts: and then shall every man have praise of God* (1 Corinthians 4:5).

Therefore, I can only hope to learn the lessons that God is trying to teach me through my relationships with others; because at the end of the day, it is important for me to examine my character and hope God is pleased with my actions as I work toward becoming more like Christ. *See to it, then, that the light within you is not darkness* (Luke 11:35). My desire is to live by example and not act on S/He-motions. *Delight thyself also in the Lord; and He shall give thee the desires of thine heart* (Psalm 37:4).

Examine yourselves, whether ye be in the faith; prove your own selves. Know ye not your own selves, how that Jesus Christ is in you, except ye be reprobates.

~ 2 Corinthians 13:5

Oftentimes, the objective of man—depending upon the convictions of his heart—when he is confronted and forced to look at himself, is to deny the truth. Instead of looking at the situation objectively, the confronter is accused of (1) exaggerating the truth, (2) blowing things out of proportion and (3) being a troublemaker. Like Abraham, the father of many nations, I AM more than a conqueror. I refuse to take on any name I AM called by people in the world unless it is the name God has called me to be, because I AM not of this world! I AM the head and not the tail. I AM above and not below. God knows my potential, thus I have high expectations that He is able, by the power at work within me, to do more than anyone else and to do for me more than I could ever ask or imagine.

Be prepared when a person speaks out openly about what he sees, feels and thinks or how he is impacted by the action or situation; the objective of the unfaithful is to discredit him in the eyes of others. If others believe the confronter is exaggerating, blowing things out of proportion and aims to cause trouble, attention is diverted from the real problem. No one seriously takes to heart what is said or is being done; the need for change is not considered, and the mayhem continues. **Be careful not to allow yourself to be limited by those in the world, but define yourself by what is in the Bible.**

Seeing then that we have such hope,
we use great plainness of speech.

~ 2 Corinthians 3:12

M&Ms

October 17, 2007

07:42 a.m.

Dear Father God,

I AM a little out of sorts today because I believe You are leading me to attend The Salvation Army's chapel service this morning. For the past seven years, I have been very selective with my time, not only as it relates to my association with others here, but as it relates to my praise and worship here. I always want my focus to be on You and not allow my surroundings or what I encounter here to hinder that focus. Knowing me as You do, You know I have a real problem with hypocrisy. My observance of my surroundings as it encompasses the action of those within the environment in which I work seems to vex my spirit, thus not allowing me to want to freely attend chapel service to worship You amongst those I believe have no real clue as to who You are through what I consider to be a false teaching.

Adamant about not offending You on any level or being disobedient, I need You to send me an earth-shattering sign concerning Your desire for me to attend this service today. In fact, my unwillingness over the past four years to participate in the chapel events was taken into consideration and counted against me, proved evident in my performance evaluation (the most unfavorable evaluation I have received throughout my many years of working), which seems ironic considering the notification approximately one week ago from the secretary of personnel (Mrs. Falin) reiterating the *optional* chapel service policy. It's a little hard to hear a sermon and attempt to focus on or receive the message when it's being delivered by those in a ministering capacity or leadership role (or anyone for that matter) who has treated you unjustly, having lost perspective of what it means to be in the world and not of the world.

11:51 a.m.

Dear God,

You never cease to amaze me! What a wonderful Father You are. While sitting and pondering on going to chapel, You sent Mary Bryant to pull my coattail at 9:20 a.m. Approaching my office door, she pops in her head and with a smile asks, "Are you going to chapel?" I let out a big sigh and said under my breath, "Oh God, I should not have shared my dilemma with her earlier." (Later, I learned, it was You who sent her for encouragement!) Nonetheless, feeling compelled to be obedient to You, I get up from my desk and go into the bathroom to pray before taking my final steps toward the elevator to go to the chapel.

Still operating under the spirit of reluctance, You sent yet another message through Grace Herring and MacDonald

Chaava. As we rode down on the elevator together, I could feel the spirit of encouragement. As Grace began to sing a song that not only spoke to my heart but to my need to please You in being obedient, I started to cry silently. Upon entering the chapel, I sat down to compose myself and You had me fix my eyes on Katie Burgmayer, who was seated at the piano, to calm my nerves.

Officer Forster, who had already started the service, had us sing a song from the hymnbook that touched my spirit in a mighty way. It was as if my mind, body and spirit were separate; however, my body and spirit were on one accord. Not much of a singer, I closed my eyes as the others sang and steadied my mind to focus on the words. My body seemed to surge with energy as my spirit danced. That was another sign from You.

Officer Forster shared a story or two and asked, "What is the second-most read book after the Bible?" *A Purpose Driven Life* was the answer. Wanting nothing more than to know my purpose or the reason for my existence, I not only purchased that book but many others like it. Anything dealing with spiritual growth, I had to get it and read it.

How beautifully the message tied into the title, M & Ms.
Who is my Master? God!
What is my Mission? Serving You!

Where I work has nothing to do with my supreme desire: serving You! However, through the will of God and by His grace, I work at The Salvation Army. Oh God, confirmation after confirmation, You speak to me through the Holy Spirit that dwells within me as the Holy Spirit within others communes with my spirit. Thank God for Officer Forster's willingness and boldness in how he delivered his sermon to speak in truth about being led by You for the Kingdom. He had us hold out our hands and look at them as he pointed out how different they were in comparison to another individual's. No two sets of hands are made alike. In some cases, not even one set of hands may be identical to the other.

As he closed, he cited the following scripture:

> *But speaking the truth in love, may grow up into him in all things which is the head, even Christ.*
>
> ~ Ephesians 4:15

I AM who I AM because of You! I AM an original! I was designed by You and strategically placed in position by You. For seven years, I have longed to get away and run from here as fast as I can. Still here beyond my wishes, I resolved my mind to deal the best way I can by separating myself from others. The more I seem to create distance and space, the more You seem to propel me right in the middle of controversy. And yet, I was perfectly designed by You to fulfill a post that obviously You feel can only be done by me.

Dear God, I thank You for Your unwavering confidence. I want nothing more than to please You. I continue to ask for the ability to remove self out of the way, hear You with clarity and act and speak with authority, without hesitation, through the Holy Spirit in accomplishing Your will for my life.

MALACHI 3:1 MINISTRIES

*Behold, I will send my messenger,
and he shall prepare the way before me: and the Lord,
whom ye seek, shall suddenly come to his temple,
even the messenger of the covenant, whom ye delight in:
behold, he shall come, saith the LORD of hosts.*

~ Malachi 3:1

October 19, 2007

Dear Father God,

Good morning! Today is Friday—the end of a workweek. With all that's going on at work and in my life these days, You know I was looking forward to this day. However, I'm sure Monday will come around quickly. So today, I ask and pray that I not only accomplish what needs to be accomplished this weekend, in accordance to Your will of course, but that I get the proper rest to be ready to tackle next week with the presence of mind, body and soul, charged with the Holy Ghost to continue to stand with You and for You with authority. Please bless me with the wherewithal, including but not limited to the entire armor of Christ to wage war on behalf of the Kingdom. Ephesians 6:11 says to *put on the full armor of God so that you can take your stand against the devil's schemes.* **I plead the blood of Jesus to be upon me, within me and between me and all evil and the author of evil, in Jesus' name!**

Last Friday, I was attending a three-day spiritual conference through the Malachi 3:1 Ministries. Oh God, what a wonderful opportunity! I recommend this teaching to each person within the body of Christ who is trying to find themselves as it relates to Your will or have lost their way and need to be encouraged. What a wonderful start to removing strongholds on your life, your person and your mind to realizing your fullest potential as it relates to your purpose in the Kingdom of God in accordance to the will of God is how I would summarize the nature of what you will walk away with by attending a Malachi 3:1 Ministries Conference! An experience, I know, I will hold onto from now until!

Malachi is one of the strongest messages on tithing in the Old Testament and is frequently used by pastors. However, it is much more than just that! Malachi is a call to repent and return to the covenant for blessings. The prophet reminds the people of what God will do for His people. But the book is also a warning of judgment. The prophet stresses that God will bless the people in judgment if they are faithful. The message is one delivered to a people who have gotten beyond the "high" of Nehemiah's revival and have succumbed to the temptations of everyday life. Malachi preaches for a return to the revival standard.

During my one-hour-and-twenty-minute drive as I returned home from the conference, I couldn't help but replay the events of the conference over and over again in my mind. I was truly sorry to see the conference end, but I viewed it as being the beginning—a new beginning. Rebirth! Learning to unlearn as I relearn in seeking Your face. Seeking a connection to You through Jesus Christ—the Holy Spirit (Ghost) that dwells within me as well as those who have accepted Christ as their Lord and Savior (John 14:17)! Understanding the importance of spiritual growth, maturity and learning through the Holy Spirit! Allowing You to work in my life through the Holy Spirit in fulfilling Your will. Awesome, awesome, awesome! I experienced a spiritual cleansing of the physical body through the Holy Spirit as assisted by the Messenger.

Malachi 3:1 Ministries not only reinforced or confirmed things for me, but they educated me on who I AM in the body of Christ as it is emphasized by Your word through the Bible. I saw and truly experienced the presence of the Holy Spirit at work through Your children. The supernatural and the spirit world, if ever I doubted it before, I now know is real; it exists in this realm (the earthly realm) as it does in the next (the spirit world). Unfortunately, this is not taught in many churches. This teaching I received through Malachi 3:1 Ministries was made possible by You. I saw, felt and knew in my heart that You were present in each one of the members of the Malachi 3:1 Ministries as well as within Your children who were allowed by You to participate in this glorious affair. (Grace be to you and peace from God, the Father and from our Lord, Jesus Christ, who gave himself for our sins, that he might deliver us from this present, evil world, according to the will of God and our Father.)

Who Is the Holy Spirit?

God the Holy Spirit is the third member of the Godhead and the only member operating in the earth today. He is called the manifested Power of God. It is His voice we hear telling us to go this way instead of that or to do this thing and not the other. It is God the Holy Spirit who performed the acts of creation that were spoken into existence with words (Jesus, the walking WORD made flesh) uttered by God the Father, who willed all things into existence.

Teaching Reference from Malachi 3:1 Ministries

www.ThisIsWorship.com
http://ronnamatthews.com

Background

Growing up, I always wondered where I fit. I have had a great deal of difficulty attempting to identify with people, places or things here on earth. What was it about me that set me apart from the rest of the world, including my immediate family? People always wanted to reshape me, change me or control me, especially on jobs. As I encountered trouble, I would run from one job to another and socialize with others as little as possible.

I never liked having to justify who I was or feeling as though I had to continuously prove myself to get ahead. Shouldn't my ability to perform my job be enough? No matter what I did, it was never enough unless the person supervising me felt they had total control over me while at work *and* away from the job. Unless I was willing to change who I was to become what or who others felt I should be, I was allowed to progress on the job; but still not at the rate of others within certain environments. As I went from one job to the other, God, it was always the same. They never had a problem giving me more than my share of work while never compensating me for all of what I was asked to do or what I was capable of doing or accomplishing.

When I was offered a position at The Salvation Army, I thought my prayers were answered and that I would no longer be subjected to persecution, unfairness or unjustness by receiving what should be rightfully mine through my performance and ability to complete my assigned tasks. One month into employment, I did not like what I was seeing. Why had God subjected me to the same treatment at the hands of Christian folks in the name of Jesus Christ who were *making a mockery of his name!* Wanting to run away as quickly as I could, I started looking for other employment, but I did not want to break the promise I made to God: to finish school and get my degree if he would make it possible for me to accomplish this defeat with no financial burden on my behalf. So I attempted to endure for as long as I could while still looking for other employment, only to be able to move from one position of The Salvation Army as the Personnel Assistant within the Office of Human Resources, earning an annual salary of approximately $25,000, to another position as Program Assistant within the same building of The Salvation Army for a separate entity, the Salvation Army World Service Office, with a starting annual salary of $36,000. Seven years later, I AM still here and enduring!

> *I marvel that ye are so soon removed from him that called you into the grace of Christ unto another gospel: Which is not another; but there be some that trouble you, and would pervert the gospel of Christ. But though we, or an angel from heaven, preach any other gospel unto you than that which we have preached unto you, let him be accursed. As we said before, so say I now again, If any man preach any other gospel unto you than that ye have received, let him be accursed. For do I now persuade men, or God? or do I seek to please men? for if I yet pleased men, I should not be the servant of Christ. But I certify you, brethren, that the gospel which was preached of me is not after man. For I neither received it of man, neither was I taught it, but by the revelation of Jesus Christ.*
>
> ~ Galatians 1:6-12

A church or body of Christ has to be extra careful about how it conducts itself in the name of Jesus Christ through false teaching. You are held accountable at the highest level when your actions go against who Christ is and what He represents. I AM still here, not because I want to be, but because this is where I'm supposed to be in accordance to Your will. You are teaching me and forcing me to stand and fight for the Kingdom. I AM experiencing in one place of employment that which I have experienced collectively at all my places of employment. The ultimate test! You are preparing me for greatness (John 14:12); the supernatural utterance of the mind and council of God that is NOT preceded by tongues and directed to the church—not the unbeliever. Oh God, You put me in a hot seat! Nonetheless, I want nothing more than to please You and do as You command.

Motive Gifts

Through a workshop entitled Motive Gifts, **Malachi 3:1 Ministries** helped me to identify who I AM as it not only relates to the Kingdom, but as it is pointed out or referenced in the Bible through the word of God. That confirmation of who I AM was also revealed to me this morning while in the car as I was driving to work.

Dear God, I realize You speak to me each and every day, however, there are days when Your message is so clear and heart piercing, leaving me in such an emotional state of joy, praise and worship as experienced during the conference! At times, it's so powerful that I feel the need to pull over or hope there is no one within my path while driving that I AM allowed to continue on my way. This morning, You allowed my life, as it is up to this point, to flash before me from the past to the present. I thought about the many tests and then I heard You say, ultimate test. That's what threw me into overdrive.

Imagine driving alongside a woman who is screaming at the top of her lungs, grabbing at her heart and stomach (which is not visible for you to see) as she rocks back and forth. What a sight! And if you can hear her in the midst of the screams, she's yelling, Oh God, Oh God, Oh God, thank You, thank You, thank You, I understand! The conference through **Malachi 3:1 Ministries** was necessary to give me a different perspective or focus of how You are using me. You are using me to reach others! Through the Holy Spirit, I have been given the gift of prophecy.

> *Follow after charity, and desire spiritual gifts, but rather that ye may prophesy. For he that speaketh in an unknown tongue speaketh not unto men, but unto God: for no man understandeth him; howbeit in the spirit he speaketh mysteries. But he that prophesieth speaketh unto men to edification, and exhortation, and comfort. He that speaketh in an unknown tongue edifieth himself; but he that prophesieth edifieth the church.*[49][1] *I would that ye all spake with tongues, but rather that ye prophesied: for greater is he that prophesieth than he that speaketh with tongues, except he interpret, that the church may receive edifying. Now, brethren, if I come unto you speaking with tongues, what shall I profit you, except I shall speak to you either by revelation, or by knowledge, or by prophesying, or by doctrine? And even things without life giving sound, whether pipe or harp, except they give a distinction in the sounds, how shall it be known what is piped or harped? For if the trumpet give an uncertain sound, who shall prepare himself to the battle? So likewise ye, except ye utter by the tongue words easy to be understood, how shall it be known what is spoken? for ye shall speak into the air.*

---

49 [51] Until the reading of 1 Corinthians 5 through the teaching of **Malachi 3:1 Ministries**, I believed I had offended God in some way because he had not blessed me with the speaking in tongues. Falling to my face, I asked God to forgive me of my ignorance as I thanked Him for loving me and seeing me as being special to Him.

There are, it may be, so many kinds of voices in the world, and none of them is without signification. Therefore if I know not the meaning of the voice, I shall be unto him that speaketh a barbarian, and he that speaketh shall be a barbarian unto me. Even so ye, forasmuch as ye are zealous of spiritual gifts, seek that ye may excel to the edifying of the church.

~1 Corinthians 1-12

I came to the realization of the Father, the Son and the Holy Ghost as being real. Using the analogy from Creflo Dollar's "The Spiritual Man" message from October, 19, 2007, You are no longer a figment of my imagination. Therefore, I no longer have time to waist worrying about what people think about me. Ignorance can be fixed! Teach me and help me always be in the right frame of mind to have the right attitude about myself. I wish to always operate and grow in the Spirit with Your objective in mind: removing self.

Oh Father God, I thank you for the Malachi 3:1 Ministries and the opportunity You have given to me in allowing us to commune as one in seeking Your face. I pray for their protection from the enemy of darkness in accordance to Your will as they continue with zeal. Please keep them in perfect health, peace and harmony.

DEVELOPING A PERSONAL RELATIONSHIP WITH GOD

October 27, 2007

Dear God,

On October 23, 2007, my supervisor cautioned me about sharing my testimonies with others. *For as the body without the spirit is dead, so also faith without works is dead* (James 2:26). It seems a number of my coworkers in my immediate office do not wish to receive these types of emails from me. Personal emails that speak directly to the heart have a way of piercing the heart to incite change! Depending upon the person reading the emails, the content may—on occasion—convict[50] the heart and the mind, which has difficulty accepting, for one reason or another, that he or she is accountable for their actions. In the same token, *God means what he says. What he says goes. His powerful Word is sharp as a surgeon's scalpel, cutting through everything, whether doubt or defense, laying us open to listen and obey. Nothing and

---

50   http://www.acts17-11.com/conviction.html

no one is impervious to God's Word. We can't get away from it— no matter what (Hebrews 4:12-13 MSG).

Since the beginning of my employment within the Salvation Army World Service Office, I have been told in a roundabout way through my supervisor (never directly) that some of the staff members were expressing a disinterest in receiving emails from me. It's ironic, but initially, all emails were work-related, so I have concluded that on some level, it has more to do with me than what the information entails.

If any man among you seem to be religious,
and bridleth not his tongue, but deceiveth his own heart,
this man's religion is vain.

~ James 1:26

On October 26, I received a written warning indicating I failed to follow instructions and violated a company email policy. As usual, when something is bothering me or I attempt to make sense of it all, I'm forced to remember and review every aspect of my life pertaining to that immediate situation that has me so puzzled. For as long as I can remember, my personality has always been geared toward dealing with people on a direct basis. I actually have this uncanny notion to treat people in the manner in which I would like to be treated as opposed to how they treat me. It's actually not in my nature to treat people as undignified as some of my coworkers have treated me or related to me. If I have a problem with a person, I believe in confronting the individual or situation in an adult-like manner—constructively!

People allow themselves to get so consumed with class, title, gender and race that they have decided who should or should not be more knowledgeable than them based on where they fit into one of the above categories. So once again, we put more emphasis on status (in the world, not of the world). A number of my staff members in higher positions see themselves as being more knowledgeable based on the position they hold. For some reason, I keep forgetting I am not seen on the same level—according to the standards of a number of my coworkers.

> *Culture dictates the environment with an emphasis on how you are perceived by others; generally, those in leadership positions! There's a ranking order or chain of command, if you will, that seems to set the stage. One, I'm not an officer or a Salvationist. Two, my title does not say, "Important Personnel." Three, I do not fit the image that's considered acceptable enough not to be asked to do odd jobs outside of my job description. Four, now I hold the worst title—troublemaker—because I refuse to allow myself to be taken for granted, and I have resulted to writing about it.*

Yet, through all my thinking and pondering, You spoke to me: "It's much more than that! They do not want to be reminded of how they have treated you or conducted themselves. No one denied anything that was written. They have a problem with the person who wrote it and refuse to see the truth. They have put themselves above you as well as others like you and feel justified in their actions. They do not want to hear about how wrong they have been by you. Remember, you are writing for Me! Each time they look at you, they have to deal with themselves. It's not about man; it's about Me!"

Oh, dear God, they have failed to realize there are levels of spirituality too! Your title is above all titles. You are the most high and I want nothing more than to please You; not man. Your command is my desire. I AM a living sacrifice striving for the highest good, not the most good.

Your faithful servant,
Ann G. Mack

BAPTISM
IT'S MORE THAN JUST GOING THROUGH THE MOTIONS!

He that believeth and is baptized shall be saved;
but he that believeth not shall be damned

~ Mark 16:16

January 8, 2008

Dear God,

As you know, I rededicated my life to You on November 20, 2007, through spiritual (Christian) experience. In speaking with my supervisor, a longtime Salvationist from birth, on Wednesday, January 2, 2008, I hope my response to his question was pleasing to You. In fact, I felt inspired knowing he wanted to attempt to understand my reasoning for what I would like to refer to as a renewed spirit as opposed to him judging me blindly.

As he began to tell me The Salvation Army's belief that salvation and commitment to God can be obtained without baptism, I felt the need to tell him I have a strong belief that there is a difference between being spiritual and religious, just as there is a difference with being hot or cold. Fortunately, there is no in-between, and the scripture speaks about being lukewarm. We should always be striving to obtain the highest good and not just "most good"! Doing the most good, to me, sounds mediocre. It tells me we are not giving our all. Going through the motions is more about being religious. Being religious, in my mind, means only existing with no sense of integrity or sincerity and just going through the motions with no commitment or real thought-provoking effort to initiate change. I view spiritualism as a form of religion but perhaps one or two steps above religion. Nonetheless, being spiritual means attempting to take God's word seriously and making a conscious effort to follow through with His every command, including baptism. You cannot serve two masters.

God, needless to say, my thoughts on the subject made him a little defensive. However, I do not desire to honor You by just existing and going through the motions. I desire to honor You by doing and showing You that I AM committed to more than just showing up for church on Sunday. So for me, being baptized this second time was my way of saying, "I AM truly ready to follow Your ways. I AM a living sacrifice in every sense of the word, and I desire to be used by You for the glorification of the Kingdom.

Thank You for having faith in me and never giving up on me.

PEACE

*Peace I leave with you, My peace I give unto you:
not as the world giveth, give I unto you.
Let not your heart be troubled, neither let it be afraid.*

~ John 14:27

June 11, 2008

Dear God,

How are you today? Fine I hope, and I am pleased with the development of Your children who are forging ahead to stay in Your will and keep Your commandments.

For quite some time—actually for as long as I can remember—I have had nothing on my mind but to know my purpose in the world. For some reason, I assumed I was not worthy of Your love, but then You spoke to me. Since that day, I have never been the same. Now I wake up each day in anticipation of hearing Your voice and seeing the presence of You. I want more of Your power, Your presence and Your influence.

Please continue to shower me with Your love and affection. Hold me tight and don't let go! I pray for Your peace; I call on it to sustain me and heal me. You said, "Peace you give me and peace you leave with me." Therefore, it is Your peace that I want; the peace in knowing that You are forever with me; the peace in knowing that I was created to be the person that I AM today; the peace in knowing that I AM growing spiritually and maturing for the Kingdom, leaning on You and yearning for You to guide me. Teach me Your ways.

How awesome You are and how awesome it is to know that I was chosen by You. You have never given up on me in spite of my hesitation and blindness to Your will. You kept me close and always reached for me as I drifted, but I never drifted too far away.

Thank You!

A PRAYER REQUEST

August 6, 2008

Dear God,

Please heighten my senses that my spiritual ears are tuned to hearing Your every command. I desire to commune with You and You with me. My objective is to move forward and never backwards, for I long to grow spiritually and exercise maturity in every aspect of my life! I wish to let go of the past by holding no grudges and releasing all negativity that may hinder my walk with You. Oh God, I ask that all obstacles or boundaries be removed or lifted. I do not want them to interfere with my relationship with You. If anything, I want to connect to You to be stronger than any bond on earth. I want to forgive those who have ever hurt me or wronged me that I may be free from things that bind me or limit me from reaching my destiny.

    I have waited so long to know You and to have You speak to me. I will forever remember the day You first revealed yourself to me. I apologize for not believing in You and doubting Your existence. I thank You for not giving up on me. I thank You for loving me enough to continue to reach out to me. Your persistence saved me.

With all my love,
Ann

FROM REVELATION TO REALIZATION

September 4, 2008

Good Morning God,

How are You today? I AM feeling great and on top of the world. After all, it was You who said I was the head and not the tail. I AM above and not below. I AM more than a conqueror. Father God, I thank You for not giving up on me and for being so patient with me. As I sit writing to You this morning, I must admit, I did not believe I would ever get to this point in my life. And I owe it all to You! You have increased my faith, renewed my mind and filled me with the Holy Spirit that keeps me connected to You. It is an awesome thing to finally know You for myself. As I look back over my life, I did not have this same awareness or deep-rooted connection to You upon my first baptism on June 30, 1995. Perhaps that is why it was so necessary for me to rededicate my life to You on November 20, 2007. I have a better understanding of Your love for me.

I thank You for revealing Yourself to me like never before. I AM sure, without a doubt, that there is more You will reveal to me over time. The supernatural presence of You and Your holy power is real. Yesterday, I attempted to explain to someone what it is to have a *revelation* that gives true meaning or confirmation to a *realization*. Wow! If only I had my tape recorder. The item that You keep prompting me to have with me at all times to be able to capture and play back over and over again my encounters with You. The incident that still blows me away even to this day was the erupting of the Holy Spirit within me during a Salvation Army World Service Office (SAWSO) corps meeting that was held on the same day a National Commissioners' Conference was also being held. To think that they actually thought I was experiencing a nervous breakdown still boggles my mind. I had such great respect and appreciation for what I thought and felt The Salvation Army represented. And I was extremely overjoyed to be associated with them as an employee to the point of thinking or believing they would have a measurable amount of influence on my spiritual growth! But instead of them helping me understand what I had experienced to embrace it, I was ridiculed by many and called a religious fanatic by another person, who happened to be my immediate supervisor; in fact, he was a long-standing acquainted Salvationist. That left me more confused than ever about their idea of Christianity as well as their leadership and relationship to God. What doctrine of religion were they following if they were not relying on Your word of truth or guidance from the Holy Spirit?

Nonetheless, within minutes of attempting to explain revelation versus realization, I was asked a question by someone else about forgiveness. In particular, "Do You forgive us when we do something wrong?" If it were not for Pastor Sharonda D. Stewart, Senior Pastor of Visionary Christian Church through S & S Ministries, taking the time to provide a one-on-one Bible study and extending an open-door policy in allowing me to attend her prophetic Saturday and Sunday worship sessions this past weekend, I would not have been able to address this question. I was in need of more specialized understanding in this area myself. Not wanting to be hypocritical, for years, I distanced myself from You because I knew You were not pleased with my choices in life. Not knowing if I ever really wanted to get married or have any children, I believed this type of thinking was considered a sin because it went against Your principles that were outlined in the Bible. (Be fruitful and multiply.) However, I never really took the time to read the Bible or study it extensively for myself for a clear understanding of Your word. I always took the word of those I sort out to preach the gospel in delivering Your word to me on Sundays to convict me.

As You are aware, my mother made sure my sister and I were introduced to the church before we could walk or talk. As I listened to the sermons, I took to heart every word that was being presented. As I became older and adapted to my flesh that was influenced by the world, I was introduced to lust, want, need and lack. These elements fueled my emotions and dictated my choices. Choices I did not feel or think were overly wrong in accordance to choices made by others. I didn't steal, cheat or lie, nor did I take pleasure in mistreating or deceiving others in any way. The choices I made, I felt to some extent, did not harm anyone but me. However, knowing what I do now, I not only hurt me, I hurt You, yet You loved me unconditionally. You continued to love me as You made several attempts to reach me in extending to me a life raft.

Having had many thoughts about forgiveness, it took me a while to understand how differently You think from man. Fortunately for us, Your ways are not like our ways. Therefore, I desire to denounce all the ways of man to think more like You. Feeling guilty about my less than Christ-like choices in life, I would not allow myself to get close to You for fear of You not loving me or forgiving me for not being perfect. In June of 1995, I had an extensive conversation with an Elder of the Holy Christian Missionary Baptist Church for All People who explained, I did not have to be perfect to be baptized. It was this misconception that kept me from taking the first step, although I knew within my heart that You were calling me. We are born sinners into a sin-infested world. We are not perfect, but we are given the opportunity to be ye therefore perfect, even as You, our Father which is in heaven is perfect (see Matthew 5:48). But, You accept us as we are and work within us, through us and around us to perfect us!

Forgetting is not as easy as forgiveness. However, it is possible to forgive without forgetting. I find that many people tend to believe that discussing a situation or issue means I AM holding on to anger that prevents me from forgiving. On the other hand, I have come to learn through You that many people refuse to accept responsibility for their actions and would, therefore, have me to believe that their issues or problems have more to do with me than it has to do with them not willing to change. As Christians, we should be able to talk openly and directly in truth and in love about the things that need to be confronted.

Father, thank You for giving me the ability to see beyond my faults and being willing to admit when I'm wrong in asking You for Your forgiveness as I release my guilt and seek to change as well as improve my way of thinking. Because my past, present and future experiences help to shape who I AM, You have taught me that forgetting is not necessary; however, for growth, forgiveness is a part of a process. In knowing who I AM, there is no need for me to hold grudges. For vengeance is YOURS!

> *He suffered no man to do them wrong:*
> *yea, he reproved kings for their sakes;*
> *Saying, Touch not mine anointed, and*
> *do my prophets no harm.*
>
> ~ Psalm 105:15

◆

> *And David said to Abisha,*
> *Destroy him not: for who can stretch forth*
> *his hand against the Lord's anointed,*
> *and be guiltless?*
>
> ~ 1 Samuel 26:9

I AM FOREVER GRATEFUL!

October 27, 2008

Dear God,

Although overwhelmed and blessed by my new challenges, I know without a doubt that You are with me. I AM so grateful for Your attentiveness to my every need. I cannot help but remember a time not that long ago when I doubted Your existence as well as Your love for me. In having a better understanding of Your word and seeing it in action, my spirit and my mind have been renewed. I walk in the confidence of knowing who I AM and being connected to You, which brings me so much joy as well as inner peace. A peace I never knew could be so intoxicating or even possible.

Verily, verily, I say unto you, that ye shall
weep and lament, but the world shall rejoice:
and ye shall be sorrowful,
but your sorrow shall be turned into joy.

~ John 16:23

Oh God, I no longer look at people the same. I do not allow man to dictate my happiness or my success. I look to You! In elevating me from one level to the next, You have delivered me from the issues of my heart and rescued me from an environment full of doctrines and actions of pseudo Christians playing church. Needing me to be Your eyes, ears and voice, You purposely subjected me to a situation You knew would vex my spirit the most. You used The Salvation Army to bring me closer to You. You knew their doctrines and false display of Christian love would bring me to the place You needed me to be to do what You needed to be done for the uplifting of Your Kingdom. I, unfortunately, did not think it was possible to experience racism to the extent or degree to which it is practiced there, especially not in a place I believed to be recognized globally as a church of God. It is obvious they have good intentions with the desire of helping others, but for all of the wrong reasons. Those are what I consider to be deadly motives. Unfortunately, I, as well as others who are in denial or are more afraid of man than they are of You, have been a witness to those ungodly and deadly motives that are driven more by greed than by righteousness.

Howbeit when He, the Spirit of truth, is come,
He will guide you into all truth for He shall not speak of himself;
but whatsoever He shall hear, that shall He speak:
and He will shew you things to come.

~ John 16:13

Discerning (or Distinguishing) of Spirits

Such hypocrisy taught me how easy it is for people to pretend to be Christians who are more influenced by the enemy of God than by Christ. Christians, even ordained ministers, wear masks! As we attempt to put a lot of emphasis on our gain here on earth, I must not forget and always keep in the forefront of my mind the gain in Heaven to be far greater. That which I cannot see is much more important than that of which I can see because that which I can see is more of an illusion than that which I cannot see. And yet, we as people allow that which we can see to consume us the most.

> *Also I set watchmen over you, saying,*
> *HEARKEN to the sound of the trumpet.*
> *But they said, we will not HEARKEN.*
>
> ~ Jeremiah 6:17

Through The Salvation Army's misconceived reputation, I assumed they would love me as a child of God and treat me accordingly. However, they afflicted on me the same pain and measure of persecution Jesus received. After it was all said and done, I realized they were, unfortunately, no different from those in the world. The pain from that ordeal could have proven to be more devastating than all of what I had encountered or experienced up to that point in my life, mainly because my expectation of a religious organization and those who proclaimed to be Christians was of a much higher level (righteous and holy) with no comparison to those in the world. However, I quickly learned that their behavior was, on the contrary, one in the same. I believed working for a nationally recognized church, the body of Christ, would be so rewarding and fulfilling that it would override all the pre-recorded, stamped images of pain and suffering through un-Christ-like behavioral actions brought against me in the past in the form of racism. And yet, this necessary process as allowed by You made me aware of the Holy Spirit that dwells within. You were equipping me to function in the gifts and ministries of the Holy Spirit as they were activated, for You did not want me to be ignorant concerning the existence or power of spiritual gifts (1Corinthians 12:1)!

> *Now there are diversities of operations, but it is the same Spirit. And there are differences of administrations, but the same Lord. And there are diversities of operations, but it is the same God which worketh all in all. But the manifestation of the Spirit is given to every man to profit withal.*
>
> ~ 1 Corinthians 12:4-7

You not wanting me to rely on what I was seeing allowed me to see what You knew to be true through the power of the supernatural. As I fixed my eyes on the physical image before me with my natural eyes, You let me see the fruit of the spirit of the uniformed ordained minister and Salvation Army officer, Lt. Colonel Daniel Starrett, through my spiritual eyes. In shock and amazement, I saw a fully clothed, grand wizard of the KKK, and needless to say, I cried within myself. However, in a matter of seconds, my crying quickly turned to laughter because I knew at that point, You wanted me to be aware of my surroundings and to know the spirits for who they were—inside and out. Not only that, You were elevating me to another spiritual level, and a change was taking place. I was being transformed through the renewing of my mind and spirit as well as being prepared for spiritual warfare. To be under the guidance and protection of the Holy Spirit to know things and see things out of the natural—but supernaturally—was like nothing I could have ever imagined.

> *Many pastors have destroyed my vineyard,*
> *they have trodden my portion under foot,*
> *they have made my pleasant portion a desolate wilderness.*
> *They have made it desolate, and being desolate*
> *it mourneth unto me; the whole land is made*
> *desolate, because no man layeth it to heart.*
>
> ~ Jeremiah 12:10-11

Forever Grateful Indeed

Thinking back to a conversation I once had with my former supervisor, Bram Bailey, I shared my excitement of knowing things no one thought I knew or I could ever know. I AM truly amazed at how easy it is for two or more people to be present at the same time, both seeing what the other sees and hearing what the other hears. However, because one is not impacted the same, he is more apt to and determined to tell you what you don't see, hear or feel. Even worse, he will attempt to tell you it's all in your head, you made it up or you are exaggerating and blowing things out of proportion. And that person, unfortunately, will expect—if not demand—you to believe as well as accept their evaluation of you that has nothing to do with the real picture. As explained, given the color of his skin or ethnicity as a Caucasian, he may never know what it's like to be discriminated against or to even know the pain of having your growth limited due to the narrow-minded view of those in a position of power who wish to hold you back by placing you in a box; because in their mind, they rank superior, and you are not worthy to receive the same opportunities afforded to them, such as annual salary increases, that others who are even less deserving and don't work as hard are granted. Regardless of the differences in our ethical and educational background as deemed by man, what about fairness and equality? What about righteousness? Nonetheless, my reward is in Heaven and God will supply all my needs. *For evildoers shall be cut off: but those that wait upon the Lord, they shall inherit the earth!*

> *I hearkened and heard, but they spake not aright:*
> *no man repented him of his wickedness, saying,*
> *What have I done? Every one turned to his course,*
> *as the horse rusheth into the battle.*
>
> ~ Jeremiah 8:6

So today and always, I AM grateful to You for many things. I have been delivered to an understanding I did not know or think was possible. *I can do all things through Christ who strengthens me.* I AM called to do great things, and my desire above all is to seek You first. I long not only to have You near and dear to me; I long to be near and dear to You! I thirst for Your presence and desire to have You speak to me, through me, in me, on me and around me. I desire to have You flow through me, in me, on me and around me. Thank You for unmasking those I needed to see beyond what they wanted me to see. I AM grateful to You for Your wisdom and knowledge. I pray for those who have found themselves to be in the same situation—present, past and future—that they overcome the strongholds and limitations placed on them by unequally yoked Christians or pretentious people allowing themselves to be ruled by darkness. Shield the righteous from the unrighteous and guard their heart that it may not be hardened or damaged by the injustices facing them. Dear God, please lend them Your strength as You fortify their heart and their mind to believe in You with full faith.

> **Side Note Added February 28, 2017:** Fear is universal and I strongly believe we all struggle with fear on different levels or to different degrees! Our greatest fear is generated by our lack of knowledge, which is nothing other than the fear of the unknown. Our experiences in relation to cultural differences, backgrounds and environmental influences contribute to our way of thinking, which ignite and control our fears. Simply put, we just have to be open minded to hearing and seeing supernaturally for a GREATER understanding of characteristics demonstrated by the actions of others, which helps to DISCERN the individual spirits within our surroundings. If we allow the Holy Spirit to penetrate our thoughts to conquer our fears, He will enlighten us to know TRUTH and aid us in conducting ourselves accordingly.

ENTERTAINING THE WRONG THINKING

*My brethren, count it all joy
when ye fall into divers temptations.*

~ James 1:2

January 18, 2009

Dear Father God,

You are so awesome to me! Once, not long ago, I assumed You heard me not. I assumed You listened not to what I had to say. Painfully, I thought You were ignoring my prayers. For years, I was void of answers and seeking truth that only You could provide to me. Today, You never cease to amaze me. You have proven every thought that I have ever had concerning Your truth and have passionately revealed it to me. Delivering me from myself, You also delivered me from people who threatened my life on behalf of the enemy: Your adversary, who wanted to destroy me and hold me forever captive. Not only did You save me from the world, You deemed me ambassador to spread the Gospel and renewed my way of thinking! For my mindset was all wrong. As more questions develop, I have no doubt You will answer those too!

Preparing for church this morning, I listened to T. D. Jakes's sermon that was aired on TV entitled, "Yet!" Connecting to what was being said, I jumped up and leaped across the room as I shouted, HOW TRUE! At that point, I realized that for years, I allowed the circumstances and situations of my past to pollute my faith (trust and confidence in God) in the present. I questioned my faith and doubted You on the basis of my circumstances as they developed. There was no evidence of You as others came against me for no apparent reason other than to limit my growth, destroy my life and to control the very essence of me. I did not look at my circumstances and count it all as joy. I did not know being rejected was a blessing and not a curse. I did not know You were about to do great things through my persecution. Not seeing beyond my circumstances, I endured much pain.

Realizing it was getting later and later, I departed from the house noting I was going to miss at least thirty to forty minutes of the service. Racing to church, I found myself succumbing to the spirit of wrong thinking as it threatened to convince me how worthless it would be to attend church so late. Ignoring the voice that was speaking in my ear, I thought how badly I needed to get to Victory Christian Ministries International to be fed by the Brazeltons (Tony and Cynthia). However, thinking how far You brought me to get where I AM today, I knew I needed to press on. All I needed to do was to get there (to church) and everything else would just fall into place. For I knew within my heart that this was where You needed me to be! I no longer doubted You were moving me from one church to another. Entering the sanctuary, I heard them singing: "God, in Your arms, You are my shelter from the storm. When all my friends were gone, You were right there all along. I have never known a love like this before. I just want to say that I love You more than anything. I love You, Jesus. I worship and adore You. Just want to tell You that I love You more than anything." At that point, it was over! I was where I belonged.

But God, You did not stop there! Knowing the issues of my heart, it was as if You had centered today's message around me, which was presented through Pastor Cynthia Brazelton's sermon entitled, "Accessing Heaven's Resources by Faith." You are just awesome indeed! When once I thought I did not matter to You, now, it seems You are quick to answer each and every question or thought that weighs heavily on my mind. Amazingly, You even hear and know the issues of my heart that I AM not aware of until I receive a message or word from You. Messages You get through to me through others, through the reading of Your word or even other books that reference the works of Kingdom, through song and through the Holy Spirit that dwells within me. In fact, there is no limit to what You can do in communicating with me once my prayers get through to You, from earth to the Heavens where You are. For example, when you led me to an answer of understanding, You did not forsake me. You directed me to a book entitled *Spiritual Warfare* by Derek Prince. This book helped me to understand the war of two opposing Kingdoms in great detail. Prayers may not always be heard by You because there's a possibility of them being intercepted by the enemy (Lucifer and his army) before they get to You. This is what prolongs my answer. It's not because You don't love me. It's not because You don't value me or think that I AM not important enough. It's not even because You are ignoring me. I entertained the wrong thinking! That's why today was so important to me—for I have questioned my faith many times.

Knowing this, that the trying of you faith worketh patience. But let patience have her perfect work, that he may be per and entire, wanting nothing. If any of you lack wisdom, let him ask of God, that giveth to all men liberally, and upbraideth not; and it shall be given him.

~ James 1:2

Oh God! Only You could use two or more people in the course of a day to deliver the same message but in a different context. Pastor Brazelton was so on point that the Holy Ghost not only showed up, it showed out and showed off. It is impossible for me to fail. You hath already given me (us) victory over the enemy. I have all I'll ever need to walk in faith. I just have to believe and keep believing and never render myself to the voice of the enemy in believing I AM defeated. *For all the promises of God in Him are yea and in Him A-men, unto the glory of God by us* (2 Corinthians 1:20). If I use my faith, I can access what has already been given to me! God, when my faith is tested, please let me waiver not! I need to be confident knowing that You have performed a good work in me, therefore, You will do this until the return of Jesus Christ (Philippians 1:6). The communication of my faith may become effectual by acknowledging every good thing that is in me that is in Jesus Christ (Philemon 1:6). I now know the importance of developing my relationship with You to increase my faith! THANK YOU for having faith in me!

JUDGING OR JUST REFUSING TO ACCEPT INIQUITY

> *In those days there was no King in Israel:*
> *every man did that which was right in his own eyes.*
> **~ Judges 21:25**

March 1, 2009

Dear God,

Having a relationship with You is about spending time with You and getting to know You as well as understanding Your likes and dislikes. It is about communicating with You and having an exchange of dialogue. It is about listening to Your every word and wanting nothing more than to please You. It is about a divine, deep-rooted connection and getting deeper into You. So deep, in fact, that what grieves You grieves me and vice versa. I did not know that such a relationship with You was ever possible. And today, I find myself not wanting to go a moment without You in my life as I seek to carry out every assignment You entrust to me.

Until recently, I did not hear many sermons or discussions concerning the importance of developing a relationship with You. People hold services and go through the motions in the pretense of being Christians, but they fail to take to heart what it is that You demand of us. Most often, the only time they seem to reverence You is when they gather together in church, and the minute they walk out of those doors, all is forgotten. And some only attend church on Sundays just to be able to say they were present, but only in body and not in spirit. They, unfortunately, take on the identity dictated by their flesh and conduct themselves in a manner that has nothing to do with You, but they are so quick to reference themselves as being Christians. Even worse, ministers who should be spreading the gospel have not only lost their nerve, they have lost their soul by not following You. They fail to take heed to Your example!

Many people have become so accustomed to wanting what they want for themselves through selfish gain that they find it so easy to live their lives according to double standards. How can individuals proclaim to be Christians and compromise their integrity to accept iniquity by going along with what they know to be wrong? And why should I be forced to watch the wicked prosper and dare not say a word? When and if I should confront the situation, I AM not only accused of being angry as if I have no right to take a stance for Your truth, but I AM accused of judging those who take advantage of others. Sitting idly by as others commit a dishonor to You while claiming to love You saddens me deeply. Not opening my mouth to reiterate what You told me in an attempt to please others only damages my relationship with You. Do I seek to please men or please You?

Upon receiving my first request from You, I allowed fear to hinder my assignment. The more You revealed Yourself to me, the greater my confidence in fulfilling Your purpose for my life. However, the pain of what I was witnessing as well as experiencing was too great for me to bear. So I asked You to deliver me from that Godforsaken place against Your will, for I had not fully completed my assignment! But Your love for me prevailed, and Your permissive will grant me my departure. Although You had distanced me physically, You had not released me from my assignment. Because I have every right to decide what untruths I AM determined not to invade my mind that goes against Your teaching, I AM not suppose to accept any lie that threatens my relationship with You.

You have taught me to see beyond the physical and accept that which others refuse to see through darkness. You have taught me not to accept anything less than a life You feel I deserve; a life You promised me in spite of what others tell me; a life full of hope as I walk into my destiny with faith, believing and trusting You every step of the way! Judging, they say! No, listening to You with all my heart and refusing to accept the iniquity as I make no excuses along the way in taking a stance against what I know to be wrong, for not only do I have the audacity of hope, but I have the audacity of faith.

And finally, after so many years of others attempting to define who I should be based on what I allowed in my life, I now know and understand that they can do no more to me than I allow. Because of Your love for me, You have wakened me from a sleep that threatened to conform me through a life of control. A control that prohibited me from questioning the exhibited actions and characteristics blatantly being displayed from within a church that opposes Your will. Others may try to and want to condemn me in an attempt to discredit my motives, but it is You, God, the Father, my Father through Jesus Christ, who has redeemed me in spite of how others wish to view me. I AM growing stronger and dying to self each and every day—transforming, not conforming! *Jesus answered him, "Truly, truly, I say to you, unless one is born again he cannot see the kingdom of God." Nicodemus said to him, "How can a man be born when he is old? Can he enter a second time into his mother's womb and be born?" Jesus answered, "Truly, truly, I say to you, unless one is born of water and the Spirit, he cannot enter the kingdom of God. That which is born of the flesh is flesh and that which is born of the Spirit is spirit. Do not marvel that I said to you, 'You must be born again.'"* (John 3:3-7 ESV).

God, I cannot thank You enough for liberating me, freeing my soul, helping me to change through the renewing of my mind and the way I think and aiding me in walking boldly with confidence for the love of my Father who has restored me in many ways!

> *Then the Lord put forth his hand and touched my mouth. And the Lord said unto me, Behold, I have put my words in they mouth.*
>
> ~ Jeremiah 1:9

God, I love You!

WHY SHOULD I GO ALONG TO GET ALONG?

But know that the LORD hath set apart him that is godly for himself: the LORD will hear when I call unto him.

~ Psalm 4:3 KJV

February 26, 2012

Dear God,

When I made the decision to rededicate my life to You approximately six to seven years ago, I made a vow and covenant promise to *obey and stand on your every word*. I was so disappointed and turned off by the number of people who proclaimed to be Christians and walked with the pretense of being followers of Christ in the presence of others. Not only did they lack the knowledge of the depth of the character of Your Son, they had the absence of His love in their hearts. Why else would it be so easy for them to deny His power and be so content with just going through the motions while playing church?

> *Wherefore lay apart all filthiness and superfluity of naughtiness, and receive with meekness the engrafted word, which is able to save your souls.*
>
> ~ James 1:21 KJV

As you are aware, whenever something troubles my heart, I not only ponder on it for a while, but I make an attempt to bring it to You in prayer. Well, last week was a grizzly bear of a week to say the least. And the topper was a rather disturbing and challenging conversation with a Christian who presumptuously stated that I made things difficult for myself by not agreeing or being willing to go along to get along. Though this is a summary of that conversation, I know You sit up high and look down low in seeing, knowing and hearing all. However, the fact that such a thing was said to me demonstrates not only this person's value of me, but that she doesn't know me at all. I place integrity and righteousness in the highest category above the position, title or grade of any person. I refuse to let myself be a hypocrite for anyone unless it is for You. And even You frown on such a thing. So NO! It is not possible for me to go along to get along. I cannot and will not because that is not who You have created me to be! And I AM sick and tired of being in the company of those who would rather sell their soul to the highest bidder if it means fitting in and getting along with those they thought could push them along if only they would turn a blind eye to the truth around them.

> *For what [is] the hope of the hypocrite, though he hath gained, when God taketh away his soul?*
>
> ~ Job 27:8 KJV

Upon attempting to know You and learn of You, I thought it would be simpler and easier to just watch those who spoke of You and visited Your house on Sundays to teach me what it meant to be a Christian. But watching them and attempting to mimic them only confused me more. As I started reading Your word for myself and seeking understanding in comprehending what I read, I realized many of those I was watching were not doers and hearers of Your word. They heard only what they wanted to hear and replaced Your meaning with their own. Not wanting to be like them, I wanted to know Your truth for myself. I wanted to be able to follow Your *every word* with such conviction and passion. I knew it was not going to be easy, so I called on You for assistance. From that time forward, You have been teaching me Yourself, and I pray for Your continued tutelage. Others, with their ulterior motives, will attempt to lead me astray without hesitation or remorse in their hearts! *He answered and said unto them, "Well hath Esaias prophesied of you hypocrites, as it is written, This people honoureth me with [their] lips, but their heart is far from me"* (Mark 7:6 KJV).

> *Therefore, he knows their deeds, he overthrows them in the night and they are crushed. He strikes them for their wickedness, in a place where people can see, because they have turned away from following him and have not understood any of his ways, so that they caused the cry of the poor to come before him, so that he hears the cry of the needy.*
>
> ~ Job 34:25-27 NET

God, I know without a doubt and with everything that I AM, You are not like any man on this earth. You would not lie, deceive me or withhold any good thing from me. It is not my desire nor my intent, today or tomorrow, to join forces with those who have lost their way! Going along to get along would mean I have turned my back on You in accepting the ways of the world system in seeking what they define as success and promotion to excel (get ahead). If they were just and fair at all, they would be willing to do the right thing for everyone because it is the right thing to do. They have never had any intentions of doing what is right but only what will deceive me into thinking they have my best interest at heart. The only person I can count on in this world or the next, if there is a next, is You and only You. Though I am truly grateful to have a job, I AM more grateful to You for who You are in ordering my steps and blessing me to be in the position to have a job, with the fortitude and presence of mind to always be willing to do the right thing in spite of friend or foe. For You are my friend, and You will never steer me wrong!

> *But if God is quiet, who can condemn him? If he hides his face, then who can see him? Yet he is over the individual and the nation alike, so that the godless man should not rule, and not lay snares for the people. "Has anyone said to God, 'I have endured chastisement, but I will not act wrongly any more. Teach me what I cannot see. If I have done evil, I will do so no more."*
>
> ~ Job 34: 29-32 NET

Closing Prayer

Lord, I pray to You in the name of Jesus Christ, Your Son, my Lord and Master and Savior. I thank You for seeing me for who I AM. And still, in spite of me, You chose me out of a bag of marbles in seeing my potential and worth. Your confidence in my ability makes me more determined than ever to please You in every way. I have come a very long way in acknowledging You and developing a relationship with You that I did not know was possible. I cannot let anyone come in between me and You. I cannot let them get in my head by questioning Your God-given assignment or purpose for my life. It is my desire to be less like them and more like You! I want to know your ways and think like You in seeing this world and the people in it as You see it.

Dear Lord, it is important for me to see the power of Your hand (big or small) moving in every aspect of my life. Please move those mountains out of my way that seek to hinder my growth in attempting to make me stumble and fall. Please cut the chains that attempt to bind me and reverse any and every curse sent to harm me; return to the sender that which he has meant for me twofold. Justice and righteousness is long overdue! I need the favor of Your love for me. So please cut down each and every stronghold at the root never to regenerate or thrive again. I decree and declare that every strong man standing in the way of my destiny be dealt with by You, for You said, Vengeance is yours. You said no weapon formed against me shall prosper, and every tongue that rises against me shall be condemned.

God, I AM trusting You, believing You and counting on Your every word. Let them see You like never before and let every spiritual wickedness in high as well as low places be revealed and rendered powerless and dethroned.

For we wrestle not against flesh and blood, but against principalities, against powers, against the rulers of the darkness of this world, against spiritual wickedness in high [places].

~ Ephesians 12:6 KJV

Amen

BROKEN, MENDED, AND SECOND WINDED

*A cheerful heart is good medicine,
but a crushed spirit dries up the bones.*
~ **Proverbs 17:22 NIV**

November 11, 2013

Dear Lord,

As I look back over my life, I was drawn to darkness and living in sin. Seduced by a world full of the walking wounded like me, I asked no questions and moved about like a puppet on a string, following instead of leading while hoping to be accepted by a world that only rejected me time and time again. Void of life with a dying soul, I struggled continuously to find my way. Identifying with no one and everyone, I quickly got lost in a sea of confusion, unaware of my actions and giving no thought to the consequences! Gullible to the lies and seeking to fit in with no real knowledge of the truth until the day I realized something was missing. And then, I could no longer go through the motions while never being truly happy of who I was becoming.

> *If you do well, will you not be accepted?*
> *And if you do not do well, sin crouches at your door;*
> *its desire is for you, but you must master it.*
>
> ~ Genesis 4:7 AMP

I was not living or growing but sinking deeper and deeper into myself with such pain, grief and despair! Tired of the rat race, I wanted much more than to be like the rest! Standing tall, I needed a balance. Seeking truth became my ultimate mission. Getting free was the number one goal at hand. Escaping my pain was the need for my survival, and forgiving those who had hurt me was a matter of life or death to dodge the dis-ease that was inevitable. In choosing life, I could not do it alone. Choosing happiness, I needed an anchor—a steady rock that would not crumble under pressure! I finally realized I needed You. I needed to believe You existed. More importantly, I needed to develop a relationship with You to get to know You for myself! So I let You in when so many others in my life had let me down.

> *The strong spirit of a man sustains him in bodily pain*
> *or trouble, but a weak and broken spirit*
> *who can raise up or bear?*
>
> ~ Proverbs 18:14 AMP

In spite of me and who I was, You loved me long before I loved You. You knew me better than I knew myself. You were always there just waiting for me to acknowledge You. All I had to do was reach for You. Lord, I AM forever grateful to You for Your persistance in life. In creating me with a purpose for a purpose, You wanted nothing but the best for me. You never gave up on me, even when I knew You not and turned my back on You while seeking to find my way through the darkness! You said You would never leave me nor forsake me (Hebrews 13:5). You were always near and never far way. You were patiently waiting for me to come to my senses in realizing my one and only true love.

Before I formed thee in the belly I knew thee;
and before thou camest forth out of the womb I sanctified
thee, and I ordained thee a prophet unto the nations.

~ Jeremiah 1:5

There I was being denied over and over again by the world, broken hearted and in need of repair! My spirit was damaged beyond recognition, and I was looking for love in all the wrong places. Looking for man to validate me only made me more vulnerable. But You, Lord, are like no other person on the face of the earth or within the entire universe for that matter! You believed in me when no one else did. You STILL believe in me! When people made attempts to tear me down, You lifted me and elevated me, and You keep on lifting me. When man speaks harsh of me, You redeem me and encourage me to go on. When I AM too bruised and tattered to go any further, You carry me and give me the strength to endure—no matter what! You said I was the head and not the tail; above and not beneath if only I would just take heed to your every command (Deuteronomy 28:12-14). Because You are a man of Your word who honors every promise ever made to me, You have confirmed Your *unconditional* love for me over and over again. Oh God, how I love thee! You sacrificed Your only Son for me. Then why should I not give my life to thee? Oh, how I want to tell the world about You, for my fire burns brightly!

> *By day the Lord went ahead of them*
> *in a column of smoke to lead them on their way.*
> *By night he went ahead of them in a column of fire*
> *to give them light so that they could travel by day or by night.*
>
> ~ Exodus 13:21

You have touched my life in such a mighty way that there are not enough words in all the universe that I could use to express, explain or to describe my gratitude, joy and yes, even the sorrow. Bittersweet is how I see Thee, but awesome indeed are You! Your *grace* and *mercy* have shown me the way! You allowed me to go through situations needed to fortify me! Situations I would have never been able to accomplish in succeeding without You. For once in my life, I AM no longer afraid to say "no" to those who try to control me, use me or abuse me. Thank You for being who You are and for allowing me to be who I AM in You! Thank You for choosing me. Thank You for being so relentless in Your pursuit of me. For I will continue to speak to the hills and all across the nations about Your goodness!

TESTIMONIES

THE INNER ME

*Stay alert and keep your eyes open because
the devil is roaming around like a hungry lion,
Desperate to find anyone he can destroy.
Stand firm in the faith and resist the devil, knowing
the believers everywhere are going
through the same things you are.*

~ 1 Peter 5:8 TCW

I feel so confused about myself
That I don't know what to do!

The evil side just won't let go,
And the righteous side is about to give up.

At battle, in war, they are tearing me apart.

My mind seems to wander from here to there.
Can you help me feel at peace with myself
Or let me deteriorate little by little until there is no more?

At times, I feel love, but then I feel hate.
Yes, for I AM fading.
Fading away, not into darkness,
But deeper into myself.

1977

ONCE WAS

*But the salvation of the righteous [is] of the LORD:
[he is] their strength in the time of trouble.*
~ Psalm 37:39

I was once that shy, introverted girl
Who always kept to herself.

Now, I feel at peace with myself
And the whole world as well.

I once had an inferiority complex
That just would not go away.

Thanks to that special someone,
I can now leave my troubles behind
And only think of what is ahead.

I no longer feel left out from the rest of the world,
For I AM who I AM
And who I AM is me.

1978

DISCERNING OF SPIRITS

*Beware of false prophets,
which come to you in sheep's clothing,
but inwardly they are ravening wolves.
Ye shall know them by their fruits.
Do men gather grapes of thorns, or figs of thistles?*

~ Matthew 7:15-16

January 2, 1996

Part I

Satan has many disguises! Once an angel and God's right hand, Lucifer was not satisfied with his position in Heaven. As a result of greed, envy and jealousy, he tried to overthrow God. Through deceit, Lucifer was able to convince some of the other angels to side with him, mostly because they were just as wicked.

*For such are false apostles,
deceitful workers, transforming themselves into the apostles of
Christ. And no marvel; for Satan himself is transformed into*

> *an angel of light. Therefore, it is no great thing if his ministers also be transformed as the ministers of righteousness; whose end shall be according to their works.*
>
> ~ 2 Corinthians 11:13-15

When God got wind of what was going on, He threw Lucifer (Satan), along with his followers, out of Heaven and sentenced them to a life in Hell. This made Lucifer very angry, and he vowed to take as many of God's children with him as he could before the end of latter days. Because Satan was an angel and the right hand of God, he knew what God knew before getting thrown out of Heaven. He was considered to be very intelligent and handsome.

Part II: A Personal Encounter

During an unfortunate time in my life, which I refer to as my wilderness period, I met a man named David Christian. He was very intelligent! He could recite the Bible from front to back or back to front and quote scriptures from beginning to end. Why not? Remember, Satan was an angel who knew the Bible too! The difference between Satan and God is Satan is not omnipresent; he can read your mind or know what is in your heart. However, he is evil, he works through deceit, and he does not have your best interest at heart. His major desire is to steal, kill and destroy.

> *Beloved, believe not every spirit, but try the spirits whether they are of God; because many false prophets*

are gone out into the world. Hereby know ye the Spirit of God: Every spirit that confesseth that

Jesus Christ is come in the flesh is of God: And every spirit that confesseth not that Jesus Christ is come in the flesh is not of God; and this is that spirit of antichrist, whereof ye have heard that it should come; and even now already is it in the world.

~ I John 4:1-3

In Rebecca Brown's book *He Came to Set the Captives Free*, she talks about Satanism and Elaine's marriage to Satan. Elaine served Satan for seventeen years before seeking God. Elaine talks about how handsome Satan looked on their honeymoon when he appeared before her surrounded by light. Toward the end of that night, he changed into a hideous, foul-smelling monster, revealing his true identity and leaving her battered and bruised.

David told me he was a doctor who worked at Howard University Hospital. He was always in church, played the organ and sang with the choir. He was very encouraging and convincing. When I was down, he knew exactly what to say to lift my spirits. His answer to everything was, "Live by faith." One night, I was having very bad pains on my left side. He prayed over me and said he had the gift to heal. While gently laying his hands on my back, he then told me, "Since you are not working a permanent position and have no health insurance, I will work out something with the hospital and add you to my policy." He said he did not think it would be a problem since we were going to be married soon, but he needed to know my social security number. Naïve but not that naïve, I refused to give him my social security number. In fact, had I not been so depressed at the time of our chance encounter or in my right mind, I would like to believe that perhaps I would have made a better judgment call.

> *Lay hands suddenly on no man,*
> *neither be partaker of other men's sins: keep thyself pure."*
> *(In other words, be careful who you let lay on hands.)*
>
> ~ I Timothy 5:22

God kept trying to warn me. He gave me all kinds of different signs. I would listen, but I failed to follow through and act. I was disobedient and very stubborn! Because of my negativity about men as a result of my previous relationships, I thought, just maybe, I was jumping to conclusions. I wanted to give him the benefit of the doubt. In addition to that, my mental state at the time was very cynical and pessimistic. Feeling numb about life, I was somewhat bitter and viewed life as not being fair at all. Today, my mental state is quite the opposite. I believe it is not life that is not fair, but the people within the world who were given life in addition to being given the ability to give life or destroy life who are not fair. They, on the other hand, do not always make the right choices to live holy and righteously. And there are those of us who tend to get caught in their web of deceit.

Part III: Endless Signs

David was very good at living a lie and telling lies. People get so good at telling lies that they lose track of what's real and what isn't. If you are not careful, you'll find yourself playing out the lie in an attempt to not only make the lie believable to others but to yourself as well. What measures are you willing to take to make your lie believable? David would go to work every morning—or so I thought—wearing a lab coat and stethoscope around his neck. Wearing a costume is like wearing a mask to disguise the real you! Some evenings, he would come to my apartment with endless stories of procedures he had performed in the operating room. He even cried one evening—real tears—because he was unable to save a little girl who was in a severe car accident. This story, I know now, was made up. He said she died on the operating table while under his care. He literally cried like a baby! I remember one other evening, he was upset because he had to break and reset the legs of a baby who was having difficulty learning to walk as a result of a deformity. He talked about how angry he was at the parents for allowing the paralysis for going so long without seeking treatment.

One afternoon, during a severe snowstorm, I called the hospital to make sure he had arrived safely. Of course, I was told there was no one on the hospital staff by the name of David Christian. When I confronted him, he got very angry and asked if I remembered the name of the person I had spoken to. Needless to say, he was extremely angry at me for failing to get the name of the operator who had incompetently handled my call. He actually stated he was going to make an investigative inquiry to have the person fired for giving out false information and poorly performing her job. What difficulty it must be in trying to keep up with such a charade!

When David showed up at my apartment in a brand new car (the second new 1995 car in over two months), I made a note of the license plate number and called a friend to run a check on the tag number for me. That search yielded an outcome I was not ready to receive. The car was not registered to him; it was registered to a woman who lived in Accokeek, Maryland. As I collected information, I filed it away until it was an appropriate time to follow up on it. However, I confronted David about the car, being careful not to let it slip that I had a friend run a check on the tag. He said his cousin (a woman) was not able to make her car payments. In helping her salvage her credit rating, he indicated he had offered to assume her note in exchange for allowing her to assume his note since it was much lower than hers. Admirable! Too good to be true! Would you believe, the following month, he showed up with the first car again? (I'll explain; keep reading.)

Concerned for my well-being, a close friend insisted on running a full police report to determine whether or not David had any outstanding warrants or a criminal record. Only I needed to get from him what I had refused to provide to him earlier: his social security number. With so much doubt and uneasiness, I don't know why I just did not consider ending the relationship at that point. Upon inquiring about his driver's license (in hopes of obtaining the social security number), I indicated I needed a copy of his driver's license to add him to my insurance policy as a beneficiary. His reply: "I don't want to benefit from your death." (Admirable? Yes! But, unfortunately, I still had nothing concrete to go on.)

On the day David and I were scheduled to move into a newly constructed, single-family home on April 5, 1995, he conveniently became unreachable. Retrieving all the information I had gathered and stored for safekeeping, I decided to conduct my own investigation. Borrowing my father's car, I drove to Accokeek, Maryland. Attempting to sustain some sense of my sanity for peace of mind, it was important for me to uncover the truth. Taking a deep breath, I politely said to God, *You have been trying to warn me as well as prepare me for something, but I have been too stubborn to listen. I allowed my mind to be deceived. Please help me bounce back. Please do not allow this situation to devastate me to the point of a slow recovery.* I then told myself that no matter what, I would be strong. THAT WAS GOD!

After the completion of my investigation, I uncovered the following: David Christian married Renee Funn on April 5, 1995. However, he had not divorced his first wife, Diane Christian, of sixteen years. In fact, David was a bigamist who was married to many women in a successful con scheme in which his wife, Diane, was an accomplice. He was wanted on a felony charge in Virginia and made a living preying on single, naïve, unhappy, grief-stricken, fed-up-with-life, depressed women.

1. Due to an unlawful termination, I was awaiting the outcome of a pending lawsuit. Disturbed by the circumstances of the discharge, it was a painful experience that I could not readily discuss with anyone and I decided to pursue a case against my previous employer. This was the initial motive or incentive for David and Diane Christian's con involving me.

2. David successfully obtained my personal information to include my creditors. By accessing this information, he was able to not only contact my creditors, but he also attempted to set up other accounts in committing fraud. (I was amazed to find out just how insecure and unorganized our world systems are for others to obtain and access your credit. Ironically, it is easier for a person to illegally commit fraud against you than it is for you to get it cleared up.)

3. Although I was unemployed and in between temporary assignments and barely surviving to make a living, he was trying to convince me to quit the only source of income I had at the time (a 24-hour-a-week job) and commit myself financially to a new car and home, which I refused. He said God intended man to be the head of household; the woman was to be obedient and serve her husband. He even attempted to point out scriptures to substantiate his claim and insisted that this was the major downfall of so many marriages/relationships.

As stated before, he went to church faithfully. The rest will blow you away!

I pulled out the address and number of the woman who lived in Accokeek, Maryland, Renee Funn. After leaving a note and several messages, she finally returned my call after being prompted, warned and urged by her mother (who was the pastor of the church David attended) to return home as soon as possible from her honeymoon. Yes, she married David. I felt the need to share with her the information that I had uncovered.

I was able to convince her I was telling the truth by presenting her with the full name, number and address of the wife he was still married to for over sixteen years (who was living in the house in Ft. Washington, Maryland, that he not only took me to on several occasions and claimed was his, but it was the same house he supposedly was going to use as collateral for the new house). I also provided to her the name and number of the police officer I consulted and the name and number of the two car dealerships that had contacted me earlier. They called to say my information was listed on file as a point of contact or reference for the woman who was present with David Christian at the time of sale for the two vehicles. They had already repossessed the green 1995 Volkswagen Passat and were in the process of repossessing the white 1995 Volkswagen Jetta; both cars of which were in her name. I proceeded to instruct her to call each of the credit bureaus to request a fraud protection alert be put in her file for all her accounts and to ask them to take action to specifically investigate any open accounts in her name for the possibility of fraud.

During my personal investigation and visit to the home of David and Diane Christian, I noted mail addressed to Renee Funn on the dinette table. Oddly enough, the name on the envelope did not match Renee's physical address of record (in Accokeek, Maryland) as opposed to it having a Ft. Washington, Maryland address. Unfortunately, David was able to convince Renee to quit her job, sign for both cars unknowingly and co-sign for a new house. Renee, like many women, wanted to be loved and appreciated by a good man. However, for one reason or another, some of us look for love in all the wrong places and fail to do our homework before we commit our souls.

Renee and her parents were convinced that David was a very good, upstanding and hardworking gentleman. Someone, unlike her previous husband, who represented himself as being a God-fearing man; but David was anything but! Wanting so much to believe he was who he said he was, Renee put David on a pedestal to be the head of her world. So she had no reason to believe he would deceive her when he would simply point to what and where she should sign on the dotted line without reading the content for herself. What she didn't realize is he was using her identity and that of others to acquire material possessions. In addition to that, David was using her cell phone and ran the bill up to $1,000—the same phone he told me was given to him as a gift from his mother.

Conclusion: Test the Spirits and Rely On the Holy Spirit to Guide You

As things began to unfold, I learned David was never employed at the hospital as a doctor or in any capacity for that matter. Yes, I visited him at the hospital. Many hospitals do not have a secured system or staff to monitor the comings and goings of outside people. Well, Howard University Hospital didn't at the time. So David roamed the hallways of the Howard University Hospital sporting his lab coat and stethoscope while pretending to be a doctor. He would also view medical tapes of operating procedures in an effort to brush up on his technique in preparation for his scheduled, make-believe surgeries. In addition to visiting David at the hospital, I also visited him at his home in Ft. Washington, Maryland, where I greeted a woman who I was led to believe was his sister. When she and I met, David introduced her to me as being his sister and she didn't say anything to the contrary.

And, much later, as the plot started to unravel and I came to my senses to do some personal investigating on my own, I learned the woman at the home in Ft. Washington was actually his wife of sixteen years. Now, according to her, she and David had three children together; but he was unemployed and homeless! Was this Satan or a con artist? You tell me! One is as bad as the other. They both deal in deceit. **Be vigilant, alert and sober at all times.**

Yes, I survived this ordeal with God as my healer who is able to restore and deliver us from anything! Some would say I was lucky, but I would say that luck had nothing to do with it. It was God who rained down on me and poured a blessing to give me grace. I am truly blessed indeed to have my mental sanity intact! No one can tell me that God was not with me throughout all of this! And to Him, I owe everything! So again, I say, no regrets, no anger and no unhappiness—only joy and peace of mind in knowing from whom my strength comes!

I can do all things through Christ

Who strengthens me!

Side Note or Background Information, Added January 1, 2009: How did I come to meet David or get involved with him? After finding myself unemployed for the second time in my life due to no fault of my own, I fell into a deep depression. The thing that devastated me the most was the circumstances surrounding my termination. My supervisor handed me a document that stated I was being terminated because they believed I lied about the death of my grandmother. However, upon handing me the document, my supervisor indicated she knew my grandmother died. Unfortunately, my termination had more to do with me not allowing management to change me or control me through the aid of a Jezebel spirit. Prior to a planned merger and business acquisition between Group Health Association and Humana, my supervisor made many failed harassment attempts to get me to conform or resign. Surprised by my own resilience, it was obvious I wasn't as easily intimated or fearful as anticipated by management.

Losing my hair at the age of fourteen was a really low blow to my self-esteem. I endured many years of reinventing my self-image. First, I had to see myself differently and adjust my way of thinking to accept my hair loss, and I had to deal with how others perceived my lack of hair. I went from wearing head wraps and wigs to hats or not wearing anything at all on my head to conceal my baldness. So conforming meant having to go backwards to a time and place when I felt ashamed of who was or had become. And, I was just beginning to accept who I was to include the hand I had been dealt to be comfortable in my own skin.

As mentioned earlier, sometime before being terminated, my supervisor said she wanted to talk to me about my appearance in the eyes of white people. She went on to say my look served to make a militant statement that others found to be defensive and intimidating. Calmly, I indicated, "My hair loss is not by choice. It is the result of a medical illness referred to as Alopecia. As an employee, and in addition to being a customer or member of this healthcare organization, you have full access to my medical records. Medical records, I might add, that could be easily reviewed at any time by anyone within this establishment without my prior knowledge or approval! Had you bothered to consult me directly about the issue or my medical records, you would have been well informed to know my hair loss has nothing to do with a style or statement I was intending to convey, as you have accused. Besides that, I do not see how my lack of hair has anything to do with my ability to do my job. I will not let you or anyone else undo what has taken me years to accomplish: learning to love me, like me and accept me for me in spite of my hair loss!"

From the date of my termination (January 1994) until the death of my brother in August of the same year, I wallowed in self-pity and relived the incident surrounding my termination over and over again in my head to the point where I resented how I was approached. I not only let it eat me up inside, I let it undo what took years and years for me to accomplish. I was beginning to lose confidence in myself and question God. I became angry and consumed with what was going on in my life to the point of neglecting others who needed me to be there for them. I went through life just going through the motions, void of self and detached from my feelings until I received a call from my brother who was hospitalized. During that call, he revived me. He died before I could get to the hospital to see him.

Attempting to pull myself up but still not quite myself, I pleaded to God to send me some help—a religious help meet (mate). (Always remember, there is a difference between the religious and spiritual!) I was tired of going through life alone. If it was inevitable for me to suffer in this cruel world, otherwise known as the devil's playground, I did not want to have to do it alone. Not understanding that Satan hears all requests, I took the bait upon meeting David Christian. Satan's plan was to destroy me and devastate me some more or even worse, kill me! So, during a very vulnerable time in my life, like Job, I became a target for ill-gotten gain. You see, I actually met David prior to the death of my brother; but there was no interest on my part for him as a suitor or getting romantically involved with anyone. After my brother's passing, which added one more troubling thing to my plate, I let my guard down.

Job's First Test

One day the members of the heavenly court came to present themselves before the LORD, and the Accuser, Satan, came with them. "Where have you come from?" the LORD asked Satan. Satan answered the LORD, "I have been patrolling the earth, watching everything that's going on." Then the LORD asked Satan, "Have you noticed my servant Job? He is the finest man in all the earth. He is blameless—a man of complete integrity. He fears God and stays away from evil." Satan replied to the LORD, "Yes, but Job has good reason to fear God. You have always put a wall of protection around him and his home and his property. You have made him prosper in everything he does. Look how rich he is! But reach out and take away everything he has, and he will surely curse you to your face!" "All right, you may test him," the LORD said to Satan. "Do whatever you want with everything he possesses, but don't harm him physically." So Satan left the LORD's presence.

~ Job 1:6-12 NLT

Ladies, we must not be too quick to be in a relationship as a result of loneliness or for the mere desire to satisfy the flesh. Society teaches us to believe that we should be married and with children by a certain age. You must not allow yourself to give in to the wrong thinking. Ask the hard questions and wait on the Lord to supply all your needs.

A Gracious Let Down

Amazingly enough, while attempting to rent some movies from Blockbuster this evening, I overheard a conversation between a man and a woman. The man approached the woman using a pick up line. The woman, evading the man's advances in a direct gracious way, let him down easy. Refusing to accept the rejection and just walk away, the man decided he would throw God into the mix by attempting to insult her stance on premarital sex. In fact, he told her if she truly believed in God, then she should trust Him with her life in believing He would protect her by not allowing her to contract AIDS upon getting involved in a relationship and attending to the physical (lustful) needs of a man—her man to be exact.

Remembering David Christian, it was hard not to say anything or go to the woman's defense. As I moved in closer, the woman told the man, "God and the Bible are very clear about fornication. Sex is the last thing on my mind when I meet someone new. We need to connect spiritually and mentally. If sex is the only thing on a man's mind when we meet, then oh well, he just needs to move on."

Bravo!

HELP ME!
I'VE FALLEN, AND I CAN'T GET UP!

*And let us not be weary in well doing
or grow weary in doing what's right before God:
for in due season we shall reap, if we
faint not or don't give up.*

~ **Galatians 6:9 KJV**

January 2, 1996

Part I

I am reading a book entitled, *Help Me! I've Fallen and I Can't Get Up*, by T. D. Jakes, and already into page 13, it is enlightening indeed. The more I read, the more I wanted to share with you. There are so many thoughts, so many answers and so much joy. Do you know what it's really like to be faced with adversity and later realize you may have brought it on yourself? Mainly because you failed to be obedient to God on the basis of your choices in life? Do you remember Jesus' wilderness experience? He did not allow Himself to be deceived by Lucifer, His adversary. He made the right choice! In T. D. Jakes's book entitled *Water in the Wilderness*, he describes the wilderness as a place of dying—a place where all the things that cause you to stumble in your walk with God are killed. The Lord sometimes leads you to the wilderness on purpose. He feels it is the only time and place where He can finally speak to you or get through! To get your undivided attention, God may find it necessary to isolate you and destroy all things that stand in the way of you and Him having a relationship. However, as you lean closer to God, Lucifer, your adversary, will be more determined than ever to disrupt that union and lead you astray. Can you imagine getting hit with one adversity after the other before you've fully recovered from one? Well, unfortunately, if you had no clear understanding of spiritual warfare, this would be the best way to describe it: one jolt after the other.

> *The few troubles we're having at this moment are not to be compared with the far more important glorious future. We're not looking at things we can see, but at things unseen by humans. What we see around us is temporary and will soon be destroyed, but that which can't be seen now will last forever.*
>
> 2 Corinthians 3:17-18 TCW

Part II

My Wilderness Experience: January 1994 – June 1995

Each summer, my parents would give my sister and I no choice but to stay in the city during school breaks. Therefore, our summers were spent equally divided between North and South Carolina. Comparably, It was like getting a taste of the best of both worlds—modern and traditional living. Washington, D.C., was what I considered to be modern and North and South Carolina were traditional. Talk about a cultural, well-rounded experience! During the early part of my childhood, there was no indoor plumbing or electricity in North or South Carolina. The outdoors was fully equipped with an outhouse and a water pump (the kind that needed to be primed by first adding a little water and then pumped vigorously to get anything out). At night, a kerosene lamp or candles were used as a source of light to see or read by. We took baths in a tin tub that was filled with heated water. Have you ever picked cotton or dried tobacco? We were exposed to that as well. My grandparents played an important part in our upbringing.

My mother, upon receiving a call that her mother had taken ill, immediately dropped everything to travel to Wilson, North Carolina, to be by her side. On Friday, January 7, 1994, my mother called me around 3:00 a.m. to tell me my grandmother had just died. Having been partially raised by both sets of grandparents on my mother's side (North Carolina) as well as my father's (South Carolina), there was a bond that served to occupy nothing but fond memories in my heart and mind for them.

My Wilderness Events

- January 7, 1994 — My grandmother went home to glory.

- January 8, 1984 — My father had a severe asthma attack and had to be rushed to the hospital.

- January 9, 1984 — My transmission went out on my car, and I ended a thirteen-year relationship that turned ugly toward the end.

- January 25, 1984 — I was unlawfully terminated. (In my mind, earning an annual salary of $35,000 with no college degree, as well as having the ability to work since age fourteen, was pretty good. But to go from $35,000 to unemployment for the second time in a five-year period is rough!)

- August 11, 1994 — I lost my twenty-four-year-old brother to AIDS. My baby brother; it was like losing my own son. (Still unable to get together from losing my job, I didn't spend much time with my brother before his death. That I regret!)

- November 28, 1984 — I lost my grandfather (spouse to the grandmother who died in January).

- December 1, 1984 — I was in a car accident. My car was totaled. I was hit so hard from the passenger side, I couldn't get out of the car on the driver side. (This was the first luxury used car I owned, out of a total of four cars that actually had a working heating source since age twenty-one, which were all purchased by me with no cosigner. It was a 1986, fully loaded Buick Regal with cloth seats that were purchased in 1989. I was riding in style. See how easy it is to get caught up in material things?)

- March 31, 1995 — I gave up my apartment to marry and live with Satan. On April 5, 1995, the day I was to move into a new home with Satan, he married someone else. I had already given my rental office my thirty-day notice. I was packed and moved out. How in the world is one able to maintain bills and rent during unemployment (twice) and give up an apartment for a man? Sorry men, I know how this must sound, but you would have had to have been there to experience my ordeal to understand. However, if the situation were reversed, I am sure you would feel the same way. And this man's last name was Christian. Talk about not being able to discern the spirits. The circumstances surrounding this situation are better than the Soaps! If I hadn't personally experienced it, I wouldn't believe it myself.

While in the Wilderness, Jesus fasted for forty days and He became extremely hungry. Then the devil confronted Him by disguising himself as an angel from heaven surrounded with light. He told Jesus that now that His fast was over, his Father had given Him permission to use His divine power to turn one of the desert stones into bread. "If you are the Son of God, that should be no problem," Satan said.

~ Matthew 4:2-3 TCW

Part III

Life throws us all some sort of curve(s). And in the end, if we have faith, we will survive. It's a stage of growing, learning and developing to another level (hopefully higher). *I can do all things through Christ who strengthens me.* Please always remember that! God will not put any more on you than what you can bear. Boy, have I grown! God told me I was stronger than I thought, and I feel great. No regrets, no remorse and no unhappiness. When we go through certain things in life and look back on them, we often ask, why? But ask yourself: If it had been different, would I have obtained the knowledge I now have?

Looking Back - Worshipping False Idols

- The more money I made, the more I wanted to earn. Each and every job became my life; an idol for replacing God in my life. I couldn't get up on Sunday to go to church, but I would get up on Sunday to go to work if there was a need for me to be there.

- That car could take me everywhere I wanted to go but not to church. There was a time when, if I didn't make it to church, I would read my Bible, watch Rev. Price, or listen to gospel music most of the day. That too came to pass.

- I would lock myself in my apartment away from everybody, including God. Friends who saw what was happening tried to talk to me about God. I wouldn't listen and would reply, "I don't want to talk about God. I'm angry." Have you heard of a pity party? Well, I was beyond that.

Remember the wilderness? A place where all the things that cause you to stumble in your walk with God are killed: job, car, apartment. Did He break me down? He wore me out! Did I not retreat to my prayer closet? You bet I did! I got on my knees and poured out my soul. A day later, I reached for the phone to call a friend and invited myself to accompany her to church—my Father's house.

Part IV

What a glorious time! My girlfriend, Janet Galloway, planned a wonderful Sunday for me. She arrived at my mother's bright and early to take me to the early morning Sunday service at the Holy Christian Missionary Baptist Church for All People. Immediately following the Sunday service, we were planning to ride to Jessup, Maryland, for breakfast and visit her cousins, Gwen and Rebe. Gwen was actively serving in the military and lived in Jessup, Maryland. Rebe was visiting Gwen from Texas. Upon entering the house, we were greeted by Gwen's family and Rebe. As we approached the dining room, we engaged in conversation, and I discussed the loss of my hair. I also indicated it was somewhat difficult accepting the loss of my hair; however, over time, and in spite of my recent termination, I had endured. Suddenly, Gwen jumped up and departed upstairs to her room.

At that moment, Rebe told me she traveled from Texas to be with her sister, Gwen, because she was worried about her. Gwen was diagnosed with cancer, and her method of treatment was chemotherapy. She also said, "My sister is a little vain when it comes to her hair. But when you walked through the door, I knew she was going to be okay. God sent you! Thank you for sharing your story about your hair loss. When my husband and I left the house to get on the highway, God told me I forgot my Bible. My husband, quite like myself, has learned not to question God when told to do something. Being obedient, he politely got off at the nearest exist and we turned around to go back to the house to get my Bible. So now it is time for me to do something for you."

Looking puzzled, I could not imagine what that could be. Upon opening her Bible, she asked me some questions about my personality, and before I could answer the question in its entirety, she would start reading from certain passages that actually described me. I didn't understand how that was possible, but I later learned she was prophesying and sharing her spiritual gifts—the gifts of healing, teaching and deliverance. As she continued to flip through the pages of the Bible, she began to speak to me about my character and explained the following: Spiritual growth is a continuous process! Bad things happen to good people no matter how many measures you take to avoid trouble. It is not your understanding of the situation or encounter that is important; it's God's will and your purpose for being which may often bring about discipline through pain. You despise hypocrisy, which is why you haven't been baptized yet. You believe in truth and fairness. You value sincerity. You are a special and unique person. You think you need to be perfect to get baptized. No one is perfect, and God's been trying to reach you for quite some time. It's time for you to stop running and fulfill your purpose. You have to be careful whom you eat from. You are a part of a spiritual war. Satan will stop at nothing to prevent you from obtaining your blessings. As she touched me, I began to shake, and then there was a sense of warmth, calmness and peace. I left feeling overjoyed about my experience and empowered. She told me she knew of my difficulty determining the meaning of the scriptures as it is written in the King James version, and I was not unlike many others in that area as she encouraged me to look around for a Bible to reference with an English translation of hard truths. What a wonderful and joyous experience. (For additional information, please read the letter to the Commissioner of The Salvation Army as instructed by God.) That night, I had the most peaceful sleep I had had in a long time. I slept like a baby and woke up the next morning feeling rejuvenated and alive.

> *This lasted for seven years. Then suddenly my reason returned and I was able to think like a human being again. I stood in the open field and looked up to heaven and praised the Most High God. I praised and honored the One who lives forever and ever, His kingship never ends. He rules in the affairs of men from generation to generation. All the people in the world are like a drop in the bucket to Him. He does what He pleases among the hosts of heaven and among the inhabitants of the earth. No one has the power to stop Him or the wisdom to question what He does. At the same time that my reason was returned to me, my advisers, counselors and leading officials came out looking for me and gave me back my Kingdom with all the power and glory that I had had before. My people welcomed me with open arms and honored me more than ever. So now I, Nebuchadnezzar, king of Babylon, praise and honor the God of heaven and glorify the King of kings, whose ways are right and just toward everyone, but who also humbles those who are lifted up by pride and power.*
>
> ~ Daniel 4:34-37

It took a while for God to reach me, so He kept sending others to minister to me. He tried everything! There was nowhere I could go to run from God or His messages. Walking down the street, I was approached by a woman wearing all white, who told me everything was going to be okay. Walking into a store, which was directly across from Howard University on the corner of Harvard and Georgia Avenue, called The Blue Nile to purchase herbs, the gentleman behind the counter who assisted me with my order, told me, "You are stronger than you give yourself credit for. You suffer many losses within the course of a year. Can you imagine losing your entire family in one day? You are going to be okay because God is with you."

That was amazing, but I had difficulty understanding how He could know so much about me. Not understanding the supernatural power of God, it took me nearly a year before I went back to that store for anything. Knowing me as He did, God knew He had to put me in an environment or place where I needed to be still long enough for Him to get through to me. His plan was to make me listen and take notice. Allowing my employment with the ICMA Retirement Corporation, He surrounded me with children of God who were already employed there. They, unfortunately, were being oppressed, but in spite of their circumstances, they knew who they were within the Kingdom of God. He used my immediate supervisor, Vanessa Waller-Jones; she would bring me biblical literature to read and walk me through it in case I had any questions. That was the first step, but it didn't end there. Next, somehow, I became a part of an email mailing list of coworkers who shared the gospel. Lastly, I had to ask God to help me get up, only to find He had never left me. He was there all the time. That's the powerful, supernatural strength of God—sending **reinforcements** to help me through it.

So the Israelites left Soccuth and continued east until they got to Etham on the edge of the Wilderness and set up camp there. During the day, the Lord went ahead of them hidden in a pillar of cloud to show them the way. He also shaded them from the hot desert sun. At night He kept them warm by turning the same cloud into a pillar of fire to give them light. So the pillar of cloud was in front of them by day and it became a pillar of fire by night. And the Lord was always with them.

~ Exodus 13:2-22

Talk about lessons in living! I am truly blessed. There is no other way to explain it. I have inner peace as I'm steered toward God.

SEEKING TO KNOW MY PURPOSE

February 5, 1999

Today I asked a question; a question often asked and for which I so desperately need an answer. What is my purpose? What is my destiny or God's plan for my life? I seem to always find myself in situations that I often wonder how I ended up in. For as long as I can remember, I've always worked at places that were filled with confusion and caused me a great deal of frustration. Why is it so difficult for me to fit in? I always seem to have that problem! So seek, I must!

While speaking to a coworker, I heard myself say, "I know God does not put more on us than what we can bear. But it would be different, or I would feel different, if I had as much confidence in myself as God must obviously has in me. If only I had a little more insight into what my involvement is or the work needed to be performed by me to fulfill His will, it might make things a little easier. I think not knowing contributes to my pain of going through my trial or the task of my mission.

However, I'm sure Jesus' pain must have been far greater. Not only His, but God's as well. He lost His only Son. *So who am I?*

As I read over what I've stated above, I have to wonder if knowing would make it much easier for me to accomplish my task or if it would create more fear. I was once told that if God did reveal His plan, we might not like it. Let me explain! What God chooses for us or what He wants for us may not be what we want or would choose for ourselves. But I believe knowing in advance would sure make me feel better.

Thinking back, I have to wonder how many lives I have touched in the working environments I perceived to be hostile. Was I drawn to these situations purposely? Were these situations or environments of my choosing and is that why time spent there seemed so difficult? Did God allow these things to happen to prove a point? Were they lessons of growth? Did I fulfill His wish or meet His expectations? Was His will carried out?

In the beginning of my employment with an organization called Kajax Engineering, Inc. (KEI), a black-owned corporation in Roslyn, Virginia, I saw an opportunity for growth within Human Resources. The opportunity for growth in Human Resources is probably still there, but I truly do not believe that is my purpose. For the past couple of months (even years), I have been searching for answers that only God can provide. Tonight, I may have received my answer, at least to why I was drawn to KEI. While watching an episode of *Touched by an Angel*, I began to cry in the first five minutes of the segment. Wow, just listening to the narrative of the upcoming show brought tears to my eyes! By the end of the show, I had thoughts that I was employed at KEI to reach someone who was possibly experiencing great emotional distress or growing pains similar to what I was experiencing. Even as I wrote down these thoughts that reveal what is weighing so heavily on my mind, I began to take note of many emotions plaguing me:

- The joy of knowing God is using me;
- The fear of, perhaps, failing Him; and
- Hurt, because I know that in order to reach this person, I must experience the pain of what needs to be expressed.

But on the other hand, I know I am going to be all right because God is working on me as well. I must learn to trust in Him, depend upon Him and talk to Him more. Though I was excited to be working for a black-owned company for the first time in my career, I was also dissatisfied by what I had observed to be the norm in many independently owned establishments: a growing lack of integrity. Being assigned to the Human Resources Department, I saw a number of disturbing discrepancies. On the payroll, there were people who never reported to work—not once—but received a bi-weekly paycheck. And there were others, from my understanding, who were terminated on the basis of irreconcilable differences, but due to clauses in their contracts, they had the ability to receive a salary until an undisclosed date, which was being rendered to them bi-weekly as well. Within one year's time, the CEO increased his own salary from $100,000 to $500,000 a year, in addition to his brother's—also an employee—receiving of regular payout bonuses. Seeing this type of business activity not only makes me nervous, but it is a sign of a possible buy-out or planned closure. As time went on, I saw and witnessed more than I cared to.

Was I here to merely observe or was it God's objective for me to learn what not to do as it pertained to unethical business practices?

> **Note Added September 23, 2010:** Approximately one year later, on February 20, 2000, to be exact, I was told my position as Human Resources/Personnel Specialist was being abolished, but I was welcome to apply for a lower position as Administrative Assistant. Refusing to compromise my level of integrity on one too many occasions resulted in a management decision to terminate me. Not long after my departure, KEI was sold to another organization that resulted in a reorganizational structure, a number of layoffs (including the Director of Human Resources) and a change in the company's name.

Everything happens for a reason, and God always has a bigger plan!

SHARING AN EXAMPLE OF GOD'S FAVOR IN MY LIFE

August 16, 2007

As you may or may not be aware, I experienced an accident that occurred on June 7, 2007, involving a tow truck company. As a AAA member, I called for a tow truck and the dispatched company was Able Towing. As my car was being hooked to the back of the tow truck to be lifted on the bed, the winch snapped and my car fell off the bed of the tow truck. Upon impact, it rolled backwards, slamming into the front of a parked, four-door Black Dodge Stratus.

During that time of the morning, there was no one out who could witness the incident except for me and the tow truck driver, who was yelling hysterically while I screamed. However, given my personality, I left a note for the owner of the Dodge Stratus disclosing what had happened and how to reach me. As of August 3, 2007, I was receiving approximately two to three calls a day from the owner who was trying to reach a resolution between the Able Towing Company and AAA. To my surprise, she was not overly angry with me—she actually sympathized with me and attempted to work with me to get results—but she was starting to get on my nerves.

After making several attempts to speak with the owner of the Able Towing Company, AAA referred us to the insurance company (Claims Management Services, Inc.) representing Able Towing. I explained in a written statement and forwarded to Able, AAA and the Claims Management Services that my objective was not to receive compensation for myself. It was to make sure (1) the owner of the Dodge Stratus was compensated for damages sustained to her vehicle, (2) the necessary repairs were made to the tow truck preventing such an incident from happening to anyone else or (3) the truck be removed from the street all together.

Fortunately but reluctantly, I am truly learning the world we live in and how no one cares about the little people—except for God! There is an extreme struggle for power and control regardless of the moral position. And companies in today's society seem to benefit and prosper at any and all cost while not being willing to take social responsibility for inappropriate, unethical business practices. After receiving a return call from the insurance company representing AAA and the Able Towing Company, I was left feeling numb and distraught—especially after being told my car was not worth anything. Yes, my car was old. And yes it had been purchased used nearly six years ago from The Salvation Army through an employee-closed auction and bidding offer. To make matters worse, I was told my "car was valued even less because it was declared a total loss in 2003 as a result of a previous accident" in which I was not at fault.

> As a result of the 2003 accident, my insurance company, Nationwide Mutual, did not want to pay to get my car repaired, so they declared my car a total loss; in my opinion, it was repairable and still in excellent driving condition as well as safe to be on the road. When I purchased the vehicle, a 1992 in 2001, it only had 60,000 miles on it. I accepted the check for the assessed value minus the salvage amount for me to buy it back from Nationwide Mutual. I took the car to a reputable auto-body repair shop. My car ran great, and considering how far it was pushed through an intersection (while stopped at a red light waiting for the light to change) into the back of a mid-size van by an older model, black Cadillac that was driven by a young teenager, it was built like a tank. I drove my car from the scene of the accident, and he had to have his Cadillac towed. There was no damage to the front of my car, but there was some damage to the back bumper. The Cadillac, on the other hand, was in pretty bad shape. The front end was lying in the street, and the radiator was exposed. Amazingly, given the impact, I was not physically hurt in any way. That was God and the angels assigned to me!

Wow! Disappointed and frustrated that no one took into consideration that I could have been killed or that there was still a tow truck operating in the vicinity of the Washington, D.C., metropolitan area that was unsafe, I made numerous calls to the Department of Transportation, the Federal Highway Administration, and the National Highway Traffic Safety Administration; I was determined to get someone to take my claim seriously. After making the decision to contact every Maryland, D.C., and Virginia council member, I finally received some guidance on how to proceed. This D.C. councilwoman was so concerned that she not only instructed me on how to proceed, but she directly contacted someone within the D.C. Office of Regulatory Affairs on my behalf.

Within minutes, I received an email and a follow-up call from the D.C. Office of Regulatory Affairs who advised me they were in receipt of my complaint and an investigation was underway. From that investigation, I learned the tow truck failed inspection the day before my incident and it was not properly licensed to be on the street. The owner of towing company will receive a $2,000 fine and be ordered to cease operation of the truck in question until it receives the appropriate repairs and the proper licensing.

I am truly blessed to receive favor from God in allowing these satisfactory events from beginning to end. It seems God has allowed me to see the quick results of His power. Just when I felt helpless and I was about to give up and give in, He felt my pain. I just needed to exercise faith. The owner of the Black Dodge Stratus received the maximum payment for the necessary repairs needed to correct the damages she sustained to her vehicle. What a glorious VICTORY!

JUDGING OTHERS
A THOUGHT FOR THE DAY!

August 24, 2007

It's unfortunate we presume to know all there is to know about a person and are more apt to spread negative notions or ideas because they don't fall in the category of what we perceive to be true as opposed to taking a long hard look at ourselves. No one has all the answers, but we should at least attempt to respect others by allowing them to live their life according to how they see fit. It's not about you! It's about them, their walk, and being accountable for every action in the eyes of God.

So ask yourselves, am I living up to the standards of God? Am I working toward allowing myself to be molded in accordance to the characteristics of Christ? Judge yourselves before you judge others.

> *Do not judge, so that you may not be judged.*
> *For with the judgment you make you will be judged,*
> *and the measure you get. Why do you see the speck in*
> *your neighbor's eye, but do not notice the*

log in your own eye? Or how can you say to your neighbor, Let me take the speck out of your eye, while the log is in your own eye? You hypocrite, first take the long out of your own eye, and then you will see clearly to take the speck out of your neighbor's eye.

~ Matthew 7:1-5 NRSV

IGNORANCE

If you [claim ignorance and] say, "See, we did not know this," Does He not consider it who weighs and examines the hearts and their motives? And does He not know it who guards your life and keeps your soul? And will He not repay [you and] every man according to his works?
~ **Proverbs 24:12**

September 17, 2007

How often I keep forgetting that ignorance comes in all shapes, sizes, colors and denominations. The plight of my faith is wanting so much to believe that people are not generally cruel or filled with hate and malice. Unfortunately, due to many prejudices, false beliefs or misconceptions people have about an array of many different things, they are driven by ignorance and don't even realize it. The irony is they fear the unknown or that which they do not understand, and for the most part, they don't make any attempts to understand or find out the truth. They would rather remain ignorant to the truth (Proverbs 18: 2).

> *Believing in our hearts that who we are is enough*
> *is the key to a more satisfying and balanced life.*
>
> ~ Ellen Sue Stern, motivational speaker and writer

Today, like no other day, I recognize the Holy Spirit that dwells within me (Acts 4:31); it is real. Because of God, I am on my way to being what He has intended me to be and not what man thinks I should be. I have inner joy and peace regardless of my surroundings and the limitations that people attempt to place upon me.

> *Ye have not chosen me, but I have chosen you,*
> *and ordained you, that ye should go and bring forth fruit,*
> *and that your fruit should remain: that whatsoever*
> *ye shall ask of the Father in my name,*
> *He may give it you.*
>
> ~ John 15:16

Sharing my morning experience: This morning, like always, I walked into the 7 Eleven for a cup of coffee. When the store is overly crowded, I normally have the exact amount ($1.31) in my hand and pay for my coffee upon entering as opposed to on the way out. The line always seems to be much longer and a little more chaotic as I'm leaving the store. Because of my hair loss, I'm still aware of the stares and comments (mostly more negative than positive due to the fear of the unknown). Therefore, I'm not afraid the cashier will forget I paid for the coffee on the way in and attempt to accuse me of stealing a $1.31 cup of coffee on the way out. You cannot help but notice the bold, black, bald-headed woman (and all her glory) who stands before you! I've learned to use what many people would see as a disability or disadvantage as an advantage and a blessing. That does not mean I don't wake up some mornings and still ask God why He has allowed this medical condition that has been bestowed upon me. And then I am reminded, "God does not put more on you than what you can bear." With that in mind, I suck it up and keep on pushing with hurt and pain in tow. That which does not kill you makes you stronger!

As I began to fix my coffee, the man standing next to me was angry and outraged at the laughter being directed at me. He said some not-so-pleasant, choice words in my honor to my adversaries and wanted to know why I wasn't reacting. I looked at him and said, "I'm used to ignorance. Why react and give them that satisfaction? In fact, I'm stronger by not reacting." He looked at me and said he would feel stronger if he busted some heads. I said, "Thank you, not necessary!" I then walked over to the group of men and said, "Good morning. How are you today?" As they held their heads down in shame, they replied, "Good morning. Fine!" I turned and walked back to the coffee counter and proceeded to continue to fix my coffee. I looked at my protector and said, "Good-bye. Have a great day." He replied, "I hope you have a peaceful day and go with God in love." I replied, "Thank you, I would like to consider myself as being a very spiritual person. That's why I didn't react the way the devil would have wanted me to." He looked at me, smiled and nodded with approval as he said, "I understand."

> *These things have I spoken unto you,*
> *that ye should not be offended.*
>
> ~ John 16:1

Walking toward the door to leave, God reminded me of another incident that took place in that same spot at that same 7 Eleven (a little shy of one year ago). A seven- or eight-year-old little girl looked at me and asked her mother if I had cancer just like her grandmother. The mother looked at me and said, "I am teaching my daughter not to stare at people or make assumptions. Therefore, I am teaching her to ask questions. Is it okay if she directs her questions to you?" Offering my approval, I explained, "My condition is medically related, and my hair fell out when I was fourteen years old. Unfortunately, my hair has not grown back since that time, but I am not receiving chemotherapy." A treatment I was sure her grandmother was receiving to destroy the disease that was causing her grandmother's sickness.

As I started to leave, I turned to say good-bye and noticed the little girl was crying. I looked at her mother and asked what was wrong. She said her daughter was sad and hurting because she knew people would laugh and stare at me all the time and possibly say mean things to me to hurt my feelings because I have no hair. *Remember the word that I said unto you, The servant is not greater than his lord. If they have persecuted me, they will also persecute you; if they have kept my saying, they will keep yours also* (John 15:20). As I walked toward the little girl, she grabbed me and hugged me as she continued to cry. What a big heart in such a little person! She was giving me God's love! I told her, "Everything is going to be all right. It's been hard, but I've grown to be very strong, inside and out. And I know you are strong too. Just like your mother and your grandmother. I don't worry about people staring at me or laughing at me. When you get older you will understand. Dry your eyes and be strong for your grandmother. When you get home, tell her how much you love her." God wants us to live by faith and trust Him with our hearts, not our eyes!

> *Intelligence and character!*
> *That is the goal of true education.*
>
> **~Dr. Martin Luther King Jr.**

Oh, what a wonderful feeling to know that you are surrounded by God's grace and love. I truly know what is meant by being blessed and highly favored! Trials come on every hand, but I feel like going on! Tomorrow morning, I plan to go to that same 7 Eleven.

Finally, let no one cause me trouble,
for I bear on my body the marks of Jesus.

~ Galatians 6:17

"One's education can take many turns and twists in the road, but pursuing self-education or enlightenment can bring rich rewards."

REPUTATION VERSUS CHARACTER

"Be more concerned with your character than your reputation, because your character is what you really are, while your reputation is merely what others think you are."

~ John Wooden

November 4, 2007

The Salvation Army National Headquarters recently developed and released a blogging policy that speaks to their position and their right to block any blogs being posted through the use of their server that attempt to ruin or distort the reputation of The Salvation Army.

The word *fair* may not be in the Bible, but the word *just* most certainly is!

My experiences are my experiences, and my experiences are real. My experiences may be similar or different to those of others. They are situations or events that have taken place in my life. Depending upon how my experiences have affected me, they can and have generated feelings of good and bad. No one (!) can tell me the events or situations in my life did not happen, nor can they tell me that I am wrong in how I perceive them in relation to the impact they have had on my life. Unless you are able to trade places with me and walk in my shoes, you cannot know the depth or to what extent of my pain or joy was contributed by those experiences or how they have impacted me spiritually or emotionally—good, bad or indifferent. Nonetheless, I can only hope and pray that my experiences (negative or positive), which pierce my soul and contribute to my character (that which is the very essence of who I am), do not hinder my growth or cause me to drift away from God.

Reputation covers the outside. It is defined by one's perception or opinion in observance of your actions or demeanor.

Character grows from within. It is defined by who and what you are made of on the inside; your nature.

What is most important? Your image (reputation) or your character? If you are willing to openly take a look at your actions and commit yourself to taking full responsibility for those actions, only then are you willing to listen intently to what is being said by me (or others who have found themselves in this same position) to bring about change and much needed healing. If you have no intentions of considering anyone else other than yourself, thus allowing self (ego) and the outside world (in the world, not of the world) to influence your character (not Christ-like), then you have no right to tell me that I cannot share my experiences with others because you are afraid of how it may look to the outside world. *Therefore, since we have seen the mercy and graciousness of God and have been called to share the good news of Christ with others, by His grace we will not lose heart* (2 Corinthians 4:1). You can, however, object to me using what is considered to be company equipment to share my experiences, but you and only you are responsible for your reputation! God sees and knows all, regardless of what is exposed to the outside world.

> *They that observe lying vanities forsake their own mercy.*
> *But I will sacrifice unto thee with the voice of thanksgiving;*
> *I will pay that that I have vowed. Salvation is of the Lord.*
>
> ~ Jonah 2:8-9

So what about God's reputation? Have you given any thought to how you distort or ruin His reputation based on your actions? As a church or body of Christ, you have the power to touch a number of lives and make a difference. You can induce a positive influence or a negative one. Have you given any thought to the souls you have betrayed or failed by not honoring God's word?

> *As ministers of the gospel, we are not dishonest; we don't play church politics or falsify the word of God to please others. We recommend ourselves and our ministry to everyone's conscience by practicing the truth as if we were in the actual presence of God.*
>
> ~ 2 Corinthians 4:2

THE ASSIGNMENT

November 9, 2007

There was a time in my life when I believed God was not listening to me. He did not see me as being important nor did I exist to Him at all. Unfortunately, society teaches us to rely on instincts because the scientific mind cannot relate to nor understand that which it cannot see. Through the Holy Spirit, I am learning not only to trust that which I cannot see, but also to believe what I cannot see as being the most important above all.

> For I know the plans I have for you. [I know the thoughts that I think towards you, says the Lord, thoughts of peace and not of evil, to give you a good hope at the end.] Plans to prosper you and not to harm you. Plans to give you hope and a future. Then you will call upon me and come and pray to me, and I will listen to you.
>
> ~ Jeremiah 29:11-13

On Sundays, while sitting in church, I would observe the congregation praising, shouting, rejoicing, dancing and speaking in tongues. Experiencing this early on as a child, I had no idea what was going on, but I was never afraid. My grandfather, sensing my confusion one Sunday, told me, "Don't worry! It is nothing to be afraid of, and when it happens, nothing and no one else around you will matter." As I became older and understood this behavior to be the presence of God through the Holy Spirit, I assumed God was not pleased with me for some reason, because He had not blessed me in such a way.

In my quest for seeking God and wanting to know or understand religion, I learned the most important thing of all. Religion has nothing to do with God! Religion, essentially, is a systematic order or set of man-made rules and guidelines that dictate how one should worship. Religion is a classification or label created by man to define God as we attempt to place Him in a box or category of an affiliated denomination of comfort. For me, aspiring to be like Christ is about being spiritual. There is no limit to the power of the Holy Spirit. You cannot confine God! Yet, we not only attempt to confine God but each other as well—over and over again!

> *For false christs and false prophets will appear and perform signs and miracles to deceive the elect. [For there will rise false christs and lying prophets, and they will show signs and wonders, and mislead, if possible, even the chosen ones.] Truly I say to you, this nation will not pass away until all these things happen. Heaven and earth will pass away, but my words will not pass away. Be alert always!*
>
> ~ Mark 13:22-31

Because I had encountered so many "Christian" folks who had confessed with their mouths to be one thing but presented themselves through their actions to be another, I did not want anyone to tell me God existed; I needed and wanted to experience Him for myself. I am stubborn and hardheaded when it comes to believing what is told to me. So I have this need to review, investigate or research the facts to substantiate what is told to me—especially when I see so many around me who are prospering (getting ahead) and are corrupt, vindictive or just evil. And, given my character or personality, I am normally an impatient person by nature, which makes it difficult for me to understand the concept or importance of waiting on God.

Righteous art thou, O LORD, when I plead with thee: yet let me talk with thee of thy judgments: Wherefore doth the way of the wicked prosper? Wherefore are all they happy that deal very treacherously? Thou hast planted them, yea, they have taken root: they grow, yea, they bring forth fruit: thou art near in their mouth and far from their reins. But thou, O LORD, knowest me: thou has seen me, and tried mine heart toward thee: pull them out like sheep for the slaughter, and pre them for the day of slaughter.

~ Jeremiah 12:1-3

When I received what was and is my assignment from God, I could not believe just how simple or easy it was to have a real relationship with Him. And to think that He would entrust such a task to me is out of this world, to say the least. I was a person who doubted His existence because my prayers were not answered immediately or according to my timetable! I was a person who avoided confrontation and adversity at all cost. God will and can use the most unlikely person to get His point across. Today, I am learning to listen intently, be obedient and "be strong in the Lord and stand in the power of His might" (Ephesians 6:10).

> *Dear brothers and sisters, when troubles come your way, consider it an opportunity for great joy. For you know that when your faith is tested, your endurance has a chance to grow. So let it grow, for when your endurance is fully developed, you will be perfect and complete, needing nothing.*
>
> ~ James 1:2-4 NLT

God surely has a sense of humor!

As mentioned previously, during a Salvation Army World Service Office (SAWSO) annual staff meeting on November 29, 2006, I had a wonderful experience through the Holy Spirit during the receiving of devotion, which was delivered by Thebisa Chaava. I just could not understand why God would allow me for the first time to experience what I did in the middle of a staff meeting surrounded by all my coworkers who thought I was having a nervous breakdown or losing my mind; not to mention, a Commissioner's conference was going on in the next room. (I actually had no knowledge of the Commissioner's conference that was being held on the same floor as the SAWSO staff meeting until approximately two weeks after having my spiritual experience.) Talk about having mixed emotions! When the Spirit hits you—more like moves you—there is nothing you can do but surrender.

There I was trying to be reserved and attempting to fight the will of the Spirit while trying to make sense of what was happening. My mind was telling me one thing, and my body was doing another. When I realized I could not contain it, my intellect told me, for the sake of embarrassment given the expressions on the faces of everyone who was in the room with me on that day, I needed to leave the room. But the Holy Spirit had other plans! Thinking back, it was like something from out of a cartoon script. I leaped out of my chair, let out a big yell (more like laughter) and headed for the door. I attempted to open the door, and the Spirit closed it. So there I was—as it must have looked to the others in the room—opening and closing the door until I was finally able to slip through it. Little did they know, I could not explain what was happening to me either but what a joyful feeling to know God truly loves me. I just felt He picked a bad time to show it. However, there is no right or wrong time as far as God is concerned. It's called God's time, and He was preparing me and getting me ready for flight or fight (spiritual warfare). I am still flying high.

Ironically, the assignment was initially given to me on October 27, 2006 (a year ago), and unfortunately, I have been slow to act. Upon arriving to work on Monday morning, October 22, 2007, I was extremely charged with a positive attitude. I could not help but think about how different I was feeling. This is what I would consider to be the renewing of one's mind and spirit. As I thought about all the negative things I had endured on the job, I was void of anger. What a wonderful feeling to know a releasing had truly occurred through the Holy Spirit during the Malachi 3:1 Ministries conference. Just the thought of that makes me want to shout and spread the news of how God has worked in my life, through my life and around my life. God has not allowed me to go through what I go through not only expecting me to learn and grow through my experiences, but expecting me to share my experiences in teaching and bringing others to Him that they may experience Him as I do. I began to cry with joy!

My supervisor approached me at 9:26 a.m. and asked me not to send out my testimonies because people did not want to receive them. "I am glad you are excited about God, but not everyone wants you to share it with them. Just send it to me and no one else." (He never said exactly who it was that had expressed a disinterest; no one had expressed it to me. In fact, some stated they appreciated my willingness to share my testimonies because it gave them hope. It was viewed as being encouraging.) Oh God, my objective is to be obedient to You and follow Your instructions as commanded and doubt not my faith or Your confidence in me.

By allowing a spirit of fear to intervene, yet again, with my assignment, I was flustered and discouraged after receiving a written National Headquarters Employee Warning Notice on Friday, October 26, 2007. Knowing me as He does, in all my stubborn ways and hard-headedness, God knew He needed to regenerate me. A week later, on Friday, November 2, 2007, God sent me five messages of confirmation or reassurance. Not one, but five, to get me back on track. *And the word of the LORD came unto Jonah the second time, saying, Arise, go unto Nin'-e-veh, that great city and preach unto it the preaching that I bid thee* (Jonah 3).

About Message(s): Please understand and always remember, messages can come in many forms. God can use anyone or anything to speak to you to get His message across.

Messages I Received:

1. The thought for the day received via email through heresathought@ragan.com reads: The truth is not simply what you think it is, it is also the circumstances in which it is said and to whom, why and how it is said. Vaclav Havel, Czech President and playwright.

2. Issue 4, Volume 1, November 2007 Monthly Newsletter: Received from a friend. The article that spoke to me was entitled *A Blessing in Your Storm*.

   > *We can rejoice, too, when we run into problems and trials, for we know that they help us develop endurance. And endurance develops strength of character, and character strengthens our confident hope of salvation.*
   >
   > ~ Romans 5:3-4 NLT

3. October 2007 issue of the Eric L. Farrell & Will Holmes, Jr. Collaborations: "Ministry of Poems." The introduction reads: "The question of this poem should leave you

with this: Do you want to follow the crowd or do you want to follow the truth?" (Oddly, I did not receive this issue at the beginning of October but on November 2, 2007. Was that not God!)

4. The Victorious Daily Word by Pastor Wil Nichols was just as powerful. He called it, "The Battles of Spiritual Warfare: Wrestle to Always Win, Not to Keep From Losing." Some people go through life trying to keep from losing. They never take risks, they play it safe and they never even try because they don't want to lose. But, trying to keep from losing means that you will never win; and if you will never win, then ultimately you will lose. And so it is with spiritual warfare.

5. A visit from an out-of-town Salvation Army officer yielded a message I'm sure she was not aware she was passing on. I secretly retreated to the restroom to engage in prayer and tell God I understood as I thanked Him. She spoke to me about being sent to The Salvation Army and chosen for an uncomfortable assignment.

Listening to God on November 4, 2007, I rose early at 3:00 a.m. to receive His message and get it all down on paper before He instructed me for the fourth time on which church He wanted me to attend. (Remember what was stated above. God deals with each of us differently and in accordance to our personality. So He knows me well—better than I know myself! He had given me three messages previously through people I had met that had either encouraged me or invited me to attend this same church before.) As I arrived for service at the First Baptist Church of Glen Arden, I noted the parking lot was excessively empty, but I proceeded to park and go inside to be seated. Upon reading the program, that highlighted SHABACH! Ministries Inc. Day, I noted the scripture Ephesians 6:7: *With goodwill doing service as to the LORD, and not to men. I began to cry because I knew I was in the right place.* Anxiously waiting for the service to begin, I questioned what was taking so long. In asking the woman who was seated in front of me at the time, I learned I had arrived a whole hour before service was to begin. God wanted to make sure I was present and on time. The focus of the sermon was Jonah.

> *Then Jonah prayed unto the LORD his god out of the fish's belly, And said, I cried by reason of mine affliction unto the Lord, and He heard me; out of the belly of hell cried I, and though heardest my voice. For thou hadst cast me into the deep, in the midst of the seas; and the floods compassed me about: all thy billows and thy waves passed over me. Then I said, I am cast out of thy sight; yet I will look again toward thy holy temple. The waters compassed me about, even to the soul: the dept closed me round about, the weeds were wrapped about my head. I went down to the bottoms of the mountains; the earth with her bars was about me for ever: yet hast though brought up my life from corruption, O LORD my God. When my soul fainted within me I remembered the LORD: and my prayer came in unto thee, into thine holy temple. They that observe lying vanities forsake their own mercy. But I will sacrifice unto thee with the voice of thanksgiving; I will pay that that I have*

*vowed. Salvation is of the LORD. And the LORD spake
unto the fish, and it vomited out Jonah upon the dry land*

~ Jonah 2:1-10

I have committed myself to God, the Father, the Son and the Holy Ghost. My first baptism took place in April of 1995; however, I desire to recommit my faith through Christian experience and the re-dedication of my spirit through baptism as I become a member of the First Baptist Church of Glen Arden. Father God, my Lord and Master, I yearn for You in the highest and worst way possible. I am Yours! Do with me as You will.

*And Jacob was left alone; and there wrestled a man with
him until the breaking of the day. And when he saw that he
prevailed not against him, he touched the hollow of his thigh;
and the hollow of Jacob's thigh was out of joint, as he wrestled
with him. And he said, Let me go, for the day breaketh.
And he said, I will not let thee go, except thou bless me.*

~ Genesis 32:24-26

OBEDIENT TO GOD

November 19, 2007

A quote from Erin L. Wikle's article found in The Salvation Army's *New Frontier*, October 12, 2007, Volume 26, Number 18; page 21:

> **Don't Lose Your Voice! If God is not dead, if his word is still very much so alive, then the days of prophecy and revelation are not over. Rise Up! God is speaking and we must be obedient to listen, receive and deliver his word.**

Character is made by what you stand for; reputation, by what you fall for.

Robert Quillen (1887–1948),
publisher and humorist

On Friday, November 9, 2007, I was accused of being angry[51] due to the content and tone in my rendition of "Reputation versus Character." The Salvation Army advertised a writing contest in an attempt to get the employees to participate by submitting something for their newsletter. My article as directed and inspired by God was written to emphasize the difference between reputation and character and to show how character was more important. They not only took offense to it in refusing to publish it, but they threatened to write me up for a disciplinary action. Nonetheless, the tone of the article is no different from the tone or content found in Psalms or Proverbs.

Angry? What about hurt or in pain and suffering? What about heartbroken? *Come unto me, all ye that labour and are heavy laden, and I will give you rest* (Matthew 11:28). I have been given an assignment that serves as my mission from my Master and Savior. Unbeknownst to me, I have been put in a position not of my own choosing—at least not directly! I applied for a position to work at The Salvation Army National Headquarters; but I had no idea that God would have much more in store for me. To that end, it is my desire to be obedient and follow through!

> *The fear of the Lord is the beginning of knowledge,*
> *but fools despise wisdom and instruction.*
>
> ~ Proverbs 1:7

---

51   Psalm 69:24 AMP: *Pour out Your indignation on them, And let [the fierceness of] Your burning anger overtake them.*

God gives me the topic and supervises the content. He has given me a multitude of talents—talents I cannot contribute to a classroom setting or scholar of teaching other than that of Jesus Christ Himself. Society and those in position of power or authority would have me believe that I need to obtain a degree that identifies me as being knowledgeable in a certain area before I am allowed to perform and receive compensation or recognition for a specific skill or task. But God has revealed a God-given talent in which the reward is much greater than any compensation man would be willing to grant me. I do not need to be qualified as a pastor or minister by man to preach the gospel and evangelize on behalf of God. I'm simply a child of God being led by the Holy Spirit!

The Spirit of the Lord God is upon me, Because the Lord has anointed and commissioned me To bring good news to the humble and afflicted; He has sent me to bind up [the wounds of] the brokenhearted, To proclaim release [from confinement and condemnation] to the [physical and spiritual] captives And freedom to prisoners, To proclaim the favorable year of the Lord, And the day of vengeance and retribution of our God, To comfort all who mourn, To grant to those who mourn in Zion the following: To give them a turban instead of dust [on their heads, a sign of mourning], The oil of joy instead of mourning, The garment [expressive] of praise instead of a disheartened spirit. So they will be called the trees of righteousness [strong and magnificent, distinguished for integrity, justice, and right standing with God], The planting of the Lord, that He may be glorified.

~ Isaiah 61:1-3 AMP

And He gave some, apostles; and some, prophets; and some, evangelists; and some, pastors and teachers.

~ Ephesians 4:11

If you denounce the existence of the Holy Sprit, then you denounce the existence of Jesus Christ, the Son. And if you denounce Him, you denounce the presence of God! You cannot and should not, if you are a true Christian, acknowledge one and not the other! You cannot camouflage it forever. At some point, you have to deal with God. It is He who is angry. He not only feels my pain but the pain of many countless others who are and have found themselves to be where I am today. And I am most grateful to Him from which my strength comes as well as the opportunity to serve Him. Through God, my wounds are being healed. *And he said, Ab'ba, Father, all things are possible unto thee; take away this cup from me: nevertheless not what I will, but what thou wilt* (Mark 14:36).

STANDARD(S)[52]

[1]An acknowledged measure of comparison for quantitative or qualitative value; criterion; norm.
[2]A degree or level of requirement, excellence or attainment.
[3]A requirement of moral conduct.

In attempting to lower my standards just to fit in according to the standards of society or the majority, I find I have allowed myself in the past to be taken advantage of by those in my personal life and workplace who wish to control me by any

---

52 http://www.thefreedictionary.com/standard

means necessary through abuse, racism, discrimination and many other prejudices or hang ups that man possesses. Friends and those who truly know me have often told me I may never get married and be forever single unless I am willing to lower my standards; no one may be able to measure up to the high standards I have set for myself, which is why I am harder on myself than others are on me—including God. And it is He, God, who keeps reminding me to not be so hard on myself! My standards and desire is to be loved by others as they love themselves and anything less, including a double standard (us, them, me and not all), is unChrist-like! The truth is the truth! And ye shall know the truth, and the truth shall make you free (John 8:32). It should not be watered down or sugarcoated. Are you familiar with the phrase, "things that hurt instruct"?

JUSTICE[53]

1) Fairness *or fair handling*, 2) moral rightness *or impartiality*, 3) a scheme or system of law in which every person receives his or her due from the system, including all rights, both natural and legal; *due reward or treatment*.

- **Social Justice**[54] – The fair and proper administration of laws conforming to the natural law that all persons, irrespective of ethnic origin, gender, possessions, race, religion, etc., are to be treated equally and without prejudice. (Also think in terms of civil rights.)

---

53   http://legal-dictionary.thefreedictionary.com/justice
54   http://www.businessdictionary.com/definition/social-justice.html

> Taking on the ever-changing meaning of just and fair as it relates to a society, thus becoming impartial, because it does not take into consideration *all* instead of only what is significant to the power base. It is, generally, thought of as a society that affords or voids individuals and groups fair treatment and a just share of the pie (benefits). Benefits not in equal size of that which is extended or enjoyed by the majority.

- **Society**[55] - A group of human beings broadly distinguished from other groups by mutual interest, participation in characteristic relationships, shared institutions and a common culture. (There's that word again—culture!)

The Politics of It All

In today's society, politics has a big role in how things are done, and unfortunately, the truth is never handled in a direct, head-on fashion. The truth is normally swept under the rug as it is diffused for damage control while things continue in the same direction with no thought ever being given to the truth to implement change. Most people are comfortable living in the dark because that is much easier than dealing with the truth or confronting it directly; so normally, they give up trying or give in.

---

55 *Webster's II New College Dictionary*, Houghton Mifflin Company, 2001, 1999, 1995; p. 1047

This is the basis for the repeat of history—the shifting of or reverting back to the past, which is why there seems to be a high increase in religious wars and hate crimes fueled by discrimination, prejudices and racism. People are allowing their false beliefs to dictate their character and call it truth. Why is it hard to believe that the information you were once fed as truth is far from the truth. And for some reason we have stopped seeking to know what is truth. So now we enter into a time where there is a great divide.

How can we continue to strip one another of dignity and self-respect while compromising our integrity and call it truth? Then we masquerade that false truth by covering it up and calling it politics as we take advantage of the poor or less fortunate. We rig elections and appoint people into office, not based on their character or moral code for considering all of humanity but based on a select few who feel they have the right to not only be in power but decide on the distribution of wealth not considering all of humanity. I view that as a sign of greed and corruption in high places.

Even so hath the LORD ordained
that they which preach the gospel should live of the gospel.

~ 1 Corinthians 9:14

As the stage is set by the rulers of this world, religion seems to position itself next in line. Where is the separation of church and state? Does a separation still exist? It is getting much harder each season to distinguish between the two. Church leaders sell their soul by getting involved in politics in a less-than-Christ-like way, and the faces begin to look all the same. So what about "in the world, not of the world?" That begins to look even more confusing to those who are seeking truth.

> *As ministers of the gospel, we are not dishonest; we don't play church politics or falsify the word of God to please others. We recommend ourselves and our ministry to everyone's conscience by practicing the truth as if we were in the actual presence of God.*
>
> ~ 2 Corinthians 4:2

> *Many pastors have destroyed my vineyard,*
> *they have trodden my portion under foot,*
> *they have made my pleasant portion a late wilderness.*
>
> ~ Jeremiah 12:10

Faith-Based Initiative

In 1996, Congress passed a welfare reform legislation, Charitable Choice, that permitted religious groups who assisted and counseled welfare recipients (and made their religious message an integral part of their work) to receive government funding. During President Bush's term, he endorsed and campaigned for something called the "faith-based initiative." A number of political and social leaders turned toward religious or "faith-based" organizations to assist or even take over the administration of social welfare functions that were previously handled by the government, including but not limited to welfare benefits, prison reform, and drug and alcohol treatment. Al

Gore and Bush both endorsed Charitable Choice and argued for its expansion to other religious groups that worked with the homeless or troubled youth. (The Salvation Army is President Bush's largest religious organization/faith-based supporter.)

The benefits of being identified as a faith-based organization: A participating faith-based organization retains its independence from government, including control over the definition, development, practice and expression of its religious beliefs. The government cannot require a religious organization to alter its form of internal governance or remove religious art, icons or symbols to be eligible to participate. A religious organization may consider religious beliefs and practices in their employment decisions.[56] Under the faith-based initiative or classification, as it was originally written, **Religious institutions are exempt from the nondiscrimination requirements of Title VII and other anti-discrimination laws.** You would have to read the Executive Order #13279[57] and the House Bill #1054 to see how I came up with that conclusion.

---

56   The Salvation Army began in 1865. The first female general was Booth's daughter, Evangeline Booth, serving from 1934 to 1939. Eva Burrows was the second female general in 1986. Few blacks have served as the top officials of majority white U.S. religious bodies, including The Salvation Army. The Salvation Army appointed a black leader for its U.S. operations on May 12, 2006, which was the first time a black church official has led the predominantly white, evangelical denomination in this country. Politics? Things that make you go hmmm!

57   Executive Order 13279; https://www.gpo.gov/fdsys/pkg/FR-2002-12-16/pdf/02-31831.pdf and https://www.congress.gov/bill/109th-congress/house-bill/1054/text.

On October 12, 2007, day two of the Malachi 3:1 Ministries conference I attended, Elder Ronna Matthews talked about culture and how the world changes according to whoever is in charge. **Culture affects the tone of an atmosphere.** You cannot limit the spirit or box God in, but it's amazing to see how easy it is for people or an organization to attempt to limit your growth based on culture. It is also unbelievable to see and think that a body of Christ, an army that has confessed to believe and wishes to work for and with God in fulfilling His will to reach others as an operating symbol of the church, is so divided that only a few acknowledge and know the Holy Spirit (Ghost). My prayer and desire is that all within and throughout The Salvation Army who truly seek God and wish to know Him be allowed to experience that part of Him, the Son and the Holy Spirit that dwells within each of us and that they be given the opportunity to worship Him freely with no limitation on the Spirit. Oh dear God, Your presence is needed in a very mighty way.

> *Culture is always a collective phenomenon; it is at least partly shared with people who live or have lived within the same social environment. In other words, it derives from one's social environment, not from one's genes. Culture is learned, not inherited! It can be viewed as a programming of the mind that distinguishes the members of one group or category of people from another. Culture should be distinguished from human nature on one side and from an individual's personality on the other.*
>
> ~ Based on Geert Hofstede's Model of Culture[58]

---

58   http://scholarworks.gvsu.edu/cgi/viewcontent. cgi?article=1014&context=orpc

Doubt Not Your Faith!

Waking one morning on October 6, 2007, I heard God say, "Doubt not your faith!" In retrospect, I was feeling a little distraught about my experiences within The Salvation Army National Headquarters for the past seven years, most specifically with their teachings and how it must have and has affected others. *For it is commendable if a man bears up under the pain of unjust suffering because he is conscious of God* (1 Peter 2:19). I remember thinking about the importance of being familiar with the organizational culture of an establishment for a clearer understanding of that working environment. Where did I hear the term *organizational culture* before? And why was it so important for me to make the connection? In remembering my degree that God made possible for me to obtain in Business Management, which the Salvation Army World Service Office refuses to acknowledge I have, God also brought to my mind a course I had the pleasure of taking, entitled Organizational Theory, Behavior and Management. Unfortunately, if a person does not seek to know God personally for him or herself, there seems to be an underlying organizational culture within The Salvation Army that could be instrumental in causing one to doubt their faith; especially those who find that they are or have been treated unfairly or unjustly by Christian folks within a "church" and unfortunately fall into a trap by the enemy in which you not only doubt your faith, but you refuse to trust God or rely on Him for guidance and understanding (answers) through these most important times. Father God, let thy will be done on earth as it is in Heaven and bring about peace and insurmountable knowledge and wisdom to those who have been easily confused by what they see, have seen and feel as well as felt through what could be considered to be a false teaching about what it really means to worship and seek You. More awareness should be given to how actions discount belief, especially when it is done in the name of Jesus Christ and teaches to reinforce His false character.

> *Fight the good fight of faith, lay hold on eternal life,*
> *whereunto thou art also called,*
> *and hast professed a good profession before many witnesses.*
>
> ~ 1 Timothy 6:12

Reporting to The Salvation Army for orientation on August 21, 2000, I was given a document to sign that stated the following: "I am signing this document acknowledging that where I work is a church and I will conduct myself accordingly." Because I tend to take each thing that is ever said or done literally, I began to question whether or not The Salvation Army is truly a church or operating under the premise of an illusion reinforced by a lot of religious dogma and double standards. So I decided I would begin to seek God more! Ask and you shall receive, said the Lord.

Historical Background

Growing up, my mother always told my sister and I that we would never have anything to worry about if we lived our lives according to the Ten Commandments and went to school and received good grades. She also said those good grades would give us the opportunity to get a good job to aid us in excelling in whatever career we chose. Unfortunately, she never told us you could do all these things and still be met by opposition and obstacles designed to keep you from succeeding in ways you thought possible. Therefore, it was extremely hard to believe that you did not have to do anything to anyone to direct physical pain toward them for them to inflict pain upon you. Just being who you are is enough for some people to attempt to impose their will upon you through their false beliefs they hold as truth.

Being victimized, persecuted or made to look like a villain in the eyes of others is never easy to accept or deal with unless you are an individual who enjoys pain (a masochist). So I often found it hard to forgive those who had deliberately hurt me for no sound reason other than the color of my skin, appearance or gender. Pain inflicted upon you by an organization as a tactic of control to bring about a sense of conformance is an example of the impact of culture within a working environment. The invisible scars developed over the years through hurt and pain from others left me feeling numb and doubtful. I was stripped of my integrity, dignity and self-respect while being left to feel useless and inferior to the person causing the pain. Watching others going through the same thing was even more painful.

My Assignment: Today, my assignment from God is much clearer.

> *O Lord, rebuke me not in thine anger, neither chasten me in thy hot displeasure. Have mercy upon me, O Lord; for I am weak: O Lord, heal me; for my bones are vexed. My soul is also sore vexed; but thou, O Lord, how long? Return, O Lord, deliver my soul: oh save me for thy mercies' sake. For*

in death there is no remembrance of thee: in the gave who shall give thee thanks? I am weary with my groaning; all the night make I my bed to swim; I water my couch with my tears. Mine eye is consumed because of grief; it waxeth old because of all mine enemies. Depart from me, all ye workers of iniquity; for the Lord hath heard the voice of my weeping. The Lord hath heard my supplication; the Lord will receive my prayer. Let all mine enemies be ashamed and sore vexed: let them return and be ashamed suddenly.

~Psalm 6:1-10

Oh let the wickedness of the wicked come to an end; but establish the just: for the righteous God trieth the hearts and reins. My defence is of God, which saveth the upright heart. God judgeth the righteous, and God is angry with the wicked every day.

~ Psalm 7:9-11

MESSENGERS OF GOD

I know thy works, and thy labour, and thy patience, and how thou canst not bear them which are evil: and thou hast tried them which say they are apostles, and are not and hast found them liars:

~ **Revelation 2:2**

August 13, 2008

Many months after my departure from The Salvation Army, I still tried to make sense of their deceptive nature. I found it hard to believe a religious (proclaimed to be Christian) organization could be so negative and hypocritical. *Having a form of godliness, but denying the power thereof: from such turn away* (2 Timothy 3:13). Upon preparing for work and leaving the house for the train station, my mind was consumed with thoughts. With that experience still weighing heavily on my mind, I found myself replaying events of certain situations in my head over and over again. I just could not believe that such an organization of people would risk defying God by their actions and think that they could possibly escape going to Hell if they continued on such a path of iniquity. How could they serve two masters and call themselves Christians?

> *And hast borne and hast patience,*
> *and for my name's sake has laboured and has not fainted.*
> *Nevertheless I have somewhat against thee,*
> *because thou hast left thy first love.*
>
> ~ Revelation 2:3-4

I could feel the pain in my heart; however, I noticed there was something else as well. There was a sense of joy and peace in seeking to understand my existence as well as the purpose of God in allowing me to experience what I did while working at The Salvation Army. Approaching the platform of the train station to take that journey to my new place of employment, I was greeted by a young lady who commented on my hat. As we started to talk a little more, she said something that was very interesting. She indicated she had noted a change in the energy of the atmosphere in 1984. In fact, it was so overwhelming to her spirit that she was determined to leave the Washington, D.C., area and relocate to Houston, Texas, to continue her career path. Putting her plan in action, she actually left but later returned to the D.C. area in 2003, at which time she noticed the presence of that energy not only still existed, but it had increased to a higher level of intensity.

Remember therefore from whence thou art fallen,
and repent and do the first works;
Or else I will come unto thee quickly,
and will remove thy candlestick out of his place,
except thou repent.

~ Revelation 2:5

If you are spiritually aware of your surroundings and tuned in to God, you would be amazed about what is revealed to you. It is like having an interpersonal radar system that prepares you for what is to come, so you'll be better equipped to deal with it. The more we talked, the more we shared information and I noted God was allowing His children to enlighten one another about what they had observed. God, knowing I was seeking to understand more about Him, orchestrated a chance meeting with a woman who could steer me in the right direction for answers. In sharing her experience as a pastor's wife, I shared my experience of working for a religious organization that could have destroyed me spiritually by pushing in a direction away from God rather than toward God. Intrigued by my encounter with this woman, I found it extremely hard to discontinue our conversation when I arrived at my stop. In fact, I rode past my stop to two more stops before getting off the train to double back to my destination, but not before she asked if I had the word with me. I pulled out my Bible and she proceeded to point something out to me in Revelations 2:6. It was the word *Nicolaitans*. She told me to research that word and to make sure I included it as a part of my next topic.

> *But this thou hast,*
> *that thou hatest the deeds of the Nicolaitanes,*
> *which I also hate.*
>
> ~ Revelation 2:6

Wow, God sends us messages at the most unexpected times from the most unexpected people. When I am puzzled and am in need of understanding, He sends me a message from Heaven to enlighten me. God is awesome indeed! He helped me to understand why I was viewed as being a religious fanatic by some and thought to have had a nervous breakdown by others when I experienced the **quickening** of the **Holy Spirit** (Ephesians 2:1-5) during the reading of a prayer and scripture that was being presented by a coworker prior to the beginning of a Salvation Army World Service Office core meeting (also noted or referred to as their annual retreat.) Had they themselves possessed the right spirit, they would have recognized and welcomed the visitation from God. *Thou hast granted me life and favour, and thy visitation hath preserved my spirit* (Job 10:12).

Revelation 2:6 - Ephesus – Nicolaitans[59]

Nicolaitans = *nicáo* (to conquer) + *láos* (people)

Nicolaitans: anyone with a dominating and manipulating spirit. They seek to influence and control others in very subtle ways, including using intimidation. They have been known to use

---

59 http://www.spiritandtruth.org/teaching/Book_of_Revelation/14_Revelation_2_1-11/webshow/index.htm?16

religion and events or major, life-changing causes to pressure people into movements. Hate the deeds: **God hates the evil deeds and false** doctrine (Revelation 2:13). **We must separate hatred for the sin from hatred for the sinner. Believers are to have no fellowship with unfruitful works and expose them** (Ephesians 5:11; 2 John 1:9).

- Nicolaitans: **Teachings may be related by association to Balaam** (Revelation 2:14-15).

1. An early cult that followed or perverted the teachings of Nicolas (Acts 6:5).
2. Denotes a group who taught an unnatural distinction between clergy and laity.

- **Laity:** the ordinary people who are involved **with a** church but who do not hold official religious positions[60] (and thought to be untrained).[61]

---

60 http://dictionary.cambridge.org/us/dictionary/english/laity
61 http://www.todayifoundout.com/index.php/2012/02/origin-of-the-term-layman/

THE GRACE OF GOD
GRACE IS ACTIVE AND MEANS FAVOR! GRACE IS POWER!

For I say, through the grace given unto me, to every man that is among you, not to think of himself more highly than he ought to think; but to think soberly, according as God hath dealt to every man the measure of faith.

~ Romans 12:3

This testimony is in no way meant to condemn or belittle the accomplishments of The Salvation Army; that is not how God operates. *But as we were allowed of God to be put in trust with the gospel, even so we speak; not as pleasing men, but God, which trieth our hearts* (Thessalonians 2:4). He uses people, places, things and situations to discipline us through love and truth by allowing things to happen that incite change. *But all things that are reproved (exposed) are made manifest by the light: for whatsoever doth make manifest is light* (Ephesians 5:13). We can adhere to His teaching and make a conscious effort to reposition ourselves, or we can continue to spiral out of control away from God's purpose for our life or the path He has intended for us. But it is your choice; *for them that honour me I will honour, and they that despise me shall be lightly esteemed* (1 Samuel 2:30)!

October 1, 2008

Toxic Environments

Toxicity is not limited to a poison chemical, fume or gas that invades the body or an environment through the atmosphere. A toxic environment can be one that is consumed by evil and unrighteous works whereby negative energy is released into the atmosphere thus having the ability to contaminate the spirit of others. Have you ever entered a room and sensed evil or knew within your spirit that the environment you just entered was not conducive to your health? Can you imagine an environment so toxic that it not only suffocates you, it alters your character or changes your way of thinking to mirror the negativity that surrounds you? If you are not careful and know not from where your strength lies, the kind, loving, Christ-like character you once possessed before entering such an environment can cause you to conduct yourself outside of the will of God to fit in and to be accepted. Such darkness can devour you and weaken your spirit while subjecting you to a slow spiritual death. *God is light and in Him there is no darkness at all* (1 John 1:5)! The spirit you allow yourself to entertain is the spirit to which you give power and control over your life, and you release it on others. Did you know your attitude can influence or alter the energy in an environment? Any environment that poses a threat to your spirit can prove to be very detrimental to your mental, physical and spiritual health.

> *Grace be to you and peace from the Father,*
> *and from our Lord Jesus Christ.*
> *Who gave himself for our sins,*
> *that he might deliver us from this present evil world*
> *according to the will of God and our Father.*
> *To whom be glory for ever and ever.*
> *Amen.*
>
> ~ Galatians 1:3-5

As I encounter negativity, the more likely I am to retreat. I feel the need to decompress and rid (cleanse) myself of it and pray the invasion does no real damage to my soul. The greater the adversity, the greater my desire to limit my association with those within that environment. Have you ever been in the presence of an individual whose spirit was so grotesque that it left you feeling weak and drained of all your energy? Have you ever left a particular environment or encountered certain people that, upon your departure from their presence or that atmosphere, all you wanted to do was retreat to a place of rest? At the end of the day, you are left feeling mentally drained or depressed and have no idea as to why. You may even notice an increasing amount of headaches. A similarly environmentally hazardous situation cannot only diminish your physical health; it can possibly even induce a stroke. Like breathing in toxins that fill up the lungs and get dispersed to other parts of the body causing illness, being exposed to negative spirits day in and day out that surround you in darkness threatens to absorb your light as it diminishes your soul; you become engulfed with sickness, which then leads to death. *For thou hath delivered my soul from death: wilt not thou deliver my feet from falling, that I may walk before God in the light of the living?* (Psalm 56:13) *And we all, with unveiled face, continually seeing as in a mirror the glory of the Lord, are progressively being transformed into His image from [one degree of] glory to [even more] glory, which comes from the Lord, [who is] the Spirit* (2 Corinthians 3:18 AMP).

From Glory to Glory; New Devil, New Level

Making assumptions about those who proclaimed to love God left me open and ill-prepared for having to be aware of spiritual warfare with other Christians. Oftentimes, that which we do not expect to exist or experience in certain environments may become a reality. And unfortunately, you may find yourself having to deal with those issues beyond your belief on a daily basis. However, the outcome is always up to you! You can fall prey to humanism (having more faith in man's ability than having faith in God's ability) whereby you choose to handle the situation on your own, or you can ask God for help. Confused by what others wanted me to believe in correlation to what I misunderstood about God as well as myself, I did not have enough faith, confidence or trust in God to believe He could help me. Over the years, in viewing my surroundings, I began to lose hope. It seemed those without integrity were always winning and getting ahead while those who struggled to do the right thing were losing the battle and falling further behind. Asking for the ability to discern, through the activation and manifestation of the Holy Spirit, I have been allowed to see more clearly.

> *Ask and it will be given you; seek, and you will find;*
> *knock and it shall be opened onto you.*
> *For everyone that asketh receiveth;*
> *and he that seeketh findeth;*
> *and to him that knocketh it shall be opened.*
>
> ~ Matthew 7:7-8

Satan (aka Lucifer, the ruler of darkness who was once considered to be the angel of light in Heaven before he allowed himself to be consumed by pride and went against God) does not discriminate against whom he is willing to use to defy God. I have come to learn that there are many religious people in the world who attend church and go through the motions on the outside but lack Jesus in their hearts. That is why it is so easy for them to do what is wrong rather than for them to do what is right. And they will attempt to justify their actions according to their own understanding and reasoning regardless of the word of God. God's love cannot and should not be used as an excuse to operate in perversion. There is truly a difference between just going to church or fellowshipping with others and having a relationship with God. For quite some time, I believed we were all God's children. Today, I now know and understand we were all created by Him; in spite of this, we are, by far, all children of God. Just as God knows His children, Satan knows his as well. An ordained minister may give the illusion that He is a man of God on the outside, but the darkness of his heart and the example of his fruit will truly reveal his spirit. *As a man thinketh, so is he in his heart!* It is possible for a wolf to hide amongst sheep. Therefore, it is most important for you to be vigilant and sober at all times and be prepared for spiritual warfare—even in the church. Just as equally important, you need to know that those who claim to know God do not necessarily have a relationship with Him *at all*.

> *Beware of false prophets,*
> *which come to you in sheep's clothing,*
> *but inwardly they are ravening wolves.*
> *Ye shall know them by their fruits.*
> *Do men gather grapes of thorns, or figs of thistles?*
>
> ~ Matthew 7:15-16

Envision being so ecstatic, to the say the least, about receiving an offer of employment from an establishment or business you not only recognized as being a leading Christian organization in the United States, but you were allowed to recollect a favorable childhood memory that brought joy to your heart and peace to your mind whenever your subconscious released it. Falling to my knees, I thanked God for giving me the opportunity to be reunited with the church that gave me refuge so long ago. Most evenings after school, I would retreat to the Salvation Army Corps in my neighborhood for assistance with my homework or just to hang out in a comforting and nurturing environment. The culture of The Salvation Army at that time is nothing like the culture I was allowed to witness for the seven years of my employment with them. Therefore, reporting to work for the second day, I felt I had gone back in time to a culture with overbearing, chauvinistic men who regarded women as being second-class citizens with no voice. Were they not aware of the energy that such an environment could create? The environment disturbed me and grieved me the most as I noticed the blatant racism and prejudiced attitudes with oppressive tendencies throughout the National Headquarters. So there I was, feeling depressed, hurt and trapped in a building that is viewed or labeled as being a church to the outside world and giving the illusion that those who operate it are sincere and committed to upholding God's covenant. The major difference is, they operated more in accordance to the standards *of* the world than they did *outside* of the world (in accordance to the word of God). *Love not the world, neither the things that are in the world. If any man love the world, the love of the Father is not in him* (1 John 2:15). When you are given the opportunity to be a part of what you consider to be the mandate of God, your involvement or association on an intimate or personal level with that church not only exposes you to the people responsible for the church's development and growth, your spirit man (The Holy Spirit) awakens you to the truth surrounding you.

I will instruct thee
and teach thee in the way which thou shalt go:
I will guide thee with mine eye.

~ Psalm 32:8

The Salvation Army is a non-profit, religious organization or church that is moving more in the direction of being the largest philanthropic organization in the United States and abroad. During an employee's initial day and orientation, they are presented with a document that states, "I am signing this document acknowledging that where I work is a church and I will conduct myself accordingly." Nonetheless, the weekly Wednesday morning chapel services were considered to be non-mandatory and rightfully so. My employment with The Salvation Army National Headquarters began seven to eight years ago in August of 2000 in the Human Resources Department. In January of 2003, I accepted a position with the Salvation Army World Service Office (SAWSO)[62] still within the building of the National Headquarters. However, different in the manner of business, The Salvation Army's culture is merely the same, whether it falls under the leadership of the eastern, western, central or southern territory, though they are politically registered as a 501(c)3 organization. Under the guidelines of one jurisdiction to the next, the laws governing the 501(c)3 incorporation are indeed the same, thereby giving The Salvation Army as a whole, exemption from federal income tax with the possibility of being further determined not to be a private foundation within the meaning of section 509(a) of the same Internal Revenue Code. Such a 501(c)3 registry also affords The Salvation Army exemption from abiding by certain federal laws like discrimination. According to the terminology of a Salvationist-born employee (a person who has taken an oath to follow The Salvation Army doctrine), whose intent was to enlighten me about the division as I witnessed it, this was not considered to be discrimination on the basis of race but on

---

62   https://sawso.org/sawso/history_of_blessing

the basis of class, thus attempting to justify it in making it more acceptable as opposed to being unlawful.

> *Knowing that a man is not justified by the works of the law, but by the faith of Jesus Christ, even we have believed in Jesus Christ, that we might be justified by the faith of Christ, and not by the works of the law: for by the works of the law shall no flesh be justified.*
>
> ~ Galatians 2:16

A person who is operating under the influence of negative spirits (demons) does not necessarily limit his attacks to just one person or group; there is no rhyme or reason that makes absolute sense as to who he will choose as his next prey or victim. In other words, there is no such thing as loyalty as far as he is concerned. Though you may not be the target of his abuse or rage initially, as you team up or become allies with him, you allow yourself to be used to oppress others. When you have successfully succeeded at helping him with his personal agenda, it is just a matter of time before he turns on you, making you next on the list to receive his wrath. This is what I call selling your soul to the devil. You, without hesitation or doubt, joined forces with another in doing what you knew to be wrong, but you participated anyway.

With toxic leaders at the helm playing god, abusing power and worshiping false idols, exemption from federal laws gives them the protection under the government to break these laws at will, with no justice to those who find themselves being victimized. Though you would assume an organization that was initially started in 1865 in accordance to the vision of one man, William Booth, as a result of his love for the Lord, would have no need to be held accountable for social ethics or responsibility to the people by the government. On the contrary, The Salvation Army is protected by the government, which allows them to exercise unfairness time and time again. It is apparent the government did not take into consideration the possibility of such abuse under its protection prior to putting such a law into action. Or did it? This is, in essence, an example of a reason for our declining economy today. Laws are written to enable corporations to prosper illegally while people, mostly the poor or less fortunate, suffer through exploitation.

> *He that committeth sin is of the devil;*
> *for the devil sinneth from the beginning.*
> *For this purpose the Son of God was manifested,*
> *that he might destroy the works of the devil.*
>
> ~ 1 John 3:8

After learning more about The Salvation Army in accordance to what I was allowed to see from the inside, the less I wanted to know. Given the hierarchy structure (or chain of command) of the Salvation Army, which mirrors the hierarchy of the military, officers of The Salvation Army are rotated from one post to another within as well as outside of the United States. Therefore, I find it extremely hard to believe that those at the top have no knowledge of the unfair, immoral and unethical business practices that take place at various locations throughout The Salvation Army. For example, I found it hard to believe that the high-ranking military officers had no prior knowledge of the abuse at Abu Ghraib. Do you really believe that the soldiers—who were blamed and sentenced for such an incident and conducted themselves in such an undignified manner and degraded their humanity as well as those they abused at Abu Ghraib—would have taken the chance of jeopardizing their careers by photographing the injustices they committed toward others without the blessing of those who commanded them? In such a dictatorship-structured environment, if the person at the top is not in their right mind, it is possible for him to be ruled by his flesh in how he commands his post.

> *Whosoever is born of God doth no commit sin;*
> *for his seed remaineth in him:*
> *And he cannot sin, because he is born of God.*
>
> ~ 1 John 3:9

Being influenced by the wrong spirit or controlled by the wrong character in a position of power and authority, without having a strong constitution (exercising self-control, self-restraint and self-discipline) or being mature enough to handle the responsibility of the position, regardless of the situation, has caused many to abuse that power. Those who are driven by power and abuse may see themselves as God; however, they do not conduct themselves in accordance to the character of Christ (God) but to the anti-Christ. This unfortunate behavior becomes the norm that sets the stage or culture for the environment and trickles downward. Some are able to resist the urge to follow suit through the renewing of their minds, but others may be too weak to resist, thus becoming more like those they fought so hard not to emulate. The disparaging treatment funnels downward and all around. My heart goes out to those Salvation Army officers who genuinely love the Lord and have made a sacrifice and a commitment to upholding the will of God. They find themselves in an extremely difficult situation, considering their investment of time, that now binds them to The Salvation Army as a way of life until retirement, thus subjecting them to the officers who have put satisfying their flesh above God's laws as a way of life.

> *I marvel that ye are so soon removed from Him*
> *that called you into the grace of Christ unto another gospel:*
> *Which is not another, but there be some*
> *that trouble you and would pervert the gospel of Christ.*
>
> ~ Galatians 1:6-7

When money changes hands, the value is always the same regardless of who handles it. Money gives you undue power and control. Depending upon your values, it can drive you to operate outside of the will of God. Those who crave it will do all within their power to obtain it, manipulate it and use it for their own selfish gain. To deceive you into thinking they have good intentions in applying it accordingly, they will redirect just enough of it to convince you they are sincere.

In a world full of hate that has been centered on racism and discrimination for far too long, minorities or those who practice other religions do not have to be liked or respected to be employed by The Salvation Army or any organization for that matter that honors a similar culture. They are merely needed and used as a visible and identifiable object or tool (marketing strategy) to attract or target the corresponding population for the purpose of receiving donations. Given my experience with racism, the absence of diversity within an organization would display the nature of that organization's culture or view of exclusion. However, should I see people within an organization who I am able to identify with, I am more likely to believe the organization promotes a hiring practice that is void of discrimination and welcomes diversity. I myself found it difficult and painful to believe that such a reputable religious organization that claims to love God would love money more and despise me even more while subjecting me to double standards in the name of the Lord.

> *He therefore that despiseth, despiseth not man,*
> *but God, who hath also given unto us his Holy Spirit.*
> *But as touching brotherly love ye need no that I write unto*
> *you: for ye yourselves are taught of God to love one another.*
> *And indeed ye do it toward all the brethren which*
> *are in all of Macedonia: But we beseech you,*
> *brethren, that ye increase more and more.*
>
> ~ 1 Thessalonians 4:8-10

During a meeting, a current Salvation Army minister stated what motivated his decision to join The Salvation Army. Unfortunately, it had nothing to do with a spiritual commitment or love for God. He was motivated by his flesh—a desire to pursue a woman who was a part of The Salvation Army who had since become his wife. Because his love for God was missing prior to him joining The Salvation Army, his foundation as a Christian was also lacking. This world government has put laws in place that exempt churches from certain laws but legally classifies the church as a business; therefore, man sees it as a way of life for obtaining status. But those who truly love the Lord take God's business seriously. And there is a very distinct difference between *choosing to serve* God as opposed to *being chosen by* God. However, both require you to be equally willing to commit your life to the perfect will of God in developing a relationship with Him. Developing and cultivating a relationship with God connects you to the heart of God, thus enabling you to see His truth more clearly. When you are chosen by God, you are called to action. It is not about being passive; it's about hearing the cry for souls and acting upon that call to direct those souls to God; not away from God. Upon choosing to serve God, you need to make sure you come with the right intentions, the right motives and be willing, ready and able to resist the temptations of the devil. There is no time to play or to be pretentious in any area of your life. What's your mission? Serving God, your flesh or man?

Or do I seek to please men?
For If I yet pleased men,
I should not be the servant of Christ.

~ Galatians 1:10

LAUGHTER IS GOOD FOR THE SOUL

October 7, 2008

Sharing my adventure:

Attempting to help a fellow coworker, but also anxious to leave work for the day (on Monday, October 6, 2008), I turned to run back to the office to get her some water for her to take her medicine. Down I went! My heel of my left shoe slid against the wet floor as if I was deliberately trying to do a split—something I have never been able to do even if I wanted to. My keys went one way while my purse went another. As I hit the floor, all I could think about was, "Why wasn't I limber?" Experiencing some pain, but not much, I laughed. What a sight! As my coworker and another acquaintance came to my rescue, I asked them to let me lay there for a while—just long enough to regain my composure and let any pain settle! Besides, can you imagine a seventy-year-old woman and a woman in a scooter trying to pick me up off of the floor?

What was even funnier was the coworker I was attempting to help made a mad dash for the elevator as I was still trying to pick myself up because she needed to catch the last train. She yelled down the hallway, "I am so sorry Ann! Are you sure you are all right? I need to try to catch my last train." I laughed even more. As I made it to the first floor to exit the building, I could see a little silhouette of her shadow and her scooter as she kept turning around to make sure I was well on my way. I'm actually glad she did not miss her last train.

At the end of a busy day, we all need laughter. However, it would be nice if it was not at my expense. Nonetheless, if I can't laugh at myself, then who can I laugh at? Why do we go through life being so uptight about everything? We can be serious and still have fun. For some reason, we have truly forgotten how to live.

As I move today, feeling some reminder of my incident, I laugh to myself between the pain! For the most part, I'm okay.

Loving life,
Ann

BE MINDFUL OF WHAT YOU ASK

October 15, 2008

On this day, God brought to my remembrance an incident that took place the Sunday before Thanksgiving in 1996; to be exact, it was November 24, 1996. I went to church and attended every service that day. Have you ever had one of those moments in life where nothing seemed to be working no matter what you did right? The more I attempted to work things out, the worse they seemed to get. My spirits were low, and I was feeling lost and forgotten by God.

Needing a word from God, I started out early to attend the 8:00 a.m. service. After service was over, I didn't feel any better, so I opted to stay for the 11:00 a.m. service. Trying to fill up on the Holy Ghost, I even opted to stay after the 11:00 a.m. service for the afternoon service. Finally, at about 3:30 p.m. or 4:00 p.m., a surge of energy swept through my body and lifted my spirits.

On the way home, I remembered receiving a call from my mother who had not heard from me in a week. Her message stated, "Gwen, where are you? Are you okay? If you don't drop by, I would normally at least hear from you by phone. Call your mother! Let me know you're okay!" I decided to visit my mother, but upon arriving at her house, I didn't see her car in the parking lot. At any rate, I thought I would let myself in with my key and leave her a note. As I entered her apartment, I noticed how quiet it was and thought how appropriate it would be to pray.

Kneeling and engaging in prayer and conversation with God, I became overwhelmed. I began to cry and asked God why wasn't He hearing me or answering my prayers. "Did I do something that displeased You? Are you there? Can You at least drop something out of the sky and hit me on the head so I know You're there? I don't understand! I just need a sign from You!" Pulling myself together, I realized I still had not written the note to my mother. In a brief note, I wrote, "Mom, I got your message. I came by to say hello and to let you know I was okay."

Exiting my mother's building, I noted my car was not where I had parked it. That was one more thing to add to my mood to bring me down some more. Who would steal my old, beat-up car? I started running around in circles acting like a crazy person. I started shouting and murmuring to myself. Oh God, not my car! Boy was I angry.

Because I didn't live far, I decided I would walk home. And then it hit me! Where is my purse? I had left my purse in the car with my keys and identification. My mother told me to stop leaving my purse in the car. Now, I have to hear her tell me she told me so. Thinking all sorts of things, I ran home, screaming and shouting some more. There better not be anybody in my apartment! Satan, I am tired of you messing with me. If it's a fight you want, then it's a fight you'll get.

Can you imagine calling Satan out to a fight? What was on my mind? How was I going to get in my apartment with no keys? By the time I reached my apartment, I was out of breath. And then I heard a small voice say, "Look in your pocket. Your door keys are there!" Oh yea! Still freaking out as I approached the door of my apartment, I had decided I was going to look for my car. For some reason, calling the police had slipped my mind. I changed my clothes, put on a pair of tennis shoes and grabbed the metal bar to my weights to use as a weapon to defend myself (if needed). As I crossed Suitland Parkway, a car approached me. It was my mother.

My mother:	Girl, what are you doing running down the parkway? What is wrong with you?
Me:	Mom, they stole my car.
My mother:	And what are you planning to do? Why are you running through the street like a mad woman? Lord, I have some crazy kids. Did you call the police? You didn't pay much for the car at all. You might even get more than what you paid for it and be able to get something better.
Me:	I didn't think about that. I'm just angry. I was already feeling down. I haven't had the car that long. I'm just getting back on my feet.

My mother:	And? At least you have feet! Girl, I'm taking you to the house to call the police. You should have reported the car stolen as soon as you noticed it was gone.

By the time I arrived at my mother's, I was calm. However, after having to call the police at least five times before someone took me seriously enough to send a scout car for a written report, I was mad all over again. On my fifth or sixth call, I asked the dispatcher, "Where is the scout car to take down my stolen car report? If I were calling you from Georgetown, 16th Street or Connecticut Avenue, someone would have been here by now. Because I'm calling you from South East Washington does not mean I'm not as important or my issue is not as great a concern. Do I need to be present when they finally get here?

Dispatcher:	Yes. Where are you going?
Me:	I'm going to do the police's job for them and find my car. They can talk to my mother to get a report.
Dispatcher:	They are on their way. In fact, they should be right outside now. I apologize for the wait. We have had a busy day, and the computer is down. We were unable to check your tag and put it in the computer.
Me:	(Looking out the window.) Is that them riding up and down the street? Where are they going? They passed the apartment.

Dispatcher: Can you go outside and flag them down, please?

While this was going on, I could hear my mother in the background. "Girl, if you don't calm your butt down…" I still hadn't told her that my purse was in the car. Exiting the building and getting the attention of the officers, they parked and came over to take my report. Already in a foul mood, I asked, "What took you so long? It doesn't make any sense for me to have to place a call as many times as I did for me to get some assistance."

Police: Miss, we apologize. This seems to be the day for stolen cars. You cannot believe how many calls we've been on today alone, and our computers are down. Is your tag number V83-172?

Me: Yes! If your computers are down, how did you get the number?

Police: Because, Miss, we've had your car before you noted it was stolen! We were on patrol and spotted some suspicious looking characters. They must have assumed we were on patrol looking for the stolen car when they started to crouch down in their seats. We made a U-turn to approach them, and they took off down an alley in a high-speed chase. We followed in pursuit, which led us to a dead-end street. They jumped out of your car, ran on foot and climbed a fence. Unfortunately, we lost them when they jumped the fence.

All of a sudden, I started laughing. I laughed so hard that I was crying and almost wet my pants. The two police officers looked at me as if I had lost my mind. One of them said, "That was truly a quick change. A minute ago, you were biting our heads off, and now you're laughing. Did we miss something?" I replied, "Yes! If you heard the story, you would probably laugh too. I asked God for a sign, and He gave me one, but I didn't expect it this way." At any rate, the recovery of my car within minutes after it was stolen—before I had even realized it was missing, and reported it to the police—was God's way, in my mind, of Him letting me know He was forever present!

Me:	Where is my car now?
Police:	Miss, your car is at the precinct.
Me:	How much is it going to cost me to get it back?
Police:	Miss, it's not at the impound lot. We have it in the parking lot of the police precinct. It is waiting for you to come and pick it up. We just have to show you how to start it. They hot-wired it using a screwdriver. You have to unplug the battery to start it and unplug the battery to turn the car off.

Me:	I laughed again and then I asked about my purse.
Police:	Your purse! What about your purse!
Me:	It was in the car seat along with my Bible and my club that I didn't use.
Police:	Miss, you had a club, and you didn't use it in addition to you leaving your purse in the car?
Me:	I know! I could have prevented the theft if I only used the club, but I didn't plan to be in the apartment that long. I got carried away with my prayer. Did you notice if they took anything else or did any other damage?
Police:	Miss, it looks like they broke into your trunk.

Oh no! There goes my converter I just purchased. As the police escorted me to the precinct to get my car, one of the officers asked if I knew I had a hot car.

Me:	Hot car! What do you mean?
Police:	Do you know what type of engine you have in this car?
Me:	No! But the person I purchased the car from tried to tell me. Because I'm not

	into cars and the only thing I care about is getting from point A to point B, I didn't listen, and it didn't register.
Police:	Well, Miss, you have a racing engine in this car. These are the type of cars people steal and strip just for the engine. Are you also aware that your rims are approximately $350 to $500 dollars apiece?
Me:	I laughed again and said I only paid $1,000 for the car.
Police:	Well, Miss, do you realize you can sell the rims for close to, if not more than what you paid for the car? You might want to get some wheel locks and use your steering club next time. Oh, and by the way, please try not to leave your purse in the car anymore. You sure are lucky.
Me:	No, I'm blessed!

Arriving to get my car, I noticed my purse was missing and so was my Bible. I had to take off from work on Monday and use leave to call my bank, to include each of my creditors. What a disappointment! I was not interested in having to stand in the long line at the motor vehicle department to get another driver's license. If only I had used my club and removed my purse. What a headache! In between making calls to the bank, I heard a small voice say, call your office and check your voicemail. I thought to myself, who would call me on the weekend? Everyone who knows me knows I don't work on the weekend.

Tuesday morning, I arrived at work bright and early. I just knew there was going to be a number of items piled up and waiting for me since I wasn't in the day before. Listening to my messages, a man's voice said, "Honey, this is Mr. Johnson. I came in on Sunday from the Chateau after shaking a leg, and I found your purse on the sidewalk outside the building where I live. Honey, call me and come get your purse. I think everything is here. I didn't take anything. The contents of your purse were spilled out all over the sidewalk. I just followed the trail as I picked everything up. Please call me as soon as possible to get your purse."

Wow! I couldn't stop laughing to save my life. Tell me God does not have a sense of humor. On Thursday, which was Thanksgiving morning, I attended church with a big, bright smile. That morning, they opened the floor for the congregation to give a testimony and share what they were thankful for. Even though I was reluctant to tell my story, in obedience to God, I moved forward to share my testimony. There wasn't a dry eye in the church, especially when I lifted my purse in the air and told them I wouldn't be leaving it in the car anymore. And not only that, but everything was there: credit cards, bank book, driver's license and the only two dollars I had left after attending three services on Sunday. But needless to say, I didn't get my Bible back.

An elder of the church stood up and asked me, "What lesson did you learn?" The moral of this story is, be very careful what you ask God and always be specific. Otherwise, you just might get what you asked for—a sign.

(*After getting my steering column replaced, I drove around for two to three weeks determined not to look in the trunk to reaffirm what I knew was missing. Finally, I mustered up enough courage. There was my $200 converter. I assume they were not able to get the trunk open when they broke the lock. You can't tell me God isn't good!*)

Thank you for allowing me to share.
Ann G. Mack

TOUCHED BY GOD AND LED BY THE HOLY SPIRIT

The righteous cry, and the Lord heareth,
and delivereth them out of all their troubles.
The Lord is nigh unto them that are of a broken heart;
and saveth such as be of a contrite spirit. Many are the
afflictions of the righteous: but the Lord delivereth him out of
them all. He keepeth all his bones: not one of them is broken.

~ **Psalm 34:17-20**

November 19, 2008

How deep is your love? There is nowhere I can run or hide from the love of God. God's love is pure and unconditional. He loves us dearly and wants nothing but the best for us. He desires to have all of us saved and come to the knowledge of truth (1 Timothy 2:4). Yet, He does not intend to control us, which is why He gave us the gift of free will. It is His hope, however, that we use that gift wisely in making the right choices. When and if we should stray, He will welcome us back with open arms, though you must know He is true to His word, for our wrong choices are not without consequences. Never changing and never wavering, He is the same yesterday, today, tomorrow and always. Instructions for living are ideal, if only we are willing to follow Him by saying what we mean and doing what we say with integrity and honesty all the way. But to the contrary, like running water, our minds have a tendency to flow out of control as we make no commitment to do what's right. Perhaps if people came with instructions, having to interact with them would be much simpler. The label could read: Please do not detach, for I come with instructions that reveal many truths I wish to hide but have no choice in keeping them inside. There is no secret to what God can do! Little did I know or think in a million years that God would use the very thing that irked me the most to convict me and use it to teach me, as well as others, through hypocrisy.

> Let your love be sincere (a real thing);
> hate what is evil (loathe all ungodliness, turn in horror from wickedness), but hold fast to that which is good.
>
> ~ Romans 12:9 AMP

Understanding there is no such thing as a perfect place, situation or person (other than the one who died for our sins), does not excuse us of our wrongdoing or give us the right to continue to conduct ourselves immorally or unethically just because we can. Being human, as you might so eloquently put it, should compel us to being more consciously aware and adamant about striving to be more like the man of God and not the anti-Christ. Are you serious about your walk with God, or are you playing church? Do you know the difference between what it means to be genuine in comparison to being a counterfeit? Are you in love with the lifestyle that you are able to benefit from as a result of the church's legal status while failing to heed to the word of God? Do you truly believe everyone is living in darkness and is not being revealed the truth by way of the light through the Holy Spirit? Do you believe the supernatural is not real because you yourself have not experienced it?

Jesus, fortunately, is the savior to many people; however, He is not recognized by many of them as their Lord! Whatever you do, work at it with all your heart because when working for the Lord, not for man, you will receive an inheritance from the Lord as a reward. Remember always, it is the Lord Jesus Christ you are serving and not man (Colossians 3:23-25).

I am thy servant;
give me understanding,
that I may know thy testimonies.

~ Psalm 119:125

People disappointed me and left me wanting as well as needing so desperately to distance myself from them (2 Corinthians 6:17) as much as possible. But for some reason, I needed to cling to the idea that not all people were cruel or uncaring. Determined not to pick up their bad habits by adding to those I already possessed, I set out with passion to seek God and get to know Him deeply for a true understanding of how *He* needed me to be and not how man wanted me to be as He attempted to confirm or justify his untruths about who or what I should be! Was there no one I could trust to live up to doing and saying what they would or would have the conviction of heart and the courage to do what they knew was right, fair and just? Broken promise after broken promise. And when you start using the word Christian (Christ-like) lightly, without giving any real thought to its meaning and failing to acknowledge your actions based on what you teach others who are seeking truth, I would get a chill that numbed me and pierced my soul. Therefore, this not only affirmed my decision to create some distance, but it confirmed why it was important for me not to trust people, and I found it increasingly difficult to trust those who claimed to love God!

And without controversy great is the mystery of godliness: God was manifest in the flesh, justified in the Spirit, seen angels, Preached unto the Gentiles, believed on in the world, received up into glory.

~ 1 Timothy 3:16

My experiences involving people early on in life revealed I could not believe or trust what people said. I had encountered people who had no problems saying one thing and immediately doing another with no sense of forgiveness or remorse while looking me in the eye and confessing to be a Christian. You cannot believe just how angry this made me! The thing that seems to get under my skin is a person's unwillingness to say three simple words—"I am sorry"—in addition to them pretending to be something they are not. *For if a man thinks himself to be something, when he is nothing, he deceives himself* (Galatians 6:3). With a **spirit of competitiveness**, as human beings, we often want so much to be right even when we are wrong! And at all costs, many times, we are not willing to admit when we have made a mistake! All God wants is for us to take responsibility for our actions and be willing to confess our faults one to another as well as repent before Him with all sincerity (and supplication) in our hearts! In addition, He wants us to extend love to one another as He loves us. Ironically, we seem to have no problem pointing out the mistakes of others or judging one another, but fail to judge ourselves by using that same rule of measurement we direct toward others.

> *So I've discovered this truth:*
> *Evil is present with me even when I want to*
> *do what God's standards say is good.*
>
> ~ Romans 7:21 GW

We should always make a conscious effort to do what is right as well as desire to do what is right even if it is the furthest thing from our mind. Doing what you know to be right in the midst of trouble or peer pressure, regardless if everyone around you, including those in high places, is doing what you know to be wrong. You cannot give any thought to others' false sense of belief that it is better to lie about your indiscretions or lay blame on others because you have a problem taking responsibility for your actions. This taught me about the ability of people to wear masks. On the other hand, it taught me the significance of being able to discern the spirits.

A faithful witness will not lie:
but a false witness will utter lies.

~ Proverbs 14:5

After waiting many years in anticipation of receiving a miracle or a word from God in answer to my prayers, I found myself amongst double-minded Christians who made a living as ordained ministers while deceiving many people. As a Christian, how can you say or believe that one person is less worthy than another to receive or have the same opportunities as others, including you? Did God not feel that you were worthy for Him to sacrifice His only Son for you to be free?

Feeling I had reached my rope's end, I told God I didn't understand this world or people's warped sense of what it meant to be holy, true and Christian. Confused by what I was seeing, I started to doubt God as well as myself. I thought I was a good person who constantly went out of her way to help others above and beyond the call of duty. Should that not account for something? And yet, the more I distanced myself from others, the more adversity I seemed to have encountered. Why was I still on the less receiving end and having to prove I was worthy over and over again? I thought my search for a meaningful and satisfying occupational position was over. Finally, there would be no more moving around until the day I can retire. Oh no! More roadblocks, hurdles and people who wish to limit me and confine my growth in accordance to what they want me to have or be. God, are you punishing me for something I did? If so, can you at least tell me what it was so I can attempt to correct it? What would you have us do? What do you expect from me?

Neglect not the gift that is in thee, which was given thee by prophecy, with the laying on of the hands of the presbytery. Meditate upon these things; give thyself wholly to them; that thy profiting may appear to all. Take heed unto thyself, and unto the doctrine; continue in them: for in doing this thou shalt both save thyself, and them that hear thee.

~ 1 Timothy 4:14-16

The following is a message I received from a coworker, Charles Bryant (aka Lordy B.), on January 22, 2009, entitled, "Spiritual Gifts."

Romans 11:29, Amplified Bible For (*God's gifts and His call are irrevocable or permanent.*) [He never withdraws them when once they are given, and He does not change His mind about those to whom He gives His grace or to whom He sends His call.] God is not an Indian giver when it comes to giving you a gift or a call. For all that God does in our lives is all divinely orchestrated out for usage at His appointed time. So don't become weary in well-doing, for in God's appointed time, you shall reap if you faint not or lose heart. So keep on keeping on! God's Word says that He will perfect that which concerns you. So be encouraged and never stop doing what you're doing. For everyday you are changing behind the scenes. For your life is on the increase in your God, and your time of being brought out into the spotlight of God's expression is on the rise!

Amen

Attending the Salvation Army World Service Office's (SAWSO) annual core week staff meeting, I received an unexpected visit from the Holy Spirit while seated at a round table with coworkers in the conference room. As previously stated, on Wednesday, November 29, during the receiving of a devotion being delivered by Thebisa Chaava, I began to rock back and forth as tears started to well up. Trying desperately to understand what was happening, I also felt the need to attempt to regain my composure. Feeling a little embarrassed, I stood to my feet rather abruptly, let out a big yell (more like laughter) and ran for the door. Like something from out of a cartoon script, attempting to get the door open was very comical indeed. It was as if there were two entirely separate wills, mine and the Holy Spirit's. I wanted to escape the conference room, and the Holy Spirit wanted me to stay. As I attempted to open the door, the Holy Spirit closed it. There I was, having a spiritual tug of war with the Holy Spirit opening and closing the door until I was finally able to slip through it but not before hitting myself in the face with the door. Making my way out into the hallway of the fourth-floor conference rooms, I fell to my knees in acknowledgment of what was on the heart of God. Feeling overwhelmed, excited and puzzled at the same time, while still attempting to understand what was happening, I had an awesome, real-life, out-of-body experience.

> *For the time is come that judgment must begin at the house of God; and if it first begin at us, what shall the end be of them that obey not the gospel of God?*
>
> ~ 1 Peter 4:17

God allowed me to ascend to get a full view of what was happening. So there I was, confused and watching myself on the floor in a fetal-like position, while my soul hovered from above. Not only was I able to see everything, I was allowed to hear and feel even more. Many issues of my heart flashed before me as I engaged in an open conversation with God. Crying out loudly for all to hear, I was disturbed by the less-than-Christ-like actions of those who presented their employees with a document during orientation that stated, "I am signing this document to acknowledge that where I work is a church and I will conduct myself accordingly." However, I had witnessed an unfavorable display of character by Salvation Army officers to honor a policy or rule they enacted for others to follow by disregarding it themselves. A building they labeled as being a church that lacked the compassion, conviction and commitment of souls to reach souls in directing them toward Christ. Though they spared no expense in a materialistic kind of way in the cosmetic representation of the two buildings owned by The Salvation Army, as plush as the National Headquarters is, I could hear footsteps on the carpet. That was the supernatural power of God alerting me that someone was coming. It was as if all my senses were heightened! Still crying out to God, I indicated, "There is much evilness and wickedness within this building they presume to call a church. These are not Christians; they have lost sight of what's important. They have lost touch with the true concept of what it means to be in the world, but not of the world. They are operating like a cult! How can they be allowed to continue in this manner? These hypocrites are disgracing Your name and pretending to love You."

Be not deceived; God is not mocked:
for whatsoever a man soweth, that shall he also reap.
For he that soweth to his flesh shall of the flesh reap corruption;
but he that soweth to the Spirit shall of
the Spirit reap life everlasting.

~ Galatians 6:7-8

Hearing the footsteps quickly approaching, I asked God to let it be Mary Bryant (a coworker and a dear friend I knew was of a right spirit) and not Major Patricia Kiddoo. Screaming on the inside as I saw it was Major Kiddoo, I asked God not to let her touch me. As she kneeled beside me, she whispered, "Ann, you must be quiet. You have to keep those comments to yourself and be careful not to let anyone hear you. I am going to pray for you and ask that you find God's peace within."

As she stretched out her hand, I flinched and pleaded to God under my breath, "Please don't let her touch me. Please keep her away from me and protect me from the spirit of negativity that influences her as well as the many others within this building. If anything, do not let that spirit invade me. Let the spirit (the Holy Spirit) that is upon me to come upon her to hopefully transform her." Proceeding out loud, I said, "God, please protect and shield me from any negativity and harm by clothing me in the entire armor of Christ fully equipped from head to toe in the helmet of salvation, the shoes of good news, the breastplate of righteousness, the sword which is His word and the shield of faith. Shield my heart!" Though my heart was saddened, I did not want it to harden as a result of the abuse or what I was seeing in my surroundings that did not meet with

God's approval or His teaching of Christianity. Nor did I want to be a cold or bitter person even though I was being exposed to unrighteousness.

> *Purge me with hyssop, and I shall be clean:*
> *wash me, and I shall be whiter than snow.*
>
> ~Psalm 51:7

Placing her hand on me, my body started to tense up as I started to rock and sob even more. As she began to pray, I started to pray out loud. The louder she got, the louder I got. "God, I understand I am purposely put in this current situation to fulfill Your will. I need Your continued strength along with the wherewithal to accomplish what You want. This pain is great, and still I try to maintain a sense of professionalism while attempting to remove self and hold my ego at bay. Please continue to bind my tongue and flow through me. You know me, but they haven't a clue who I am. They don't know who I am."

The Major cried out and began to say, "Ann, please forgive me. I'm sorry. I didn't know. Please forgive me for the things I've done to you in the past. Thank you for your prayer. You helped me. You helped me to remember things I had forgotten." She handed me some tissue and began to cry. Then she jumped up and ran into the bathroom coughing and purging as I continued on my knees in prayer. *Draw nigh to God, and He will draw nigh to you. Cleanse your hands, ye sinners; and purify your hearts, ye double minded* (James 4:8).

At that moment, God told me someone else was coming, and He needed me to get up; however, not until He told me it was okay to do so. Upon receiving his prompting for me to get up, He told me to go into one of the empty conference rooms to the right and sit a while. He knew I was going to need a few minutes to get over the initial shock of what I had just experienced; not to mention, attempt to rationalize and process it all in my head.

> *I know that, whatsoever God doeth,*
> *it shall be for ever: nothing can be put to it,*
> *nor anything taken from it: and God doeth it,*
> *that men should fear before Him.*
>
> ~ Ecclesiastes 3:14

I have watched many science fiction movies, but this was no movie. It was real life—my life. Still rocking, I thought, "amazing," and then I began to direct my questions to God. As phenomenal as it was, I was still searching for an answer. I just could not understand why God would allow me for the first time to experience what I did in the middle of a staff meeting surrounded by all my coworkers who, I later learned, thought I was having a nervous breakdown. Having mixed emotions in addition to feeling embarrassed, I returned to the staff meeting to tell my supervisor I needed to be excused for the remainder of the day. He told me to take all the time I needed.

Returning to my office instead, I sat in the dark. As I was still rocking and reliving the whole incident, in walk Grace and Mary to check on me. While sharing my thoughts with them, they helped me to understand that nothing happens by chance when God is involved. I may not understand why God chose to allow this display of the quickening of the Holy Spirit in the manner in which He did, but it was part of a plan that would unfold in time. *There is a season and a time to every purpose under the Heaven* (Ecclesiastes 3:1). It was not for me to understand; it was important that I obey. At that moment, God reminded me of something else. Initially, I was given an assignment on October 27, 2006. A command, if you will, to write a letter to the Commissioner of The Salvation Army National Headquarters with a delivery date of November 15, 2006, in which I was also instructed to include and reference what was said or stated earlier during my encounter with the Holy Spirit. More than sixteen days later, I was not in compliance with God's request. In fact, I was hesitant and disobedient; therefore, I needed more convincing.

> *Write the things which thou has seen,*
> *and the things which are, and the things*
> *which shall be hereafter.*
>
> ~ Revelation 1:19

God confirming what I knew to be true also confirmed something else to each of us. We were connected and in place for a reason only God was knowledgeable about; however, He revealed the significance of the number three as it related to the Kingdom of God (the Holy Trinity and the balance of energy within SAWSO). Imagine seeing with the naked eye—in the natural—a ball of energy or life force, the Spirit of God! Envision an unattached sparkle or peck of illuminating light travel from one person to the next as you are allowed to feel (and see) the presence of God as He passes through you and *from you to two to three persons to form a triangle in showing you how you are connected!* Feeling what I knew I could not deny, with a look of amazement, I looked at both Grace and Mary to note they felt the same. Grace immediately began to tell me she was sorry for fighting me all this time. For the first time since my employment there, she was allowed by God to see me through His eyes—a child of God sent to The Salvation Army on a mission. In fact, we each had a very important purpose; however, for me to do what I was sent to do, we needed to cooperate by not getting in each other's way. That would mean we were in God's way, thus preventing the work of the Kingdom. Upon this great revelation, Grace began to cough and purge as I immediately handed her my trashcan. *And some of them of understanding shall fall, to try them, and to purge, and to make them white, even to the time of the end: because it is yet for a time appointed* (Daniel 11:35). Talk about having mixed emotions! Oh my God, was this not, truly, a day to remember?

> *Before I formed thee in the belly I knew thee;*
> *and before thou camest forth out of the womb I sanctified thee,*
> *and I ordained thee a prophet unto the nations.*
> *said I, Ah, Lord God! Behold, I cannot speak: for I am a child.*
> *But the Lord said unto me, Say not, I am a child:*
> *for thou shalt go to all that I shall send thee,*
> *and whatsoever I command thee thou shalt speak.*
>
> ~ Jeremiah 1:5-7

> "God created even secular work to meet human needs. Man began to divide work into spiritual and non-spiritual terms which introduced a form of dualism in the third and fourth centuries. But God never secularized our work. He desires our work to be viewed as worship."
>
> ~ From the wisdom of Minister Darrick D. McGhee

After being accused of being a religious fanatic by someone who should have been familiar with the awakening of the Holy Spirit as referenced in the Bible, I was starting to feel very vulnerable and overly sensitive to everything. Not to mention, I was still dealing with the fact that many believed and had alleged that I had a nervous breakdown. Succeeding at avoiding everyone for approximately two weeks and refraining from going to The Salvation Army lunchroom, I learned a National Commissioner's conference was being held in one of the other conference rooms outside of where the Holy Spirit had rendered me helpless to my flesh. Nonetheless, taking heed to my visitation from God, I completed my letter on December 3, 2006, to the commissioner of the National Headquarters as instructed. Again, God showed me His sense of humor! When the spirit of the Lord hits you or comes upon you (moves you), there is nothing you can do but surrender and throw your hands up. Being allowed by God to see yourself through His eyes immediately delivers you from strongholds. By connecting to His heart,

I felt His pain as He felt mine. More importantly, I also felt His joy as He imparted His peace. I was a vessel being used as a living sacrifice. I cannot begin to tell you just how free I felt and so loved by God.

> *And let us not be weary in well doing:*
> *for in due season we shall reap, if we faint not.*

~ Galatians 6:9

A Special Note:

I received a response dated January 2, 2007, from Lt. Colonel Judy Falin, the National Secretary for Personnel, regarding my letter to the Commissioner entitled, *A Living Testimony*. Her response read:

Dear Ann,

I am in receipt of your December 3rd communication to Commissioner Israel Gaither who has designated me to respond. Please write me and let me know the specific areas of concern you have addressed either orally or in writing with Major Patricia Kiddoo and/or Lt. Colonel Daniel Starrett.

Kind Regards,
Signed Lt. Colonel Judy Falin

Upon the receipt and reading of the letter from Lt. Colonel Judy Falin, I was instructed by God to do nothing. He had already given me a command, which I had honored. *Speak unto them all that I command thee and be not dismayed at their faces, lest I confound thee before them* (Jeremiah 11:16). My assignment, although important, was a simple one. Sound the alarm. Sound the trumpet! *To whom shall I speak, and give warning, that they may hear? Behold, their ear is uncircumcised, and they cannot hearken: behold, the word of the Lord is unto them a reproach; they have no delight in it* (Jeremiah 6:10). The Salvation Army leadership for the most part is aware of all that goes on there (the good and the bad). Those who complain are retaliated against; employees are terminated or coerced into resigning; officers are deployed to locations outside of the United States or remote areas not of their choosing; complaints are ignored; change is not welcomed or recommended.

> *Thine own wickedness shall correct thee,*
> *and thy backslidings shall reprove thee:*
> *know therefore and see that it is an evil thing and bitter,*
> *that thou hast forsaken the Lord thy God,*
> *and that my fear is not in thee,*
> *saith the Lord God of hosts.*
>
> ~ Jeremiah 2:19

TRUST GOD IN SPITE OF WHAT YOU SEE

*For what is a man profited,
if he shall gain the whole world, and lose his own soul?
Or what shall a man give in exchange for his soul?*
~ **Matthew 16:26**

What is it about people who are more apt to believe the credibility of one person and not another, knowing nothing of the facts or the truth? For far too long, out of fear, I allowed others around me to not only dictate my self-worth but my purpose in life as well. Why should I be more willing to forgive your actions against me when, if given half the chance, you would not hesitate to wrong me again and again? *Because God loves me and tells me vengeance is His!* (Romans 12:19) And yet, I am expected time and time again to be the resilient one. *Because God loves me and reminds me of His preparation for Kingdom living!* Should I not be expected to defend myself or voice my disappointment when you attempt to lie on me or strip me of my self-respect and dignity? *Because God loves me and tells me if I allow you to tear me down, He will tear me down and remind me of how strong I am!* Would you not do the same if the role was reversed, or have you decided my life and who I am is nothing in comparison to who you are as dictated by society? *However, God tells me He loves me as He reminds me of my purpose!* Perhaps you feel it is your right to continue to degrade me and control me on the basis of gender, age, race or even your position, including culture, religion, language, education, skill or sexual orientation in accordance to society. *But God not only whispers in my ear in that still loving voice as He tells me I am special to Him, He reminds me that He created me!*

And thou, son of man, be not afraid of them,
neither be afraid of their words,
though briers and thorns be with thee,
and thou dost dwell among scorpions:
be not afraid of their words, nor be dismayed at their looks,
though they be a rebellious house.

~ Ezekiel 2:6

The world we live in seems to be dominated by people who are driven by iniquity (moral turpitude or sin and wickedness), which has many confused and unwilling to see right from wrong. Though they try to convince me that there is nothing wrong with their sinful nature, everything within me tells me not to give in or give up, believing that it is better to thrive in being righteous. However, everything I see and all that I have endured tells me not to believe. The thoughts in my head of the pain and the hurt of things past and present are easier to grasp than something that is not visible to the naked eye. And what are more real are the thoughts regarding a conversation I had with a Salvation Army supervisor that seem to play over and over again in my head. How dare he commence to tell me that the unfair treatment within The Salvation Army being experienced by me and other employees has more to do with class than it does race or discrimination, as if any unfair treatment, if not racially motivated, is politically OKAY! And yet under the same breath, he urged me to excuse the less-than-righteous behavior of an ordained minister as being normal, which made it even more impossible for me to attend The Salvation Army chapel services. There was no way I could force myself to sit through a sermon being delivered by someone who was serving two masters and living a double life. How could I see the word, hear the word and understand the word if those speaking the word were not living the word? And I am expected to pretend they truly loved the Lord?

Speaking the word and not applying it to your life does nothing for your soul. Therefore, it is no surprise to me that The Salvation Army would seek the legal assistance of this world system; a New York federal court ruling in October of 2005 granted The Salvation Army the legal right to fire employees and not to hire persons who practice a religion that is different from their religious beliefs; this is a form of discrimination. Although The Salvation Army receives most of their money for social services from the government, this ruling was considered to be a major court victory for the Bush administration. But Jesus showed love to all people of any race and any age including those who hated Him. *Christ is all and in all everything and everywhere, to all men, without distinction of person!* (Colossians 3:11 AMPC). The Bible also declares we should love our neighbors like we love ourselves. In fact, if you review John 15:11-15 within the Message Bible, it states: *I've told you these things for a purpose: that my joy might be your joy, and your joy wholly mature. This is my command: Love one another the way I loved you. This is the very best way to love. Put your life on the line for your friends. You are my friends when you do the things I command you. I'm no longer calling you servants because servants don't understand what their master is thinking and planning. No, I've named you friends because I've let you in on everything I've heard from the Father.*

> *This is a true saying,*
> *If a man desire the office of a bishop, he desireth a good work.*
> *A bishop then must be blameless, the husband of one wife,*
> *vigilant, sober, of good behavior, given to hospitality, apt to teach.*
> *Not given to wine, no striker, not greedy of filthy lucre;*
> *But patient, not a brawler, not covetous.*
>
> ~ 2 Timothy 3:1-3

Based on what I was seeing and witnessing as the pain of my sorrow, I refused to believe anything differently, unless I was blessed by God to see and experience something else. In reality, I know what God represents. I know that He is everything that is good and decent in my life. I know that He loves me equally because the Bible tells me He is no respecter of persons; He shows no partiality (Acts 10:34). Every thought of what was good and pleasing to me about God's love for me was questioned as I examined or witnessed the demonstrated behavior and actions of those who wanted me to believe they were Christians who loved the Lord. And yet, for seven years, I was forced to watch the extent of that love embrace double standards, which have nothing to do with God's principles. As I viewed my surroundings, I found it harder and harder not to see the deception and dismiss it as having no bearing or impact on my life. Frustrated by what I was seeing, I had great difficulty understanding how those who claimed to be Christians could refuse to acknowledge a culture within a church that regularly demonstrated un-Godly principles and be okay with it as they attempted to convince me that it was all in my head. The oldest trick of the enemy is to convince you that it is you who is delusional as the iniquity continues and nothing changes.

> *But thou, son of man,*
> *hear what I say unto thee;*
> *be not thou rebellious like that rebellious house:*
> *open thy mouth, and eat that I give thee.*
>
> ~ Ezekiel 2:8

Nearly eight months after my departure from The Salvation Army, I was instructed by the Holy Spirit to view The Salvation Army National Headquarters' updated website and note the inclusion of their acknowledgement and belief in the Holy Spirit to the outside world—an obvious attempt to dispute and discredit what I wrote and know to be true! However, the written acknowledgment of a belief means nothing if it is not acted upon and applied accordingly to your everyday life. I know all too well from my employment with The Salvation Army that people are more than capable of living a lie to project an image to meet a desired outcome. As I attended church Sunday morning (on November, 30, 2008), I asked God to remove the pain of what I know to be true about The Salvation Army and let not my memories from that time in my life bring about more tears or sorrow. Nonetheless, when I think of those who I have left behind, my heart aches knowing there have been no changes to an outdated culture that still threatens to enslave the mind and limit the spirit through oppressive abuse and control.

Who is there even among you that would shut the doors for nought? neither do ye kindle fire on mine altar for nought, I have no pleasure in you, saith the Lord of hosts, neither will I accept an offering at your hand.

~ Malachi 1:10

My hope and prayer for them, should they not be able to escape physically for healing to commence, is they be granted through God and the Holy Spirit that dwells within them the ability to escape spiritually and mentally from the ties that bind. I also hope and pray that they rely on the courage from within to allow the Holy Spirit to guide them and draw them closer to God in seeking and cultivating a relationship with Him in spite of what they see. And hopefully, one day soon, change will begin to take place within The Salvation Army to mirror a loving God who is no respecter of persons in consideration of all people.

But unto you that fear my name shall the Sun of righteousness arise with healing in his wings; and ye shall go forth, and grow up as calves of the stall. And ye shall tread down the wicked; for they shall be ashes under the soles of your feet in the day that I shall do this, saith the LORD of hosts.

~ Malachi 4:2-3

The Uprooting of a Family Under False Pretense

Approximately three years ago, in the early part of 2005, the Salvation Army World Service Office (SAWSO) had the need to recruit for the position of an HIV-AIDS program advisor. In an effort to prove a point that my unfair treatment was solely due to a sub-class category rather than race, my supervisor, the program coordinator (Bram Bailey) of SAWSO, approached a longtime, childhood friend (Thebisa Chaava) who lived in Zambia. Aside for her association as a Salvationist, she was highly regarded for her expertise and knowledge in the area of HIV-AIDS. In fact, Thebisa Chaava is qualified, competent and probably the most experienced CCE-CC (Community Capacity Enhancement through Community Conversation) facilitator and instructor. She carries the title "Master Trainer," and she is sought after by programs across Africa and beyond. Finalizing his selection and extending the offer of employment, my supervisor was adamant about making sure his choice for the HIV-AIDS position was granted and accepted by management, in spite of the resistance from Major Patricia Kiddoo, who was second in command within SAWSO at the time and two other SAWSO-employed, female program advisors (Holly Christofferson and Claire Boswell) who had issues with him going outside of the United States to fill the position.

At the conclusion of a Chaava family discussion, this family of five had entered into an agreement to join their extended Salvation Army family in the United States by taking a leap of faith and embark upon a new adventure; they sold everything, including their vehicle, and left their home in Zambia to relocate to Virginia for what they thought would be a gratifying opportunity for each family member. Unaware of the blatant racism and cultural challenges they would face from their Salvation Army peers, as well as the growing intense racial and cultural differences present within the United States as a whole, unfortunately, they walked into an environment that opposed their employment long before their arrival. Though no one should have to get used to such opposing behavior under any circumstances, least of all in a Christian organization, if you are not familiar with this system of mental and physical hatred, it would prove to be a very devastating and demoralizing culture shock.

Regardless of your accomplishments, however big or small, there are people in the world who are unfortunately driven by bigotry and refuse to see or acknowledge what God sees and knows about you to be true. Thebisa's very talented, gifted and God-fearing husband, Macdonald Chaava, who worked alongside his wife on previous Salvation Army Corps projects, is a qualified medical sciences lecturer and project manager with additional experience in community mobilization, specializing in monitoring and evaluation processes. With the hope that both of them were being employed by The Salvation Army or the Salvation Army World Service Office, as eluded to them in prior discussions before their departure from Zambia, they had no need to think they would not be in good company. Unlike many husband and wife teams who just so happen to be Salvationists—meaning they follow and believe in the religious doctrine of The Salvation Army—they had dual positions of employment waiting for them upon their arrival (or at least one was created for them with little to no waiting period). Since the arrival of the Chaava family to the United States, they have been met with one opposition after the other, more so from within The Salvation Army and have seen and experienced exactly what I know to be true. A truth I would not wish upon anyone—not even my greatest enemy.

And have no fellowship with the unfruitful works of darkness, but rather reprove them.

~ Ephesians 5:11

Blinded by Darkness

Subconsciously, my supervisor did not want to believe what he already knew to be true or at least he did not want me to be right about what I painfully knew to be true. Being a person of color with any degree would not be viewed as acceptable in this so-called religious, non-profit working environment to be seen as a professional and valued employee to excel in equal standing as our white counterparts. Having a Bachelor in

Business Administration was not acknowledged; although, I was led to believe that having something greater or in the profession of a Technical Writer with a concentrated discipline in the area of social or clinical work would grant me more opportunities for promotions within SAWSO during the time I was an employee there. But it did not keep them from asking me to consider doing some grant for them—without any additional compensation. So I declined! Then they proceeded to attack my ability to write intelligent and meaningful proposals. However, I was commissioned by God to do what man told me I could not do—write!

> *Then the Lord answered me and said,*
> *"Write the vision and engrave it plainly on [clay] tablets*
> *So that the one who reads it will run."*
>
> ~ Habakkuk 2:2

I wonder if the first highest-ranking African American officer in the history of The Salvation Army (as of 2006) would agree or disagree with the prevailing double standard culture. However, much is revealed when people do not think they are being watched! As quiet as it is kept, a few of the employees who were present during the time of the announcement concerning the appointment of Commissioner Gaither to The Salvation Army National Headquarters were witness to the unfavorable behavior of the officers as they huddled in corners, whispering and protesting his arrival; they didn't give any thought to his accomplishments, position and title, which is similar to the current behavior and attitudes of those who have condemned the potential of the first elected African American president of the United States before he was officially sworn into office.

I am sure, without a doubt, those reading this will attempt to deface me as they continue to deny what they know to be true as opposed to taking ownership of their mistakes for accountability. I was always reminded by Major Patricia Kiddoo not to air out the dirty laundry of The Salvation Army for the world to see as I witnessed those in the higher-ranking positions (officers and employees alike) never hesitating to redirect blame whenever necessary, even if they were the responsible party for whatever went wrong.

A Personal Observation:

- Thebisa Chaava's reputation is not based on shallow techniques in the Holy Spirit; she is a Bible-based instructor who SAWSO/TSA should have taken care of but failed to do so.

- When the Chaava Family came to the United States, they had a savings of $35,000, which they have had to exhaust to cover the gaps created by the faulty Salvation Army administration systems. Three years after their arrival, they have officially been granted permanent residence in the United States.

- As stated above, The Salvation Army should have extended to the Chaava Family conditions similar or equivalent to staff they send overseas to serve, but instead, they changed those conditions with no prior notification (after the family had departed Africa) and presented them with a totally empty relocation package that left them exposed to the negative effects of a vibrant economy.

In the words of MacDonald Chaava: "It is a fact that the Lord has come through for us each and every time. We do not complain and we do not keep any bitterness within us, but that is not to say we would wish our situation for anyone else. For that reason, it is also a fact that we support you in your reflections through writing." They are truly a family who lives by faith, which means doubting nothing and relying on God for everything!

Found in Old Saint Paul's Church
Baltimore, Maryland
Dated 1692

DESIDERATA[63]

(Latin meaning: desired things)

Go placidly amid the noise and the haste, and remember what peace there may be in silence. As far as possible, without surrender, be on good terms with all persons. Speak your truth quietly and clearly; and listen to others, even to the dull and the ignorant; they too have their story. Avoid loud and aggressive persons; they are vexatious to the spirit.

---

[63] http://www.stpaulsbaltimore.org/wp-content/uploads/2015/02/desiderata-pamphlet.pdf

If you compare yourself with others, you may become vain or bitter, for always there will be greater and lesser persons than yourself. Enjoy your achievements as well as your plans. Keep interested in your own career, however humble; it is a real possession in the changing fortunes of time.

Exercise caution in your business affairs, for the world is full of trickery. But let this not blind you to what virtue there is; many persons strive for high ideals, and everywhere life is full of heroism. Be yourself. Especially do not feign affection. Neither be cynical about love, for in the face of all aridity and disenchantment, it is as perennial as the grass.

Take kindly the counsel of the years, gracefully surrendering the things of youth. Nurture strength of spirit to shield you in sudden misfortune. But do not distress yourself with dark imaginings. Many fears are born of fatigue and loneliness. Beyond a wholesome discipline, be gentle with yourself. You are a child of the universe no less than the trees and the stars; you have a right to be here. And whether or not it is clear to you, no doubt the universe is unfolding as it should.

Therefore be at peace with God, whatever you conceive Him to be. And whatever your labors and aspirations, in the noisy confusion of life, keep peace in your soul. With all its sham, drudgery, and broken dreams, it is still a beautiful world. Be cheerful. Strive to be happy.

You do not have to be a part of an order to appreciate it or the content!

If thine enemy be hungry, give him bread to eat; and if he be thirsty, give him water to drink: For thou shalt heap coals of fire upon his head, and the LORD shall reward thee.

~ Proverbs 25: 21 –22

Bless them which persecute you: bless and curse not. Rejoice with them that do rejoice and weep with them that weep. Recompense to no man evil for evil. Provide things honest in the sight of all men. If it be possible, as much as lieth in you, live peaceably with all men.
Dearly beloved, avenge not yourselves, but rather give place unto wrath: for it is written, Vengeance is mine; I will repay, saith the Lord. Therefore if thine enemy hunger, feed him; if he thirst, give him drink: for in so doing thou shalt heap coals of fire on his head. Be not overcome of evil, but overcome evil with good.

~ Romans 12:14-15, 17-21

WHAT WOULD JESUS DO?

January 19, 2009

God brought to my remembrance the scenario that took place while I was in the employment of The Salvation Army:

Today, unfortunately, is no different from any other day. One of my coworkers within the Salvation Army World Service Office, who just loves to flex her muscles by attempting to show me who the real boss is, apparently got up on the wrong side of the bed again this morning. I am truly convinced that she goes to bed at night and gets up in the morning thinking of ways she can make my life just as miserable as hers. Now don't get me wrong, there are days when she has her good moments, but I never know from one day to the next which personality she will decide to graciously adorn me with.

Initially, I assumed we were getting along; she, being a practicing Buddhist, took the time to share information concerning her religion with me, only to find out I was not the average Christian who was driven by religiosity (legalistic dogma) who knew nothing about other religions or only about one way in which people worshipped in accordance to their idea of God. In fact, it is not by belief to believe that my way is the only way or the best way. It's just right for me. However, also interested in the metaphysical power or spiritual association of crystals (gemstones), I attended her temple to see the large display of crystals housed there and found the whole experience to be quite enlightening. For some reason, I assumed my less-than-judgmental religious mindset that did not take on the view of "my religion is better than yours" would foster mutual respect and an opportunity for us to celebrate as well as embrace our differences rather than using them to belittle one another. This, unfortunately, was not the case. It seemed I could do nothing right as far as she was concerned. Even when I made great accomplishments at work, they were overlooked or not considered to be valued in any way.

Speaking to my supervisor about the situation, he surprisingly was made to believe that it was *me* who was less than accommodating when it came to her; it was me who lacked the ability or willingness to forge an ideal working relationship. Nonetheless, he did reveal that their conversation had uncovered something else. It seemed that she once occupied a position of the same capacity as mine in providing administrative support to an office or group of coworkers during her career history, and she was treated in a less-than-favorable manner. Still holding onto the memories from that ordeal, which must have resulted in a mind trauma, she was insistent upon making me feel as uncomfortable and miserable as she was made to feel while working in that environment. Looking at my supervisor in a very puzzling manner, not meaning to be disrespectful in any way but attempting to get him to see the logic in what he shared with me, I asked, "And you would still have me to believe that our inability to get along has more to with me than it does her? You, having all the facts disproving my less than willingness to get along with others, would rather put this on me. Why? Because the status and position of one is valued more highly than the other, even when the one in the higher position is clearly wrong! Or could this be about something else? As a Christian and lifelong Salvationist, should you not have reminded her that it is unlawful to do tit for tat, and not to mention, that her previous ordeal had nothing to do with me at all? And, vengeance is his, said the Lord!"

What would Jesus do? He would treat people in the manner in which He wanted to be treated rather than in the manner in which He was being treated. Besides, the treatment she endured from others in her past has nothing to do with me in her present. In asking to be forgiven by God, it is also required by us to forgive those who have trespassed against us and pray for healing.

The Message: Never give the devil his satisfaction by playing into his hands! My mother had this saying when I was growing up: Always treat the devil with kindness and never stoop to his level. The objective is to bring him up to your level. That's what Jesus would do!

HIDDEN AGENDAS AND UNGODLY MOTIVES

For whatsoever is born of God overcometh the world: and this is the victory that overcometh the world, even our faith.

~ 1 John 5:4

February 23, 2009

Approximately three to four months after my employment as a Personnel Assistant within The Salvation Army National Headquarters (TSA-NHQ), I received a visit from a gentleman named Steve Boyer. Thinking he had come from his office on the first floor within the Department of Finance to see me on the fourth floor, I just knew he had a question pertaining to Human Resources; however, that was not the case. He came, specifically, to ask me if I was a Christian. God, preparing me in advance for my response to a question He knew was going to be directed at me, spoke to me a day or so earlier; or perhaps it was the same day. With puzzlement and amazement, I knew God was smiling upon me as I lifted my head to give Steve my undivided attention and direct eye contact. I spoke clearly as I stated, "The word 'Christian' denotes, to me, Christ-like. So if you are asking me if I'm like Christ, then I will have to say no. I have aspirations of being like Christ and I work toward accomplishing that goal each and every day. Unfortunately, a number of us are too quick to attach labels to ourselves and not give any thought to its true meaning. And more importantly, we fail to conduct ourselves accordingly in a manner that defines the character of the meaning of the word Christian." Somewhat speechless and still standing in the doorway of my office, Steve said, "I see you have given this some thought." I replied, "Yes," and Steve turned and walked out. Little did I know, this was the beginning of a test that would later reveal the true purpose of my existence and shed some light as to why God had ordered my steps in orchestrating this plan for me to be at The Salvation Army.

> *And he said, Ab'-ba, Father,*
> *all things are possible unto thee;*
> *take away this cup from me: nevertheless not what I will,*
> *but what thou wilt:*
>
> ~ Mark 14:36

Call me naïve, but I had much faith in those who called themselves Christians, not giving any thought to them being just men. I assumed those who used the word Christian to apply it to themselves had taken much care to investigate its true meaning to walk as Christ did by examining themselves wisely. Or at least they would put forth much consideration to exercise their conscience in being determined to pattern their life after the word of God. When you make the decision to join a church that represents the body of Christ, you pledge your life to become a part of an organization that is recognized throughout the United States and abroad for the works that should mirror Christ's love for *all*. Should you not take that position seriously? Having great expectations to finally be connected to those who not only said they were Christians but knew what it meant to be Christ-like gave me hope—initially. I thought that through them, I would learn the ways of God. However, I was disillusioned by their attempts at doing the right things and quickly learned it was for all of the wrong reasons with clearly all of the wrong motives. Failing me not, God intervened by showing up, touching my heart and taking me by the hand to teach me what He needed me to know—to see through my experiences and see through His eyes. What better teacher in the world is there other than God Himself? I saw things, heard things, felt things and realized so much through the revelation of God. While others made a mockery out of His name, He was determined not to allow me to be deceived any longer.

Call unto me, and I will answer thee,
and shew thee great and mighty things,
which thou knowest not.

~ Jeremiah 33:3

God helped me to understand the importance and difference of not doing the right thing with the wrong motives. He taught me to examine the fruits of a person's heart in spite of what they wanted me to believe, which made it very clear to me that the issues of the heart are revealed through the fruit. He indicated He could not stress enough the character of a man through his heart based on the display of his actions. As a man thinketh in his heart, so is he! Therefore, He cautioned me to know and observe the difference between what it means to be spiritual as opposed to being religious. Being religious is about dogma or adhering to a set of rules, regulations or guidelines formulated by man with the sole purpose of dictating how you should worship God or to whom you should worship, which oftentimes has nothing to do with the true essence of God. Being spiritual is about recognizing the spirit (the Holy Spirit) and allowing it to lead you in praising and worshiping God as well as the appropriate (Christ-like) way in which to regard others with love. Religion is taught with limits; you cannot limit the spirit or put God in a box. You cannot confine God to movement or limit His works through you, in you or around you. Religious people have a tendency to pervert the word of God and interject their own understanding or reasoning to justify their belief(s). And more often than not, false truths reinforce their commitment to their belief(s) as they demonstrate unChrist-like actions bordering on hate (ungodly motives) and not love. As we allow ourselves to operate in the world, if we are not careful, the world can influence hidden agendas and ungodly motives. Stubbornly, most of us see only what we want to see and refuse to believe that which we truly see. We hear what we want to hear and refuse to accept that which was actually heard and stated in truth. We feel what we want to feel and refuse to acknowledge or accept that our emotions merely cloud our judgment. We are told the truth, but in disbelief of the truth, we are quick to believe the lie.

Hear now this, O foolish people, and without without understanding; which have eyes, and see not; which have ears, and hear not.

~ Jeremiah 5:21

Upon accepting a position with the Salvation Army World Service Office (SAWSO), I was excited to know there would be an annual retreat or core meeting away from the office. These meetings were aimed at giving us, SAWSO, a wonderful opportunity to bond and work out issues. In addition, I viewed them as a collective effort to improve our working relationships and explore ideas on how we could possibly do a better job to serve the public or those in need. Unfortunately, there was much bickering at times and an unwillingness to listen to or incorporate ideas or suggestions voiced by employees in lower level positions. On occasion, I also noted the reluctance of the headstrong employees amongst us to listen to Major Harden White, SAWSO's previous department head who was a very fair man in his approach to everything. As I observed the dynamics of what was taking place at these retreats, I often wondered how it was possible for SAWSO to accomplish as much as they had to successfully still be in business. If we allow ourselves to get stuck on titles or positions that a person holds, with an unwillingness to view them as being able to contribute something worthwhile to the discussion, how would we be able to consider a diverse population that represents us all to be able to assist them in all fairness? We don't! There was a recognizable undertone or attitude dictating a god complex with the determination of who was considered to be worthy enough to receive assistance from The Salvation Army with an emphasis on the level of recognition or valued exposure the organization could obtain with the right positioning. This was a completely different concept from what I considered to be a helping hand; it was more about politics than helping others. And as a rule, before finalizing plans to pursue a proposal or fundraising effort, SAWSO needed to obtain the approval of The Salvation Army or the International Headquarters on Queen Victoria Street in the City of London.

> *My bowels, my bowels!*
> *I am pained at my very heart; my heart maketh a noise in me;*
> *I cannot hold my peace, because thou hast heard,*
> *O my soul, the sound of the trumpet, the alarm of war.*
>
> ~ Jeremiah 4:19

Working late one afternoon and being the only person still remaining in SAWSO, I received a visit from Lt. Colonel Sharon Ulyat who took a seat in my office. I'm ashamed to say, I initially paid no attention to Mrs. Ulyat as I continued to work on my project in an effort to complete it as soon as possible to be able to depart for the evening like all the rest of the SAWSO team. Besides, I had grown quite accustomed to not being regarded by many of the officers to warrant receiving as much as a simple hello during my tenure at The Salvation Army, in spite of them claiming to be Christians. Mrs. Ulyat was doing some last-minute follow-ups before she and her husband, Lt. Colonel Richard Ulyat, embarked upon their retirement. Sharing her excitement with me, she told me how happy she was to be leaving The Salvation Army after all these years. At that moment, I realized this was a genuine visit and a need for her to speak to someone concerning her experiences in truth with love. For the first time, I understood not every Salvation Army officer was satisfied or in agreement with the negative direction and lack of display of Christianly love within The Salvation Army. And upon their exit, there was a sense of liberation from having to hold their peace concerning the unChrist-like actions they found themselves being forced to overlook. Mrs. Ulyat and I had more in common than I realized. She indicated the only reason she did not express more of her concerns as openly as she did was because of her husband, who she loved dearly. She also indicated she had been written up many times for speaking out. A woman after my own heart! And now it was Major Harden White's turn.

And I will give you pastors according to mine heart, which shall feed you with knowledge and understanding.

~ Jeremiah 3:15

The 2005 retreat was held from August 9 through August 12 at the Willow Valley Resort in Lancaster, Pennsylvania. What an eye-opening experience to a greater level of church politics within The Salvation Army; it was a moment of truth. A retirement dinner took place in honor of Majors Harden and Marilyn White to give us the opportunity to wish them farewell before they embarked upon their new and wonderful adventure called living life to the fullest on a different time schedule. Joining us was Lt. Colonel Larry Bosh and his wife, Lt. Colonel Mary Petroff, Francis McDonnell and daughter, Fiona. The Salvation Army planned a larger celebration for the Whites, however, only a select few were allowed to attend. Major White had extended an invitation to each of the SAWSO staff members to attend the big Salvation Army celebration, but he was instructed by leadership to disinvite us. At any rate, Major White shared what I considered to be a political strategic plan to bankrupt SAWSO into non-existence. It is my belief that God spoke to Major White's heart, and through the Holy Spirit, he revealed truth to us with love. The unfortunate direction and events within SAWSO is confirming a truth that no one wants to acknowledge except those who set the action in motion. A person who has nothing to lose during his retirement dinner stands before you and tells you he was purposely sent to head a particular department with direct orders to cripple its operations and today, in spite of all of what you see or all that has been presented to you, you still refuse to believe the truth. Ironically, the scripture identified on the inside of each agenda package for the 2005 SAWSO retreat was Colossians 1:12-14 and 17.

> *Giving thanks unto the Father, which hath made us meet to be partakers of the inheritance of the saints in light: Who hath delivered us from the power of darkness and hath translated us into the Kingdom of his dear Son: In whom we have redemption through his blood, even the forgiveness of sins: And he is before all things and by him all things consist.*
>
> ~ Colossians 1:12-14, 17

Major White's conscience would not allow him to deliberately displace a group of people just because he was given a command from man as a political ploy to do so. *Study to shew thyself approved unto God, a workman that needeth not to be ashamed, rightly dividing the word of truth* (2 Timothy 2:15). Instead, he assumed full responsibility for those under his leadership by honoring the word of truth and preparing for a rainy day. Being frugal, he managed to devise a plan to compensate his staff in the event of an emergency to provide them each with a severance package, should the need arise. However, Major White knew his departure would open the door for The Salvation Army to carry out their original plan to bring in an officer who would succeed at destroying SAWSO where he himself had failed. Opting to choose the lesser of two evils, Major White even made a last minute attempt to recommend Major Patricia Kiddoo as his replacement to head SAWSO. And how would I know that? I was asked to type the letter of recommendation, which I held in the strictest of confidence. Nonetheless, The Salvation Army elected to fill Major White's post with an individual many officers made reference to as being a bull in a china shop. And Major Kiddoo remained the second in command though there was an unhealthy pairing that often had her retreating to the restroom in tears, with Grace Herring as her confidant. Honestly, I did not think it was possible for Major Kiddoo to meet her match.

> *But a prophet of the Lord was there, whose name was O'-ded: and he went out before the host that came to Sa-ma'-ri-a, and said unto them, behold, because the Lord God of your fathers was wroth with Judah, he hath delivered*

them into your hand, and ye have slain them in a rage that reacheth up unto heaven.
And now ye purpose to keep under the children of Judah and Jerusalem for bondmen and bondwomen unto you: but are there not with you, even with you, sins against the Lord your God?

~ 2 Chronicles 28: 9-10

Ironically, the less-than-secretive discussions surrounding the lunchroom table eluded to side bets amongst Christians concerning how long it would take for SAWSO's new department head to own up to his reputation for destroying everything he touched. The Salvation Army leadership beyond the command and authority of the national commander, Commissioner Israel Gaither, made the decision to deliberately deplore and count on the personality and reputation of a man, Lt. Colonel Daniel Starrett, who precedes him based on his history of excessive spending habits that far exceeded the financial expectations of the Western Territory as well as IHQ when he was stationed there—a reputation and pattern of spending that The Salvation Army was hoping to manipulate by directing Lt. Colonel Daniel Starrett toward SAWSO in an effort to push TSA's political agenda to bankrupt SAWSO. In addition, Lt. Colonel Starrett unwillingness to follow orders as he continues to do things his way has created an even bigger problem that's undoubtedly brought more attention to The Salvation Army than their history of discriminatory business practices. Therefore, the demise of SAWSO as planned is not going as smoothly or as quickly as

TSA anticipated. So needless to say, The Salvation Army has lost their leverage to manipulate the situation any further.

In the words of T.D. Jakes, "When experience becomes tradition, it becomes dangerous. Therefore, experience does have its liabilities." Over time, experience becomes practice, and practice makes perfect. But what happens when you perfect your wrongdoing? Somehow, you become convinced that your wrongdoing, which is outside of the will of God, is in some way right. After a while, you tend to lose track of right from wrong, but you fail to realize that playing Russian roulette opens a doorway to Hell that is not going to be so easy to close. The Salvation Army, through its past practices in how they have conducted their business, has been very successful in getting away with what falls outside of the character of Christ. However, in the case of The Salvation Army's liabilities, such as unethical business practices and God's children being treated unfairly and discriminated against, they have gone unanswered for quite some time.

The most important thing in the world to a Christian or a body of Christ should be the will of God! **NOT MY WILL; NOT YOUR WILL BUT THE WILL OF GOD.** And what unnerves me the most is the blatant disregard of an organization to follow the will of God as it seeks to push its own selfish, ambitious agenda by changing the rules and justifying it by calling it "business." The Salvation Army has an uncanny desire to live by its own rules. Its man's business, not God's, to separate and divide God's people with the use of negative influences in the world—a form of business that has taken on a world view driven by pride and greed that you would be willing to compromise God's laws! You have been very instrumental in seeking man's court of law to dispute God's word. And even worse, you perverted God's word into untruths and imposed those untruths upon God's children, leaving them spiritually wounded as vulnerable prey to the enemy of God. When a problem arises, it should be dealt with appropriately. Consideration for correcting the problem should be an option. A person committing the wrong should not be transferred and unleashed upon others to receive the same infractions. Similar to how the Catholic church dealt with child molesters, rotating the individual from one parish to the next and not treating the disease or the illness only makes matters worse.

THE SALVATION ARMY MISSION STATEMENT

The Salvation Army, an international movement, is an evangelical part of the universal Christian Church (the Body of Christ that is incorporated through baptism by the Holy Spirit). **The word universal implies to all or worldwide meaning many. In short, it would pertain to a diverse population; however, diversity is not recognized nor honored by The Salvation Army. Nonetheless, diversity is, indeed, a good thing, but disunity is not.** Its message is based on the Bible. **And yet The Salvation Army seems to compromise God's word, the Bible, to incorporate a world view that contradicts the teaching of God's laws.** Its ministry is motivated by the love of God, **but fails to extend or display God's love towards all of humanity.** Its mission is to preach the gospel of Jesus Christ and to meet human needs in His name without discrimination. **On the contrary, the gospel of Jesus Christ is not preached with love, it is taught in a rather condescending manner with the aid of double standards and discriminatory practices throughout The Salvation Army.**

Note:

1. The church, which is the body of Christ, is the temple of God. *And He is the head of the body, the church: who is the beginning, the firstborn from the dead; that in all things He might have the preeminence* (Colossians 1:18).

2. The baptism by the Holy Spirit is the means by which believers in Christ are incorporated into His body. *For by one Spirit are we all baptized into one body, whether*

we be Jews or Gentiles, whether we be bond or free; and have been all made to drink into one Spirit (1 Corinthians 12:13).]

3. The baptism by the Holy Spirit began on the day of Pentecost after Christ's resurrection. *For John truly baptized with water; but ye shall be baptized with the Holy Ghost (Spirit) not many days hence* (Acts 1:5). See also, Acts 2:1-4; 11:15-17. Therefore, the church began on the day of Pentecost after Christ's resurrection.

WHEN THE WORLD SPILLS OVER INTO THE CHURCH!

"Give thanks unto the LORD, call upon his name, make known HIS deeds among the people."

~ 1 Chronicles 16:8 KJV

November 28, 2012

Revised December 2, 2012

God's word through biblical instruction, should *we* take the opportunity to consider it seriously, guides us through all TRUTH! It carefully spells out what God expects of us and points out what we should expect from the world to not be deceived by the Prince of Darkness. However, a number of us do not believe in Heaven (angels) to consider Hell (demons), which makes it even more difficult to discuss the ramifications between good (righteous behavior) and evil (unrighteous behavior). Some of us comprehend that which is written as intended by God, but some of us miss the message entirely and become condemned or destroyed for lack of knowledge, wisdom and understanding.

For they that are after the flesh do mind the things of the flesh;
but they that are after the Spirit the things of the Spirit.
For to be carnally minded is death;
but to be spiritually minded is life and peace.
Because the carnal mind is enmity against God:
for it is not subject to the law of God, neither indeed can be.
So then they that are in the flesh cannot please God.

~ Romans 8:5-8

If we were to humble ourselves and seek God's face like never before—above all else—in bringing to Him all matters of the heart, God Himself will provide all we need. First, we must be willing to acknowledge His word (all of it), accept Christ as our Lord and Savior, surrender our carnal minds to His will and ask the Holy Spirit to be the dominant force in our lives—**over our flesh**. Then we should ask questions in all sincerity in requesting God's knowledge, wisdom and understanding to lead and guide us while being extra careful not to lean to our own understanding. For the carnal mind cannot fully understand the things of the spirit, and we should in no way attempt to predict or to know God's limit. By not conforming or succumbing to the ways of the world but renewing our minds to think like Christ through the Holy Spirit, we are made aware of the things of God to change our hearts to include complete repentance, forgiving ourselves and others.

And every spirit
that confesseth not that Jesus Christ
is come in the flesh is not of God:
and this is that spirit of antichrist,
whereof ye have heard that it should come;
and even now already is it in the world.

~ 1 John 4:3

Repentance is about confessing with our mouths but being committed through our hearts to living holy and believing in the Father, the Son and the Holy Spirit! It is not just about saying what will and should be, but doing and putting into action a right mindset with complete follow through and endurance. That means taking into consideration the entire concept of what is truly meant by **in the world, but not of the world**. There is the world's system (way or viewpoint) of doing things and then there is God's way (standards) of doing things. And when we, *God's children*, allow the things of the world to spill over into the church, we have invited trouble in the name of darkness to also enter our hearts and minds.

Set your affection on things above,
not on things on the earth.

~ Colossians 3:2

♦

*Love not the world,
neither the things that are in the world.
If any man love the world, the love of the Father is not in him.*

~ 1 John 2:15

God Is Nothing Like Man

The world uses and encourages discriminative and prejudicial practices, such as favoritism, racism, nepotism and oppression as a means of control; these are less-than-godly principles when dealing with people! *That there should be no schism in the body; but that the members should have the same care one for another* (1 Corinthians 12:25). Man views himself and others according to their position, title and net worth for exercising power over others in deeming who he thinks should be considered worthy, important and of value in the name of a false validation system. Some choose their profession in the same way they choose their material possessions—as a symbol of status in an attempt to project a certain image to the world. Unfortunately, in somewhat of the same manner, some may choose to be ministers or pastors for the reason of wanting to feel important and to rule or be the head over others. So you see, as in the world, it may have very little or nothing to do with choosing God out of love and a commitment to reaching souls with the right motive. Or it could quite simply be misguided, egotistical emotions getting in the way as the delivery of God's word or the intended message is tainted. Should you be gifted (blessed) with spiritual knowledge, wisdom and understanding in developing discernment, God will reveal the heart of each spirit to you in exposing hypocrisy and false prophets. This is why God instructs us through 1 John 4:1 to *believe not every spirit, but try the spirits whether they are of God: because many false prophets are gone out into the world.*

> *There is therefore now no condemnation to them which*
> *are in Christ Jesus, who walk*
> *not after the flesh, but after the Spirit.*
>
> ~ Romans 8:1

Everything man is not, God is more! Unlike man, God does not limit us and He does not expect you to limit Him. God is no respecter of persons. He, very lovingly and with divine care, extends the same opportunity to everyone (Judeans, Gentiles, Jews and Samaritans alike). He does not forcibly impose anything upon us, but through the encouragement of free will, He, with patience, gives us the choice to choose our own path. However, although He is a patient man, He can be quite persistent in His pursuit of you. Nonetheless, He will never leave you nor forsake you, and in return, you should never take Him for granted. He loves you unconditionally, and He will not fail to give you the adequate training to equip you to be victorious. Knowing you better than you know yourself and wanting nothing less than the best for you, God will not attempt to limit your growth or withhold any good thing from you. Instead, He may push you beyond your comfort zone or your perceived limit of yourself while attempting to stretch us as He encourages us and prepares us to come up higher in Him to the inner court beyond the veil.

> *Serve the Lord with reverent awe*
> *and worshipful fear; rejoice and be in high spirits*
> *with trembling [lest you displease Him].*
>
> ~ Psalms 2:11

The Shepherd of the Church

Pastoral leaders, teachers, Apostles (Bishops), prophets, Evangelists and children of God are called to come away from the world (depart from iniquity [sin]) and view the world through the eyes of God (connected to His heart). That does not mean for us to take a stance or view with arrogance that we ourselves are above reproach. No man but one (Jesus Christ) is perfect. And yes, we all fall short of the glory of the Lord; however, as leaders and children of God (a body of believers), we are held accountable to a higher standard. God's standard! We are expected to conduct ourselves not as those within the world but in accordance to a spirit of excellence! It's about patterning yourself after the character of Christ and improving your mindset with sincere intent! Twenty-four seven, day in and day out—without hesitation!

> *For all that is in the world, the lust of the flesh,*
> *and the lust of the eyes, and the pride of life,*
> *is not of the Father, but is of the world.*
>
> ~ 1 John 2:16

Each of us is created by the heavenly Father with a purpose for a purpose! Each of us is just as important, worthy and valued by our heavenly Father. Each of us has an important job to do or role to play in the building and uplifting of the Kingdom. Many of us are called, but so few of us are chosen. Why? Because we tend to lose our way as we become too consumed by the world and adapt to the things of the world. We fail too often to take heed to God's caution for us not to think of ourselves as being higher than we ought to. God is no respecter of persons, and if we truly are following His lead and answering His call, we are to be no respecter of persons either! That does not negate the position in which He has called us to perform, but we should be careful not to view our title and position according to those within the world. You must be mindful to not become bigheaded or puffed up. God does not like that!

> *Whoever is patient has great understanding,*
> *but one who is quick-tempered displays folly.*
>
> ~ Proverbs 14:29 NLT

To be an effective leader and teacher, you must be sensitive to *God's heart* and able and willing to view each individual (male and female) equally. You must be willing to humble yourself to relate to each individual regardless of their level of education and not in accordance to the world's system of educational definition or interpretation. You must be willing to meet the spiritual need of each individual at their level of comfort and possess the ability to escort them not just to your level of growth and potential but to God's! Because it is not about you; it is all about God, *His Kingdom* and righteousness. It is about reaching souls and ushering them to salvation.

> *For after that in the wisdom of God the world*
> *by wisdom knew not God, it pleased God by the foolishness*
> *of preaching to save them that believe.*
>
> ~ 1 Corinthians 1:21

Taking into consideration the diversity of each and every individual across every area or scope of their life, including yours, you should also be willing to recognize those who have exceeded your level of spiritual growth or maturity to be able to embrace them and allow them to teach you as well. Even in a leadership role, it is possible for you not to have all of the answers or pieces to the puzzle of God's knowledge, wisdom and understanding. If we are willing to work together in unity under the umbrella of God's Kingdom, where one is lacking, we can glean from each other as a body. A good leader should always be in a flexible position to teach as well as to be taught by others and *through* others. You should never feel that you know all there is to know about life, living and ministry (or any given subject for that matter). Otherwise, God cannot fully and effectively use you to **His greatest potential for your life**. You should never limit God or the potential of others (e.g., those within your congregation) to be used or sent by God!

> *Hearken, my beloved brethren,*
> *Hath not God chosen the poor of this world rich in faith,*
> *and heirs of the Kingdom which he hath*
> *promised to them that love him?*
>
> ~ James 2:5

Those Who Are Sent

God's children of light are sent out into the world of darkness to ignite (or encourage) change and to impact the atmosphere. But imagine traveling a million light years from your home to another planet or location. The success of your transport is contingent upon a systematic process that allows you to be seen in the natural (by earthly eyes). This process is called a "birthing," which is complete when your heavenly body (spirit) is redeveloped over a period of nine months in the womb of a woman (your earthly mother to earthly parents), which is not unlike the birthing of God in His natural (human) form, Jesus Christ. Being separated from our heavenly Father and creator, it takes some of us a lot longer to recall the history of our previous home to include our purpose and our God-given assignment. Over time, through a series of life events called tests (trials and tribulations), we encounter experiences designed to wake us from our slumber (darkness). Some are revived (restored) and move onward to fulfill God's will in reaching our destiny while others may have a little more difficulty bouncing back. Thus, they adapt to the world's system and never follow through with God's plan for their life.

> "Before you Gentiles knew God, you were slaves to so-called gods that do not even exist. So now that you know God (or should I say, now that God knows you), why do you want to go back again and become slaves once more to the weak and useless spiritual principles of this world?" Stand fast in the liberty that has made you free.
>
> ~ Galatians 4:8-9 NLT

As mentioned above, many are called but so few are chosen because we allow ourselves to lose sight of the mission. We fail to resist the wiles of the devil (Lucifer, Satan, the adversary). We give in to the enjoyment of that which excites our flesh instead of guarding our minds and girthing our loins with truth (Ephesians 6:14). We too, readily and easily, go through the motions of repenting (and change); but, deep down, it is just an illusion. So we become robots while holding on to everything the world has to offer and we bring the characteristics of the world into the church. (To name a few: the Jezebel spirit [controlling], a spirit of competitiveness, jealousy and division.) We even fail to realize those who have been sent to speak to us on behalf of the Lord to bring us a word of caution or correction. Why? Because they do not fit the world's image of worthiness! Too many of His children are being led astray and scattered about (Jeremiah 10:21, 23:1-2; Ezekiel 34:12). What we do not seem to realize is, God sees all, knows all and will judge each and every person according to his or her heart.

(Of whom the world was not worthy:)
they wandered in deserts and in mountains,
and in dens and caves of the earth.

~ Hebrews 11:38

When things are brought to my attention and I feel I may not have given the best answer or response, by way of *clarity*, the Holy Spirit always nudges me and gives me guidance, to include the right words to say. One of the things God has been dealing with me the most is the need for me to view things with objectivity by taking myself out of the equation. In fact, one morning upon leaving the house, I started crying as if someone had literally beaten me with an ugly stick. I could not quite understand or put my finger on the issue because there were several issues concerning my then place of worship. So I asked God, "How do I do what you command or ask of me?" And He said, "Emotional detachment!"

> *I will instruct you and teach you the way you should go;*
> *I will counsel you with my eye upon you.*
>
> ~ Psalm 32:8

Unfortunately, we allow ourselves to get more attached to people than we do to God. If we are not careful, that association can influence our judgment. Each of us was purposely sent here for a reason, meaning we have all been given the opportunity to receive a source of funding by way of being employed in the natural through the world system. But there is another reason why we are truly where we are and what positions we occupy. We have been allowed to meet and interact with those we have had the pleasure of connecting with. We are used by God to teach others in the same manner in which we are expected to learn. It is a *mutual* exchange, whether or not we wish to believe it, accept it or acknowledge it. *If we live in the Spirit, let us also walk in the Spirit. Let us not be desirous of vain glory, provoking one another, envying one another* (Galatians 5:25-26).

They drew names at random to see who would do what. Nobody, whether young or old, teacher or student, was given preference or advantage over another.

~ 1 Chronicles 25:8 MSG

You have to ask yourself what you are hoping to accomplish through your ministry and the expectation from others. Does your friendship or association interfere with what God is calling you to do? We want to give people more credit than they deserve; we put too much stock or trust in people to do the right thing. And when they let us down based on our perceived expectation, we feel out of sorts, wounded and hurt. People are people regardless of who they are in relation to their position, title or religious affiliation. We all fall short! But you have to be willing to separate yourself and ask God to bless you with sight beyond sight and the ability to carry out your assignment—no matter what! Even if it costs you some friendships!

I understand and acknowledge that there is an extreme darkness (or negative force) at work in the world. I also understand the influence and impact it can have on each individual. However, you must be willing to see it (observe it), dissect it and study it to honestly identify (discern) the characteristics. Then you have to be able to openly and honestly ask yourself if you, too, have started to notice any form of these characteristics within yourself to combat them spiritually. From the smallest of the smallest to the greatest visibility! Some of us are able to point out things in others that we are not willing to see in ourselves, but if the darkness exists in any form, you have to also understand how it works, spreads and takes hold. The longer a person is in a particular environment of darkness, the greater the hold, but deliverance is possible. If you are not being fed and growing spiritually in accordance to God's will (not man's), you may have to distance yourself from a situation, even if it means finding another place of worship, to look at it differently to be able to assist where needed.

*In whom the god of this world
hath blinded the minds of them which believe not,
lest the light of the glorious gospel of Christ,
who is the image of God, should shine unto them.*

~ 2 Corinthians 4:4

Christian Friend or Foe?

For a very long time, I have been very discouraged by others' view of Christianity. It can be quite disheartening and makes you wonder which book they are referencing. And then I came to learn how easy it is for people to make up what they are willing to believe or disbelieve along their spiritual journey. Because they are unwilling to change, they will even select a place of worship that does not encourage or teach the importance of being a doer and a hearer in applying God's principles to their life. They gather with others who only pour into the sanctuary on Sundays, and when they depart from the church, all is forgotten. They cannot even begin to tell you what the sermon was about, least of all the scripture from which the context was taken.

Listen, O isles, unto me; and hearken, ye people, from far; The LORD hath called me from the womb; from the bowels of my mother hath he made mention of my name. And he hath made my mouth like a sharp sword; in the shadow of his hand hath he hid me, and made me a polished shaft; in his quiver hath he hid me; And said unto me, Thou [art] my servant, O Israel, in whom I will be glorified. Then I said, I have laboured in vain, I have spent my strength for nought, and in vain: [yet] surely my judgment [is] with the LORD, and my work with my God.

~ Isaiah 49:1-4 KJV

People have become so accustomed to using the word "Christian"; it's similar to how they approach the word(s) "friend" or "friendship." Everyone who calls you a friend is not your friend. Not everyone who calls themselves Christians know enough about the character of Jesus Christ to even denote the derivative of the **Christ**ian root word. Do you remember when Christ was in the wilderness and He was approached by Satan, who was disguised as an angel surrounded by light? It was all a part of a master plan to deceive Jesus and to get Him to be disobedient to God! So do not be discouraged nor question your value or God when He deems you worthy to be used by Him to deliver a word or message to others.

Oh yes, you shaped me first inside, then out; you formed me in my mother's womb. I thank you, High God—you're breathtaking! Body and soul, I am marvelously made! I worship in adoration—what a creation! You know me inside and out, you know every bone in my body; You know exactly how I was made, bit by bit, how I was sculpted from nothing into something. Like an open book, you watched me grow from conception to birth; all the stages of my life were spread out before you, The days of my life all prepared before I'd even lived one day.

~ Psalm 139:14 MSG

◆

But God hath chosen the foolish things of the world to confound the wise; and God hath chosen the weak things of the world to confound the things which are mighty.

~ 1 Corinthians 1:27

Testimonial Conclusion

***The Letter and Spirit of the Law*[64]**: Through persecution and, later, conditioning by those who live according to the world's system, I bought into the lies of me being less than worthy because I lacked the desired image and education from a school *they* did not deem as being prestigious enough to qualify me for acceptance instead of rejection. As time went on, I learned other groups called cliques were also forming to impact division to a greater degree with the aid of peer pressure. Refusing to be recruited to jockey for a placement in one of these groups, I found myself standing alone on the sideline. So I, like many others, started second-guessing myself and being extremely

---

64 http://rcg.org/questions/p162.a.html

hard on myself to the point of self-condemnation in attempting to figure out the difficulty of my fit amongst the masses. The more I tried to identify with others, the less likely my need grew to be accepted by others. Although many have disputed and will continue to dispute how God uses me, I too have struggled with understanding and accepting how God is using me. But I have struggled even more with trying to accept those in the world who have allowed themselves to be so easily misguided and deceived by the world's system against all of what God has spelled out for us through His word.

The world, which is the devil's playground, develops laws, rules, regulations, policies and guidelines that do not encourage, enforce or maintain a high standard of justice and equality for all. Instead, people are allowed, by way of double standards, to avoid having to adhere to any of those laws, rules, regulations, policies and guidelines as they dance to the tune of much lower standards. Then you have those (like me) who are not deemed worthy to possess a certain skill or ability and successfully benefit from it unless we receive the appropriate blessing, approval or validation from man. Amazingly, we take that same attitude, behavior and worldly viewpoint into the church in how we interpret, teach and redirect God's word to obtain our (personal) desired outcome in manipulating others like those in the world for a little bit of power and control. If you teach wrong, the information or message is received wrong then perceived wrong and in turn, relayed to others wrong!

I cannot begin to tell you how often I have been told by people, including God's children, that, "When in Rome, do as the Romans do." And at the same time, I am hearing in my inner ear and feeling a tugging in my gut as the Holy Spirit reminds me to be vigilant and sober in scoping out the law of the land and reiterates, "In the world, not of the world!" I cannot tell you just how much joy I felt in my heart at that precise moment to understand and be reminded of my position and assignment God has entrusted to me. Just as there are varieties of gifts but the same spirit, each assignment, purpose and calling is indeed different (diverse in complexity at various levels and positions with the same importance) but necessary as a whole for the appropriate alignment and realignment of **Kingdom business**! The church is much more than a building of brick and mortar. *You* are the church! I AM the church! You must work on getting your house, the church, in order for the return of our Lord and Savior. He is looking for and coming back for a church without a spot or wrinkle.

> *Wherefore, beloved, seeing that ye look for such things, be diligent that ye may be found of him in peace, without spot, and blameless.*
>
> ~ 2 Peter 3:14 KJV

The key is, with God's wisdom, knowledge and understanding comes discernment! Seek the Father and put your complete trust in Him, being sure to never forget Jeremiah 17:5: "Thus says the LORD: 'Cursed is the man who trusts in man and makes flesh his strength, whose heart departs from the LORD'" as you encounter others along the journey of your spiritual growth. Exercise emotional detachment and obedience to His word and

His calling on your life, listening to what it is He commands of you and follow through with doing and saying what He tells you to in spite of what others think! For obedience is far greater and better than sacrifice. God will never steer you wrong. *Hearken, my beloved brethren, Hath not God chosen the poor of this world rich in faith, and heirs of the Kingdom which he hath promised to them that love him?* (James 2:5) When it is time to move onward and forward to the next level, you will know it!

Today, like never before, I am more aware of who I am and what it is I am called to do! I am not fully walking in it, but I am attempting to move in the right direction by making sure I encourage you! God is truly an awesome and powerful source of inspiration!

And we know that all things work together
for good to them that love God,
to them who are the called according to [his] purpose.

~ Romans 8:28 KJV

I would like to leave you with a message I received from a movie, *A Christmas Snow*, while watching a Christian network called Daystar. To all during this Christmas holiday, I pray you each obtain the gift of faith that you will have a love for God in your heart; friendship that will teach you to love others deeply; family that you will embrace no matter the circumstance; peace, that you will enjoy life to its fullest and have a full heart, forgiveness, that you will discover the healing and restoring power of forgiveness.

MINISTRY GIFTS
~ Ephesians 4:11 ~

	RESPONSIBILITY	NATURAL MANIFESTATION
Apostle	Doctrine and Discipline	Enjoys building things: projects, businesses, etc.
Prophet	Discern and Proclaim God's Word.	Has a keen (sometimes problematic) sense of Justice.
Evangelist	Present the Gospel of Christ to the lost.	Enjoys direct contact with people. Most are successful salesmen.
Pastor	To care for the everyday needs of the church family.	Enjoys serving. Loves to have people come to their home.
Teacher	Instruct the Church in the practical application of God's Word.	Is able to explain complex issues in a way that even a child can understand.

http://www.apostle.org/lectures/ffm.htm

Now there are diversities of gifts, but the same Spirit. And there are differences of administrations, but the same Lord. And there are diversities of operations, but it is the same God which worketh all in all. But the manifestation of the Spirit is given to every man to profit withal. For to one is given by the Spirit the word of wisdom; to another the word of knowledge by the same Spirit; To another faith by the same Spirit; to another the gifts of healing by the same Spirit; To another the working of miracles; to another prophecy; to another discerning of spirits; to another divers kinds of tongues; to another the interpretation of tongues: But all these worketh that one and the selfsame Spirit, dividing to every man severally as he will. For as the body is one and hath many members and all the members of that one body, being many, are one body: so also is Christ.

~ 1 Corinthians 4-12

Nine Fruits of the Spirit

Galatians ~ But the fruit of the Spirit is love, joy, peace, long-suffering, gentleness, goodness, faith, meekness, temperance: against such there is no law.

TAKE CARE OF GOD'S TEMPLE

For he that eateth and drinketh unworthily, eateth and drinketh damnation to himself, not discerning the Lord's body. For this cause many [are] weak and sickly among you, and many sleep.

~ 1 Corinthians 11:29-30

November 1, 2013

The year was 1967, and the first-attempted black Barbie doll, Francie, was introduced to the world of little girls. Imagine her dressed in a beautiful wedding gown decorated with multi-colored gemstones that resemble the foundations of the wall of the city as referenced in Relations 21:19-20 GWT which states: *The foundations of the city wall were beautifully decorated with all kinds of gems: The first foundation was gray quartz, the second sapphire, the third agate, the fourth emerald, the fifth onyx, the sixth red quartz, the seventh yellow quartz, the eighth beryl, the* ninth topaz, the tenth green quartz, the eleventh jacinth and the twelfth amethyst. And, her shoes are also covered in gemstones and her necklace, earrings and engagement ring or wedding band all match as they sparkle brightly. Knowing the possible value of collecting such a doll and that it could prove to be worth a pretty penny somewhere down the line, you would be so inclined to put her away for safe keeping. But due to the health problems of the one you intend to bless with such a purchase, you hesitate to wonder if her allergies, asthma and hay fever would prevent you from being able to surprise her with a gift you know she would appreciate with all her heart. Can you imagine the child's frustration in knowing she cannot join in on the fun with other children her age because playing with dolls causes an allergic reaction with the possibility of her breaking out in hives and limiting her ability to breath? Being exposed to the doll's hair brings about the same symptoms or reaction to being around dogs, cats and grass during a cookout in the park. Like no ordinary child, she has to be extra careful about what she comes in contact with through the elements of the air and her surroundings because something as simple and normal as the enjoyment of life could easily compromise her immune system!

In thee have they discovered
their fathers' nakedness: in thee have they humbled her
that was set apart for pollution.

~ Ezekiel 22:10 KJV

No longer that seven-year-old who was often quite sickly growing up for one reason or another, I have easily forgotten the need to be mindful of what may wreak havoc upon my body, called God's temple. Although my current health challenges are a little different than they were from age seven until midway into my teen years, other factors due to menopause and aging bones, through a process called the change of life, has taken center stage. Of course, I no longer have baby teeth that get recycled to regenerate another stronger set later down the road. So, if I fail to take care of this set without proper cleaning and consideration to my hygiene, then they are indeed gone forever. After breaking a leg or having a sprained ankle, I no longer heal as quickly as I once did before menopause. Something as simple as drinking a cold glass of milk is no longer a possibility without being able to keep it in my stomach for very long. Within seconds of swallowing it, I can actually hear it churning in my stomach before it starts to curdle. So, today, I am what you would call lactose intolerant. Enjoying a big bowl of butter pecan ice cream with chocolate syrup has its ups and downs; but I do it very carefully with cayenne pepper.

Our bodies are very complex! The body was designed by God with the ability to regenerate cells and heal itself naturally, if we are mindful of what we ingest. Fruits, vegetables and various flowers or plants provide an ample supply of natural vitamins and minerals to flow freely through the body as they are absorbed, stored and multiplied, or reproduced and carried from cell to cell by a process called osmosis and diffusion. Over the years, however, this process has been reduced or compromised by the influence of toxins or chemicals and other foods that are not acceptable to my body and interfere with the normal healing sequence to aid in the breakdown of certain cells, muscles, tissues and bones.

> *Better [is] a dinner of herbs*
> *where love is, than a stalled ox*
> *and hatred therewith.*
>
> ~ Proverbs 15:17 KJV

Once young but now old, I was also once blind, but now I see! That which was once a priority or interest no longer reigns supreme in my life. I can no longer use ignorance as an excuse for not knowing that which is important to God. My entire way of thinking should shift to incorporate those things that are important to God as being my main focus. It is not important for me to fit my thoughts and actions into the world's view of success by following the patterns and norms of those within the world just to say I am great. I must readjust my way of thinking to commit myself and actions to fall in line with God's mandate and purpose for my life. If I am able to say out of my mouth, *It is not about me, it is about God,* how much truth does that statement contain? If I say out of my mouth, *For God I live and for God I die,* am I truly willing to commit myself to God's will in sacrificing my own? The time is now for me to act upon those things that need to be changed **permanently** in implementing and carrying out God's mandate and purpose for my life in a radical way, regardless of the acceptance or understanding of others!

> *Then said I, Lo, I come*
> *(in the volume of the book it is written of me,)*
> *to do thy will, O God.*
>
> ~ Hebrews 10:7 KJV

Early Monday morning, on October 28 of this year, a coworker Steve and I were having a conversation about my decision to consult with God on every issue of my life before moving forward. We were interrupted by another coworker, Sherry, who always felt the need, for one reason or another, to challenge me on everything! Not fully aware of the full content of our discussion, she wanted to weigh in on my response to Steve's question. Feeling a little agitated, I answered her a little abruptly and reiterated, "I consult with God about everything!" In challenging my comment, she asked, "Did God say you could drink that coffee?" (which I was holding in my hand, by the way).

Just to give you a little background: My initial conversation with Steve, minutes before we were interrupted by Sherry, was in reference to my interest in precious gemstones, to include why I do the things I do. So I explained the meaning of each ring on my fingers in association with the gemstones on the Breastplate of Aaron as referenced in Exodus 28. And I shared how delighted I was to be working on my next God-given assignment to write my second book, *From What Tribe Were You Birthed: Understanding the Significance of Aaron's Breastplate*. But before getting started, I asked God to give me some clarity about the original twelve gemstones and their rightful order.

To that end, God has been talking to me about every aspect of my life, including the increased negativity I encounter within my working environment (or general surroundings). While I'm mindful of the impact of this present darkness to my soul, it is God who reiterates the importance of me keeping a level head. On that day, at that particular time and moment, He was cautioning me about keeping my flesh under subjection in not allowing the **spirit of offense** to get the upper hand. In other words, I was being scolded and reminded not to take a defensive posture in rising up and becoming combative or letting the individual nor the incident get under my skin. So I humbly quoted some scripture references and retreated to my desk while allowing God to minister *His peace and His calm* for a satisfying response unto Him. For I am learning, it is no longer important for me to prove anything to anybody in my own strength.

When you realize you are called and chosen by God to accomplish Kingdom business on His behalf, you have to be willing to set yourself apart in allowing God to lead you—no matter the situation. Before I go any further, let me first say that there is no reference to drinking coffee or smoking cigarettes as being a sin in the Bible. And neither is there a reference to women being limited to wearing dresses as opposed to wearing pants to church to worship the Lord or fellowship with others. Tradition and religiosity have dictated patterns and norms handed down from generation to generation that have nothing to do with God within the context in which they are prematurely being taught. However, exercising wisdom and using discernment is very important. So, unbeknownst to Sherry, I was previously diagnosed as having osteoporosis. As a woman who has already reached the full menopausal stage, which means there is an increasingly declining drop in estrogen along with a drop in calcium, it would be beneficial for me to eliminate my intake of any and everything that would deplete my existing bone mass. Therefore, my choice to continue to consume caffeine or sodas did not come without a price.

Four weeks prior to Monday, October 28, I was doing so well! Initially, I took the advice of a chiropractor, Dr. Marcia Boyce-Levi, who introduced me to a twenty-one-day detoxification that aided my decision and ability to change my daily diet. Not only had I cut out all caffeine and sodas, I had limited my consumption of red meat and pork. I was starting to lose weight, I was sleeping better at night and I had even started to notice a glow and luster to my skin. With one incident at work, I purchased a cup of coffee that reintroduced a taste and craving to my flesh. I even joked about falling off the wagon! Well, that following Tuesday (October 29), God started talking to me in a language He knew I would understand to honor His expectation once and for all. Leaving work Tuesday evening, I had difficulty walking from the building to the subway. Reaching my car, I wondered where I had stored my crutches and my cane for getting around more comfortably. My head may be hard at times, but God's language, called PAIN, gets through all the time! First, He was subtle in giving me the opportunity to make the right choice. Then, He was patient in waiting for me to exercise judgment. Then, He exercised longsuffering in waiting for me to draw upon His wisdom. Then He said, "Enough is enough; let's do this the hard way." So He turned up the heat! Which would you prefer: the easy way or hard way?

As I went from the couch to the bed trying to find a position that was conducive to the least amount of pain, I tossed and turned throughout the night, getting little to no sleep at all. God wanted me to not only feel the pain; He wanted me to concentrate on it in order to choose between Him and the pain. On Wednesdays, I have a standing appointment with Dr. Levi, and I was too ashamed to tell her how much I (unintentionally and undeliberately) undermined her efforts in working with the Lord to restore my vessel. But as a child of God and chosen vessel herself, she knew. Nonetheless, she still ministered to me with love and patience in offering encouragement and healing to my body and spirit. Later that night, through Dr. Boyce-Levi, God lessened my pain while allowing me to sleep as He reminded me of what He expected. Throughout the following day (Thursday, October 31), I was reminded of Paul and his thorn in his side. As I walked more freely with minimal to no pain, I was reminded of **God's power, glory, miracles, signs and wonders!** If you were to supernaturally feel my pain, in great detail with the same intensity, you would truly understand why **obedience is better than sacrifice.** No more caffeine, no more coffee and no more sodas is my higher goal; and I have lessened my intake of these products tremendously to be able to see a divine difference!

> *And this I pray, that your love may abound*
> *yet more and more in knowledge and [in] all judgment;*
> *That ye may approve things that are excellent;*
> *that ye may be sincere and without*
> *offence till the day of Christ;*
>
> ~ Philippians 1:9-10 KJV

A Summary of the Pain: Imagine receiving a bone density test results that shows you have abnormally decreased bone in your spine, pelvis and right and left hip areas. You are told to be very careful and mindful in how you bend, stoop and lift up. Imagine being so fragile that you are told that, should you pick up anything the wrong way, you could literally break your back. You are then instructed on what things to eat or take in the way of vitamins and minerals to help strengthen your bones as well as what things are best not to consume at all. You even conduct your own research and are quite knowledgeable about holistic healing in various areas, which was gifted to you by God to help others. But you fail to take heed to your own advice and jeopardize God's ability to use your vessel for the uplifting of the Kingdom. Your bones begin to deteriorate more and more to the point of the thigh bone feeling disjointed and out of place. You just know it has dropped down out of its nesting place thus preventing you from walking, sitting on the toilet and lying down. It hurts to the touch and is deeply pained and inflamed when your upper thigh comes into close proximity of the toilet seat. You want to cry out in anger, and you have no one to blame but yourself. The miracle is knowing just how much pain and discomfort you endured when, a day or two later, it was as if it never happened. You cannot tell me God ain't bad! So *what do I do with my pain*? Be obedient to God and proclaim liberty to the captives!

An excerpt from Dr. Charles F. Stanley's *Work of the Believer*: God bestows upon His followers gifts tailored to each one's ordained assignments. The Holy Spirit reveals our calling and we're to give our best effort. Of course, no matter what the task may be, the result will be worthless unless the Father breathes life into it. In other words, we are entrusted with God-appointed work. He assigns the duty, provides the skills and causes growth. The Lord deserves all of the glory. We are blessed simply to be a part of His plan.

Suggestion: Be obedient to God; prayer; vitamin D3, calcium, magnesium and zinc; a reliable, dedicated, passionate and God-fearing practitioner like Dr. Boyce-Levi (nutritionist, chiropractor, teacher and life coach). **Reference:** http://www.standardprocess.com/Standard-Process/Purification-Program

THE REALITY OF IT ALL

For those who are living according to the flesh set their minds on the things of the flesh [which gratify the body], but those who are living according to the Spirit, [set their minds on] the things of the Spirit [His will and purpose]. Now the mind of the flesh is death [both now and forever—because it pursues sin]; but the mind of the Spirit is life and peace [the spiritual well-being that comes from walking with God—both now and forever]; the mind of the flesh [with its sinful pursuits] is actively hostile to God. It does not submit itself to God's law, since it cannot, and those who are in the flesh [living a life that caters to sinful appetites and impulses] cannot please God.

~ Romans 8:5-8 AMP

WHAT IS YOUR REALITY?

*Such things are only a shadow of what is to come
and they have only symbolic value;
but the substance [the reality of what is foreshadowed]
belongs to Christ.*

~ Colossians 2:17 AMP

March 30, 2017

There is a great deal of negativity in the world, which is created and directed by the influence of darkness. Some people refuse to acknowledge reality to see it in its absolute form! I know the acceptance of truth can prove to be life shattering—if you DO NOT allow yourself to unlearn to relearn by re-evaluating all your thought patterns. But the reality of a truth can be richly liberating when you make a vow to keep an open mind to view your surroundings with great objectivity. With much determination, I prefer to acknowledge and to accept truth to free myself from living my life in denial of all that's going on around me, even if I am not directly impacted by the events.

Many people tend to close their eyes to what is going on around them; especially if they are not directly affected by the outcome. But it is very difficult for me to observe unfairness of any kind and not speak on it or write about it as a watchman who was put in position by God to honor my purpose, regardless if others agree or not! *On your walls, O Jerusalem, I have appointed and stationed watchmen (prophets), Who will never keep silent day or night; You who profess the Lord, take no rest for yourselves, And give Him no rest [from your prayers] until He establishes Jerusalem And makes her a praise on the earth* (Isaiah 62:6-7 AMP).

In John W. Newton's book, *A Pen Named Man: Our Purpose*, he states: "As a human being you develop your greatest satisfaction in life through interactions with other people." Honestly speaking, because people can be so hurtful, l wouldn't mind living on a secluded island as a place of refuge when being around people becomes a little unbearable for me. I could simply do all my shopping online and have my purchases shipped or delivered by airmail. I could always work from home. However, I truly believe we are tested and evaluated by God based on our interactions with others; because we all play a very important role or part in each other's development and life lessons. Each time I open the Bible to read or study it, I run across something that leaves me speechless in confirmation of how we are connected and given significant responsibility by God! For instance, let's take a look at Ezekiel 3:17-19 from The Message Bible:

> *Son of man, I've made you a watchman for the family of Israel. Whenever you hear me say something, warn them*

for me. If I say to the wicked, 'You are going to die,' and you don't sound the alarm warning them that it's a matter of life or death, they will die and it will be your fault. I'll hold you responsible. But if you warn the wicked and they keep right on sinning anyway, they'll most certainly die for their sin, but you won't die. You'll have saved your life.

Practice makes perfect! We just have to stop trying to convince folks that the experiences that make up their reality is not true because we haven't experienced their truth to be impacted the same.

Therefore, we must practice being better stewards over that which belongs to the Lord. *The earth is the Lord's and everything in it, the world and all who live in it* (Psalm 24:1 NIV). *For if we go on willfully and* deliberately sinning after receiving the knowledge of the truth, there no longer remains a sacrifice [to atone] for our sins [that is, no further offering to anticipate], *but a kind of awful and* terrifying expectation of [divine] judgment and the fury of a *fire and* burning wrath which *will consume the adversaries [those who put themselves in opposition to God]* (Hebrews 10:26-27 AMP).

What exactly is a pattern or lifestyle?

> ▸ Pattern[65]: Consistent and recurring characteristic or trait that helps in the identification of a phenomenon or problem which, in turn, serves as an indicator or model for predicting its future behavior.

---

65 http://www.businessdictionary.com/definition/pattern.html

- Lifestyle[66]: a set of attitudes, habits, or possessions associated with a particular person or group.

As human beings, we often shy away from being open and honest with one another about who we really are underneath the masks we present. When I was working near Union Station, I would see various homeless people upon entering or exiting the station. I cannot seem to walk past a homeless person or someone in need without feeling remorseful and wanting to help in some way. Whatever I could give or share, I would do freely to include a warm smile or a heartfelt hello. One day during lunch, a middle aged white man approached me to say, "You always speak, smile and offer what you can. Do you know I'm a racist? I don't like your kind, but you still stop and spend time with me. You will stop when many others including my own kind keep going. Because of you, I am ashamed! Can you forgive me? I see light all around you." I looked at him and started to shed tears as I said yes and walked away. I, unfortunately, don't remember seeing him anymore after that day; but I looked for him. Not once did he disrespect me; he was never rude or unpleasant in any way. Perhaps he was an angel! He touched my heart that day and even as I write to share this story, which I had forgotten, there are tears streaming down my face.

When people actually reveal who they are, it's hard for them to convince you of anything else after you see what you need to see for yourself with your own heart! After observing my heart, the man in the above story revealed his heart to me. The action

---

66 http://www.dictionary.com/browse/lifestyle

of one individual can change the heart of another if we are willing and open to the possibility of seeing and accepting truth.

Food for Thought

Understanding the make-up and functionality of man is very important; **I LIVE IN A BODY, I HAVE A SOUL, I AM SPIRIT!** The only place where limitation begins is in my mind, and I do not have to allow the limitations that others attempt to place upon me as a form of control to hold me in bondage or at a certain level to dictate my place of being. Where others see me or intend for me to see myself is not where I have to be or live within my mind, heart and spirit!

Your mind, unfortunately, cannot distinguish between a real event and something you think about in your mind. Scripture tells us, as a man thinks (within his mind), so is he within his heart. That's why it is so important for us to guard our thoughts. And we must always be mindful of the conversations we entertain to be careful not to incorporate someone else's thoughts into our mind (brainwashing).

Whatever belief you hold within your subconscious becomes your reality; but if you rely on the Holy Spirit, He will take you by the hand and guide you into all the truth (full and complete truth) there is (see John 16:13)!

HISTORY: YOURS OR MINE?

For whatsoever things were written aforetime were written for our learning, that we through patience and comfort of the scriptures might have hope.

~ Romans 15:4

November 27, 2014

Revised March 30, 2017

If you were to take a nice long and hard look at the word "history," you would see two entirely different words: **"his"** *and* **"story."** If you were to think about it, it truly makes a lot of sense. Is my story your story or your story my story? No, not exactly! My story hinges on my experiences and your story, I am sure, also is linked to your experiences. But for some reason, because many people find it hard to believe a truth as it relates to me, they want to rewrite my story! In fact, they are often adamant, and sometimes indignant, on insisting that they can tell me that my story is a lie. And if I allow that manipulation and intimidation to take place, I am denying my existence and myself. Why?

Because for years I agonized over my reason for being, down to the exact year, month, day and time of my birth! I questioned my purpose as it related to the heart God gave me; a heart so easily broken and hurt by the level of unrighteousness in the world! And I could not seem to bring myself to do to others what was so easily done to me. I would cry often and ask God why He had given me such a heart that prevented me from being like so many others in the world who gave no thought to their actions or their consequences. During the unfolding of my true identity, God revealed the answer to so many of my questions. In particular, He said I was not created to be like everyone else; I was fashioned with a *sensitive* heart for Him and others!

See, if you were not present during my experiences and in sync with my spirit to feel the impact these experiences have had on me as they touched my heart, my mind and my soul like the experiences of my ancestors, then who are you to tell me that my story is a lie? Or could it possibly be that you were a negative part of my experiences, therefore, wanting people to see you not as the person you were or are, but as the person you thought you had become? Yes, your past is your past; however, it is still a part of who you are! Especially if you attempt to lock away secrets deep within your darkness where you think they are safely tucked away and hidden. *For there is nothing hidden that will not become evident, nor anything secret that will not be known and come out into the open (Luke 8:17 AMP).*

Unfortunately, throughout time, people have attempted to rewrite history to deny the existence of God, Heaven and Hell. Often, as man begins to tamper with things to erase history by redirecting or restructuring his lies to resemble a false truth, he misses something! You must be willing to see out the hidden treasures (or clues) in the midst of the darkness by starting at the beginning to learn who you were created to be!

Food for Thought: How to govern yourself accordingly! The nature of the testing or the strategy in the wilderness:

▶ Your wilderness could also be the Battlefield!

God, knowing that the enemy comes to steal, kill and destroy while using individuals within your dimension, puts you into position to withstand the wiles of the devil. But these individuals in the flesh (earthly bound) are being influenced by spirits from another dimension (without physical form or bodies). Therefore, you have to figure out a way to program your way of thinking (mindset) to govern yourself for dealing with what's directed at you, being mindful to conduct yourself at all times in accordance with the expectation of God.

So, the trick is governing your will, emotion and intellect for <u>NOT</u> responding or reacting outside of the WILL OF GOD for your life!

IMAGE

*So God created mankind was in his own image,
in the image of God he created them;
male and female he created them.*

~ Genesis 1:27 NIV

November 30, 2016

This topic was first laid on my heart approximately six months ago or more, but it has taken me until now to follow through in seeking direction from the Holy Spirit to put pen to paper to record the message and share it with you. My definition or understanding of the word "image," at best, was tainted by man's worldview as it pertains to appearance and reputation, which left me, unfortunately, struggling with my thoughts. But God's ways are not ours and our ways are not His; however, as Children of God we must attempt to renew our way of thinking to resemble that of the Lord's! Scripture refers to it as having the mind of Christ!

Let's start off by entertaining a thought! What if someone told you they were interviewing candidates for a very important position, but they were seeking to fill it with someone or anyone possessing the right image? What would that look like? And how would that actually make you feel, knowing you were the most qualified, but the less likely one to be selected on the basis of you not fitting that image? So, what did the Hiring Manager exactly mean when he said the "right image"? Especially when the Bible states we were all created in the image and likeness of God our Father and Creator!

Elaborating further to go a little deeper, aren't we all tripart beings, thus possessing a (1) spirit, (2) body and (3) soul? God is Spirit! He birthed himself through Immaculate Conception on earth in the form of a man; a human being possessing a body, spirit and soul! In the beginning was the word (God, the Father and Spirit) and later, the word dwelled among us in the appearance of the living word (Jesus, the son of God). In death, God the Father and the son gifted us with the Holy Spirit and eternal life through Salvation. And yet, we still refuse to see the importance of what we have been given to see beyond the surface of a superficial mindset or carnal thinking in how we view one another. Yes, the previous sentence can be viewed as being redundant; but it was worded exactly as it is to emphasize a point for clarity. Man views things from the outside while God takes into consideration the entire package from the inside out with great emphasis on the heart of the matter.

Now, I would like to encourage you to close your eyes and exercise your mind through visualization. Spirit, in essence, is neither male nor female. There is no outer shell or material substance to influence the mind seduction of the flesh. Spirit is a mass or substance of pure energy inside and out; a life force or source equally shared by that which is living or dead. Energy can be directed or absorbed! Meaning, it has the potential to achieve its purpose.

What is potential? Possessing a quality or capacity (ability) to fulfill one's purpose. It can be a latent or undeveloped resource (potential) leading to future success. Nonetheless, we were all created by God as having the same untapped inner and limitless potential!

The Bible, should you choose to read it and apply it to your life, is very clear about who God is in addition to His expectations of us. The first step is to read it, study it to show ourselves approved and rightly divide the word of truth. When I consider that last part, I believe it is about interpretation and comprehension. However, not necessarily about a feeling or your point of view, but allowing yourself to be guided by the Holy Spirit to know God's intended purpose based on His character, which is far greater than our limited understanding of image. Spirit has no boundaries; the sky is the limit! And I can do all things through Christ who strengthens me! Never let anyone coerce you into believing your potential has no value because they are not willing to acknowledge it! Their loss, not yours!

Reference:

The term "image of God" occurs three times in the Bible. In Genesis 1:26-27 and 9:6, we find out that man is created in the image of God. In 2 Corinthians 4:4, we see the phrase used in reference to Jesus who is the "image of God."

Food for Thought:

- What is character versus reputation?

- What is image if it lacks the "image of God" (substance or character)?

- What about integrity? Where does it fit in your definition of image?

TRANSFORMATION

*And be not conformed to this world:
but be ye transformed by the renewing of your mind,
that ye may prove what is that good, and acceptable,
and perfect, will of God.*

~ Romans 12:2

October 13, 2015

They say life is not fair! However, how can a gift of life that was given to us from God not be fair? Technically, fairness has nothing to do with life; it is directly related to the actions of people and the choices we make that impact the outcome of our lives. We have grown rather accustomed to attempting to justify our actions with the intent of making ourselves feel good about not holding ourselves accountable for anything we do. Our willingness to be gullible in believing and allowing ourselves to be influenced by those who operate outside of the will of God has altered the direction of our moral compass to change the definition of morality. In other words, we have made wrong right and right wrong and told ourselves it is perfectly normal to do so! But what is normal?

We don't ask the right questions. We stop reading the word of God for ourselves. We don't study to show ourselves approved by God, but we seek the approval of man on the basis of what He is able to reward us in accordance to the world's standards. We literally sell our souls to align ourselves with darkness, and the deeper we transcend into that darkness, the more difficult the incline toward the light becomes. This is mainly because we stop thinking for ourselves as we begin to lose our identity, which is instrumental in setting us apart to embrace our uniqueness. And should you resist blending in or fitting in, just know the challenges become a little more intense and frequent as a wearing-down tactic is administered to uproot you from your post (your God-ordained position) in Him.

Unfortunately, some people are just as naturally evil as others are naturally good—deep down to the bone. The objective is to be **righteous** and **holy**, forever doing what is right in your heart no matter the circumstances, and following our God-given example, Jesus Christ, as it relates to God and His righteousness—not man's ideology! To be transformed, step away to see and renew your way of thinking. Transformation is always possible through Christ from the inside out, and God expects it! We simply cannot get caught up in the world's way of doing things. That's why God tells us in Romans 12:2 to be transformed by the renewing of our minds.

By taking me from a place of unbelief to belief, God has given me the opportunity to share my spiritual journey with you. Not as someone who is perfect or who has all the answers, but as a person who has undergone a sense of change—a transformation or state of metamorphosis. This book references that change which has not always been easy or steady. There have been steep hills and rocky terrain! It has been an extreme challenge to keep my focus, but my motive and will has been to please God—not man—while going through the fire, no matter how painful it can be.

> *But now, this is what the Lord, your Creator says, O Jacob, And He who formed you, O Israel, "Do not fear, for I have redeemed you [from captivity]; I have called you by name; you are Mine! "When you pass through the waters, I will be with you; And through the rivers, they will not overwhelm you. When you walk through fire, you will not be scorched, Nor will the flame burn you. "For I am the Lord your God, The Holy One of Israel, your Savior; I have given Egypt [to the Babylonians] as your ransom, Cush (ancient Ethiopia) and Seba [its province] in exchange for you. "Because you are precious in My sight, You are honored and I love you, I will give other men in return for you and other peoples in exchange for your life.*
>
> *~ Isaiah 43:1-4 AMP*

SHARING MY THOUGHTS ON THE SUBJECT OF MY EDUCATION, CAREER AND GOD

September 26, 2010

Revised September 21, 2015

My mother always directed my focus toward getting a good education although she did not envision education beyond high school! She did believe that getting good grades and being an honor student throughout my grade school experience would get me a very good paying job. However, I felt going to college and obtaining as much knowledge and education as possible would help me obtain more than just a job. I wanted a career that would sustain me to succeed beyond retirement and old age! So school became a way of escape for me. It was an opportunity to get lost in books to forget my troubles at home and later at work. I thought equality, education and the pursuit of a career was the American Dream and opportunity was granted to all! I made the assumption that man was capable of learning from his past mistakes to treat all men and women as being equal, and all my dreams would fall into place if I trusted man to do the right thing. But I unfortunately gave man too much credit as I watched mankind lie, cheat and exploit others on their way to the top. No, not everybody starts out this way, but they soon get confused as they allow themselves to be seduced by the world to be all they can be!

Throughout my life, I have drowned myself in my studies and my work, not knowing it would be used as part of God's plan to propel me toward my destiny. I pursued education and jobs for career growth above developing relationships with my family and God. Socializing and developing friendships took a back seat as well because I had a general succession plan for my growth and getting ahead! I kept finding myself surrounded by people within various organizations, including governmental, who wanted me to prove myself (my worth) over and over again, even after I had succeeded at putting in the necessary time and energy to fulfill the tasks thrown at me. There were countless long working hours, missed lunches and sacrificed weekends with family and friends to get projects accomplished for others with very little to no appreciation. The more I did, the more that was expected of me, and my growth for excelling in an area of my choosing did not work in my favor as I had hoped. For some, when you do not fit the image of the status quo, having the necessary talents, skills and know-how to execute your assignments as deemed by man will not necessarily make any difference in being promoted or allowed to excel in business or your career choice once you have served your usefulness in being manipulated. Nonetheless, little did I know, God was setting me up in allowing all of what I was experiencing and obtaining through work and school assignments to be an intricate part of my spiritual growth for His glory. He was preparing me for a career with Him and for Him through my failed belief in man.

God does nothing by happenstance! Everything is either orchestrated or allowed by Him with divine purpose in keeping with Romans 8:28, which states, "And we know that all things work together for good to them that love God, to them who are the called according to *his* purpose." Once I began to take into consideration God's plan for my life over what I thought I wanted, the world's ability to seduce me no longer had the influence to rule over me. Man, who lacks the love of God in his heart, will attempt to deceive you into believing he has integrity and your best interest at heart, all while making promises he never intends to keep unless there is something in it for him. Man rationalizes his unrighteous thinking as he plots, schemes and plans his elevation over your demise. Lacking wisdom, knowledge and understanding to see beyond man's reputation to know his character, I was naïve to think I could blend in and be accepted for who I am amongst those who operate outside of the will of God.

God expects me not to be afraid (2 Timothy 1:7) of speaking up and letting those around me know that I know they are deceitful. It is easy for people to walk by you, hold a conversation with you and smile in your face when they do not think you truly see them for who they are as they attempt to deceive you time and time again. But, it is a lot harder for them when they know you know. Then they attempt to figure out ways to justify their wrongdoing by deceiving others into believing that the person they deceived not only deserved it but lacked the skills or willingness to do anything about it. Then the real games begin—the spiritual warfare! They deny you meaningful training and details with the attempt to hold you in a position they feel you are more suited for by design. The design is based on what position they are in to abuse their power and control to limit your growth. But God is awesome! He never leaves you in the dark! Half the battle, for me, is being able to see. The other half is conducting myself accordingly and not to fall for the traps while attempting to keep my focus on God.

Choosing God is my greatest reward! Following His lead as I let things divinely play out enriches my life of success. God's plan for my life is strategically orchestrated through the events (good, bad and indifferent) He has allowed and the people He purposely positioned around me for the benefit of grooming me for the Kingdom. God is the Father of my universe. He is all-knowing, omnipresent and magnificent! He knows more about me than any person on the face of this earth, including myself. He knows what is going to take place, how it will play out and the beginning and end of each step of my life. And yet, He still makes several attempts to direct me in all thy ways. Why? Because He loves me unconditionally and wants nothing but the best for me! Amazingly, in spite of all my foolishness, He has never given up on me. Pursuing me, He relentlessly and patiently waited on me to come out of darkness to realize my purpose. God truly coordinates time and space for our life.

WORK ENVIRONMENTS

WORKPLACE BULLYING AND VIOLENCE ARE SERIOUS ISSUES!

September 17, 2013

In the wake of the aftermath yesterday, I wonder if those in positions of leadership and power are still refusing to address the many issues within workplace environments. Why do we insist on waiting to seriously address outstanding issues until "something rotten in the state of Denmark" takes the countless lives of innocent people? And as I watched one segment of the news upon my arrival home from work, I was extremely unnerved by the comment of one reporter who had the audacity to make light of the situation! Yes, employees have had supervisors they were not entirely pleased with all throughout their working careers, but for the past four to five years, something else has been taking place—an elevated presence of workplace violence that others have insisted on demising and sweeping under the rug.

The active shooter who was responsible for the incident that occurred at the navy yard yesterday cannot give an account of his side of the story. And I am more than certain that no one at this point is willing or able to muster up any compassion for the entire situation to want to know what took place besides him losing his job that would trigger a response or action of violence. My heart not only grieves for those who were caught in the crossfire, it bleeds for the shooter as well. I have experienced workplace bullying and could not have imagined being subjected to any type of workplace abuse in my adult life. It can be just as devastating observing such an act of bullying being done to others as it is to experience it yourself. Especially while those in position of leadership to implement change in ensuring a safe workplace environment for all only encourage a culture that embraces and condones the behavior in acceptance of what they have deemed to be a normal and welcoming leadership style. But I say and will continue to say, "Workplace bullying is unacceptable at any level!"

WORKPLACE BULLYING IS UNACCEPTABLE!

Now therefore, behold, the cry of the children of Israel is come unto me: and I have also seen the oppression wherewith the Egyptians oppress them.

~ Exodus 3:9

October 10, 2010

As I prepare for church this morning, I am reminded of the ways in which God is using me to accomplish His will. I am truly grateful, appreciative and remorseful all at the same time. Remorseful because I can remember a time I not only ran from God and what He had to offer me, but I doubted His existence. Grateful because in spite of me and my past, God still loves me (John 15:13) and wants nothing but the best for me. Appreciative because God never stopped trying to reach me! In creating me for a purpose with a purpose, He was persistent in His approach in making sure I received my inheritance. Persistent to the point of revealing Himself to me and allowing me to see myself through His eyes! Oh God, my passion for You this day is nothing like I would have imagined. *Great [is] my boldness of speech toward you, great [is] my glorying of you: I am filled with comfort, I am exceeding joyful in all my (our) tribulation* (2 Corinthians 7).

Ordering my steps while rebuilding my confidence, trust, belief and faith in Him, God was training me to be fearless and teaching me to fight for the uplifting of the Kingdom. Finally, unselfishly yielding myself to Him, He gradually enlightened me to His plan for my life. Then I realized God was (and is) with me always as I gladly accepted my assignment in knowing God was deliberately putting me in situations (sending me to places where there was darkness to be His light [John 9:5]). Once I was in, God gave me no way out as He forced me to stand and fight. *For ye have not received the spirit of bondage again to fear; but ye have received the Spirit of adoption, whereby we cry, Abba, Father* (Romans 8:15). This is not a time for passivity!

> *Who art thou that judgest another man's servant?*
> *to his own master he standeth or falleth.*
> *Yea, he shall be holden up:*
> *for God his able to make him stand.*
>
> ~ Romans 14:4

Entering the church this morning, my spirit soared as always and took off into orbit. Such powerful sermons; two for the price of one! They fit perfectly together. No one but God could have set this up! Pastor Deborah Heath spoke on

"Suffering: Why Me Lord?" and Bishop Raymond Horton III spoke on "Evil Down on the Inside." Many times, I wondered if people gave any thought to the impact of their actions as directed toward others. Do evildoers recognize the suffering they impose upon others that resulted from their selfishness? Do people in positions of power realize their less-than-favorable leadership skills have nothing to do with being a good leader? Being in a position *of* authority is about learning how to be *in* authority. Leading is more than just setting a course of direction and influencing others to follow that direction by way of bullying. It is about leading by way of motivating people and empowering them to be effective leaders themselves. Leading has more to do with character and integrity than being popular. Leading is about being a good example for others to follow: a role model. Is there no one in a position of power and authority who is committed to doing the right thing in making sure all are held accountable for their actions? Regardless of who you are, we all have to answer to someone! Your actions (good or bad) have consequences. Each action is the equivalent of sowing a seed. And each seed eventually reaps a harvest. *From what I have seen, those who sow evil will reap evil and those who deliberately or undeliberately cause trouble to others will get it back* (Job 4:8). If undeliberate, unmerited favor can be granted or given from the Lord. For He is able to see your heart, but you should be willing to ask for and seek forgiveness! All things should be followed or handled decently and in order.

Learning I had the opportunity to leave the employment of The Salvation Army National Headquarters to return to the government sector after so many years of working in the private sector was God shining down on me. This was a desire God was honoring on my behalf through my obedience. However, little did I know that at the time, this was an example of God's *permissive will* to release me from a present situation but not from my God-ordained assignment! So God paved the way for me to be considered for and selected to receive a challenging career intern position (CIP) with the U.S. Department of Energy. Excited to leave the lion's den and embark upon a new adventure, I did not realize I was entering another lion's den in continuance of doing my Father's business. For I had not matured spiritually enough to understand the nature or importance of a God-given assignment. From glory to glory, new level new devil! For to whom much is given, much is required!

> *So I returned,*
> *and considered all the oppressions that*
> *are done under the sun: and behold the tears of*
> *[such as were] oppressed, and they had no comforter;*
> *and on the side of their oppressors [there was] power;*
> *but they had no comforter.*
>
> ~ Ecclesiastics 4:1

Approximately six months after starting my new position at the U.S. Department of Energy, I noted a number of disturbing events within the office of Learning and Workforce Development that trickled downward and left a presence of its thickness throughout the entire building. Observing my surroundings revealed more than I had expected or cared to see. And God was allowing me to meet others within various agencies, departments or divisions who shared their testimonies concerning the darkness they were encountering. It was then that I understood my assignment to be the same no matter where I went until God was ready to reassign me or charge me with another. Being absent from one environment and present in another only revealed the difference in people according to their physical appearance. What was common were the dark spirits surrounding them and influencing their actions. So yet again, I found myself to be in the company of those within a working environment who were more concerned about exerting control through fear and bullying tactics than accomplishing the goals and objectives of the organization. And of course, they deny any wrongdoing. *All the ways of a man [are] clean in his own eyes; but the LORD weigheth the spirits* (Proverbs 16:2).

> *There is no fear in love;*
> *but perfect love casteth out fear*
> *Because fear hath torment. He that feareth*
> *is not made perfect in love.*
>
> ~ 1 John 4:18

As this unfavorable behavior escalated, it became apparent this was the organizational culture that was allowed and delegated downward. It had become the norm for those who had been here the longest. No one should have to get used to dealing with and accepting disparaging behavior from anyone! Having had my share of hostile working environments, I found it necessary to rebuke the influence of demonic spirits as directed at me (and others) by exposing them, addressing the issues and confronting it head-on. However, those in positions of power who abuse their authority to oppress and bully others do not take too kindly to resistance! In fact, they often solicit assistance from others in lower positions to help fuel and carry out their personal agenda to wage war, create confusion, divide and conquer. But as a child of God who was purposely assigned to shake things up, I must be careful not to allow myself to be used as a pawn by evildoers to wreak (inflict) havoc (mayhem and foolishness) upon another. Even at the cost of persecution in being threatened with the possibility of receiving low performance (evaluations) ratings! Nonetheless, as relentless as God was in His pursuit of me, I must, according to the will of God, cry out for change and righteousness to prevail.

> *For the vineyard of the LORD of hosts*
> *[is] the house of Israel, and the men of Judah*
> *his pleasant plant: and he looked for judgment,*
> *but behold oppression; for righteousness, but behold a cry.*
>
> ~ Isaiah 5:7

In order for delayed change to take place, each of us must be willing to take an active involvement in manning the post to which we were assigned by God. You are to act boldly, with no hesitation, to be an effective arm of the body of Christ. Should you fail to move out when called or instructed to carry out what is given to you, the task at hand will get accomplished with or without you. God will simply deploy a more willing participant by ushering them to the front line and move you to the rear until you are ready (or not). For God is teaching me (as well as others) to be a spiritual warrior and take not lightly the ways of this world. Yielding to God is about having the understanding of doing my Father's business and wanting nothing more than to please Him. It is about remembering the condition of my soul prior to being set free! It is about having insurmountable inner joy and peace that cannot be given to me by man. It is important to be vigilant. I must be able and ready to examine the spirits and know them by their fruit to escape the trap of being pulled in and consumed by darkness. In the world, not of the world! Are you allowing your environment to affect your spiritual growth?

A Spiritual Analogy of the Workplace:

1. Government ▶ Politics ▶ Control ▶ People (abuse of power) ▶ Personal Agendas ▶ Prejudices ▶ Fueled by Information ▶ Truth or False Truth ▶ Impact ▶ Mind ▶ Strongholds

2. U.S. Department of Energy ▶ Energy ▶ Portals ▶ Spirits ▶ Influence ▶ People (abuse of power) ▶ Impact ▶ Mind ▶ Strongholds

Government: An organization or agency through which a political unit exercises its authority (abuse of power), controls and administers public policy and directs and controls the actions of its members or subjects.

Energy is fluid and flows very freely. It gives life to the living and the dead. Spirits are a form of energy. Other different forms of energy include kinetic, potential, thermal, gravitational, sound, elastic and electromagnetic energy.

WHAT KIND OF PERSON ARE YOU?

Put them in mind to be subject to principalities and powers, to obey magistrates, to be ready to every good work. To speak evil of no man, to be no brawlers, but gentle, shewing all meekness unto all men. For we ourselves also were sometimes foolish, disobedient, deceived, serving divers lusts and pleasures, living in malice and envy, hateful, and hating one another.

~ Titus 3:1-3

October 17, 2010

Bishop Raymond Horton III, the father and leader of Unity Life Christian Ministries, gave us a word that was out of this world! No one but You, dear God, could know the heaviness of my heart upon leaving work on Friday evening following the events that took place that day. Leaving the office to exit the building, I asked You to forgive me if I acted out of character in displaying a personality that was unpleasing to You. It is my deepest desire not to allow my flesh to get the better of me in an environment that seems to display so much disharmony and great discord on a daily basis.

Peace I leave with you, my peace I give unto you: not as the world giveth, give I unto you. <u>Let not your heart</u> be troubled, neither let it be afraid.

~ John 14: 27

The tension in this building (U.S. Department of Energy Headquarters) is very high. And the negative energy is so thick, you can cut it with a knife. People are attacking one another as if it is a competitive sport that life and living is dependent upon or a fashionable new game that adds years to their life. Watching all of this take place right in front of my eyes vexes my spirit and makes me want to run and hide. Being sensitive to the presence of the spirit—that which is in the atmosphere that seems to have taken hold of so many saints and sinners alike—Your children who claim to know You should be better equipped to withstand the influence of the enemy or at least recognize a behavior or fruit that does not mirror the characteristics of Christ! Even within Your children themselves!

But let all those that put their trust in thee rejoice: let them ever shout for joy, because thou defendest them: let them also that love thy name be joyful in thee.

~ Psalms 5:11

Seeing this so often makes me extremely angry! *Be ye angry, and sin not: let not the sun go down upon your wrath: Neither give place to the devil (an opportunity)* (Ephesians 4:26-27). And then I must remember to grab hold and sin not through my anger. Bridle (Psalm 39:1) or muzzle my mouth I must, but I get mad enough to fight. Fight not as the world is so accustomed to doing, but be that spiritual warrior that God has called me to be. Listening to one of the speakers on Saturday (October 16, 2010, at the Breakthrough Conference) deliver a very well-thought-out and detailed teaching on spiritual warfare, I remembered how important it is for me to always remember where I am but also who I am. At all times, I must be focused on serving the Lord! And yet at times, I am so naïve about this world and the people in it that I let my mind forget that there is a war going on and that we are in our last days. For this is not a time for me to forget! This is a time for me to take my rightful place and get into position. This is a time for me to learn all Your ways, Father God! Teach me! For prayer is the key.

> *Stand in awe, and sin not:*
> *commune with your own heart upon your bed,*
> *and be still. Selah.*
>
> ~ Psalm 4:4

Prayer, dear God, should be my first and only defense in times of trouble. I should not allow my emotions to get the better of me through my mind as the enemy sends reinforcements my way to knock me off my perch. Because I spoke out on behalf of the oppressed, I was accused of making excuses for them. Replying, I said, "I guess I'm just compassionate!" I was so angry I could cry. Lately it doesn't take much to make me cry! *Rivers of waters run down mine eyes, because they keep not thy law* (Psalm 119:136). When I heard Bishop Horton speak on being compassionate or it being necessary for us to have compassion one for another, dear God, I knew You heard my cry. For there is truly a big difference between having Christ-like compassion and man's definition of what he perceives compassion to be!

Awake to righteousness, and sin not;
for some have not the knowledge of God:
I speak [this] to your shame.

~ 1 Corinthians 15:34

For the enemy is truly busy running to and fro seeking whom he may devour. It is he who sends out his army to influence those who are weak—those who have not yet guarded themselves on every side! If there is the slightest opening, he will not hesitate to slip in and steer the mind in accordance to the ways of the world. He knows how easy it is for them to get puffed up and beat on their chest. I am man, I am woman, I am the king of this jungle, hear me roar! That ego is what drives them and leads them to seek control at any cost—even at the cost of their salvation!

Love (Charity) is patient
(long suffering) and kind. It doesn't envy (or boast),

> *and it doesn't focus on itself (selfishness)*
> *or puff up (egotistical) with its own importance.*
>
> ~ 1 Corinthians 13:4 TCW

Where is the love? God reminds us often of his most important commandment. To put it simply, love your neighbor as you love yourself. *Do not seek revenge or bear a grudge against anyone among your people, but love your neighbor as yourself. I am the Lord* (Leviticus 18:19 NIV). Deuteronomy 6:5 tells us we should love God with all our heart, our soul, our mind and our strength. If there is any part of my heart that is in immediate need of repair or convicting, I ask and pray for God to cut out the bad parts and circumcise my heart, that it be anew, fresh and pure, and delight in the ways of the Lord. It is wrong for me to despise any man for his wrongdoing, but if the spirit consumes and influences the mind of a person to commit sin and trespass against me, I will despise it and pray for the person. Oh God, let not my heart or my mind be led by my flesh in dealing with any situation. Let me not stumble when strife and confrontation comes my way. Let me continue to pray for the weary and attempt to shield myself in the process from fiery darts. Please! Keep me humble and separated from those who wish to harm others intentionally or unintentionally. Though I should count it all as joy, should I fall into divers temptation (James 1:2), I will also pray I do not fall into being used by one to oppress another.

> *Depart from me, ye evildoers:*
> *for I will keep the commandments of my God.*
>
> ~ Psalm 119:115

We need to consider the character of Christ in all we do! What kind of person are you? Are you living and striving to be Christ-like through the examples of your actions? Do you tear down or lift up? "He that loveth not knoweth not God; for God is love" (1 John 4:8).

AM I NOT MY BROTHER'S KEEPER?

*And the LORD said unto Cain,
Where [is] Abel thy brother?
And he said, I know not:
[Am] I my brother' Keeper?*

~ Genesis 4:9

October 24, 2010

God did it again! Before leaving to go to church this morning, something was put in my spirit that led me to sit and immediately type out what was in my heart. Little did I know, a similar topic about us being our "Brothers' Keeper" would be given to and referenced by Brother Fred A. Wilson Jr. through the Holy Spirit, with emphasis put on Hebrews, Chapter Five, for his seven-minute sermonette. That word pierced my spirit like you wouldn't believe!

*And if he shall neglect to hear them, tell [it] unto the church:
but if he neglect to hear the church,
let him be unto thee as an heathen man and a publican.*

~ Matthew 18:17

My spirit has been vexed for many years concerning the condition of today's churches and the nature of so-called Christians. In fact, God dropped in my spirit a month or two ago the need for me to "Defend not the church but the character of Christ." Every week, it seemed I was engaging in conversations concerning not only the state of churches but the lack of true Christianity as displayed by God's children. Oh my goodness! One day I was so drained and saddened that I came home and cried until I got a headache. I told God I was finding it extremely difficult to have such conversations that left me feeling heartbroken and worn down. I was encountering individuals left and right who were expressing their feelings to me about church folks. This also became their excuse for not wanting to attend church.

*Those who continue to behave like Jezebel
I will not protect from the plague of death.
Then the church will know that I search
everyone's heart and mind,
and I will repay each one for what he has done.*

~ Revelation 2:23 TCW

Having had this same view, once upon a time, I could truly relate to what was being shared with me. However, that was the old me. That was the me that did not know nor realize I could have a relationship with God. That was the me that did not know I could connect with Jesus in a supernatural way. That was the me that did not understand the importance of not looking at the people in the church for my salvation. The me today understands it is not about people nor is it about me. It is about God! It is about me following the one who was sent to reconnect us all to the Father. It is about studying to show myself approved! It is about me learning to be more like Christ in character.

> *Listen carefully.*
> *Some who are worshiping with you are serving Satan.*
> *They claim they're true sons of Abraham,*
> *But they're not. They are lying,*
> *And someday I will make them come and bow at your feet*
> *And acknowledge that I have loved you.*
>
> ~ Revelation 3:9

As I looked upon the world, I was finding it exceedingly difficult to distinguish the believers from the nonbelievers. I thought being a Christian was a full-time, around-the-clock job. I thought it was a position one should value and take seriously twenty-four hours a day, seven days a week, including while sleeping. It is not something you consider on Sunday and neglect throughout the remainder of the week. This is why God tells us it is important to understand and know the difference between being in the world and not of the world. As a bringer of light into dark places, we should be prepared to change the atmosphere according to the will of God. But through mistaken identity, a number of us have it all wrong. We are conducting ourselves in situations to be less like Christ as we allow ourselves to be driven by our flesh and we are sending a horrible message to lost souls who need to be directed toward Christ rather than away from Him. It is your responsibility to be a disciple—a fishers of men.

> *And he (Jesus) saith unto them (the disciples),*
> *Follow me, and I will make you fishers of men.*
>
> ~ Matthew 4:19

I once heard a congressman who is a minister say he was told by those he serves with as a member of the House that there was no place for a minister in politics. Wrong! Being a believer of Christ, the Son of the Father who created us all, should be the first order of business. Everything else should follow afterwards. Accepting a worldly position as a judge, lawyer, secretary, administrative assistant or a human resources employee should not interfere with you being a Christian. It should, however, dictate the stance you take in how you conduct yourself within that worldly position. At all times, you should be a person of integrity with strong values and morals in keeping with the character of Christ.

> *Happy (blessed) is the man who doesn't*
> *take advice(counsel) from the ungodly, who doesn't*
> *participate in the ways of wicked men(sinners) and*
> *who doesn't criticize others, [2]but who*
> *delights in the law of the Lord.*
>
> ~ Psalms 1:1 TCW

Finding myself on more than one occasion being treated unjustly and oppressed by those in positions of power and authority, not to mention by so-called Christians, it is not a situation I would be inclined to wish on anyone. Given the condition of my heart and my unwillingness to allow myself to be bullied or intimidated into bringing about distress to others, I have been known to grieve when others are being taken advantage of or bruised. On one Saturday (November 7, 2009) morning, God woke me from a deep sleep, only to allow me to connect with the spirit of a coworker whose heart was heavy.

Being used as an empath, I was allowed to feel this coworker's deepest pain. As I cried out, I not only noted I was lying in a fetal position, I was clinching at my heart and stomach as I sobbed uncontrollably while seeing the vision of this young woman in my mind. Attempting to gain my composure and make sense of it all, God prompted me to get up to write her a letter of apology on behalf of those who had contributed to her pain. Not only was I instructed to send this letter to her, I was instructed to provide a copy to everyone in our office. Questioning God about what was being asked of me, I knew it was important to be obedient. So I jumped to my feet to begin writing what I was hearing: LOVING DEEPLY IS THE OPPOSITE OF GRIEVING! The correspondence was written to my grieving coworker in support of what she was going through along with a copy to each person within our office or division.

Approximately two weeks later, my supervisor and "pretend" mentor met with me to discuss the letter. No one seemed concerned for the young woman's pain or the part they played in contributing to her grief as a result of her persecution.

She was accused of using the death of her son as an excuse to be absent from work while continuously being persecuted for not being able to bounce back or put it all behind her as quickly as others felt she should. But there is no time limit or perfect process for grieving! Upon being asked why I felt the need to defend her, I replied, "I am following orders as they were given to me by God." Why? Because, I am my brother's keeper! And workplace bullying is unacceptable!

A copy of the actual correspondence:

FROM: Ann G. Mack
TO: HC-21 Training Division (Undisclosed recipients)
DATE: Monday, November 09, 2009 10:42 AM
SUBJECT: **LOVING DEEPLY IS THE OPPOSITE OF GRIEVING!**

As a child, before encountering a truth called cruelty through experience and learning about the history of my ancestors, I wanted so much to believe in my heart that this world we live in was filled with people who have love and compassion for one another. Naively, I still want to believe that the world we live in is not as cruel as it appears to be. Especially given the fact that America claims to be built or founded upon biblical or Godly principles. However, not many know what it is to be Christ-like, kind, caring or sincere to act with sensitivity towards another human being.

If a wise man contendeth with a foolish man,
whether he rage or laugh,
there is no rest.

~ Proverbs 29:9

As individuals or people who are as diverse in our thinking as we are genetically, we differ in many other ways as well in accordance to how deeply we love. And with that same degree of passion that may not be recognized by most, grieving for a loved one could easily render you to a catatonic state of mind. If God loves us unconditionally and if as people (Christians), we are told to love our neighbors as we love ourselves, why is it so impossible for others to believe that a mother who has lost a child (son) cannot lose a part of herself in the process?

> *Keep they heart with all diligence;*
> *for out of it are issues of life.*
>
> ~ Proverbs 4:23

Knowing and sympathizing with the loss of your son, I did not realize until Friday that he was not taken from you by natural causes through sickness or illness. He was, unfortunately, taken from you by the hands of another human being, which indeed, in my opinion, intensifies your pain. Learning this not only brought me pain, it brought tears to my eyes as I found it difficult to contain my emotions as I struggled to regain my composure. Therefore, I commend you for attempting to take each day at a time as it comes to conquer your loss by not giving up or giving in to your hurt regardless of how challenging it may be.

As a person who has lost three members of my family all in the same year (1994), to include my baby brother to AIDS who was more like a son than a brother, in addition to being terminated that same year from a job for not having any hair, no one can tell you how deep an emotion can penetrate your very soul and render you helpless to not wanting to go on with your life. And until they experience this hurt or deep pain for themselves—a pain I live with everything day—no one can tell you how you should feel when it comes to grief or love.

(Mental and physical pain can co-exist or exist alone. A mental [psychic] pain can also prove to be much greater than a physical pain beyond any ones comprehension!) Simply telling or expecting a person to accept loss or death and get over it is not acceptable. Nor is it an appropriate approach to take, because it only adds to your grief by asserting what I consider to be a form of mental abuse that only deepens the pain.

> *Confess your faults one to another,*
> *and pray one for another; that ye may be healed.*
> *The effectual fervent prayer of a righteous man availeth much.*
>
> ~ James 5:16

Today, I wish to offer my sincere apology for those who know not what they do, but pray they leave you alone to let you live your life to grieve according to what's in your heart as opposed to them presuming to know what you should feel. I also pray God gives you divine peace through and through in helping you with your loss no matter how long it may take.

Many Blessings,
Ann

A FACT-FINDING INVESTIGATION

*Write the things which thou hast seen,
and the things which are,
and the things which shall be hereafter;*

~ **Revelations 1:19 KJV**

February 12, 2012

Resulting from a workplace bullying and harassment claim as addressed by Aleta (Haynes) Clark, a fact-finding investigation was scheduled to determine the validity of her case. Depending upon what people are willing to disclose (the truth or a lie) and desperately want concealed (the truth), a fact is just that: a fact with no evidence of truth, but a fact can also be twisted and manipulated with the use of a spider web in spinning a story that benefits those with more to hide or lose. Thus, giving them (her abusers) the opportunity to be more empowered at doing what they do with the aid of a ruling that gives them a justified reason for their cunning and crafty behavior. Partners in crime are gloating about the intended and successful terrorizing of a coworker while plotting and scheming ways to destroy her spirit! How can a fact-finding investigation be the very substance or source of a ruling intended to uncover or expose the truth but only serve to unleash more wrath upon the victim(s)?

> *Men are nothing but a mere breath; human beings are unreliable.*
> *When they are weighed in the scales,*
> *all of them together are lighter than air.*
> *Do not trust in what you can gain by oppression!*
> *Do not put false confidence in what you can gain by robbery!*
> *If wealth increases, do not become attached to it!*
> *God has declared one principle; two principles I have heard:*
> *God is strong,*
> *and you, O Lord, demonstrate loyal love.*
> *For you repay men for what they do.*
>
> ~ Psalm 62:9-12 NET

If a department, division or agency is noted for such a history of activity (abuse of power, position and authority), it is very easy to show that the presence of a pattern and growing culture exists, but only if others are truly sincere and ready to explore options to bring about change directed at developing a more cohesive and safe working environment for all! Just submitting a "no harassment or bullying tolerated" statement or document *with no intent* of launching a full-on investigation, mandatory training and counseling programs are not the answer, especially when it is happening more frequently throughout the building at all levels as if the water is laced with some mind-altering serum to induce psychotic, demon-possessed behavior.

> *Let them be ashamed and confounded together*
> *that seek after my soul to destroy it;*
> *let them be driven backward and put*
> *to shame that wish me evil.*
>
> ~ Psalm 40:15 KJV

Ironically, about one month prior to the scheduled fact-finding investigation interviews with some of the key players cited or voiced in Aleta's workplace bullying and harassment claim, an altercation (more specifically, a fist fight) ensued that resulted in one female employee hitting another within Human Capital Management (HC-22). Because this would add too much validity to Aleta's claim in exposing such a hostile environment, which indeed exists, no official report was filed by the manager(s) concerning the incident. Therefore, it was conveniently concealed from any and everyone who mattered. However, news spreads like wildfire if there is anything unfavorable to be told. A number of employees were whispering amongst themselves about the incident across the departments as it became known. However, no one was willing to voice what they knew and had witnessed over time as being prevalent. Instead, they joined forces with others in an attempt to make Aleta look like the problem for not getting in line to willingly accept her abuse for the enjoyment and entertainment of her peers.

> *The wicked watcheth the righteous,*
> *and seeketh to slay him.*
>
> ~ Psalms 37:32 KJV

Records and files, if accurately used to capture data objectively (truthfully), should be included as part of an investigation. The Union, labor relations and Equal Employment Opportunity (EEO) could and should be consulted if what one seeks is the absolute truth and not an attempt to conceal or cover up that which is true. What about the use of surveys? Not just any survey with no special meaning, but one directed at addressing the real issues with straight questions. One whereby each employee within HC-20 to all of HC and the *entire* U.S. Department of Energy can also participate anonymously, if necessary, with no fear of retaliation in speaking the truth about what they have encountered, witnessed or experienced indirectly as well as directly to be effective in correcting an injustice from the root. And why not take it another step further by including all federal government agencies?

> *Lest there should be among you man, or woman, or family, or tribe, whose heart turneth away this day from the LORD our God, to go [and] serve the gods of these nations; lest there should be among you a root that beareth gall and wormwood; And it come to pass, when he heareth the words of this curse, that he bless himself in his heart, saying, I shall have peace, though I walk in the imagination of mine heart, to add drunkenness to thirst: The LORD will not spare him, but then the anger of the LORD and his jealousy shall smoke against that man, and all the curses that are written in this book shall lie upon him, and the LORD shall blot out his name from under heaven.*
>
> ~ Deuteronomy 29:18-20 KJV

As I mentioned to the fact-finding investigator who was assigned to address the claim voiced by Aleta, after working within the area of human resources for nearly twenty years in the private sector, I was not naïve to believe or think this investigation was to benefit her or bring her any relief. It was merely a fishing expedition, if you will, directed at figuring out a way to appease her, disprove her claim and to find out what she had (if anything) that she could actually use outside of the measures in place in winning her case if she took the liberty of filing an official lawsuit. In other words, it was risk management at its best—protecting the organization and not the victims; it was a way to conceal from those on the outside what was happening within. Politics and survival!

> *For, behold, the day cometh, that shall burn as an oven;*
> *and all the proud, yea, and all that do wickedly,*
> *shall be stubble: and the day that cometh shall burn them up,*
> *saith the LORD of hosts, that it shall leave*
> *them neither root nor branch.*
>
> ~ Malachi 4:1 KJV

As a matter of fact, considering the nature in which the interviews were conducted, how can you receive a favorable outcome on the part of the plaintiff if there are less protagonists than there are antagonists willing to speak the truth? After the closing of my interviewing session, I received for my review a summary of what was deemed to be my responsive dialogue with the investigator; it failed completely to represent my stance as being on the side of Aleta. Instead, it was written to drive a more desired outcome to disprove the truth. So I took the liberty of addressing this issue and I submitted a replacement summary in my own words to the investigator and a copy to Aleta for her file.

The Lord judges the people; judge me, O Lord,
and do me justice according to my righteousness
[my rightness, justice, and right standing with You] and
according to the integrity that is in me.

~ Psalm 7:8 KJV

In seeing this type of workplace terrorism all too often within an organization, it always trickles down unless an association exists with the right connections (clique, group, team of power and authority). Such activity cannot exist or flourish within an environment if it is not allowed. And at the onset of its awareness, just like any issue, it needs to be dealt with immediately and not pushed under the rug or it will only escalate with no hope of restoration. So in the meantime, everyone walks around avoiding the existence of the great, big elephant in their path. Because they have not always walked the straight and narrow path themselves, they have joined an alliance or allegiance with the aggressors in avoidance of or concealing the loom of darkness over their heads that threatens to reveal some of their secrets should they take a stance for doing what is right. But in saying or doing nothing or taking responsibility for their actions in holding themselves accountable, if not now, they will be held accountable at a later date, and then it will be too late to dodge the inevitable destination of their soul for eternity.

*And, behold, I come quickly;
and my reward [is] with me, to give every man
according as his work shall be. I am Alpha and Omega,
the beginning and the end, the first and the last.
Blessed [are] they that do his commandments,
that they may have right to the tree of life,
and may enter in through the gates into the city.*

~ Revelations 22:12-14

Prayer

Dear Father God, it is my hope, desire and prayer in the name of Jesus Christ that Aleta Clark and many others like her who are and have experienced such destructive and ruthless behavior at the hands of her enemies receive Your wisdom, knowledge and understanding of the "what, why and how." Let them not lose hope or stop expecting righteousness to prevail in any given situation in spite of those within her immediate environment that have succumbed to doing that which is not right and gloat about it for far too long. Aleta should never feel ashamed of having a heart after Your own heart. She will lose no sleep or worry or fret about the events of the troubled. And she will continue to extend to them the grace and mercy they have not shown her, for she is much greater than them all in spirit, mind and body. Continue to protect her O'Lord as You reveal yourself to her as only You can! Let her see the power of Your hand as You move out on her behalf in bringing this situation to a close—once and for all—according to Your will. For You know the thoughts that You think toward her, thoughts of peace, and not of evil, to give her an expected end.

One of victory with no feelings of malice toward anyone though they deserve it! For you will repay all in rewarding them according to their deeds. Amen!

TO SOLVE THE BIG PROBLEMS, SEE THE BIG PICTURE

Thus saith the LORD; cursed [be] the man that trusteth in man, and maketh flesh his arm, and whose heart departeth from the LORD.For he shall be like the heath in the desert, and shall not see when good cometh; but shall inhabit the parched places in the wilderness, [in] a salt land and not inhabited.Blessed [is] the man that trusteth in the LORD, and whose hope the LORD is.For he shall be as a tree planted by the waters, and [that] spreadeth out her roots by the river, and shall not see when heat cometh, but her leaf shall be green; and shall not be careful in the year of drought, neither shall cease from yielding fruit.

~ Jeremiah 17: 5-8 KJV

February 12, 2012

This topic, unfortunately, has been one of the most difficult to date in which to write and reflect upon as instructed by God.

Through His word, He tells me (us) *not to fret because of evildoers nor be envious of the workers of iniquity. For they shall soon be cut down like the grass and wither as the green herb* (Psalm 37:1-2). While driving this past holiday (Columbus Day) weekend, I felt the need to pull over to the side of the road to have a deep cry and conversation with God concerning my present situation as it relates to my God-given assignment. I know without a doubt, God is preparing me for my next season and level of promotion. Until I complete this assignment, I cannot move onward and transition to the next one without first being tried, tested and confirmed! Although I am excited to be promoted by God (James 1-9), I have mixed emotions about my next level in encountering a new devil (figuratively). This current one has been quite challenging to say the least; but to whom much is given, much is required (Luke 12:48)! After all of what I have experienced and endured while being blessed to see another birthday (age fifty-two on September 23, 2012), I do not know why I am still surprised or appalled by the increased darkness and wickedness in the world that is directed by demonic forces to influence man. Though **I have nothing to fear**, is not the world on earth the devil's playground?

> *For, behold, the darkness shall cover the earth,*
> *And gross darkness the people:*
> *but the LORD shall arise upon thee,*
> *And the glory shall be seen upon thee.*
>
> ~ Isaiah 60:2

I know the answer to that question all too well! But I guess the most disheartening part is witnessing it all as people display a blatant disregard and level of disrespect for the civil liberties or human rights of another human being. These people use politics (or power play), disloyalty, cruelty and corruption in the name of success (on the basis of spiritual warfare) with no remorse or repentance for change! Oh my goodness! Coming back into the federal government in 2008, I had such high hopes and great expectations concerning my future career growth in the area of human resources and my current working environment—only to be sadly disappointed, again, by people and their need for power and control! After leaving the employment of the government sector approximately four times, only to return to the same nonsense and lack of righteous leadership, why did I think it would be any different this time around? Faith! Because I *know; therefore that the LORD thy God, HE is God, the faithful God, which keepeth covenant and mercy with them that love HIM and keep HIS commandments to a thousand generations* (Deuteronomy 7:9 KJV). For He is nothing like man, and it was He who opened the door to allow me to return when I did!

The heart [the human mind] is deceitful above all things, and desperately wicked: who can know it?

~ Jeremiah 17:9

We seem to be living in a very scary time and place whereby **character, integrity, responsibility and accountability** take a back seat to the level of emphasis placed on the perceived position of power a person holds. In a government structure, that level of power and control can also symbolize or be significant to the grade of a position and title, thus dictating a false sense of importance. This form of practice is also displayed in the private sector, but I naïvely viewed the government as being synonymous with **principle** (ethical standard: a standard of moral or ethical decision-making). Wrong! *For our wrestling is not against flesh and blood, but against the **principalities**, against the **powers**, against the **world-rulers of this darkness**, against the spiritual hosts of **wickedness** in the heavenly places* (Ephesians 6:12, *emphasis added*).

> *For I say, through the grace given unto me,*
> *to every man that is among you, not to think of himself*
> *more highly than he ought to think; but to think soberly,*
> *according as God hath dealt to every man the measure of faith.*
>
> ~ Romans 12:3

The higher the position, the greater the power and the control or **influence** which enables some to abuse their power while manipulating the laws, rules and regulations to misrepresent truth! Why? Just because they feel they can through a false sense of entitlement that comes with power and influence! How? The influence of their power and position may deceitfully and greatly impact the outcome of whom and what others are willing to believe or value as truth! This truly explains the widespread corruption throughout our government and the entire world. Just recently, I was made aware of the possible source or entry of darkness (unlawful and cultish influences) into a corporation or organization. What an astounding revelation to learn it begins in the Human Resources Department and spreads throughout the organization from there!

> *I the Lord search the mind, I try the heart,*
> *even to give to every man according to his ways,*
> *according to the fruit of his doings.*
>
> ~ Jeremiah 17: 10 AMP

Quack, quack! If it looks like a duck and sounds like a duck, there is no way anyone can make me believe that it is not a duck! A major problem I have, which could be viewed as an advantage or disadvantage, is having an analytical mindset that never turns off. So why is it okay for some to start out at a lower level and work their way up while others are deliberately held at a certain level by those who have no intention of letting them excel? Why do we attempt to limit others from obtaining that which we want? Shouldn't we want for others that which we want for ourselves? Shouldn't we celebrate the life and growth of each and every human being? So why do we dispense so much wasted time and energy in attempting to set others up for failure? Because we want power and control, or as one sister-in-Christ put it, "Human beings are grossly flawed!" Some are just broken (damaged), lost (confused) and in need of reprogramming! For instance, just days ago, I had a discussion with a coworker who, during a previous staff meeting, blatantly verbally attacked me and accused me of not doing my part. Of course, "doing my part" would mean I would not resist her attempts to bully me into doing what she and others with her same mindset think is beneath them; but it is perfectly okay for them to delegate to me while making themselves feel more important than they are within an environment that encourages that type of behavior. Have you ever worked in an office where there were more chiefs than Indians or more cooks in the kitchen than there were qualified chefs? A place where everybody wants to be a supervisor and give you orders, yet they lack the leadership and interrelationship skills needed to be successful at it; but they strive just the same as dictated by a prevailing hierarchical organizational culture that looks the other way until they get exposed (unmasked) and suffer financially!

> **Example #1:** As indicated above, in frustration of not being able to excel or receive the necessary training to get noticed as being skilled to do something else outside of the administrative capacity, I found myself being pigeon-holed in, I left the employment of the federal government a total of four times prior to 1985. After obtaining a four-year degree in Business Management, I returned to the federal government by way of the Career/Corporate Intern Program in 2008 with the hope of excelling within HR as a Program Analyst. But once again, I found things had not changed all that much within my 23-year absence to note the existence of the same patterns and obstacles from which I tried to break free!

Let me start by saying, there is nothing wrong with clerical or administrative work and many have started out at lower levels in their career with the hope and dream of becoming the best they can be in the area of their choosing. But that is it in a nutshell! Each and every individual should have the option to choose for him or herself the direction of their career path. And should you later decide to choose another avenue or path in which to succeed, it should be your choice to do so. You should never feel pressured or limited by others into thinking or believing your potential for greatness does not exceed beyond their scope or view of who they think you should be or who you really are! For instance, management's intent was to utilize me as an Administrative Assistant, but they created obstacles to keep me within their reach with no room for growth. Their objective was to prevent me from fulfilling the requirements needed to successfully complete the two-year career intern program. But God in all His infinite wisdom is awesome! He always steps in and intervenes on your behalf to redirect that which was meant for evil to work in your favor. Just four months shy of completing the first year of the two-year program, I was able to successfully meet the criteria (for reaching the 50 percent in compliance mark) needed to obtain my next grade regardless of the obstacles set in place to engineer a failure! Pressing forward, I was determined not to give up or give in to the limitations of those within my surroundings. Their deliberate attempts to trip me up only ignited the fire within me to meet the criteria of the second year to successfully complete all of the requirements needed for the Career Intern Program to become a permanent federal government employee with a total of ten years of service to date.

For therefore we both labour and suffer reproach, because we trust in the living God, who is the Saviour of all men, specially of those that believe.

~ 1 Timothy 4:10 KJV

Things Are Not As They Seem

Looking at things on the surface according to the image (or illusion) of that which is being projected to those on the outside, you would think we have everything together! Unfortunately, we are further away from being together than we are at being closer to having everything worked out. Everything nowadays is done quick, fast and in a hurry—what I consider to be a "microwave society." That is our main problem! We want everything *yesterday* with no commitment to training, knowledge, sharing or research (observational analysis) before forging ahead with a plan; not to mention, with no attention to detail, follow up or follow through, there are a number of broken systems within the government that need to be addressed!

Who [is] a wise man and endued with knowledge among you? Let him shew out of a good conversation his works with meekness of wisdom.

~ James 3:13 KJV

When President Obama made reference to the "Private Industry or Sector" being all right, people wanted to condemn him for making a statement with great merit. The government has been spiraling out of control for quite a long time with no counter measures for ensuring accountability. Based on my personal observational analysis of the government in general and not just the U.S. Department of Energy (DOE), in the way of staffing and recruitment, there is an inferior federal government compensation and performance evaluation system compared to the private sector—in some cases—due to insufficient budget resources as much as it is due to excessive waste. Waste of financial and material resources affects the budget in the name of overspending and carelessness. Meanwhile, there's an unequal distribution of wealth and training opportunities. People in positions of leadership with the decision-making authority to approve who is allowed to receive training for promotion and upward mobility opportunities have a displayed history of deliberately impeding the advancement of an employee—an apparent practice or strategy to delegate meaningless tasks needing little to no skill to keep them at a desired level or position! Some are overloaded with tasks (unequal distribution of work assignments) in carrying out the load of others who lack a particular skill or refuse to perform particular tasks.

Example #2: Amazingly, while in a staff meeting a little less than a month ago, an acting director actually stated he did not need to be as knowledgeable or skilled in the same areas as those he supervised. He then went on to say he just needed to be in a position to delegate tasks. Wow! What would you contribute that statement to be: authority, ignorance or arrogance? For me, I come from a different school of thought. I believe a supervisor should be as knowledgeable as those he or she supervises (and more). A supervisor should be in a position to think on his feet, think under pressure and be willing as well as able to function in every capacity of those under his leadership. He should be able to answer the tough questions or at least know where and to whom to ascertain the answer. But he should also be in a position to confirm his answer or response by citing examples and references for teaching and empowering others he supervises to step in and step up when he is absent.

Example #3: To put my foot in my mouth, I also believe the government is very top-heavy; this is, in part, due to the concept of what is termed as the "good old boy network" that causes inadequate training or a lack of qualified employees in managerial and essential positions. One of the disadvantages of being top-heavy is that it often results in conflicting and competing priorities. Not to mention, a number of higher-graded employees are reluctant to perform what they consider to be "lower-graded" functions in such a time as this when the economy and budget constraints bring about a hiring freeze. Many government employees are not being cross trained like they are in the private sector to multi-task and handle other responsibilities or areas of concern to compensate for unexpected absences or hiring crises.

Example #4: On Friday, July 22, I participated in the Best Places to Work Action Planning Workshop as facilitated by the Partnership for Public Service. As mentioned during that session, unless the problems within the agency are taken seriously to determine where the necessary change is needed and that change is implemented, the energy and effort dedicated to the workshop would just be a waste of time. First you have to be willing to acknowledge and admit a problem does indeed exist. Then you have to be willing to ask the hard questions to get to the root of the problem. Then you have to be willing to determine a strategy for fixing the problems and be committed to implementing those strategies to bring about change—a temporary, superficial fix for the sake of image by giving the illusion that change is not going to work (at least not for very long).

To combat staffing and recruiting issues, those responsible for the hiring process should consider outside training that's comparable to meeting today's employment challenges for attracting and maintaining qualified employees. Suggestive training would include continued education in keeping with the changing demand in the workforce. The Society for Human Resource Management offers a number of resource tools and certification for HR professionals.

The ongoing challenges DOE faces in its project management efforts have kept the department's contract and project management functions on the GAO[67] (U.S. Accountability Office) High Risk List since 1990. In the area of project management, it wouldn't be unheard of to research the practices utilized by other agencies to compare their success rate to include the recurring issues and differences surrounding how business is or should be conducted within DOE's HR office (see "Quality Assurance" below).

---

67 The U.S. Government Accountability Office (GAO) is an independent, nonpartisan agency that works for Congress. Often called the "congressional watchdog," GAO investigates how the federal government spends taxpayer dollars. The head of GAO, the Comptroller General of the United States, is appointed to a fifteen-year term by the president from a slate of candidates Congress proposes (see http://www.gao.gov/about/index.html).

Example #5: Can you imagine being close to finishing high school and looking forward to continuing your education on a higher level while attempting to seek meaningful employment to assist with meeting those goals? I met a young lady who began working at DOE during the summer months before her last year in high school as a part of STEP (Student Temporary Employee Program). She later found out she could return to the employment of DOE through SCEP (Student Career Employee Program) while pursuing higher education as a college student. Due to the mismanagement of the CIP, STEP and the SCEP, a decision was reached to abolish these programs and replace them with one called Pathways (or the Pathways Internship Program).[68] This young lady refused to give up hope as she forged ahead to see if she qualified for continued employment under Pathways.

Can you imagine her disappointment, frustration and anger when she learned on a Tuesday that Thursday would be her last day employed through DOE, especially after she thought she had been converted over to the Pathways program? Not to mention, the appropriate action (SF-52) or documentation was never put into place to decrease her hours from full-time to part-time and vice versa to meet the change in her school schedule. This meant she was put into a leave without pay (LWOP) status that later interfered with her not being able to accumulate any leave that could

---

68 https://www.opm.gov/policy-data-oversight/hiring-information/students-recent-graduates/reference-materials/pathways-programs-handbook.pdf

have potentially benefited her when she was let go rather abruptly. Should she have the opportunity to return to the federal government at a later date, her record will show a damaged leave status due to incompetence, simple neglect or a lack of training concerning the system for generating and processing personnel actions. (This same, unfortunate lack of commitment or work ethic also prevented the full-time, permanent employment of a highly decorated candidate within the Wounded Warriors Program.)

Organizational Culture

Organizational culture, whether right or wrong, is the personality of a department, division, agency or organization. **Culture** is comprised of the prejudices, assumptions, values, norms and tangible signs of people and/or members within an organization as well as their personal idiosyncrasies and behaviors. Depending upon how observant one is or how close one may be to situations being displayed or experienced within an organization, a person does and is able to soon sense the particular culture of an organization. **Culture** is taught, enforced and re-enforced over time and varies according to the change in leadership as to what is allowed and by whom.

> *Dear brothers and sisters, if another believer is overcome by some sin, you who are godly should gently and humbly help that person back onto the right path. And be careful not to fall into the same temptation yourself. Share each other's burdens and in this way obey the law of Christ. If you think you are too important to help someone, you*

are only fooling yourself. You are not that important. Pay careful attention to your own work, for then you will get the satisfaction of a job well done and you won't need to compare yourself to anyone else. For we are each responsible for our own conduct. Those who are taught the word of God should provide for their teachers, sharing all good things with them. Don't be misled - you cannot mock the justice of God. You will always harvest what you plant. Those who live only to satisfy their own sinful nature will harvest decay and death from that sinful nature. But those who live to please the Spirit will harvest everlasting life from the Spirit. So let's not get tired of doing what is good. At just the right time we will reap a harvest of blessing if we don't give up. Therefore, whenever we have the opportunity, we should do good to everyone—especially to those in the family of faith.

~ Galatians 6:1-10 NLT

Negative organizational culture, if not challenged, can thrive, fester and poison a previously healthy environment. Why? Because practice makes perfect, and most people become comfortable with their wrongdoing or sin nature. This type of unhealthy culture may be distinctly difficult to express for some, but everyone knows it when they recognize it. However, through fear and intimidation, they may not choose to acknowledge it openly or speak up or out about it because many people find it easier to go along to get along instead of giving thought to accountability or responsibility! Once it gets into the heart of an individual, it takes root and grows like a virus or toxic substance flowing through the air to reach its full contamination potential. As people move onward from one organization to another, somewhat like those who are indoctrinated and deployed by the military from post to post, they take that same mindset and culture with them to be pushed upon or forced on others wherever they go. Because my driving force is the word of God in carrying out His mission and mandate for my life, I cannot allow my mind to take hold of what my heart through God does not approve. This is why I keep holding out for the hope and belief that not all people are without a righteous soul to do good and not evil regardless of their atmospheric (environmental) influences!

> **Example #6**: Let's take the electoral process for instance. Every four years, a new person is voted into office as the president of the United States. Depending upon which party is elected (Democrat or Republican), laws are changed or influenced to mirror the political views of that individual or administration. If you are willing to take an objective look at the turn of events as they have played out and impacted our nation over the years, your analysis with the appropriate components should show the decisions governing what laws are enacted (or enforced) have nothing to do with what is right or wrong in relation to moralistic content but merely in accordance to the power base and benefit of certain classes of people in feeling elite—never with the consideration of the impact of humanity as a whole in all fairness or equal justice for all!
>
> **Example #7**: Question seven (also know as the Gaming Expansion Referendum) on the ballot of the upcoming

November 2012 election is very controversial. The question/referendum reads: Do you favor the expansion of commercial gaming in the State of Maryland **for the primary purpose of raising revenue for education** to authorize video lottery operation licensees to operate *table games* as defined by law; to increase from 15,000 to 16,500 the maximum number of video lottery terminals that may be operated in the State; and to increase from 5 to 6 the maximum number of video lottery operation licenses that may be awarded in the State and allow a video lottery facility to operate in Prince George's County?[69]

Gambling is an illegal act or crime that, should you be convicted of committing it, does not come without a price or the attachment of jail time. However, when it becomes a political ploy, it gets renamed (legalized) and attached to a "world-class resort casino" for the benefit of greed at the expense of the people. Why should our need for educational funding to improve our schools and ensure the future of our children be contingent upon us voting "yes" to the development of an establishment for gambling to enable the rich to get richer from our hard-earned dollars? Why should the generation of wealth through the creation of more jobs be contingent upon us voting "yes" to the development of an establishment for gambling to enable more division within an already dysfunctional family structure? Where there is gambling, there is alcohol and possibly prostitution—the generation of more crimes. Why can't

---

[69] http://towncourier.com/urbana/gaming-expansion-question-wins-most-confusing-referendum/

there be a separate question on the ballot to represent all three categories (expanding construction of gambling facilities [if warranted], creating jobs, increasing the education budget), if in fact what we the people are in need of is truly taken into consideration by our government and those in position of power with the influence to redirect change for equal distribution of wealth and everything else?

For [there is] no faithfulness in their mouth;
their inward part [is] very wickedness; their throat [is]
an open sepulchre; they flatter with their tongue.

~ Psalm 5:9 KJV

The spirit of DENIAL is a very powerful thing! Many people refuse to see or accept the obvious as displayed by a growing pattern of events. For some, the truth is too hard to swallow, so they walk around in darkness refusing to see the light. Some may see or feel what others do not. Each person is wired differently in how they receive and process information. Therefore, our experiences are different based on how we are impacted, and some are more intensely affected than others. That does not mean what I am experiencing, seeing, feeling and being so greatly impacted by is all in my head just because you choose not to acknowledge what is going on within the world around you. While time stops for some, time actually keeps on revolving and moving forward for others and can prove to be just as real as it is painful. When my eyes are open by way of a new revelation, my mind has a tendency to race to catch up with what my spirit already knew but needed confirmation to believe.

As stated to a former supervisor, I truly want to believe that there are many righteous people in the world. However, resulting from fear and the need to fit in or to belong, they are not willing to trust God (Psalm 37:3) enough to stand up and fight for righteousness. Nonetheless, I cannot, by any means, allow myself to disregard what I know God expects of me and therefore cannot mimic the actions of those as dictated by an unhealthy organizational culture to fit in or go along. Those who usually follow the crowd normally get lost in the crowd, and soon after, they get left behind or pushed to the side by the crowd.

> **Example #8:** There have been numerous complaints about workplace bullying or a pattern of disruptive and unacceptable behavior within the HR division of the DOE and the federal government as a whole. Many incidents of workplace violence go unreported because employees are reluctant to get involved. **Keeping silent about workplace violence will not make the problem go away**. In fact, under-reporting of such incidences only increases the risk of such violent disturbances by ignoring the warning signs for early intervention and prevention. The overall analysis of a two-day, DOE fact-finding investigation, as conducted by Mr. Jonathan Kaufmann (Esquire) from July 21–22, 2010, resulted in an inconclusive verdict. Meaning, the outcome recorded and filed stated there was no evidence in support of a workplace-bullying claim brought forth by Aleta Clark (Haynes). However, an Equal Employment Opportunity (EEO) claim was filed against DOE by another employee about two years later citing some of the same allegations: harassment and a violation of her civil

and human rights by allowing the disparaging treatment to take place within the training division of HR. That case proved to be one of substance as rendered on behalf of the plaintiff (SH). In the meantime, Aleta Clark, who failed to pursue her claim outside of the DOE chain of command, is still being bullied by those within her immediate working environment on the basis of retaliation. Another pattern that others refuse to acknowledge does exist!

The LORD saw how great the wickedness of the human race had become on the earth and that every inclination of the thoughts of the human heart was only evil all the time. The LORD regretted that he had made human beings on the earth and his heart was deeply troubled. So the LORD said, "I will wipe from the face of the earth the human race I have created—and with them the animals, the birds and the creatures that move along the ground—for I regret that I have made them." But Noah found favor in the eyes of the LORD.

~ Genesis 6:5-8 NIV

Example #9: A black female director (DOE employee, GS-15 level) also found herself impacted by this hostile workplace environment. She felt threatened to the point of taking an employee in an administrative support (GS-11) capacity to accompany her to some of her meetings. This employee would position herself inconspicuously in the rear of the meeting location to have a full view of her surroundings while engaging in silent prayer on behalf of her supervisor. In the event these men who were so accustomed to raising their voices, a finger or a fist were compelled to do much more, she would have a witness. Ironically, instead of this director choosing to fight to let this behavior be known to the appropriate entities for change, she accepted it by becoming a part of it in doing to others what was done to her. What a vicious cycle! This explains the number of EEO settlement agreements being ordered by presiding judges to plaintiffs (those without fear who are tired and willing to fight the injustice—disparaging behavior flourishing all over the building).

BUSINESS 101: First, let's revisit the concept of the "good old boy network"! In government and politics, which go hand-in-hand, there is a lot of palm greasing and unhealthy alliances. Contracts are developed and extended with the association of those connections to the "good old boy network" with not much thought given to the actual organizational need; meaning, you must determine if the objectives of the servicing contract correspond with meeting the mission of the organization before it is finalized. Or, you must initially set up a trial contract with at least two to three servicing organizations for comparison and not on the basis of relationship because he or she is a former acquaintance. There are many examples of this type of partiality, with Halliburton being the major one.

1. Conflict of interest.

2. A service was provided and overpayment was extended.

3. Was the payment recovered and returned to be used where it was otherwise needed?

4. Or was the cost like many others written off at the expense of the tax payers?

5. Was the service that was provided adequate?

6. Did it meet the objectives of the overall mission?

7. And where does it stand now, thus keeping in mind the stability and quality measures?

Example #10: There are a number of actively used computer database systems throughout DOE. That means there are a number of servicing contracts in maintaining them. Has anyone evaluated the cost in comparison to the benefit? Can these systems be linked to communicate from one to the other, or are they independent and stand-alone systems? In following up to ascertain the answer to my previous question, I reached out to our Enterprise "Energy" IT Service Center to learn the compatibility of our existing software systems, such as the DOE address book, MS Outlook, People, CHRIS, DOEinfo and BI/IDW. Aside from hearing shared information I wish not to repeat, I learned most of the systems within DOE are stand-alone. Therefore, there would be no way to get them to communicate across DOE to eliminate duplication for better accuracy.

A human resources information system (HRIS) should capture all pertinent information pertaining to an employee (past and current) for generating queries and retrieval of reports. Once the report is generated, man-hours should not have to be used to add or delete information from a report that was intended to serve as a contact list in identifying HC/HR or DOE employees. That would denote the database system to be inadequate or that there was a breakdown in the process pertaining to how the system was being utilized. (If it isn't broken, don't fix it. But if it is not working, then obviously, it's broken and in dire need of repair or replacement with something newer and better!)

When considering the establishment of a business, a decision should be made to determine the key positions or functions needed to ensure the successfulness of meeting the goals, objectives and missions of an agency, department or organization. **As technology advances around us, we should be flexible to advance with it in considering the best-qualified candidates for each position.** There should be skilled and qualified IT (information technology) subject-matter experts to advise those in decision-making positions of authority about the state-of-the-art resources best suited for the agency. But those in leadership positions should be knowledgeable in this area as well or at least be willing to admit what they do not know and secure enough to be willing to explore the advice received from their subject-matter experts. In addition, they should be willing to obtain the training for themselves as well as others to function accordingly within an ever-changing, technological culture that is equipped to consider cyber security measures.

The first departments or divisions for consideration should be HR and IT, which may vary depending upon the nature of the business. However, you should never forget your key personnel, including the receptionist and clerical or administrative staff!

A business practice called "outsourcing," which was made easier by a bill (North American Free Trade Agreement) that was written and passed by a Democratic majority when former president Bill Clinton was in office, has several drawbacks. The bill encouraged the A-76 and the overall contracting out of certain functions and services that would have been extended to permanent, in-house FTE (full-time equivalent) positions, such as those of clerical and administrative in nature within the government. One of the major causes of the increase in bullying for some of those who have been impacted by the disparaging, abusive behavior is the managerial decision to outsource!

Outsourcing[70]: The government, along with other private organizations, viewed this business practice as an opportunity to avoid burdensome regulations, high employment and real estate taxes and adsorbent energy costs. The real incentive, in my opinion, was a way to cut down on health insurance and labor union contracts by eliminating or targeting certain blue-collar positions. Wikipedia references outsourcing as reducing the need to hire and train specialized staff in addition to reducing capital and operating expenses, which I believe was the main objective and an opportunity, by way of greed, to ensure higher payout in bonuses to those in leadership and head supervisory or management positions of power and control.

Example #11: I am sure each and every individual wants the opportunity to either grow in their career or to consider other developmental options in trying their hand

---

70   http://www.businessweek.com/stories/2006-01-29/the-future-of-outsourcing

at excelling in other labor categories. This was my main reason for being adamant about returning to school to pursue higher education and a degree in business management. It was an attempt to increase my income, improve upon my capacity for learning and to consider a career outside of the administrative field.

When I embarked upon my first human resources position, I did not know what to expect. Then I became excited about the opportunity to learn, grow and interact with people. I welcomed being cross-trained for a need to multi-task as the go-to person concerning all things HR. From posting internal and external vacancy announcements to processing health-related benefit plans, administering 401(k) payouts, answering various questions and providing guidance wherever possible in meeting the needs of the employees, was and still is a fulfilling and rewarding challenge. With the right balance, it can prove to be a never-boring and always-learning venture to developing the appropriate skill sets for starting your own business. However, over the years, I have witnessed the revamping of HR divisions to be anything but encouraging the employees to be all they can be to empower them. Even the renaming, in my opinion, to Human Capital Management (HC or HCM) sounds more controlling, exploitive and limiting rather than developmental! For some reason, when I hear the term Human (people) Capital (assets) Management (control), what comes to my mind is ushering in cattle for the slaughter in observation of the disjointed HR practices of late—especially within DOE.

HUMAN RESOURCES: Webster's Dictionary refers to human resources as being a department within a company or institution that looks after personnel records, company benefits, hiring and training of employees. But I like to think of it as being much more than that! The primary universal human resource is labor. Labor constitutes skilled people who operate and function in a capacity for an organization in aiding to recruit others in meeting the corporate goals and objectives. This skilled set of professionals should be knowledgeable and instrumental in making sure the continuity of business operations meets the standards and compliance of local, state and federal laws. HR is the face of an organization or the central operating catalyst—the liaison between the company owner(s), leadership and its employees. It is the department that can make or break a company or institution easily by not making its employees aware of the rules, regulations and company policies. If the rules, regulations and company policies are not enforced and taken seriously, along with the goals and objectives for attempting to maintain a diversified and trained staff, the dysfunctionality of HR can greatly impact the success of an organization. Today, HR has come a long way and may incorporate fields of study, such as program management, organizational/industrial psychology (which is behavioral in nature), employment/business law and employee (human) relations with a flair for customer service. In addition to the above subjects and the right financial background or aptitude for investing and retirement planning, there are many opportunities within the area of human resources. The key is being in the right place at the right time and blessed to find an organization that values people and their skill sets enough to be willing to consider their potential for career growth and encourage it. But instead of receiving the purity of the law as related to human resources, I received the manipulation of policies and standards.

Example #12: Since my initial entry into the government sector in 1978, the manner in which employees are selected has changed, but much improvement is still needed. Not all employees are being selected because of their skill level for certain positions. Positions are being filled using outdated position descriptions that lack the necessary content needed to express the core qualifications needed to successfully meet the objectives of the position in comparison to the title and tasks. Position descriptions need to be reviewed and rewritten (reclassified) often enough to actually spell out or capture the defined roles and responsibilities needed for the perspective candidate to perform the duties of their designated job 100 percent in keeping with the advancement of technology and processes.

Quality assurance (QA) is the act or process of putting in place systems or processes for providing the best possible products or services. It corresponds with or is related to quality control whereby certain measures are put in place to test, evaluate and monitor products and services for accuracy as well as ensuring dynamic customer service. As technology advances, the economy changes, the need for manpower fluctuates and the manner in which products are produced or serviced starts to evolve. All of these impacting factors (to include resources and training) should be considered and improved upon as deemed absolutely necessary. **Quality of service** is best measured through customer satisfaction questionnaires, which are designed to capture an unbiased and objective view of business operations.

Lack of project reviews: Because accountability and responsibility go hand-in-hand, projects, in my opinion, are not being properly managed or reviewed for quality assurance. In this fast-paced, microwave society, adequate time is not being devoted to measuring and evaluating systems and practices being utilized to reach a desired outcome. Generally speaking, technology is advancing too quickly for man to keep up, and valuable steps are being eliminated and adequate personnel resources are being impacted. Those who take the initiative to do what it takes to obtain adequate training and seek viable resources are being overtaxed because others are not pulling their weight.

There is an increased unwillingness to utilize something as simple as a checklist or check sheet to ensure all "i's" are dotted and "t's" are crossed. This may add more work and become too time consuming for most, but it will lessen cost over the long run. (This observational analysis was included as part of my homework assignment. Root Cause Analysis-Corrective Action Plan [CAP] of 2008.[71]

TRAINING: The *Government Employees Training Act* or *GETA* became law in 1958. It was established to give federal agencies the general authority for employee training, including

---

71   http://management.energy.gov

the use of non-government training resources, to meet identified training needs which otherwise could not be met with existing governmental programs and facilities. GETA was amended in 1994 to broaden the considered area of training resources for government employees. However, as indicated above, not everyone is allowed the same training opportunities. That which is written into law and regarded as a policy or guideline looks good on paper, but is obsolete if it is not honored or enforced as an actively used governing rule for guidance and direction to promote equality. Tabulated training costs: With a more adequate database system, the monitoring and tracking of training in relation to dollars could be simplified.

> **Example #13:** Although the creation and completion of Individual Development Plans (IDP) are encouraged, not everyone gets the opportunity to pursue the developmental training they desire for advancement. Prior to being reassigned to the Business Office of HCM, I had the pleasure of processing training requests for DOE employees. I noticed some of the same individuals receiving training regularly, but I also saw there was no measurement in place for making sure each employee within DOE received equal training according to a set, budgeted amount geared towards training for all employees. Why not generate a policy for determining a set dollar amount for each employee per fiscal year directed towards development training? While working for an organization called Robbins-Gioia, I was responsible for monitoring and tracking the training budget. Each person was allotted $1,500 to $3,000 per year towards their individual training. This did

not include their cost in travel expenses. But, if the training was locally obtainable, each person was encouraged to lower the cost by seeking a training vendor within their immediate, geographical area. Of course this was reviewed on a case-by-case scenario depending upon the level of training needed to successfully execute the desired tasks or functions in meeting the mission of the organization.

To every [thing there is] a season,
and a time to every purpose under the heaven:

~ Ecclesiastics 3:1 KJV

Due to the number of discrepancies and delayed processing times for carrying out some of the HR-related actions, the lack of knowledge and training is a very big factor. Many individuals are hired and given no formal training or allotted an ample transition period in which to get up to speed with what is expected of them. Too often, employees are trained by other employees who know less than they do. If you are trained wrong, you learn wrong, with no point of reference for confirming what you know or should know to successfully complete a task in a timely and efficient manner. Besides that, I truly would like to believe that a lack of training and not deliberate malice is the motivation or reason for the number of inadequacies throughout the department.

Example #14: Upon returning to the federal government and being processed during my orientation, I was placed in the incorrect retirement category. After researching the policy for myself by way of the OPM (Office of Personnel

Management) website, I made several attempts over the course of two years to get it corrected. I had no success until I finally reached out to Secretary Chu, but not before attempting to go up the HC chain of command for assistance. According to the policy, I was eligible for a correction provided the error was noted and changed prior to the third year of my entry date. Each person I spoke to within HR interpreted the policy incorrectly and told me, in writing, I needed to be in the incorrect retirement category for three or more years before it could be corrected.

Shouldn't you make an attempt to correct an error as soon as you note an error was made? Being in a FERS status versus a CSRS status meant a reverse of certain deposits. Could the lack of training in this area or lack of concern initially be the reason why there is such a delay in retirement payouts?

Example #15: Initially hired as a program analyst GS-0343 series, I was constantly denied training that would enable me to fully perform in the position. Upon being reassigned to HC-1.5, my position description was revised to reflect the title of "management analyst," although the classification series was still the same as that of a program analyst. The objective was to include language corresponding to a 0301, 0318 or 0399 classification series[72] with the intent

---

72   Position classification is a process through which federal jobs (i.e., positions) are assigned to a pay system, series, title and grade or band, based on consistent application of position classification standards. See https://www.opm.gov/policy-data-oversight/classification-qualifications/.

of further denying me training beyond the clerical and administrative duties being delegated to me in an effort to keep me at a desired level and grade with no potential for growth. This is a strategic tactic I have experienced or witnessed too often as directed at many employees in my same situation. In part, this is due to the introduction of outsourcing or contracting out of clerical and administrative functions (mainly blue collar positions at lower salary levels). Some employees are forced (bullied) into performing these functions as a result of budget constraints or misappropriation of funding.

The Condition of the Heart

During a word at a work Bible study session, as presented by Michael Vernon Kelsey Sr. of New Samaritan Baptist Church, he asked if it was easier or harder to do the right thing! The responses were very interesting, but what he did not know about me was the number of conversations I have had with God concerning that very same thing. In fact, I used to question God often about the *heart* He gave me. A heart I did not appreciate because it would not allow me to treat people as unjustly and unkindly as they were compelled to treat me. After each and every cruelty I suffered at the hands of others, I would think of what I wished I could have said or done in response to their grave inhumanity towards me. But God, through the conviction of my heart, would not let me as I struggled to understand why it was so difficult for me to commit a wrong act even if it was justified. As time went on and I spent more time with God in seeking His face, He would speak to my heart and reveal many things to me. The choices we make helps to determine the condition of our heart. In 2 Chronicles 16:10, it says, "For the eyes of the Lord run to and fro throughout the whole earth to shew himself strong on behalf of them whose heart is perfect toward Him." In Proverbs 4:23, it says "Keep thy heart with all diligence; for out of it are the issues of life." This includes what we think about, care about, what we choose to do and where we choose to go. What causes an individual to quickly lay down his or her spiritual duties and embrace the fleeting things of the world? Their **HEART**!

> *Search me, O God, and know my heart:*
> *try me, and know my thoughts:*
> *And see if there be any wicked way in me,*
> *and lead me in the way everlasting.*
>
> ~ Psalm 139:23-24

Galatians 6:4-5 teaches us, "Make a careful exploration of who you are and the work you have been given and then sink yourself into that. Don't be impressed with yourself. Don't compare yourself with others. Each of you must take responsibility for doing the creative best you can with your own life" (MSG). But God, I guess what I do not understand or am not able to find in my heart to believe is how easy it is for one individual to turn their back on a cry for help from his brother or sister! How is it possible for people to be consciously aware of what they know in their heart is an immoral act and turn a blind eye to it all while denying the existence of what they see or know to be a true injustice? Not to mention, they complain about an injustice being done to them, but allow themselves to be influenced to commit that same wrongful act to another and possess no moral compass for **repentance**. I find it to be so difficult to fit in or to follow for the sake of getting along with those who seem to have no problem doing that which I know goes against what God commands of me (or all of us for that matter) to be and to do! I cannot in good faith sit idly on the sidelines and witness injustice being done to others as well as myself and do nothing in making my objection known. For it is important for me to be faithful to God concerning what I have been called to do and be! Therefore, I want to scream from the top of my lungs and say, "No more! Enough is enough! How dare you!"

> *[He that is] first in his own cause [seemeth] just;*
> *but his neighbour cometh and searcheth him.*
>
> ~ Proverbs 18:17 KJV

Example #16: About two months ago, a female employee within the DOE Headquarters building fell in the hallway while walking with another employee on their way to a meeting. She hit the floor so hard her doctors indicated her injuries to be more serious than they initially thought. Falling flat on her back on a concrete surface, she suffered a sprained back and disk injury. Prior to her fall, she was already experiencing a great deal of discomfort due to osteoporosis: thinning bones in various areas of her body with arthritic complication. She is actually blessed to not have suffered a broken back, but her injuries are quite serious and gravely painful, which are not being viewed as such by those who are responsible for receiving and processing her supporting medical documentation. Once her forms were received by her HR (Human Capital Management) coworkers, they were delayed and altered to exclude pertinent information needed to assist the Labor Department in making an objective decision concerning her continued workman's compensation benefit and ruling. This egregious act prolonged her return to work and impeded her care for a successful and speedy recovery.

You shall not repeat or raise a false report; you shall not join with the wicked to be an unrighteous witness. You shall not follow a crowd to do evil; nor shall you bear witness at a trial so as to side with a multitude to pervert justice.

~ Exodus 23:1-2

Conclusion

Change and correction is unfortunately long overdue! If problems or issues are not addressed at the onset, it sends a very unsettling message to those on either end of the spectrum. It tells those on one side that there is no such thing as truth, righteousness or fairness. It tells those on the other side that the only way is with dishonesty and brute force at all cost, even at the expense of ruining the reputation of an organization; and it's okay!

As seasons change, so does the shift within the atmosphere! For quite some time now, there has been a shift according to the influence of the power base on earth. That influence which has been more negative in nature has attempted to interfere with people's civil liberties (human rights) thus giving more power to companies and organizations. So in turn, the term or concept of conflict resolution has been one-sided. In the name of risk management, many companies and organizations attempt to use a conflict resolution process to ascertain the validity of a person's claim before it gets to EEO. During this process, they attempt to learn what substantiating proof one might have at winning their claim. Then they start to put measures in place to not only discredit the individual, but they also attempt to impede any damaging information disclosing the truth a person may have as a viable case against them. Therefore, in many cases, the organization will go through great lengths to protect those in managerial, supervisory or leadership positions who are committing wrongful acts against an employee to figure out ways to keep the employee quiet about what is going on. In many cases, the person in the higher-ranked position does not receive a reprimand for his disparaging actions, nor does he receive training to prevent his behavior from getting any worse. Doing nothing to objectively divert the shifting only gives those who commit the disparaging act against the employee a false sense of power and excuse to feel untouchable and invisible for taking no responsibility at all. Another example of a shift in the atmosphere is the impact it has had on borrowers and lenders within the past ten years. This can be monitored by the start of and increased foreclosures. Not only that, but lenders have recently been noted to deliberately engage in wrongful acts against homeowners. Under the leadership of our current president, this administration has been directed to attempt to restore order to the homeowner.

In order to receive justice, people (you) must be willing to fight the good fight of FAITH. You must be willing to pursue a course (plan) of action that may not be easy or swift. **It will call for us to draw near to God, rely on His strength and seek His wisdom, knowledge and understanding *in every area of our life* for direction and guidance.** For His word states, "My people are destroyed for lack of knowledge" (Hosea 4:6). That in the natural also equates to our occasional unwillingness to educate ourselves according to our rights and do our part so God can do His part! You must also be willing to review your surroundings and take into account the history and structure of its power base or the influence thereof to determine whether to pursue an option for reprieve outside of the normal chain of command that's put in place to limit you.

Take, for instance, the newly recent housing development: Under a settlement between the federal government's major regulators, the Office of the Comptroller of the Currency (OCC), Federal Reserve and mortgage lenders, independent reviewers will review the homeowner's file. They will determine if the homeowner suffered financial harm, including not obtaining an affordable mortgage payment or losing their home resulting from lender caused errors, misrepresentations or other deficiencies. The independent consultants will decide whether the homeowner should receive cash compensation up to $125,000, a return of the foreclosed property or another remedy, such as cancellation of the foreclosure.

In reading an announcement entitled, "Celebrate Conflict Resolution Day!" I had to laugh. How can we celebrate what is not being taken into consideration? To reach a resolution, first we must we willing to acknowledge the problem, and then we must be committed to reaching a mutual solution in solving the conflict with both parties in mind. If a serious commitment was made to holding people accountable for their actions and a beneficial change was implemented to ensure a safe and healthy workplace environment to protect the nature or manner in which business was conducted with fewer casualties of war, then I could—in all honesty—celebrate, unless I am celebrating **knowing that HE who gives us all life lives and see all!**

> *All unrighteousness is sin:*
> *and there is a sin not unto death.*
>
> ~ 1 John 5:17

Note

- **New level** – When I speak of a new level, I am speaking of a different plateau in one's learning and growth. To be promoted rather than demoted is truly a great reward in itself. But you must also be willing to take into account the wisdom, knowledge and understanding you gain from transitioning from one position to another even if it is just a lateral move.

- **New devil** – Many people do not put themselves in a position to think, learn and grow on their own. They have the tendency to rely more on technology as well as the knowledge of others pertaining to what they are willing to believe or accept as being the truth. You have to be willing to look at everything with an open mind and objective view. Research and study for yourself to grasp the meaning and depth of what you should know.

Just as there are many degrees or levels in positioning, there are many influences in the world with varied levels of power. Figuratively speaking, a new devil is a spirit of influence at a higher level than the one before it. Just like the military structure of hierarchical ranking comes with more power of influence and control, there is that same hierarchical ranking amongst those within the spirit world or realm (angels on the side of God and those on the side of Lucifer, the devil). Once you pass your spiritual test in succeeding or transitioning to a higher level, do you honestly think that Lucifer will reassign one of his minions that you already defeated in spiritual warfare?

Overcoming sinful attitudes and behaviors starts with **genuine repentance**, which has three aspects:

1. *Conviction* – The Holy Spirit will reveal the areas in which we have sinned and convict us of wrongdoing. Through scripture, the Spirit shows us God's standard and what needs to change. Repentance begins with understanding where we have gone astray.

2. ***Contrition*** – The next step, grieving over our iniquity, is followed by confession to the Lord. Genuine sorrow arises from the knowledge that we have sinned against Him. In contrast, human unhappiness often comes from being caught misbehaving. Other times, we are miserable because of where our choices have led us, or we feel ashamed that people know about our sin. True contrition is followed by humble confession.

3. ***Commitment to Act*** – Real repentance is complete when we wholeheartedly pledge to turn around our old behavior and move toward righteousness. God knows we will not live perfectly, but He looks for a surrendered heart that diligently seeks to obey Him by living holy.

Corruption

- dishonesty for personal gain; dishonest exploitation of power for personal gain

- depravity; extreme immorality or depravity

- undesirable change; an undesirable change in meaning or another error introduced into a text during copying (displaying) past actions[73]

- The act of wrongdoing on the part of an authority or powerful party through means that are illegitimate, immoral or incompatible with ethical standards.

---

73   Definition via http://www.bing.com

▸ Corruption often results from patronage and is associated with bribery.[74]

Forms of corruption vary but include bribery, extortion, cronyism, nepotism, patronage, graft and embezzlement. While corruption may facilitate criminal enterprise such as drug trafficking or money laundering, it is not restricted to these activities. The activities that constitute illegal corruption differ depending on the country or jurisdiction. For instance, certain political funding practices that are legal in one place may be illegal in another. In some cases, government officials have broad or poorly defined powers that make it difficult to distinguish between legal and illegal actions.

▸ **Political corruption:** The use of legislated powers by government officials for illegitimate private gain. Misuse of government power for other purposes, such as repression of political opponents and general police brutality, is not considered political corruption. Neither are illegal acts by private persons or corporations not directly involved with the government. An illegal act by an officeholder constitutes political corruption only if the act is directly related to their official duties.

▸ Worldwide, **bribery** alone is estimated to involve over one trillion U.S. dollars annually. A state of unrestrained political corruption is known as a **kleptocracy** (alternatively *cleptocracy* or *kleptarchy*), meaning "rule by thieves."[75]

---

74 Definition via http://www.businessdictionary.com
75 Information via http://en.wikipedia.org/wiki/Politics

ATTACHMENT 1

Description: My personal observational analysis as presented to Mr. Jonathan Kaufmann (Esquire) after the completion of my questioning RE: The Fact Finding Investigation, July 2010.

Recap:

What makes one department or organization different from another? The policies, guidelines, goals, methodologies, missions and plans (culture)! Unfortunately, not many government employees view their environment or function of the organization as a business. Ethical vs. unethical: The business practices exercised or utilized in one office and not another could make a world of difference and cripple an organization.

1. What sets the stage within an organization to dictate the underlying behavior?

    > The culture! Whether right or wrong or appropriate or inappropriate for a business setting. If it is wrong or inappropriate, and it is not challenged or questioned, it can strive, fester and possibly get worse, thus leaving the victims

to be continually pressured and oppressed by the victimizer.

> Why? Because practice makes perfect, and most people become comfortable with their sin or wrongdoing because it contributes to a false sense of power.

> Who are the victimizers? Those in position of power, higher-grade positions or those in association with others who have given them the power to be bullies.

2. What could be the underlying problem?

> The dinosaurs vs. newcomers with innovative ideas.

> Those with work experience vs. those with education.

> Those who are comfortable with their level of knowledge vs. those who are continual or avid learners.

> Those who are afraid of change vs. those who embrace change.

Why not embrace education and experience? Why not be willing to learn from each other? Experience is education, and education is experience!

This behavior of abuse and hostility within the workplace is also not an isolated event within Human Capital Management. It is a problem throughout DOE as well as government agencies outside of DOE. For example, on July 15, 2010, I met and spoke with a young lady from another department within DOE who I learned through her body language and our conversation was experiencing a similar situation that had been going on since the beginning of her employment through the Career Intern Program in 2008. As we were standing in the subway line, she indicated she was hypoglycemic and working in an environment that uses threats of affecting her next promotion to a GS-12 should she resist or refuse to continue working at an unethical pace which involved assignments of those at a GS-14 level while missing lunch, working through lunch and forgetting to take her much-needed medication. (In line, she was fidgety and feeling faint because she hadn't had anything to eat. I regret that I neglected to get her name, but I have thought of her often and pray that what she is encountering in her office does not have an adverse effect on her health any more than it has already.)

On another note: Thoughts about an issue that needs to be addressed!

Depending upon the nature of a person, when you become comfortable with where you are, you do not want to review other ways of reaching an outcome or a better solution, such as observing other methods. This feeling can be expressed in a very intimidating manner and threaten the enthusiastic newcomer whose only desire is to make a contribution to the department, agency or organization in keeping with the current advancement in technology and competition.

1. **Problem #1**: Not many old-timers or "dinosaurs" want to be moved from the now to the future. They tend to resent newcomers with different ideas or concepts for doing things, where different ways have the same outcome but possibly in a shorter timespan. They want newcomers to conform instead of transform.

> I was once yelled at and told, "You are trying to tell me something that I already know; I've been here for a long time." Knowing how something was done previously, a year, two years or even three years ago, does not mean the method or the policy in how it is done now has not changed, especially if you are not willing to familiarize yourself with the changes as they occur.

2. **Problem #2**: The old timers who are comfortable and set in their ways may not want to learn anything new. Instead of taking the time or putting forth the effort to try their hand at learning, some feel they lack the aptitude for learning new equipment or programs and may unfortunately feel threatened or intimated about growth and change. Being intent on doing things their way, they may prevent those who want to learn from

obtaining the training needed or desired to compete with the best and brightest. (This happens a lot!)

3. **Problem #3**: Feuds between managers (or leadership) at higher-leveled positions pose even more of a problem. Lower-leveled employees get caught in the crossfire. The fight or the agenda to prove to one another that they are not going to be told what to do when it concerns the direction of their leadership as a head of a department or division gets in the way and becomes more important than the work that needs to be accomplished for the success of the office. Once a bully, always a bully, and bullies normally turn on each other if they do not have a willing participant for them to direct their rage towards.

What people do not tend to realize is, if you allow yourself to be manipulated into bullying (oppressing) others, it is just a matter of time before you find yourself on the receiving end of the abuse. Then the cycle begins again.

The problem: Depending upon who you are, staying in a hostile or abusive environment or relationship makes you an angry and bitter person over time! Such an environment can have a negative impact on your health and your spirit. If not careful or strong willed enough to resist, you will and can also become a victimizer to do to others what was done to you. Hurt people sometimes hurt people, and fitting in becomes easier than resisting.

4. **Problem #4**: Those that become comfortable in their wrongdoing have a tendency to justify their behavior as being right. When those who are being abused attempt to resist, the abuser uses his power of authority to convince the abused that they are to blame; then, they get written up or receive false performance evaluations. This tactic is a strategy to keep the abused quiet and position them to take even more abuse. It is an attempt to discredit them in the eyes of those who could possibly offer them moral support. It is an attempt to get others not to believe the abused about the unfair and abusive treatment. It is a tactic to continually tear down the abused and create doubt.

ATTACHMENT 2

PM Systems and Practices
Homework Assignment
March 2009

SIGNIFICANT TO THE U.S. DEPARTMENT OF ENERGY:

Root Cause Analysis Corrective Action Plan (CAP) 2008
Document can be found at http://management.energy.gov

1. **Cause 1**: (list): Federal Personnel—DOE does not have the adequate number of federal contracting and project management personnel with the appropriate skills (e.g., cost estimating, scheduling, risk management, and technical) to plan, direct, and oversee project execution.

    > Insufficient budget resources

    > Conflicting and competing priorities

- Inferior federal government compensation compared to the private sector
- Inadequate defined roles and responsibilities
- Inadequate training

2. **Cause 2:** (list): Requirements Management – DOE has not ensured that its project management requirements are consistently followed. In some instances, projects are initiated or carried out without fully complying with the processes and controls contained in DOE policy and guidance.

   - Conflicting guidance and priorities
   - Lack of adequate personnel resources
   - Inadequate training
   - Lack of failed project reviews

3. ***Do you think the corrective action plan proposed for your Cause 1 and 2 will be effective? Why or why not?***

In review of corrective measures 2 and 8 as they relate to the root causes identified above, any action of change for improving a situation would be most effective with the right commitment to overseeing and complying with the processes and controls contained in the (DOE) policy, procedural and guidance manuals. However, I have noted that many policies are not tested for clarity before they are put into action. Not all departments have developed a viable up-to-date training needs analysis to determine the number of qualified (skilled) personnel on board before they recruit other personnel. Quite possibly, the current personnel could be moved around a bit to fill positions that are best suited for them as well as the department/agency before finalizing a need to obtain more employees thus giving the current employees an opportunity to change careers. I do not believe checklists are being utilized as outlined in corrective measure #8. What type of contingency plan is in place to monitor the ownership responsibility of the project management personnel as outlined or documented relating to "defined" roles, responsibilities and authorities before the individual is assigned to a project?

For example: I received a call from an individual who wanted to know what courses an employee should take to meet the requirements for being a COR/COTOR/COTR. An employee who took the initial training and obtaining a certification ten (10) years ago was not obtaining what was needed by taking the refresher course to satisfactorily perform the functions of his job as a COR/COTOR/COTR today. Therefore, the Office Administrator was given the task to research what level of training and certification was needed for the entire office to be in compliance with the requirements. This was not noted until after the employee spent viable time on a project (i.e., after a performance baseline was established) that did not produce the desired outcome or quality of work performed.

4. **For your number 1 (highest priority) recommendation from Question 1, what obstacles do you see with**

implementing that recommendation? What would have to occur to make it happen?

The highest area of improvement needed is Human Resources. This observation is not one in relation to human error; however, it is on the basis of how systems need to be evaluated and change implemented for improving processes. Unfortunately, the guidelines governing the CIP/CCIS curriculum have not been finalized or operated consistently across DOE. When the decision is made to employ an individual as part of the CIP and courses have been identified, a budget should be worked out to cover that individual's training as outlined in the curriculum for the entire two-year period. The employee should not be penalized in any way should management or their employing agency fail to consider a budget for their training as specified in the curriculum guidelines as a reference for their guidance.

<u>Training</u>: Training does not seem to be applicable or considered for everyone and viewed differently for higher level employees as opposed to lower level employees. Everyone should be given the same opportunity to grow regardless of their career level in accordance to the GETA.

AWARENESS

*Keep a cool head. Stay alert.
The Devil is poised to pounce, and would like nothing better than to catch you napping. Keep your guard up. You're not the only ones plunged into these hard times. It's the same with Christians all over the world. So keep a firm grip on the faith. The suffering won't last forever. It won't be long before this generous God who has great plans for us in Christ—eternal and glorious plans they are!—will have you put together and on your feet for good.
He gets the last word; yes, he does.*

~ 1 Peter 5:8-11 MSG

May 6, 2011

Revised November 9, 2015

We are all sinners who were born into sin, but we do not have to give in to sin by practicing and living it! Nor do we have to allow the influences of a diseased and dark world to fulfill its single, solitary objective to separate us from the love of God as we unconsciously idolize sin. If that task is accomplished, then it truly demonstrates the manifested evidence of us suffering from an infectious, diseased soul that is drunk off the power of darkness; a withered and dying soul that is void of humanity and tricked into thinking you are in control with each taste of power—like a drug—drifting deeper and deeper into the abyss by the disillusionment of right and wrong! You are fully seduced by the adversary and the things of the world while your flesh dominates and interferes with your will to live an eternal and glorious life with the Father who created you! In turn, you seek to destroy everything in your path by taking what you will, inflicting pain on others and giving no thought to the damaging consequences of your actions. Although many of us are considered to be the walking wounded who are blinded by darkness to the truth around us, we (people in general) are not expecting others to be the wiser—especially those who believe themselves to be far above you in their way of thinking, education and position in life for you to have any power to stop them in their tracks.

> *Say ye not, A confederacy,*
> *to all [them to] whom this people shall say, A confederacy;*
> *neither fear ye their fear, nor be afraid.*
> *Sanctify the LORD of hosts himself; and [let] him*
> *[be] your fear, and [let] him [be] your dread.*
>
> ~ Isaiah 8:12-13

On the basis of my thinking and writings, I have been accused of or viewed by many as being a conspiracy theorist. Yes, I know we *all* view things differently; that's because we *all* are wired differently in our thinking as perceived by what we see or don't see! You see the glass as being half empty, and I may see that same glass as being half full. I believe, without a doubt, that there is a God in Heaven who sits up high and looks down low upon *all* that is going on in the world. I have been allowed to experience Him for myself to know He is real; I am as much a part of Him as He is of me, through the existence and connection of the Holy Spirit who lives deep within my being to see the manifestation of His hand moving all around me! I am in agreement with the Father, the Son and the Holy Spirit, who are one and the same but are performing in different capacities, positions and uniqueness just as I am unique to Him! You not being able to see what I see does not equate to what I see as being untrue. It simply means I am more sensitive to my surroundings to be able to discern that which you cannot see, are not willing to see under the surface or are hoping I do not see to know what you already know to be true as you attempt to deceive me. Therefore, I will not allow your attempts to derail me from moving forward in acceptance of my inheritance and God-ordained assignment.

Who would you rather be? A person who is able to see with your eyes wide open or one who can only see with your eyes wide shut while allowing yourself to be deceived by everything and everyone around you? What if you had the ability to see in 3D while relying on the Lord to direct your every step and be willing to utilize discernment and welcome God's gift of knowledge, wisdom and understanding to see the world in a panoramic view through His eyes? Be open-minded to seeing the natural in the supernatural, but through Christ, receive the generous gift of His life to accept and embrace who you were created to be through this precious gifting and calling! It is a call to acknowledge an urgent task of spreading the gospel (good news) to others who are willing to listen, receive and walk by *faith* in obedience and trust in the Lord regardless of their nationality, social status or position in life. *It's news I'm most proud to proclaim, this extraordinary Message of God's powerful plan to rescue everyone who trusts him, starting with Jews and then right on to everyone else! God's way of putting people right shows up in the acts of faith, confirming what Scripture has said all along: "The person in right standing before God by trusting him really lives"* (Romans 1:16-17 MSG). Therefore, being labeled a strange and weird outcast that many tend to blackball and ostracize on the basis of their personal agenda or perception can be a good thing! Why? Because Psalm 4:3 states, "But know that the LORD hath set apart him that is godly for himself: the LORD will hear when I call unto him."

Being fully awake to discern your surrounding environment is truly a whole lot better than being fully asleep or half awake. Being fully awake is a sign of being fearless! People who do not want to see the truth for what it really is are the ones who are easily influenced by lies and negativity, causing them to be fueled by their own fears! If those living in fear refuse to see and acknowledge truth, oh well! You just simply need to continue to pray while being fully armed with more ammunition—being fully awake and not falling for the tricks and the schemes of the enemy. Each and every person on earth is uniquely made by God. We are uniquely special to Him on the basis of our purpose and God-given assignments. Even if you find yourself surrounded by total darkness, you *must not compromise* what you know to be true just to fit in and to be accepted by those who do not understand you! If we as believers, who are committed to following Jesus, aren't willing to say the hard things to those in our lives, who will? God has put us into position in our families, our workplaces and even our neighborhoods to share the truth in love.

> *Since they didn't bother to acknowledge God, God quit bothering them and let them run loose. And then all hell broke loose: rampant evil, grabbing and grasping, vicious backstabbing. They made life hell on earth with their envy, wanton killing, bickering, and cheating. Look at them: mean-spirited, venomous, fork-tongued God-bashers. Bullies, swaggerers, insufferable windbags! They keep inventing new ways of wrecking lives. They ditch their parents when they get in the way. Stupid, slimy, cruel, cold-blooded. And it's not as if they don't know better. They know perfectly well they're spitting in God's face. And they don't care—worse, they hand out prizes to those who do the worst things best.*
>
> ~ Romans 1:28-32 MSG

When you are able to see clearly and possess the ability to articulate your observation both verbally and in writing, those around you will attempt to discredit you in any way they can to influence others to disbelieve you! But, when God is in the mix and you have rightfully aligned yourself with Him, He will unveil (uncover), reveal (expose) and unmask TRUTH. He will, quite frankly, spoil the plot and plans of the enemy every time.

You just have to be patient, and when the time comes, every one of us will have to face the consequences of what we have done in this life!

> *God will pay back to each person according to his deeds [justly, as his deeds deserve]: to those who by persistence in doing good seek [unseen but certain heavenly] glory, honor, and immortality, [He will give the gift of] eternal life. But for those who are selfishly ambitious and self-seeking and disobedient to the truth but responsive to wickedness, [there will be] wrath and indignation. There will be tribulation and anguish [torturing confinement] for every human soul who does [or permits] evil, to the Jew first and also to the Greek, but glory and honor and inner peace [will be given] to everyone who habitually does good, to the Jew first and also to the Greek. For God shows no partiality [no arbitrary favoritism; with Him one person is not more important than another.*
>
> ~ Romans 2:6-11 AMP

The Spirit of Elitism

Elitism is defined as the belief that certain persons or members of certain classes or groups deserve favored treatment (sense of entitlement) by virtue of their perceived superiority, as in intellect, social status or financial resources to control, rule or dominate others. Many people who are in positions of leadership, often see themselves as gods, putting themselves far above those who are "below them" in certain positions or capacities to exploit, manipulate, intimidate and abuse at will—all under the disguise of control and the ability to conceal truth from others. *For I say, through the grace given unto me, to every man that is among you, not to think [of himself] more highly than he ought to think; but to think soberly, according as God hath dealt to every man the measure of faith* (Romans 12:3).

To add insult to injury, on Saturday, April 30, 2011, a Hazmat Team was deployed to the U.S. Department of Energy (DOE) Headquarters building, located at 1000 Independence Avenue, SW in Washington, D.C., to investigate a particularly harmful package or substance. It is not clear as to the nature of the substance, how it happened to appear or who initially discovered it other than the possibility of it being transported through the weekend mail. However, when employees arrived to work on Monday, May 2, 2011, there was no mention of the events that took place that weekend. There was no warning or notification of any kind as a precautionary measure to alert the DOE employees of a potentially dangerous chemical substance spreading throughout the atmosphere of their working environment should they start to experience any symptoms or allergic reactions. As people all over the building started to get sick and began to react to the smell or existence of an airborne substance that caused, for some, headaches, tightness in the chest, closing throat, burning flesh, itchy skin rashes, hives and blisters, they would report to the nurses station one-by-one for care. Upon being attended to by the nursing staff, they were questioned about their apparent condition or symptoms that persisted and varied in which they were administered allergy medication, aspirin, EpiPens and oxygen due to difficulty breathing. On the following day, Tuesday, May 3, 2011, as the substance still lingered and more were affected, another Hazmat Team was deployed to the building of the U.S. Department of Energy between 7 and 8 p.m. for yet another sweep of what they knew to already be present on Saturday, April 30, 2011, during the initial sweep of the building.

Upon complaining about feeling ill or experiencing an allergic reaction to something within the atmospheric existence of the building, some employees were made to feel as if it were all in our heads or that we were making it all up (exaggerating) just to get attention. Unfortunately, many possibilities were given to us to downplay what really took place and still, not once—to this day—were we given full disclosure (to my knowledge) to the possible threat of anthrax or a fraction of some chemical that was delivered to and released within the building in the same manner as a number of schools throughout the Washington metropolitan area within that same timeframe. Instead, as a "risk management strategy" the three (Mack, Lewis, Lanning) out of four (Allan-Benard) individuals who were impacted the most on the fourth floor of the Office of Chief Human Capital Officer (CHCO) were called into an office by the then deputy CHCO, the HR director, and the head of the DOE Security Team to be interrogated as if they were criminals who devised a scheme to release the chemicals ourselves. On another scale, we were told that there was nothing to worry about; otherwise, none of them would be present in the building.

As a secondary measure, I was called into a second meeting by the then chief learning officer and told that he thought it was strange that only four out of an entire office of over one hundred people were the only ones to make mention of being affected by a foreign substance floating throughout the surrounding environment of our workplace. As I mentioned to him, each and every person is different based on our physiological makeup or medical limitations, to include how our bodies process the elements in the air. Some people are more sensitive than others to suffer from asthma, hay fever and allergies, especially if a person has a medical history of issues with respiratory illness. What affects one individual may not necessarily affect another. And we were not the only four affected; there were others, but they were reluctant to openly say anything at all! Immediately following that discussion where his intent was to influence me to believe me I was in the wrong, a mandatory meeting was called to order within the large conference room in which much of our conversation was shared with others—word for word—to ease their tensions.

I was extremely livid by the entire scenario and how very little to no concern for the safety of others was taken into consideration. And not once were there any reports given to the employees concerning the arrival of the Hazmat Team on that Saturday prior to the Monday the employees returned to work. Instead, we were told numerous, bogus stories or possibilities for feeling ill or experiencing allergic reactions:

- The U.S. Department of Agriculture, as well as other federal government agencies, had a reported infestation of bedbugs. Therefore, the employees who had allergic reactions could have been bitten by spiders, fleas ticks or other insects possibly inhabiting the U.S. Department of Energy.

- There was also some talk of the walls being painted on Friday night; and although they used a low-grade, harmless and fumeless paint, one of the ingredients or properties was latex, which could have caused some of the allergic reactions.

- We were also told about the possibility of other elements circling through the building due to the air vents connecting outside, such as pollen, since this was "allergy season" for some.

Is the safety of people not important? What happened to accountability, full disclosure or people first? Shouldn't we have been readily given information to make us aware of how to handle the situation or given an option not to report to work on Monday until the authorities were able to guarantee everything was cleared and under control? Just as second-hand smoke has been proven to be just as deadly or harmful to others as the one doing the actual puffing, breathing in and being exposed to any chemical circulating in an immediate environment can be deadly or harmful to folks with silently long-lasting effects over time. The building should have been evacuated for a certain number of days to ensure the employees' safety.

Aside from that, my major concern was for the well-being of my mother who was diagnosed with stage 4 lung cancer the day before Thanksgiving in November of 2010. She was undergoing radiation and chemotherapy, which was extremely taxing to her immune system; therefore, she was hospitalized for brief periods due to complications with her immune system. As her caregiver, I was already a little distraught from the possibility of losing my mother to this disease. In addition, I needed to be sure my contact or exposure to certain elements within the DOE building was not harmful to her in any way. This was my mother! So why wouldn't she be my major concern? Why wouldn't the handling of the entire matter anger me or others, for that matter? It then became my responsibility, for the love of my mother, to take the necessary precautions to get a full blood panel screening after experiencing tightness in my chest, coughing, burning skin and body rashes. Although we are considered to be expendable, the life of any human being is very important!

Conclusion

When I first started working at the U.S. Department of Energy in January of 2008, I had such great and high expectations concerning my new working environment. I was extremely excited to return to the employment of the federal government to continue a career in human resources after a twenty-three-year period of working in the private sector; however, something was terribly wrong. Each day I reported for work, my spirit wrestled and grieved in agony for the souls around me to the point of me finding it increasingly unbearable to be there. Many days, I would retreat to the bathroom in tears to pray and to engage in conversation with God for answers about what I was experiencing. No matter what part of the building I was in, no one seemed to be happy or at peace as I began to note a very thick blanket of darkness fueling the rapidly increasing hostile environment. The more I resisted and voiced what I was experiencing and seeing to others, the more they denied it—and the attacks on me grew. Crying out to God, I attempted to wrap my head around why He would usher me into such a vexing environment.

Finally, God revealed His plan as He opened my eyes to the encasing environment, which was intended to teach me about **spiritual warfare**! The U.S. Department of Energy, which God referred to as the "headquarters of demonic activity," was to be my ultimate training ground, and He wanted me to be *fully* aware of my surroundings! They say experience is the best teacher, and I had been thrown into an arena with a bunch of wolves, similar to Daniel in the lion's den—with no warning. But God was also teaching me to rely solely on Him throughout my entire process of meet and greet. I was being given a crash course of sink or swim without a floatation device of any kind—so I thought! As time went on, I learned God was my life-preserving vest.

God is nothing like man that He should lie to you—ever! He values *all* life and honors *all* of His promises! When He created us, He equipped us *all* with the same potential and opportunities in life; however, it is up to us to stay on track while evading captivity to the enemy. To do this, you have to be willing to protect yourselves by putting on the whole armor of Christ. When you enlist in the military, there is a possibility of being sent to war. When and if that happens, you need to be prepared to be a casualty and a victor. Should you ever find yourself in the position of a casualty, that does not necessarily equate to you being a prisoner of war who is not capable of getting free! You have to be committed to changing your way of thinking and renewing your mind in order to see things differently. Call those things that are not as though they were (Romans 4:17)! You have to be willing to choose a viable side and source to take an immovable stand. You have to be able to see yourself walking on the water with the one who said He would not leave you nor forsake you (Matthew 14:22 – 36 and Deuteronomy 31:6)!

Yes, the things of the world look so inviting, and there are countless things (material objects) available for the taking to excite the flesh! But why would you compromise your soul for temporary satisfaction to join forces with those who would turn their backs on you in a heartbeat for the right price? Why would you align yourself with the dark forces of this world and those who have no integrity and sincerity for your well-being or others? Do you realize that when you became a Christian, your body became a temple for the Holy Spirit to live in? His presence in you is a gift to you from God (1 Corinthians 6:19)! He has given us free will! In other words, man is a free agent, and he has the right to choose his own path and follow his own mind when it comes to judging his decisions in this world! Nonetheless, God is very direct and straightforward as it relates to His expectations concerning our ability or willingness to choose what is right over that which is wrong in relation to His word. He will never force His will upon us or use manipulation, trickery or deceit, like man does. God will move out of our way to allow us the opportunity to set ourselves up and love us just the same! And yet, we as human beings push way beyond boundaries each and every day in an attempt to reason with God about our actions as if we are negotiating some sort of contract. Having free will does not give us the right to rewrite the law set before us at every given opportunity to justify our wrongdoing.

Lessons Learned

1. Seek ye first the Kingdom of God and all His righteousness, all else will be added unto to you (Matthew 6:33). Know who you are in Him and Him in you. No matter what is going on around you, keep your focus on the Lord, and He will prevail in due time.

2. That which is done in the dark will soon come to light (Luke 8:17). God never wants us to be too surprised about anything, but you have to be in the right position and posture to hear, see and receive. God will reveal the unknown to you to keep you abreast of what is going on around you.

3. Just as you are encouraged to study the word of God to show yourself approved (2 Timothy 2:15), you must be willing to study your environment to avoid being deceived.

4. Stay humble and never allow yourself to be compromised by influence. People often think that they are getting away with what they do behind the scenes, and no one is the wiser. But after you have done all you can to stand, just continue to stand and hold your ground. God sees everything!

5. Be anxious for nothing (Philippians 4:6).

6. Not that I speak in respect of want, for I have learned in whatever state I am in to be content. I know both how to be abased and how to abound; everywhere and in all things, I am instructed both to be full and to be hungry, both to abound and to suffer need. I can do all things through Christ which strengtheneth me (Philippians 4:11). But godliness with contentment is great gain (1 Timothy 6:6).

7. And we know that *all* things work together for good to them that love God, to them who are the called according to this purpose (Romans 8:28).

EXIT INTERVIEWS

ICMA RETIREMENT CORPORATION (RC)
EXIT INTERVIEW

1996

This form is to be completed by each associate who has resigned employment with RC; it should be returned to human resources before the last day of employment. All information will be held in the strictest of confidence. A circle or check mark should be used where appropriate.

1. **What reasons led to your decision to resign your employment with RC?**

   ▶ My experience here at RC has not been totally pleasant. I have noted as well as observed double standards and rules that were created and engineered to control certain people while allowing others to break them.

   ▶ The managerial style at RC dictates: Even if the manager is incorrect, the manager is always right.

- I was told by one senior administrative assistant (AA) that she thought it was absurd that she could not be out with her sick baby, who was running a fever, and feel confident that her job was being "perfected" in her absence by me.

    > No one is perfect

    > Why would someone expect you to "perfect" a job in their absence when they themselves had not perfected their job? That's a tall order to fill.

2. **Did your training provide you with enough information regarding your job?**

    No! No formal training was received in which to perform my position as the administrative assistant floater. I pretty much taught myself from trial and error. A perfect example—I taught myself Word Perfect for Windows.

    If no, please list what additional training would have been helpful.

    - PowerPoint and Harvard Graphics would have been helpful. I made a request to have PowerPoint added to my system after I realized I would have difficulty attending the classes to enhance or increase my skill level. This would have at least given me the opportunity to train myself.

        > Steve Nordholt uses Harvard Graphics to produce slide presentations.

> Girard Miller uses PowerPoint to produce slide presentations. On my own merits: When asked unexpectedly by Girard if I knew PowerPoint, I said no, but if given the opportunity, I'm sure I wouldn't have a problem accessing the system to produce a draft for your work. Then Kristine could finalize it when she returns. So I did, and he was impressed. So was I.

NOTE: As the AA floater, I am expected to function in the capacity of providing support to both Steve Nordholt and Girard Miller in the absence of their designated, full-time AAs.

3. **Would you say your workload was overwhelming, varied but challenging, challenging or light and/or not challenging?**

   My workload varied from light to heavy from day-to-day, but it was never challenging. The most challenging was dealing with the various personalities and mood swings and trying not to let others ruin my day.

4. **What did you like most about working at RC?**

   Learning how the stock market works; hot stocks vs. aggressive stocks is what I liked most about working at RC.

5. **What best helped you achieve your goals?**

   Having the opportunity to save and invest in what helped me best to achieve my goals.

6. **What did you like best about your work environment?**

   No comment! N/A

7. **Please rate your employment with RC in terms of the factor below:**

   - **Experience gained**   Poor
   - **Job satisfaction**   Fair
   - **Salary**   Fair:

     During my evaluation period, I was told that I qualified for an increase in pay. However, because I was getting a higher salary than what the Human Resources Department assumed or thought initially, I was told I would not and could not get an increase.

   - **Benefits**   Fair

     Caliber of Supervisor - Vanessa Waller-Jones, immediate supervisor (Good; has very little authority)

8. **Please rate our Human Resources Department**

   Rating the Human Resources Department is tough to do; especially taking into consideration that I was told by a human resources employee (not Vanessa) that because I worked within the Human Resources Department:

- I should consider myself as being above other RC employees, and

- I should not socialize with anyone outside of the Human Resources Department.

That statement (being discriminatory) goes against my belief as well as my integrity. I was raised to consider everyone as being equal—no matter what position they held. In addition, I was taught to never consider myself as being better or above another human being. More qualified maybe!

9. **In what areas does RC need to improve?**

   Managerial and interpersonal skills need improvement. Additionally, more consideration, recognition and compensation need to be given to lower-grade-level associates. It's the little people who keep RC in business, because they're the most productive. (It is very surprising that RC has not been investigated by the EEOC. Ironically, there is a department within RC that refers to itself as the "slave quarters" which is a reflection of how they're treated.)

10. **What can we do to retain you in our employ?**

    At this point, unfortunately, nothing. I made the final decision to leave when I returned from a doctor's appointment one evening between 6:00 – 6:15 pm to find crumbs all over my desk and on the floor as the result of someone tossing a dirty, aluminum sheet cake pan that had the remains of peach cobbler from an HR-hosted luncheon/meeting. If I had not returned to the office that evening, it would have sat on my desk all night! The proper thing to do would have been to take it to the kitchen and place it in the sink. This display of disparaging behavior was an example of my worth! Though I was not present to participate in the festivities, I was treated as the hired help and expected to clean up the mess.

11. **Would you recommend RC as an employer to work for?**

- If they had no other job lined up.

- Depending on the nature of the position and the disposition of the person or persons who was assigned to supervise them.

September 7, 1998

MAILED TO THE OFFICE OF:
Christopher R. McCleary
Chairman and CEO
USinternetworking, Inc.
410 Severn Avenue, Suite 403
Annapolis, MD 21403

RE: **Exit Correspondence**

Dear Mr. McCleary,

Too often, many people leave a company not having the opportunity to express or explain their experiences and reasons for leaving. Mainly because they feel no one will listen. In relation to human nature, you're more likely to take the word of that person who's in (a position of) power and exhibits the most control. And what emphasis do we put on power or how most would define it: prestige, money and status? Where does fairness or truth fit in? What about integrity?

I contemplated long and hard about whether to write this letter. Am I angry? No! It's about principle and commitment. Not to mention wasted time. So what do I hope to accomplish? Nothing other than to be heard!

There were a number of discussions between Brenda Woodsmall and I prior to me giving my resignation on Thursday, August 27, 1998, that centered on my initial interview (which I feel was very misleading). Pursuant to those discussions, I mentioned to Brenda that had I known the position was salaried (exempt) instead of hourly (non-exempt), I would never have agreed to accept the position.

Yes, during the interview, she did mention there would be long hours. However, she failed to mention the exempt status of the position. And if not discussed during an interview, it's normally indicated on an offer letter. One might understand the need to work long hours on occasion, but the problem arises when long hours become an expected (by the employer), everyday occurrence, and the employee's long commute of 45 minutes to an hour is not taken into consideration.

In accepting the position, my deciding factor was based upon what I considered to be an opportunity to advance as a human resources specialist, which is how the position was presented to me. However, I found myself performing day-to-day duties as an administrative assistant. And to my surprise, during that last discussion which took place for over an hour on Thursday, a number of things were revealed to me after I told her I felt I was moving backwards versus forward. Yes, she did state I would be wearing many hats; but the emphasis was on human resources specialist with growth potential ... not administrative assistant.

Me: Now correct me if I'm wrong, but if I'm expected to come before you truthfully during an interview to discuss my qualifications and capabilities to perform a particular task, then shouldn't you be upfront with me about what it is I'm coming into and exactly what you're offering?

Brenda: You are! In fact, my main focus or intent in hiring you was to have you perform as my Administrative Assistant."

Me: Okay. (Direct confirmation of deception! Yes, I had been misled and accepted a position under false pretense.) Why would I leave a non-exempt Personnel Specialist position earning $36,000 (having my own office and two months away from an annual review (8 percent increase) to accept an exempt Administrative Assistant (however per my offer letter, a Human Resources Specialist) position earning $35,000 with the possibilities of no advancement?

Brenda: Because you work in the HR department, and considering the nature of your job in handling confidential/sensitive material, these positions are always exempt.

Me: Brenda, there was a similar situation with my previous employer. My supervisor learned from an EEO Labor conference that was position should be non-exempt; not exempt.

Brenda: What did they do?

Me: They switched me right away, gave me retro pay for some of the additional hours and let me take some time off for the rest.

Brenda: I've been in personnel for over 25 years. I've never encountered anyone like you nor have I ever had a problem like this. I don't know how things are done in your world, but in my world, this is how it is. If we pay you on an hourly basis for each hour worked, you wouldn't get paid for those two days you were out sick or the day you had an emergency involving your car. And how do I know you were really sick?

Me: It's normally customary for an employee to have sick leave and vacation leave. And according to my offer letter, I get two weeks vacation. You can deduct the three days from that.

Brenda: USi is not a normal company. We don't do things like other companies. There isn't a sick leave policy. That's the difference in being exempted—we're paying you for the three days.

Me: Okay.

Brenda: I don't like your attitude. In fact, I don't like how you handled the whole situation from the beginning. A number of people, including vice presidents and managers, weren't specifically hired to do what they were doing either, but they came to work every day joking about it and still smiling.

Me: Do I not have the right to be disappointed if I feel I was misled during an interview considering what I gave up thinking what I was gaining? Am I not a separate entity with different thoughts and ideas? And how another person deals with a particular situation has nothing to do with me; there's no comparison.

Brenda: Vince Romano told me you expressed an interest in applying for the secretarial position within his department. He can't hire anybody; there's a freeze. If you can't perform as my AA, what makes you think you can perform as his AA and do a better job? And you make a lot of mistakes. I could sit at your desk and do your job just like that (while snapping her fingers) and do it better than you.

Me: Yes, I did make mistakes. I'm not going to deny that I didn't. But I also knew why I was making the mistakes. No, it was not intentional. I was trying to perform a job that I went into with a different vision of what I would be doing and, at the same time, feeling betrayed while trying desperately to turn a bad situation around. How would you feel?

Yes, I did speak to Vince Romano about his future plans. Why not? The opportunity presented itself, and I was performing some secretarial duties for him anyway. And if I'm going to perform a task as an Administrative Assistant, I should have the opportunity to knowingly apply for the position having the option to accept or decline of my own free will verses how it was done.

Brenda: Do you dislike the people you work with?

Me: I don't dislike anyone.

Brenda: That's not what I asked you. Do you have a problem with your co-workers? Why do you isolate yourself from HR and other USi employees? You didn't go to Todd's going away lunch.

Me: Brenda, as I stated before, I don't dislike anyone. You knew why I wasn't going to Todd's lunch. In fact, I spoke to Todd and extended a personal good-bye. I also explained why I wouldn't be able to attend his going away lunch with the HR department. He knew I was involved in a car accident and had scheduled an appointment during my lunch break to meet with the claims adjuster to access the damage.

Brenda: What about the all-hands meeting? Maybe that's how you are. You don't seem to socialize with others. You're not a part of my team. How do you suppose we fix it? Or it may not be fixable.

Me: I don't know. It's up to you. I can leave. I'm not pleased with the outcome or the fact that I left a company thinking I was coming here for advancement in learning and growth opportunities aside from what I was bringing as a personnel specialist as outlined in my resume and discussed during the interview. However, I am not an unsociable person. I do have problems initially warming up to people I don't know. But for the most part, considering my short tenure here, anyone could tell you I'm not unapproachable.

Brenda: Did you call the company you left?

Me: Yes, I called them. I had a conversation with someone who stated I could come back and that they hired someone for my old position, but they could find something else for her to do. I told them no. I didn't want the same thing done to her that was done to me. That's not right. So now I'm trying to make the best out of an unpleasant situation and do what I can to boost my morale and turn things around within myself.

Brenda: You've only been here two months. You haven't given it enough time. Look at Linda. Do you know she started out as my secretary? You know how much money she and Maria Melton make? They both used to work for me. That's what I do. I take people and have them work under me to learn from me. And when they leave, they become managers. I'm feeling very uncomfortable about this. Why don't you think about what you want to do and let me know on Monday if this situation is fixable.

Me: Okay.

After returning to my desk, I found it more difficult to concentrate. And given the conversation between Brenda and I, there would be a definite strain on our working relationship.

As stated in my resignation letter, however short, I'm glad to have had the opportunity to work within a start-up organization and see it in the beginning stages from a business prospective.

Sincerely,
Ann G. Mack

KAJAX ENGINEERING, INC.
EXIT INTERVIEW

February 20, 2000

I would like to take this opportunity to say thank you. Oftentimes, it's very hard to leave an environment or people who have touched you in one way or another, but sometimes, we are not meant to stay in one place too long. When you've reached your limitation of possible growth, whatever your focus (for me, it's not always about monetary value), living *without* focus is only existing. And when you feel the environment you're placed in no longer has anything to offer but negativity and unfairness, that's when you know it is, indeed, time to go. Should you wait too long before making that move, you may miss your window of opportunity and find yourself amidst confusion. If you can't be the solution to a problem, then you may want to consider removing yourself from the problem. Oppression is a state of mind, not a reality!

During my tenure here, I've had the pleasure of working with and being allowed to meet some really great people. And I can honestly say it's been a learning experience—some good and some bad. But nevertheless, because our experiences provide growth and add to our character, one can only hope that those experiences bring upon lessons of achievement while not allowing the negative experiences to strip us of our dignity, self-respect or character. It's truly insulting and frustrating when a person uses his or her position and authority to try to manipulate you into thinking or believing what they wish to project, all because they refuse to accept responsibility for their actions. Unfortunately, it's always much easier to lay blame on others rather than examine yourself.

After being told that I have a negative presence or force that drove three managers (Lisa Bell, Katherine Sayer and Marlon Lobban) away, I had to ask myself, "If I possess such power, then what am I doing here?" Was that the same negative presence or force that drove others within the HR department away? Just to mention a few—Claudia Romero, Mary Abougadareh, Theresa Ross and Charlie Johnson—let's not forget about them. Should I take credit for those losses as well?

Your best defense is knowledge! You should make it a point to always question what is being told to you and learn the laws that govern your rights! Never assume anything and take the time to observe your surroundings to include the personalities of those within your environment. Know thyself and have faith in the creator—not man.

Best wishes to you all!
Ann G. Mack (A very positive presence)

EXIT INTERVIEW

Department:	Position:
SAWSO, Program Division	Program Assistant →Admin Specialist → Admin Assistant

Department Head	Length of Service at SAWSO	From Jan 13, 2003 - Jan 18, 2007
Lt. Colonel D. S.	Length of Service at TSA-NHQ	From Aug 20, 2000 - Jan 10, 2003
Seven years and five months total within The Salvation Army		
Man may demote you, but God lifts you every time and promotes you!		

Reason for Termination

(check one and/or circle the appropriate reason/answer):

Resignation - Was resignation due to (circle one): physical condition, family situation, returning to school, securing a better position or another reason.

▶ I was offered and accepted a career intern training position in line with my degree in business management at the U.S. Department of Energy.

If resignation was due to securing a better position, is the new position (circle all that apply): the same kind of position with the same duties and level of responsibility, a totally different position, a position with more responsibility, a position with upward mobility, a position with more hours, or other?

▶ This position is a combination of all the things I've accomplished during my tenure here but with more concentration in the area of human resources as a program analyst on a managerial level.

What is the title of the new position?

▶ The title of my new position, as indicated above, is program analyst. However, my experience here has taught me that "the value and emphasis of what a person does should not be placed on the title of the position." It should be placed on the accomplishments and responsibilities actually carried out by the employee. In fact, given the nature of this business, more care and commitment should be directed at achieving fairness with an intent of doing the highest good for all; not the most good.

▸ **How can two people with college degrees be given the same job description in the same department but have different titles with greatly varying salaries?**

Layoff - Was layoff due to (circle all that apply): temporary work, reduction of staff, reduction of work hours, or another reason (please specify):   *N/A*

Was employee offered a transfer?

❑ Yes or ❑ No   *N/A*

Transfer - was transfer due to (circle one): location, a better position, or another reason?   *N/A*

Leave of Absence - was leave due to: a physical condition, family situation, or another reason: *N/A*

Training

▸ Who explained the job to the employee and how was it done? *N/A*

▸ Was the employee given a job description?

❑ Yes or ❑ No   *No comment*

▸ Did the employee feel the training was adequate? *N/A*

▸ How could your initial training have been improved? *N/A*

Financial

- How did the employee feel about his/her salary and raises? **N/A**

- What part did salary play in the employee's decision to leave? **None**

   Salary, solely, was never the issue. Abuse equated to abnormal use was the deciding factor as well as the inequality. This is not an employee-friendly environment unless you are a Salvationist, relative or associated with a former officer having ties to The Salvation Army befitting an accepted or approved image. Character examination as it relates to the organizational culture should be reviewed. There's no compassion!

   How can two people in the same department, both with college degrees be given the same job description, but with different titles and vary greatly in salary?

Supervision

Please rate your supervisor in the following areas as **Excellent, Good, Fair or Poor**.

1. Demonstrates fair and equitable treatment
2. Provides appropriate recognition
3. Resolves complaints/problems in a timely manner
4. Informs staff of matters pertaining to work

5. Encourages employee input

6. Gives clear instruction

7. Evaluates fairly

8. Other (specify): *Responding N/A to each category!*

9. Did the employee feel comfortable in taking any complaints or problems to his/her supervisor? *N/A*

10. Did the employee have any problems with his/her supervisor? *N/A*

11. Was the employee given goals/objectives with his/her evaluations? *N/A*

12. What suggestions does the employee think would be most helpful to his/her supervisor? *N/A*

Organization as a place to work. On a scale of 1 to 5 (1 being the lowest and 5 being the highest), how would you rate the following aspects of your employment with The Salvation Army National Headquarters?

Opportunity for advancement:	*1*	
Feedback regarding performance:	*N/A*	
Physical working conditions:	*5*	

Salary:*	Could be better, fair and equal across the board! How can two people in the same department, both with college degrees be given the same job description, but with different titles and vary greatly in salary?	
Vacation:	Okay	
Sick time:	Okay	
Health insurance benefits:	Okay	
Pension plan:	Employee pension not equivalent to that of the officers.	
Feeling of belonging:	1	
Other (specify):	N/A	

Who was the most helpful person the employee worked with at National Headquarters?

▸ **God, the Father, the Son and the Holy Spirit!**

What did the employee like best about National Headquarters?

▸ **Meeting the employees I've had the opportunity and pleasure of working with and getting to know.**

What would make you interested in returning to work at National Headquarters?

▸ **Character examination as it relates to the organizational culture should be reviewed. There's no com-**

passion! During the orientation of an employee, he or she is obligated to sign a document acknowledging that where they work is a church, and they should conduct themselves accordingly. This doctrine should be followed by all, including the officers across the board, and not just directed at the employees to be used as a measurement of control. More thought should be given to the statement "in the world, not of the world."

Summary

- What did the employee like best about his/her job? *N/A or no comment*

- What did the employee like least about his/her job? *N/A or no comment*

- What could we have done to make the job better? Easier? *N/A or no comment*

SCHOOL ASSIGNMENTS

THIS IS MY STORY, THIS IS MY SONG

**Prepared on March 19, 2001
For African American Art History**

While reading a copy of a publication titled, "How to Answer the 64 Toughest Interview Questions," I pondered over number 27 for a long time: Who has inspired you in your life and why? What a coincidence! The theme of my African American Art History class project is the contributions of African Americans (or blacks) to civilization. African Americans have made considerable accomplishments, remarkable strides in the arts, business, education, politics, and have held vital roles in shaping America while making history along the way. However, over the years, there have been many attempts to deny African Americans their own history, including schoolbooks with no mention of blacks and historical records rewritten to exclude blacks, thus repeatedly robbing them of their heritage. In addition, we (African Americans) have allowed a stereotypical view (or views) based on the perception(s) of others, which are stemmed from their fear of that which is different, to divide us to the point that a number of us are unaware of the major contributions of our ancestors to world's civilization.

So who inspires me? Those African Americans who struggled to make a difference and are constant reminders that nothing is impossible if we try. Harriet Tubman was a remarkable woman. For over 10 years, Harriet Tubman, made numerous trips from the North into the South to rescue slaves and plot their escape by way of the Underground Railroad. Having been a part of the first graduating elementary class named in honor of Harriet Tubman (the Harriet Tubman Elementary School in Washington, D.C.), I heard countless stories about her and viewed her, along with others, as spiritual soldiers of war in relation to the many trials and tribulations they faced.

The National Association for the Advancement of Colored People (NAACP) was created in 1909 to work for the abolition of segregation and discrimination in housing, education, employment, voting and transportation to oppose racism and to ensure blacks their constitutional rights. Today, the NAACP is seen in a different light under a new leadership. Kweisi Mfume (his name meaning, "conquering son of kings") became president and chief executive officer on February 15, 1996, after being unanimously elected to the post by the NAACP Board of Directors. Within his rein as president, he has raised the standards and expectations of the NAACP branches nationwide and has worked with the NAACP volunteers across the country to help usher in a whole new generation of civil rights leaders across the country. Nevertheless, there have been other NAACP leaders and associates, including one of the founders (W.E.B. Du Bois), who made numerous sacrifices; for example, Medger Evers who lost his life on June 12, 1963, as a result of his passionate views and fight for racial equality.

In an effort to promote greater awareness of African American achievements, Dr. Carter G. Woodson announced the institution of **Negro History Week**, which coincided with the birthdays of Abraham Lincoln and Frederick Douglas on February of 1926. In 1976, the observance was expanded to "National African American History Month," in honor of the nation's bicentennial.

The Black Arts Movement was the creative companion to the Black Power Movement of the 1960s and 1970s. The Harlem Renaissance was not an organized movement; it was a period of creativity among African American writers, artists, musicians and entertainers. It was a time of explosive and energetic artistic expression.

People like Edmonia Lewis gave us sculpture by breathing life into historic, heroic figures, and Jacob Lawrence, through his paintings, depicted the migration of African Americans from the South to the North in search of social and economic freedom. Arthur Ashe and Althea Gibson taught us we could play tennis and be successful at it. Wilma Rudolph, Jesse Owens and Carl Lewis taught us we could run and hurdle in fashion with grace and style, paving the way for others like Florence Griffith Joyner, and Jackie Joyner-Kersee. Before Mohammed Ali, there was Jack Johnson. He was the first black to hold the heavyweight boxing championship of the world and was often referred to as the "great white hope." Alice Walker and Alex Haley wrote stories that focused on the lives of African Americans and their ability to survive and triumph as strong, undiminished human beings. Before Michael Jordan, there was Wilt Chamberlain and Julius Irving who brought new meaning to pro basketball.

Again, I ask, who inspires me? The scientific achievements as well as discoveries made by African Americans are endless—from the invention of the gas mask and the traffic light to the first successful open-heart surgery and the first neurosurgeon to successfully separate Siamese twins joined at the head. From the Underground Railroad and the Civil War to the Harlem Renaissance and the Civil Rights Movement, we have come a long way and have endured much! Where would Washington, D.C., be without Benjamin Banneker? Despite injustice and intolerance, they opened doors giving us vision while renewing our confidence.

Civil rights leaders like Dr. Martin Luther King tried to advocate nonviolence and left us with great speeches that told us stories about the history of our ancestors while trying to get us to unite. Dr. King's challenges towards segregation and racial discrimination in the 1950s and 1960s helped convince many white Americans to support the cause of civil rights in the United States. After his assassination in 1968, Dr. King became a symbol of protest in the struggle for racial justice.

And now, I would like to leave you with an excerpt from Maya Angelo's *Souls of My Sisters*, which always brings to my mind visions of Angela Davis.

> *"Someone was hurt before you, wronged before you, hungry before you, frightened before you, beaten before you, humiliated before you, raped before you...yet, someone survived."*

I CAN!
A PERSONAL AND PROFESSIONAL DEVELOPMENT PLAN

Prepared on March 20, 2001
For Personnel Management

Before graduating from high school, my initial goal was to become a psychiatrist. I had even mapped out the amount of time it would take to accomplish my task and decided it would be best to choose a university that had a medical school. Considering my dedication towards various areas of study throughout grade school, I was an exceptional student in English, math and science earning high marks; honor student. So the possibilities were endless, and this aided in my acceptance to each school I had applied to, and MIT expressed an interest. So what happened?

After narrowing down one school, I decided on Lincoln University because it was the only school that was talking money, initially. However, on the day I was to leave for Lincoln, I had not received my detailed proposed award letter assuring me assistance with the payment of my education. In anticipation of the outcome, I was determined not to resign from my job unless the response was favorable, and I had no idea of what to expect.

*I can
do all things
through Christ which strengtheneth me.*

~ Philippians 4:13

I WILL
(Written by: Sandra R. Taxton-Hicks)

Drained is how I feel; drained of life's energies. Drained of hope and destiny.

Come up, I say to myself; come up higher.

Reach the depths of greatness;

Attain, o self, I say to me.

Believe, wake up, o self, and believe; believe in life again for it has *much* to offer …

This dismal crypt that now contains me is only a temporary stop for me; I *will* move on to bigger and brighter tomorrows.

Right now, I am touched by afflictions – Afflictions which wrongly believe that they have overtaken me – But oh no – that is *not* to be. I am not out for the count!

I will show them that I have a new wind and I will mount up with wings as an eagle and conquer!

Still not giving up on my dream to attend college, I enrolled at Strayer (a business school in lieu of a university) until transferring to the University of the District of Columbia because the tuition was lower. As a result of the schools being structured differently (in comparison, a quarter system versus a semester system), I felt my time at Strayer was uneventful. A number of my accomplished credits from Strayer were not accepted nor did they meet the course hour requirement in accordance with the university-wide requirement. As my frustration increased, I attended school off and on allowing pressured working environments, personal issues and the idea of making money (what I considered to be pretty good for a person with no degree) to interfere with my long-range plan to seek higher education. I lost sight of what was important.

Money will buy a bed but not sleep; books but not brains; food but not appetite; finery but not beauty; a house but not a home; medicine but not health; luxuries but not culture; amusements but not happiness; religion but not salvation; a passport to everywhere but heaven.
~Anonymous

After all I've been through, I still have joy. Can you imagine how hard it must be for many people to not only be able to say that phrase but to believe with all their being, in spite of everything, there's still hope? At the end of my second unemployment experience, I was introduced to a position within the area of human resources as a personnel assistant and found it to be a very rewarding and mentally satisfying experience. As a result of personal experiences (work and non-work related), I was always fascinated by law and was more intrigued by employment law in accordance with the impact it has had on my life.

Don't be afraid to look at your faults.
(Yoruba Proverb)

Even though we know there is always room for improvement, we tend to shy away from criticism. Our egos tell us we are being attacked and quite naturally we want to strike back. In order to be whole, healthy beings, we need to know all there is to know about ourselves. Sometimes that information must come from others. This may mean admitting that we are not always right and knowing it is okay to make a mistake. A mistake, an error, a poor choice or bad decision does not equal "there is something wrong with me." It means you are on your way to being better. We do not make mistakes on the basis of race or color. We make them because we are human. When we acknowledge our errors and face up to our shortcomings, no one can use them against us.

~ Unknown

After finding myself unemployed for the third time, I disappeared to a dark, distant and familiar place in hopes of seeking refuge from the outside world. This secret place provides solitude while searching for answers on how to get my life back on track. However, in the interim, I reflected back and evaluated the events of my life. Each period of unemployment seemed to be more challenging than the previous upon seeking employment. Twenty-three years later, I've grown to believe everything happens for a reason. Some of us are a little slow at making the right decisions or in choosing the right path to follow, so we have to be steered in the right direction. We are only limited by how far our thoughts can take us, and when we connect with the all-powerful mind of God, we are unlimited; WE CAN! I CAN! YOU CAN!

> *Did I not tell you that if you believed,*
> *you would see the glory of God?*
>
> ~ John 11:40

In today's society, as technology advances and the curriculum for various studies increase or change, so does the need for one to have a degree or certification in various fields. In looking through the classified section, there's evidence of that need. I also noted the request or requirement for individuals to have BS degrees for secretarial and administrative positions. In having the potential to do almost anything if I apply myself, I made a conscious decision to go back to school to pursue my degree with a concentration in the area of human resources or personnel management.

> *This is the beginning of a new day. God has given me this day to use as I will. I can waste it or use it for good. What I do today is very important because I am exchanging a day of my life for it. When tomorrow comes, this day will be gone forever, leaving something in its place I have traded for it. I want it to be gain, not loss—good, not evil. Success, not failure, in order that I shall not forget the price I paid for it.*
>
> ~ Unknown

In any given situation, your best defense is knowledge! I can sit and allow the past to consume me; I can put the past behind me while choosing to ignore it; or I can embrace it while learning and growing from it. Because our experiences provide growth and add to our character, one can only hope and pray that those experiences bring upon lessons of achievement while not allowing the negative experiences to strip you of your aspirations, dignity or self-respect. My current desire and determination to obtain my degree stems from the need to fulfill a spiritual debt and confirm within self, I can!

STRESS AND ITS PRESENCE IN THE WORKPLACE

**Prepared on April 17, 2001
For Organizational Theory and Behavior**

Stress is a poorly understood and unpredictable disorder that affects a number of people in many different ways. Because life is filled with stress, it is considered to be an unavoidable consequence of life. In other words, without stress, there would be no life. There's good (positive) stress and bad (negative) stress. Appropriate and controllable stress provides interest and excitement and motivates the individual to greater achievement, while a lack of stress may lead to boredom and depression. However, on the other hand, stress can make people vulnerable to illness.

Stress can be a short-term (acute) or long-term (chronic) symptom depending upon the circumstances. Acute stress is the reaction to an immediate threat, commonly known as the "fight or flight" response. The threat can be any situation that is experienced, even subconsciously or falsely, as a danger.[76] Memories of past threatening or dangerous events can also evoke feelings of stress. Once the body determines it is out of danger and the threat has passed, the response slows, lowering the levels of stress hormones back to normal, and the body relaxes. Chronic stress is the reaction to psychological pressures, such as relationship problems, loneliness, continual deadlines, or financial worries.

According to a study conducted by the National Institute for Occupational Safety and Health (NIOSH), stress in the workplace or job-related stress has become a common and costly problem in American organizations, leaving few workers untouched.[77]

What Is Stress?

Stress is defined as mental and physical tension or a strain caused by one's perception of an event (stressor), triggering physiological, biochemical, or psychological changes in the body. Stress is synonymous with change. Anything that causes a change in one's life that alters a daily routine causes stress. It does not matter if it's a "good" change, or a "bad" change; they both evoke feelings of stress. However, too little stress.

Stress is when you are worried about getting laid off your job, worried about having enough money to pay your bills or worried about your mother when the doctor says she may need

---

76 http://californiacardiovascular.com/prevention/stress.html.
77 http://www.cdc.gov/niosh/docs/99-101/

an operation. In fact, to most of us, stress is synonymous with worry. Excessive worry is a major element in the vicious cycle of tension. If it is something that makes you worry, then it is stress. When you find your dream apartment and get ready to move, that is stress. If you break your leg, that is stress. Good or bad; if a change occurs in your life, it's generates some feeling of stress as far as your body is concerned.

The Physical Responses to Stress

- Response in the brain: The body's response to stress is somewhat like an airplane readying for takeoff. Virtually all systems—the heart and blood vessels, the immune system, the lungs, the digestive system, the sensory organs and brain—are modified to meet the perceived danger and affect each person differently. In response to stress revoking stimulus, the body's release of adrenaline triggers a secretion of a steroid hormone known as cortisol. This process speeds up the heartbeat, supplies extra glucose for energy, and thickens the blood as a defense mechanism in an effort to suppress the immune system. The body can handle a big jolt of stress, but continued or frequent exposure to stressors weakens one's immune cells and invites illness.[78]

- For example, at the age of 14, I was diagnosed as having alopecia. The word "alopecia" is derived from the Greek word *alopex*, which means baldness. Unfortunately,

---

78 http://www.testmyhormones.com/saliva_cortisol_test_AM_PM_patient_info.html

during that time, there were no studies conducted to determine the actual cause of Alopecia and little was known on how to treat or cure it. Therefore, it was explained to me as the following: When the brain detects there is an illness or foreign object in the body upsetting the natural order or impeding health, it sends a signal releasing antibodies. The antibodies are produced to seek, search and repair the damage to the body in an effort to heal itself. However, due to a nervous disorder brought on by stress and anxiety when I was young, there were no foreign objects in the body. So supposedly, in my case, the antibodies attacked each other, causing shock to the body and my hair to fall out. Twenty-six years later, I've learned to cope with stress differently. However, there has been no positive change in hair growth.

- The Response of the heart, lungs, and circulatory system: The heart rate and blood pressure increase instantaneously in response to stressful situations. Breathing becomes rapid, and the lungs take more oxygen. Blood flow may actually increase 300 to 400 percent, priming the muscles, lungs, and brain for added demands. In addition, spleen discharges red and white blood cells, allowing the blood to transport more oxygen.

- The Response of the Immune System: The immediate effect of stress is to dampen parts of the immune system. In addition, certain factors in the immune system—important white blood cells—are redistributed, much like soldiers to potentially critical areas. In the case of stress, -boosting troops are sent to the body's front lines where or infection is most likely, such as the skin, the bone marrow, and lymph nodes.[79]

- Response in the Mouth and Throat: During stress, fluids are diverted from nonessential locations, including the mouth, causing dryness and difficulty in talking. In addition, can cause spasms of the throat muscles, making it difficult to swallow and fight infection.

- Response in the Skin: Stress commonly results in cool, clammy sweaty skin and in tightening of the scalp that makes the hair seem to stand on end. The skin is cool because blood flow is diverted away so it can support the heart and muscle tissues. As a result, physical capacity is and blood loss is reduced in the event of injury.[80]

- Metabolic Response: Stress shuts down digestive activity, a nonessential body during short-term periods of physical exertion or crisis.[81]

---

79 floridaheartcpr.com/uploads/**stress**_and_**stress**_mgt.docx
80 http://health-f1.co.in/acuteDiseases.php
81 http://www.destresswellnesscenter.com/html/What_is_Effect_of_Acute_Stress.htm

Job-Related Stress

Workplace stress costs businesses billions of dollars a year in staff turnover, errors, accidents, increased workers compensation and even theft to support drug or alcohol habits. From a 1996 survey directed towards its members, the Employee Assistance Professional Association (based in Arlington, Virginia) found that stress ranked second only to family crisis as to why those members contacted the organization for assistance.

Be aware of workplace stressors; the most significant one being a lack of control or feeling powerless to change a given situation. Along with workload, change, whether favorable or not, is another stressor, whether because there is too little (boredom) or too much (exhaustion). Job politics can be stressful when you refuse, deny, or respond ineffectively to the "game." Interruptions, conflicting demands, procrastination, ineffective delegating, and poor organizational and time management skills only add pressure to one's workday (Tea & Coffee Trade Journal; May 20, 2000).

The Effects of Job-Related Stress

Stress on the job can reduce your effectiveness by impairing concentration, causing sleeplessness, and increasing the risk for illness, back problems, accidents, and lost time. Work stress can lead to harassment or even violence while on the job. At its most extreme, it can place such a burden on the heart and circulation that it may even be fatal. Stress experienced as a result of the job is particularly likely to become chronic because it is such a large part of daily life. In fact, work stress has repeatedly been associated with an increased risk for cardiovascular disease (NIOSH; 1999). The Japanese even have a word for sudden death due to overwork; it is called *Karoushi* (Multinational Monitor; June 2000).

In this age of downsizing, a lack of job security is also a major cause of stress. Additional stressors include long hours, time spent away from home and family, office politics and conflicts between workers, wages that are not commensurate with levels of responsibility, and—in this competitive society—unrelenting and unreasonable demands for performance. While working within a Human Resources office of a company in Roslyn, Virginia, I often found it necessary as a result of unreasonable demands and work overload to report to work as early as 6:30 am, work through lunch and end my day at 8:00 p.m. (in some cases, later). In less than a year, along with no change in salary or compensation for overtime, I noted I had become increasingly irritated, less motivated and found very little job satisfaction. In realizing the negative change in my attitude, not to mention the frequent headaches, I made a conscious effort to only put in eight-hour days. Unfortunately, I made the decision too late! As a result of failing health, I was hospitalized and placed on disability for nearly eight weeks while recovery from surgery. Six months later, after I returned to work, I was laid off.

Early Warning Signs of Job Stress

- Headache
- Sleep disturbances
- Difficulty in concentrating

- Short temper
- Upset stomach
- Job dissatisfaction
- Low morale

Studies on Stress

Some studies indicate that the people who are most likely to experience stress in the workplace are those who feel they have no control over their circumstances. This is likely to occur in an organization that lacks effective communication and conflict-resolution methods; one that doesn't invite employees to participate in making decisions, allow creativity or where employees lack control over their responsibilities.

The National Institute for Occupational Safety and Health defines job stress as "the harmful physical and emotional responses that occur when the requirements of the job do not match the capabilities, resources, or needs of the worker" (NIOSH; 1999). For example, studies report the following:

- One-fourth of employees view their jobs as the number one stressor in their lives. (Study conducted by the Northwester National Life.)
- Three-fourths of employees believe the worker has more on-the-job stress than a generation ago. (Study conducted by the Princeton Survey Research Associates.)

- Problems at work are more strongly associated with health complaints than are any other life stressor. More so than even financial problems or family problems. (Study conducted by the St. Paul Fire and Marine Insurance Company.)

The Cornell University researchers have found some kinds of stress (good stress) will keep people on the job; other kinds (bad stress) will make them look for the exit door (HR Focus; April 1999). "Bad" stress includes office politics, red tape, and a stalled career. "Good" stress includes challenges that come with increased job responsibility, time pressure and high-quality assignments. The study concluded that when employees perceive that stressful situations will bring them value such as money, new skills or promotion, they tend to see them in a better light and consequently will remain on the job.

Four Myths about Stress

You know how great it feels to clean out a cluttered attic, basement or closet? Give yourself the same treatment by blasting through stressors that can sap your energy (Top Performance; February 2001).

Myth #1: **Everyone experiences stress the same way.** Stress is different for each person. What bothers one person may be fine for another. Everyone responds to life events in his or her own way.

Myth #2: **All stress is bad stress.** Stress is a natural part of life. It encourages us to strive to improve and challenge ourselves. *Managed* stress is part of a happy life. *Mismanaged* stress makes you unhappy and stressed out.

Myth #3: I cannot do anything about stress. Just because stress is a part of life, it does not mean you have to let it rule your life. You can learn ways to manage stress effectively:

- Take brisk half-hour walks every day, or do other regular exercises.

- Get plenty of sleep (seven to eight hours per night is the recommended minimum).

- Take time out for yourself. Read, practice a hobby or do something you enjoy.

- Pamper yourself, but be certain not to overindulge in anything.

Myth #4: I feel fine, so I'm not experiencing stress. Take a step back and look at your habits. Do you tend to overeat and have trouble maintaining a healthy weight? Can you never find time to exercise? Do you smoke? Are you tired all the time? All of these can be signs of too much stress. Try tackling one lifestyle change at a time and learn some stress management techniques that can help you along the way.

Stress Management

Stress management programs teach workers about the nature and sources of stress, the effects of stress on health and personal skills to reduce stress. Stress management training may rapidly reduce stress symptoms such as anxiety and sleep disturbances; it also has the advantage of being inexpensive and easy to implement.

The 1999 annual benefits survey by the Society for Human Resource Management (SHRM) showed an increase in company programs directed towards helping employees reduce stress, stay healthy and improve upon their ability to cope with difficult work situations. Two-thirds provide Employee Assistant Programs (EAP), 56 percent have wellness programs and 21 percent provide stress reduction programs. EAPs are one of the most effective programs, but their use could be much higher if managers continually promoted them.

In contrast to stress management training and EAP programs, some companies try to reduce job stress by bringing in a consultant to recommend ways to improve working conditions. This approach is the most direct way to reduce stress at work. It involves the identification of stressful aspects of work (e.g., excessive workload and conflicting expectations) and the design of strategies to reduce or eliminate the identified stressors. The advantage of this approach is that it deals directly with the root causes of stress at work. Bringing workers or workers and managers together in a committee or problem-solving group may be an especially useful approach for developing a stress prevention program.

Conclusion: Like it or not, stress is an inevitable part of life. How you deal with it, though, makes the difference in your wellbeing. The process of learning to control stress is lifelong and will contribute to better health, as well as a greater ability to succeed. The key to controlling stress is to do simple re-energizing exercises regularly. Scheduled break times during the day will help recharge you every day. Taking a stroll during your lunch break may not be as relaxing as a weeklong vacation in the mountains, but it will certainly help diminish your stress level. That way, when your vacation finally does come around, you'll be better able to enjoy it and reap the rewards of a totally rested and recharged psyche.

Fairfax County Public Library Database
General Reference Center Gold (GPIP)

SOURCE MATERIALS:

1. "Good Stress, Bad Stress." HR Focus 76.4, April 1999: 4.

2. Madison, Devon. "Can Your Job Make You Sick?" Psychology Today 33.6, November 2000: 14.

3. Mehri, Darius. "Death by Overwork." Multinational Monitor 2.6, June 2000: 26.

4. Minter, Stephen G. "Too Much Stress?" Occupational Hazards 61.5, May 1999: 49.

5. Mowday, Richard T., and Robert I. Sutton. " Organizational Behavior: linking individuals and groups to

organizational contexts." Annual Review of Psychology 44, 1993: 195.

6. Newton, Virginia L. "Learning to Chill Out." Association Management, 52.2, February 2000: 132.

7. Sykes, Claire. "Say, Yes to Less Stress." Tea & Coffee Trade Journal, 172.5, May 20, 2000: 113.

8. "Stress at Work." Health and Human Services Department (HHS); National Institute for Occupational Safety and Health (NIOSH) (1999): 1-25.

9. Verespej, Michael A. "Stressed Out." Industry Week, 249.4, February 21, 2000: 30.

10. Wah, Louisa. "The Emotional Tightrope." Management Review, January 2000: 38.

Websites

1. <http://www.cdc.gov/niosh/jobstres.html>

2. <http://www.ivf.com/stress.html>

3. <http://www.stress.org>

4. <http://www.teachhealth.com/>

5. <http://www.webmd.lycos.com/content/dmk/dmk_article_53246>

STRESS-BUILDING BELIEFS - A SIMPLE TEST

Perfectionism

- Do you feel a constant pressure to achieve?
- Do you criticize yourself when you're not perfect?
- Do you feel you haven't done enough no matter how hard you try?
- Do you give up pleasure in order to be the best in everything you do?

Control

- Do you have to be perfectly in control at all times?
- Do you worry about how you appear to others when you are nervous?
- Do you feel that any lack of control is a sign of weakness or failure?
- Are you uncomfortable delegating projects to others?

People Pleasing

- Does your self-esteem depend on everyone else's opinion of you?
- Do you sometimes avoid assignments because you're afraid of disappointing your boss?

- Are you better at caring for others than caring for yourself?
- Do you keep most negative feelings inside to avoid displeasing others?

Competence

- Do you feel you can never do as good a job as other people?
- Do you feel your judgment is poor?
- Do you feel you lack common sense?
- Do you feel like an impostor when told your work is good?

Your answers indicate potential roadblocks to a stress-free work life. Challenge these beliefs. Experiment. Try acting in a way that is opposite to your usual behavior. Then, evaluate the results. For example, if you feel overburdened because of a need to control, delegate a task and observe the consequences.

Become aware of how your stress-building beliefs affect your behavior. Replace them with more realistic and less stressful thoughts.

REPARATIONS

Prepared on April 30, 2001
For African-American Art History

In a past newspaper article regarding an apology to China for a mid-air collision between a U.S. spy plane and a Chinese fighter jet, Republican Senator Kay Bailey Hutchison of Texas was quoted as saying, "We have apologized many, many times in history. The United States is always ready to apologize when we are at fault. However, we should never apologize unless we find that we were at fault and we should never be 'demanded' to apologize."

So why is there so much controversy and difficulty for the United States to extend an apology to African Americans for the role they played in the history of slavery? Didn't the government take part in promoting, fostering and supporting the slave trade? Were they not responsible for legitimizing the institution of slavery and profiting from it? So are they saying they are not at fault? Or perhaps, they object to an "inferior" race demanding an apology?

Is a debt owed to the descendants of black people who helped build this country but spent their lives in forced servitude? Blacks suffered unrelenting exploitation, daily humiliation and torture; sexual abuse of men, women and children; annihilation of ancestral culture; denial of education and economic development; loss of control over one's person and the moral destruction of an entire people. And yes, the institution of slavery as it was defined then has since ended. However, is it not true that the consequences of the crime of slavery continue to manifest? So with that said, I must agree with Minister Preston Muhammad (Iowa representative of Minister Louis Farrakhan and The Nation of Islam):. "From emancipation to the present, sons and daughters of ex-slaves not only inherited the ill-effects of such massive and deeply-rooted damage, we carry the legacy of having suffered the worst of mankind's inhumanity to man."

On the African continent alone, flourishing civilizations were destroyed, and millions of Africans were forcibly removed from their homes, thus reducing the land and the people to a pattern of poverty and underdevelopment, which is also evident today. Is it not obvious that although the approach is different, the concept hasn't changed and is still visible?

Most of the case laws on reparations concern the compensation for specific losses such as the destruction of property, buildings, ships and so on. A number of agreements have been made under the British Foreign Compensation Act of 1950, and a tribunal was set up to make awards from the sums made available in an effort to right the wrong involving many thousands of claimants whose property had been expropriated.

For this purpose, lump sum settlements were made by Bulgaria, Poland, Hungary, Egypt and Romania. So how does this work?

> *For example, the order made under the British Foreign Compensation Act of 1950 provided that the Foreign Compensation Commission should treat as established, any claim relating to certain property in Egypt which had been sequestrated by the Nasser government if the applicant was the owner "or is the successor in title of such owner," making it plain that the children and the grandchildren of the original dispossessed owners were entitled or eligible to present a claim.*[82].

In 1981, a U.S.-Iran Claims Tribunal was set up for a similar purpose. It is therefore clear that the concept of reparations is firmly established and actively pursued by states, on behalf of their injured nationals, against other wrong doing states. There are other direct precedents for the payment of reparations, such as the following cases:

- Japan has made reparation payments to South Korea for acts committed during the period of invasion and occupation of Korea by Japan.

- Most recently, the United Nations Security Council has passed a resolution, binding in international law, requiring Iraq to pay reparations for its invasion of Kuwait.

---

82 http://www.shaka.mistral.co.uk/legalbasis.htm

- The German government has paid $60 billion to settle claims from victims of Nazi persecution.

- Restitution was made to the Aleut residents of various Alaskan islands "in settlement of U.S. obligations in equity and at law, for injustices suffered and unreasonable hardships endured while those Aleut residents were under U.S. control."

- Various groups of Eskimos, Native Americans, Aleuts and survivors of a 1923 massacre in a predominantly black Florida town have also received restitution—combined, more than $1 billion.

- In Australia, the government has apologized for its treatment of Aborigines after an official inquiry called it genocide. Compensation is being negotiated.

- In 1988, the United States Congress passed the Civil Liberties Act, which was designed to make restitution to Japanese Americans on the basis of losses sustained due to "any discriminatory act of the U.S. Government based upon the individual's Japanese ancestry during the wartime period." A total of $1.2 billion, or about $20,000 for each claimant (roughly 60,000 survivors), was paid. Canada followed with its own apology and a $230 million reparations package to Japanese Canadians.

There is no legal barrier to prevent those who still suffer the consequences of crimes against humanity from claiming reparations, even though the crimes were committed against their ancestors. The Civil Liberties Act in regards to the Japanese began by stating the basis for reparations in clear terms, which could be applied with the greatest relevance to the claims of Africans and their descendants:

1. Make restitution to those individuals of Japanese ancestry who were interned (detained or confined, especially in wartime) and extend apologies on behalf of the people of the U.S.

2. Acknowledge the fundamental injustice of the evacuation, relocation and internment of U.S. citizens and permanent resident aliens of Japanese ancestry during World War II.

3. Make more credible and sincere any declaration of concern by the U.S. over violations of human rights committed by other nations."

In considering the above information, one should not only be able to identify a second category of reparations, but they should also see the relevance of its importance in regards to the pain and suffering imposed by one group on to another. This is where a state has accepted the responsibility to make restitution, not just to other states, but to a group of people within its own borders whose rights have been violated. The acknowledgement of an illegal and unethical action to control, degrade, genocide and enslave another human being regardless of the time or era in which it took place and atoning for it.

Unfortunately, the mention of the word *slavery* causes most people to run for cover or dismiss it as an irrelevant factor in the redemption of black and white America. The word *racism* is just as disregarded. If America is to be redeemed, she must come to grips with this great horror and cancer of herself.

So will we ever be able to get past it? No, not as long as there is a double standard and especially not until we recognize the problems that exist today, openly acknowledge the problems and are willing to work towards a solution as a nation to heal the body, the mind and the spirit.

MY IDEA OF UTOPIA

Prepared on October 24, 2001
For Public Personnel Management

The *Catholic Encyclopedia* defines **utopia** as a term used to designate a visionary or an ideally perfect state of society. The American Heritage Dictionary refers to utopia as the following:

1. Any condition, place or situation of social or political perfection.

2. Any idealistic goal or concept for social and political reform. Sir Thomas More was the first to reference this term in the early 16th century in his writings.

3. "Utopia" is a deliberate combination of two words: eutopia + outopia.[83] In Latin, *eutopia* means "nice place" and in Greek it means "good place." In the Greek *outopia* means "no place," but there was no reference for it in Latin.

---

83 http://www.bachelorandmaster.com/literaryterms/utopia.html#.WOLL4yDyuUk

> Eutopia[84] (pronounced yoo-toh-pee-uh): a place in which human society, natural conditions, etc., are so ideally perfect that there is complete contentment; a nice place.

Nonetheless, it combines the mythical and non-existent with the promise of happiness. Today, it is referred to by scientists or idealists as a study of socialism that attempts to explain the philosophy of striving for the best life attainable that should be a part of the human culture. This basic philosophy can be one global element of common sense and common purpose in an otherwise complex and fragmented world governed by people who seek total control of everything and everyone, but fail to judge themselves in accordance to the same guidelines they create and reference in demanding compliance and conformity from us or others. In every aspect of my life, I tend to see examples of this behavior in various individuals I encounter. There is a need to "play God," yet people fail to exercise moral control over self while operating in accordance to a mindset dictated by society (this world system) that speaks to "Do as I say and not as I do!" instead of, "Do unto me as I would do unto you!"

Upon hearing the word utopia, I drifted to a distant place known only to me as a perfect place where there is no evidence of poverty, disease, mental anguish or immorality. This place in my subconscious could be equated to "Heaven on earth" but in a different realm. There are deep blue oceans filled with creatures that have not become extinct due to man's disrespect for their existence. Seas and streams filled with an abundance of nev-

---

84 http://www.dictionary.com/browse/eutopia

er-ending seafood at no charge. The land has not been overrun with buildings and factories or seized and overthrown by governments who protect those who want to control the natural resources for selfish gain at the expense of orchestrating wars in an effort to take what they want at will. There is an ample consumption of livestock or animals that are free to roam in the forest of beautiful trees, plants and flowers where they are not hunted by man just for sport. The sky is clear, and the air is crisp and void of pollution. I picture an environment filled with many races of people with the same opportunities and agenda with no focus or thought to the difference in skin color. No one is considered to be inferior or superior. All are treated equally, and there is an equal distribution of wealth. A world filled with hope, peace and justice for all in the pursuit of happiness. Laws are not made by a select few, considered to be the majority to subject conformity amongst the minority, because there is no separatism or double standards in utopia.

Unfortunately, reality sets in, and I become consciously aware of where I am as I review my surroundings and attempt to take into consideration my personal experience and the role or participation of my ancestors **to the contribution of civilization** and their plight in this world. My heart becomes heavy, and I immediately begin to engage in conversation with God trying to understand why things are as I perceive them to be and why this contributes to my disillusionment about the importance of family, friends, education, technology, employment or industry, economics and our government. What it is versus what it isn't or should be. What would I change? In utopia, anything is possible!

Family

The idea of being able to pick my family members is very appealing to me. Unfortunately, although blessed, I have endured a number of hardships growing up that have caused me to trust or rely on no one, *including* my family. In essence, it is not entirely a bad thing. It has made me aware of my surroundings and the people I encounter while allowing me to attempt to identify the varied degree of personalities that manifest within an individual that could possibly camouflage themselves as being a friendly entity. So on a daily basis, I pray and ask God to bless me with the ability to discern. And with that in mind, I don't use the word friendship lightly. In fact, I am able to count my true friends on one hand. However, in utopia, each person is interconnected and related to each other spiritually as well as mentally **with each other's best interest at heart**. There's a body of one with the same objective and goal.

Education

Because the continuation or completion of my college degree has been contingent upon the availability of financial support, training or education of any kind for developmental advancement or pleasure is free in utopia. I feel education on any level should be made possible by the state in which an individual claims residence. And the concept of education or the knowledge obtained from an educational institution can be misleading. Having something on paper to confirm your intelligence level is not needed in utopia. Each person is brilliant in his or her own right, and they are viewed as being just as equally capable of making a contribution to the growth of civilization regardless of their IQ, race, sex or sexual orientation. And, in utopia, education and training are readily available to all who are interested!

Employment

In lieu of my current place of employment, I have finally learned that it does not matter where you work. You may still encounter or be subjected to an unfair working environment that is governed by individuals who set standards or rules and break them at will in accordance to favoritism and office politics. **It's not necessary *what* you know but *who* you know that tends to contribute to your advancement in today's working environment.** Given my experience, prior to my current place of employment, you would think that I would have grasped that concept at least six years ago when I found myself unemployed because I refused to allow my supervisor and upper management to force me into conformity during their attempt to strip me of my dignity, self-respect and character as a result of being different and choosing to accept my faith. I made a conscious decision in 1988 to no longer wear a wig and accept my inability to grow hair due to a medical illness. So instead of being judged by my ability to perform my job, my appearance was viewed as being offensive and as an attempt to be militant. Although I was without a job, God shielded my heart, my soul and my mind throughout that whole ordeal while strengthening me spiritually.

In utopia, no one has to worry about finding a job. We're born with an immeasurable amount of wealth, knowledge and freedom. Many members of a whole; uniquely made with a purpose for a purpose. Created to possess various gifts and talents and working together as a team toward accomplishing the same objective. **Free from mental, physical and monetary bondage.**

Spiritualism

I thought upon accepting this position, things would be different here. Even in a religious organization, where people view themselves as true Christians, they allow themselves to be consumed by worldly things and lose sight of the bigger picture. They still strive for control over another being and make unjust, irrational judgments against each other. Nonetheless, because I believe all things happen for a reason, I have been placed here to learn a very valuable lesson. We all fall short of the grace of God.

Over the years, I have questioned my views and beliefs about my own Christianity and have learned that I'm no different from anyone else. We're all human, and no one is perfect. However, I've learned the difference between being religious, a Christian (Christ-like) and spiritual. Which one are you? **I see myself as a spiritual being striving to do the will of God while consciously trying not to judge others.**

In utopia, a perfect world, all religious beliefs are able to coexist in appreciation of the God who resides within each of us while demonstrating divine love for all. God is Spirit and we, as individuals, are spirit beings first and foremost.

Conclusion

So in my utopia, there is no free will that practices hypocrisy. Thus, the word *hypocrisy* does not exist in utopia. And where there is no hypocrisy, there is no room for technology or governments whose only **purpose** is to exercise control and confine people to a standard of living that goes against God's plan.

WRONGFUL TERMINATION

Socialization[85], a process a new employee undergoes enabling him to become a productive part of an organization, is intended to teach him the culture of the organization as well as how "things are done or should be done." It also helps the individual to develop expectations about what the job will be like through his interactions with company contacts, thus easing his tension and allowing him to begin to feel comfortable with the requirements of his job and those with whom he must interact to accomplish that task. The successfulness of his defeat may prove to be a very exhausting and intense experience if he is not ready to explore the concept of office politics and master how it works. But first, he may want to consider making a major investment towards swimming lessons.

Organizational culture is what employees perceive and how this perception creates a pattern of beliefs, values and

---

85 Anthony, William P., Pamela L. Perrewe & K. Michele Kacmar. *Human Resource Management: A Strategic Approach*. Florida: Harcourt Brace College Publishers. 1999.

expectations.[86] Since organizational culture involves shared expectations, values and attitudes, it exerts influence on individuals, groups and organizational processes. Because culture can be created to influence the behavior of the employee in the direction management desires, it can have a positive or negative effect on the psyche of the individual depending upon his personal objective, integrity and character.

Depending upon the employee's resourcefulness and level of development during and after the socialization period, management's evaluation may be less-than-favorable and choose to exercise its option to pursue one of three basic types of termination strategies.

- The first is referred to as the *leave 'em naked termination strategy*. Employers essentially release employees from the organization without providing any protection, compensation benefits or outplacement services, and they provide no severance pay or counseling benefits.

- The second strategy is referred to as the *early retirement incentive*. It usually provides some form of inducements for employees to retire from the organization before they reach the normal retirement age. This could be viewed as age discrimination, but it's perfectly legal.

- The third strategy is referred to as a *forced resignation*. The employee is given the option of either resigning or being terminated outright. However, given the change

---

86 Matteson, Ivancevich. *Organizational Behavior and Management*. New York: Irwin/McGraw-Hill. 1999.

in guidelines governing the receipt of unemployment benefits, if you should leave (quit) a job voluntarily for any reason other than medically recommended and documented by a physician unless you are involuntarily terminated or laid off, you forfeit your eligibility to obtain this service.

During the middle part of 1993, my supervisor stated she wanted to discuss my appearance in the eyes of white people. She went on to say that my appearance was viewed as being defensive and intimidating. A couple of months later, she called me into her office to discuss a proposition. She stated she wanted to give me the opportunity to look for another job on a full-time basis. Upon asking her to elaborate, she stated she and the organization were prepared to give me three-months pay in advance in exchange for my resignation. I declined and stated, given the change in the economy and considering the number of downsizing attempts made by other organizations within the past three years, it may take me longer than three months to find another position. Therefore, unless you or the organization is willing to put in writing your proposition and guarantee my unemployment claim, I am not willing to give you resignation. If I resign, I would not be able to claim unemployment benefits. The following year, after many failing harassment attempts to get me to quit, I was terminated on the basis of allegedly lying about the death of my grandmother. I not only filed a suit for wrongful termination but for discrimination, defamation of character, punitive damages, back wages, and reinstatement.

Terminations, reduction in force, or downsizing as it is more commonly referred to today, is management's attempt, in my view, to weed out the less desirable or less productive, cut costs, induce a desired morale or behavior, instill fear, loyalty and gain control as an attempt to change the overall organizational culture or to enforce it.

My second termination in 1994, without a doubt, was very ugly, however, my third experience in 2000 was not as devastating. Nonetheless, because I showed reluctance to change or lacked the ability to be molded or conform, I was terminated. Can you imagine being told by your supervisor that she wanted you to change the view or perception that others have of you? Impossible! At least I thought so. Pursuant to her, I was being terminated because I wasn't considered to be a team player, and to top it off, they did not have enough work to keep me busy. Wow, that was truly a lie. I was in the office most mornings before the crack of dawn because I had so much work to do. Most evenings, I was the only person in the office working while others either left at their regularly scheduled quitting times or earlier. There were times I neglected family, friends and even myself for the sake of completing a task that just could not wait until tomorrow.

My first termination in 1990 was due to a decline in the economy. Who would have thought a bank could and would go bankrupt? Bad investments and overspending! Or was it a ploy for management or top executives to retain more and shell out less?

"Wrongful termination" is a term that generally refers to a person being fired when they should not have been. It can be very misleading because many terminations that people think of as being "wrongful" are not necessarily illegal, depending upon the wording or the stated reason given for terminating the person. Nonetheless, the stated reason is not necessarily the actual reason, but it may be hard to prove unless the employers dictate otherwise. In other words, the employer may have acted morally wrong but was not exposed as having been legally liable.

Wrongful termination can result in an employer being held responsible for back wages with interest, reinstatement of employment and often for punitive damages assessed as a deterrent to other employers. Examples of wrongful termination:[87]

- ▸ If the employer directs a worker to violate any law, ordinance, regulation or statute, the employer cannot legally fire that employee for refusing such a directive.

- ▸ If the employee complains about what he or she reasonably perceives as a violation of law, like late-payment of wages, failure to pay overtime or workplace safety issues, and is fired in retaliation, that would also constitute an actionable claim for wrongful termination.

Under common law, the phrase "at-will employment" normally relating to non-union, private sector employees describes the relationship between employer and employee that exists without a written contract or other agreement guaranteeing job security. This means the employer has the right to terminate your employment at any time, for any reason (fair or

---

87   http://www.leefeldmanlaw.com/wrongfultermination.html

unfair) or for no reason, as long as the reason is not illegal—even if your performance has been outstanding. It also means that you, as an employee, can quit your job at any time for any reason. Or, if you choose, you do not have to give a reason for quitting, but you must be prepared for the outcome of your actions if your reason(s) do not meet with your employer's satisfaction. In addition, you should be aware of the double standard in regards to how they may treat you in not giving you ample notice, but you will be expected to give them at least a two-week notice. In some cases, depending upon the nature of your work, you may be asked to stay for a month prior to your last of employment.

Even if the employee is at-will and does not have job security, workers are still protected from termination for illegal reasons. Upon seeking legal counsel when an employee is terminated, the first question asked is whether the employee is protected by a job security system, such as civil service, a collective bargaining agreement (union), academic tenure or other promises of job security made by the employer. If the employee has job security, the employer must have a good cause for terminating the employee.

Each state has different laws regulating the employment relationship and no two states may have exactly the same laws governing those policies. However, most states have statutes created by state legislatures prohibiting discriminatory discharge based on race, religion, sex, national origin, age and disability. In addition, most states have specific statutes prohibiting certain kinds of discrimination not covered by federal law, for example, with respect to sexual preference or marital status. Therefore, there are many federal and state laws that make reasons for adverse employment action illegal.[88] To reiterate the above, a person cannot or should not be fired for unlawful reasons:

1. **Discrimination** based on race, age, gender, religion, disability, sexual orientation or national origin. Discrimination claims generally fall into two categories: disparate treatment and disparate impact.

    > **Disparate treatment** - the employer intentionally discriminates against an individual or a group belonging to a protected class.

    Example: Johnson Controls, Inc., a battery manufacturer located in Wisconsin, had an employment policy that eliminated women under seventy years of age from performing certain jobs in the making of batteries unless they could produce proof that they were infertile. The company argued that it was just trying to protect its workers since all the prohibited jobs involved prolonged exposure to lead. The U.S. Supreme Court disagreed and labeled the company's policy a clear-cut example of sex discrimination. [89]

    > **Disparate impact** - occurs when an employer has a policy that on the surface seems neutral, but

---

88 http://www.prairielaw.com/articles/article.asp?channelId=14&articleId=1111

89 Brown, Gordon W. and Paul A. Sukys. (1997). *Business Law With UCC Applications* (9th ed.). New York: McGraw-Hill.

which has an unequal and unfair impair on the members of one or more of the protected classes.

Example: An employer who requires all employees who work in the warehouse to be six feet tall and to weigh at least 180 pounds may have discriminated against women under the doctrine of disparate impact. Although the criteria seem neutral on the surface, they would exclude disproportionately and would thus have an unfair impact on them.[90]

> **Sexual harassment** - a type of sexual discrimination, generally falls into two categories: quid pro quo or hostile work environment. Quid pro quo occurs when a supervisor makes unwelcomed sexual advances toward a subordinate or suggests that the subordinate trade sexual favors for preferential treatment.

> Hostile work environment occurs when misconduct; such as, sexually explicit comments, photographs, pictures, cartoons, jokes, posters, or gestures, pervaded the workplace to the extent that conditions become distressing, offensive or hostile.

Employers are liable for acts of sexual harassment by one employee against another employee if the employer (or any supervisor) knew or should have known about the

---

90 Brown, Gordon W. and Paul A. Sukys. (1997). *Business Law With UCC Applications* (9th ed.). New York: McGraw-Hill.

conduct and failed to take reasonable steps to prevent it. Employers are also liable if they fail to implement harassment policies designed to effectively prevent such conduct.

2. **Personal injury** - If firing the employee violates a fundamental, public policy, or if the employer negligently or intentionally causes the employee some kind of personal injury, the employer may be liable for damages for emotional distress or punitive damages, in addition to being liable for the employee's economic losses.

3. **Defamation** - If the employer told the world that an employee had been fired for possessing illegal drugs when in fact the employee had not been in possession of drugs.

4. **Retaliation** - When an employer terminates an employee that complains of sexual harassment and is then subjected to unwarranted work-related criticism and disciplinary actions, or an employee who refuses to participate in hazardous work.

If your termination is considered unlawful, you may recover some or all of the following: lost wages, lost benefits, emotional distress damages, punitive damages, reinstatement, promotion and attorney fees. Thus an employee who wishes to sue for wrongful termination must and should be able to show either[91]:

---

91 http://www.uchastings.edu/plri/96-97tex/jury.htm#I.
percent20Introduction

1. that his employment contract, either expressly or implicitly, included a promise that he would not be fired without cause (*contract cases*); or,

2. that his employer fired him for a reason that violates a fundamental policy expressed in the state and/or federal statutes or constitution (*public policy cases*), including laws against unlawful discrimination (*discrimination cases*), or

3. that the employer committed a tort, like defamation, invasion of privacy or intentional infliction of emotional distress (independent tort cases).

Within the Washington metropolitan area, Virginia state laws are considered to be the harshest. An employer in the state of Virginia has the ability to terminate an employee without a good reason. In fact, on February 16, 2000, my employer stated they were terminating me because they did not have enough work to keep me busy. However, prior to my termination, I was reporting to work as early as 6:30 am, working through my breaks (including lunch) and leaving as late as 9:00 pm as a result of my workload. The termination came about because I refused to no longer come in on the weekends. Not to mention, I was a salaried employee when I should have been classified as an hourly employee. When I inquired about the difference, I noted a change in my supervisor's disposition towards me.

Facts

- Private lawsuits alleging discrimination in the workplace more then tripled during the 1990s.

- The average large corporation pays an estimated $6.7 million to investigate, defend, and either settle or pay judgments for sexual harassment claims.

- In 1998, nearly 10 percent of federal employment discrimination cases had judgments in excess of $10 million.

- The average wrongful termination jury award in California is $1.3 million.

- Cases may take years from the time a complaint is filed until the case is finally resolved.

Nationwide, lawyers are suing and enforcing employees' rights at an increasingly high rate because of jobs terminating without good cause.[92] A clear case of wrongful termination may be when an employee is terminated and then replaced by one or more other persons receiving salaries of a combined or lesser pay than the terminated employee received which is common practice.[93] Cover-ups are another way employers try to protect themselves. Reports indicating false tardiness, false customer and coworker complaints and false poor work standards can be seen in the employees' personnel files.

---

92 http://www.legalpitfalls.com/employerbenefits.htm
93 Ibid.

BONUS

WHAT IS THE NATURE OF A SCRIBE?

Now go, write it before them in a table, and note it in a book, that it may be for the time to come for ever and ever:

~ Isaiah 30:8 KJV

February 5, 2012

For nearly four weeks leading up to Sunday, January 29, my spirit was especially vexed by the things I saw or was witnessing as being contrary to the manner in which we are requested by God to conduct ourselves as followers of Christ. So much in fact that I allowed my mind this weekend to get the better of me as I pondered intensely, cried out to God and slept off and on in anticipation of some much needed answers concerning my God-given purpose for being at the U.S. Department of Energy (DOE). *I have seen all the works that are done under the sun; and, behold, all [is] vanity and vexation of spirit* (Ecclesiastes 1:14). Instead of things getting better and calming down, I was still seeing and encountering things that have been evident since the first day of my arrival on January 22, 2008. But at this juncture, the playing field or battleground is increasing with a number of unsuspected players (souls) or impacted people; and I so desperately want out of this situation! But when you are sent on assignment or to a location (Adullam) as part of a curriculum needed to complete your (spiritual) training, you are there until you accomplish the task at hand unless you wash out, tap out, give up or give in to the opposing forces within your surroundings! Divine assignments are not necessarily comfortable (meaning they do not feel good); but you have to have an unshakeable, unmovable, made-up mind (transformed) and heart for the law of the spirit of life in Christ Jesus.

Now the things which I write unto you, behold, before God, I lie not.

~ Galatians 1:20 KJV

Example #1: My current working environment, which in essence may actually be just a sample of what others may be enduring in their workplace elsewhere, leaves a lot to be desired in the number of challenges demonstrated by the characters and behaviors of people I come in contact with on a daily basis. Just everyday people no different from you and me on the surface—regardless of their titles and the positions they hold, the size of their salary, grade or bank accounts, the cars they drive or the houses they live in—but very different in accordance to the condition of their hearts with varied priorities and personal agendas! Some truly have a heart for God, some proclaim to be Christians but still lack the knowledge, some haven't a clue about Christianity at all but seem curious, and some just don't care one way or the other while others pretend to be knowledgeable about everything under the sun with no apparent direction. But nonetheless, some of them may even be the same people you meet and greet on Sundays in your neighborhood church. And unfortunately, there is one parody I have heard stated often by one of my coworkers that others have become to accept or either ignores: "These are 'DOE Christians.' They only reference or call on the Lord when it suits them." Ironically, this is not a practice that is only isolated to DOE. There is a growing culture of the walking wounded (lost souls) who lack the knowledge or desire to learn the true ways of God and be committed to follow it to the letter. Some may even know the word to include the knowledge of what is required to obtain Kingdom results, but simply infiltrate themselves into the church of God in doing his or her job as a Jezebel; the work of the adversary to confuse you.

> *When they are ashamed*
> *of all that they have done, make known to them*
> *the design of the temple, its pattern, its exits and entrances,*
> *and its whole design –all its statutes, its entire design,*
> *and all its laws; write it all down in their sight,*
> *so that they may observe its entire design*
> *and all its statutes and do them.*
>
> ~ Ezekiel 43:11 NET

Upon laying my head down most nights within the last couple of weeks, I tossed and turned while thoughts of a phrase danced repeatedly in my mind. Wrestling with God, similar to Jacob in Genesis 32, I was not going to let go until He blessed me with a clear understanding of "What, how and WHY!" God is so awesome! I love Him with every beat of my heart. When you are blessed with the ability of objective observation to include the discernment of wickedness and spirits [demons, angels and children of darkness, invisible spirits without a body that influence others] and the presence of darkness, you should not fear it. You should embrace it and see it as an advantage rather than a disadvantage though it can be somewhat overwhelming at times. However, no one will be able to convince you that what you see, you don't see; what you know, you don't know; what you feel you don't feel and most of all, what you have experienced that's imprinted on your heart is just an illusion or a figment of your imagination. Though they will try, you know it is and was all real as based on the God honest truth and gifting through the Holy Spirit to see the light!

> *If ye then, being evil,*
> *know how to give good gifts unto your children,*
> *how much more shall your Father which is in heaven*
> *give good things to them that ask him?*
>
> Mathew 7:11; Luke 11:13

We have a tendency to live our lives according to our flesh, but God calls us to live according to the Spirit. Not just any spirit, but in alignment with His spirit! And I have noted the presence of dark spirits at work that makes me wonder why it is so easy for many around me to be a part of it to literally deny it. Are they blind (2 Corinthians 4:4) to it or does it serve a purpose in providing a fleshy emotional pleasure of ecstasy? In the same manner in which I am satisfied and pleased in doing a good deed or the will of the Lord, there are others who feel satisfied in doing a bad deed. If you view the Maslow Hierarchy of Need Theory, it does not point out from a psychological standpoint just how differently wired we are from each other. Some people may even witness a wrong being done to another, but out of fear will rather allow themselves to be a part of the morally and unlawful oppression to escape the same being directed at them.

Example #2: A coworker who was almost in tears approached me with a confession and a testimony. Having been at DOE for approximately 30 years, experiencing and being the center of entertainment for those who get pleasure from wrongdoing tends to alter your perception as well as your heart. She actually indicated she was sorry for the part she played in terrorizing (bullying) one of her coworkers. She took part because she was wrongly happy to see a new person come into the department to get what she was experiencing herself for years that she welcomed the break (refuge) from it. Her participation was a way to make others think and feel she was on their side in the hope that they would leave her alone. *So I find it to be a law (rule of action of my being) that when I want to do what is right and good, evil is ever present with me and I am subject to its insistent demands* (Romans 7:21 AMP). Have you heard the saying, "Hurt people hurt people"? And there is another saying I like better: "Be careful to never become what you hate." Why? This behavior is the start of one vicious cycle! More importantly,

God calls us to resist the devil, his temptation and all his wiles and watch him flee.

> *Blessed [is] the man*
> *that endureth temptation: for when he is tried,*
> *he shall receive the crown of life, which*
> *the Lord hath promised to them that love him.*
>
> *~ James 1:12 KJV*

◆

> *Put on the whole armour of God,*
> *that ye may be able to stand against the wiles of the devil.*
>
> *~ Ephesians 6:11 KJV*

Example #3: Standing in the Subway line on the ground floor of DOE, I noted a woman who was acting rather abnormal. Focusing on her I thought, "Am I standing too close in her space? If so, perhaps, I should give her more room!" But that only resulted in more back-and-forth movement. As she approached the server in placing her order, the young person waiting on her indicated, "You're much later today." She said, "Yes, I haven't eaten and I haven't had the opportunity to take my medicine. I'm diabetic and I'm experiencing low sugar." Having a father who almost slipped into a diabetic coma, I now understood exactly what was going on. So, I turned to her to say, "That's not good! You need to make sure you eat and you definitely need to make sure you take your medicine. You could pass out on this floor and slip into a diabetic coma!" With watered eyes, she indicated she was working in an office full of men who were bullying her and taking advantage of her since the day she arrived in 2008 as a Career Intern participant. Similar to myself, as part of the Career Intern Program, she came in the door as a GS-09 with the opportunity to excel to a certain grade potential upon completion of training and satisfactory performance ratings. But she found herself being delegated to complete assignments directed at GS-14s and to attend every meeting scheduled. Being away from her desk so often did not afford her the opportunity to gather information for generating reports and analyses in a timely manner to meet her deadlines. She was threatened not to make waves by complaining or reporting their behavior to anyone because they could adversely affect the progression of her growth potential and no one would believe her to do anything about it anyway. *This is very a serious trend or pattern and belief of the enemy to incite fear, thus giving him the opportunity or advantage to keep abusing you!*

As individuals, our tolerance levels of endurance and for overcoming obstacles is very different! Some of us are able to ride out the storm on the battlefield as we wait on the Lord while others run on empty with no reserve of faith or belief! We are worn down, torn down, broken, bruised and tattered so we go along to get along with the antagonist. We are to trust in our heavenly Father. He will not only be our mighty refuge and shield, but He Himself will take care of the antagonists for us: *"Vengeance is Mine, I will repay,"* says the Lord God (Romans 12:19). Through a series of events, God not only stilled my mind to show me the existence of a historical pattern involving some of the same people who have been there for years, He showed me the spread of this infection throughout the entire building. He specifically tells us that we have not, because we ask not (James 4:2). We set our sights on the things outside of His Kingdom and make many attempts to acquire those things in conforming to the ways of the world.

> An **antagonist** *(*from the Greek word *grammateus,* which means scholar or professional writer; synonyms: opponent, competitor, adversary, enemy and rival) is a character, group of characters or institution, represents the opposition against which the protagonist must contend. In other words, a person or a group of people who team up to oppose the main character or the main characters. In the classic style of a story wherein the main plot consists of a hero fighting a villain, the two can be regarded as protagonist and antagonist, respectively.
>
> "Hard-core antagonists cannot be reasoned with because they lack the emotional stability to understand."
>
> An excerpt from *Antagonists in the Church: How to Identify and Deal with Destructive Conflict* (Augsburg Publishing House, 1988; page 29).

Playing Church Through Infiltration

The church or the concept of church is not a failure; the individuals in the church who have forsaken God and His doctrine in not being hearers and doers of the word have failed both the church and God! You should not judge all churches or Christians to be the same. For just as we have many members (cells, parts, limbs) in (and on) *one* body, respectively, all those members do not operate in the same function (Romans 12:4). God encourages *unity* among His children to work as a team (body of Christ) in accomplishing a common goal (for the uplifting of the Kingdom). He does not encourage separatism, nepotism, fascism, racism or chauvinism; no isms or schisms of any kind!

> *Ye stiffnecked and uncircumcised in heart and ears,*
> *ye do always resist the Holy Ghost:*
> *as your fathers [did], so [do] ye.*
>
> ~ Acts 7:51 KJV

Many churchgoing people have not, for whatever reason, caught ahold of that principle or concept. Letting the world dictate their actions according to their flesh, they often choose their church based on its reputation, status (in the community or political affiliation for *power*) and size of the congregation rather than its teaching. Some even hold positions in the church aimed at adding value to whom they want people to believe they are rather than becoming who they should be within the body of Christ. That is why it is so easy for them to conform to a behavior outside of the church within their working environment and everyday life unrepresentative of the fruit they should bear in resembling the character of Christ. Nevertheless, there should be no difference in your character as a participatory member of a church, in the workplace or anywhere if you are a true believer and follower of Christ. Being a Christian is a lifestyle you present twenty-four seven—even in your sleep!

Yes, we are living breathing human beings in an earthly body that is governed by our flesh subject to making mistakes. But we were also given an example in which to follow. Jesus Christ, the Son of God, who walked this earth in His human form that was also governed by flesh! And though He was tempted (Matthew 4:1, Mark 1:13, Luke 4:2) by the prince of darkness (Lucifer, Satan, Devil, the Antichrist, the Adversary, the Prince of this World), He stayed the course in pursuit of His destiny (road to Zion) according to the will of His Father.

The LORD looked down from heaven upon the children of men, to see if there were any that did understand, [and] seek God.

~ Psalm 14:2

It is not all that impossible for the enemy to infiltrate the church. As individuals, you are and should represent the church! Nonetheless, the church as perceived by a number of people is a physical building (brick and mortar) comprised of and occupied by an array of people with different emotions. Some well (whole) and some not so well (sick and wounded). Some attending on pretense (just going through the motions) and refusing to denounce their old ways with a reprobate mind. Some attending with the desire to get closer to the Lord with a transformed mind. Therefore, the angel of darkness is able to infiltrate people first through their minds and through their hearts. Then he is able to possess them through the body to influence and control you completely. Unless you have the ability to discern spirits, study the *word of truth* (Bible) to show yourself approved and actually read it for yourself, you are left at a disadvantage. That is why it is important for you to develop a relationship with God, believe and welcome the Holy Spirit into your life for guidance and direction.

> *Ye therefore, beloved, seeing ye know*
> *[these things] before, beware lest ye also,*
> *being led away with the error of the wicked,*
> *fall from your own stedfastness.*
>
> ~ 2 Peter 3:17 KJV

Empowerment Versus Power

People who have become comfortable with the world system like to feel powerful and not necessarily empowered! There is a very big difference between possessing power and being empowered. Being empowered is having the innate desire to learn how something is done and do it—having the desire to be mentally stimulated and grow. It is the understanding that growth and learning is a continuous, lifelong event. Not wanting to rely on or depend on anyone or anybody for accomplishing a task or getting a job done could be seen as being self-sufficient—having the ability to do a job and see it through from start to finish and not pushing it off on someone else. But you should also be willing to accept the opportunity to work with others (who are operating under the influence of the right spirit) as part of a team effort to accomplish a task. Keep in mind, not everybody who offers to assist you has the right motive (1 Peter 5:8).

> *But sanctify the Lord God in your hearts:*
> *and [be] ready always to [give] an answer*
> *to every man that asketh you a reason of the hope*
> *that is in you with meekness and fear:*
>
> ~ 1 Peter 3:15

And then there are those who strive on power and will do almost anything to get it. Having the need to feel in control of a person, place or thing at all cost. The need to feel more important and powerful than they ought to is what directs them to abuse their false sense of power and take advantage of others. Getting too comfortable in that high-minded position and feeling you are above reproach or unaccountable for your actions leads you down a darker path—possibly down a path of no return. Having the wrong concept of leadership and leading through a form of bullying (terrorism), dictatorship (fear) and unlawful tactics (injustice and unfairness) in satisfying an urge of pleasure in doing bad (evil, wicked) deeds. With this power, they are also able to seduce, tempt and manipulate others to join forces in carrying out their agenda of iniquity.

> *Traitors, heady, highminded,*
> *lovers of pleasures more than lovers of God;*
>
> ~ 2 Timothy 3:4 KJV

Ironically, evil spirits often work in packs, meaning they never attack alone. They normally double-team you. You could have two or more people who have a deep-rooted dislike for each other, but given the nature of their spirit (darkness), they will band together to come up against you to kill your spirit!

> *And so, since they did not see fit to acknowledge God or approve of Him or consider Him worth the knowing, God gave them over to a base and condemned mind to do things not proper or decent but loathsome, Until they were filled (permeated and saturated) with every kind of unrighteousness, iniquity, grasping and covetous greed, and malice. [They were] full of envy and jealousy, murder, strife, deceit and treachery, ill will and cruel ways. [They were] secret backbiters and gossipers, Slanderers, hateful to and hating God, full of insolence, arrogance, [and] boasting; inventors of new forms of evil, disobedient and undutiful to parents. [They were] without understanding, conscienceless and faithless, heartless and loveless [and] merciless. Though they are fully aware of God's righteous decree that those who do such things deserve to die, they not only do them themselves but approve and applaud others who practice them.*
>
> ~ Romans 1:28-32 AMP

Called to Challenge

When things are revealed to me by God beyond the surface (supernaturally in the spirit), which is different from what others may see in the natural with their physical eye, I can only attempt to share that information with them (only when released by God to do so) and graciously move on when it is not readily received. Therefore, I have been cautioned by God not to spend any unnecessary time or energy defending that which He has brought to my attention with anyone! I am to graciously humble myself and accept to agree to disagree without getting confrontational or combative. But under no circumstances am I to allow what others don't see to compromise what God has blessed me to see or my God-given assignment. For I am to stay focused and open to seeing beyond the surface in understanding and acknowledging a truth that is bigger than both you and me! But when you take a question or concern to God, you need to make sure you are ready for the answer in addition to your instructions! Are you familiar with the comment, "Be careful what you ask (or wish) for because you just might get it?"

And whatsoever we ask, we receive of him,
because we keep his commandments,
and do those things that are pleasing in his sight.

1 John 3:22 KJV

Monday, January 30, at approximately 7:10 a.m., upon reaching the L'Enfant subway station in transit to work, I received a rhema word so profound that it could not possibly be from anyone else but God! Especially since I was being challenged to act outside of my comfort level or zone! In particular, I was being called to challenge those who challenged the word of God and His children. Those who were comfortable in their sin or wrong doing (iniquity) to think the things they did in the dark or in secret were unnoticeable by man. For God sits up high and looks down low. He sees all and knows all!

A Quote from Joyce Myers's Teaching:

*If you do not learn
to think like God thinks and say what God says,
there is no hope of you having victory in your life.*

Was this the first revelation knowledge of my purpose or God-given assignment? No, but this was the first time it was confirmed to this extent with such intensity. So there I was, standing in the middle of the subway station looking perplexed and telling God, "You have got to be kidding me! No, please!" Attempting to pull myself together, I managed to get to the escalator only to drape myself across it as I started to cry while riding up to make my exit. Before leaving the mall area of L'Enfant Plaza, I needed to take a seat to process what I heard. Still in awe, I needed to share this information with a dear friend, Mary Bryant. Because she knows me better than anybody with the exception of God Himself, I knew she would understand what I was feeling. And she did understand, but she also added some confirmation of laughter while saying, yes Jeremiah.

*Take thee a roll of a book and write therein
all the words that I have spoken unto thee against Israel,
and against Judah and against all the nations,
from the day I spake unto thee, from the days of Josiah,
even unto this day.*

~ Jeremiah 36:2

Have you ever been called to do something you were so adamant about not wanting to do, but felt you had no other option or way of getting out of it? Why? Because obedience is better than sacrifice! And if you truly love God with all your heart and all your might, you will be obedient to His *every* word (2 Corinthians 2:9). He will never ask anything of you to harm you—only to prosper you. So I was being reminded of a plan God had for my life that had been set in motion long before I was conceived within the womb of my biological (earthly) mother (Jeremiah 1:5), simply to challenge unrighteousness by exposing the truth as it is brought to my attention with the stroke of a pen—taking notes, writing it down and making it plain for all the world to see.

> *Blessed [are] they that keep his testimonies,*
> *[and that] seek him with the whole heart.*
>
> ~ Psalm 119:2 KJV

A DEEPER HURT

There is no need to fear when times of trouble come, even though surrounded by enemies! They trust in their wealth and boast about how rich they are, yet not one of them, though rich as kings, can ransom his own brother from the penalty of sin! For God's forgiveness does not come that way. For a soul is far too precious to be ransomed by mere earthly wealth. There is not enough of it in all the earth to buy eternal life for just one soul, to keep it out of hell.

~ Psalms 49:5-9 TLB

May 19, 2014
Revised May 21, 2014

Tomorrow is promised to no man or woman! Life as we know it on earth will soon cease to exist as it did during the days of Noah and the flood; but not by water (see 2 Peter 3:10) this time around! For approximately one month or so, I have felt a deep-rooted hurt or ache that is anchored in the very pit of my soul.

The soul can be best defined or described as being the **immortal** entity or spiritual part of one's self, which separates from the human body after death. The Hebrew word for soul is *nephesh* and in the Greek, it is called *psūchē*.[94] Regardless of its true origin, I cannot seem to shake this feeling. This hurt is not comparable to the pain I have endured over the years as caused by the people I have encountered throughout the environment of my experiences! It is a type of grieving or mourning for the living! It is an unselfish love for the soul of others in not wanting to see them perish. Why? Because I believe—aside from worshiping the Lord—that this is the sole purpose, vein or bridge of my existence. To connect to the Spirit of our Father, the one who has given us all life! And, to take ahold of that which is most important to Him by pushing past or beyond my personal pain or mental anguish from desperately wanting to loathe a species of selfless people who have hurt me—only to pray for their souls as an intercessor. *For there is one God and one Father of us all who is above all (sovereign over us all), pervading all and living in us all* (Ephesians 4:6)!

We, unfortunately, live in a **sin-infested world** comprised of a volatile (explosive, unstable, forever unpredictable) and diverse race of people who for some reason do not seem to believe in "Heaven or Hell." What other reason could there be for their short attention spans or detachment to taking responsibility for their actions in not considering the possibility of their souls being condemned to living out eternity in Hell? How can they deliberately not draw from their intellect to acknowl-

---

94 http://biblehub.com/topical/s/soul.htm

edge truth! The very thing that they deem as being so important (intellect and education) for getting ahead in life like rats in a maze only to neglect using it to its fullest potential to be able to pull themselves from a deep dark and illusive state of mind called <u>slumber</u>. *For if God spared not the angels that sinned, but cast them down to hell and delivered them into chains of darkness to be reserved unto judgment (2 Peter 2:4)*, what should your fate be for your arrogance? So wake up and arise! The time is near; the time is now for you to hear the voice of the LORD to embrace the light and receive salvation!

> *And I, the Lord, will punish the world for its evil,*
> *and the wicked for their guilt and iniquity;*
> *I will cause the arrogance of the proud to cease*
> *and will lay low the haughtiness of the terrible*
> *and the boasting of the violent and ruthless.*
>
> ~ Isaiah 13:11 AMP

As I observe people and take into consideration the history of this world relative to our track record for attempting to make wrong right, I want to hold on to the hope and belief that it is never too late for things to turn around or for people to change! But it seems the more people are seduced or influenced by this world's system, the less likely they are to take heed to their immoral decay. *Their moral understanding is darkened and their reasoning is beclouded. They are alienated (estranged, self-banished) from the life of God with no share in it; this is because of the ignorance (the want of knowledge and perception, the willful blindness) that is deep-seated in them, due to their hardness of heart to the insensitiveness of their moral nature. In their spiritual apathy, they have become callous and past feeling and reckless and have abandoned themselves a prey to unbridled sensuality; eager and greedy to indulge in every form of impurity that their depraved desires may suggest and demand* (Ephesians 4:18-19). In the meanwhile, my hurt—to include others like me—grows deeper as we pray continuously without ceasing for not only a change, but a divine awakening.

> *What good will it be*
> *for someone to gain the whole world,*
> *yet forfeit their soul? Or what can anyone*
> *give in exchange for their soul?*
>
> ~ Matthew 16:26 NIV

As creatures of habit, we tend to pick and choose that which we wish to adhere to by testing the waters to see what we think we can get away with—with the least complication (or insult to injury to ourselves)—thus avoiding the consideration of others, including God. Then we reason with ourselves and others in justifying our wrongful actions in accordance to the extent or degree of measuring right and wrong while still operating outside of the will of God. But, *do not be deceived, deluded or misled; God will not allow Himself to be sneered at (scorned, disdained, or mocked by mere pretensions or professions, or by His precepts being set aside.) He inevitably deludes himself who attempts to delude God. For whatever a man sows, that and that only is what he will reap* (Galatians 6:7).

BORN TO DIE

*For to me, to live is
Christ and to die is gain.*

~ **Philippians 1:21 NIV**

August 18, 2014

When you actually consider the process or concept of life and death, we were not meant to occupy space in the physical realm while on earth forever! Just as Christ who is referenced as being the second Adam, He was born to die *to save us from ourselves.* We who are born in this world are also born to die to self—both in the physical and the spiritual. We are three-part beings; first and foremost born of **spirit** which is housed in a **body** (made up of flesh, blood and bone) possessing a **soul**. The spirit is that part of God within us, which returns to Him when our body has served its usefulness. Our body that was created from dust returns to the earth in the form of dust, meaning the body, one day ceases to function and dies while our spirit transcends back to our heavenly Father.

All go to the same place;
all come from dust, and to dust all return.

~ Ecclesiastes 3:20

Early Sunday morning on August 17, 2014, at exactly 2:02 a.m., my mother—born Ruby Hinnant Mack on July 20, 1936—took her last breath after a three-year battle with cancer. She was a child of God who was born on this earth with a purpose. She wasn't perfect, but neither am I. Yes, we had our ups and downs, but what relationship does not take hits to evolve into an everlasting union? Throughout the years of my life, I had the pleasure of learning more and more about this person who was my mother and to appreciate what she had instilled in me. She was a very special and soft-spoken individual who had a very loving, caring and forgiving spirit. She unselfishly gave much of herself, and she made many sacrifices for those she loved. At times, I felt she made too many sacrifices for those who weren't deserving and appreciative. However, she showed no evidence of any regrets and never looked back as she spoke to me often about the importance of forgiveness. Even in her diminished state, she still found time to put others before herself and wanted nothing but the best for those around her.

As stated above, I know we are not meant to live here on earth forever. But, you can never really be ready or prepared to see the person who has given birth to you depart from you. Determined to succeed and live life, she was truly a fighter who refused to give up since the day God introduced her to me as my mother. And I saw much more of that determination when she was diagnosed in November of 2010 with stage 4 lung cancer.

She learned of her diagnosis the day before Thanksgiving and wanted as many of us as possible to pull together for a Thanksgiving Dinner at a restaurant, at which time she shared the unpleasant news. It was her spirit in how she accepted and handled her illness that gave me the strength to endure. For her to have held on for as long as she did was truly a blessing. I am just grateful to have had the opportunity to be with her up until she took that last breath of transitioning to be with the Lord. In the onset of her illness, she refused to let anyone take her to her chemotherapy or radiation treatments. And even after her road to recovery became long, discouraging and a little difficult toward the end, she still always threatened me with talks of getting in her own car to drive herself wherever she needed to go.

I consider that our present sufferings
are not worth comparing with the glory
that will be revealed in us.

~ Romans 8:18 NIV

Just hours after her death, I began to dial her number, and upon realizing she would not be there, I forced myself to fall asleep. I am sure there will be plenty more days of me reaching out for the phone only to remember the Lord took her home to be with Him. Like any child, I am sure I am going to deeply miss spending time with my mother and pulling up a chair to watch a daily episode of the soaps or hear her tease me about my weight. We used to joke about who had gained more weight than the other, and she would playfully refer to me as "whale tail" in that child-like, soft voice of hers. She had a beautiful smile and wonderful sense of humor! The cancer spread to her lymph nodes and then to her bones. Just weeks before her passing, she asked me, "Why does God keep leaving me here? And I responded, "Tell Him what you want, and He will give you the desires of your heart. If you are ready to go, just let Him know." God finally answered her request; she went peacefully and many family and friends gathered around her those last three days! She is no longer suffering and she is no longer in pain. If God grants me just half her strength, strong will and tenacity, I will be A-okay.

A TIME FOR EVERYTHING!

There is a time for everything, and a season for every activity under the heavens: a time to be born and a time to die, a time to plant and a time to uproot, a time to kill and a time to heal, a time to tear down and a time to build, a time to weep and a time to laugh, a time to mourn and a time to dance, a time to scatter stones and a time to gather them, a time to embrace and a time to refrain from embracing, a time to search and a time to give up, a time to keep and a time to throw away, a time to tear and a time to mend, a time to be silent and a time to speak, a time to love and a time to hate, a time for war and a time for peace.

~ Ecclesiastes 3:1-8

FIGHT, TAKE FLIGHT OR FREEZE

Fight the good fight of faith, lay hold on eternal life, whereunto thou art also called, and has professed a good profession before many witnesses.

~ 1 Timothy 6-12

October 21, 2014

When I first started to hear "Fight, take flight or freeze," I was very puzzled! I didn't know if it was a message directly related to me or a subject matter (title) referenced for me to speak on later—until God made His expectation very clear. He told me He was giving me one option while taking away two: (1) my option to take flight (run from trouble) and (2) my option to freeze (stand still and do nothing). So that leaves me with only the option to fight. Many want us to believe Christ was meek and passive (according to their interpretation). But according to God's interpretation, being meek is exuding *power under control*. And Christ knew when to speak, what to say, what to do, how to do it and how to be still (freeze) when absolutely necessary! Unfortunately, we have allowed the enemy to push us in a corner and to deceive us about many things.

> *The meek will HE guide in judgment:*
> *And the meek will HE teach HIS way.*
>
> ~ Psalms 25:9

Growing up, I always took the low road. I never wanted to rock the boat or hurt anyone's feelings. I always neglected myself and opted to forfeit what I wanted or needed just to make others happy in getting their way. How many times have you heard "'Vengeance is mine,' said the LORD" being redirected at you by others as a result of you attempting to resist their control over you? Many who do not know the word and have not made a conscious commitment to following the Lord's example do not waste any time quoting the scripture to work in their favor against you. That's why it is very important to develop a **relationship with the Lord** for yourself, study the word and to allow the Holy Spirit to give you **revelation**. In fighting the good fight of **faith**, it is about believing in yourself and **trusting in the Lord** to see you through. But you have to be willing to listen to Him intently as He guides you and instructs you on what to do. Then you have to be willing to follow His instructions to the letter to carry out the assignment(s) He entrusts to you. He may push you outside of your comfort zone by telling you to take a stand, when in your past, you often took the approach to run, hide or just cry in letting others walk all over you. He may tell you to speak up and speak out—to no longer keep silent. He may tell you to put something in writing and send it out to share it with others on a particular issue you have never considered taking on. He may even tell you to comfort the enemy at every turn, thus putting yourself in the line of fire to receive more attacks.

> *Jesus went straight to the Temple*
> *and threw out everyone who had set up shop, buying and*
> *selling. He kicked over the tables of loan sharks and the stalls of*
> *dove merchants. He quoted this text: My house was designated*
> *a house of prayer; You have made it a hangout for thieves.*
> *Now there was room for the blind and crippled to get in.*
> *They came to Jesus and He healed them.*
>
> ~ Matthew 21:12-14 MSG

As a child of God who is anointed and appointed with a special mission, you can no longer sit quietly on the sidelines doing nothing. In due season (the right timing), God raises up an individual or individuals by equipping them for battle (spiritual warfare) and sending them out for a specific task (or to a particular post) to uproot, tear down or pull down (See Jeremiah 1:10). Indeed, the weapons we fight with are not the weapons of the world. On the contrary, they have divine power through the Holy Spirit to demolish strongholds (2 Corinthians 10:4). We must claim our rightful positions! Decree and declare with humbleness says the Lord! We must take up our cross and walk with **boldness** to scope out the land as prophets of the most high God! It's time to move out as in the days of the old when John the Baptist was present (see Matthew 11:12-13)!

What Is a Stronghold?

A stronghold is a faulty thinking pattern based on lies and deception, which could also result in others placing limitations upon you to keep you in a box. Deception is one of the primary weapons of the devil on the basis of perception and interpretation; it is the major building block for developing strongholds and limitations. What strongholds can do is cause us to think in ways (outside of the will of God) that block us from receiving God's best. For example, James 5:16 sates, *"Confess to one another therefore your faults (your slips, your false steps, your offenses, your sins) and pray [also] for one another, that you may be healed and restored [to a spiritual tone of mind and heart]. The earnest (heartfelt, continued) prayer of a righteous man makes tremendous power available [dynamic in its working]."* However, if you think you have to confess all your sins to *everybody* you have ever wronged in your life, this could possibly take you forever to accomplish and could send you on a downward, self-condemning spiral (to feel awful and extremely guilty), thus bringing about doubt and unforgiveness. You should, however, take every offense to God in prayer in seeking His wisdom, His knowledge and His understanding for moving forward. Why? Because not everyone is at a level of spiritual maturity to handle your confession or transparency! Let God guide you all the way!

*And take THE HELMET OF SALVATION
and the sword of the Spirit, which is the Word of God.*

~ Ephesians 6:17 AMP

SELAH!

CHURCH HURT IS REAL!

If God gives such attention to the appearance of wildflowers—most of which are never even seen—don't you think he'll attend to you, take pride in you, do his best for you? What I'm trying to do here is to get you to relax, to not be so preoccupied with getting, so you can respond to God's giving. People who don't know God and the way he works fuss over these things, but you know both God and how he works. Steep your life in God-reality, God-initiative, God-provisions. Don't worry about missing out. You'll find all your everyday human concerns will be met.

~ Matthew 6:30-33 MSG

August 28, 2015

Revised September 3, 2015

Do you know "church hurt" can be the most devastating and deadly of any and all forms of hurt for some people? Why? Because there are people, including myself, who have come to church in search of refuge from the outside world. Therefore, it is not unheard of for the behavior of the world to be infused in the church. When we come to church, many of us do not expect to encounter the same spirit of division or Jezebel greeting us at the altar! But, we have, unfortunately, succumbed to the ways of the world and have taken that outside behavior into the church with us. However, as leaders who have taken on the role of "pastoring" the church, we should be putting forth an effort to withstand the wiles of the devil in how we conduct ourselves as messengers of God.

> The collateral damage (from church hurt) negatively affects the ministry and outreach of the church, too, and some churches never recover. Recognize that the behavior that brought such devastation to your heart is not much different than the hurt any of us can encounter in the workplace, marketplace, or home. The difference is we don't expect God's people to behave like those without Christ in their lives. The church is the one place almost everyone agrees should be safe, accepting, forgiving, and free from conflict and pain. Yet in most churches at least some elements of strife, conflict, and hatred creep in and tarnish that ideal.
>
> https://www.gotquestions.org/hurt-by-church.html

We should be working toward growing in spiritual maturity. We should possess a knowledge and lifestyle unlike those who are coming to the church for refuge. We should be living examples, mindful of God's agenda and His word in working toward accomplishing our divine, assigned missions on behalf of the Lord as opposed to building a reputation for ourselves. What about our character? Does it resemble the character of Christ? What are we teaching others by way of our character and behavior?

We question terrorism! But we have not given any thought to the true meaning of that word to note our unrighteous, terrorist behavior with no regard for the hurt we cause others. People are hurting and seeking hope while others have lost complete faith in humanity and the church. But their hope and faith should never be put in man. Man will disappoint you every time! Our faith should be put in God; *He is love*. He said He would never leave us nor forsake us. It is man who makes empty promises. It is man who seeks to belong and will do any and everything necessary to fulfill a need of self-realization at the expense of others. But as followers of Christ, we should not think as the world thinks. *Don't deceive yourselves. If any of you think you are wise in the ways of this world, you should give up that wisdom in order to become really wise* (1 Corinthians 3:18).

By setting your sights on the world, you have become confused in your thinking. You see the wicked getting ahead as they trample you to climb to the top. The more wrong they do, the more they are rewarded and promoted. They go through life not being held accountable for their actions, causing them to think there are no consequences. When you lose your footing or moral compass, your actions start to mirror the actions of the world. Putting ourselves on that same pedestal, we start to see ourselves as giants. We forget about saving souls and conduct our services with the need to excite the senses to hold the interest of people. We plan programs to entertain and compete with other churches just to pull in a larger crowd. No one is paying attention to God's word falling on good soil. No one is paying attention to the blessing of the offering for a plentiful harvest.

Where's the deliverance? Where's the power and the presence of the Lord? What about the miracles, signs and wonders? People are hurting! Many are called, but few are chosen, and those of us who have chosen to serve the Lord on the basis of free will must make sure that we are following His example (1 Peter 2:21). Otherwise, you are out of order! None of us are without sin or blemish and must make sure that we, ourselves, have been delivered, healed and set free from the challenges of that which threatens to hold us within captivity. Meaning, if we are finding it difficult to manage or deal with unresolved issues, we should know when it is time to step down or move back—temporarily or otherwise—in an attempt to keep from hurting others or to keep from scattering the sheep (Jeremiah 23:1 and Ezekiel 34).

MATTHEW 22:34-36 MSG
The Most Important Command

When the Pharisees heard how he had bested the Sadducees, they gathered their forces for an assault. One of their religion scholars spoke for them, posing a question they hoped would show him up: "Teacher, which command in God's Law is the most important?" Jesus said, "'Love the Lord your God with all your passion and prayer and intelligence.' This is the most important, the first on any list. But there is a second to set alongside it: 'Love others as well as you love yourself.' These two commands are pegs; everything in God's Law and the Prophets hangs from them."

COVERING

*Woe to the rebellious children,
saith the Lord, that take counsel, but not of me;
and that cover with a covering, but not of my spirit,
that they may add sin to sin.*

~ Isaiah 30:1 KJV

September 6, 2015

Everyone within the body of Christ does not believe the same thing to the same degree or extent of the word. Why? Mainly because each and every person is wired differently in our thinking and comprehension of the word! We are at different levels in our thinking when it comes to our belief in Him and the word. We are at different levels of spiritual maturity, but we are all called and encouraged to study to show ourselves approved, rightly dividing the word and being not ashamed of our covering. Our covenant is with God, not man. However, I will attempt to honor and be respectful of the person who is in position of leadership to rule as governed by the covering of us all. God commands us to assemble regularly to worship Him in spirit and in truth (Hebrews 10:25-27).

> *But [the time is coming when] the earth*
> *shall be filled with the knowledge of the glory of the Lord*
> *as the waters cover the sea.*
>
> ~ Habakkuk 2:14

Many have been taught to believe the shepherd of the church was and is God's delegated authority and ambassador who communicates God's messages to the masses. Authority is granted (and allowed) to all men from God. However, more responsibility may be given to some than others; it is important for us to be mindful of our roles and perspective positions as ordained by God. We were *all* created by Him for a purpose with a purpose. We *all* have a part to play as part of a whole. Disobeying the shepherd is like disobeying God, but our divine objective should be to please God and not man—if man is operating outside of the will of God.

> *And be not conformed to this world:*
> *but be ye transformed by the renewing of your mind,*
> *that ye may prove what [is] that good, and acceptable,*
> *and perfect, will of God.*
>
> ~ Romans 12:2

There have been times when I readily believed and followed all of what was told to me without questioning a single word. I simply went with the flow until I found out differently and was greatly disappointed or frustrated by what I received and followed that later turned out to be wrong! Unfortunately, much of what we are told, believe and follow, as it relates to the church, is taught as a result of tradition and religiosity which stems from characteristics of the world that's introduced to the church in the name of control. We must be mindful to evaluate every teaching to ensure it lines up with the word of God! *God's word is very clear!* He provides us with explicit instructions and principles (the law of the Lord) in which to follow should we take the time to read and to study them faithfully! God's word is liberating; it encourages freedom from bondage and legalism. When what we learn threatens to hold us in captivity, it is not of God and proves to be false teaching.

> *But there were also false prophets among the people, just as there will be false teachers among you. They will secretly introduce destructive heresies, even denying the sovereign Lord who bought them—bringing swift destruction on themselves. Many will follow their depraved conduct and will bring the way of truth into disrepute.*
>
> ~ 2 Peter 2:1-2

Although it is equally important for us to withstand the wiles of the devil, it is also believed that finding the right church to attend is about finding the right covering and protection. We must not give in to the temptation that is wisely disguised to deceive us! Each and every time I hear someone tell me I need a covering, I shrink as if the Holy Spirit is warning me not to store that information into my thoughts or my heart. While giving me *revelation,* God reminded me that He is my covering and directs me to various scriptures of reference. *We are Christ's body, and individually members of it* (1 Corinthians 12:27). *For just as we have many members in one body and all the members do not have the same function, so we, who are many, are one body in Christ, and individually members one of another* (Romans 12:4-5). Put in the proper context, *God has put all things under the power of Christ, and for the good of the church HE has made Him the head of everything* (Ephesians 1:22). When considering and choosing the right church, the environment should believe in the Bible and teach the Holy Ghost while trusting and leaning on the Lord to deliver, heal and set the captives free, baptizing in the name of the Father, the Son and the Holy Spirit!

He is also head of the body, the church;
and He is the beginning, the firstborn from the dead,
so that He Himself will come to have first place in everything.

~ Colossians 1:18

References:

Cover (or covering): To shelter; to protect; to defend.

http://bibleresources.org/head-coverings/

http://www.eskimo.com/~scoleman/cover.html

http://www.bible.ca/interactive/worship-10-weekly-attendance.htm

Not forsaking or neglecting to assemble together [as believers], as is the habit of some people, but admonishing (warning, urging, and encouraging) one another, and all the more faithfully as you see the day approaching. For if we go on deliberately and willingly sinning after once acquiring the knowledge of the Truth, there is no longer any sacrifice left to atone for [our] sins [no further offering to which to look forward]. [There is nothing left for us then] but a kind of awful and fearful prospect and expectation of divine judgment and the fury of burning wrath and indignation which will consume those who put themselves in opposition [to God].

~ Hebrews 10:25-27 **AMP**

APPENDICES

December 19, 1994

Seventh-Day Adventist Head Quarters
12501 Old Columbia Pike
Silver Spring, Maryland 20904

I am very disturbed by an encounter I had with an affiliated member (Wanda Marable) of your church. It is with sadness that I write this letter out of anger in hopes of seeking some understanding. Because I was always taught that you should forgive your enemies (trespassers) and pray for their sins, for the past 11 months, it has been a constant struggle to forgive or forget and least of all pray. I can't seem to let go!

How can a person refer to her or himself as a Christian and repeatedly crusade to attack or destroy another person with no remorse? Is the teaching of one religion so different from another that it teaches hatred in the name of Christianity? I have so many questions. I understand that it is morally wrong to take a life, and that's why many religions condemn or frown on abortion. However, no one is perfect, and we sometimes make irrational choices while not giving any thought to the possible outcome. However, if one chooses abortion and is inflicted with pain and suffering (e.g., hemorrhaging), would you say, "Anyone who chooses abortion as a means of birth control deserves any suffering—even death—as a complication"? Do we not have a responsibility to teach the importance of life through the understanding of the word in the Bible of any religion? Do we have the right to judge others?

One afternoon, a coworker walked over to my office to tell me he saw another coworker entering the ladies' room. Because she looked rather pale, he decided to come to me to ask if I would check on her. Entering the bathroom, I found Natalie nearly unconscious. She indicated she was hemorrhaging due to the complications of an abortion. I ran to my desk to call the hospital and Natalie's mother and learned from Ms. Marable that she was aware of the abortion. Referring to Natalie as PWT (poor white trash), she indicated she deserved to be punished for using abortion as a means of birth control. Regardless of a person's stance on abortion, Natalie is a person who was in need of help.

At the age of 15, I was diagnosed as having alopecia; however, I started to lose my hair at age 14. (As if my other problems were not bad enough.) The word "alopecia" comes from the Greek work *alopex* which means baldness or loss of hair. Can you imagine how devastating it is for a 15-year-old to find out that she is losing her hair permanently? Can you imagine the pressures at such an early age? By age 17, I was completely bald, and by age 21, I had no body hair of any kind except for my eyelashes. By that time, I had developed alopecia universalis, which is considered to be complete or total loss of body hair. There are three stages of alopecia:

1. alopecia areata - area baldness or loss of hair in patches,

2. alopecia totalis - total baldness in one localized area, and

3. alopecia universalis - the most severe.

In June of 1988, I decided to take full responsibility for my happiness. Therefore, I decided not to allow society to dictate how I should live my life. I felt that, no matter what, we were all created by God, and we each had a purpose or a reason for being. I began to realize that with the loss of my hair came the strength and the will to survive. I had determination, character, dignity and self-respect. I was no longer going to feel ashamed of not having any hair. I was going to accept the life that was given to me and be thankful for the ability to help others.

I knew my task was not going to be an easy one, but I kept telling myself that people are not necessarily shallow or ignorant because they want to be. They only fear the unknown, and out of the unknown comes ignorance. They just need a little guidance and understanding—a teacher of belief. I also decided not to wear a wig to hide behind. I began to rationalize. What is hair? Does hair make the person? Should a person's abilities be measured by the presence of or lack of hair? *It's not what's on the outside, but what's in the heart.* The first week was the hardest. I cried every morning before leaving the house. In one breath, I would ask God for strength and endurance, while in another breath, I would curse God for punishing me (condemning me to experience hair loss through an illness). I couldn't understand what I had done that was so bad. As time went on, I apologized to God for cursing him, and I began to appreciate the person I had become as a result of losing my hair.

I was always told that sometimes, in order to learn and attain the good, we would have to experience the bad to appreciate the outcome. And until recently, I thought I had conquered those negative forces (strongholds) in my life that were trying to defy my faith in God. But they have resurfaced causing me once again to question my destiny. But I must remember and understand that there is another force on earth as powerful or as impactful as God.

This is the devil's playground. He will stop at nothing to undermine God through the eyes of his children. And no matter what obstacles of negativity are put in our way, we must be strong and believe that God would let no one harm his children. But when a person repeatedly attacks another while verbally announcing their belief in God, I have to doubt the purpose of mankind and this planet we call EARTH.

Wanda Marable's beliefs as a Christian distorted my views or interpretation of what constitutes a Christian in any religion. Each and every deliberate and malicious act or statement she made was followed by her saying four words: I am a Christian. And she would state that phrase with such conviction! At any rate, I refused to wear a wig because I vowed to love myself and help others. I refused to deny who I was and denounce my heritage like so many others. I was determined not to let others control me because I vowed to take full control of my life and full responsibility for my actions. As a result of choosing to live my life in the manner stated above, I feel I was falsely terminated, and the death of my grandmother was used as a farce by Wanda Marable as stated on my exit documents.

Trying to forgive,
Ann G. Mack

> **Note Added January 19, 2009:** After reading this letter for the first time in years, I can feel the pain of my circumstances as I reflect back to my state of mind during this time. Much wiser and more knowledgeable about the importance of developing a relationship with God, I now know that many people pervert (misinterpret) God's word for the justification of their own reasoning or understanding outside of His will. In spite of their actions, I must keep a cool and level head by not allowing the adversary to drive a wedge between me and God. Exercising my faith, I should trust and have confidence in God to see me through regardless of the circumstances or the situation.
>
> **Note Added September 25, 2010:** Although very angry for quite some time about the particulars of that ordeal, I found it extremely hard to believe God would let another human being just like me (of flesh and blood) to decide my fate, especially when I had no control over the loss of my hair due to a medical condition. Nevertheless, after learning the importance of excusing (forgiving) my trespassers and releasing them, I hold no malice in my heart for Wanda Marable. In fact, I pray for her spiritual maturity and hope she has developed a relationship with God to include the presence of the Holy Spirit in her life for her personal guidance and growth.

December 15, 2006

Harpo Productions, Inc.
Attn: Ms. Oprah Winfrey
110 N. Carpenter Street
Chicago, IL 60607

Dear Ms. Winfrey,

How are you today? Fine I hope. I hope, as of this date, you not only received my first letter with the enclosures, but that you have had the opportunity to read and digest the contents. I am extremely tired but for a good reason. I have been up most nights until 2 or 3 am typing, crying, rejoicing and releasing while trying to capture everything on paper through my writing. In fact, I didn't go to bed at all for two nights straight. Amazingly, I still managed to get up by 5:30 am to prepare myself for work. I guess this is the true meaning of running on adrenalin.

Once I placed everything in the mail, as instructed to do so, by midnight before the full moon, I assumed I was finished. Apparently not so! Upon awakening Friday morning (12/8/06), I was told to write some more. Unfortunately, I didn't cover other points I was supposed to cover. So when He said everything, I guess He truly meant *everything*. And as usual, I tend to hesitate as opposed to acting quickly when called upon by God.

Not because I intend to make Him angry; I just want to make sure I'm hearing Him correctly.

On Sunday (12/10/06), I needed more confirmation. After listening to Fred Price, T.D. Jakes and one other minister personality on TV, I decided I should attend service at the Church of Two Worlds, a 100-year-old spiritualist church in the Georgetown, D.C., area where one receives healing, prayer and messages from the spirit world through mediumship and a sermon. During the service, the pastor told me, "You need to stop hesitating when given an instruction. You are on the right path and you are embarking upon another spiritual level. This is your spiritual journey."

As if I didn't cry and shout enough that morning after watching my favorite ministers, I cried some more—tears of joy. That was my answer. The service was right on point. During the sermon, the pastor spoke about asking for things and receiving them: "Ask and you shall receive; ask and it shall be given." But once we receive the gift, we don't know what to do with it or how to act upon it accordingly. I asked for discernment and to be used by God to fulfill His will, however, I didn't take into consideration what that could truly mean. So here I am! I'm like a little kid in a toy store for the very first time. The excitement of realizing my purpose is so overwhelming. The connection with God, the creator, that I've yearned for, for so long, is finally here. And the first thing I do is hesitate. Actually, I've always been connected but not like this. So here I am once again, attempting to be obedient and follow instructions as they are presented to me by God; hence, this second letter to you. It's as puzzling to me as I'm sure it is to you.

Still reluctant to follow through with the second request and disturbed by something that took place at work on Wednesday, I went to a spiritual/herbalist store in northeast Washington. Upon walking in, the older woman said, "Hello baby, it's been a long time." Low and behold, I received more messages. I was told I needed to stop panicking. The younger woman in the store said, "When you hear that voice or get an instruction, just ask, 'Are you of God?' And when it involves writing or typing, let your fingers do the work. Do not spend time trying to read and reread to edit. Because when you do that, you tire yourself out and may lose something in the translation or the opportunity to be used. Don't worry about the spelling or the flow of the content. Just put it down as it is given to you." Talk about the supernatural being real and coming to life for me right in front of my eyes. The presence of God being revealed to me like never before! What an extreme honor.

> Below are excerpts from a book I read, *The Gospel of Thomas: A Guidebook for Spiritual Practice*. I tend to keep a pad with me and write down interesting quotes or useful lessons for my life.
>
> - There is both bad and good peace. Peace is fine when it is the fruit of justice, but it is not fine when it condones injustice.
>
> - Recognize what is in front of you, and what is hidden from you will be revealed. There is nothing hidden that will not be revealed.

The Salvation Army (TSA) has had a number of claims brought against them by employees who have been subjected to discriminatory (abusive) practices over the years. By way of luck, not to mention, excelling at being deceitful as well as having adequate legal representation, The Salvation Army has managed to absolve themselves from taking responsibility for their actions. I assume that's why I've been given this task, which truly frightens me, but I fear God more. Ironic isn't it? Nonetheless, should you go online to gather information by entering: Salvation Army + lawsuits, Salvation Army + class actions, Salvation Army + officer's last name, or Salvation Army + discrimination, you will uncover what I see regularly as an employee of the Army.

However, I'm sure there have been a number of other incidences (or things) not reported by others as a result of fear or intimidation through manipulation. In fact, Patricia Poe, an African American, female employee since 1995, with an adequate food handling certificate, was passed over for a promotion to the head food handler/supervisor position in her division after the retirement of her previous supervisor, Coreen Watkins—also an African American female. Coreen's replacement was filled by a Caucasian male, Larry, who I believe is a former TSA officer. However, having nothing against Larry personally, he lacks the appropriate qualifications to be operating in the position. Therefore, the operation of the kitchen is functioning under Pat's license. Unless Larry has obtained his own within the past two weeks, this is a major violation and could result in a fine.

> These issues aren't just about race. It's about injustice. It's about people in positions of power taking advantage of those without power. It's about an organization that has put themselves in a position of playing God that contradicts who God is and the character of Jesus Christ. It's about a hidden practice that has endured for many years while others are being oppressed. If the oppressed are weak and don't know the true God, this practice reinforces untruths in teaching what Christ is not as opposed to who He is!

My previous HR replacement, Laura Ahern (a Caucasian female), called me one evening crying. Upon noticing the phone extension and the name, I neglected to answer the phone. I allowed the answering machine to pick up the call. After checking the message and indicating it was a distress call, I returned the call immediately. As Laura answered the phone, she asked, "Ann why did you leave this position? I can't seem to do anything right according to Dorrie. She seems to speak so highly of you and keeps comparing me to you whenever I seem to have difficulty completing an assignment she has given me." Not being able to contain my laughter, I laughed and said, "And all this time I thought Dorrie was a racist. She's just miserable and unhappy. It's nice to know she's just plain prejudice and not selective about it." Suddenly, Laura's crying turned into laughter. Then I responded, "Now do you feel better?" I told her to call me any time but to be careful because the phone conversations were being recorded. She thanked me and said she was told not to contact me or speak to me under any circumstances. I responded, "Yes, I'm sure. I was told who I could and could not socialize with as well. It's about control." Laura, feeling much better and relieved, said, "I wished I had contacted you before now. You are so organized and made my job very easy. You have notes on how to do things everywhere. You also have outlines of comments that took place. At first I didn't understand, but it is so clear to me now." Again, before hanging up the phone, I told her to feel free to call me any time but to be extremely careful in doing so. Then I gave her my cell phone number and said we could get away for lunch whenever she needed a friendly voice. We later learned we had a number of things in common to include being mystified by the science of metaphysics. Prior to her departure from The Salvation Army, she gave me a bracelet, which I wear proudly. It's my evil eye protector. That's how she saw me—as her evil eye protector. Talk about *blessings beyond your expectation* being bestowed upon us by God in allowing the paths of certain people to cross upon our journey.

> Organizations and people in power or people in general who continuously commit wrong acts against others and get away with it, do so because it becomes easier and easier to do so each time; the more they succeed at it, the more practice they have at accomplishing that task. It then becomes a way of life or habit. But in this case, they present themselves as a non-profit religious organization that proclaims to be faith-based (Christians or ordained ministers). Environments without grace retain and multiply unresolved sin issues. (TrueFaced, Bill Thrall and Bruce McNicol, 2003.)

I'm beginning to wonder whether or not The Salvation Army is operating as a secret society like the Illuminati and pretending to be a Christian organization. Anything's possible! And perhaps not all of the officers are aware of its true origin. At least, I would like to think that not all of them knowingly joined up with an organization that is deceiving people to obtain donations. The Salvation Army may have been established by

William Booth and his daughter under good pretense and flourished as a recognizable church, but something seems to have changed and gone extremely wrong over the years. Or perhaps I'm just being naïve. As some officers retire, they become a little more outspoken and have expressed their concerns or disapproval of what the Army represents under the surface. But should they speak against the current power structure, some of them have been known to be written up. (This information was shared with me by an officer on her way out. As previously referenced, working very late one evening, Lt. Colonel Sharon Ulyat noted I was still there and walked down to my office and had a seat. Not once did she have a casual conversation with me prior to this day. I was amazed to know she actually recognized me. At any rate, she said some things that made me wished I had captured the entire conversation as a confirmation of the growing darkness within The Salvation Army.)

> *God has given you one face, and you make yourselves another.*
>
> Hamlet, Shakespeare

Since the naming of The Salvation Army as executive in the will of a millionaire who left them millions, they have begun to campaign through TV and radio commercials for more donations by speaking to individuals about the importance of having a will. It was presented to teach you how and why you should have a will, and hearing it myself, I placed a call to receive more information. I'm sure it's legal, but something about a Christian organization campaigning in this matter leaves a bad taste in my mouth. Please see the enclosed (attachment). There was an introductory letter that accompanied the enclosure, but unfortunately, I threw it away.

On Friday, December 1, during the SAWSO Core week, a coworker delivered the devotions for that day entitled, "Alert! Immediate recall of humans." Her presentation was very moving. It touched me deeply. I jumped out of my chair and quickly walked towards the door; upon reaching the opening, the Holy Spirit was not going to allow me to contain what I was feeling. I shouted, "Oh God!" Once I made it outside the doorway, I fell on my knees and rocked back and forth as I began to cry—sobbing and praying. Hurt and in pain from what I was observing, which seemed to be getting worst with the new appointees, I yelled out, "How wicked and unChrist-like these people are! God, they are not Christians. They can't be. This is not a church; it is an illusion."

The assistant executive director, Major Patricia Kiddoo, appeared and kneeled down beside me and began to whisper, "Ann, you have to keep those comments to yourself and be careful not to let anyone hear you. I am going to pray for you and ask that you find God's peace within." I flinched because I didn't want her to touch me. I didn't want her to pray for me. So I began to speak to God out loud in hopes of overshadowing her prayer. I asked God to protect and shield me from any negativity and harm by clothing me in the entire armor of Christ, fully equipped from head to toe in the helmet of salvation, the shoes of good news, the breastplate of righteousness, the sword which is His word and the shield of faith. I continued by asking God to shield my heart. And although it was saddened, I did not want it to harden from the abuse or by what I was seeing in my surroundings that did not meet with His approval or teaching of Christianity. Nor did I want to be a cold or bitter person regardless of what I was being exposed to.

As the Major touched me, I asked God under my breath not to allow the spirit of negativity and evilness to penetrate me through her. However, I asked that He allow the Holy Spirit within me to penetrate her and transform her. I continued my prayer out loud to God: "I understand I am purposely put in this current situation to fulfill Your will. I need Your continued strength along with the wherewithal to accomplish what You want. This pain is great, and still I try to maintain a sense of professionalism while attempting to remove self and hold my ego at bay. Please continue to bind my tongue and flow through me. You know me, but they haven't a clue who I am. They don't know who I am." The Major cried out and began to say, "Ann, please forgive me. I'm sorry. I didn't know. Please forgive me for the things I've done to you in the past. Thank you for your prayer. You helped me. You helped me to remember things I had forgotten. She handed me some tissue and began to sob. Then she disappeared into the bathroom as I continued on my knees in prayer. At that moment, I knew this was confirmation of what God was requested of me! I cannot begin to tell you just how free I felt and so loved by God.

If you are aware of the recent events surrounding The Salvation Army, then you know that the current commissioner is the first black, high-ranking officer in the history of The Salvation Army. Not wanting to take anything away from the accomplishments of Commissioner Gaither, I wonder if maybe his commissioning at this time is political in nature. Prior to his commissioning and arrival to the National Headquarters, the Army had a company-wide diversity workshop training centered on the number of discrimination complaints and lawsuits that were surfacing against them. I believe this was a ploy to silence the rumors and lay it to rest in the eyes of the stakeholders. The Salvation Army's major source of funding comes from donations.

> *As a man thinketh in his heart, so is he.*
> *A man is literally what he thinks,*
> *his character being the complete sum of all his thoughts.*
>
> ***As a Man Thinketh*, James Allen**

Given the history of African Americans, there are many like O.J. Simpson and Condoleezza Rice in the world who turn a deaf ear to the number of issues surrounding our past that still hunt us as a race as long as they feel they have broken the color barriers and are able to blend in. My objective is not to belittle them or their accomplishments, because in knowing the history, I also understand it was easier for some to just go along. But at what price? Doing the right thing is never easy, but doing the right thing is better for the soul. And I can honestly say, I sleep well at night. When I'm able to get to sleep that is. I'm not sure if Commissioner Gaither is aware of all the problems within the Army or if he is just going along for the recognition and opportunity of feeling as though he has finally arrived at that level of acceptance by "White America."

Commissioner Gaither, unlike previous commissioners in his position, is personally being promoted by The Salvation Army as their front-and-center golden boy. Image is everything! He recently released a book and gave an interview to The Washington Post after November 15, 2006. And considering the current economy as well as the number of national disasters that's diverted funding directly from the Army, the commissioning of an African American does not only help dispel the rumors of discrimination and racism, it's a great marketing tool to give the illusion of change in hopes of increasing donor spending. I believe I was given November 15 as my target date to deliver the first letter to delay the release of his book until these issues were addressed. Because I hesitated, more people are being deceived while others continue to be hurt and abused by the Army's style of leadership. Perhaps the submission of the letter to the commissioner in a timely manner would have triggered some chain of events to introduce change for the better in keeping with the contents of the book before being released.

As I indicated in the my previous letter to Commissioner Gaither, I began working at The Salvation Army National Headquarters on August 21, 2000, in the Human Resources Department with a staff of two employees: my supervisor, the director of HR, and me, the personnel assistant. I witnessed a number of hiring and termination practices on the basis of nepotism, favoritism, discrimination and racism. In fact, my supervisor acknowledged she knew it must be hard for me to sit in the position of personnel assistant and see all of what I did. Employees often confided in me about things going on in their department.

I spoke to my supervisor on behalf of an individual, Linda Vetrano, after her case was presented to me. However, I was told to stay out of it. I couldn't understand how a human resources representative could knowingly allow an employee to be railroaded in such a manner and not give any thought to EEO issues or the rights of an employee being violated. Linda, on the basis of her religion, did not celebrate Christmas, birthdays, etc., and she expressed her offensiveness to a picture that hung in the hallway outside of her office. It was a familiar picture of a little girl being escorted to school by the National Guard, and above her head was the "n-word." I could see the picture in someone's home as a part of their personal or private collection, or perhaps even in an office stowed away in a corner. But not in the opening of a hallway where others may find it offensive or a painful reminder of their past! Reluctantly, the picture was removed, but not without retaliation. As previously mentioned, Linda, unfortunately, suffered from MS. The constant harassment induced a great deal of stress, and the stress hindered her health. The greater the stress, the more her health was compromised and the more time she missed from work. On the day they called her in to terminate her, she quit; the picture was remounted and returned to the hallway. I'm learning there are two kinds of people in HR: those who represent the company or organization at any cost and those who represent the employee and the organization as they evaluate the situation fairly. As time went on, it became more unbearable for me to stay at the Army or in the position of Personnel Assistant.

Never having had much of a problem in the past seeking employment, I decided it was not time for me to consider an employment change for other job opportunities. I would receive calls for scheduled interviews in addition to being called for a second overview. Always close but never close enough. My objective was to leave the Army, but my frustration with my search prompted me to apply for other possibilities within the Army. For a while, that didn't look promising. When an opening became available within the Salvation Army World Service Office (SAWSO), a separate entity of the Army that was established in 1977, I expressed an interest in the program assistant position. Upon being offered the position, I accepted it because there was an opportunity to travel overseas and assist the overseas TSA locations in implementing systems for effective financial reporting. I quickly learned that they had no intentions of allowing me to travel overseas. Although the salary was much higher than what I was earning as the personnel assistant, they misrepresented the position as a lure. In the meantime, the personnel assistant position was filled by a Caucasian female with no previous HR experience at a higher salary than what I was earning in the position.

During a meeting for SAWSO and TSA National Headquarters employees (non-officers), we learned there would be no raises or cost of living increases this year or possibly the next for some time to come. However, the officers had not curtailed their spending habits; employee increases would interfere with them enjoying the lifestyle that they have become accustomed to. In the meantime, they conducted a salary compensation survey through The Salvation Army Eastern Territory's HR and legal departments to justify not giving raises. They revised the job descriptions of each employee by demoting them in title and eliminating some of their responsibilities to meet a lower classification and salary level. Of course, the minorities within the company were affected the most.

However, in SAWSO, there is a total staff size of thirteen individuals, two officers and eleven non-officers. Nonetheless, six of the non-officer staff members have received a 6 to 8 percent increase with the exception of one who is a newly hired employee. However, the support staff, including myself, will not get anything. The head financial accountant, who was considered to be a godly and fair man, attempted to express his disappointment about management's decision not to reward us all for our performance. The retaliation for his willingness to speak up on behalf of others resulted in him being overlooked to receive an increase as well. The support staff is currently waiting to obtain a copy of our revised job descriptions in addition to a performance evaluation, which has not been conducted in nearly 10 years or more within SAWSO. And yes, the support staff of three are minorities—we're all black. Upon completion of the revisions, we will be reclassified as clerks as opposed to our current titles (program assistant, cash accountant and office manager, respectively) based on salaries in the South under The Salvation Army's Southern Territory pay scales with no emphasis on our physical location here in Washington, D.C.

Prior to this change, I was asked if I had any interest in working within the Finance Department which would give me the opportunity to receive more training outside of the secretarial field in addition to an increase in salary or extra pay based on the possibility of earning overtime. However, Lt. Colonel Daniel Starrett, the newly appointed executive director as of January 2006, has decided to hire someone from the outside to fill the position in finance who just so happens to be a Caucasian male. This disappointed me greatly and confirmed my belief of him having a racist and chauvinistic spirit; but, it also prepared for me what to expect!

Not to mention, I observed a number of discrepancies, such as personal charges on corporate credit cards that are coded as hidden, business-related expenses and expense reports showing inflated charges made by family members on the basis of nepotism. Attempting to reconcile an account involving a Psychosocial Trauma Counseling project in India and Indonesia that was awarded to my supervisor's brother-in-law, I noted and corrected calculations with a difference of over 15 to 25 thousand dollars being reported on one of the financial reports. Sadly, I happened to mention out loud that I thought it was a form of money laundering, so of course they don't want me to see anything else.

Not taking the necessary steps to oversee and properly manage the construction of some houses being rebuilt in the tsunami areas, the contractor produced less than adequate housing for an adsorbent amount. In one area, houses had been constructed and placed in a less than sound location. Should it rain, the erosion would cause the houses to slide off the land down a cliff. Because I recorded more than satisfactory minutes during a meeting held on May 23, 2006 (this is the actual day I experienced my stroke), covering the outcome of progress in the tsunami areas, I have not been asked to be present at any of the future meetings.

> The Army is extremely protective about keeping certain information private; especially that which hinges on unethical business practice. We all make mistakes; if things are not deliberately done, there should be no issue. However, attempts should be made to develop solutions. Because the Army is very adamant about staff not sharing information with family or friends, they implemented a new phone system and computer-monitoring software within the past six to seven months. All calls are recorded, and all computer activity is mirrored or replicated stroke per stroke. So not only are we careful not to say anything at our desks, we reluctantly are out of ear range in fear of being overheard talking to each other in disbelief about what we see.

As mentioned previously, Major Harden White told us during his retirement dinner in August 2005 that he was sent to SAWSO approximately ten years ago to bankrupt the division and put it out of business. However, his sense of integrity and love of God would not allow him to act in such a dishonorable and immoral manner. He refused to be the cause of employees (people) being out of a job by deliberately mismanaging funds. The politics within the Army dictates the demise of SAWSO due to the large influx of donations and government funding—money the Army feels could be directed through donations to them directly. So based on his track record for undisciplined and excessive spending, the current executive director is steering SAWSO down that path. According to his reputation, which seems to follow him, The Salvation Army International Headquarters as well as the TSA California location could not afford him. In fact, there seems to be some talk as to how long it would take for him to accomplish what he was sent to do. (See HIDDEN AGENDAS AND UNGODLY MOTIVES.)

To expedite the demise of SAWSO, Lt. Colonel Starrett employed two retired officers to conduct audits in India. Initially, failing to submit an official labor contract form and scope of work outlining their services as a protocol, they were intending to collect payment or a fee and hide the expense under other line items to avoid providing social security numbers in an effort of defrauding the government. This can easily equate to tax evasion! I wonder if this is a normal practice at other TSA locations as well. By challenging Lt. Colonel Starrett, the Finance Department objected to the continued use of the retired officers and suggested utilizing a reputable accounting firm with experienced auditors to make an adequate analysis not subject to biases or the possibility of covering up discrepancies.

Money raised for Katrina and the tsunami disasters sat in the bank for quite some time before it was actually released and utilized as it was intended, due to disagreement between the four major territories that argued about its distribution. The longer the money sits, the more interest it accrues and the more disposable income the Army has for investments or to be utilized by officers who may be skimming. Unfortunately, there are a host of financial problems in Malawi. And approximately one year ago, there were financial problems involving the Republic of Georgia project. A large amount of money was unaccounted for. As a non-profit organization, TSA has several investments, including property in various areas in and outside of the U.S. For instance, a natural gemstone or crystal store and land in India aside from their usual thrift stores. Unfortunately, in the U.S., they were reported as being selective or discriminatory concerning what geographical areas (based on zip codes) they would target or avoid in obtaining goods for their thrift stores. (A story about this was featured on the news several months ago, so I shouldn't be too surprised about foul play. However, I was very disappointed!)

Not able to conceal my voice about the unfairness and the reluctance they display in instituting change to incorporate better business practices, I'm being shunned. And my refusal to allow myself to be used as a servant of man doesn't help any either. Previously, I was asked to go to the home of a female Caucasian coworker to retrieve her personal mail while she was on vacation for a month. In addition, I was instructed to sort through her mail, open bills she referenced and make payments using checks she left for me. I indicated I would do it just this once but never again in the future, and I was told it was considered other duties as assigned. Unfortunately, they had forgotten my previous experience was in HR, but that did not keep them from making other requests:

- My supervisor indicated he should have me go shopping for clothes for his wife, which I ignored, and after his third or fourth request, he finally gave up asking.

- Given my exceptional organizational skills, my supervisor indicated he should have me come to his house to clean up and organize his closets for him and his wife. I refused.

- Given my ability to sew, which is a hobby, my supervisor wanted to bring some items in for me to alter. I suggested he take those items to the dry cleaners that provided those services for a fee.

- I've been asked to pick up various individuals from Dulles, BWI and National Airport. Upon indicating my job description did not reference chauffeuring, I was told my response was not acceptable. However, again, they forgot my previous experience was in HR.

- On occasion, I would clean the office refrigerator and microwave but discontinued when I noted it was not a shared responsibility.

- When it was noted I was the first person in the office, I was asked to have coffee ready when everyone arrived in the mornings. The first time I made coffee and they complained that it was too strong or not the right mixture in accordance to their expectations, I told them, "My mother always said, 'If you want something done right, then you should do it yourself.'"

- When my supervisor asked me to dust his office, I told him I could not understand how easy it was for them to continue to ask me to do things outside of my job description—things they would expect me to do for them, but I was sure they would not consider doing those same things for me.

I truly don't have a problem going above and beyond the call of duty, but I do have a problem with being taken advantage of or people feeling as though I should wait on them. I wouldn't even mind if there was a level of respect, integrity and honesty being demonstrated. I can't help but feel I'm going backwards in time and there's a hidden agenda or objective to teach me my place—or at least an attempt at breaking me into submission. I often find myself sitting in disbelief that at age 46, in 2006, this could be happening at a religious organization. Then I have to remember, Christianity was once used to keep us enslaved. They say history repeats itself, but slavery and indentured servitude is going back just a little too far for me. The more things change, the more they stay the same.

Sincerely,
Ann G. Mack

Trust in the Lord with all your heart and don't depend on your own understanding. Put the Lord first in everything you do and He will direct your life. Don't think of yourself as being so wise. Respect the Lord and stay away from wickedness. If you do this, it will bring health to your body and give strength to your bones. Honor the Lord with your wealth and give Him the first of your harvest. Then He will bless you, and soon your barns will overflow and your grape presses will be full. My child, don't reject the discipline of the Lord or resent being reprove by Him. The Lord takes pains to discipline those He loves, just as a loving father cares about what kind of a man who finds true wisdom and the man who grows in understanding.

~ **Proverbs 3:5-13 CW**

[For the purpose of this letter, scriptures have been taken from the Clear Word (CW) and King James (KJV) Bibles.

December 3, 2006

Commissioner Israel Gaither
The Salvation Army National Headquarters
615 Slaters Lane, PO Box 269
Alexandria, Virginia 22313

Subject: A Living Testimony

Dear Commissioner Israel Gaither,

Because I truly believe everything happens for a reason, I have a tendency to examine and analyze everything while attempting to see the spiritual connection. So please understand, this letter does not bring me any great pleasure nor is it an intended vindictive or malicious act. I am merely attempting to, reluctantly and out of obligation, obediently carry out what I feel I am being called to do! In realizing what was being asked of me, I agonized over it for days in hopes of trying to make sense of it all. I told God I wanted to be sure I was hearing Him correctly. More importantly, I wanted to be sure that it was not my ego talking!

Jude, the servant of Jesus Christ, and brother of James, to them that are sanctified by God the Father, and preserved in Jesus Christ, and called.

~ Jude 1:1

While driving to work on Friday, October 27, I received my confirmation. It hit me like a ton of bricks; I didn't know what to do. It took every ounce of energy I had within me to focus on my driving and safely continue onward without incident. I began to cry uncontrollably—sobbing like a baby as I began to speak to God. Do you realize what you are asking me to do? There could be unfavorable consequences for me! What about me? Have you given any thought to the fallout for me? What would I put in the letter? He replied, "You are going to write about you. You are going to express how your experiences have impacted you." "God, why me?" I asked. "This man is a stranger. You want me to tell the commissioner—someone I don't know other than the occasional hello, good morning or good night—if I should see him at all, my trials, tribulations and pain?" Like thunder, the reply was, "YES!"

> *Write down everything I show you.*
> *This includes what is happening now*
> *and what will happen in the future.*
>
> ~ Revelation 1:19

Fearing the wrath of God as I do, I sometimes get a little beside myself and have to ask Him to forgive me for mouthing off. It took me a while to understand I should never question Him. But oftentimes, it is so hard not to. *Trust in the Lord with all your heart and don't depend on your own understanding* (Proverb 3:5). As I drove into the garage and found a parking space, I desperately tried to compose myself in an attempt not to bring any attention to myself. It was obvious I had been crying;

I was hyperventilating. Trying to process it all, I sat in the car for quite a while in a daze. Throughout the day, I received two more confirmations in the form of spiritual gifts. Talk about mixed emotions! I was overwhelmed with joy and sadness at the same time. I just couldn't seem to get past thinking about the possible outcome, especially since I understood there could be grave consequences by man resulting from its content, but I had to trust God.

> *We know that God will make everything*
> *that happens to us in this life come out*
> *to our eventual good, as long as we trust Him and remain*
> *true to the purpose for which He called us.*
>
> *~ Romans 8:28*

Still trying to think of a way I could get around not having to compose this letter, I told myself I would just ignore the request. Perhaps I would be able to find another job to avoid it all together. No chance of that! Ignore God? Not only did I miss the actual target date of November 15, 2006, I believe I missed a blessing. The following day, on November 16, I received notification from a prospective employer indicating they had decided to go with a different candidate. All I could do was laugh. God was truly dealing with me. I was receiving affirmation after affirmation and confirmation after confirmation, not to mention, my acknowledgment of realization and revelation.

Don't be afraid of them,
for I am with you and will protect you.
I, the Lord, have spoken.

~ Jeremiah 1:8

The request was clearer than ever, but I still feared the consequences. No one seems to like whistleblowers or those who stand for truth. A person doing wrong doesn't want to be told by anyone they are being unfair. (For example: Let's look at the security guard who was instrumental in shedding some light on the Watergate scandal. That man found it very difficult to get a job of any kind after that. Instead of him being seen for his courage and good nature, he was persecuted.) When you refuse to go along with a program or system put in place by those who wish to dominate any given situation for their own selfish gain and you speak out because it goes against your morals and values system, then you become a target. Unfortunately, those that are corrupt are never satisfied with what they have; they want more, more, more.

> *One day, everything that is covered up will be uncovered and everything done in secret will be made known to everyone. There is nothing you can whisper to each other in the dark or say secretly that won't be known as if shouted from the rooftops. You can't hide things from God. I'm talking to you as my friends. Don't be afraid of what people will do to you. If you're arrested for my sake and they kill you, they've only killed your body but they can't touch your soul. The only One to fear is God, who has power over your body and soul. In the end,*

He can destroy both. Yes, you should fear Him. But don't think of Him as being harsh. Instead, look at how He cares for the sparrows. You can buy five of them for just pennies, yet your heavenly Father doesn't forget even one of them. In fact, He knows the number of hairs you have on your head. So don't be afraid. You're worth more than thousands of sparrows. I want to assure you that whoever is not ashamed to acknowledge me as his Lord, I will acknowledge him before the whole universe.

~ Luke 12:2-8

While at a gas station in Washington, D.C., on Friday, November 24, I was approached by a cab driver who greeted both me and my mother and said he needed to say something to me. As he began to speak, he said, "When I am given a thought, I just have to spit it out. You have a very kind heart. You are a beautiful woman. I am a Muslim, so I don't speak to many people. You are special and unique. You have to do what you were asked to do, or you will miss your blessings. I don't know where this is coming from, and I don't understand, but there you have it." I told him I understood perfectly and replied, "It's a message from God, and it confirms what I know I must do. Thank you very much!" If my mother was not in the car with me, the waterworks would have started. I explained my plight to my mother, and she said she understood.

I have had many conversations with God about my purpose being revealed to me. There had to be a reason for all this pain and suffering. There was no way it was all in vain. Finally, recognizing my purpose as it relates to the will of God, I now understand why I am subjected to various situations—both good and bad—based on my sense of desire for equality and social fairness across the board. Therefore, I can only assume my personality, in accordance with my handling of events as well as my willingness to address issues openly by looking at them as being a living testimony that is to be shared with others, is also a major factor. I guess my life is one, big, open book.

> *Only by the grace of God am I what I am now.*
> *His grace was not given to me in vain,*
> *because since accepting His grace,*
> *I've worked harder than any of the apostles.*
> *Yet, I'm not the one who did the work,*
> *but God's grace which was with me.*
>
> ~ 1 Corinthians 15:10

Speaking of my personality, God helped me to appreciate who I AM. A person with a deep-rooted desire to do unto others as I would have them do unto me! I believed that as long as you did what you were suppose to do by honoring man's laws as well as God's commandments, you could co-exist on this physical plane with no problems, hurt or pain; in other words, no harm would come to you. There would be no merit for retaliation or bad behavior towards you; you were safe. What a naive person I was, and to some extent, I still am. Many have tried to change me by questioning my personality and making assumptions that are not true because they fail to understand me. I also had difficulty understanding *myself*. In fact, for a long time, I couldn't understand why it was difficult for me to be mean and nasty to others even if they deserved it.

> *Above everything else in life,*
> *guard the affections of your heart;*
> *the emotional attachments you make*
> *determine the direction of your life.*
>
> ~ Proverbs 5:23

After every unkind, unfair or vindictive and malicious act imposed upon me by others, I didn't understand why my heart wouldn't allow me to react in the same manner towards them. I remember crying out to God asking Him why he gave me such a heart—a heart filled of compassion, conviction and commitment for always wanting to do what is right; a heart that wouldn't allow me to sleep or get a moment's rest when I responded or acted out of character by displaying a behavior that was less-than-favorable; a heart that refuses to allow me to compromise my sense of integrity! I believe in the correct order of things and everything that is good.

> *As surely as God lives, who refuses to give me justice*
> *and who has made me taste bitterness of soul; as long as*
> *I live and the breath of life He has given me fills my lungs,*
> *I will not speak wickedly, and my tongue will utter no deceit.*
> *I will never admit to having turned against God as you have*
> *charged. I will insist on my faithfulness to Him until the day I*
> *die. I will maintain my integrity and never let go.*
> *My conscience will not reproach me.*
>
> ~ Job 27:2-6

Every Sunday, come rain or shine, whether I wanted to go or not, my mother would make my sister and I get up and go to church. At the end of each Sunday school service, the pastor would pick an individual from each study group to interpret the lesson. For some reason, I was always selected, and I took up most of the time as the elders of the church encouraged me to deliver a summarized sermon. Shying away from the spotlight, I convinced my mother to direct my sister and I to another church. As time went on, I would drift from one church to another only to be singled out again and again to participate in one way or another—mainly speaking in front of the congregation to deliver a prayer or to read and interpret a scripture. From church to church I went, and unaware of the Power of the Holy Spirit, I would break down and cry upon entering each church. I thought because the church was a holy place, I didn't belong, and my crying was a sign of me being reproved.

> *If the Spirit of God who raised Jesus Christ from the dead dwells in you, then He who raised Christ from the dead will also raise you from the dead through the same Holy Spirit, who's already in you.*
>
> ~ Romans 8:11

I remember sharing this thought with the mother of my closest friend, Mrs. McIlwain, who grabbed me and wept as she held me close while saying, you poor child. That's the Holy Spirit! Your Spirit inside of you rejoicing because you're home each time you enter church. It's God telling you how much he loves you. You are truly blessed. You are transcending into another level—a spiritual level. Oftentimes, we forget certain memorable moments of our lives or traumatic experiences that have impacted us in some way until something triggers them and brings them to the surface. It wasn't until now that I remembered that very important moment.

I can face any situation with
Christ who gives me strength.

~ Philippians 4:13

Being an introvert and losing my hair between the age of 14 and 15 as a result of a medical condition referred to as alopecia caused me to withdraw even more. I put up invisible walls all around me. I wouldn't allow myself to attend or participate in special gatherings with family or friends; I didn't socialize with anyone at school or work for fear of having to explain my hair loss. My circle of friends was very limited. I spent many years trying to understand why God would allow such a thing to happen and often asked, "Why was He punishing me?" Hadn't He done enough damage by not hearing my prayers and granting my wish to make my father stop drinking? To a child who is told many stories growing up about a God who answers all prayers and the importance of always doing the right thing, can you understand why I would find it difficult to believe His existence when those prayers at such an early age went unanswered.

Their maidens will dance and be glad,
and so will their men, both young and old.
I will turn their mourning into gladness and
give them comfort and joy instead of sorrow and pain

~ Jeremiah 31:13

And throughout the years of my life, I was being afflicted with yet another issue—one right after the other—along with experiencing racism and discrimination. Unfortunately, discriminatory conduct and deliberate discriminatory actions committed by consciously prejudice individuals are often hidden (masked) and orchestrated to appear unintentional in the workplace while the oppressed are intimidated into believing they are overly paranoid, exaggerating or blowing things out of proportion. In essence, they are manipulated into believing that what they see, they don't see or what they feel, they don't feel.

Moral decay will be so prevalent that
most people won't even know what love is,
but those who stand firm until the end will be saved.

~ Matthew 24:12-13

My mother raised my siblings and me with good values, morals and beliefs. She always told us, you should never stare at anyone; it's not polite. If you don't have anything good to say then don't say anything at all. No matter what, respect your elders. Always treat the devil with kindness. Honor the Ten Commandments and pray. And as long as you went to school and obtained a good education, everything else would fall into place, and you will be able to find a good job with no problems. However, she never prepared us for racism or the effects of discrimination!

As a civilian with the federal government working for the navy from August 1979 through January 1983, I went home in tears every evening. I was the center of racial jokes and discrimination almost every day. I found it hard to believe that men in uniform, dressed to represent the United States, had no regard for the feelings of another human being—a woman. Me. Such cruelty and abuse! God forbid I should leave any food on my desk; they would pour it out and leave the empty container or wrapper in the center of my desk to taunt me. One day, I returned from the restroom to find they had pierced a metal letter opener through my doughnut.

While I prepared to leave the office for the day, they would wait until I had gotten halfway down the corridor towards the exit doors and would deliberately call me back to give me something else to do to delay my departure by one to two hours just because they could. This was a Friday ritual. I was very young and didn't have any knowledge of how to address the issue with anyone. Who would listen? My pride would not allow me to let them see just how upsetting their actions were towards me or how I was affected. And I definitely would not give them the satisfaction of seeing me cry.

When opportunities for advancement presented itself, I would never hesitate to apply for the position. Each time, I was either told I didn't have the experience or I needed more education. There were times when my application was intentionally disregarded, lost or misplaced without a thought. However, I was always given the task of training the new person in the position I was told I didn't have the qualifications to perform. As I obtained more knowledge or education, the qualifying criteria for the position would change. Eventually, I resigned from the government and went into the private sector. Unfortunately, I encountered some of the same problems.

> *Your work won't be easy for you,*
> *because you'll be like sheep walking in the midst of wolves.*
> *You must be wise as snakes and innocent as doves.*
>
> ~ Matthew 10:16

Little did I know this was just the beginning! My greatest challenge, so it seemed, came about when I was terminated from a job in 1994 because the new leadership that had resulted from a buyout or merger could not deal with me being bald and not wearing a wig. It was not the "appropriate" image for an employee at a healthcare organization. I made a conscious decision not to use the wig as a crutch by attempting to eliminate it in 1988. I truly found out just how cruel and abusive people could be. They would make all sorts of comments. And one person actually had the nerve to approach and ask me what I would do if he smacked me upside my head. I guess I should be grateful he didn't act on it before verbalizing it. Talk about having to develop a strong exterior as well as a strong interior. Walking out of my apartment in the mornings became an unwelcomed event. I would cry each morning in preparing to face the world without my wig. I was determined not to allow society to dictate how I was going to live my life.

> *Cast all your anxiety on him*
> *because he cares for you.*
>
> ~ 1 Peter 5:7

According to my immediate supervisor, they assumed I was shaving my head to make a militant statement, and she was given the task of expressing to me how my appearance was perceived in the eyes of white people. Man looks on the outward appearance, but the Lord looks on the heart (1 Samuel 16:7). They failed to realize, it was not by choice. Nor did they understand that my refusing to hide my baldness was the ending of a chapter in my life that marked the beginning of a new one for me!

> **A Special Note:** Recognizing the impact of my hair loss, I wrote a letter in December 1988 or in the early part of 1989 to the *Oprah Winfrey Show* asking them to consider airing a show that would be instrumental in educating her viewers and others about alopecia since she had such a worldwide audience. I received a response in March of 1989 thanking me for the idea but received no other correspondence about the final decision. I think being involved directly somehow would have been good therapy for me. However, ironically, the topic was aired on the *Oprah Winfrey Show*—I believe during my employment with the company that terminated me or shortly after my termination. One of my coworkers saw it and taped it for me. What a blessing; I cried throughout the whole segment of that show while watching it! Unfortunately, I cannot seem to locate that tape today, but it was truly an emotional and inspirational liberating moment for me. (A copy of the response is included in the Appendix).

Because I had spent many years in pain over losing my hair and trying to work out how to handle it, I resented God for allowing a person of flesh and blood—no different from me—to decide my fate; especially, after I had finally accepted my hair loss and the possibility of it never growing back. This ordeal not only caused me to question God but the true meaning of Christianity. After every abusive, unkind or unfair statement or act made by my supervisor, she would claim to be a Christian. Can you imagine what that did to me? I sat down and took a long hard look at myself as I began to analyze my life in accordance to the things I had experienced up to that point. Could I have been wrong all these years about the true nature of Christianity as well as the character of a person who proclaims to be a Christian? This was the very first wrongful action directed at me by someone who actually confessed to being a Christian. In seeking to research this information, I wasn't sure of what source to use.

False christs and false prophets will proclaim themselves.
The devil will give them power to work miracles,
miracles which will almost convince
even the righteous. I'm telling you all this
ahead of time so you won't be deceived.

~ Matthew 24:24

Unfortunately, during this stage of my life, in spite of all my previous biblical lessons, I wasn't used to using the Bible as a reference tool in the same manner as I would reference a dictionary or other books for knowledge in an effort to increase my education or gain wisdom. So the Holy Spirit intervened. While sitting at my computer, I began to type out a letter to God explaining how I was feeling.

> August 28, 1993
>
> Dear Lord,
>
> Every day I am tested by the DEVIL! Sometimes in the image of himself and sometimes in the image of a Christian. But I must often remember that he is not a Christian of the world, nor is he a Christian as we know him. He does not come before me as a follower or worshiper of You but merely as a tool of the Devil to defy my faith and belief in You. You brought me through many trials and tribulations. You have stood with me through the tests of time. For now I am strong and I will survive.
>
> Thanks for Your guidance and the will to survive.
>
> Ann G. Mack
>
> ***Sometimes trials come on every hand,***
> ***but I feel like going on!***

After the completion of that letter, I couldn't believe I had actually typed what I was reading. I began to cry because I knew that was a message *to* me and *for* me. Utilizing my book sense,

I attempted to define the word Christian that denotes "Christ-like." Determined to push on although I was in so much pain, I went to work each morning and worked as diligently as I had since the day I was hired, only to receive many more months of on-the-job harassment and abuse. In the end, because I had refused to give them my resignation as previously requested, they developed a reason to terminate me.

Unfortunately, it took me a while to realize that my being terminated marked the beginning of yet another chapter bringing me closer to God, and through this ordeal, He taught me the meaning of wilderness. During this period in my life from January 1994 through June 1995, I was forced to do a lot of soul searching, praying, humbling, crying and reading.

Everyone who tries to appear great will one day be humbled, and everyone who humbles himself will one day be honored.

~ Luke 14:11

◆

While in the Wilderness, Jesus fasted for forty days and He became extremely hungry. Then the devil confronted Him by disguising himself as an angel from heaven surrounded with light. He told Jesus that now that His fast was over, His Father had given Him permission to use His divine power to turn one of the desert stones into bread. "If you are the Son of God, that should be no problem," Satan said. But, as famished as He was, Jesus recognized who was tempting Him to save Himself. So He answered, The Scripture teaches that man is not to put physical survival before obedience to God's word. I will not use my divinity to ease my lot on earth.

~ Matthew 4:2-4

January 7, 1994:	My grandmother passed away.
January 8:	I received an emergency telephone call from an EMT who was calling to tell me my father had suffered a severe asthma attack, and they were rushing him to the hospital. Because he was unable to speak and I was listed as the next of kin in an emergency situation, I needed to meet them at the hospital.
January 25:	I was terminated and given a written justification for my dismissal that read I was being terminated because management believed I lied about the death of my grandmother. But as my supervisor handed the documents to me, she contradicted the written statement by saying she knew my grandmother died.
August 11:	My 26-year-old brother passed away due to complications from AIDS. Unfortunately, he had received approximately three blood transfusions before he told us, his family, he had AIDS. And because

I was still distraught about the previous events in my life, I didn't spend time with him near the end of his life. Prior to his death, he called me from the hospital to tell me he knew something was really wrong with me because he had been hospitalized for nearly a month and his big sister still had not come to see him. He called to console me and tell me how much he loved me. He told me how much he admired me and looked up to me although he had never expressed this to me before. He told me how proud of me he was about how I handled not having any hair and other issues I had encountered. He told me he learned a lot from me. He also said he knew that whatever problems facing me at the moment, I would get through it. Then he told me he understood I may have pneumonia, and because I didn't have any health insurance, he was going to call my mother to tell her to give her his bankcard and pin number so I could get the medical attention I needed.

November 28: My grandfather passed away. He was the husband of my grandmother that passed away in January.

December 1:   Preparing to travel to North Carolina for my grandfather's funeral, I was involved in a car accident that resulted in a total lost of my vehicle. This ordeal threw me into an immediate mental shock.

March 30, 1995:   Preparing to get married and move into a home that didn't exist, I gave up my apartment that I'd occupied since 1986 to move in with my mother. In addition to everything else above, within my wilderness, my vulnerability allowed me to confide in a man I believed was sent from God in answer of a prayer. His name was David Christian. I later learned how easy it is to be deceived by those who disguise themselves as angels from Heaven who are surrounded with light; however, I got out before being tangled in his weave of deception. This lesson not only confirmed the importance of Matthew 4, it taught me the true meaning of the laying on of hands (that's another story for another chapter).

Lay hands suddenly on no man,
neither be partaker of other men's sins; keep thyself pure.

~ 1 Timothy 5:22

Trying to function through it all, I was like a walking zombie with no feeling of life—just going through the motions and having what my former pastor would refer to as a pity party. Little did I know or recognize that I was in a deep depression until God said, enough is enough. God reminded me of an earlier conversation I had with him. I told him that losing my hair and accepting that loss would be the greatest challenge of my life. And if I could accomplish that great victory, I felt I could deal with anything I would ever have to face in life. Talk about challenges! I began to cry and laugh at the same time while telling God I understood. And then the phone rang.

> *Accept the lessons He's trying to teach you,*
> *and lay up His words in your heart.*
>
> ~ Job 22:22

It was a former supervisor, Connie Wright, inviting me to meet her for lunch. Over the years, she had grown to be a good spiritual friend. We met at a nearby restaurant in Chinatown. Upon my arrival, she handed me a Bible and told me she wanted me to read the book of Job. Can you imagine my response? I replied, "I have a Bible!" "Yes," she said, "but I want you to have my Bible." "Why?" I asked. She responded, "Because you remind me of Job, and it would be such a blessing if you would take my Bible to read Job again, in its entirety. Ann, you are very special and you don't realize just how special you are. God selects those who are able to handle certain situations and uses them as living testimony to others. That's how I see you. I don't know anyone who could have gone through what you have and survive it all like nothing has happened. Yes, I'm sure you're hurting, but you haven't given up. That's the beauty of it all!" While trying to hold back the tears, I retreated to the bathroom to get myself together so I could return to enjoy my lunch.

> *I still feel bitter against God for allowing all this to happen. He seems to be against me in spite of my groaning. If only I knew where to find Him and how to go where he is, I would state my case before Him and fill my mouth with arguments in my favor. I would want Him to answer me and I would carefully consider what he had to say.*
>
> ~ Job 23:2-5

After reading Job as I had promised, I set out to find another church home and was later introduced to the Holy Christian Missionary Baptist Church for All People by a dear friend, Janet Galloway. Janet not only offered to give me a ride that first Sunday, she invited me to attend dinner immediately following the service to meet her relatives who were gathering to greet another family member (Rebe) who had traveled from Texas to Washington, D.C. While sitting around the table, we engaged in a conversation about hair. Not knowing one relative (Gwen) was undergoing chemotherapy, and my being oblivious to the side effect which is hair loss, felt comfortable and openly encouraged to discuss my hair loss as well as a number of prejudicial issues that impacted my life. As I began to share my hurt and pain as humorously as I could, Gwen jumped up from the table and ran upstairs. Still unaware of what was going on, Rebe thanked me for my testimony. She then proceeded to say, when you walked in the door, I knew my sister was going to be okay. I can drive back to Texas and not worry about her! God told me who you were and what I needed to do. He sent you here to help and now I need to help you. She pulled out her Bible and shared her spiritual gifts; the gift of healing, teaching and deliverance.

*Christ through the Holy Spirit gave us
the gifts that God determined.
Some were gifted to be apostles, others to function as prophets,
still others to be evangelists and others to be pastors or teachers.*

~ Ephesians 4:11

As she flipped through the pages of the Bible, she began to speak to me about my character and explained the following: Spiritual growth is a continuous process! Bad things happen to good people no matter how many measures you take to avoid trouble. It is not your understanding of the situation or encounter that is important, it's God's will and your purpose for being, which may often bring about discipline through pain. You despise hypocrisy which is why you haven't been baptized yet. You believe in truth and fairness. You value sincerity. You are a special and unique person. You think you need to be perfect to get baptized. No one is perfect, and God's been trying to reach you for quite some time. It's time for you to stop running and fulfill your purpose. You have to be careful whom you eat from. You are a part of a spiritual war. Satan will stop at nothing to prevent you from obtaining your blessings. As she touched me, I began to shake, and then there was a sense of warmth, calmness and peace. I left feeling overjoyed about my experience and empowered. She told me she knew of my difficulty determining the meaning of the scriptures as it is written in the King James Version. She encouraged me to look around for a Bible to reference with an English translation of hard truths. To put me back on the path that God had intended for me, she recommended some reading material to assist me with my journey for healing and understanding. She also told me, *as more are needed, you will be drawn to them because God knows your personality for seeking knowledge through books. However, He has already given you what you need.*

So, for a greater understanding, I began reading the Bible as well as the following books as instructed:

- By Rebecca Brown:
  - *He Came to Set the Captives Free*
  - *Prepare for War*
  - *Becoming a Vessel of Honor*
- By T. D. Jakes:
  - *Help Me, I've Fallen and I Can't Get Up*
  - *Water in the Wilderness*
  - *Why? Because You are Anointed*
- *The Color Complex* by Kathy Russell, Midge Wilson and Ronald Hall
- *Living with Racism* by Joe R. Feagin and Melvin P. Sikes

That night, I had the most peaceful sleep I had had in a long time. I slept like a baby and woke up the next morning feeling rejuvenated alive.

> *I want you to have the same inner peace that I have; not the kind of peace that the world gives, but that abiding peace with the Father that only I can give. Don't be afraid of Him, because He loves you.*
>
> ~ John 14:27

In having a better understanding of my wilderness, a place where all the things that cause you to stumble in your walk with God are destroyed, I believe the Lord—dealing with each one of us differently—purposely leads us to the wilderness by allowing a chain of events to take place, thus isolating us while bringing us to a quiet place to make us humble while strengthening us in preparing us to fulfill His will. God does not kill off people to punish another, but can you imagine what it is like to get hit with one adversity after the other, which includes the death of three loved ones in the same year before you have had the opportunity to fully recover from one to the next? I guess this is what is truly meant by the phrase, "That which does not kill you, makes you stronger."

> *For we wrestle not against flesh and blood, but against principalities, against powers, against the rulers of the darkness of this world, against spiritual wickedness in high places.*
>
> ~ Ephesians 6:12

On June 30, 1995, I got baptized for the second time. For some reason, I believed that things would get better following my baptism; my trials and tribulations would be over. However, I quickly learned that seeking God does not cover our heads from the storm nor arm our hearts against the darts and daggers of many a pain, anxiety and care. The disturbance that forms around us is a very small matter if there be a better thing, such as rest within.

> *When I saw what was happening, I remembered what the Lord had said, John is baptizing people with water, but you will see people baptized with the Holy Spirit.*
>
> ~ Acts 11:16

In 1998, after leaving a company called KEI, I found myself unemployed for the third time in my life. I fell on my knees and yelled out to God, "Now what? I do not want to see any harm bestowed upon anyone, but my pain is so great that just once I would like to see those who hurt me get hurt in the same way. What lesson(s) are you trying to teach me? I have gone through this three times! There are people who have not experienced unemployment—not once. What didn't I get the first and second time around that I have managed to miss again? God, I refuse to believe that everyone in the world is so wicked and evil. Hope keeps me alive! I cannot allow myself, even at the direction of a supervisor in hopes of keeping my job, to display a character that is mean, relentless and cruel to others. Being mindful not to make God angry, although I was angry, I told Him I needed some answers.

Strangely enough, you'll find yourself blessed even when people insult you, persecute you and lie about you because you have accepted me. When this happens, be glad, because it shows that your name is written in heaven and that your reward will be waiting for you there. Remember, the prophets were treated no differently. If you hold on to these values, you will be the salt of the world. But if you let go of these values, you'll be like tasteless salt. What good is tasteless salt? The only thing you can do with it is to throw it out on the road to walk on. With these values, you'll be like a city built on a hill, visible to everyone who passes by.

~ Matthew 5:11-16

Attempting to sit quietly in hopes of receiving an answer, my mind wandered, and I remembered the following incident:

Claudia Romero is a bright and spiritual young lady who, like me, was seeking to know God and had many questions. She was working on obtaining her citizenship and going to school at night in addition to continuously working on improving her English. I was given the unofficial task of supervising her and one other person, which served two purposes. Based on the employment laws, a person in a supervisory position could be classified as being exempt, meaning not eligible for overtime. However, by it not being written or disclosed in my job description, they not only got away with not paying me overtime, but they paid me a lower salary compared to a managerial position. And unfortunately, I was just too tired to fight it. It was easier to put it out of my mind.

Nevertheless, because I had many ideas about organizing the personnel files that were in disarray for quite some time prior to my employment there, the responsibility was given to me. If the HR Department (a staff of approximately nine to ten employees) as a whole were committed to working together as a team, this task would have been accomplished in record time. There were files everywhere—complete and incomplete—on the floor and on top of the filing cabinets as well as in the filing cabinets. I was instructed by my supervisor, the daughter of a minister, to use pressure as a tactic of forcing Claudia to give up her weekends to come in and work on the filing system every weekend to meet the target completion date as discussed between the director of HR and the CEO. I never understood how people in authoritative positions who haven't a clue about the nature of a job and how much time it would actually take to accomplish it realistically could make decisions and not consult those who actually do the work.

Unfortunately, my eagerness to treat people in the manner in which I would want to be treated and voice that openly always seem to get me in trouble. For some reason, I felt the need to tell a woman, my supervisor, whom I had witnessed pick up an office chair in the middle of a meeting and throw it across the room, that I wasn't brought up that way. And more importantly, my character and sense of integrity would not let me conduct myself in such a manner. I could not supervise an individual in the same manner in which I was being supervised. Before I could stop myself, the damage was done. If she could breathe fire, I would have been toast.

> *So just communicate with people honestly by letting your "Yes" mean yes and your "No" mean no. Taking an oath to confirm what you say is one of the devil's ways to create suspicion between people.*
>
> ~ Matthew 5:37

◆

> *Treat other people the way you would like them to treat you. That's what the law and the prophets are all about. Don't follow the crowd. The pathway to destruction is wide and well traveled.*
>
> ~ Matthew 7:12-13

Approaching Claudia, I explained my position and indicated I would come in with her on the weekends to help. Although she appreciated my offer, she was concerned about me; I was exempt from receiving overtime. I told her my conscience would not allow me to put that burden of completing that task solely on her. And any good supervisor would not expect the person they are responsible for supervising to do what they themselves are not willing to do. I told her I thought it should be a team effort; we could get more done. She hugged me and asked if all working environments were this hostile. Searching for a positive response, I told her it was impossible for me to give her hope when I was lacking it myself. At that moment, I felt as though I had failed her as well as God. Not wanting to cry in front of her, I excused myself and went into the bathroom to pray. That following Saturday, she gave me a book entitled, *Jesus CEO: Using Ancient Wisdom for Visionary Leadership* by Laurie Beth Jones.

> *Admit our faults to each other and confess your sins to God. Pray for each other, and if it's God will, the sick among you will be healed. The fervent prayer of the righteous man has tremendous power.*
>
> ~ James 5:16

Remembering that small detail, which brought us closer together as friends, made me want to call Claudia to see how she was doing, and then I heard a voice say, "school." I cried out, school! Yes, you are your happiest when you are learning. How do you suppose I do that with no job and no money? At least not enough to pay for school, rent and groceries! I thought, Okay, because I had a habit of starting things and not finishing them before going on to the next project or I would get tired, give up and quit, I made God a promise. I promised I would not only register for school, I would continue the curriculum with no interruption until I obtained my degree. And then God said, "Where is that notice you received a couple of weeks ago?" I replied, "What notice?" "The one you received about a free tuition program for D.C. residents." Upon locating the notice, I followed through by obtaining more information pertaining to the qualifying criteria for the program. With much resistance that centered on bureaucracy and neglectful politics, I wrote many letters outlining the numerous problems I was encountering to Mayor Anthony Williams and the Director of the Department of Employment Services.

Side Note: If you tell me a program exists by extending an offer and I meet all of the qualifying criteria, don't give me the run around when you had no intentions of keeping your word. Why bother to send out the notices? Fortunately, it didn't take me long to figure out how the system works. A need is determined through a study or analysis and written up as a formal justification. A budget is determined and generated. If the budget is not utilized as initially set up, it will be redistributed and used in other areas or cut the following year. More likely, it will serve as hefty bonuses for upper management (selfish gain).

Towards the end, I was indirectly awarded approximately $8,000 from the D.C. government to continue my education. From my understanding, I struck a nerve and made a lot of people angry. I had previously completed two years towards a business management degree at the University of the District of Columbia (UDC) and had only two more years to go. Acknowledging God was making a way for me to attend school with no financial burden, I had to make good on my promise. The next objective was finding employment with those who valued higher education in addition to encouraging that growth.

Think before you speak and don't make any rash promises to God that you can't keep. God is in heaven and owns the whole universe. You're only a creature living on one little planet. Recognize your place, be humble and don't play games with God by making promises you don't intend to keep.

~ Ecclesiastes 5:2

When I received the offer of employment from The Salvation Army National Headquarters (TSA-NHQ) as the HR assistant, I was enrolled as a full-time student at UDC. Assuming this new venture was God's answer to a prayer and Him smiling down on me, I broke down in tears and thanked God for making this possible. I saw this as being an end to over-controlling supervisors (or managers) who abuse their power of authority by subjecting their staff to double standards and unfair treatment of "do as I say and not as I do" in addition to the invisible color barriers and limitations that minorities are told no longer exist. Finally, I had a position with a company or organization that would acknowledge and recognize my talents and skills while promoting me and compensating me accordingly and not holding me back due to their prejudices or stereotypical prejudgments based on me being a woman or black. This would be a respectable working environment managed and operated by those who value biblical principles. I felt truly blessed and honored. Having some previous association with or knowledge of TSA, I was overjoyed to have this opportunity to work at an establishment that made such a wonderful impression on my life when I was younger.

During grade school, I was one of the first groups of children to attend the Harriet Tubman Elementary School upon its completion in the late 1960s. Having the privilege during this time to attend a school that was named after one of the most important women in black history also afforded me the opportunity to learn about my heritage. The teachers at this school made sure they not only educated us about English, reading and arithmetic, they gave us an enormous amount of information about us as a race of people and enlightened us about the plight of black people in America. They taught me to be proud of who I am and to appreciate the accomplishments of my ancestors—those who made numerous attempts to institute change.

> **Side Note:** Although very young at the time, I actually remember the death of Martin Luther King and the riots that immediately followed the news of his demise as it spread across the nation.

> I have a dream that one day this nation will rise up and live out the true meaning of its creed: "We hold these truths to be self-evident that all men are created equal." I have a dream that one day on the red hills of Georgia, the sons of former slaves and the sons of former slave owners will be able to sit down together at the table of brotherhood… Let freedom ring from every hill and molehill of Mississippi. From every mountainside, let freedom ring…when we let it ring from every village and every hamlet, from every state and every city, we will be able to speed up that day when *all* of God's children, black men and white men, Jews and Gentiles, Protestants and Catholics, will be able to join hands and sing in the words of the old Negro spiritual: *Free at last! Free at last! Thank God Almighty, we are free at last!*
>
> ~ Dr. Martin Luther King, Jr.

Not having any other race of people to identify with in my community, the first contact I had with other races came about through school: white teachers who traveled outside of their comfort zone to be educators in black communities and TSA officers or volunteers who were committed to their mission by offering their services as tutors. These officers and volunteers worked at a community recreation center near the Harriet Tubman Elementary School. Going to this center filled me with much warmth and was the highlight of my day; they provided moral support or just a kind word.

Starting my position at TSA on August 21, 2000, the adjustment from being a full-time to a part-time student while still managing to hold a 12 to 16 credit class load a semester was overwhelming and challenging. In fact, the position I actually applied for was a part-time, secretarial/administrative assistant position. But, given my previous experience, I was asked to consider the open position in human resources. Considering my ability to be direct and upfront, a trait I developed much later in life resulting from my life experiences and one that many people lack nowadays, I openly expressed my desire to finish school and shared information pertaining to the promise I made to God. I indicated that although school was my number-one priority, my studies would not interfere with my performance or prevent me from successfully carrying out the responsibilities of the HR position. However, I needed to leave on time each evening to make it to class, which is why, initially, I was seeking part-time employment. Therefore, my agreed upon hours were from 8:00 am to 3:30 pm.

> **Side Note**: Upon registering for school and attempting to continue my education over the years, I always had difficulty being allowed to leave work on time to make it to my classes. Advancing my career and accomplishing such

a great feat as getting my degree was always compromised if it was to be done through the week; overbearing supervisors wanted me to know they were in charge. This was extremely frustrating and always reminded me of that old adage of being set up to fail.

Human nature is a wonderful thing! Early on, there were no problems or conflicts, but issues developed as time went on. I began to get last-minute work requests between 3:00 and 3:15 pm. Sound familiar? I did my job well—too well. I believe I did my job better than what was initially expected. In fact, I received a compliment: I don't understand how you are able to do all of what I give you when the two individuals before you always had difficulty. There was some amazement about my ability to complete my work assignments in a timely manner; not to mention, I was staying on top of my schoolwork. The more I did, the more work I received. It is not humanly possible for anyone to work at a pace that was set for me on a daily basis. I was like the energizer bunny. Feeling frustrated about feeling the need to consistently prove myself after two years, I needed a change. My mental psyche was being affected, and I was starting to lose faith.

Feeling distraught and physically, mentally and spiritually drained, I would retreat to the restroom often to engage in prayer and conversations with God. God, not again! I am truly not understanding this. I thought I was finally home—a place of employment I could retire from. Why am I here? I'm not liking what I see. Are these really Christian folks? Please come rescue me. Tell me something, please.

> *Be tolerant of one another and forgive*
> *whatever grievances you have against each other,*
> *even as Christ has forgiven you.*
>
> ~ Colossians 3:13

The world is a very diverse place comprised of many people with different cultural backgrounds who pose an array of beliefs. Unfortunately, mainly out of fear or due to the unknown, we have allowed ourselves to make assumptions about people, ideas or things that may or may not be correct, but we apply these notions to our beliefs. And these beliefs contribute to the development of our character. If we are open to the possibility that some of our belief systems were formed based on improper thinking or information, there may be a need for an overhaul of these beliefs, and change is warranted. After many years of adapting to a particular belief system, some of us have difficulty incorporating change and are not willing to replace fiction or a myth by fact. We, therefore, feel the need to validate our negative beliefs and attempt to make them true by manipulating the situation or people for justification. We just have to be willing to unlearn to relearn and let go of preconceived belief systems.

You don't need to accept the implied limitations of your past, your education or the social conditions in which you were born. Too often, we accept the limitations of our past or the ones that are imposed upon us by others.

After obtaining my degree in December 2002, I applied for and was offered a program assistant position within the

Salvation Army World Service Office (SAWSO). This position not only offered a higher salary, it introduced me to missionary work, and I was given a number of challenging tasks; something I thrive on. Have you ever noticed just how energized you feel when you start a new position? You jump right in; you willingly participate in discussions and offer suggestions for implementing systems to make the office run more smoothly until you are greeted with resistance and possible resentment. Some people don't like organizational change and feel you are overstepping or overreaching. They don't necessarily want you to use your brain, so they begin to give you assignments (like things outside of your job description), while telling you they fall under the category of other duties as assigned, that dictate their view of where you should be. And when I verbally express or point out the directed unfairness, the reply is always, "Life is not fair." My mother used to always say, "Two wrongs don't make it right."

> *Jesus looked at them and said, The important thing for you to be careful about while I'm gone is not to be deceived. Many will come and preach in my name, claiming to be sent by me, and others will even claim the right to take may place. Many people will be deceived by them, not knowing which way to go. Before the end comes, there will be an increasing number of indescribable wars and threats of wars, but don't be discouraged or give up your faith, because God has to let some of these things happen.*
>
> ~ Matthew 24:4-6

Coming into The Salvation Army, I was given a document that stated, I am signing this document in acknowledgment of where I work as being a church, and I will conduct myself accordingly. I can't begin to tell you how warm that made me feel. What a blessing! It actually reinforced my belief of fair and equal treatment enjoyed by all and an opportunity for nurtured spiritual growth. Spiritual growth was obtained but not in the way I had expected. It came at the expense of hurt and pain mainly from employees and officers in authoritative positions who, contrary to what I signed, did not conduct themselves as if they were in a church. Concluding my first year at The Salvation Army, I was depressed by the actions of those I thought should have taken the concept of Christianity more seriously. And yet I managed to continue for six years—not because I wasn't trying to leave, but because this is where God wanted me to be!

In 1989, the vice president of underwriting called me into his office and asked me to take a seat. He began to say, "Ann, you need to learn to slow down and pace yourself. When I give you something to do, please take your time. Don't rush!" Looking at him in utter amazement, I had to pinch myself as he continued, "Yes, I know you can't believe I just said what I did. Unfortunately, you will run into managers and supervisors (people in general) in various positions at other corporations who will take advantage of your good-natured work ethics and willingness or need to excel at everything you do to get the job done. I'm telling you this for your own good. I appreciate you and thank you for trying so hard. They will attempt to use you up and refuse to compensate you for all you do while, at the same time, paying someone else more for less than half of the amount of work and effort you produce and still expect more from you." Talk about a heart-to-heart talk! As years went on, I found he was completely right. However, I didn't think that would be true here.

> *Next, I took a careful look at all the injustice and oppression that goes on in this world. Those who are oppressed cry out for help, but no one seems to pay attention. They have no power to change their situation, because power is in the hands of the oppressors. When I saw this, I realized that those who have died are better off than those who are still alive. Looking at it another way, I concluded that those who haven't been born yet are even better off than those who have died or those who are still alive, because they've never seen the injustice and oppression that goes on in this world.*
>
> ~ Ecclesiastes 4:1-3

Susan Watson, a former employee who was also a former officer, attempted to acknowledge these concerns pertaining to behavior being contradictory to the biblical doctrine through a sermon. She was suspended and later terminated, I assume, on the grounds of being deemed insubordinate. Is ministering not the delivery and revealing of truth?

> *A ruler delights in honest people and values a man who speaks the truth.*
>
> ~ Proverbs 16:13

Abuse can best be defined as any disregard for one's rights, individuality, spiritual beliefs or privacy. My tolerance level for pain has always been very high, however, the mental psyche can only take but so much, and when there is a drain on the spirit, disease manifests. I never truly realized just how much the body, mind and spirit are impacted by multiple attacks of abuse. In fact, I've received so much abuse within my six-year tenure at TSA while trying to maintain a level of professionalism, thus in an attempt to remove self (ego) out of the mix (i.e., not take things personal), I became numb. On May 23, 2006, I experienced a Transient Ischemic Attack (T.I.A.), otherwise known as a mild stroke, which medically put me at risk for the possibility of having a full stroke. However, I don't intend to claim a full stroke or sickness of any kind!

A man's spirit and his will to live sustains him when he's sick, but if that goes, then all hope is gone.

~ Proverbs 18:14

When an organization schedules a mandatory meeting introducing a new concept or idea referred to as "Doing the Most Good" and takes that opportunity to discuss the importance of their staff (officers and non-officers) not sharing any information with outsiders (including their family and friends) about what goes on within that religious (faith-based) organization, it sends a clear message. Instead of recognizing the low morale and attempting to uplift them by offering hope, the organization is more concerned about the image of the company than they are about the staff. Where's the humanity? Charity starts at home. People do not leave organizations; they leave leaders.

> *Nothing you do is a secret. Your heavenly Father knows everything, and whatever you do for Him will be made known. You can't hide a thing from Him. Everything you do will be brought out into the open.*
>
> ~ Luke 8:17

I'm learning that spiritual growth, indeed, is continuous but not impossible. People are human beings, each possessing a spirit and a soul. God has given us each free will: a choice to be good (righteous) or bad (evil). A church is a building or a shell that's operated as a business and filed on record with the government as being a non-profit, religious organization or institution that is managed by people who proclaim to be Christians. The word Christian denotes being Christ-like—possessing conviction, a strong constitution and striving to do what's right at all times. All too often, people are quick to address themselves by titles of prestige and power that fail to coincide with the needed character and willingness to truly fulfill the commitment of that position. Religion is a system of beliefs or guidelines that governs the manner in which one worships; it has nothing to do with being spiritual. You cannot limit the Holy Spirit.

> *The angels were singing, "Holy, holy, holy is the Lord God of hosts. The earth is full of His glory."*
>
> ~ Isaiah 6:3

In accordance to what I have observed, The Salvation Army is operated as a business in comparison to a Roman empirical system with plantation tendencies. In addition, the excessive spending by some to meet personal wants, not needs, seems to display a loss of discipline in addition to a lost perspective of the meaning to "although in the world, not of the world." There is an invisible line that exists to represent the separation of church and state.

Love not the world, neither the things that are in the world. If any man love the world, the love of the Father is not in him. For all that is in the world, the lust of the : but he that doeth the will of God abideth for ever.

~ 1 John 2:15-17 KJV

God, Jesus Christ himself, led by example with compassion, commitment and truth. He treated everybody the same without prejudice or discrimination. Being a Christian takes work, but it's about being committed to doing the right thing and willing to change as well as being able to admit when you are wrong. It's not life that's not fair; it's the people in the world who were given life as well as possessing the gift to give life that aren't fair. Actions speak louder than words, and sermons are best taught by displaying them; seeing is believing. I'm sure God did not intend for His children, who call themselves Christians, to operate in a position of authority in the name of Christianity to abuse that power for their own selfish gain while oppressing others or subjecting them to unjust behavior because they can. I truly do not understand how there really is no limit to how much human beings can hurt each other as well as themselves and not give it a second thought. People can be so cruel, relentless and unconscionable. When my spirit is vexed, my soul cries out!

> **Paul T. P. Wong, PhD, Clinical Psychologist:** Why do the wicked prosper, while the innocent suffer? Justice and fairness are worth fighting for, because these ideals are essential for human survival and for making life worth living. **We all have to die, but we can choose not to die in vain. In fact, we can accomplish more in death than in life, if we choose to die for a worthy cause that is larger than we are -- justice, integrity, and love for others. Such sacrifice will confer meaning retroactively on the life that precedes its noble end.**

In all thy getting, get understanding.

Finally, I get it.

It's not about me.

It's about God and His will on earth!

Filled with the Holy Ghost.

On fire and sanctified!

Dear Heavenly Father,

I would like to take this opportunity to pray to You on behalf of the many countless people as well as myself who have been abused and oppressed at the hands of others. Please send comfort and Your peace as well as healing for the body, mind and spirit. May we not lose sight of what's important but draw from Your strength as You continue to bless us with the wherewithal to stand firm and be forever committed to fulfilling Your will.

Shield our hearts that it may not grow bitter or harden from the pain and suffering, for the circumcision of our heart is mighty. May we have a renewed spirit of abundant life and trust in You always!

Amen

P.O. BOX 909715, CHICAGO, ILLINOIS 60690

Mar 3, 1989

Dear Ann:

Thanks for writing and suggesting a topic for The Oprah Winfrey Show.

We are always looking for new ideas and subject material. I appreciate your valuable input.

I have forwarded your letter to the producers for further consideration.

Thanks for helping to make The Oprah Winfrey Show #1.

Best wishes,

Oprah Winfrey

OW:mq

May 15, 2000
Mayor Anthony A. Williams
Government of the District of Columbia
441 4th Street, N.W.
Washington, D.C. 20001

RE: Tuition-free Career Training

Dear Mayor Williams:

Given my personality and my upbringing, I normally accept things at face value, and I don't make waves. However, given my experiences, I've learned to always ask questions and never make assumptions. And most importantly, I never leave anything to chance. So out of frustration, disappointment and the need for clarity, I write this letter.

When I learned of your program for tuition-free training for D.C. residents (involving high-demand occupations quickly developing in the Washington area), pursuant to receiving the correspondence announcing the opening of The New Information Technology Career Center on January 10, 2000, little did I know at the time that my interest would be more of a personal nature. Nevertheless, due to my recent unemployment, I was ecstatic to learn I could receive training for various occupations considering my disappointment surrounding my job search in my area of interest (human resources) because I lack the "now" requested required credentials (such as a degree or certification). I not only thought the training would lift my spirits but also offer endless possibilities that would enable me to rejoin the workforce with greater resources.

For many, the thought of being unemployed can be a very devastating experience. And the whole process of having to venture out to obtain suitable employment can be just as overwhelming, not to mention it's mentally and physically draining. In following up on various leads for employment in correlation to my background or skill level, I noted a number of the employers are looking to fill these positions with candidates possessing a BA or BS degree. Although I am confident I would be able to perform the duties as outlined in these classified ads, my lack of credentials limits my chances of even being considered for many of the positions.

When I called the number (1-877-319-7346) on the card to schedule an appointment, there was an automated message that gave additional information pertaining to one-stop career centers in the D.C. area. After I placed a call to the Naylor Road One-Stop Center, I was instructed to report to their location on March 8, 2000, at 9:00 am to take a TABE test. After learning I met the initial requirement, I was instructed to attend a scheduled orientation on April 24, 2000, at 9:00 am and bring the following documentation:

1. Birth certificate

2. Social security card

3. Copy of last pay stub (proof of income and state taxes)

4. Proof of residency (utility bills)

5. Copy of latest college transcript

During that orientation on April 24, 2000, I learned the following:

1. Ms. Almeita Johnson was no longer an employee there at that location.

2. I was given partially incorrect information: A copy of my high school diploma was needed and not the latest copy of my college transcript. However, the copy of my transcript from Strayer College indicated the name of my high school and graduation date. Nonetheless, I returned the following morning with my high school diploma and a copy of the grades I received from the ninth through the twelfth grade.

3. In the absence of Ms. Johnson, there was one case manager—Mr. Carlton Morrison, who I found to be very helpful—servicing the needs of over 600 individuals with no assistance. Therefore, it was important for us to cooperate fully by paying close attention to the rules governing the program, take good detailed notes, complete all paperwork accurately and forward at least two copies of the requested documents to alleviate confusion and speed up the process. He also stated and urged that the longer it took us to comply, the longer the process; so if we were interested in registering by the next available session in any curriculum in accordance to the process period, it was important not to

wait until the last minute to meet all the requirements of the program.

Initially, I wanted to take advantage of the training offered for Oracle Network Administration in hopes of receiving certification. However, once Mr. Morrison learned of my background in Human Resources, he felt there was an occupational demand and suggested I seek training more beneficial to that area.

After being referred to Ms. Virginia B. Howerton (Program Director at the University of the District of Columbia Community Outreach and Extension Services in correlation to the Dislocated Workers Program) to fulfill the "basic education skill requirement," I learned I could pursue my bachelor's degree in business administration versus the associate if I was nearly 75 percent in completion of receiving the bachelor's. I was encouraged to meet with the dean or chair of the department for additional information. So I proceeded to meet with the department chair, Professor Hany H. Makhlouf. Based on that conversation, I forwarded to Ms. Howerton the outline of courses needed to complete my studies. Once she completed the bid sheet or training cost analysis for approval, I forwarded the information to Mr. Morrison. Despite the applauded efforts of Mr. Morrison, just when I thought I had met all of the requirements or followed each guideline governing the program to receive the necessary training, I was faced with another dilemma or roadblock. Mr. Morrison consulted his superior (a DOES manager), which to my surprise was a very disturbing conversation. Mr. Morrison, not aware I was within hearing range, was accused of being sentimental because he was in favor of me completing my degree.

Overall, the manager felt if I was able to find previous employment without a degree, then he didn't feel it was necessary for me to seek one now. Not only did I consider that to be an insulting statement but a very narrow-minded view of higher education for a person in his position. In addition, I learned I needed to produce a detailed listing of my job search to confirm my efforts. No problem—I kept an updated log on a computer disk I carried in my purse with my resume.

Initially, when I walked into that office, I had a ray of hope, but now I'm feeling disoriented and disparity. And what do I hope to accomplish by writing this letter? In meeting all the requirements of the program, I provided the following additional items:

1. Layoff notice from Kajax Engineering, Inc.
2. A detailed listing of my job search to confirm my efforts.
3. Clippings from the classified section of the Washington Post indicating a degree is required for various positions (including some clerical/secretarial positions).
4. Documentation (correspondence dated 4/27/00) from Ms. Howerton.
5. Letters of recommendation indicating credit worthiness and pass work ethics.

Taking into consideration, the approval process timeline (at least 30 days pursuant to Mr. Carlton), I have a number of questions as listed below:

1. What is the actual purpose of the tuition-free training program?

2. Aside from residency, income requirement and being dislocated, who is the program extended to?

3. Do you or a representative from your office oversee the program or meet with a representative from the Department of Employment Services (DOES) and the Dislocated Workers Program to evaluate the effectiveness of the program?

   > Does someone check the status of the enrollees to make sure there is a level of fairness across the board?

   > b.Do you solicit feedback from the perspective and current participants?

4. Should I expect to receive written or verbal documentation stating my standing or position in the program?

5. If denied, will I receive notification as to why within the confines of the rules and regulations (aside from the personal views of a DOES employee)?

Sincerely,

Ann G. Mack

April 29, 2000

Gregory P. Irish, Director
Department of Employment Services
500 C Street, NW
Washington, D.C. 20001

RE: Tuition-free Career Training

Dear Mr. Irish,

I am forwarding additional background information for your review to substantiate my claim and the need for your guidance and assistance. Upon my visit to the Naylor Road One-Stop Career Center on April 24, 2000, I learned the following:

1. Ms. Johnson was no longer an employee at that location.

2. I was given partially incorrect information: A copy of my high school diploma was needed and not the latest copy of my college transcript. However, the copy of my transcript from Strayer College indicated the name of my high school and graduation date. Nonetheless, I returned the following morning with my high school diploma and the grades I received from the 9th through the 12th grade.

3. In the absence of Ms. Johnson, there was currently one case manager (Mr. Carlton Morrison—who I found to be very helpful) now servicing the needs of over 600 individuals with no assistance. Therefore, it was important for us to cooperate fully by paying close attention to the rules governing the program, take good detailed notes, complete all paperwork accurately, and forward at least two copies of the requested documents to alleviate confusion and speed up the process. He also stated and urged that the longer it took us to comply, the longer the process; so if we were interested in registering by the next available session in any curriculum in accordance to the process period, it was important not to wait until the last minute to meet all the requirements of the program.

I apologize for the inconvenience, and I'm not trying to overkill, but I feel I'm at a dead end. Any assistance and attention to this matter would be greatly appreciated. Thanks in advance.

Sincerely,

Ann G. Mack

August 20, 2004

Washington City Paper
2390 Champlin Street, NW
Washington, D.C. 20009
ATTN: Mr. Brian Montopoli
Or Current Writers/Editors

**RE: Volume 23, Number 33 dated August 22-28, 2003
- Article, "Have We Got a Job for You?"**

Dear Mr. Montopoli,

Unfortunately, this letter is extremely overdue—about a year in fact. I had the pleasure of reading the above article which brought tears to my eyes because it painfully reminded me of my experience with the Department of Employment Services (DOES). Therefore, I am writing to express my appreciation as well as my thoughts on the subject.

I also commend Councilmember David Catania's sense of integrity and willingness to speak openly about the mismanagement of DOES as well as its organizational dysfunction at various levels from the top to the bottom. However, I doubt his openness or your article sparked any initiatives from the mayor or Mr. Parish to produce change. A year later,

- What measures are in place to monitor or evaluate the effectiveness for improvement?

- Is Mayor Williams willing to address the problems and make a conscious as well as committed effort to introduce change?

For a favorable outcome, should one ever find themselves in an unfortunate situation that dictates they utilize the services of the D.C. DOES, I caution them to mentally prepare themselves to not only deal with the unprofessional attitudes (I'm not here to work or to exercise integrity; I'm here to collect a paycheck while being careful not to rock the boat and to make the mayor, the director and DOES as a whole look good by giving the appearance we care and are trying to help others!), but to keep a journal detailing their contacts and be persistently annoying as a follow-up tactic.

From my experience, the few positions filled by those within DOES who possess integrity and business ethics are unable to follow through successfully in assisting others honorably because they are often managed by others that lack the above attributes. In addition, if they pretend to care and openly voice their observance of unfairness (i.e., rock the boat), they become frustrated by the systems (or lack of systems) in place, conform and follow suit in an effort to keep their jobs while others that have been labeled a non-team player are transferred (willingly or unwillingly) or leave all together for other employment.

Having been a victim of the DOES bureaucracy, I whole-heartedly sympathize with those mentioned in your article as well as those you do not know about. From my experience, I—without a doubt—believe the political system that governs the operation of DOES (as well as other government agencies in the district and at the federal level) is truly functioning as it was intended. In my opinion, the DOES fails to serve the purpose of empowering those in need, at least not for the past eight to ten years. It merely assists in ensuring the failure of the less desirable or lower political class while giving the false pretense of providing a public service of equality enjoyed by all.

If a public service is offered or an empowerment program is introduced and I take the initiative based on interest and desire for improvement or change for self by attempting to obtain that assistance, I would not expect to get the run around. And if I go the extra step to learn about the qualifying factors or policies in place governing that program and I am in compliance with the guidelines meeting those qualifications, I would definitely not expect to get the run around. However, if a system was not designed to operate as you were led to believe and you are consistently met with adversity after crossing your "t's" and dotting all your "i's," the objective of the program is not to assist and encourage but the opposite: to discourage you and hope that you are too illiterate to know the difference. Hence, you give up, and the cycle begins again with the next unsuspecting, poor soul.

Nonetheless, due to my persistence (annoyance to others), I reluctantly received assistance and completed my degree in business management from UDC in December of 2002, partially through the D.C. free tuition assistance program. Please see the attached documentation detailing the events of my experience with DOES.

Concerned,

Ann G. Mack

December 6, 2007

Charles Grassley, Ranking Member
United States Senate
House Committee on Finance
Washington, D.C. 2007

RE: Your letter of November 5, 2007,
      to Creflo Dollar Ministries
      Tax-exempt Donations Made to
      Religious Organizations

If in fact recent articles and news reports regarding possible misuse of tax-exempt donations made to religious organizations has caused some concerns for the Finance Committee, then why not *take a look at all religious, non-profit and faith-based organizations.* The first organizations on the list should be those who have repeatedly used those donations to contribute to the extremely adsorbent lifestyle afforded by those at the executive levels. Does this mean you are also monitoring such organizations as the United Way, given their previous factual use and abuse of taxpayers' hard-earned wages that were donated for the assistance of humanitarian aide? Or perhaps you endorse the president's faith-based initiative that gives certain organizations the opportunity, should they sign on, to take advantage of the poor as they get richer under the protection of the government at the expense of humanitarian aide!

For example, why would an establishment that claims to have been a church *[The Salvation Army]* since the beginning of its inception, in 1865 to be exact, feel the need to circulate a petition amongst its staff in solicitation of signatures in promoting and advancing the church's political stance or views that they not only endorse the president's candidacy but his faith-based initiative as well? Considering the definition and objective of a church, does not its very existence spell out the belief in a higher power, God, as a derivative of faith? Or does this action on the basis of politics clearly define its hidden agenda and spell out the evident and blatant pretense of giving the people what they want through manipulation and falsehood, similar to the work of a magician who uses trickery and disillusionment into fooling people into thinking what they want them to believe? So clearly, there is no longer a separation of church and state, and *there never was*; only when it is beneficial to those who are driven by greed.

Let us take a look at politics! Those in office or in power based on a majority vote or stealing of votes, especially in this current (Bush) administration, desire the people to believe that they are being heard and that an attempt is being made to give the people what they want with their best interest in mind. It is the illusion of false hope and promises of humanity to gain something in return! So is it safe to say (or you would say assume) that The Salvation Army is to the president (or the Republican Party) what Halliburton is to Bush and this administration (the Republican Party)? Considering Halliburton was allowed to cheat the government, get away with it to suffer no unreputable damage and still operate under the same ethics as Enron while continuing to thrive, did the government intervene on behalf of the employees of Enron or the executives who benefited from the blatant mismanagement and laundering of employee savings? That was handled all wrong and at the expense of those who lost everything, rather than at the expense of those who stole everything.

Politicians surely make strange bedfellows, or should I say *appropriate bedfellows*, at the cost of winning unearnestly! I guess this confirms how an internationally famous or well-known establishment that's registered as a church, 501(c)3, but operated more like a cult is able to practice discrimination with the blessing of the government (majority leaders) and get away with it regardless of what is presented to the outside world through the media while other churches that are without a doubt known for helping minorities *to include all people* are being persecuted because they have not once been in the media and implicated as violating the rights of others. Is it safe to say or assume that the churches being targeted or looked at, such as the Creflo Dollar Ministries, did not and do not influence its congregation in areas of politics that meet with the approval of the power base nor have elected to sign-on in agreement with the faith-based initiative? Perhaps such ministries are credited with helping too many of the underlings like education, and empowering them to make their own decisions based on the facts is more of a threat to the direction of upcoming elections and the attempt to cripple these churches is mainly the agenda.

Have you requested to review the financial records and audit reports of The Salvation Army? A non-profit organization (Oops, I mean a church!) that owns many properties throughout the U.S. and outside of the U.S. and is considering establishing a bank in India or Indonesia. An organization with a sub-entity, the Salvation Army World Service Office that was established in 1977 with the pretense of honoring the concept of separation of church and state, that recently misplaced or lost over $400,000 dollars of the taxpayers' hard-earned, donated wages towards the tsunami disaster in 2007 through the use of an International Assets Holding Corporation called International Global Currencies Ltd. to transfer U.S. dollars and government funds. We are in the middle of a war! How do we confirm the money did not fall into the wrong hands? All precautions should be taken to ensure the ability of tracking and confirming the transfer of funds from the U.S. to overseas locations—in the same manner in which the government should have instituted a better management plan for securing the military items that are now missing and are probably in the hands of the enemy to use against us in this war. With the technology that we seem to push so quickly to keep track of each other in America like illegal wire-tapping and satellite surveillance, we sure have a difficult time with the overall corruption of those we appoint and place in positions of power and authority in the name of politics which is truly and clearly our downfall. Why worry about terrorists abroad when we do enough here to terrorize each other in the name of the American dream?

In addition to the above, The Salvation Army miscalculated or misreported employee earnings to the Internal Revenue

Service for 2004 and 2005. Imagine receiving a letter from the Internal Revenue Service indicating you owe back taxes, including interest and penalties, on money you did not receive (earn) in payment. Unfortunately, some individuals are not that organized, or they panic when they receive such a letter even if they are not in the wrong. In fact, they do not put up a fight or take the time to defend themselves and take financial responsibility for something they are not legally bound by. The Finance Department of the Salvation Army World Service Office received correspondence from the Internal Revenue Service indicating a miscalculation or misreported earnings of over $100,000 for 2004 or 2005. This information, as it turns out, was not reported to the Internal Revenue Service by the Washington, D.C. office but through the New York location. Why would the New York location have pertinent information pertaining to employees working at a D.C. location if the two locations are entirely different and registered as two entirely different corporations only tied to one another in name only—for example, with two different Employer Identification Numbers (EIN)?

Opposed to what we would like for our children and other unsuspecting naïve minds to believe, justice in our society has nothing to do with right or wrong. It has more to do with how much money or power one has to be able to afford the most convincing attorney, an illusionist, to plead a case. Or the ability of a powerful person with the right connections to call in a favor or grease palms. There are a lot of *innocent* people in jail because they didn't have the right representation, and there are a lot of criminals walking around free because they had the best representation that influence and money could buy. Remember

Chappaquiddick[95]! But a great deal of time was devoted to the attempted impeachment of President Bill Clinton for his sexual scandal. However, he did not murder anyone. Nonetheless, one is just as bad as the other and *sin is sin*! And let's not forget about the number of Catholic priests who never received punishment for molesting children. The Catholic Church never requested or demanded a list of the names and known acts committed by priests for which a payment was made to the families of the victims.

On another note, given the nature of your request for documentation over a period of three years from 2004 through 2007, one month is not an appropriate amount of time.[96] Look at the amount of time that is given to known violators of human rights crimes committed against blacks by whites; for instance, crimes the KKK committed in the 1950s and 1960s that were not publicized. Why did it take so long for the legal judicial system to sort justice for the families of the black children who were burned in a church in the 1960s? By the time the government got around to prosecuting their attackers, those that committed the crime were too old to serve the sentence that befitted the crime due to their illnesses and ages. The families that suffered during the Black Wall Street massacre still have not received any justice for the crimes committed against them. This clearly shows the importance of people relating to race as defined by the government and the so-called judicial system. And today, you are allowing The Salvation Army to discrimi-

---

95   http://www.history.com/this-day-in-history/incident-on-chappaquiddick-island
96   http://media.npr.org/documents/2007/nov/grassley/dollar.pdf

nate against non-English-speaking individuals, which does not make a great deal of sense to me. Were they not required to complete an application form that's written in English? Were they not requested to complete a testing and recruitment process for the position in English? Is it safe to say they completed the assignment or work and now The Salvation Army no longer has need for their services because the hard part of the assignment was accomplished? Or is it safe to say they have not been able to completely cover up their accents to go undetected or have complete command of the English language in accordance to the standards set by those that are ruled by prejudiced means?

What does the latter have to do with the main topic of this letter? Everything! It speaks to history and a pattern (the modus operandi) of the government as it embodies aspects of politics and how things are handled and covered up—repeatedly. *Organized crime is organized crime, and corruption is still defined the same regardless of who the players are! Some are just better at it than others with the law on their side.*

Cordially,

A concerned citizen for legal and social justice for all; not just for the select few.

    c: Creflo and Taffi Dollar
       World Changers Church International
       Creflo Dollar Ministries
       2500 Burdett Road
       College Park, GA 30349

REFERENCES

DEFINITIONS

- **Double Standard(s)** - a set of principles that applies differently and usually more rigorously to one group of people or individual than another in the same situation under the same circumstances.

- **Racism** - a belief system hinging on racial/cultural prejudice and discrimination supported by institutional power and authority; designed to overtly or covertly limit advancement opportunities by keeping certain individuals at a particular level regardless of their training or education and qualifications to successfully perform at a higher level that may afford them higher wages.

- **Prejudice** - an assumption (stereotype) or prejudgment in favor of or against a person (gender and/or appearance), a group, an event, an idea (beliefs) or a particular thing.

- **Discrimination** - the process of responding to a person differently by imposing unfair or unfavorable treatment upon him/her or denying a person or group equal opportunities stemming from biases or prejudices or stereotypes based on that individual's or group's gender, race, age, religion (beliefs), sexual orientation, social class or national origin. **Specific types of discrimination:**[97] age, culture (National Origin), disability, ethnicity, gender, harassment, pregnancy, race/color, religion, retaliation, sexual orientation/ genetic information, sexual harassment.

- **Oppression** - an act to rule in a non-diplomatic, dehumanizing way oftentimes coupled with unjust harshness whereby those being oppressed become high-risk candidates for emotional or physical collapse.

---

97   https://www.eeoc.gov/laws/types/

DIVERSITY BY DESIGN

DEFINITIONS

Culture – predominating attitudes and behaviors that characterize how a group functions or behaves.

Ethnocentrism – A belief demonstrated through a display of behavior that your group (or race) is inherently superior to that of another group (or race). Taking a subjective view that your way is the best way or your race is better.

Minority – generally characterized as being an outsider; however, a minority status can fluctuate depending upon the social dynamics occurring at the time. Once perceived to be merely a racial distinction, it is a term that's used to describe a group that represents a relatively smaller percentage of the overall population.

Prejudice – occurs when you make prejudgments about an individual with little or no absolute knowledge. For example, if you have had a bad experience with an individual, you may prejudge others of the same class, race or group based on your bad experience.

Stereotypes – rigid and generally negative beliefs that people use to categorize members of a group (race) who share general characteristics. (Biases and bigotry are based on uninformed stereotypes.)

http://www.aclu.org/religion/govtfunding/16103prs20040224.html

- NYCLU Sues The Salvation Army for Religious Discrimination Against Employees in Government-Funded Social Services for Children (2/24/2004)

- NYCLU Calls on State Officials to Audit The Salvation Army Employment Practices (1/14/2004)

- Pittsburg Tribune-Review by Mark Houser [mhouser@tribweb.com or (412) 320-7995]

- Sunday, April 29, 2007: The Salvation Army sued in Boston for firing non-English speakers, employs none here.

- "The Equal Employment Opportunity Commission (EEOC) sued The Salvation Army this month (April) in U.S. District Court in Boston saying a Framingham, Mass., thrift store violated the civil rights of two female Hispanic immigrants. The lawsuit is the second the EEOC has filed against The Salvation Army involving its English-only rule."

http://www.hispanictips.com/2007/04/02/eeoc-sues-salvation-army-discrimination-against-hispanic-employees/

▶ "Under EEOC's guidelines and English-only rule violates the law unless the employer can provide a legitimate business justification for forcing employees to stop speaking their native language. The Salvation Army presented no such justification," said Estela D'az, trial attorney for the EEOC's New York district office, in a written statement Friday.

http://www.freerepublic.com/focus/f-news/1825568/posts
http://www.wsfa.com/global/story.asp?S=6445581

http://www.westword.com/1995-04-19/news/segregated-salvation/

http://www.nyclu.org/news/nyclu-settlement-ensures-salvation-army-will-not-discriminate-using-government-funds

FROM REVELATION TO REALIZATION

http://center-of-hope.blogspot.com/2008/11/salvation-army-lawsuits.html

http://transcripts.cnn.com/TRANSCRIPTS/0704/26/ldt.01.html

Http://www.aclu.org/religion/govtfunding/16103prs20040224.html

http://www.hispanictips.com/2007/04/02/eeoc-sues-salvation-army-discrimination-against-hispanic-employees/

HIDDEN AGENDAS AND UNGODLY MOTIVES

http://www.salvationarmyusa.org/usn/www_usn.nsf/vw-text-index/85256ddc007274df85256b76006fa193?opendocument

http://www.fractallywrong.com/?p=172

http://www.westword.com/content/result/issue:207713

FIGHT, TAKE FLIGHT OR FREEZE

http://www.raystedman.org/thematic-studies/spiritual-warfare/pulling-down-strongholds

http://www.greatbiblestudy.com/strongholds.php

LETTER TO CHARLES GRASSLEY, Ranking Member

United States Senate, House Committee on Finance

http://media.npr.org/documents/2007/nov/grassley/dollar.pdf

http://media.npr.org/documents/2007/nov/grassley/copeland.pdf

http://media.npr.org/documents/2007/nov/grassley/hinn.pdf

http://media.npr.org/documents/2007/nov/grassley/meyer.pdf

http://media.npr.org/documents/2007/nov/grassley/white.pdf

http://media.npr.org/documents/2007/nov/grassley/long.pdf

http://www.npr.org/templates/story/story.php?storyId=16860611

http://www.cbsnews.com/news/senate-panel-probes-6-top-televangelists/

http://www.nbcnews.com/id/40960871/ns/politics-capitol_hill/t/televangelists-escape-penalty-senate-inquiry/#.WKJKffkrKM8

OBEDIENT TO GOD

http://www.socialjusticesolutions.org/2013/01/15/the-definition-of-social-justice/

REPARATIONS

http://afroamhistory.about.com/arts/afroamhistory/mbody.htm

http://www.commonlink.com/users/carl-olsen/RASTAFARI/NOI/Muhammad-002.html

http://www.directblackaction.com

http://www.geocities.com/CapitolHill/8533/apology.html

http://www.house.gov/tonyhall/pr145.html

http://www.mydrum.com

http://www.pbs.org/newshour/bb/race_relations/july-dec00/reparations.html

http://www.plebispsyche.com/hr29_1867.html

http://racerelations.about.com/newsissues/racerelations/library/weekly/aa051200a.htm

http://saxakali.com/urafrican/reparationslinks.htm

http://sites.netscape.net/reps4slavery2000

http://www.swagga.com/reparation.htm

http://www.thefence.com/debate.asp?forumid=133

http://www.udayton.edu/~race/03justice/AfAmlaw02.htm

http://www.udayton.edu/~race/02rights/slave01.htm#Databases

http://web.africa.ufl.edu/asq/v2/v2i4.htm

TO SOLVE THE BIG PROBLEMS, SEE THE BIG PICTURE

http://www.businessdictionary.com/definition/organizational-culture.html

https://www.torbenrick.eu/blog/culture/organizational-culture/

https://archive.org/details/Ballot_Question_7_Gaming_Expansion_in_Maryland

TRUST GOD IN SPITE OF WHAT YOU SEE

http://www.npr.org/templates/story/story.php?storyId=4945299

UTOPIA

https://archive.org/details/utopiainlatinand00moreuoft

http://www.bl.uk/learning/histcitizen/21cc/utopia/utopia.html

https://en.wikisource.org/wiki/Catholic_Encyclopedia_(1913)/Utopia

http://www.encyclopedia.com/social-sciences-and-law/political-science-and-government/political-science-terms-and-concepts-94

http://www.thesaurus.com/browse/utopia

WORKPLACE BULLYING IS UNACCEPTABLE

https://www.magellanassist.com/media/122419/october-2015_bullying-awareness.pdf

WRONGFUL TERMINATION

Anthony, William P., Pamela L. Perrewe & K. Michele Kacmar. (1999). *Human Resource Management: A Strategic Approach.* Florida: Harcourt Brace College Publishers.

Brown, Gordon W. & Paul A. Sukys. (1997). *Business Law: With UCC Applications.* Ohio: Glencoe/McGraw-Hill.

Matteson, Ivancevich. (1999). *Organizational Behavior and Management.* New York: Irwin/McGraw-Hill.

http://www.business2.com/webguide/0,1660,50486,FF.html

http://employment-law.freeadvice.com/firing/action_wrongful_termination.htm

http://www.frascona.com/resource/jhl494wt.htm

http://homepages.uhwo.hawaii.edu/clear/laws6.html

http://jobsearchtech.about.com/library/weekly/aa080601.htm

http://www.leefeldmanlaw.com/wrongfultermination.html

https://www.nela.org/

http://www.nerinet.org/dismissals.shtml

http://home.pacbell.net/netlaw/el2.htm#Part5

http://www.prairielaw.com/articles/article.asp?channelId=14&articleId=1111

http://www.protectingrights.net/Discrimination_Harassment.html

http://www.sexualharassment-discriminationhotline.com/wrongfultermination.htm

http://www.uchastings.edu/plri/96-97tex/jury.htm#I.percent20Introduction

SUGGESTED GENERAL READING

1. *Seeing the Unseen: Preparing Yourself for Spiritual Warfare*

   › Author: Joe Bean

   › **ISBN-10:** 1582292736 and
   ISBN-13: 978-1582292731

2. *Sensitivity of Heart: How to Be Sensitive to The Father, His Word and One Another*

   › Author: Kenneth Copeland

   › **ISBN-10:** 0881147117 and
   ISBN-13: 978-0881147117

3. *The Supernatural Power of a Transformed Mind Expanded Edition: Access to a Life of Miracles*

   › Author: Bill Johnson

   › **ISBN-10:** 0768404207 **and**
   ISBN-13: 978-0768404203

BIBLICAL REFERENCES

Unless otherwise indicated, scripture quotations are from the Holy Bible, King James Version. All rights reserved.

Scriptures marked AMP are taken from the Amplified Version®. Copyright © 2015 by The Lockman Foundation. All rights reserved.

Scriptures marked ERV are taken from the Easy-to-Read Version®. Copyright © 2006 by Bible League international. All rights reserved.

Scriptures marked ESV are taken from English Standard Version®. Copyright © 2001 by Crossway, a publishing ministry of Good News Publishers. All rights reserved.

Scriptures marked GW are taken from the God's Word to the Nations®. Copyright © 1995 by Baker Publishing Group. All rights reserved.

Scriptures marked MSG are taken from The Message®. Copyright © 1993, 1994, 1995, 1996, 2000, 2001, 2002. Used by permission of NavPress Publishing Group.

Scriptures marked NASB are taken from the New American Standard Bible®. Copyright © 1960, 1962, 1963, 1968, 1971, 1972, 1973, 1975, 1977, 1995 by The Lockman Foundation. Used by permission.

Scriptures marked NIV are taken from the New International Version®. Copyright © 1973, 1978, 1984, 2011 by Biblica, Inc.™. All rights reserved.

Scriptures marked NKJV are taken from the New King James Version®. Copyright © 1982 by Thomas Nelson. All rights reserved.

Scriptures marked NLT are taken from the New Living Translation®. Copyright © 1996, 2004, 2007, 2013 by Tyndale House Foundation. All rights reserved.

Scriptures marked NET are taken from the NET Bible® copyright ©1996-2006 by Biblical Studies Press, L.L.C. http://netbible.com All rights reserved.

Scriptures marked NRSV are taken from the New Revised Standard Version Bible, copyright © 1989 the Division of Christian Education of the National Council of the Churches of Christ in the United States of America. Used by permission. All rights reserved.

Scriptures marked TLB are taken from The Living Bible copyright © 1971 by Tyndale House Foundation. Used by permission of Tyndale House Publishers Inc., Carol Stream, Illinois 60188. All rights reserved. The Living Bible, TLB, and The

Living Bible logo are registered trademarks of Tyndale House Publishers.

Scriptures marked TCW are taken from The Clear Word Bible copyright © 1994 by James Blanco, Review & Herald Publishing. All rights reserved.

ABOUT THE AUTHOR

Ann Gwen Mack, a native Washingtonian, was born on September 23, 1960, to Ruby H. and James S. Mack. Through life's lessons and challenges, she was determined to push beyond the boundaries and limitations she encountered to prove to herself that she could indeed accomplish what others believed and always told her she could not do. After finding herself unemployed for the third time, she made a conscious commitment to go back to school to pursue a degree in business management with an emphasis on human resources, business, and employment law!

Spending most of her life church hopping, Ann spent a great deal of time in church attempting to get closer to God because she believed there was much more to life than the pain, the ups and downs, the world had presented. God's persistence to bring her through every trial and tribulation has given her the push she's needed to endure with divine determination.

In August of 2010, Ann yielded to the call on her life to minister the Gospel, which led to the beginning of her first God-ordained writing assignment, the first edition of *What Do I Do With My Pain?* She went on to write her second book, entitled *From What Tribe Were You Birthed?: Understanding the Significance of the Breastplate of Aaron*.

To contact Ann, email her at author_ann@anngwenmack.com